ANALYSIS AND DESIGN OF ALGORITHMS

[Conceptual Approach]

Anuradha A. Puntambekar

M.E. (Computer)

Formerly Assistant Professor in

P.E.S. Modern College of Engineering,

Pune

Analysis and Design of Algorithms

First Edition : December 2020

Published by :

Amit Residency, Office No.1, 412, Shaniwar Peth, Pune - 411030, M.S. INDIA
Ph.: +91-020-24495496/97, Email : sales@technicalpublications.org
Website : www.technicalpublications.org

ISBN 978-93-332-2386-7

9789333223867

PREFACE

The importance of **Analysis and Design of Algorithms** is well known in various engineering fields. Overwhelming response to my books on various subjects inspired me to write this book. The book is structured to cover the key aspects of the subject **Analysis and Design of Algorithms**.

The book uses plain, lucid language to explain fundamentals of this subject. The book provides logical method of explaining various complicated concepts and stepwise methods to explain the important topics. Each chapter is well supported with necessary illustrations, practical examples and solved problems. All the chapters in the book are arranged in a proper sequence that permits each topic to build upon earlier studies. All care has been taken to make students comfortable in understanding the basic concepts of the subject.

Representative questions have been added at the end of each section to help the students in picking important points from that section.

The book not only covers the entire scope of the subject but explains the philosophy of the subject. This makes the understanding of this subject more clear and makes it more interesting. The book will be very useful not only to the students but also to the subject teachers. The students have to omit nothing and possibly have to cover nothing more.

I wish to express my profound thanks to all those who helped in making this book a reality. Much needed moral support and encouragement is provided on numerous occasions by my whole family. I wish to thank the **Publisher** and the entire team of **Technical Publications** who have taken immense pain to get this book in time with quality printing.

Any suggestion for the improvement of the book will be acknowledged and well appreciated.

Author

A. A. Puntambekar

Dedicated to God.

SYLLABUS

1. Basics of Algorithms and Mathematics

What is an algorithm ?, Mathematics for algorithmic sets, Functions and relations, Vectors and matrices, Linear inequalities and linear equations. **(Chapter - 1)**

2. Analysis of Algorithm

The efficient algorithm, Average, best and worst case analysis, Amortized analysis, Asymptotic notations, Analyzing control statement, Loop invariant and the correctness of the algorithm, Sorting algorithms and analysis : Bubble sort, Selection sort, Insertion sort, Shell sort, Heap sort, Sorting in linear time : Bucket sort, Radix sort and Counting sort. **(Chapter - 2)**

3. Divide and Conquer Algorithm

Introduction, Recurrence and different methods to solve recurrence, Multiplying large integers problem, Problem solving using divide and conquer algorithm - Binary search, Max-Min problem, Sorting (Merge sort, Quick sort), Matrix multiplication, Exponential. **(Chapter - 3)**

4. Dynamic Programming

Introduction, The principle of optimality, Problem solving using dynamic programming - Calculating the binomial coefficient, Making change problem, Assembly line-scheduling, Knapsack problem, All points shortest path, Matrix chain multiplication, Longest common subsequence. **(Chapter - 4)**

5. Greedy Algorithm

General characteristics of greedy algorithms, Problem solving using Greedy algorithm

- Activity selection problem, Elements of greedy strategy, Minimum spanning trees (Kruskal's algorithm, Prim's algorithm), Graphs : Shortest paths, The knapsack problem, Job scheduling problem, Huffman code. **(Chapter - 5)**

6. Exploring Graphs

An introduction using graphs and games, Undirected graph, Directed graph, Traversing graphs, Depth first search, Breadth first search, Topological sort, Connected components. **(Chapter - 6)**

7. Backtracking and Branch and Bound

Introduction, The eight queens problem , Knapsack problem, Travelling salesman problem, Minimax principle. **(Chapter - 7)**

8. String Matching

Introduction, The naive string matching algorithm, The Rabin-Karp algorithm, String matching with finite automata, The Knuth-Morris-Pratt algorithm. **(Chapter - 8)**

9. Introduction to NP-Completeness

The class P and NP, Polynomial reduction, NP-completeness problem, NP-hard problems. Travelling salesman problem, Hamiltonian problem, Approximation algorithms. **(Chapter - 9)**

TABLE OF CONTENTS

Chapter - 2 Analysis of Algorithms (2 - 1) to (2 - 106)

1 Basics of Algorithms and Mathematics

Syllabus

What is an algorithm ?, Mathematics for algorithmic sets, Functions and relations, Vectors and matrices, Linear inequalities and linear equations.

Contents

1.1 Introduction

An algorithm, named for the ninth century Persian mathematician **al-Khowarizmi**, is simply a set of rules used to perform some calculations, either by hand or more usually on a machine. In this subject we will refer algorithm as a method that can be used by the computer for solution of a problem. For instance performing the addition, multiplication, division or subtraction is an algorithm. Use of algorithm for some computations is a common practice. Even ancient Greek has used an algorithm which is popularly known as Euclid's algorithm for calculating the greatest common divisor of two numbers.

Basically algorithm is a finite set of instructions that can be used to perform certain task. In this chapter we will learn some basic concepts of algorithm. We will start our discussion by understanding the notion of algorithm. And for understanding how to write an algorithm we will discuss some examples.

1.2 What is an Algorithm ?

GTU : Dec.-10, Winter-15, Marks 3

In this section we will first understand ***"What is algorithm?"*** and ***"When it is required ?"***

Definition of algorithm : The algorithm is defined as a collection of unambiguous instructions occurring in some specific sequence and such an algorithm should produce output for given set of input in finite amount of time.

This definition of algorithm is represented in Fig. 1.2.1.

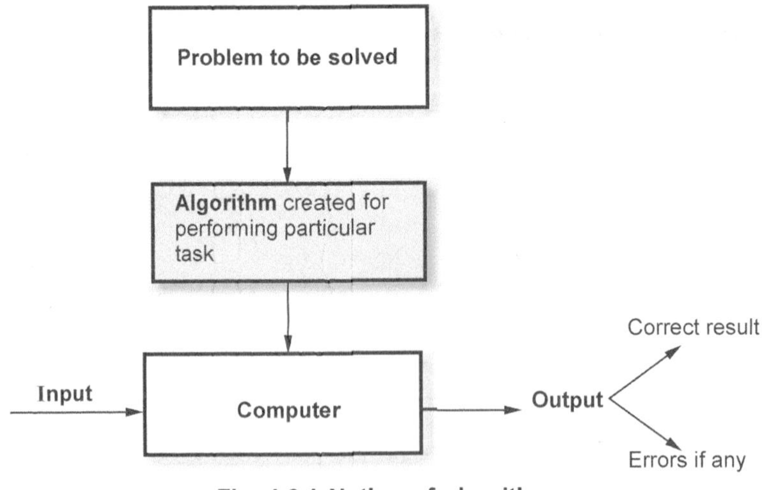

Fig. 1.2.1 Notion of algorithm

After understanding the problem statement we have to create an algorithm carefully for the given problem. The algorithm is then converted into some programming language and then given to some computing device (computer). The computer then executes this algorithm which is actually submitted in the form of source program. During the process of execution it requires certain set of input. With the help of algorithm (in the form of program) and input set, the result is produced as an output. If the given input is invalid then it should raise appropriate error message ; otherwise correct result will be produced as an output.

1.2.1 Properties of Algorithm

Simply writing the sequence of instructions as an algorithm is not sufficient to accomplish certain task. It is necessary to have following properties associated with an algorithm :

1. **Non-ambiguity :** Each step in an algorithm should be non-ambiguous. That means each instruction should be clear and precise. The instruction in an algorithm should not denote any conflicting meaning. This property also indicate the *effectiveness* of algorithm.
2. **Range of input :** The range of input should be specified. This is because normally the algorithm is input driven and if the range of the input is not been specified then algorithm can go in an infinite state.
3. **Multiplicity :** The same algorithm can be represented in several different ways. That means we can write in simple English the sequence of instructions or we can write it in the form of pseudo code. Similarly for solving the same problem we can write several different algorithms. For instance : for searching a number from the given list we can use sequential search or a binary search method. Here *"searching"* is a task and use of either a *"sequential search method"* or *"binary search method"* is an algorithm.
4. **Speed :** The algorithms are written using some specific ideas (which is popularly known as logic of algorithm). But such algorithms should be efficient and should produce the output with fast speed.
5. **Finiteness :** The algorithm should be finite. That means after performing required operations it should terminate.

1.2.2 Issues in Writing an Algorithm

There are various issues in the study of algorithms and those are :

1. How to devise algorithms ?

The creation of an algorithm is a logical activity and one cannot automate it. But there are certain **algorithmic design strategies** and using these strategies one can create many useful algorithms. Hence mastering of such design strategies is an important activity in study of design and analysis of algorithms.

2. How to validate algorithms ?

The next step after creation of algorithms is to validate algorithms. The process of checking whether an algorithm computes the correct answer for all possible legal inputs is called **algorithm validation**. The purpose of validation of algorithm is to find whether algorithm works properly without being dependant upon programming languages. Once validation of algorithm is done a program can be written using corresponding algorithm.

3. How to analyze algorithms ?

Analysis of algorithm is a task of determining how much **computing time** and **storage** is required by an algorithm. Analysis of algorithms is also called **performance analysis**. This analysis is based on mathematics. And a judgment is often needed about better algorithm when two algorithms get compared. The behaviour of algorithm in best case, worst case and average case needs to be obtained.

4. How to test a program ?

After finding an efficient algorithm it is necessary to test that the program written using the efficient algorithm behaves properly or not. Testing of a program is an activity that can be carried out in two phases - **i) debugging** and **ii) performance measuring** (profiling). While debugging a program, it is checked whether program produces faulty results for valid set of input, and if it is found then the program has to be corrected. Thus by debugging thoroughly the program is corrected.

Profiling is a process of measuring time and space required by a corrected program for valid set of inputs.

1.2.3 How to Write an Algorithm ?

Algorithm is basically a sequence of instructions written in simple English language. The algorithm is broadly divided into two sections -

Algorithm heading
It consists of name of algorithm, problem description, input and output.

Algorithm body
It consists of logical body of the algorithm by making use of various programming constructs and assignment statement.

Fig. 1.2.2 Structure of algorithm

Let us understand some rules for writing the algorithm.

1. Algorithm is a procedure consisting of heading and body. The heading consists of keyword **Algorithm** and name of the algorithm and parameter list. The syntax is

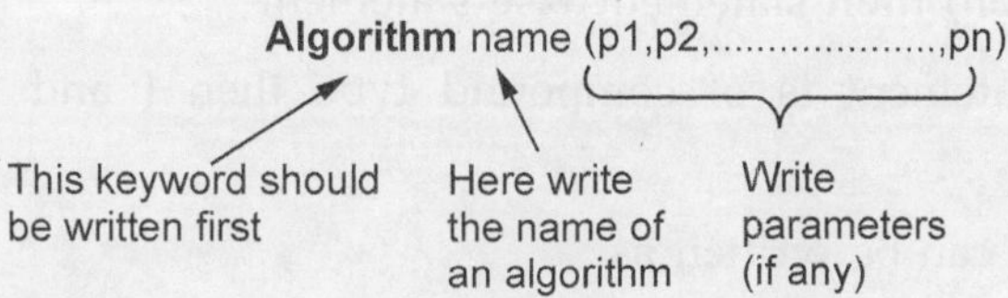

2. Then in the heading section we should write following things :

```
//Problem Description :
//Input :
//Output :
```

3. Then body of an algorithm is written, in which various programming constructs like if, for, while or some assignment statements may be written.
4. The compound statements should be enclosed within { and } brackets.
5. Single line comments are written using // as beginning of comment.
6. The **identifier** should begin by letter and not by digit. An identifier can be a combination of alphanumeric string.

   It is not necessary to write data types explicitly for identifiers. It will be represented by the context itself. Basic data types used are integer, float, char, Boolean and so on. The pointer type is also used to point memory location. The compound data type such as structure or record can also be used.
7. Using assignment operator ← an assignment statement can be given.

   For instance :

```
Variable ← expression
```

8. There are other types of operators such as Boolean operators such as true or false. Logical operators such as **and, or, not**. And relational operators such as <, <=, >, >=, =, ≠

9. The array indices are stored with in square brackets '[' ']'. The index of array usually start at zero. The multidimensional arrays can also be used in algorithm.

10. The inputting and outputting can be done using **read** and **write**.

    For example :

    write("This message will be displayed on console") ;

    read(val) ;

11. The conditional statements such as if-then or if-then-else are written in following form :

    if (condition) **then** statement

    if (condition) **then** statement **else** statement

    If the **if-then** statement is of compound type then { and } should be used for enclosing block.

12. **while** statement can be written as :

```
while (condition) do
{
        statement 1
        statement 2
            :
            :
        statement n
}
```

While the condition is true the block enclosed with { } gets executed otherwise statement after } will be executed.

13. The general form for writing for loop is :

for variable ← $value_1$ **to** $value_n$ **do**

```
{
        statement 1
        statement 2
            :
            :
        statement n
}
```

Here $\textbf{value}_1$ is initialization condition and $\textbf{value}_n$ is a terminating condition.

Sometime a keyword **step** is used to denote increment or decrement the value of variable. **For example :**

```
for i←1 to n step 1        ← Here variable i is incremented
{                            by 1 at each iteration
        Write (i)
}
```

14. The **repeat - until** statement can be written as :

```
repeat
        statement 1
        statement 2
            :
            :
        statement n
until (condition)
```

15. The **break** statement is used to exit from inner loop. The **return** statement is used to return control from one point to another. Generally used while exiting from function.

Note that statements in an algorithm executes in sequential order i.e. in the same order as they appear-one after the other.

Some Examples

Example 1 : Write an algorithm to count the sum of n numbers.

```
Algorithm sum (1, n)
//Problem Description : This algorithm is for finding the
//sum of given n numbers
//Input : 1 to n numbers
//Output : The sum of n numbers
    result ← 0
    for i ← 1 to n do i ← i+1
        result ← result+i
 return result
```

Example 2 : Write an algorithm to check whether given number is even or odd.

```
Algorithm eventest (val)
//Problem Description : This algorithm test whether given
//number is even or odd
//Input : the number to be tested i.e. val
//Output : Appropriate messages indicating even or oddness
if (val%2=0) then
        write ("Given number is even")
else
        write("Given number is odd")
```

Example 3 : Write an algorithm for sorting the elements.

```
Algorithm sort (a,n)
//Problem Description : sorting the elements in ascending order
//Input : An array a in which the elements are stored and n
//is total number of elements in the array
```

```
//Output : The sorted array
for i ← 1 to n do
for j ← i+1 to n – 1 do
{
 if(a[i]>a[j]) then
 {
        temp ← a[i]
        a[i] ← a[j]
        a[j] ← temp
 }
}
write ("List is sorted")
```

Example 4 : Write an algorithm to find factorial of n number.

```
Algorithm fact (n)
//Problem Description : This algorithm finds the factorial
//of given number n
//Input : The number n of which the factorial is to be
//calculated.
//Output : factorial value of given n number.
if(n ← 1) then
        return 1
else
        return n*fact(n – 1)
```

Example 5 : Write an algorithm to perform multiplication of two matrices.

```
Algorithm Mul(A,B,n)
//Problem Description : This algorithm is for computing
//multiplication of two matrices
//Input : The two matrices A,B and order of them as n
//Output : The multiplication result will be in matrix C
for i ← 1 to n do
  for j ← 1 to n do
    C[i,j] ← 0
        for k ← 1 to n do
      C[i,j] ← C[i,j]+A[i,k]B[k,j]
```

Example for Practice

Example 1.2.1 : *Design recursive algorithm for computing* 2^n *for non-negative integer using the formula* $2^n = 2^{n-1} + 2^{n-1}$

Review Questions

1. *What is an algorithm ? Explain various properties of an algorithm.* **GTU : Dec.-10, Marks 3**
2. *Define the term - algorithm.* **GTU : Winter-15, Marks 2**

1.3 Designing of an Algorithm

GTU : May-12, Marks 6

In computer science, developing an algorithm is an art or a skill. And we can have mastery on algorithm development process only when we follow certain method. Before actual implementation of the program, designing an algorithm is very important step.

Suppose, if we want to build a house we do not directly start constructing the house. Instead we consult an architect, we put our ideas and suggestions, accordingly he draws a plan of the house, and he discusses it with us. If we have some suggestion, the architect notes it down and makes the necessary changes accordingly in the plan. This process continues till we are happy. Finally the blue print of house gets ready. Once design process is over actual construction activity starts. Now it becomes very easy and systematic for construction of desired house. In this example, you will find that all designing is just a paper work and at that instance if we want some changes to be done then those can be easily carried out on the paper. After a satisfactory design the construction activities start. Same is a program development process.

If we could follow same kind of approach while designing and analyzing the algorithm then we can have successful implementation for complex problems also. Let us list the **"What are the steps that need to be followed ?"** while designing an algorithm.

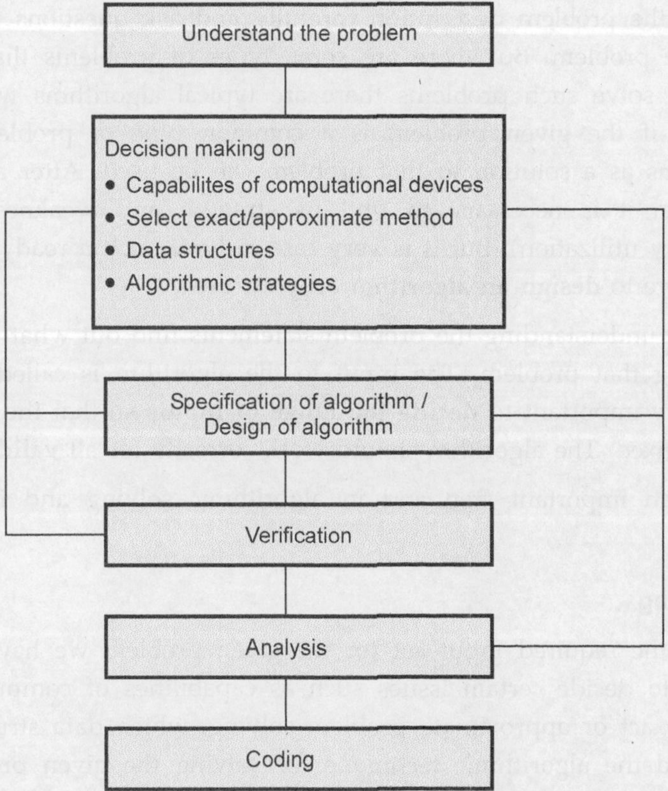

Fig. 1.3.1 Algorithm design steps

These steps are -

1. Understanding the problem.
2. Decision making on,
   a. Capabilities of computational devices
   b. Choice for either exact or approximate problem solving method.
   c. Data structures.
   d. Algorithmic strategies.
3. Specification of algorithm.
4. Algorithmic verification.
5. Analysis of algorithm.
6. Implementation or coding of algorithm.

Let us now discuss each step in detail

1. Understanding the problem

This is the very first step in designing of algorithm. In this step first of all you need to **understand the problem** statement completely. While understanding the problem statements, read the problem description carefully and ask questions for clarifying the doubts about the problem. But there are some types of problems that are commonly occurring and to solve such problems there are typical algorithms which are already available. Hence if the given problem is a common type of problem, then already existing algorithms as a solution to that problem can be used. After applying such an existing algorithm it is necessary to find its strength and weakness (For example, efficiency, memory utilization). But it is very rare to have such a ready-made algorithm. Normally you have to **design an algorithm on your own**.

After carefully understanding the problem statements find out what are the necessary inputs for solving that problem. The input to the algorithm is called **instance** of the problem. It is very important to **decide the range of inputs** so that the boundary values of algorithm get fixed. The algorithm should work correctly for all **valid inputs**.

This step is an important step and in algorithmic solving and it should not be skipped at all.

2. Decision making

After finding the required input set for the given problem we have to analyze the input and need to decide certain issues such as capabilities of computational devices, whether to use exact or approximate problem solving, which data structures has to be used, and to find the algorithmic technique for solving the given problem. This step serves as a base for the actual design of algorithm.

a. Capabilities of computational devices

It is necessary to know the computational capabilities of devices on which the algorithm will be running. Globally we can classify an algorithm from execution point of view as **sequential algorithm** and **parallel algorithm**. The sequential algorithm specifically runs on the machine in which the instructions are executed one after another. Such a machine is called as Random Access Machine (RAM). And the parallel algorithms are run on the machine in which the instructions are executed in parallel.

There are certain complex problems which require huge amount of memory or the problems for which execution time is an important factor. For solving such problems it is essential to have proper choice of a **computational device** which is **space and time efficient**.

b. Choice for either exact or approximate problem solving method

The next important decision is to decide whether the problem is to be solved exactly or approximately. If the problem needs to be solved correctly then we need **exact algorithm**. Otherwise if the problem is so complex that we won't get the exact solution then in that situation we need to choose **approximation algorithm.** The typical example of approximation algorithm is travelling Salesperson Problem.

c. Data structures

Data structure and algorithm work together and these are interdependent. Hence choice of proper data structure is required before designing the actual algorithm. The implementation of algorithm (program) is possible with the help of algorithm and data structure.

d. Algorithmic strategies

Algorithmic strategies is a general approach by which many problems can be solved algorithmically. These problems may belong to different areas of computing. Algorithmic strategies are also called as algorithmic techniques or algorithmic paradigm.

Algorithm Design Techniques -

- *Brute force :* This is straightforward technique with naive approach.
- *Divide-and-conquer* : The problem is divided into smaller instances.
- *Dynamic programming :* The results of smaller, reoccurring instances are obtained to solve the problem.
- *Greedy technique :* To solve the problem locally optimal decisions are made.
- *Back tracking :* This method is based on the trial and error. If we want to solve some problem then desired solution is chosen from the finite set S.

In this subject, we will discuss these algorithmic strategies and see how to solve certain problems using these strategies. Various algorithmic strategies are classified according the design idea that the particular algorithm adopts. And if using certain design idea the particular problem is getting solved then that problem belongs to corresponding algorithmic strategy.

3. Specification of algorithm

There are various ways by which we can specify an algorithm

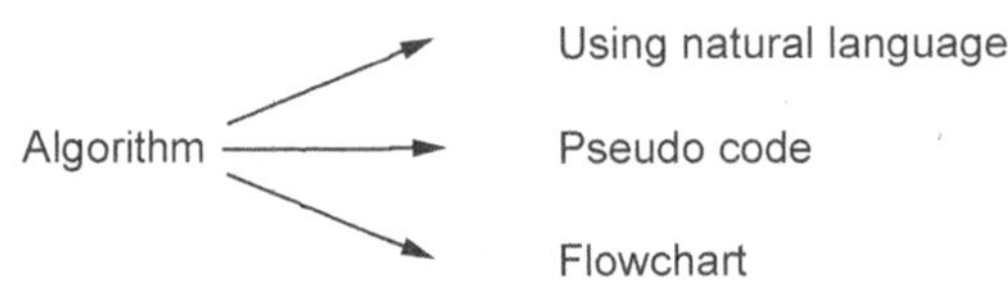

It is very simple to specify an algorithm using **natural language**. But many times specification of algorithm by using natural language is not clear, and there by we get brief specification.

For example : *write an algorithm to perform addition of two numbers.*

Step 1 : Read the first number say a.

Step 2 : Read the second number say b.

Step 3 : Add the two numbers and store the result in a variable c.

Step 4 : Display the result.

Such a specification creates difficulty while actually implementing it. Hence many programmers prefer to have specification of algorithm by means of **pseudo code**.

Pseudo code is nothing but a combination of natural language and programming language constructs. A pseudo code is usually more precise than a natural language.

For example : *Write an algorithm for performing addition of two numbers.*

```
Algorithm sum(a,b)
//Problem Description This algorithm performs addition of
//two integers
//Input : two integers a and b
//Output : addition of two integers
c ← a+b
write (c)
```

This specification is more useful from implementation point of view.

Another way of representing the algorithm is by **flowchart.** Flowchart is a graphical representation of an algorithm. Typical symbols used in flowchart are -

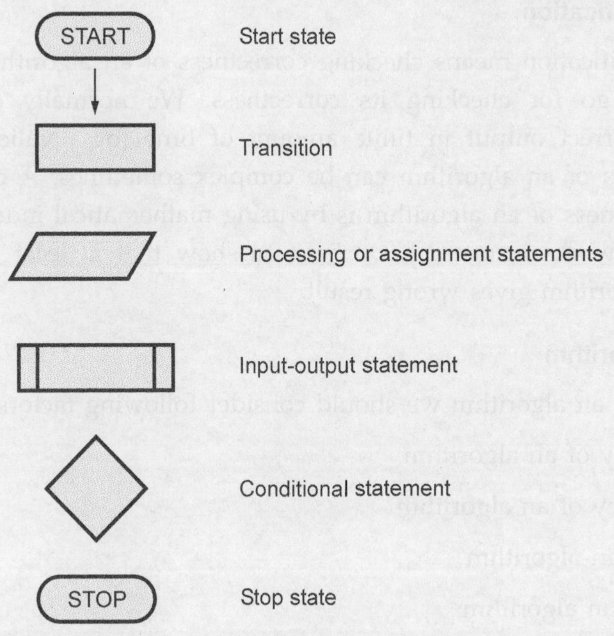
START
Start state
Transition
Processing or assignment statements
Input-output statement
Conditional statement
STOP
Stop state

For example

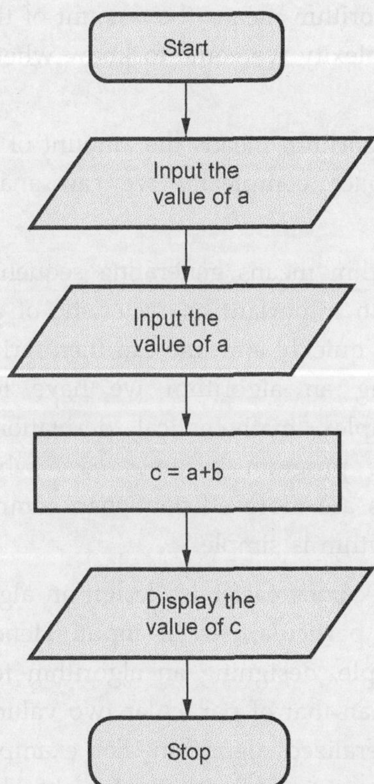
Start
Input the
value of a
Input the
value of a
c = a+b
Display the
value of c
Stop

4. Algorithmic verification

Algorithmic verification means checking correctness of an algorithm. After specifying an algorithm we go for checking its correctness. We normally check whether the algorithm gives correct output in finite amount of time for a valid set of input. The proof of correctness of an algorithm can be complex sometimes. A common method of proving the correctness of an algorithm is by using mathematical induction. But to show that an algorithm works incorrectly we have to show that at least for one instance of valid input the algorithm gives wrong result.

5. Analysis of algorithm

While analyzing an algorithm we should consider following factors -

- Time efficiency of an algorithm
- Space efficiency of an algorithm
- Simplicity of an algorithm
- Generality of an algorithm
- Range of input.

Time complexity of an algorithm means the amount of time taken by an algorithm to run. By computing time complexity we come to know whether the algorithm is slow or fast.

Space complexity of an algorithm means the amount of space (memory) taken by an algorithm. By computing space complexity we can analyze whether an algorithm requires more or less space.

Simplicity is of an algorithm means generating sequence of instructions which are easy to understand. This is an important characteristic of an algorithm because simple algorithms can be understood quickly and one can then write simpler programs for such algorithms. While simplifying an algorithm we have to compute any predefined computations or some complex mathematical derivation. Finding out bugs from algorithms or debugging the program becomes easy when an algorithm is simple. Sometimes simpler algorithms are more efficient than complex algorithms. But it is not always possible that the algorithm is simple.

Generality sometimes it becomes easier to design an algorithm in more general way rather than designing it for particular set of input. Hence we should write general algorithms always. For example, designing an algorithm for finding GCD of any two numbers is more appealing than that of particular two values. But sometimes it is not at all required to design a generalized algorithm. For example, an algorithm for finding roots of quadratic equations can not be designed to handle a polynomial of arbitrary degree.

Range of inputs comes in picture when we execute an algorithm. The design of an algorithm should be such that it should handle the range of input which is the most natural to corresponding problem.

Analysis of algorithm means checking the characteristics such as : time complexity, space complexity, simplicity, generality and range of input. If these factors are not satisfactory then we must redesign the algorithm.

6. Implementation of algorithm

The implementation of an algorithm is done by suitable programming language. For example, if an algorithm consists of objects and related methods then it will be better to implement such algorithm using some object oriented programming language like C++ or JAVA. While writing a program for given algorithm it is essential to write an optimized code. This will reduce the burden on compiler.

Example 1.3.1 *Define an algorithm. What features does one look for in a good computer algorithm ? When an algorithm is said to be correct ? When an algorithm is said to efficient ? Can an abstract algorithm be directly implemented ? If yes, how ? If not, what is its use ?*

GTU : May-12, Marks 6

Solution : Algorithm and its features : Refer section 1.2 and 1.2.1.

Correctness and efficiency : Refer section 1.3(4) and 1.3(5).

An abstract algorithm can not be implemented directly. This kind of algorithm gives the abstract view of what is to be implemented. It does not specify how to do the things. Hence abstract algorithm is only useful for knowing the structure of the implementation, and not the actual implementation.

Review Questions

1. *What are the steps that need to be followed while designing an algorithm ?*
2. *What do you understand by the term algorithmic strategies ? Name some commonly used strategies.*
3. *Explain the concept of pseudo code with some example.*
4. *Define the terms - i) Time complexity and ii) Space complexity.*

1.4 Mathematics for Algorithmic Sets

Set is defined as collection of objects. These objects are called **elements of the set**. All the elements are enclosed within curly brackets '{' and '}' and every element is separated by commas. If 'a' is an element of set A then we say that $a \in A$ and if 'a' is not an element of A then we say that $a \notin A$.

Typically set is denoted by a **capital letter**. The set can be represented using three methods.

1) Listing method

The elements are listed in the set.

For example : A set of element which are less than 5. Then,

$$A = \{0, 1, 2, 3, 4\}$$

2) Describing properties

The properties of elements of a set define the set.

For example : A set of vowels. Hence here vowel is a property of the set which defines the set as :

$$A = \{a, e, i, o, u\}$$

3) Recursion method

The recursion occurs to define the elements of the set.

For example : $A = \{ x \mid x \text{ is square of } n\}$ where $n \leq 10$.

This defines the set as :

$$A = \{0, 1, 4, 9, 16, \ldots\ldots\ldots 100\}$$

Subset : The subset A is called subset of set B if every element of set A is present in set B but reverse is not true. It is denoted by $A \subseteq B$. For example $A = \{1, 2, 3\}$ and $B = \{1, 2, 3, 4, 5\}$ then $A \subseteq B$.

Empty set : The set having no element in it is called empty set. It is denoted by $A = \{ \}$ and it can be written as ϕ(phi).

Null string : The null element is denoted by ε or $\wedge$ character. Null element means no value character. But ε does mean ϕ.

Power set : The power set is a set of all the subsets of its elements.

For example : $A = \{1, 2, 3\}$

Then power set : $Q = \{\phi, \{1\}, \{2\}, \{3\}, \{1,2\}, \{1,3\}, \{3,2\}, \{2,3\}, \{1,2,3\}\}$

The number of elements are always equal to 2^n where n is number of elements in original set. As in set A there are 3 elements. Therefore in power set Q there are $2^3 = 8$ elements.

Equal set : The two sets are said to be equal (A = B) if $A \subseteq B$ and $B \subseteq A$ i.e. every element of set A is an element of B and every element of B is an element of A.

For example :

A = {1, 2, 3} and B = {1, 2, 3} then A = B.

|A| denotes the length of set A. i.e. number of elements in set A.

For example : If

$$A = \{1, 2, 3, 4, 5\} \quad \text{then}$$

$$|A| = 5$$

1.4.1 Operations on Set

Various operations that can be carried out on set are -

i) Union ii) Intersection

iii) Difference iv) Complement.

i) $A \cup B$ is union operation - If

$$A = \{1, 2, 3\} \quad B = \{1, 2, 4\} \quad \text{then}$$

$A \cup B$ = {1, 2, 3, 4} i.e. combination of both the sets.

ii) $A \cap B$ is intersection operation - If

$$A = \{1, 2, 3\} \quad \text{and} \quad B = \{2, 3, 4\} \quad \text{then}$$

$A \cap B$ = {2, 3} i.e. collection of common elements from both the sets.

iii) A – B is the difference operation - If

$$A = \{1, 2, 3\} \quad \text{and} \quad B = \{2, 3, 4\} \quad \text{then}$$

A – B = {1} i.e. elements which are there in set A but not in set B.

iv) $\overline{A}$ is a complement operation - If

$\overline{A}$ = U – A where U is a universal set.

For example :

If $U = \{10, 20, 30, 40, 50\}$

$A = \{10, 20\}$

then $\overline{A} = U - A$

$= \{30, 40, 50\}$

1.4.2 Cartesian Product of Two Sets

The cartesian product of two sets A and B is a set of all possible ordered pairs whose first component is member of A and whose second component is member of B. The cartesian product is denoted by A × B.

$$\therefore \quad A \times B = \{\{a, b\} \mid a \in A \text{ and } b \in B\}$$

For example : Let A = {a, b} and B = {0, 1, 2}

then the cartesian product of A and B is,

$$A \times B = \{(a, 0), \ (a, 1), \ (a, 2), \ (b, 0), \ (b, 1), \ (b, 2)\}$$

1.4.3 Cardinality of Sets

The cardinality of the set is nothing but the number of members in the set.

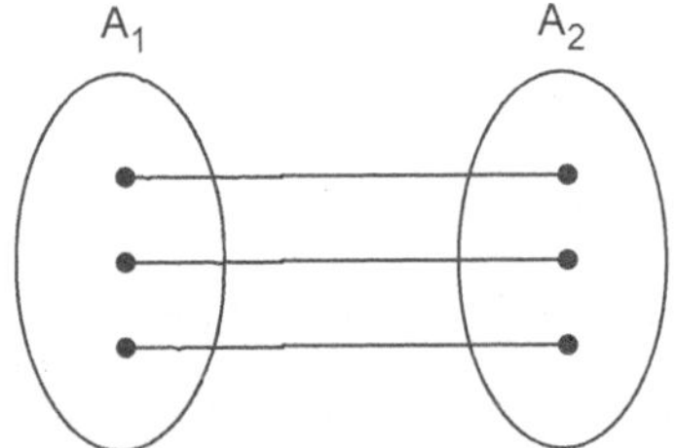

Fig. 1.4.1 Cardinality of two sets

These sets A_1 and A_2 have the same cardinality as there is one to one mapping of the elements of A_1 and A_2. The different cardinalities of set can be - one to one, one to many, many to one, many to many.

1.4.4 Sequence

The sequence means ordering of the elements of the set in some specific manner. For instance : {0, 2, 4, 6, 8} is a sequence which denotes the even numbers.

1.4.5 Tuple

An ordered pair of n elements is called tuple.

For example :

{10, 20} is a 2-tuple of pair

{10, 20, 30} is 3-tuple.

Review Questions

1. *Define the terms - i) Subset ii) Empty set iii) Power set iv) Tuple.*
2. *Explain four operations that can be performed on set.*
3. *What is cardinality of set ?*

1.5 Functions and Relations

GTU : Dec.-11, May-11, Winter-15, Marks 3

1.5.1 Functions

Function can be defined as the relationship between two sets. That means using function we can map one element of one set to some other element of another set. A function is a relation but a relation is not necessarily a function.

A function can be denoted using a letter f. If $f(x) = x^3$ then we say that f of x equals to x cube, then we can have,

$$f(2) = 8$$
$$f(5) = 125$$
$$f(-1) = -1$$

and so on.

1.5.1.1 Basic Terminologies

IF D is a set then we can define function as,

$$f(D) = \{ f(x) \mid x \in D \}$$

If we map some element to some other element then it can be denoted as ,

$$f : D \rightarrow R \quad \text{i.e.} \quad x \rightarrow x^3$$

If set D consists of all the real number then

D = {1, 2, ... } is a **domain**.

The functions are denoted in terms of its mappings.

For example Let, D = {1, 2, 3, 4} and $f(x) = x^3$.

Then the range of f will be R = { f (1), f (2), f (3), f (4) }

= { 1, 8, 27, 64 }

If we take Cartesian product of D and R then we obtain

F = { (1, 1), (2, 8), (3, 27), (4, 64) }

Thus a function can be represented using Cartesian product of its domain and range.

Example 1.5.1 *Find the domain and range of the following relation. Is this relation a function* $\{(2, 9), (3, 14), (4, 21)\}$

Solution : In above given set a relationship between certain x's and y's is a relation. Hence all the x values denote the domain and all the y values denote range. Therefore -

Domain : { 2, 3, 4 }

Range : { 9, 14, 21 }

We can observe the x and y pair to get the relationship. Note that, if x = 2 then $y = x^2 + 5 = (2)^2 + 5 = 9$. This holds true for all the x and y pair in given set. Hence we can define a relation as a function as $f(x) = x^2 + 5$.

Example 1.5.2 *Determine the domain of the given function :*

$$y = \frac{x^2+x-5}{x^2+3x-10}$$

Solution : Here domain means all the values of x that are allowed to take. For this function, the only care that has to be taken is that, the function should not produce divide by zero error. If the denominator equals to zero, then divide by zero error will occur, hence

$$x^2+3x-10 = 0$$

$$(x+5)\ (x-2) = 0$$

$$\therefore \quad x = -5 \quad \text{or} \quad x = 2$$

Hence **domain will be all those values of x that are not equal to – 5 or 2.**

- **Quantifiers :**

Quantifiers - In predicate logic the quantifier is a kind of operator which is used to determine the quantity.

There are two types of quantifiers -

Universal quantifier and **extential quantifier.**

Universal Quantifier - Any quantifier that starts with "$\forall$" is **universal quantifier.** $\forall x$ means **for all x.** This quantifier is used as a prefix to a predicate.

For example : $\forall x Bx$ means for all x, Bx.

For example : "All girls are intelligent" could be transformed into the propositional form as $\forall x\ B(x)$ where

- B (x) is the predicate denoting x is intelligent.
- The universe of discourse is only populated by girls.

Extential Quantifier - Any quantifier that starts with "$\exists$" is an **extential quantifier.**

$\exists x$ means **there exists an x such that ...**

This quantifier is used as a prefix to a predicate.

For example : " Some cars are red in color" could be transformed into the proportional form an $\exists x\, B(x)$ where

- B (x) is the predicate denoting x is red in colour
- The universe of discourse is populated by cars of various colours.

1.5.2 Relations

Relationship is a major aspect between two objects, even this is true in our real life. One object can be related with the other object by a 'mother of' relation. Then those two objects form a pair based on this certain relationship.

Definition : The relation R is a collection for the set S which represents the pair of elements.

For example : (*a*, b) is in R. We can represent their relation as ***a* R b**. The first component of each pair is chosen from a set called domain and second component of each pair is chosen from a set called range.

Properties of Relations

A relation R on set S is,

1. Reflexive if iRi for all i in S.
2. Irreflexive if iRi is false for all i in S.
3. Transitive if iRj and jRk imply iRk.
4. Symmetric if iRj implies jRi.
5. Asymmetric if iRj implies that jRi is false.

Every asymmetric relation must be irreflexive.

For example : If A = { *a*, b } then

Reflexive relation R can be = { (*a*, *a*), (b, b) }

Irreflexive relation R can be = { (*a*, b) }

Transitive relation R can be = { (*a*, b), (b, *a*), (*a*, *a*) }

Symmetric relation R can be = { (*a*, b), (b, *a*) }

Asymmetric relation R can be = { (*a*, b) }

Equivalent Relation

A relation is said to be equivalence relation if it is **reflexive, symmetric and transitive**, over some set S.

Suppose R is a set of relations and S is the set of elements.

For example : S is the set of lines in a plane and R is the relation of lines intersecting to each other.

Example 1.5.3 *Determine whether R is equivalence relation or not where*

$$A = \{0, 1, 2\}, \; R = \{(0, 0), (1, 0), (1, 1), (2, 2), (2, 1)\}$$

Solution : The R is reflexive because (0, 0), (1, 1), (2, 2) $\in$ R.

Where as R is not symmetric because (0, 1) is not in R whereas (1, 0) is in R.

Hence the R is not a equivalence relation.

Closures of Relations

Sometimes when the relation R is given, it may not be reflexive or transitive.

By adding some pairs we make the relation as reflexive or transitive.

For example : Let { (a, b), (b, c), (a, a), (b, b) }

Now this relation is not transitive because (a, b), (b, c) is there in relation R but (a, c) is not there in R so we can make the transitive closure as

{ (a, a), (b, b), (a, b), (b, c), (a, c) }

We can even define reflexive closure and symmetric closure in the same way.

Review Questions

1. *What is relation ? Explain equivalence relation.* **GTU : Dec.-11, Marks 3**
2. *Explain the term quantifiers.* **GTU : May-11, Winter-15, Marks 2**
3. *Explain the concept of domain and range.*
4. *Give various properties of relations.*

1.6 Vectors

A vector A is a collection of n tuples.

For example $A = (a_1, a_2, a_3, \ldots\ldots, a_n)$

where a_i are called the **components** of A.

Equal vectors :

If there exists two vectors namely, A and B and if both the vector contain same number of components and if corresponding components are equal then vector A = B. i.e. vector A and B are equal.

Zero vector :

Let $A = (a_1, a_2, a_3, \ldots, a_n)$ be a vector and if $a_i = 0$ then vector A is called **Zero vector.**

Addition of two vectors :

For addition of two vectors, the number of components in both the vectores must be the same. The sum A + B is a vector obtained by adding corresponding components from A and B.

$$A + B = (a_1, a_2, \ldots, a_n) + (b_1, b_2, b_3 \ldots, b_n)$$

$$= (a_1 + b_2, a_2 + b_2, a_3 + b_3, \ldots, a_n + b_n)$$

Multiplication of vector by scalar :

By multiplying each component of vector by a scalar the product is obtained.

Let k be a scalar then the product can be

$$k \cdot A = k(a_1, a_2, \ldots a_n)$$

$$= k_{a_1}, k_{a_2} \ldots k_{a_n}$$

Similarly, $-A = (-1)A$ and $A - B = A + (-B)$

Also, $k(A + B) = kA + kB$ where A and B are vectors.

Dot product :

The dot product or inner product of vectors $A = (a_1, a_2, a_3 \ldots, a_n)$ and $B = (b_1, b_2, b_3 \ldots, b_n)$ is denoted by A·B. It can be defined as follows -

$$A \cdot B = a_1 b_1 + a_2 b_2 + a_3 b_3 + \ldots + a_n b_n$$

Length of a vector :

A length or norm of the vector, A is denoted by || A ||. It is

$$|| A || = \frac{\sqrt{A \cdot A}}{\sqrt{a_1^2 + a_2^2 + \ldots + a_n^2}}$$

1.7 Matrices

In mathematics, an **array** is rectangular representation of numbers.

For Example :

$$A = \begin{bmatrix} 11 & 12 & 13 \\ 8 & 7 & 5 \\ 15 & 20 & 25 \end{bmatrix}$$

Alternate representation is with the help of parenthesis instead of box brackets.

$$A = \begin{pmatrix} 11 & 12 & 13 \\ 8 & 7 & 5 \\ 15 & 20 & 25 \end{pmatrix}$$

The horizontal lines in a matrix are called **rows** and vertical lines are called **columns.** The number in the matrix are called **entries** or **elements** of matrix.

The **size** of the matrix can be specified with m rows and n columns. It is denoted as **m × n** or **m-by-n**, where m and n are called its dimensions.

Row vector and column vector

A matrix with one row is called **row vector** and matrix with one column is called **column vector**.

$$\begin{bmatrix} 10 & 20 & 30 \end{bmatrix} \qquad \begin{bmatrix} 11 \\ 12 \\ 13 \end{bmatrix}$$

Row vector

Column vector

1.7.1 Basic Terminologies

1) Zero Matrix :

A zero matrix is a matrix with all its entries being zero.

For example : $0_{2,2} = \begin{bmatrix} 0 & 0 \\ 0 & 0 \end{bmatrix}$

2) Identify Matrix :

The identity matrix or unit matrix of size n is a square matrix having one's on the main diagonal, and zero's elsewhere.

The identity matrix is denoted by I.

For example :

$$I_1 = [1],\ I_2 = \begin{bmatrix} 1 & 0 \\ 0 & 1 \end{bmatrix},\ I_3 = \begin{bmatrix} 1 & 0 & 0 \\ 0 & 1 & 0 \\ 0 & 0 & 1 \end{bmatrix}$$

If we multiply any matrix A by unit matrix then the resultant matrix is the same matrix A.

3) Square Matrix :

If the number of rows and number of columns of any matrix are same then we say that the matrix is square matrix.

1.7.2 Operations on Matrix

Various operations that can be performed on matrix are -

1. Addition 2. Multiplication 3. Transpose

1) Addition of two matrices

Let, A and B are the two matrices of same size. Then the addition of these two matrices will be addition of each corresponding element.

For example :

$$A = \begin{bmatrix} a_{11} & a_{12} & a_{13} \\ a_{21} & a_{22} & a_{23} \\ a_{31} & a_{32} & a_{33} \end{bmatrix}$$

$$B = \begin{bmatrix} b_{11} & b_{12} & b_{13} \\ b_{21} & b_{22} & b_{23} \\ b_{31} & b_{32} & b_{33} \end{bmatrix}$$

$$A + B = \begin{bmatrix} a_{11}+b_{11} & a_{12}+b_{12} & a_{13}+b_{13} \\ a_{21}+b_{21} & a_{22}+b_{22} & a_{23}+b_{23} \\ a_{31}+b_{31} & a_{32}+b_{32} & a_{33}+b_{33} \end{bmatrix}$$

2) Multiplication of two matrices

For multiplication of two matrices, width of first matrix equals to height of second matrix. That means a matrix A with $\mathbf{m \times n}$ can be multiplied with matrix B having $\mathbf{n \times p}$ size. Then the size of resultant matrix is $\mathbf{m \times p}$.

For example :

$$A = \begin{bmatrix} 1 & 2 \\ 3 & 4 \\ 5 & 6 \end{bmatrix}_{3\times2}$$

$$B = \begin{bmatrix} 10 & 11 & 12 \\ 13 & 14 & 15 \end{bmatrix}_{2\times3}$$

The multiplication $A \times B$ can be done by multiplying a row by a column.

$$A \times B = \begin{bmatrix} 1*10+2*13 & 1*11+2*14 & 1*12+2*15 \\ 3*10+4*13 & 3*11+4*14 & 3*12+4*15 \\ 5*10+6*13 & 5*11+6*14 & 5*12+6*15 \end{bmatrix}$$

$$A \times B = \begin{bmatrix} 36 & 39 & 42 \\ 82 & 89 & 96 \\ 128 & 139 & 150 \end{bmatrix}$$

Note that the size of resultant matrix is $3\times \boxed{2\times 2} \times 3 = \mathbf{3\times 3}$

Properties of matrix multiplication

Let, A, B and C are the matrices and k is the scalar then,

1. $A(B + C) = AB + AC$
2. $(B + C)A = BA + CA$
3. $(AB)C = A(BC)$
4. $k(AB) = A(kB)$

3) Transpose of matrix

The transpose of matrix A is obtained by interchanging row and column. The transposed matrix is denoted by A^T. If matrix A is of size $m \times n$ then A^T is $n \times m$.

For example :

$$\text{If} \quad A = \begin{bmatrix} 10 & 20 \\ 30 & 40 \\ 50 & 60 \end{bmatrix} \quad \text{then,}$$

$$A^T = \begin{bmatrix} 10 & 30 & 50 \\ 20 & 40 & 60 \end{bmatrix}$$

1.7.3 Determinant of Matrix

The determinant of matrix A is a specific number. It is denoted by $|A|$.

- The determinant of order one matrix is

$$|a_{11}| = a_{11}$$

- The determinant of order two matrix is

$$\begin{vmatrix} a_{11} & a_{12} \\ a_{21} & a_{22} \end{vmatrix} = a_{11}a_{22} - a_{12}a_{21}$$

- The determinant of order three matrix is

$$\begin{vmatrix} a_{11} & a_{12} & a_{13} \\ a_{21} & a_{22} & a_{23} \\ a_{31} & a_{32} & a_{33} \end{vmatrix}$$

$$= a_{11}(a_{22}a_{33} - a_{23}a_{32}) - a_{12}(a_{21}a_{33} - a_{23}a_{31}) + a_{13}(a_{21}a_{32} - a_{22}a_{31})$$

Following is an important property of determinant function

For any two n square matrices A and B

det (AB) = det (A) · det (B)"

Review Question

1. *Explain the method of obtaining the determinant of matrix.*

1.8 Linear Inequalities

In mathematics, linear inequality is a statement containing <, >, <= or >=

For example : $x+y > 14$ is a linear inequality.

1.8.1 Solution to Linear Inequality

The solution of linear inequality is based on number of variables.

The solution to one variable inequality :

$3x+7 \leq 10$, the value of x gives true statement. For instance : $x = 1$ is a solution to the above given inequality.

The solution to two variable inequality :

$3x+7y - 5 \leq 17$, the value of x and y should be such that the statement remains true. The solution to above inequality is (2, 2) because $3(2)+7(2)-5 = 15 \leq 17$.

The solution to three variable inequality :

$3x+2y - 7z \leq 5$, the value of x, y and z should be such that the statement remains true. The solution to above inequality is (2, 2, 1). because $3(2)+2(2)-7(1) = 3 \leq 5$.

Key Point *Solution of an inequality is a solution that satisfies the inequality.*

1.8.2 Properties of Inequalities

1. If $x \leq y$ and $y \leq z$ then $x \leq z$.

2. If $x \leq y$ and c is some positive number then $x + c \leq y + c$.
3. If $x \leq y$ and c is negative, then $xc \geq yc$.
4. If $x \leq y$ and c is some positive, then $x + c \leq y + c$.

1.9 Linear Equations

GTU : Dec.-11, Marks 4

The linear equation is an equation containing n unknowns. A linear equation with one unknown can be given in standard form :

$$ax = b$$

Where x is unknown and a and b are constants. The solution of such equation will be,

$$x = \frac{b}{a}$$

The linear equation with two unknowns can be given in standard form as

$$ax + by = c.$$

Where x, y are unknowns and a, b and c are constants.

Example 1.9.1 *Solve $2x + 8 = 20$ for x.*

Solution :

$$2x + 8 = 20 \quad \text{(Subtract 8 from both sides)}$$

$$2x + 8 - 8 = 20 - 8$$

$$\therefore \quad 2x = 12$$

$$\frac{2x}{2} = \frac{12}{2}$$

$$\mathbf{x = 6}$$

Example 1.9.2 *If a number is increased by 9, the result is 25. Find the number.*

Solution : Assume that m be that number then we can write linear equation as -

$$m + 9 = 25 \quad \text{(subtract 9 from both sides)}$$

$$m + 9 - 9 = 25 - 9$$

$$m = 16$$

Hence the number is **16**.

1.9.1 Two Linear Equations with Two Unknowns

The two linear equations with two unknowns is in following standard form :

$$a_1 x + b_1 y = c_1$$

$$a_2 x + b_2 y = c_2$$

To solve such linear equations in order to obtain solution to unknowns, we will consider following **algorithm -**

Step 1 : Multiply the two equation by any two numbers such that resulting coefficients of at least one term will be negative of each other.

Step 2 : Perform additions of two equations.

For example :

$$5x + 10y = 15 \quad (1.9.1)$$

$$3x + 2y = 5 \quad (1.9.2)$$

Multiply equation (1.9.1) by (1.9.3) and equation (1.9.2) by − 5

$$15x + 30y = 45 \quad (1.9.3)$$

$$-15x - 10y = -25 \quad (1.9.4)$$

Perform addition of equations (1.9.3) and (1.9.4),

$$20y = 20$$

$$y = 1.$$

Now put y = 1 in equation (1.9.2), we will get,

$$3(x) + 2(1) = 5$$

$$3x = 3$$

$$x = 1$$

Thus we get a solution x = 1, y = 1 which is the unique solution.

1.9.2 Gauss Elimination Method

Gaussian elimination method is a method of solving linear system Ax = b by bringing augmented matrix, to an upper triangular form and then obtaining a solution by backward substitution method.

Example 1.9.3 *Solve the linear equation by Gauss elimination method.*

$$b + c = 2$$

$$2a + 3c = 15$$

$$a + b + c = 3$$

Solution : We will write augmented matrix as :

$$\begin{bmatrix} 0 & 1 & 1 & 2 \\ 2 & 0 & 3 & 15 \\ 1 & 1 & 1 & 3 \end{bmatrix}$$

Step 1 : Now interchange 1st and 2nd equation.

$$\begin{array}{rcl} 2a + 3c & = & 15 \\ b + c & = & 2 \\ a + b + c & = & 3 \end{array} \Rightarrow \begin{bmatrix} 2 & 0 & 3 & 15 \\ 0 & 1 & 1 & 2 \\ 1 & 1 & 1 & 3 \end{bmatrix}$$

Step 2 : Divide first equation by 2.

$$\begin{array}{rcl} a + \frac{3}{2}c & = & \frac{15}{2} \\ b + c & = & 2 \\ a + b + c & = & 3 \end{array} \Rightarrow \begin{bmatrix} 1 & 0 & \frac{3}{2} & \frac{15}{2} \\ 0 & 1 & 1 & 2 \\ 1 & 1 & 1 & 3 \end{bmatrix}$$

Step 3 : Multiply first equation by -1 and add it to third equation.

$$\begin{array}{rrcl} & -a - \frac{3}{2}c & = & \frac{-15}{2} \\ + & a + b + c & = & 3 \\ \hline & b - \frac{1}{2}c & = & \frac{-9}{2} \end{array}$$

is the third equation

To summerize

$$\begin{array}{rcl} a + \frac{3}{2}c & = & \frac{15}{2} \\ b + c & = & 2 \\ b - \frac{1}{2}c & = & \frac{-9}{2} \end{array} \Rightarrow \begin{bmatrix} 1 & 0 & \frac{3}{2} & \frac{15}{2} \\ 0 & 1 & 1 & 2 \\ 0 & 1 & \frac{-1}{2} & \frac{-9}{2} \end{bmatrix}$$

Step 4 : Multiply 2nd equation by -1 and add it to 3rd equation.

$$\begin{array}{rcl} a + \frac{3}{2}c & = & \frac{15}{2} \\ b + c & = & 2 \\ b - \frac{3}{2}c & = & \frac{-13}{2} \end{array} \Rightarrow \begin{bmatrix} 1 & 0 & \frac{3}{2} & \frac{15}{2} \\ 0 & 1 & 1 & 2 \\ 0 & 0 & \frac{-3}{2} & \frac{-13}{2} \end{bmatrix}$$

Step 5 : Multiply 3rd equation by $\frac{-2}{3}$

$$\begin{aligned} a+\frac{3}{2}c &= \frac{15}{2} \\ b+c &= 2 \\ c &= \frac{13}{3} \end{aligned} \Rightarrow \begin{bmatrix} 1 & 0 & \frac{3}{2} & \frac{15}{2} \\ 0 & 1 & 1 & 2 \\ 0 & 0 & 1 & \frac{13}{2} \end{bmatrix}$$

Step 6 : The 3rd equation gives $c = \frac{13}{3}$, if we substitute this value in 2nd equation then

$$b + \frac{13}{3} = 2$$

$$\therefore \quad b = 2 - \frac{13}{3}$$

$$b = \frac{-7}{3}$$

Now if we put value of $c = \frac{13}{3}$ in 1st equation then

$$a + \frac{3}{2}c = \frac{15}{2}$$

$$a + \frac{3}{2}\left(\frac{13}{3}\right) = \frac{15}{2}$$

$$a + \frac{13}{2} = \frac{15}{2}$$

$$\mathbf{a = 1}$$

Thus we get the solution for linear equations as $a = 1$, $b = \frac{-7}{3}$ and $c = \frac{13}{3}$

Review Questions

1. *Explain linear inequality and equations.* **GTU : Dec.-11, Marks 4**
2. *Explain the solution to linear in equality.*
3. *Explain the Guass elimination method with an illustrative example.*

1.10 University Questions with Answers

(Regulation 2008)

Dec.-2010

Q.1 *What is an algorithm ? Explain various properties of an algorithm.* **[Refer section 1.2]** [3]

May 2011

Q.2 *Explain the term quantifiers.* **[Refer section 1.5]** [2]

Dec. 2011

Q.3 *What is relation ? Explain equivalence relation.* **[Refer section 1.5]** [3]

(Regulation 2013)

Winter 2015

Q.4 *Define the term - Algorithm.* **[Refer section 1.2]** [2]

Q.5 *Explain the term quantifiers.* **[Refer section 1.5]** [2]

1.11 Short Questions and Answers

Q.1 Define the term algorithm.

Ans. : The algorithm is defined as a collection of unambiguous instructions occurring in some specific sequence and such an algorithm should produce output for given set of input in finite amount of time.

Q.2 Specify any two desirable properties of algorithm.

Ans. : 1. Non ambiguity 2. Finiteness

Q.3 What is algorithmic strategy?

Ans. : Algorithmic strategies is a general approach by which many problems can be solved algorithmically. These problems may belong to different areas of computing. Algorithmic strategies are also called as algorithmic techniques or algorithmic paradigm.

Q.4 Name five algorithm design techniques.

Ans. : 1. Brute Force 2. Divide and Conquer 3. Dynamic Programming 4. Greedy Technique 5. Backtracking.

Q.5 What is pseudo code?

Ans. : Pseudo code is a method of specifying an algorithm. It is basically a combination of natural language and programming construct.

Q.6 What are three ways of representing a set?

Ans. :

1. **Listing Method :** In this method the elements are listed in the set.
2. **Describing Properties :** In this method the properties of elements of a set are specified.

3. Recursion Method : The recursion occurs to define the elements of the set.

Q.7 List out various operations on the set.

Ans. : 1. Union 2. Intersection 3. Difference 4. Complement

Q.8 What is cardinality of set?

Ans. : The cardinality of set is nothing but the number of members in the set. The cardinality can be one to one, one to many, many to many.

Q.9 List out various properties of relations.

Ans. : Various properties of relations are - 1. Reflexive 2. Irreflexive 3. Transitive 4. Symmetric 5. Asymmetric

Q.10 What is Equivalent relation ?

Ans. : A relation is said to be equivalent relation if it is reflexive, symmetric and transitive.

Q.11 What is vector ?

Ans. : A vector A is a collection of n tuples.

For example A = (a1,a2,a3,...,an)

where ai are called the components of A.

Q.12 What is row vector and column vector ?

Ans. : A matrix with one row is called row vector and matrix with one column is called column vector.

[10 20 30] is a row vector.

$$\begin{bmatrix} 10 \\ 20 \\ 30 \end{bmatrix}$$

is called column vector.

Q.13 What is identity matrix ?

Ans. : The identity matrix or unit matrix of size n is a square matrix having one on main diagonal and zeros elsewhere.

Q.14 What is linear inequality ?

Ans. : In mathematics, linear inequality is a statement containing <, >, <=,>=. For example x+y>14 is a linear inequality.

Q.15 What is solution to linear in-equality ?

Ans. : The solution of an inequality is a solution that satisfies inequality.

Q.16 Give example of solution to linear in-equality.

Ans. : 3x+7y–5<=17, the value of x and y should be such that the statement remains true. The solution to above inequality is (2, 2) because 3(2)+7(2)–5=15<=17.

Q.17 What is linear equation ?

Ans. : Linear equation is an equation containing n unknowns.

Q.18 Specify the form of linear equation with one unknown.

Ans. : The standard form of linear equation with one unknown is

ax=b

Q.19 What is Gauss elimination method ?

Ans. : Gaussian elimination method is a method of solving linear system Ax=b by bringing augmented matrix, to an upper triangular form and then obtaining a solution by backward substitution method.

Q.20 Solve 5x+15=50 for x.

Ans. : 5x+15–15=50–15

5x=35

x=7

❑❑❑

2 Analysis of Algorithms

Syllabus

The efficient algorithm, Average, Best and worst case analysis, Amortized analysis, Asymptotic notations, Analyzing control statement, Loop invariant and the correctness of the algorithm, Sorting algorithms and analysis : Bubble sort, Selection sort, Insertion sort, Shell sort, Heap sort, Sorting in linear time : Bucket sort, Radix sort and counting sort.

Contents

2.1 The Efficiency of Algorithm

GTU : Winter-12, Marks 7

The efficiency of algorithm can be specified using **time efficiency** and **space efficiency** which is known as time complexity and space complexity

Time complexity of an algorithm means the amount of time taken by an algorithm to run.

Space complexity of an algorithm means amount of space(memory) taken by an algorithm

Importance of Efficiency Analysis

Performing efficiency analysis is important for these following two reasons -

1. By computing the time complexity we come to know whether algorithm is slow or fast.
2. By computing the space complexity we can analyze whether an algorithm requires more or less space.

Concept of Frequency Count

The time complexity of an algorithm can be computed using the frequency count.

Definition : The frequency count is a count that denotes how many times particular statement is executed.

Consider following code for counting the frequency count

```
void fun()
{
  int a;
  a=10;
  printf("%d",a);
}
```

```
void fun()
{
  int a;
  a=10; ..............................................Executes once
  printf("%d",a); ....................................Execute Once
}
```

The frequency count of above program is **2.**

Example 2.1.1 *Obtain the frequency count for the following code.*

```
void fun()
{
  int a;
  a=0;
```

```
 for(i=0;i<n;i++)
  {
     a  = a+i;
  }
  printf("%d",a); }
```

Solution :

```
void fun()
{
 int a;
 a=0; ..............................................1
 for(i=0;i<n;i++) ..................................n+1
  {
     a  = a+i; .....................................n
  }
  printf("%d",a); ..................................1
}
```

The frequency count of above code is **2n + 3**.

The for loop in above given fragment of code is executed n times when the condition is true and one more time when the condition becomes false. Hence for the for loop the frequency count is n + 1. The statement inside the for loop will be executed only when the condition inside the for loop is true. Therefore this statement will be executed for n times. The last printf statement will be executed for once.

Example 2.1.2 *Obtain the frequency count for the following code.*

OR

*Using Step count method analyze the time complexity when two m*n matrices are added.*

GTU : Winter-14, Marks 7

```
void fun(int a[][],int b[][])
{
 int c[3][3];
  for(i=0;i<m;i++)
  {
   for(j=0;j<n;j++)
   {
     c[i][j]=a[i][j]+b[i][j];
   }        }
```

Solution :

```
void fun(int a[][],int b[][])
{
 int c[3][3];
  for(i=0;i<m;i++) ...................................m+1
  {
   for(j=0;j<n;j++) ..................................m(n+1)
   {
```

```
    c[i][j]=a[i][j]+b[i][j]; ..........................m.n
  }
}
```

The frequency count = (m + 1) + m(n + 1) + mn = 2m + 2mn + 1 = **2m(1 + n) + 1**

Example 2.1.3 *Obtain the frequency count for the following code.*

```
for(i=1;i<=n;i++)
{
for(j=1;j<=n;j++)
{
c[i][j]=0;
for(k=1;k<=n;k++)
c[i][j]=c[i][j]+a[i][k]*b[k][j];
}
}
```

Dec.-2012

Solution :

Statement	Frequency Count
for(i=1;i<=n;i++)	n + 1
for(j=1;j<=n;j++)	n.(n + 1)
c[i][j]=0;	n.(n)
for(k=1;k<=n;k++)	n.n(n + 1)
c[i][j]=c[i][j]+a[i][k]*b[k][j];	n.n.n
Total	$\mathbf{2n^3 + 3n^2 + 2n + 1}$

After counting the frequency count, the constant terms can be neglected and only the order of magnitude is considered. The time complexity is denoted in terms of algorithmic notations. The Big oh notation is a most commonly used algorithmic notation. For the above frequency count all the constant terms are neglected and only the order of magnitude of the polynomial is considered. Hence the time complexity for the above code can be $O(n^3)$. The higher order is the polynomial is always considered.

Example 2.1.4 *Obtain the frequency count for the following code*

```
i=1;
do
{
a++;
 if(i==5)
break;
i++;
 }while(i<=n)
```

Solution :

Statement	Frequency Count
i=1;	1
a++;	5
if(i==5)	5
break;	1
i++;	5
while(i<=n)	5
Total	**22**

Example 2.1.5 *What is space complexity ? How algorithms can be analyzed in terms of space complexity ? Will it depend on type of instance (input) or will change ?*

GTU : Summer -14, Marks 4

Solution : The space complexity can be defined as amount of memory required by an algorithm to run.

To compute the space complexity we use two factors : **Constant and instance characteristics**. The space requirement S(p) can be given as,

$$S(p) = C + Sp$$

where **C** is a constant i.e. fixed part and it denotes the space of inputs and outputs. This space is an amount of space taken by instruction, variables and identifiers. And **Sp** is a space dependent upon instance characteristics. This is a variable part whose space requirement depends on particular problem instance. Thus space complexity is dependant upon the type of input.

Consider an example of algorithm to compute the space complexity.

```
Algorithm Sum(a,n)
{
    s : = 0.0 ;
        For i : = 1 to n do
            s : = s + a[i] ;
    return s
}
```

In the given code we require space for

```
s : = 0          ←    O(1)
For i : = 1 to n    ←    O(n)
```

```
s : = s + a[i] ;   ←   O(n)
returns ;   ←   O(1)
```

Hence the space complexity of given algorithm can be denoted in terms of big-oh notation. It is **O(n).**

Review Question

1. *Explain why analysis of algorithms is important ?* **GTU : Winter-12, Marks 7**

2.2 Average and Worst Case Analysis

GTU : Dec.-10, May-12, Marks 4

If an algorithm takes minimum amount of time to run to completion for a specific set of input then it is called **best case** time complexity.

For example : While searching a particular element by using sequential search we get the desired element at first place itself then it is called best case time complexity.

If an algorithm takes maximum amount of time to run to completion for a specific set of input then it is called **worst case** time complexity.

For example : While searching an element by using linear searching method if desired element is placed at the end of the list then we get worst time complexity.

The time complexity that we get for certain set of inputs is as a average same. Then for corresponding input such a time complexity is called **average case** time complexity.

Consider the following algorithm

```
Algorithm Seq_search(X[0 ... n – 1 ],key)
// Problem Description : This algorithm is for searching the
//key element from an array X[0...n – 1] sequentially.
//Input : An array X[0...n – 1] and search key
//Output : Returns the index of X where key value is present
for i ← 0 to n – 1 do
 if(X[i]=key)then
  return i
```

Best case time complexity

Best case time complexity is a time complexity when an algorithm runs for short time. In above searching algorithm the element **key** is searched from the list of **n** elements. If the **key** element is present at first location in the list(X[0...n–1]) then algorithm runs for a very short time and thereby we will get the best case time complexity. We can denote the best case time complexity as

$$C_{best} = 1$$

Worst case time complexity

Worst case time complexity is a time complexity when algorithm runs for a longest time. In above searching algorithm the element **key** is searched from the list of **n** elements. If the **key** element is present at n^{th} location then clearly the algorithm will run for longest time and thereby we will get the worst case time complexity. We can denote the worst case time complexity as

$$C_{worst} = n$$

The algorithm guarantees that for any instance of input which is of size n, the running time will not exceed $C_{worst}(n)$. Hence the worst case time complexity gives important information about the efficiency of algorithm.

Average case time complexity

This type of complexity gives information about the behaviour of an algorithm on specific or random input. Let us understand some terminologies that are required for computing average case time complexity.

Let the algorithm is for sequential search and

P be a probability of getting successful search.

n is the total number of elements in the list.

The first match of the element will occur at i^{th} location. Hence probability of occurring first match is P/n for every i^{th} element.

The probability of getting unsuccessful search is (1 – P).

Now, we can find average case time complexity $C_{avg}(n)$ as -

$$C_{avg}(n) = \text{Probability of successful search (for elements 1 to n in the list)} + \text{Probability of unsuccessful search}$$

$$C_{avg}(n) = \left[1 \cdot \frac{P}{n} + 2 \cdot \frac{P}{n} + \ldots + i \cdot \frac{P}{n}\right] + n \cdot (1-P)$$

$$= \frac{P}{n}[1+2+\ldots+i\ldots n] + n(1-P)$$

There may be n elements at which chances of 'not getting element' are possible.

$$= \frac{P}{n} \frac{n(n+1)}{2} + n(1-P)$$

$$C_{avg}(n) = \frac{P(n+1)}{2} + n(1-P)$$

Thus we can obtain the general formula for computing average case time complexity.

Suppose if P = 0 that means there is no successful search i.e. we have scanned the entire list of n elements and still we do not found the desired element in the list then in such a situation,

$$C_{avg}(n) = 0(n + 1)/2 + n(1 - 0)$$

$$C_{avg}(n) = n$$

Thus the average case running time complexity becomes equal to n.

Suppose if P = 1 i.e. we get a successful search then

$$C_{avg}(n) = 1(n + 1)/2 + n(1 - 1)$$

$$C_{avg}(n) = (n + 1)/2$$

That means the algorithm scans about half of the elements from the list.

For calculating average case time complexity we have to consider probability of getting success of the operation. And any operation in the algorithm is heavily dependent on input elements. Thus computing average case time complexity is difficult than computing worst case and best case time complexities.

Review Questions

1. *What is an algorithm ? Explain various properties of an algorithm.* **GTU : Dec.-10, Marks 3**
2. *Explain why analysis of algorithms is important ? Explain worst case, best case and average case Complexity.* **GTU : May-12, Marks 4**
3. *Explain : Worst case, best case and average case complexity.* **GTU : Winter- 12, Marks 7**

2.3 Elementary Operations

Elementary operations are those operations whose execution time is bounded by a constant which depends upon the type of implementation used. The elementary operations are **addition, multiplication and assignment.**

Let, for implementing an algorithm requires some elementary operations such as addition, multiplication and assignment.

Let,

a be the number of additions

b be the number of multiplications

c be the number of assignments

t1 be the total amount of time required by addition operations

t2 be the total amount of time required by multiplication operations

t3 be the total amount of time required by assignment operations

The total time required by the algorithm to execute can be expressed as,

$$t \le at1 + bt2 + ct3 \quad \text{or}$$

$$t \le \max\{t1, t2, t3\} \times \{a + b + c\}$$

Thus **t** is bounded by a constant multiple of time taken by elementary operations to execute.

Example

```
Algorithm SUM(n)
{
    //Problem Description: This algorithm calculates the sum of integers from 1 to n
    //Input: Integer values from 1 to n
    //Output: returns the sum value
    sum ← 0
    for (i ← 1 to n ) do
        sum ← sum+i
    return sum;
}
```

In above algorithm the elementary operation is **addition**. If a machine of 32-bit words is used to execute above algorithm, then all the additions can be executed directly provided n with no greater than 65535. Theoretically we consider that the additions costs for **n units.**

2.4 Asymptotic Notations

GTU : May-11,12, Dec.-10,11, Summer-13,14, Winter-14,15, Marks 6

To choose the best algorithm, we need to check efficiency of each algorithm. The efficiency can be measured by computing time complexity of each algorithm. Asymptotic notation is a shorthand way to represent the time complexity.

Using asymptotic notations we can give time complexity as "fastest possible", "slowest possible" or "average time".

Various notations such as Ω, Θ and O used are called **asymptotic notions.**

2.4.1 Big oh Notation

The **Big oh** notation is denoted by 'O'. It is a method of representing the **upper bound of** algorithm's running time. Using big oh notation we can give longest amount of time taken by the algorithm to complete.

Definition

Let f(n) and g(n) be two non-negative functions.

Let n_0 and constant c are two integers such that n_0 denotes some value of input and $n > n_0$. Similarly c is some constant such that $c > 0$. We can write

$$f(n) \le c * g(n)$$

then f(n) is big oh of g(n). It is also denoted as $f(n) \in O(g(n))$. In other words f(n) is less than g(n) if g(n) is multiple of some constant c.

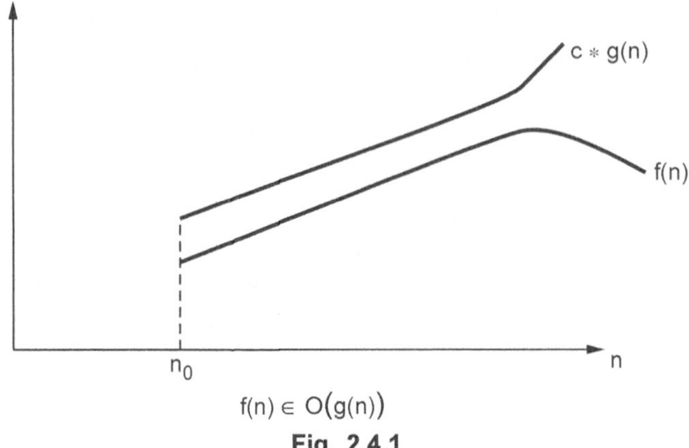

$f(n) \in O(g(n))$

Fig. 2.4.1

Example : Consider function f(n) = 2n + 2 and $g(n) = n^2$. Then we have to find some constant c, so that $f(n) \leq c * g(n)$. As f(n) = 2n + 2 and $g(n) = n^2$ then we find c for

n = 1 then,

$$f(n) = 2n + 2$$

$$= 2(1) + 2$$

$$f(n) = 4$$

and $g(n) = n^2$

$$= (1)^2$$

$$g(n) = 1$$

i.e. $f(n) > g(n)$

If n = 2 then,

$$f(n) = 2(2) + 2$$

$$= 6$$

$$g(n) = (2)^2$$

$$g(n) = 4$$

i.e. $f(n) > g(n)$

If n = 3 then,

$$f(n) = 2(3) + 2$$

$$= 8$$

$$g(n) = (3)^2$$

$$g(n) = 9$$

i.e. $f(n) < g(n)$ is true.

Hence we can conclude that for $n > 2$, we obtain

$$f(n) < g(n)$$

Thus always upper bound of existing time is obtained by big oh notation.

2.4.2 Omega Notation

Omega notation is denoted by 'Ω'. This notation is used to represent the **lower bound** of algorithm's running time. Using omega notation we can denote shortest amount of time taken by algorithm.

Definition

A function f(n) is said to be in Ω (g(n)) if f(n) is bounded below by some positive constant multiple of g(n) such that

$$f(n) \geq c * g(n) \qquad \text{For all } n \geq n_0$$

It is denoted as $f(n) \in \Omega\ (g(n))$. Following graph illustrates the curve for Ω notation.

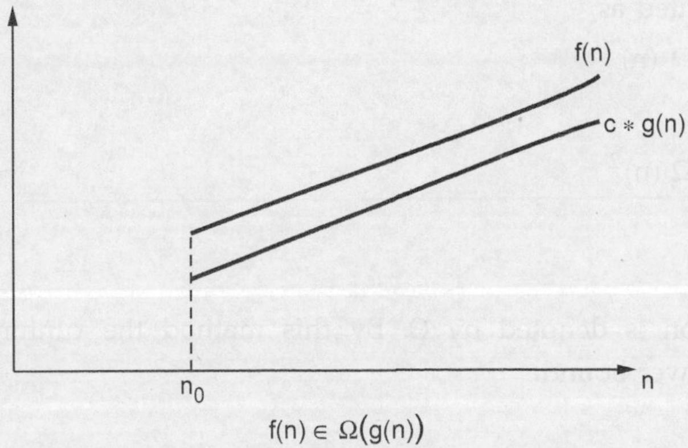

Fig. 2.4.2

Example :

Consider $f(n) = 2n^2 + 5$ and $g(n) = 7n$

Then if $n = 0$

$$f(n) = 2(0)^2 + 5$$

$$= 5$$

$$g(n) = 7\ (0)$$

$$= 0 \qquad \text{i.e. } f(n) > g(n)$$

But if $n = 1$

$$f(n) = 2(1)^2 + 5$$

$$= 7$$

$$g(n) = 7(1)$$

$$7 \text{ i.e. } f(n) = g(n)$$

If $n = 3$ then,

$$f(n) = 2(3)^2 + 5$$

$$= 18 + 5$$

$$= 23$$

$$g(n) = 7(3)$$

$$= 21$$

i.e. $f(n) > g(n)$

Thus for $n > 3$ we get $f(n) > c * g(n)$.

It can be represented as,

$$2n^2 + 5 \in \Omega\ (n)$$

Similarly any

$$n^3 \in \Omega\ (n)^2$$

2.4.3 Θ Notation

The theta notation is denoted by Θ. By this method the running time is between upper bound and lower bound.

Definition

Let f(n) and g(n) be two non negative functions. There are two positive constants namely c_1 and c_2 such that,

$$c_1 * g(n) \leq f(n) \leq c_2 * g(n)$$

Then we can say that,

$f(n) \in \Theta(g(n))$

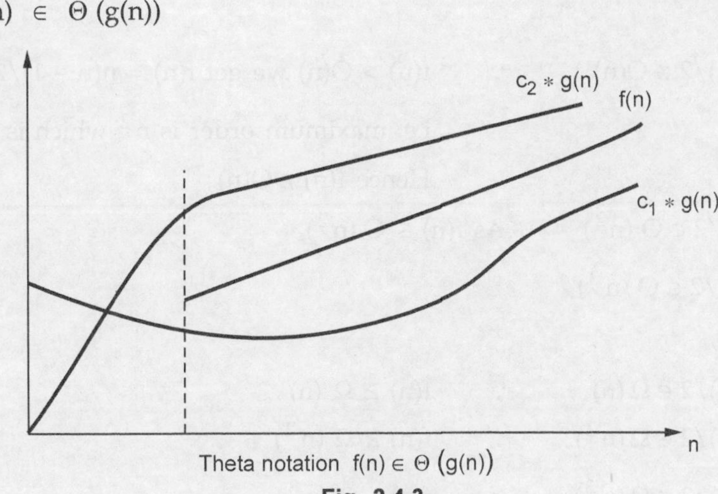

Fig. 2.4.3

Example :

If $f(n) = 2n + 8$ and $g(n) = 7n$.

where $n \geq 2$

Similarly $f(n) = 2n + 8$

$g(n) = 7n$

i.e. $5n < 2n + 8 < 7n$ For $n \geq 2$

Here $c_1 = 5$ and $c_2 = 7$ with $n_0 = 2$.

The theta notation is more precise with both big oh and omega notation.

Some examples of asymptotic order

1) $\log_2 n$ is f(n) then

$\log_2 n \in O(n)$ $\because$ $\log_2 n \leq O(n)$, the order of growth of $\log_2 n$ is slower than n.

$\log_2 n \in O(n^2)$ $\because$ $\log_2 n \leq O(n^2)$, the order of growth of $\log_2 n$ is slower than n^2 as well.

But

$\log_2 n \notin \Omega(n)$ $\because$ $\log_2 n \leq \Omega(n)$ and if a certain function f(n) is belonging to $\Omega(n)$ it should satisfy the condition $f(n) \geq c * g(n)$.

Similarly $\log_2 n \notin \Omega(n^2)$ or $\Omega(n^3)$

2) Let $f(n) = n(n-1)/2$

Then,

$n(n-1)/2 \notin O(n)$ $\because$ $f(n) > O(n)$ we get $f(n) = n(n-1)/2 = \frac{n^2 - 1}{2}$

i.e. maximum order is n^2 which is $> O(n)$.

Hence $f(n) \notin O(n)$

But $n(n-1)/2 \in O(n^2)$ As $f(n) \leq O(n^2)$

and $n(n-1)/2 \in O(n^3)$

Similarly,

$n(n-1)/2 \in \Omega(n)$ $\because$ $f(n) \geq \Omega(n)$

$n(n-1)/2 \in \Omega(n^2)$ $\because$ $f(n) \geq \Omega(n^2)$

$n(n-1)/2 \notin \Omega(n^3)$ $\because$ $f(n) > \Omega(n^3)$

2.4.4 Properties of Order of Growth

1. If $f_1(n)$ is order of $g_1(n)$ and $f_2(n)$ is order of $g_2(n)$, then

   $f_1(n) + f_2(n) \in O(\max(g_1(n), g_2(n)))$.
2. Polynomials of degree $m \in \Theta(n^m)$.

   That means maximum degree is considered from the polynomial.

   For example : $a_1n^3 + a_2n^2 + a_3n + c$ has the order of growth $\Theta(n^3)$.
3. $O(1) < O(\log n) < O(n) < O(n^2) < O(2^n)$.
4. Exponential functions a^n have different orders of growth for different values of a.

Key Points *i) O(g(n)) is a class of functions f(n) that grows less fast than g(n), that means f(n) possess the time complexity which is always lesser than the time complexities that g(n) have.*

ii) Θ (g(n)) is a class of functions' f(n) that grows at same rate as g(n).

iii) Ω(g(n)) is a class of functions f(n) that grows faster than or atleast as fast as g(n). That means f(n) is greater than $\Omega(g(n))$.

2.4.5 Order of Growth

Measuring the performance of an algorithm in relation with the input size n is called **order of growth**. For example, the order of growth for varying input size of n is as given below.

n	log n	n log n	n^2	2^n
1	0	0	1	2
2	1	2	4	4
4	2	8	16	16
8	3	24	64	256
16	4	64	256	65,536
32	5	160	1024	4,294,967,296

Table 2.4.1 Order of growth

We will plot the graph for these values.

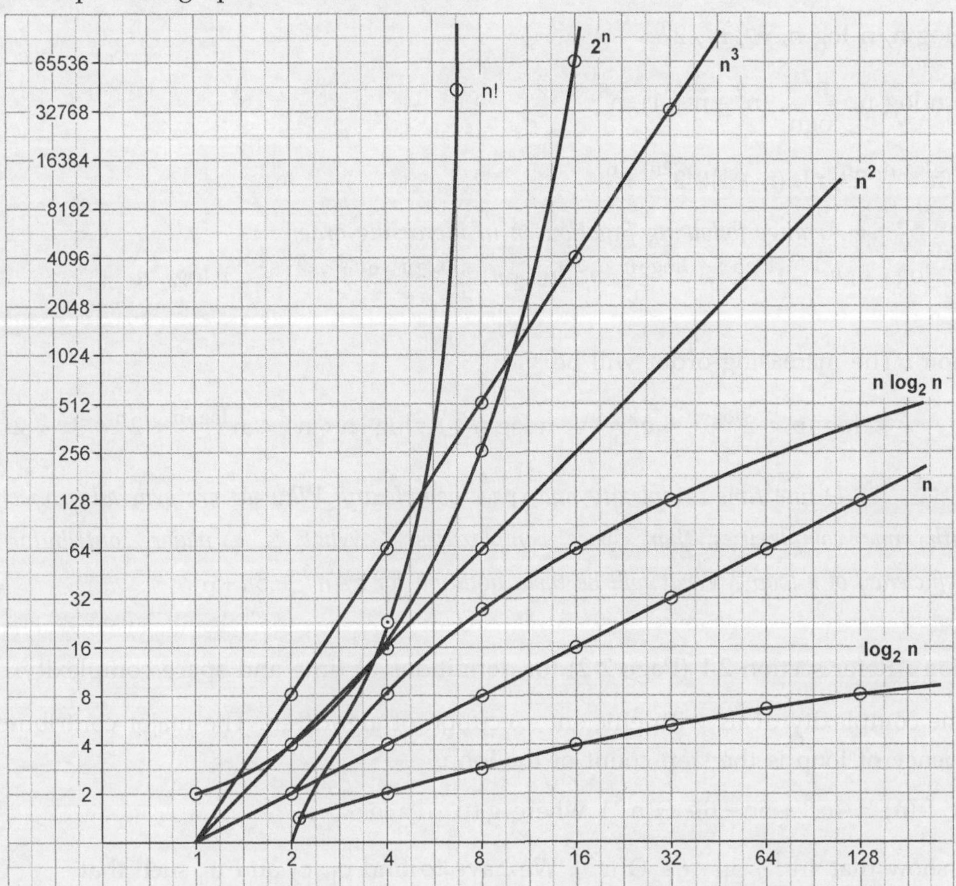

Fig. 2.4.4 Rate of growth of common computing time function

From the above drawn graph it is clear that the logarithmic function is the slowest growing function. And the exponential function 2^n is fastest and grows rapidly with varying input size n. The exponential function gives huge values even for small input n. For instance : for the value of n = 16 we get 2^{16} = 65536.

Example 2.4.1 *Arrange following rate of growth in increasing order.*

2^n, $nlogn$, n^2, 1, n, $logn$, $n!$, n^3 **GTU : Dec.-10, Marks 2**

Solution : 1, logn, n, nlogn, n^2, n^3, 2^n, n!

Example 2.4.2 *Reorder the following complexity from smallest to largest*

i) $nlog_2(n)$, $n + n^2 + n^3$, 2^4, $sqrt(n)$

ii) n^2, 2^n, $nlog_2(n)$, $log_2(n)$, n^3

iii) $nlog(n)$, n^8, $n^2/logn$, $(n^2 - n + 1)$

iv) $n!$, 2^n, $(n+1)!$, 2^{2n}, n^n, n^{logn}

Solution :

i) sqrt(n), $n \log_2 n$, $n + n^2 + n^3$, 2^4

ii) $\log n$, $n \log n$, n^2, n^3, 2^n

iii) $n \log n$, $\dfrac{n^2}{\log n}$, $(n^2 - n + 1)$, n^8

iv) $n^{\log n}$, 2^n, $n!$, $(n+1)!$, 2^{2n}, n^n

Example 2.4.3 *Arrange following functions n in increasing order :*

2^n, $\log_2 n$, n^3, $n^{\log 2n}$, $2^{\log 2n}$, $n^2 \log_2 n$, $e^{\log 2n}$, 3^n, 2^{2^n}, $\frac{1}{n}$, $n \log_2 n$

GTU : Summer-14, Marks 4

Solution : The increasing order will be,

$$\frac{1}{n} < \log_2 n < 2^{\log 2n} < e^{\log 2n} < n \log n < n^2 \log_2 n < n^3 < n^{\log 2n} < 2^n < 3^n < 2^{2^n}$$

Example 2.4.4 *Define time complexity and space complexity. Why we are generally concerned with time complexities than space complexities ? What is a major contributor for inefficiency of a loop ? What will be theta notation for :* $4n^3 + 5n + 6$ *?*

GTU : Summer-14, Marks 7

Solution : Refer section 2.1 (Page 2-2) for definitions of time and space complexity.

Time complexity deals with efficient execution of algorithm. The major contributor for inefficiency of loop is the step count of the loop.

Let, $f(n) = 4n^3 + 5n + 6 \in \Theta(n^3)$ where $g(n^3) = n^3$.

To show that $4n^3 + 5n + 6 \in \Theta(n^3)$. We have to find c_1, c_2 and n_0 such that

$0 \le c_1, g(n) \le f(n) \le c_2 g(n)$ for all $n, n \ge n_0$

We can obtain $c_1 = 4$, $c_2 = 15$ for all $n_0 = 1$ and $n \ge 1$.

as $4n^3 \le 4n^3 + 5n + 6 \le 15n^3$

Hence $\mathbf{4n^3 + 5n + 6 \in \Theta(n^3)}$ for all $n \ge 1$

Example 2.4.5 *Explain why the statement "The running time of algorithm A is at least $O(n^2)$" is meaningless. Also explain what is the smallest value of n such that an algorithm whose running time is 100 n^2 runs faster than an algorithm whose running time is 2^n on the same machine ?*

GTU : Summer-14, Marks 7

Solution : The f(n) = O (g(n) when

$$f(n) \leq c * g(n) \text{ for all } n > n_0$$

If we assume T(n) be the running time of algorithm A. The statement given in the problem say $T(n) \geq O(n^2)$.

From this we can not extract information about lower bounds and the statement also says nothing about the upper bound which could be $O(n^3)$, $O(2^n)$ etc. Hence the statement is meaningless.

We have to find smallest value of such that $100n^2 < 2^n$. Consider the values ranging 10, 11, 12, ... 20. The calculations will be,

n	$100n^2$	2^n
10	10^4	10^3 approx.
11	1.21×10^4	2.0×10^3 approx.
⋮		
14	1.96×10^4	1.64×10^4
15	2.25×10^4	3.28×10^4
⋮	⋮	⋮
20	4×10^4	10^6 approx.

At **n = 15**, 2^n exceeds $100n^2$.

2.4.6 Summation Formula and Rules used in Efficiency Analysis

1. $\sum_{i=1}^{n} 1 = 1 + 1 + 1 + \ldots + 1 = n \in \Theta(n)$

2. $\sum_{i=1}^{n} i = 1 + 2 + 3 + \ldots + n = \frac{n(n+1)}{2} \in \Theta(n^2)$

3. $\sum_{i=1}^{n} i^k = 1 + 2^k + 3^k + \ldots + n^k \approx \frac{n^{k+1}}{k+1} \in \Theta(n^{k+1})$

4. $\sum_{i=1}^{n} a^i = 1 + a + ... + a^n = \frac{a^{n+1}-1}{a-1} \in \Theta(a^n)$

5. $\sum_{i=1}^{n} (a_i \pm b_i) = \sum_{i=1}^{n} a_i \pm \sum_{i=1}^{n} b_i$

6. $\sum_{i=1}^{n} ca_i = c\sum_{i=1}^{n} a_i$

7. $\sum_{i=k}^{n} 1 = n - k + 1$ where n and k are some upper and lower limits.

Example 2.4.6 *Let f(n) and g(n) be asymptotically positive functions. Prove or disprove following.*

$f(n) + g(n) = \Theta(\min(f(n), g(n)))$ **GTU : Dec.-11, Marks 4**

Solution : To prove $f(n)+g(n) = \Theta(\min(f(n), g(n)))$

$$c_2 \min(f(n), g(n)) <= f(n) + g(n) <= c_1 \min(f(n), g(n))$$

If $\min(f(n), g(n)) = f(n)$ then

$$c_2 f(n) <= f(n)+g(n) <= c_1 f(n) \text{ where}$$

c_2 is small and c_1 is large.

Example 2.4.7 *Prove that* $(n+b)^b = \Theta(n^b), b > 0$ **GTU : Dec.-11, Marks 4**

Solution : To prove this we have to obtain two constants c_1 and c_2 in such a way that $(n+a)^b = \Omega(n^b)$ and $(n+a) = 0(n^b)$

Step 1 :

Let,

$$(n+b)^b \leq (n+|a|)^b, \quad \text{where } n > 0$$

$$\leq (n+n)^b \quad \text{for } n \geq |a|$$

$$= (2n)^b$$

$$= c_1 \cdot n^b \quad \text{where } c_1 = 2^b$$

$$\therefore \quad (n+a)^b = \Omega(n^b).$$

Step 2 :

$$(n+a)^b \geq (n-|a|)^b, \quad \text{where } n > 0$$

$$\geq (c_2' n)^b \quad \text{for } c_2' = 1/2 \quad \text{where } n \geq 2|a|$$

as $n/2 \leq n - |a|$, for $n \geq 2\ |a|$

$$\therefore \qquad (n+a)^b = 0(n^b)$$

From step 1 and step 2 we get

$c_1 = 2^b$, $c_2 = 2^{-b}$ and $n_0 \geq 2|a|$

Hence

$$(n+a)^b = \Theta(n^b) \quad b>0 \quad \text{is proved.}$$

Example 2.4.8 *Find big oh (O) notation for following :*

1) f (n) = 6993   2) f (n) = 6 n^2 +135. **GTU : Dec.-11, Marks 3**

Solution : $f(n) = O(g(n))$ where

$$f(n) < c * g(n)$$

If $c > 1$ and $g(n) = 6993$.

Then **$f(n) = O(n)$**

2) As $f(n) = 6n^2 + 135$

$$\mathbf{f(n) = O(n^2)}$$

where $c < 6$ and $n <= 2$.

This is because with these values

$$f(n) <= c * g(n)$$

holds true.

Example 2.4.9 *Answer the following,*

i) Find big theta (θ) and big omega (Ω) notation.

*1) f (n) = 14 * 7 + 83   2) f (n) = 83 n^2 + 84n*

ii) Is $2^{n+1} = O(2^n)$? Explain. **GTU : Dec.-11, Marks 7**

Solution : 1) To obtain big omega -

$f(n) = 14 * 7 + 83$ we can write it in polynomial form as

$f(n) = 2n^2 + 11n + 6$ where $n = 7$.

Now if $g(n) = 7(n)$ then

we get $f(n) > 7(n)$ Hence

$$2n^2 + 11n + 6 = \Omega(n)$$

To obtain big theta notation

We have to find out

$c_1 * g(n) \leq f(n) \leq c_2 * g(n).$

If we assume $c_1 = 7$ and $c_2 = 26$ then with n = 7,

$$7n \leq 2n^2 + 11n + 6 \leq 26n \text{ is true}$$

$\therefore$ $f(n) = \Theta(n)$ where n = 7,

$c_1 = 7$ and $c_2 = 26$.

2) $f(n) = 83n^3 + 84n \in \Omega\left(n^2\right)$

If $c_1 * g_1(n) \leq f(n) \leq c_2 * g_2(n)$ then $f(n) \in \theta(g(n))$

$\therefore$ $f(n) = \theta\left(n^3\right)$ where $c_1 = 83$ and $c_2 = 167$ with $n \geq 1$.

ii) $2^{n+1} = O\left(2^n\right)$ is true because

$2^{n+1} = 2.2^n \leq c\, 2^n$, where $c \geq 2$.

Example 2.4.10 *Check equalities (True/False) :*

$5n^2 - 6n \in \Theta(n^2)$

$n! \in O(n^n)$

$2n^2 2^n + n \log n \in \Theta(n^2 2^n)$

$\sum_{i=0}^{n} i^2 \in \Theta(n^3)$

$n^2 \in \Theta(n^3)$

$2^n \in \Theta(2^{n+1})$

$n! \in \Theta((n+1)!)$

GTU : Summer-14, Marks 7

Solution : i) $5n^2 - 6n \in \Theta(n^2)$ True because

$$f(n) = 5n^2 - 6n$$

$$g(n) = n^2$$

And $f(n) = \leq c * g(n)$ is true.

ii) $f(n) = n! = 1*2*3*4*\ldots*n$

$g(n) = n^n = n*n*n*\ldots*n$

$\therefore$ $f(n) \leq c * g(n)$ is true.

Hence $n! \in O(n^n)$ is false.

iii) $f(n) = 2n^2 2^n + n \log n$

$g(n) = n^2 2^n$

If n= 16 then

$f(n) = 2 (16)^2 (2)^{16} + 16 \log 16$

$g(n) = (16)^2 (2)^{16}$

This shows that,

$f(n) \geq c * g(n)$

Hence $2n^2 2^n + n \log n \in \Theta (n^2 2^n)$ is false.

iv) $f(n) = \sum_{i=0}^{n} i^k = 0 + 1 + 2^k + 3^k + \ldots + n^k = \frac{n^{k+1}}{k+1}$

$g(n) = \Theta(n^{k+1})$

$\therefore \sum_{i=0}^{n} i^k \in \Theta(n^{k+1})$ is true.

v) $f(n) = n^2$

$g(n) = n^3$

As $c_1 * g(n) \leq f(n) \leq c_2 * g(n)$ is true.

Hence $n^2 \in \Theta (n^3)$ is true.

vi) $2^n \in \Theta (2^{n+1})$

Let, $2^n = \frac{1}{2} \cdot 2^{n+1}$

$\therefore$ $2^n \leq 2^{n+1}$

Hence $2^n \in \Theta (2^{n+1})$ is true.

vii) $n! \in \Theta(n+1)!$

$n! = 1*2*3 \ldots *n$

$(n+1)! = (n+1) * n * \ldots 2 * 1$

$\therefore$ $n! \in \Theta(n+1)!$ is false.

Example 2.4.11 *Suppose we are comparing implementations of insertion sort and merge sort on the same machine. For input of size n, insertion sort runs in $8n^2$ steps, while merge sort runs in 64n lg n steps. For which values of n does insertion sort beat merge sort ?*

GTU : Summer - 14, Marks 5

Solution : Finding insertion sort beat merge sort means time complexity of insertion sort is less than merge sort.

$$\therefore \quad 8n^2 < 64\, n \lg n$$

$$n < 8 \lg n$$

$$\frac{n}{8} < \lg n$$

$$2^{n/8} < n$$

$$2^{n/8} - n < 0$$

$$\therefore \quad 2 \le n \le 43$$

Example 2.4.12 *Is 3 log n + log log n is O ($\log_{10}$ n) ? Is 3 log n + log log n is Ω ($\log_{10}$n) ?*

GTU : Summer-14, Marks 4

Solution : We assume n = 1000

Consider RHS

$$3 \log_2 n = 3 \log_2 n\ 1000 = 3 * (10 \text{ approx}) \approx 30$$

$$\log \log n = \log_2 (\log_2 1000) = \log_2(10) \approx 3$$

$\therefore$ 3 log n + log log n ≈ 30 + 3 ≈ 33

Consider LHS

$$\log_{10} n = \log_{10} 1000 = 3$$

As $3 \log n + \log \log n > \log_{10} n$

$$3 \log n + \log \log n \in \Omega (\log_{10} n)$$

Examples for Practice

Example 2.4.13 *Interprete the following equations :*

i) $2^n + \Theta(n) = \Theta(n^2)$ *ii)* $2n^2 + 3n + 1 = 2n^2 + \Theta(n)$

Example 2.4.14 *Show that i)* $3n+2 = \theta(n)$, *ii)* $6 * 2^n + n^2 = \theta(2^n)$

Example 2.4.15 : *Determine the asympotic order of the following functions.*

$$i)\ f(n) = 3x^2 + 5 \quad ii)\ f(n) = \sum_{i=1}^{n} i^2 \quad iii)\ f(n) = 5$$

Example 2.4.16 : *Let $f(n) = 100\ n + 5$. Express $f(n)$ using big omega.*

Review Questions

1. *What do you mean by asymptotic notations ? Explain.* **GTU : Dec.-10, Marks 2**
2. *Answer the following : Explain asymptotic analysis of algorithm.* **GTU : Dec.-11, Marks 3**
3. *Define : Big Oh, Big Omega and Big Theta notation.* **GTU : May-12, Winter-15, Marks 3**
4. *Explain different asymptotic notations in brief.* **GTU : June-11, Marks 6**
5. *Explain all asymptotic notations used in algorithm analysis.* **GTU : Summer-13, Winter-14, Marks 6**
6. *Why do we use asymptotic notations in the study of algorithms ? Briefly describe the commonly used asymptotic notations.* **GTU : Summer-14, Marks 6**

2.5 Recurrence Equation

GTU : May-12,Winter-14,15, Marks 7

The recurrence equation is an equation that defines a sequence recursively. It is normally in following form -

$$T(n) = T(n-1) + n \quad \text{for } n > 0 \quad \ldots (1)$$

$$T(0) = 0 \quad \ldots (2)$$

Here equation (1) is called recurrence relation and equation (2) is called initial condition. The recurrence equation can have infinite number of sequences. The **general solution** to the recursive function specifies some formula.

For example : Consider a recurrence relation

$$f(n) = 2f(n-1) + 1 \quad \text{for } n > 1$$

$$f(1) = 1$$

Then by solving this recurrence relation we get $f(n) = 2^n - 1$. When n = 1, 2, 3 and 4.

2.5.1 Solving Recurrence Equations

The recurrence relation can be solved by following methods -

1. Substitution method
2. Master's method.

Let us discuss methods with suitable examples -

Substitution method -

The substitution method is a kind of method in which a guess for the solution is made.

There are two types of substitutions -

- Forward substitution
- Backward substitution.

Forward substitution method - This method makes use of an initial condition in the initial term and value for the next term is generated. This process is continued until some formula is guessed. Thus in this kind of substitution method, we use recurrence equations to generate the few terms.

Example 2.5.1 *Solve a recurrence relation $T(n) = T(n-1) + n$. With initial condition $T(0) = 0$ by forward substitution method.*

Solution : Let,

$$T(n) = T(n-1) + n \quad \text{... (1)}$$

If $n = 1$ then

$$T(1) = T(0) + 1$$

$$= 0 + 1 \quad \because \text{Initial condition}$$

$$\therefore \quad \mathbf{T(1) = 1} \quad \text{... (2)}$$

If $n = 2$, then

$$T(2) = T(1) + 2$$

$$= 1 + 2 \quad \because \text{equation (2)}$$

$$\therefore \quad \mathbf{T(2) = 3} \quad \text{... (3)}$$

If $n = 3$ then

$$T(3) = T(2) + 3$$

$$= 3 + 3 \quad \because \text{equation (3)}$$

$$\therefore \quad \mathbf{T(3) = 6} \quad \text{... (4)}$$

By observing above generated equations we can derive a formula,

$$T(n) = \frac{n(n+1)}{2} = \frac{n^2}{2} + \frac{n}{2}$$

We can also denote T(n) in terms of big oh notation as follows -

$$T(n) = O(n^2)$$

But, in practice, it is difficult to guess the pattern from forward substitution. Hence this method is not very often used.

Backward substitution

In this method backward values are substituted recursively in order to derive some formula.

Example 2.5.2 *Solve, a recurrence relation*

T(n) =T(n − 1) + n ... (5)

With initial condition T(0) = 0 by backward substitution method.

GTU : Winter-15, Marks 7

Solution : $T(n-1) = T(n-1-1) + (n-1)$ ... (6)

Putting equation (6) in equation (5) we get

$$T(n) = T(n-2) + (n-1) + n \quad \text{... (7)}$$

Let

$$T(n-2) = T(n-2-1) + (n-2) \quad \text{... (8)}$$

Putting equation (8) in equation (7) we get.

$$T(n) = T(n-3) + (n-2) + (n-1) + n$$

$$\vdots$$

$$= T(n-k) + (n-k+1) + (n-k+2) + \dots + n$$

if k = n then

$$T(n) = T(0) + 1 + 2 + \dots n$$

$$T(n) = 0 + 1 + 2 + \dots + n \qquad \because T(0) = 0$$

$$T(n) = \frac{n(n+1)}{2} = \frac{n^2}{2} + \frac{n}{2}$$

Again we can denote T(n) in terms of big oh notation as

$$\mathbf{T(n) \in O(n^2)}$$

Some Examples on Recurrence Relation

Example 2.5.3 *Solve the following recurrence relation T(n) = T(n − 1) + 1 with T(0) = 0 as initial condition. Also find big oh notation.*

Solution : Let,

$$T(n) = T(n-1) + 1$$

By backward substitution,

$$T(n-1) = T(n-2) + 1$$

$$\therefore \quad T(n) = T(n-1) + 1$$

$$= (T(n-2) + 1) + 1$$

$$\mathbf{T(n) = T(n-2) + 2}$$

Again $T(n-2) = T(n-2-1) + 1$

$$= T(n-3) + 1$$

$$\therefore \quad T(n) = T(n-2) + 2$$

$$= (T(n-3) + 1) + 2$$

$$T(n) = T(n-3) + 3$$

$$\vdots$$

$$T(n) = T(n-k) + k \qquad \ldots (1)$$

If k = n then equation (1) becomes

$$T(n) = T(0) + n$$
$$= 0 + n$$
$$T(n) = n$$

$\therefore$ We can denote T(n) in terms of big oh notation as

$$\mathbf{T(n) = O(n)}$$

Example 2.5.4 *Solve the following recurrence relations :*

a) $x(n) = x(n-1) + 5$ for $n > 1$, $x(1) = 0$

b) $x(n) = 3x(n-1)$ for $n > 1$, $x(1) = 4$

c) $x(n) = x(n/2) + n$ for $n > 1$, $x(1) = 1$ (Solve for $n = 2^k$)

d) $x(n) = x(n/3) + 1$ for $n > 1$, $x(1) = 1$ (Solve for $n = 3^k$)

Solution : a) Let

$$x(n) = x(n-1) + 5$$

$$= [x(n-2) + 5] + 5$$

$$= [x(n-3) + 5] + 5 + 5 = x(n-3) + 5 * 3$$

$$\ldots$$

$= x(n-i) + 5 * i$

$\ldots$

If $\quad i = n-1$ then

$= x(n-(n-1)) + 5 * (n-1)$

$= x(1) + 5(n-1)$

$= 0 + 5(n-1) \quad \because x(1) = 0$

$\therefore \quad x(n) = 5(n-1)$

b) $\quad x(n) = 3x(n-1)$

$= 3[3x(n-2)] = 3^2 \cdot x(n-2)$

$= 3 \cdot 3[3x(n-3)] = 3^3 \cdot x(n-3)$

$\ldots$

$= 3^i x(n-i)$

If we put i = n – 1 then

$= 3^{(n-1)} x(n-(n-1))$

$= 3^{(n-1)} x(1)$

$x(n) = 3^{(n-1)} \cdot 4 \quad \because x(1) = 4$

c) Put $n = 2^k$, then

$$x(2^k) = x\left[\frac{2^k}{2}\right] + 2^k$$

$x(2^k) = x(2^{k-1}) + 2^k$

$= [x(2^{k-2}) + 2^{k-1}] + 2^k$

$= x(2^{k-3}) + 2^{k-2} + 2^{k-1} + 2^k$

$\ldots$

$= x(2^{k-i}) + 2^{k-i+1} + 2^{k-i+2} + \ldots + 2^k$

$\ldots$

$= x\left(2^{k-k}\right) + 2^1 + 2^2 + \ldots + 2^k$

$= x(2^0) + 2^1 + 2^2 + \ldots + 2^k$

$$= 1+2^1+2^2+\ldots+2^k \quad \because \quad x(1) = 1$$

$$= 2^{k+1}-1$$

$$= 2 \cdot 2^k - 1 \quad \because \quad 2^k = n$$

$\therefore$ $x(2^k) = 2 \cdot n - 1$

d) Let $x(n) = x(n/3) + 1$

Assume $n = 3^k$

$$x(3^k) = x(3^{k-1})+1$$

$$= [x(3^{k-2})+1] + 1 = x3^{k-2}+2$$

$$= [x(3^{k-3})+1] + 2 = x3^{k-3}+3$$

...

$$= x(3^{k-i})+i$$

If we put i = k then,

$$= x(3^{k-k})+k$$

$$= x(1) + k$$

$$= 1 + k \quad \because \quad x(1) = 1$$

$\therefore$ $x(3^k) = 1 + \log_3 n$ $\quad \because \; 3^k = n$ and $\log_3 n = k$

Example 2.5.5 *Prove :* $3n^3+2n^2 = O(n^3)$; $3^n \neq O\left(2^n\right)$.

Solution : The big-Oh notation denotes the upper bound of algorithm's running time. Using big oh notation we can give longest amount of time taken by the algorithm to complete.

Hence we can write

$$F(n) \le c * g(n)$$

Then $F(n) \in O(g(n))$

In short we will find the values of n,c such that

$$F(n) \le c * g(n)$$

remains true

Assume $F(n) = 3n^3 + 2n^2$

$$g(n) = n^3$$

Then for n > = 2 and c = 4 (F(n) ∈ O(g(n)) is true. That is when n = 2 and c = 4

$$F(n) = 3n^3 + 2n^2$$
$$= 3(2)^3 + 2(2)^2$$
$$= 32 \quad \rightarrow \text{L.H.S.}$$
$$g(n) = n^3$$
$$= 8$$
$$c * g(n) = 4 \times 8$$
$$= 32 \quad \rightarrow \text{R.H.S.}$$

L.H.S. = R.H.S. is thus proved.

But when

$$F(n) = 3^n$$

$g(n) = 2^n$ then let us find

$$3^n \leq c * 2^n$$

i.e. $\dfrac{3^n}{2^n} \leq c = \left(\dfrac{3}{2}\right)^n \leq c$

But there is no such value of c which is $\geq \left(\dfrac{3}{2}\right)^n$. Hence $3^n \neq 0(2^n)$. In other words $3^n < c*(2^n)$ Will never be true (However $3^n > 2^n$ always).

Example 2.5.6 *If $T_1(n) = O(f(n))$ and $T_2(n) = O(g(n))$ then show that $T_1(n) + T_2(n) = O(\max(f(n), g(n)))$*

Solution : Let there be some constant c_1 such that

$$T_1(n) \leq c_1 g_1(n) \quad \text{for } n \geq n_1 \quad \text{... (1)}$$

Similarly there will be some constant c_2

Such that

$$T_2(n) \leq c_2 g_2(n) \quad \text{for } n \geq n_2 \quad \text{... (2)}$$

Let $c_3 = \max\{c_1, c_2\}$ such that $n \geq \max\{n_1, n_2\}$

Then we can write using equations (1) and (2) as :

$$T_1(n) + T_2(n) \leq c_1 g_1(n) + c_2 g_2(n)$$

$$\leq (c_1 + c_2)(g_1(n) + g_2(n))$$

$$\leq c_3 (g_1(n) + g_2(n))$$

$$\leq c_3 \, 2 \max (g_1(n) + g_2(n))$$

Hence

$T_1(n) + T_2(n) \in O(\max(g_1(n) + g_2(n))$ is true.

Example 2.5.7 *Prove that - If $f(n) \in O(n)$ then $[f(n)]^2 \in O(n^2)$*

Solution : Let, F(n) = a(n) + c be a linear function

$$[f(n)]^2 = (a(n) + c)^2$$

$$= [a(n)]^2 + 2a(n)c + c^2$$

$$[f(n)]^2 = x^2 + 2xc + c^2 \qquad \because a(n) = x$$

By considering only highest degree of polynomial we get

$$[f(n)]^2 = O(n^2)$$

Hence if $f(n) \in O(n)$ then $[f(n)]^2 \in O(n^2)$ is true.

2) Master's Method

Efficiency analysis using master theorem

Consider the following recurrence relation -

$$\mathbf{T(n) = aT(n/b) + f(n)} \qquad \text{where } n \geq d \text{ and d is some constant.}$$

Then the Master theorem can be stated for efficiency analysis as -

Consider the following recurrence relation -

$$T(n) = aT(n/b) + f(n) \qquad \text{where } n \geq d \text{ and d is some constant.}$$

If F(n) is $\Theta(n^d)$ where $d \geq 0$ in the recurrence relation then,

1. $T(n) = \Theta(n^d)$ if $a < b^d$
2. $T(n) = \Theta(n^d \log n)$ if $a = b$
3. $T(n) = \Theta(n^{\log_b a})$ if $a > b^d$

Let us understand the Master theorem with some examples :

Example 2.5.8 *Solve T(n) = 4T (n/2) + n*

Solution : We will map this equation with

$$T(n) = aT(n/b) + f(n)$$

Now f(n) is n i.e. n^1. Hence d = 1.

$a = 4$ and $b = 2$ and

$a > b^d$ i.e. $4 > 2^1$

$$\therefore \quad T(n) = \Theta(n^{\log_b a})$$

$$= \Theta(n^{\log_2 4})$$

$$= \Theta(n^2) \qquad \because \log_2 4 = 2$$

Hence time complexity is $\Theta(n^2)$.

For quick and easy calculations of logarithmic values to base 2 following table can be memorized.

m	k
1	0
2	1
4	2
8	3
16	4
32	5
64	6
128	7
256	8
512	9
1024	10

$$\log_2 m = k$$

Another variation of Master theorem is

For $\quad T(n) = aT(n/b) + f(n) \quad$ if $n \geq d$

1. If f(n) is $O(n^{\log_b a - \varepsilon})$, then

$$T(n) = \Theta(n^{\log_b a})$$

2. If f(n) is $\Theta(n^{\log_b a} \log^k n)$, then

$$T(n) = \Theta(n^{\log_b a} \log^{k+1} n)$$

3. If f(n) is $\Omega(n^{\log_b a + \varepsilon})$, then

$$T(n) = \Theta(f(n))$$

Example 2.5.9 *Solve* $T(n) = 2T(n/2) + n \log n$ **GTU : May-12, Marks 3**

Solution :

Here $f(n) = n \log n$

$a = 2, \; b = 2$

$\log_2 2 = 1$

According to case 2 given in above Master theorem

$$f(n) = \Theta(n^{\log_2 2} \log^1 n) \qquad \text{i.e. } k = 1$$

Then
$$T(n) = \Theta(n^{\log_b a} \log^{k+1} n)$$
$$= \Theta(n^{\log_2 2} \log^2 n)$$
$$= \Theta(n^1 \log^2 n)$$

$$\therefore \quad T(n) = \Theta(n \log^2 n)$$

Example 2.5.10 $T(n) = 8T(n/2) + n^2$

Solution : Here $f(n) = n^2$

$a = 8$ and $b = 2$

$\therefore \quad \log_2 8 = 3$

Then according to case 1 of above given Master theorem

$$f(n) = O(n^{\log_b a - \varepsilon})$$
$$= O(n^{\log_2 8 - \varepsilon})$$
$$= O(n^{3-\varepsilon})$$

Then
$$T(n) = \Theta(n^{\log_b a})$$

$\therefore \quad T(n) = \Theta(n^{\log_2 8})$

$T(n) = \Theta(n^3)$

Example 2.5.11 *Solve* $T(n) = 9T(n/3) + n^3$

Solution : Here $a = 9$, $b = 3$ and $f(n) = n^3$

And $\log_3 9 = 2$

According to case 3 in above Master theorem

As $f(n)$ is $= \Omega(n^{\log_3 9 + \varepsilon})$

i.e. $\Omega(n^{2+\varepsilon})$ and we have $f(n) = n^3$

Then $T(n) = \Theta(f(n))$

$T(n) = \Theta(n^3)$

Example 2.5.12 *Solve* $T(n) = T(n/2) + 1$

Solution : Here $a = 1$ and $b = 2$.

and $\log_2 1 = 0$

Now we will analyse $f(n)$ which is $= 1$.

We assume $f(n) = 2^k$

When $k = 0$ then $f(n) = 2^0 = 1$.

That means according to case 2 of above given Master theorem.

$f(n) = \Theta(n^{\log_b a} \log^k n)$

$= \Theta(n^{\log_2 1} \log^0 n)$

$= \Theta(n^0 \cdot 1)$

$= \Theta(1) \qquad \because n^0 = 1$

$\therefore$ We get $T(n) = \Theta(n^{\log_b a} \log^{k+1} n)$

$= \Theta(n^{\log_2 1} \log^{0+1} n)$

$= \Theta(n^0 \cdot \log^1 n)$

$T(n) = \Theta(\log n) \qquad \because n^0 = 1$

Example 2.5.13 *Find the order of growth for solutions of the following recurrences.*

a. $T(n) = 4T(n/2) + nT(1) = 1$

b. $T(n) = 4T(n/2) + n^2 T(1) = 1$

c. $T(n) = 4T(n/2) + n^3 T(1) = 1$

Solution : We can solve the given recurrence using Master's theorem. It is as given below.

If $f(n) \in \Theta(n^d)$ where $d \geq 0$

then

Case 1 : $T(n) = \Theta(n^d)$ if $a < b^d$

Case 2 : $T(n) = \Theta(n^d \log n)$ if $a = b^d$

Case 3 : $T(n) = \Theta(n^{\log_b a})$ if $a > b^d$

a) $T(n) = 4T(n/2) + n$

Here $a = 4$, $b = 2$ and $f(n) = n^1$ $\therefore d = 1$

It is matching with case 3 i.e.

$$a > b^d$$

i.e. $4 > 2^1$

$\therefore$ $T(n) = \Theta(n^{\log_b a}) = \Theta(n^{\log_2 4})$

But $\log_2 4 = 2$

$\therefore$ $T(n) = \Theta(n^2)$ is the time complexity.

b) $T(n) = 4T(n/2) + n^2$

Here $a = 4$, $b = 2$ and $f(n) = n^d = n^2$.

$\therefore$ $d = 2$

It is matching with case 2 i.e.

$$a = b^d$$

i.e. $4 = 2^2$

i.e. $4 = 4$

$\therefore$ $T(n) = \Theta(n^d \log n)$

$\therefore$ $T(n) = \Theta(n^2 \log n)$ is the time complexity.

c) $T(n) = 4T(n/2) + n^3$

Here a = 4, b = 2 and $f(n) = n^3$

$\therefore \quad f(n) = n^d$

$\therefore \quad d = 3$

It is matching with case 1.

$a < b^d$

i.e. $4 < 2^3$

i.e. $4 < 8$

$\therefore \quad T(n) = \Theta(n^d)$

$\therefore \quad \boxed{T(n) = \Theta(n^3)}$ is the time complexity.

Example 2.5.14 *Solve the following recurrence equations.*

1. $T(n) = 7T(n/3) + n^2$
2. $T(n) = 4T(n/2) + \log n$

Solution: 1. $T(n) = 7T\left(\frac{n}{3}\right) + n^2$

Here a = 7, b = 3 and $f(n) = n^2$.

$\log_b a = \log_3 7 \approx 1.77$

For f(n), it matches with case 3 of Master's Theorem, i.e.

$f(n) = \Omega\left(n^{\log_b a + \varepsilon}\right) = n^2$

$\therefore \quad T(n) = \Theta(f(n)) = \Theta(\mathbf{n^2})$

2. $T(n) = 4T\left(\frac{n}{2}\right) + \log n$

Here $a = 4$, b = 2 and f(n) = log n.

$\log_b a = \log_2 4 = 2$

We find a match with cases of Master's theorem,

$f(n) = \log n = O\left(n^{\log_b a - \varepsilon}\right) = O(n^{2-\varepsilon})$

$\therefore \quad T(n) = \Theta(n^{\log_b a})$

$\mathbf{T(n) = \Theta(n^2)}$

Example 2.5.15 *Explain master theorm and solve the following recurrence equation with master method -*

1. T(n) = 9T (n/3) + n   2. T(n) = 3T (n/4) + n lgn   **GTU [IT] : Winter -14, Marks 7**

Solution : 1. By Master Theorem.

$$a = 9, b = 3, f(n) = n$$

$$n^{\log_b a} = n^{\log_3 9} = \Theta(n^2)$$

because $f(n) = O(n^{\log_3 9-\varepsilon})$ where $\varepsilon = 1$

The case 1 is applied here.

$$T(n) = \Theta(n^{\log_b a}) \text{ when}$$

$$f(n) = O(n^{\log_b a-\varepsilon})$$

Hence $\mathbf{T(n) = \Theta(n^2)}$

2. By Master Theorem,

$$a = 3, b = 4, f(n) = n\lg n$$

$$n \log_b a = n \log_4 3 = \Theta(n^{0.793})$$

$$f(n) = \Omega(n^{\log_4 3+\varepsilon}) \text{ for } \varepsilon = 0.2$$

Besides, for large n the regularity holds for c = 3/4

$$a \cdot f(n/b) = 3(n/a)\lg(n/4) \le (3/4)\ n\lg n = c\ f(n)$$

Thus case 3 is applicable

$$\therefore \quad T(n) = \Theta(f(n))$$

$$\therefore \quad \mathbf{T(n) = \Theta(n\lg n)}$$

Review Question

1. *Explain the concept of recurrence relation with some illustrative example.*
2. *State and explain the Master's theorem.*

2.6 Analyzing Control Statements

GTU : May-12, Marks 4

While analyzing the given fragment of code various programming constructs appear. Those are :

1. Sequencing
2. For loops
3. Recursive calls
4. While and repeat loops

Let us discuss the analysis process with the help of suitable examples.

1) Sequencing

Sequencing means putting one instruction after another.

For example

```
i = 10;
printf ( "% d ", i) ;
i = 10 + 5 ;
```

Here each instruction executes only once. Hence the time take by above fragment is

$1 + 1 + 1 = 3$

$\therefore \quad \mathbf{T\ (n) = 3}$

2) For loops

For loops can be simple or nested for loops. Following is a simple for loop.

Hence total frequency count is 1 + (n+1) + n + n = **3n + 2** [Note that above numbers

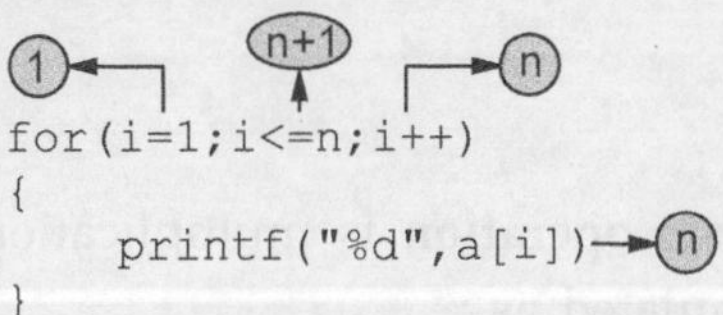

shown in shaded circle denotes number of execution]. In above example, i=1 gets executed once. The i < = n will be executed for n + 1 times. That is n times when i is really less than or equal to n (i.e. when condition is true) and one more time this statement will be executed when i becomes greater than n (i.e. when condition is false).

The statement i++ will be executed for n times. Similarly printf statement will be executed for n times.

Let us consider one more example -

The nested execution will be,

```
  (1)   (n+1)  (n)
for(i=1;i<=n;i++)
{   (1)  (n+1)  (n)
 for(j=1;j<=n;j++)
 {
      printf("%d",&a[i]);  -> (n)
 }
}
```

$$(1 + (n + 1) + n) \ * \ [(1 + (n + 1) + n) + n] = (2n + 2)\ (3n + 2)$$

$$= \mathbf{6n^2 + 10n + 4} \text{ is the frequency count.}$$

Now we can compute time complexity from the frequency count very easily. Suppose the frequency count is 3n + 2. Then just neglect all the constants and then specify the time complexity in terms of big oh notation. Hence for 3n + 2 frequency count we will get O(n) as the time complexity. Similarly if time complexity is $6n^2 + 10n + 4$, then we will get time complexity to be $O(n^2)$.

3) Recursive calls Recursion is a process in which one function calls itself.

Example 2.6.1 *Give recursive algorithm for factorial and comment on complexity of your algorithm.*

Solution : For analyzing control statements consider following algorithm :

```
Algorithm Factorial (n)
//Problem description : This algorithm computes n !
// using recursive function
// Input : A non negative integer n
// Output : returns factorial value
     if (n = 0) then
     return 1 ;
     else
     return Factorial (n-1) * n ;
```

In above algorithm the **basic operation** is multiplication. The input size is n. Hence recursive function can be formulated as :

$$f(n) = f(n-1) * n \quad \text{where } n > 0$$

We can write recurrence relation as -

$$T(n) = T(n-1) + 1$$

$T(n-1)$ ↑ These multiplications are required to compute factorial (n – 1)

1 ↑ To multiply factorial(n – 1) by n

Assume, $T(0) = 1$

$$T(n) = \underbrace{T(n-1)}+1$$

$$= [T(n-1-1)+1]+1$$

$$= \underbrace{T(n-2)}+2$$

$$= T(n-3)+1+2$$

$$= T(n-3)+3$$

$$\vdots$$

$$= T(n-k)+k$$

If k = n then

$$T(n) = T(n-n)+n$$

$$= T(0)+n$$

$$T(n) = 1 + n \qquad \because T(0) = 1$$

$\therefore$ We can say time complexity of factorial function is $\Theta(n)$.

Example 2.6.2 *Give the recursive algorithm to find Fibonacci sequence. Comment on the complexity of the algorithm.* **GTU : Dec.-10, Marks 4**

Solution :

```
Algorithm Fib (int n)
{
    // Problem Description : This is a recursive algorithm
    // to find fibonacci sequence.
        if ( n < = 2) then
                return 1;
        else
            return ( Fib (n–1) + Fib (n – 2)) ;
}
```

Complexity of algorithm

From algorithm if n< = 2 just return 1 will be executed each for Fib (1) and Fib (0).

$\therefore$ The recursive equation will be,

$$T(n) = 2 + T(n-1) + T(n-2)$$

For recursive calls Fib(n – 1) and Fib (n – 2) resp.

For Fib (3) we will have n = 3

$$\therefore \quad T(3) = 2 + T(2) + T(1)$$

$$T(3) = 2 + 1 + 1$$

$$\mathbf{T(3) = 4}$$

For Fib (4) , we will have n = 4

$$T(4) = 2 + T(3) + T(2)$$

$$= 2 + 4 + 1$$

$$T(4) = 7$$

For Fib (5) we will have n = 5

$$T(5) = 2 + T(4) + T(3)$$
$$= 2 + 7 + 4$$
$$T(5) = 13$$

Thus the complexity of fibonacci sequence is an exponentially increasing complexity.

Example 2.6.3 *Give the algorithm to solve tower of Hanoi problem. Comment on the complexity of the algorithm.* **GTU : Dec.-10, Marks 4**

Solution :

```
Algorithm TOH (n, A, C, B)
{
// if only one disk has to be moved
 if (n = 1) then
{
        Write (" The peg moved from A to C")
        return
}
else
{
 // move top n-1 disks from A to B using C
  TOH ( n-1, A, B, C);
// move remaining disk from B to C using A
TOH (n-1, B, C, A);
}
}
```

The time complexity of tower of Hanoi problem is θ (2^n).

4) While or repeat loops :

The while or repeat loops are treated just like recursive calls. While analyzing them we need to find out how many times the loop is repeated. Consider an algorithm for finding maximum value in give array.

```
Algorithm Max_Element (A[0...... n−1])
// Problem description : This algorithm is for finding
// the maximum value element from the array.
// Input : array A[0.....n−1]
// Output : returns largest element from the array.
    Max_value ←A [0]
    i ← 1 ; j ← n − 1 ;
    while ( i < j)
{
    if ( A[i] > Max_value) then
        Max_value ← A [i] ;
}
return Max_value ;
```

The input size is n and the basic operation is within a while loop, for finding larger value.

$$\therefore \quad T(n) = \sum_{i=1}^{j=n-1} 1$$

$$= (n-1) \qquad \because \quad \sum_{i=1}^{n} 1 = n$$

$$\mathbf{T(n) \in \Theta (n)}$$

Thus the time complexity of above algorithm is $\Theta(\mathbf{n})$.

Example 2.6.4 *Compare Iterative and Recursive algorithm to find the Fibonacci series.*

GTU : May-12, Marks 3

Solution : Iterative algorithm for obtaining the Fibonacci series

```
Algorithm Iter_fib(int n)
{
    f[0]=f[1]= 1;
    write(f[0],"   ",f[1]);
    for i=2; to n do
    {
        f[i]=f[i-1] + f[i-2];
        write(f[i]);
    }
}
```

The time complexity of above algorithm is O(n) as there is only one for loop required.

Recursive algorithm for obtaining the Fibonacci series

```
Algorithm fib(int n)
{

    if(n<=2)
        return 1;
    else
        return (fib(n-2)+fib(n-1));
}
```

The time complexity of above algorithm is exponentially increasing.

This shows that the iterative algorithm for computing Fibonacci sequence is more efficient than the recursive version.

Example 2.6.5 *Write an algorithm to find the maximum and minimum element in an array A storing n integers. What is the running time of this algorithm for computing the maximum element in an array of integers ?* **GTU : Summer-14, Marks 6**

Solution :

```
Algorithm Max_Min_Val (i, j, max, min)
{
    if (i = = j) then
    {
        max ← A [i]
        min ← A [j]
    }
    else if (i = j – 1)  then
    {
        if (A[ i ] < A [ j ])  then
        {
            max ← A [j]
            min ← A [i]
        }
        else
        {
            max ← A [j]
            min ← A [j]
        } //inner else
    }//outer else-if
    else
    {
        mid  (i+j)/2                        //divide the list to make
                                            // two sublists
        Max_Min_Val (i, mid, max, min)
        Max_Min_Val (mid+1, j, max_new, min_new)
        if ( max < max_new) then
            max ← max_new                   //combine solution
        if (min > min_new) then
            min ← min_new                   //combine solution
    }
}                                           //end of Algorithm
```

Analysis :

There are two recursive calls made in this algorithm, for each half divided sublist. Hence the time required for computing min and max will be

$$T(n) = T(\lceil n/2 \rceil) + T(\lceil n/2 \rceil) + 2 \qquad \text{when } n > 2$$

$$T(n) = 1 \qquad \text{when } n = 2$$

If single element is present then T(n) = 0. The time required for computing min and max will be

$$T(n) = 2\underbrace{T(n/2)}_{\downarrow} + 2$$

$$= 2[2T(n/4) + 2] + 2$$

$$= 4\,T\,(n/4) + 6$$

$$= 2(2[2T\,((n/8) + 2] + 2) + 2$$

$$= 8T\,(n/8) + 10$$

$$= 2^3 T\left(\frac{n}{2^3}\right) + (2^3 + 2)$$

$$\vdots$$

$$= 2^k T\left(\frac{n}{2^k}\right) + \left(2^k + 2\right)$$

If we put $n = 2^k$ then

$$= nT\left(\frac{n}{n}\right) + (n + 2)$$

$$= nT\,(1) + (n + 2)$$

$$= n + n + 2$$

$$T(n) = 2(n + 1)$$

By neglecting constants, we can say that time complexity of above algorithm is

$$\mathbf{T(n) = O(n)}$$

Example 2.6.6 *Develop an algorithm and program (recursive function) to calculate the GCD of two integers using top-down design. Analyze the algorithm.*

Solution :

```
#include<stdio.h>
#include<conio.h>
#include<stdlib.h>

void main(void)
{
 int a,b,ans;
 int gcd(int a,int b);
 clrscr();
 printf("\n\t\t GCD Of two integers");
 printf("\n\n Enter the two numbers: ");
 scanf("%d %d",&a,&b);
 ans=gcd(a,b);
 printf("\n The gcd of %d and %d is = %d",a,b,ans);
 getch();
}

int gcd(int a,int b)
```

```
{
int temp,ans;
if( b<=a &&a%b ==0)
    return b;
else
{
 if(a<b)
    return(gcd(b,a));
 /*the divisior should be less than divident*/
 else
    ans = a%b;
 return(gcd(b,ans));
}
}
```

Analysis : The worst case time complexity is $O(n^2)$ and average case is $O(n^2/\log n)$.

Example for Practice

Example 2.6.7 : *Perform the mathematical analysis for the following function.*

```
Algorithm count (node* head)
{
  int cnt =1;
    node * temp ;
    temp = head ;
    while (temp → next ! = head)
  {
        temp =temp → next ;
        cnt++ ;
  }
      printf (" % d," cnt) ;
}
```

Review Question

1. *What is Recursion ? Give the implementation of Tower of Hanoi problem using recursion.* **GTU : May-12, Marks 4**

2.7 Amortized Analysis

GTU : June-11, Winter-14, Marks 7

An amortized analysis means finding average running time per operation over a **worst case sequence** of operations. An amortized analysis indicates that average cost of a single operation is small if average of sequence of operations is obtained. This is true even if any one operation is expensive within the sequence. An amortized analysis guarantees the time per operation over worst case performance.

There is a difference between average case analysis and amortized analysis. In average case analysis we are averaging over all possible inputs and in amortized analysis we are averaging over a sequence of operations. An amortized analysis assumes worst-case input.

There are 3 commonly used techniques used in amortized analysis -

i) Aggregate analysis

ii) Accounting method

iii) Potential method

Key Point *The amortized cost of n operations is the total cost of the operations divided by n.*

Let us discuss each technique of amortized analysis one by one.

2.7.1 Aggregate Analysis

Aggregate analysis is a kind of analysis in which the analysis is made over sequence of n operations and these operations actually take worst case time T(n). In worst case an amortized cost per operation is T(n)/n. Let us now discuss two examples for making aggregate analysis in order to obtain amortized cost.

Example : Implementing stack as an array.

There are two basic operations in stack.

1. To implement 'push (item)' we need :

   s [top] = item;

   top ++;

2. To implement item = pop () we need :

   top – – ;

   item = s[top];

Thus push (item) and pop ( ) are the operations each running in O(1) time. This also means that cost of each operation is O(1) and for n sequences of operations the total execution time will be Θ **(n)**. Now if we write some function for performing **multiple pop** operations then **k** top objects will be removed from the stack.

```
Algorithm multiple _ pop (st, k)
{
// Problem Description : This algorithm is for
// removing k top objects repeatedly using stack.
while ((! stempty (st)) AND k! = 0)
    {
    pop (st)
    k← k – 1
    } // end if while
    } // end of algorithm
```

While stack do not gets empty the desired elements can be removed.

For example :

If we want to remove 4 elements from the stack then-

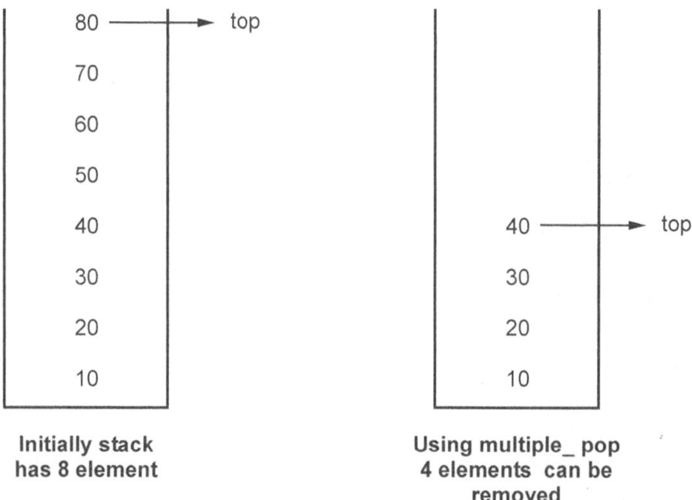

Initially stack has 8 element

Using multiple_ pop 4 elements can be removed

Empty stack after removing 4 elements

That means for the size 8 of the stack we can perform at the most 8 pop operations.

- From above given sequence of execution we can state that worst case cost for **multiple_pop** is O(n) when the size of stack is at the most n. Hence a sequence of n operations costs $O(n^2)$ because we can have O(n) multiple_pop operations costing O(n) each. The cost $O(n^2)$ is correct but not tight.
- We can broadly state that each object can be popped off once. That also means : Total number of pop = Total number of push.
- The aggregate analysis suggests to define amortized cost to be **average cost.**
- Hence average cost in amortized analysis is nothing but **average cost** of an operation = O(n)n

Example 2 : Binary counter

This problem is for implementing binary counter for a k-bit number. We will use an array **B** in which a binary number is stored. Bits ranging from 0 to k – 1.

For example :

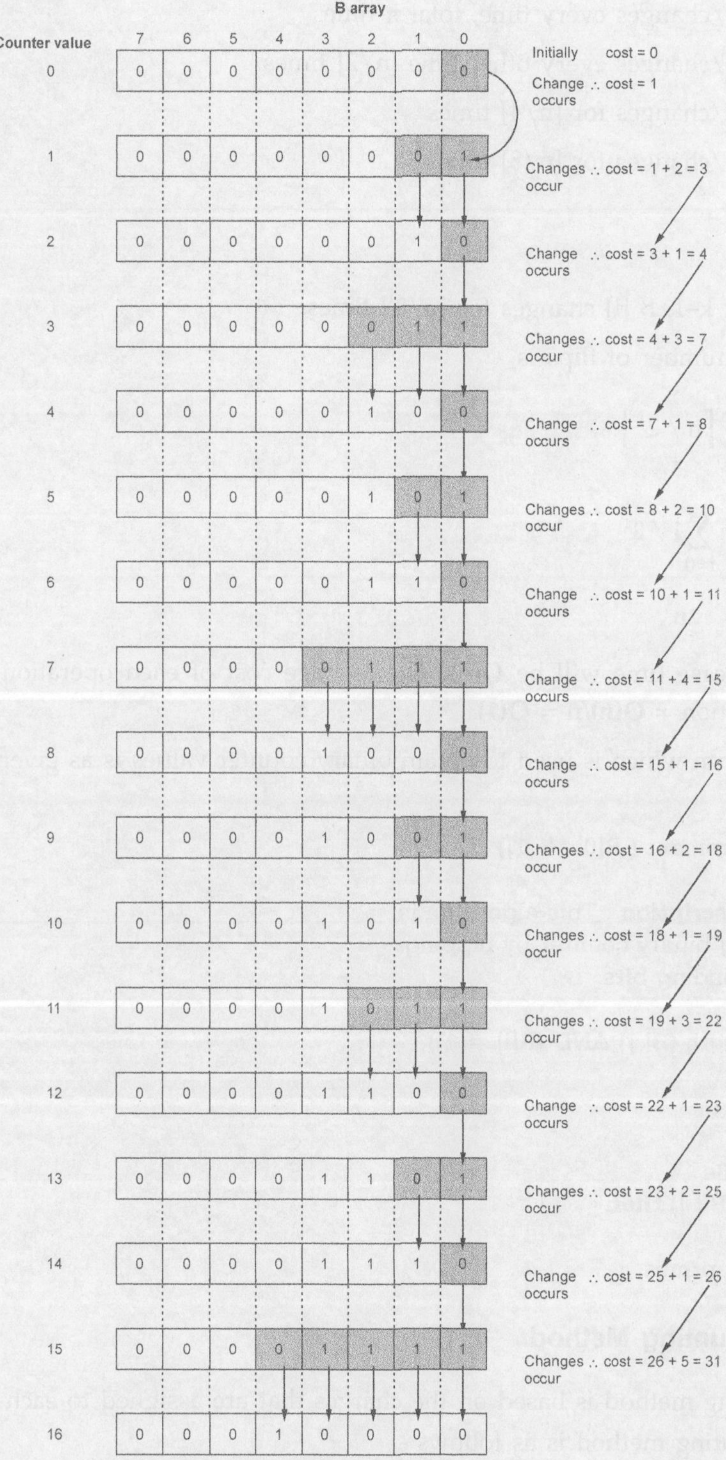

Fig. 2.7.1 8-bit binary counter

From above given counter method we can make out few observations -

B [0] flips/changes every time, total n times

B [1] flips/changes every other time [n/2] times

B [2] flips/changes for [n/4] times

B [3] flips/changes for [n/8] times

. . .

. . .

for i = 0,1... k–1, B [i] changes for $[n/2^i]$ times.

Thus total number of flips is

$$\sum_{i=0}^{k-1}[n/2^i]$$

$$< n\sum_{i=0}^{\infty}1/2^i$$

$$= \mathbf{2n}$$

The **worst case** time will be **O(n).** The average cost of each operation i.e. **amortized cost** per operation = **O(n)/n = O(1).**

The algorithm which is used to obtain binary counter values is as given below.

```
Algorithm
Algorithm Increment ( B[0... k–1])
{
// Problem Description : This algorithm is
// for obtaining binary counter by flipping
// the corresponding bits.
i ← 0
while ((i < length (B[ ]) AND (B[i] = 1))
{
B[i] ← 0
i ← i + 1
} // end of while
if (i < length (B [ ]) then
B[i] ← 1
} // end of algorithm
```

2.7.2 Accounting Method

The counting method is based on the charges that are assigned to each operation. The **idea** of accounting method is as follows -

- Assign different charges to different operations.
- The amount of charge is called **amortized cost.**
- Then there is **actual cost** of each operation. The amortized cost can be more or less than actual cost.
- When amortized cost > actual cost, the difference is saved in specific objects called **credits.**
- When for particular operation amortized cost < actual cost the stored **credits** are **utilized.**
- Thus in accounting method we can say

Amortized cost = actual cost + credits (either deposited or used up)

- In aggregate analysis method, it is **not** necessary to have amortized cost to **each operation** but in accounting method each operation must have some amortized cost.

Following are the conditions used in accounting method -

- Let c_i be the actual cost of ith operation in the sequence, and c_i' be the amortized cost of ith operation in the sequence.
- There should be -

$$\sum_{i=1}^{n} c_i' \geq \sum_{i=1}^{n} c_i$$

That means we need the total amortized cost is an upper bound of total actual cost. This holds true for all sequences of operations.

- **Total credit** $= \sum_{i=1}^{n} c_i' - \sum_{i=1}^{n} c_i$

Which should be **non negative.** Let us understand the method of obtaining amortized cost using accounting method with the help of two examples :

1) Stack operations and 2) Binary counter

Example 1 : Stack operations.

Let us first assign some charges to each stack operation.

Push (item) : = 1

Pop ( ) : 1

multiple_pop: min (st, k) where st is stack size and k is number of multiple pops. These cost are the **actual costs.**

Let us now assign amortized costs as -

push (item) : 2

pop ( ) : 0

multiple_pop : 0

Note that multiple_pop operation has variable actual cost and 0 amortized cost. Now consider some sequence of operations starting from empty stack. For now, if we push some object onto the stack then associated with it $2 as amortized cost. We then can use $1 to pay the actual cost of push and left with $1 as credit. If we go on pushing the objects the credits will get accumulated each time. Now, while popping the object each credit will be used to prepay the cost of pop operation. Thus by charging **more** on **push** operation we need **not** have to **charge** anything on **pop operation**. The same is true for multiple_pop operation. This also ensures that credits are always **non negative.**

Hence total amortized cost for n push (item), pop, multiple_pop is **O(n).** Hence average amortized cost for each operation is O(n) / n = 1

Example 2 : Binary counter

The accounting method is applied on binary counter as follows -

- Let $ 1 is the charge assigned for each unit cost.
- Let, the amortized cost of $ 2 is charged for setting a bit to 1.
- When the bit is set, then out of $ 2 we can use $ 1 to pay the actual cost and store $ 1 on the bit as credit. Thus on any point of time the set bit will have $ 1 as credit.
- When a bit is reset (i.e. changing bit to 0) the credit of $ 1 is used to pay the cost.
- Thus the amount of credit is always **non negative.**
- The total amortized cost of n operations is **O(n).**

2.7.3 Potential Method

This method is similar to the accounting method in which the concept of "prepaid" is used.

- In this method there will not be any credit but there will be some potential "energy" or "potential" which can be used to pay for future operations.
- Instead of associating potential with specific object it is associated with the data structure as a whole. The **working** of potential method is as follows -
- Let, D_0 be the initial data structure. Hence for n operations D_0, D_1, D_2.....D_n will be the data structure. Let c_1, c_2, ... c_n denotes the actual cost.
- Let Φ is a potential function which is a **real** number. $\Phi(D_i)$ is called potential of D_i.

- Let, c'_i be the **amortized cost** of ith operation

$$c'_i = c_i + \underbrace{\Phi(D_i) - \Phi(D_{i-1})}_{\text{Potential change}}$$

(c_i → Actual cost)

$$\sum_{i=1}^{n} c'_i = \sum_{i=1}^{n} (c_i + \Phi(D_i) - \Phi(D_{i-1})) \quad \text{and}$$

$$\sum_{i=1}^{n} c'_i = \sum_{i=1}^{n} c_i + \Phi(D_n) - \Phi(D_0)$$

- If $\Phi(D_n) \geq \Phi(D_0)$, then amortized cost is an **upper bound** of actual cost.
- For any sequence of operation we do not know the exact number of operations. Hence it is required to have $\Phi(D_i) \geq \Phi(D_0)$ for any value of i.
- Let $\Phi(D_0) = 0$. So $\Phi(D_i) \geq 0$ for all i.
- If **potential change** is **positive** i.e. if $\Phi(D_i) - \Phi(D_{i-1}) > 0$ then c'_i is overcharge and potential of data structure increases.
- If potential change is negative i.e. if $\Phi(D_i) - \Phi(D_{i-1}) < 0$ then c'_i is an undercharge i.e. discharge the potential to pay actual cost.

Let us now obtain amortized analysis by potential method for

1) Stack operations and 2) Binary counter.

Example 1 : Stack operation

The number of objects in the stack is the potential for the stack. So

$\Phi(D_0) = 0$ and $\Phi(D_i) \geq 0$ i.e. non negative value.

We can now obtain amortized cost of each stack operation as follows -

Push operation

$$\text{Potential change} = \Phi(D_i) - \Phi(D_{i-1})$$

$$= (s + 1) - s$$

$$= 1$$

(s + 1 means inserting one item to existing stack of size s)

$$\text{Amortized cost} = \text{actual cost} + \text{potential change}$$

$$= c_i + \Phi(D_i) - \Phi(D_{i-1})$$

$$= 1 + 1$$

$$c'_i = \mathbf{2}$$

Pop operation

$$\text{Potential change} = \Phi(D_i) - \Phi(D_{i-1})$$
$$= (s-1) - s$$
$$= -1$$

s – 1 means popping off one item from stack of size s

$$\text{Amortized cost} = \text{actual cost} + \text{potential change}$$
$$= c_i + \Phi(D_i) - \Phi(D_{i-1})$$
$$= 1 + (-1)$$
$$c'_i = 0$$

Multiple_pop

$$\text{Potential change} = \Phi(D_i) - \Phi(D_{i-1})$$
$$= k'$$

where k' = min(st, k) with k denotes number of pop and st denotes stack size.

$$\text{Amortized cost} = \text{Actual cost} + \text{Potential change}$$
$$= c_i + \Phi(D_i) - \Phi(D_{i-1})$$
$$= k' + k'$$
$$c'_i = 0$$

Thus **amortized cost** of each operation is O(1) and total amortized cost of n operations is **O(n).**

The **worst case** cost of n operations is **O(n).**

Example 2 : Binary counter

The potential of the counter after i^{th} increments is $\Phi(D_i) = b_i$ i.e. the number of 1's. Let us now compute amortized cost of an operation -

Let, there be i^{th} operation which resets t_i bits.

$\therefore$ Actual cost c_i of the operation is $t_i + 1$

$\therefore$ $\boxed{c_i = t_i + 1}$

- If $b_i = 0$ then the ith operation resets all k bits. Hence

$$\mathbf{b_{i-1} = t_i = k}$$

- If $b_i > 0$ then $b_i = b_{i-1} - t_i + 1$

From these two conditions

$bi \leq b_{i-1} - t_i + 1$

Hence potential change is

$\Phi(D_i) - \Phi(D_{i-1}) \leq b_{i-1} - t_i + 1 - b_i$

Potential change $= 1 - t_i$

$$\begin{aligned} \therefore \text{Amortized cost } c_i' &= \text{Actual cost + Potential change} \\ &= c_i + \Phi(D_i) - \Phi(D_{i-1}) \\ &\leq t_i + 1 - 1 - 1 - t_i \\ &= 2 \end{aligned}$$

The total **amortized cost** of n operations is **O(n)**

The **worst case** cost is **O(n).**

Review Questions

1. *What is an amortized analysis ? Explain aggregate method of amortized analysis using suitable example.* **GTU : June-11, Winter-14, Marks 7**
2. *What is an amortized analysis ? Explain potential method of amortized analysis using suitable example .* **GTU : Winter -14, Marks 7**
3. *Define an amortized analysis. Briefly explain its different techniques. Carry out aggregate analysis for the problem of implementing a k-bit binary counter that counts upward from 0.* **GTU : Summer -15, Marks 3**

2.8 What Kind of Problems are Solved by Algorithms ?

GTU : May-12, Dec.-10, Winter-14, Marks 7

Generally any computing problem can be solved by algorithm. There is large number of computing problems and some of them can be classified as -

1. Sorting
2. Searching
3. Numerical problems
4. Combinatorial problems
5. Graph problems
6. String processing problems.

2.8.1 Sorting Algorithm

- Sorting means arranging the elements in increasing order or decreasing order (also called **ascending order or descending order** respectively). The sorting can be done on numbers, characters (alphabets), strings or employees record. For sorting any record we need to choose certain piece of information based on which sorting can be done. For instance : for keeping the employee ID. Similarly one can arrange the library books according to the title of the books. This piece of information which is required to sort the record is called as **key**. The important property of this key is that it should be unique.

- The sorting algorithms are classified as **internal sorting** and **external sorting.** The internal sorting is used for sorting the reasonable amount of data and it can be carried out on main memory whereas the external sorting is applied to sort a huge amount of data and it can be carried out on the main memory along with the secondary memory.
- Various sorting methods are -
  1. Bubble sort
  2. Selection sort
  3. Insertion sort
  4. Quick sort
  5. Merge sort
  6. Heap sort
  7. Radix sort.
- The insertion sort, bubble sort and quick sort are comparison sort algorithms. The radix sort is counting sort algorithm in which it is assumed that input numbers are in the set {1, 2, 3........, n} then using array index the elements are arranged in ordered manner.

2.8.1.1 Bubble Sort

Bubble sort is another simplest sorting algorithm. In bubble sort, largest element is moved at highest index in the array. As the largest element moves to the highest index position it is called that element is **"bubbled up"** from its position. Hence is the name!

In the next pass, the second largest element bubbles up, then the third largest element bubbles up, and so on. After (n – 1) passes the list gets sorted. The pass $i\ (0 \le i \le n-2)$ of bubble sort can be represented as

$$A[0], \ldots, A[j] \overset{?}{\longleftrightarrow} A[j+1], \ldots, A[n-i-1] \mid A[n-i] \le \ldots < A[n-1]$$

Example

Consider the elements

70, 30, 20, 50, 60, 10, 40

We can store these elements in array as

70	30	20	50	60	10	40
A[0]	A[1]	A[2]	A[3]	A[4]	A[5]	A[6]

We will use $\overset{?}{\longleftrightarrow}$ symbol to check whether previous element is greater than next. If we found it greater, then swap them.

Pass 1 :

70	$\overset{?}{\longleftrightarrow}$	30		20		50		60		10		40
30		70	$\overset{?}{\longleftrightarrow}$	20		50		60		10		40
30		20		70	$\overset{?}{\longleftrightarrow}$	50		60		10		40
30		20		50		70	$\overset{?}{\longleftrightarrow}$	60		10		40
30		20		50		60		70	$\overset{?}{\longleftrightarrow}$	10		40
30		20		50		60		10		70	$\overset{?}{\longleftrightarrow}$	40
30		20		50		60		10		40		70

The list obtained at the end of first pass will be considered as input to second pass.

Pass 2 :

30	$\overset{?}{\longleftrightarrow}$	20		50		60		10		40		70
20		30	$\overset{?}{\longleftrightarrow}$	50	$\overset{?}{\longleftrightarrow}$	60	$\overset{?}{\longleftrightarrow}$	10		40		70
20		30		50		10		60	$\overset{?}{\longleftrightarrow}$	40		70
20		30		50		10		40		60	$\overset{?}{\longleftrightarrow}$	70
20		30		50		10		40		60		70

Pass 3 :

20	$\overset{?}{\longleftrightarrow}$	30	$\overset{?}{\longleftrightarrow}$	50	$\overset{?}{\longleftrightarrow}$	10		40		60		70
20		30		10		50	$\overset{?}{\longleftrightarrow}$	40		60		70
20		30		10		40		50	$\overset{?}{\longleftrightarrow}$	60	$\overset{?}{\longleftrightarrow}$	70
20		30		10		40		50		60	$\overset{?}{\longleftrightarrow}$	70

Pass 4 :

20	$\overset{?}{\longleftrightarrow}$	30	$\overset{?}{\longleftrightarrow}$	10		40		50		60		70

20		10		30	$\overset{?}{\longleftrightarrow}$	40	$\overset{?}{\longleftrightarrow}$	50	$\overset{?}{\longleftrightarrow}$	60	$\overset{?}{\longleftrightarrow}$	70
20		10		30		40		50		60		70
20		10		30		40		50	$\overset{?}{\longleftrightarrow}$	60	$\overset{?}{\longleftrightarrow}$	70
20		10		30		40		50		60		70

Pass 5 :

20	$\overset{?}{\longleftrightarrow}$	10		30		40		50		60		70
10		20	$\overset{?}{\longleftrightarrow}$	30	$\overset{?}{\longleftrightarrow}$	40	$\overset{?}{\longleftrightarrow}$	50	$\overset{?}{\longleftrightarrow}$	60	$\overset{?}{\longleftrightarrow}$	70
10		20		30		40		50		60		70

Now we get the sorted list as,

10	20	30	40	50	60	70

Example 2.8.1 *Sort the letters of word "DESIGN" in alphabetical order using bubble sort.*

GTU : Summer-14, Marks 7

Solution : Pass 1

D	$\overset{?}{\longleftrightarrow}$	E		S		I		G		N
D		E	$\overset{?}{\longleftrightarrow}$	S		I		G		N
D		E		S	$\overset{?}{\longleftrightarrow}$	I		G		N
D		E		I		S	$\overset{?}{\longleftrightarrow}$	G		N
D		E		I		G		S	$\overset{?}{\longleftrightarrow}$	N
D		E		I		G		N		S

Pass 2

D	$\overset{?}{\longleftrightarrow}$	E		I		G		N		S
D		E	$\overset{?}{\longleftrightarrow}$	I		G		N		N
D		E		I	$\overset{?}{\longleftrightarrow}$	G		N		N
D		E		G		I	$\overset{?}{\longleftrightarrow}$	N		N
D		E		G		I		N	$\overset{?}{\longleftrightarrow}$	S
D		E		G		I		N		S

Continuing in this manner we get the list sorted finally. It is as follows.

D	E	G	I	N	S

Algorithm

```
Algorithm Bubble(A[0...n-1])
//Problem Description : This algorithm is for sorting the
//elements using bubble sort method
//Input:An array of elements A[0...n-1] that is to be sorted
//Output: The sorted array A[0...n-1]
for i ← 0 to n – 2 do
{
 for j ←0 to n–2-i do
 {
          if(A[j]>A[j+1])then
          {
          temp ← A[j]
          A[j] ← A[j+1]
          A[j+1] ← temp
          }
 }//end of inner for loop
}//end of outer for loop
```

Analysis

The above algorithm can be analysed mathematically. We will use general plan for non recursive mathematical analysis.

Step 1 : The input size is total number of elements in the list.

Step 2 : In this algorithm the basic operation is key comparison.

```
if A[j] > A[j+1]
```

Step 3 : We can obtain **sum** as follows :

C(n) = Outer for loop with variable i × Inner for loop with variable j × Basic operation

$$\therefore \quad C(n) = \sum_{i=0}^{n-2} \sum_{j=0}^{n-2-i} 1$$

$\sum_{i=0}^{n} 1 = (n-0+1)$ using this formula we get,

$$\sum_{j=0}^{n-2-i} 1 = (n-2-i-0+1) = (n-1-i)$$

$$C(n) = \sum_{i=0}^{n-2} (n-1-i)$$

Step 4 : **Simplifying** sum we get,

$$C(n) = \sum_{i=0}^{n-2} (n-1-i)$$

$$= \sum_{i=0}^{n-2} (n-1) - \sum_{i=0}^{n-2} i$$

$$= \sum_{i=0}^{n-2} (n-1) - \frac{(n-2)(n-1)}{2}$$ ... (Refer rule 2 in section 2.4.5 for arriving at this answer)

$$= \frac{(n-1)\,n}{2}$$

$$\in \Theta(n^2)$$

If the elements are arranged in decreasing manner, the key swaps will be

$$S_{worst} = C(n) = \frac{(n-1)\,n}{2}$$

$$\in \Theta(n^2)$$

The time complexity of bubble sort is $\Theta(\mathbf{n}^2)$.

2.8.1.2 Selection Sort

Scan the array to find its smallest element and swap it with the first element. Then, starting with the second element scan the entire list to find the smallest element and swap it with the second element. Then starting from the third element the entire list is scanned in order to find the next smallest element. Continuing in this fashion we can sort the entire list.

Generally, on pass i $(0 \le i \le n-2)$, the smallest element is searched among last $n-i$ elements and is swapped with A[i]

$$A[0] \le A[1] \le \ldots \le A[i-1] \mid \overbrace{A[i], \ldots, A[k], \ldots, A[n-1]}^{\text{Last n–i elements}}$$

A[k] is smallest element

so swap A[i] and A[k]

The list gets sorted after n–1 passes.

Example

Consider the elements

70, 30, 20, 50, 60, 10, 40

We can store these elements in array A as :

70	30	20	50	60	10	40
A[0]	A[1]	A[2]	A[3]	A[4]	A[5]	A[6]
↑	↑					
Min	j					

Initially set Min j

1st pass :

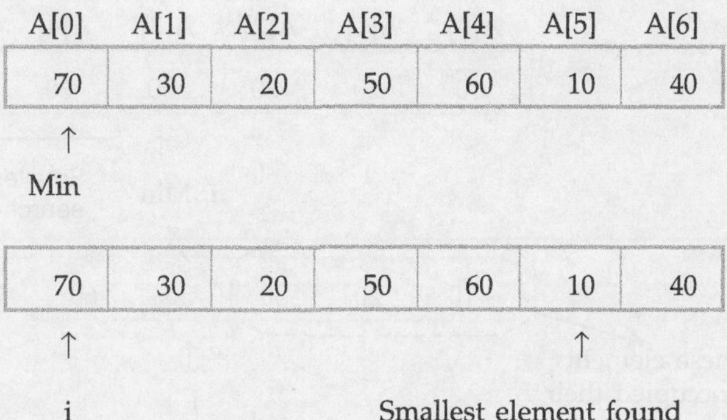

Now swap A[i] with smallest element. Then we get,

10	30	20	50	60	70	40

2nd pass :

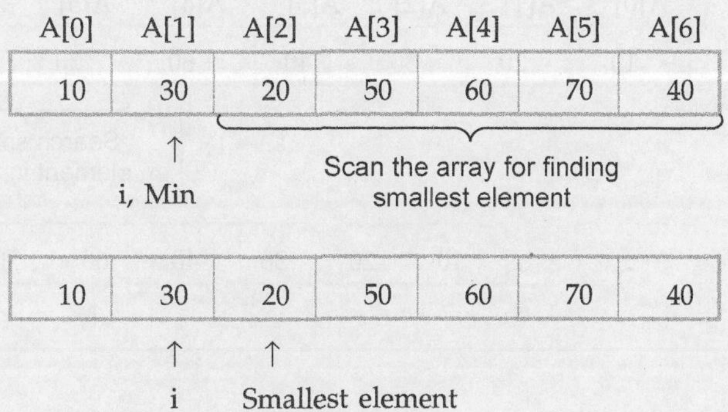

Swap A[i] with smallest element. The array becomes,

10	20	30	50	60	70	40

3rd pass :

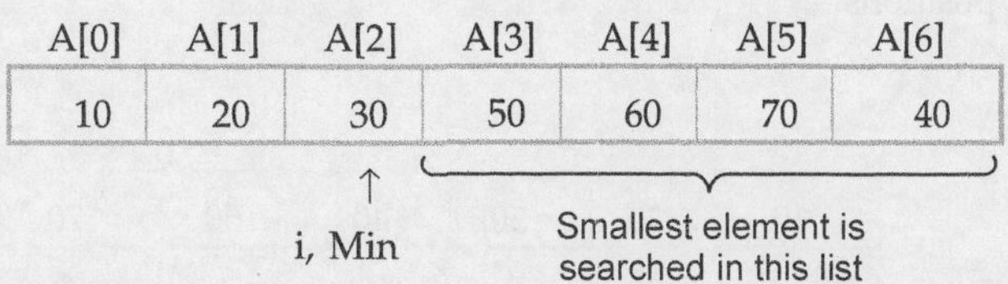

As there is no smallest element than 30 we will increment i pointer.

4th pass :

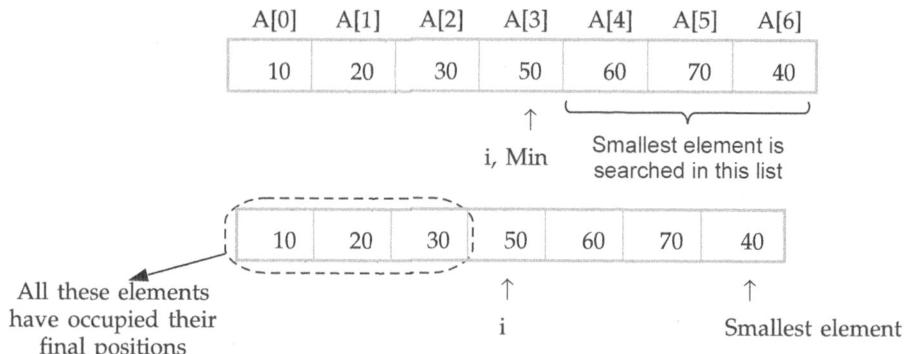

Swap A[i] with smallest element. The array then becomes,

10	20	30	40	60	70	50

5th pass :

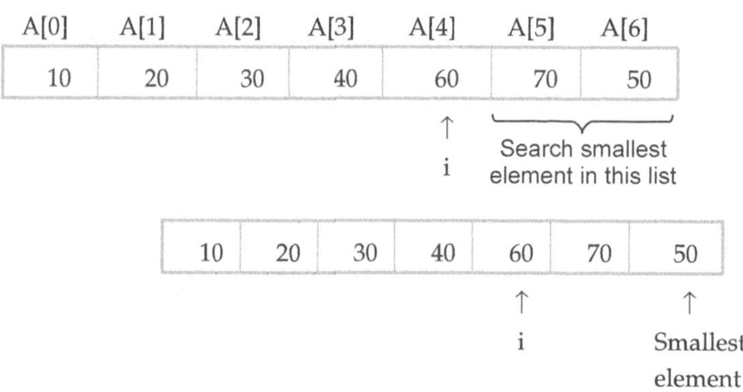

Swap A[i] with smallest element. The array then becomes,

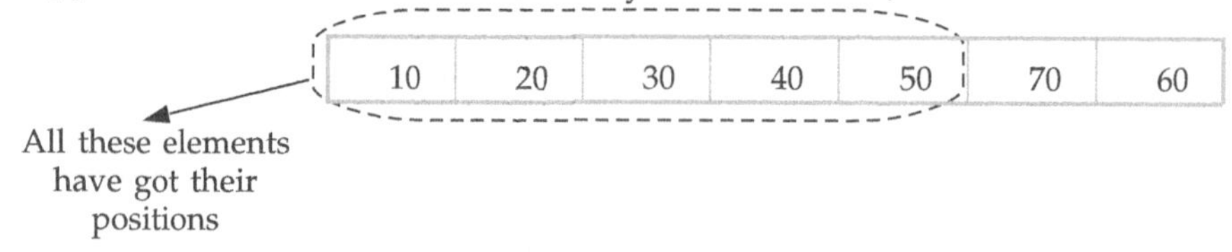

6th pass :

10	20	30	40	50	70	60

↑ i (70) ↑ Smallest element (60)

Swap A[i] with smallest element. The array then becomes,

A[0]	A[1]	A[2]	A[3]	A[4]	A[5]	A[6]
10	20	30	40	50	60	70

This is a sorted array.

Algorithm

The pseudo code for sorting the elements using selection sort is as given below.

```
Algorithm selection(A[0...n-1])
//Problem Description: This algorithm sorts the elements
//using selection sort
//Input:An array of elements A[0...n-1] that is to be sorted
//Output: The sorted array A[0...n-1]
for i ← 0 to n–2 do
{
 Min ← i
 for j ← i+1 to n–1 do
 {
         if(A[j]<A[min])then
     min ← j
 //swap A[i] and A[min]
 }//end of inner for loop
 temp ← A[i]
 A[i] ← A[min]
 A[min] ← temp
}//end of outer for loop
```

Analysis

The above algorithm can be analysed mathematically. We will apply a general plan for non recursive mathematical analysis.

Step 1 : The **input size** is n i.e. total number of elements in the list.

Step 2 : In the algorithm the **basic operation** is key comparison.

```
if A[j] < A[min]
```

Step 3 : This basic operation depends only on array size n. Hence we can find **sum** as

C(n) = Outer for loop with variable i × Inner for loop with variable j × Basic operation

$$\therefore \quad C(n) = \sum_{i=0}^{n-2} \sum_{j=i+1}^{n-1} 1$$

$\sum_{i=0}^{n} 1 = (n-0+1)$ using this formula we get,

$\sum_{j=i+1}^{n-1} 1 = [(n-1)-(i+1)+1]$

$= (n-1-i)$

$$C(n) = \sum_{i=0}^{n-2} (n-1-i)$$

Step 4 : Simplifying sum we get,

$$C(n) = \sum_{i=0}^{n-2} (n-1-i)$$

$$= \sum_{i=0}^{n-2} (n-1) - \sum_{i=0}^{n-2} i$$

$\sum_{i=1}^{n} i = \frac{n(n+1)}{2}$ using this formula

$\sum_{i=0}^{n-2} i = \frac{(n-2)(n-2+1)}{2}$

$= \frac{(n-2)(n-1)}{2}$

$$= \sum_{i=0}^{n-2} (n-1) - \frac{(n-2)(n-1)}{2}$$

Now taking (n – 1) as common factor we get,

$$C(n) = (n-1) \sum_{i=0}^{n-2} 1 - \frac{(n-2)(n-1)}{2}$$

As $\sum_{i=1}^{n} 1 = (n-1+1)$, we get,

$\sum_{i=0}^{n-2} 1 = (n-2-0+1)$

$= (n-1)$

$$= (n-1)(n-1) - \frac{(n-2)(n-1)}{2}$$

$$= (n-1)^2 - \frac{(n-2)(n-1)}{2}$$

Solving this equation we will get,

$$= \frac{2(n-1)(n-1) - (n-2)(n-1)}{2}$$

$$= \frac{2(n^2-2n+1) - (n^2-3n+2)}{2}$$

$$= \frac{n^2-n}{2}$$

$$= \frac{n(n-1)}{2}$$

$$\approx \frac{1}{2}(n^2)$$

$$\in \Theta(n^2)$$

Thus time complexity of selection sort is $\Theta(n^2)$ for all input. But total number of key swaps is only $\Theta(n)$.

2.8.1.3 Insertion Sort

In this method the elements are inserted at their appropriate place. Hence is the name **insertion sort**. Let us understand this method with the help of some example -

For Example

Consider a list of elements as,

0	1	2	3	4	5	6
30	70	20	50	40	10	60

The process starts with first element

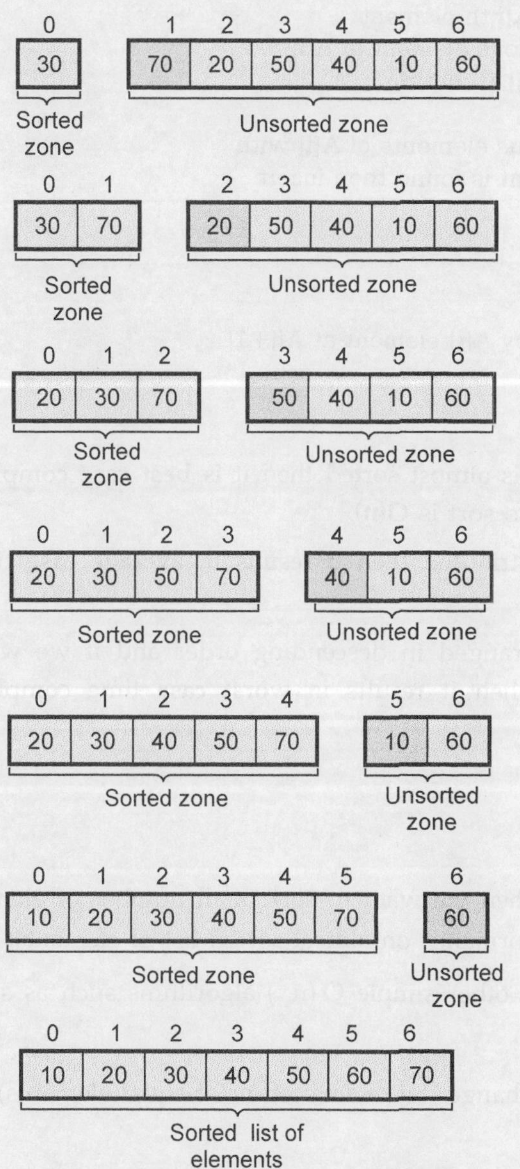

Algorithm

Although it is very natural to implement insertion using recursive(top down) algorithm but it is very efficient to implement it using bottom up(iterative) approach.

```
Algorithm Insert_sort(A[0...n-1])
//Problem Description: This algorithm is for sorting the
//elements using insertion sort
//Input: An array of n elements
//Output: Sorted array A[0...n-1] in ascending order
 for i ← 1 to n-1 do
{
        temp ← A[i]//mark A[i]th element
        j ← i-1//set j at previous element of A[i]
        while(j>=0)AND(A[j]>temp)do
        {
    //comparing all the previous elements of A[i] with
    //A[i].If any greater element is found then insert
    //it at proper position
        A[j+1] ← A[j]
        j ← j-1
        }
        A[j+1] ← temp //copy A[i] element at A[j+1]
}
```

Analysis

When an array of elements is almost sorted then it is **best case** complexity. The best case time complexity of insertion sort is **O(n).**

If an array is randomly distributed then it results in **average case** time complexity which is $O(n^2)$.

If the list of elements is arranged in descending order and if we want to sort the elements in ascending order then it results in **worst case** time complexity which is $O(n^2)$.

Advantages of insertion sort

1. *Simple* to implement.
2. This method is *efficient* when we want to sort small number of elements. And this method has excellent performance on almost sorted list of elements.
3. More efficient than most other simple $O(n^2)$ algorithms such as selection sort or bubble sort.
4. This is a *stable* (does not change the relative order of equal elements).

5. It is called *in-place* sorting algorithm (only requires a constant amount O(1) of extra memory space). The in-place sorting algorithm is an algorithm in which the input is overwritten by output and to execute the sorting method it does not require any more additional space.

C Function

```
void Insert_sort(int A[10],int n)
{
 int i,j,temp;
 for(i=1;i<=n-1;i++)
 {
        temp=A[i];
        j=i-1;
        while((j>=0)&&(A[j]>temp))
        {
         A[j+1]=A[j];
         j=j-1;
        }
        A[j+1]=temp;
 }
 printf("\n The sorted list of elements is...\n");
 for(i=0;i<n;i++)
        printf("\n%d",A[i]);
}
```

Let us now see the implementation of this method using C.

C Program

```
/*****************************************************************
     Implementation of insertion sort
*****************************************************************/
#include<stdio.h>
#include<conio.h>
void main()
{
 int A[10],n,i;
 void Insert_sort(int A[10],int n);
 clrscr();
 printf("\n\t\t Insertion Sort");
 printf("\n How many elements are there?");
 scanf("%d",&n);
 printf("\n Enter the elements\n");
 for(i=0;i<n;i++)
        scanf("%d",&A[i]);
 Insert_sort(A,n);
 getch();
```

```
}
void Insert_sort(int A[10],int n)
{
 int i,j,temp;
 for(i=1;i<=n-1;i++)
 {
          temp=A[i];
          j=i-1;
          while((j>=0)&&(A[j]>temp))
          {
           A[j+1]=A[j];
           j=j-1;
          }
          A[j+1]=temp;
 }
 printf("\n The sorted list of elements is...\n");
 for(i=0;i<n;i++)
          printf("\n%d",A[i]);
}
```

Output

```
                         Insertion Sort
     How many elements are there?5

     Enter the elements
30
20
10
40
50
     The sorted list of elements is...
10
20
30
40
50
```

Logic Explanation

For understanding the logic of above C program consider a list of unsorted elements as,

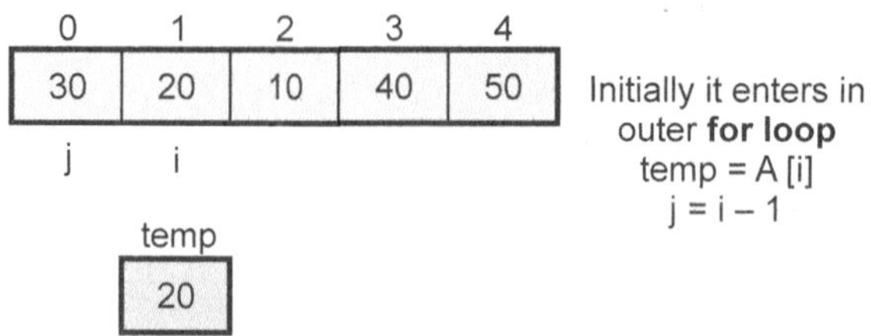

Then the control moves to **while loop**. As j >= 0 and A[j] > temp is **True**, the while loop will be executed.

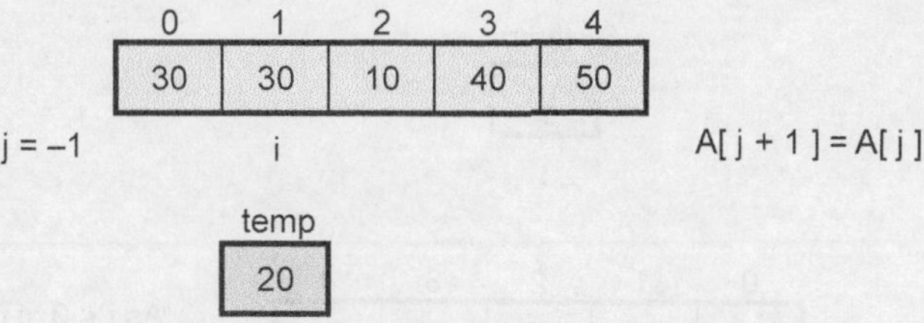

Now since j >= 0 is false, control comes out of while loop.

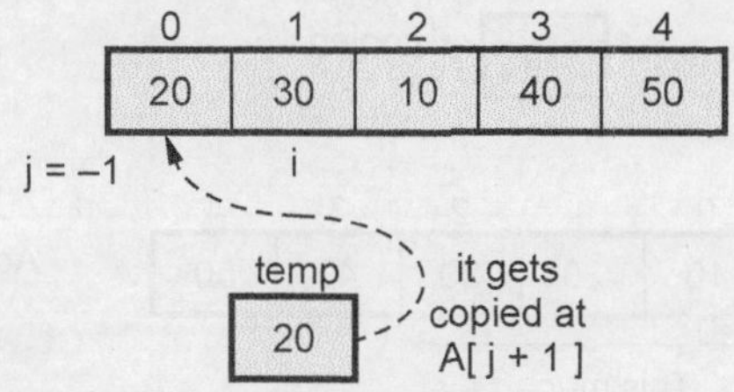

Then list becomes,

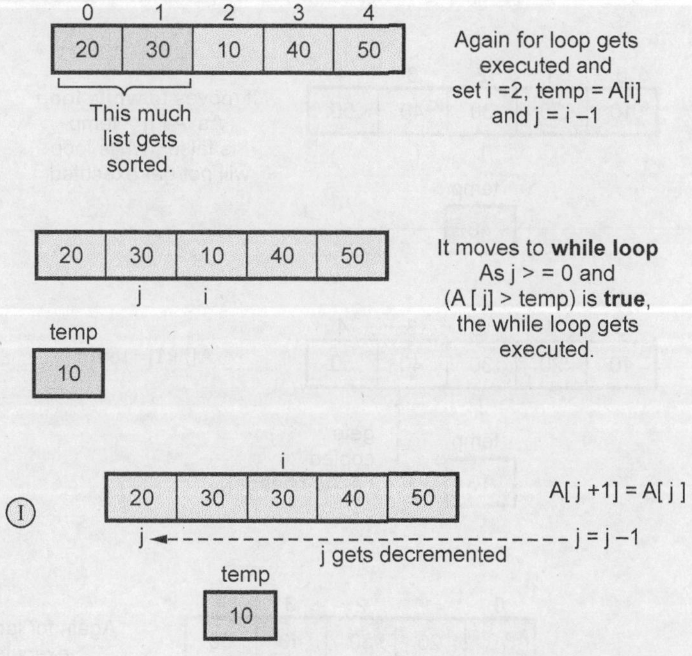

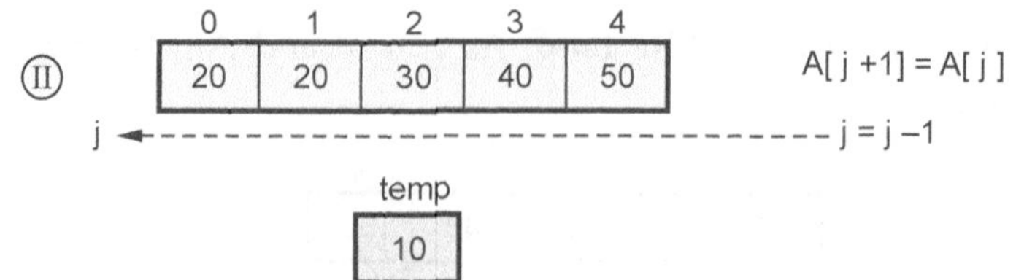

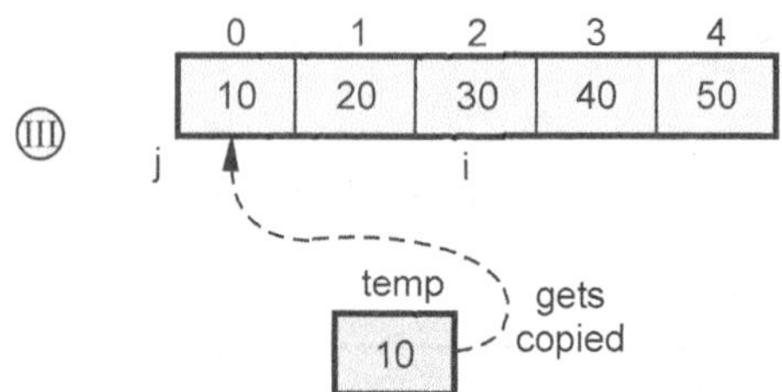

As j < 0, it comes out of **while** loop
A[j +1] = temp

Thus,

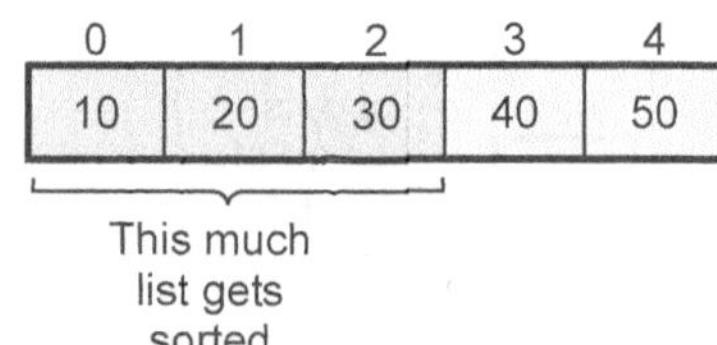

Again **for loop** gets executed.
set i = 3,
temp = A [i]
j = i –1

Then,

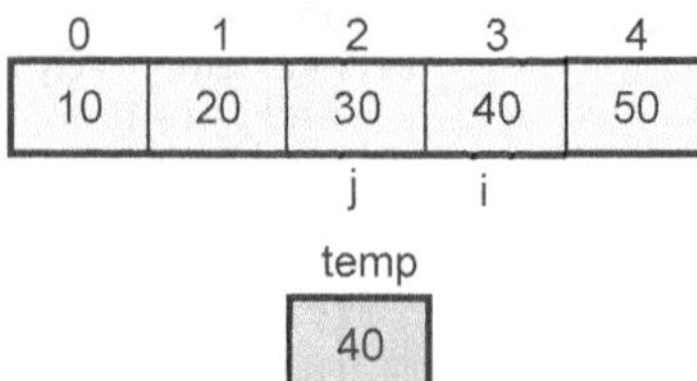

It moves to **while loop**
As A [j] > temp is false , while loop will not get executed.

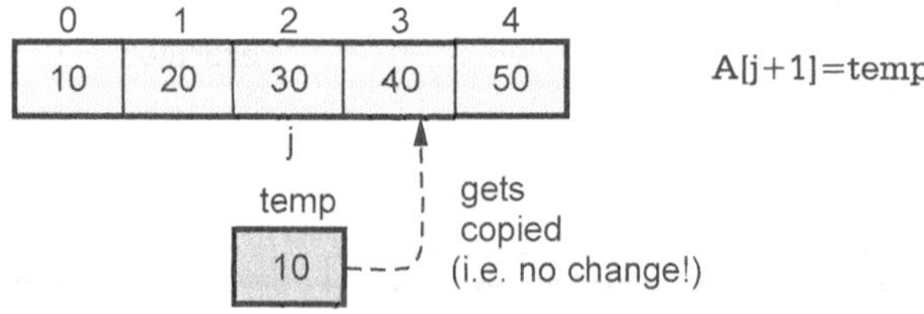

A[j+1]=temp

Then,

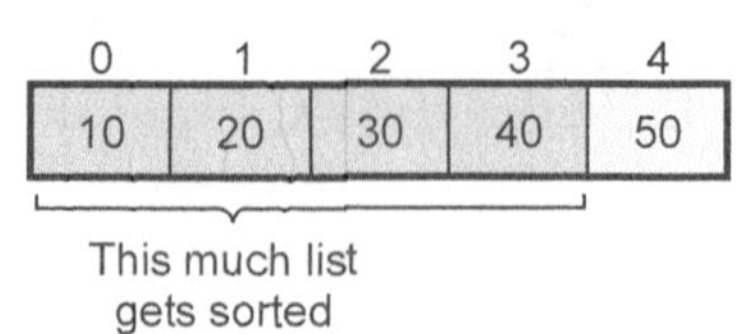

Again for loop gets executed
set i = 4
temp = A [i]
j = i –1

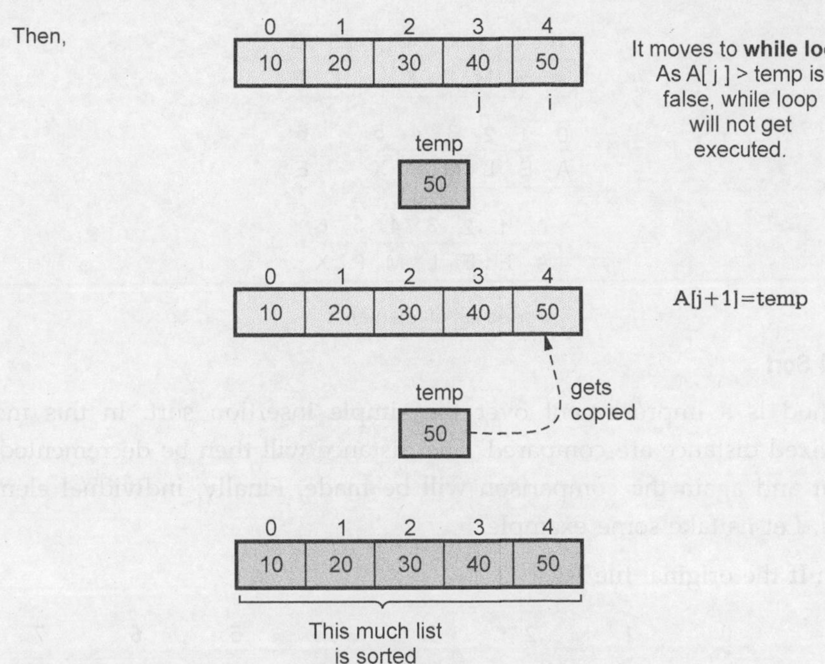

Thus we have scanned the entire list and inserted the elements at corresponding locations. Thus we get the sorted list by insertion sort.

Example 2.8.2 *Sort the letters of word "EXAMPLE" in alphabetical order using insertion sort.*

Summer-13, Marks 7

Solution : Consider the list of element as -

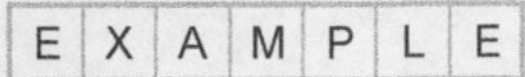

The process starts with first element.

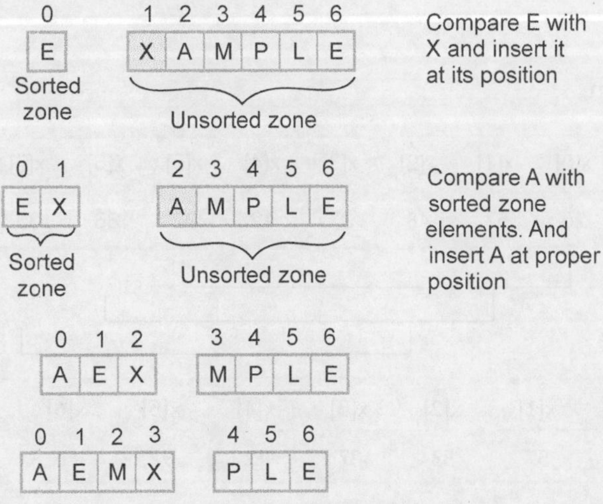

0	1	2	3	4		5	6
A	E	M	P	X		L	E

0	1	2	3	4	5		6
A	E	L	M	P	X		E

0	1	2	3	4	5	6
A	E	E	L	M	P	X

Sorted list of elements

2.8.1.4 Shell Sort

This method is a improvement over the simple insertion sort. In this method the elements at fixed distance are compared. The distance will then be decremented by some fixed amount and again the comparison will be made. Finally, individual elements will be compared. Let us take some example.

Example : If the original file is

	0	1	2	3	4	5	6	7
X array	25	57	48	37	12	92	86	33

Step 1 : Let us take the distance k = 5

So in the first iteration compare

(x [0], x[5])

(x [1], x [(6])

(x [2], x[7])

(x[3])

(x[4])

i.e. first iteration

After first iteration,

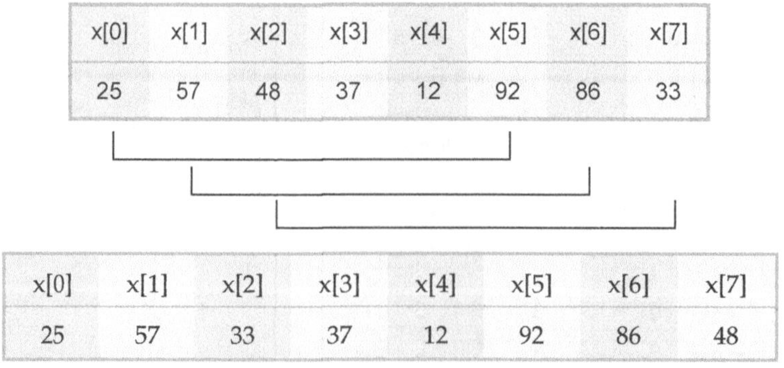

x[0]	x[1]	x[2]	x[3]	x[4]	x[5]	x[6]	x[7]
25	57	48	37	12	92	86	33

x[0]	x[1]	x[2]	x[3]	x[4]	x[5]	x[6]	x[7]
25	57	33	37	12	92	86	48

Step 2 :

Initially K was 5. Take some d and decrement K by d. Let us take d = 2

$\therefore$ K = K – d i.e. K = 5 – 2 = 3

So now compare

(x[0], x[3], x[6]), (x[1], x[4], x[7])

(x[2], x[5])

Second iteration

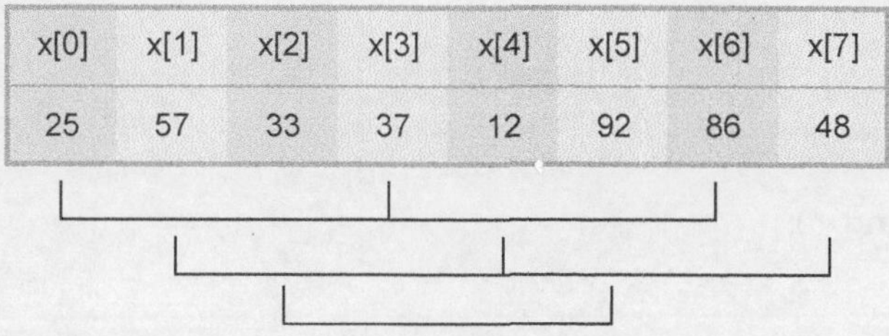

x[0]	x[1]	x[2]	x[3]	x[4]	x[5]	x[6]	x[7]
25	57	33	37	12	92	86	48

After second iteration

x[0]	x[1]	x[2]	x[3]	x[4]	x[5]	x[6]	x[7]
25	12	33	37	48	92	86	57

Step 3 : Now K = K – d $\therefore$K = 3 – 2 = 1

So now compare

(x[0], x[1], x[2], x[3], x[4], x[5], x[6], x[7])

This sorting is then done by simple insertion sort. Because simple insertion sort is highly efficient on sorted file. So we get

x[0]	x[1]	x[2]	x[3]	x[4]	x[5]	x[6]	x[7]
12	25	33	37	48	57	86	92

C Program

```
/*******************************************************************
Program for sorting  the list of elements using shell sort
*******************************************************************/
#include<stdio.h>
#include<stdlib.h>
#include<conio.h>
#define MAX 10

int main(void)
{
```

```
 void shellsort(int a[], int n);
 void Display(int a[],int n);
 int a[MAX];
 int i,n;
 clrscr();
 printf("\n\t Program for Shell Sort");
 printf("\n Enter total number of elements in an array ");

 scanf("%d",&n);
 printf("\n Enter some elements in array\n");
 for(i=0;i<n;i++)
   scanf("%d",&a[i]);
 printf("\nBefore sorting  ");
 Display(a,n);
 printf("\n");
 printf("\nAfter sorting  ");
 shellsort(a,n);
 Display(a,n);
 getch();
 return 0;
}
void Display(int a[],int n)
{
 int i;
 for(i=0;i<n;i++)
 {
  printf(" %d",a[i]);
 }
}

void shellsort(int a[], int n)
{
 int i,j,d,k,value;
 d=(n+1)/2;
 for(i=d;i>=1;i=i/2)
 {
   for(j=i;j<=n-1;j++)
   {
     value=a[j];
     k=j-i;
     while(k>=0 && value<a[k])
     {
       a[k+i]=a[k];
       k=k-i;
     }
    a[k+i]=value;
 }
```

```
 }
}
```

Output

```
    Program for Shell Sort
 Enter total number of elements in an array 10

 Enter some elements in array
10
9
8
7
6
5
4
3
2
1

Before sorting   10 9 8 7 6 5 4 3 2 1

After sorting   1 2 3 4 5 6 7 8 9 10
```

2.8.1.5 Heap Sort

Heap sort is a sorting method discovered by J. W. J. Williams. It works in two stages.

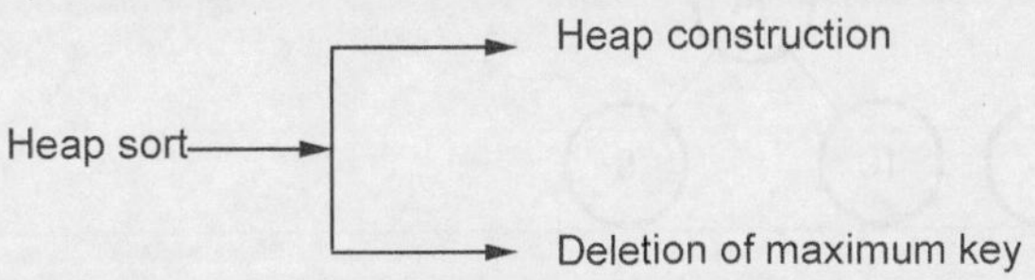

1. **Heap construction :** First construct a heap for given numbers.
2. **Deletion of maximum key :** Delete root key always for (n – 1) times to remaining heap. Hence we will get the elements in decreasing order. For an array implementation of heap, delete the element from heap and put the deleted element in the last position in array. Thus after deleting all the elements one by one, if we collect these deleted elements in an array starting from last index of array.

We get a list of elements in a ascending order.

Let us understand this technique with the help of some example.

Sort the following elements using heap sort

14, 12, 9, 8, 7, 10, 18.

Stage I : **Heap construction**

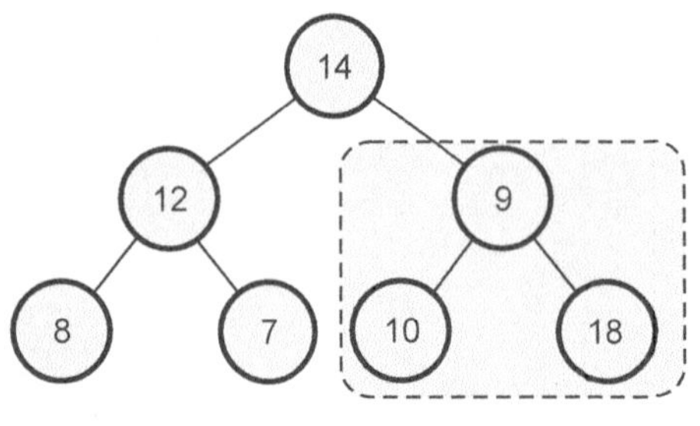

We start heapifying from bottom

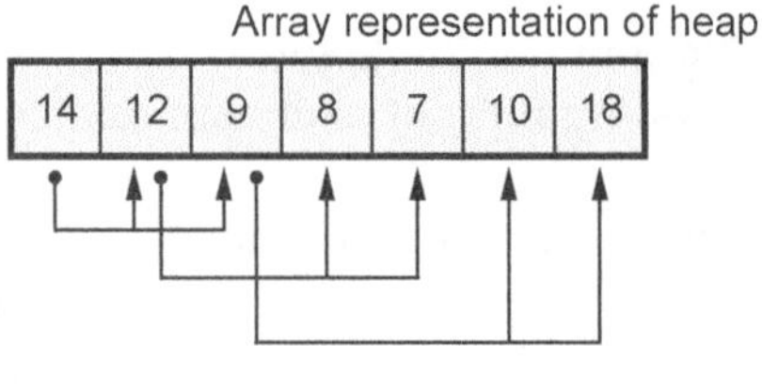

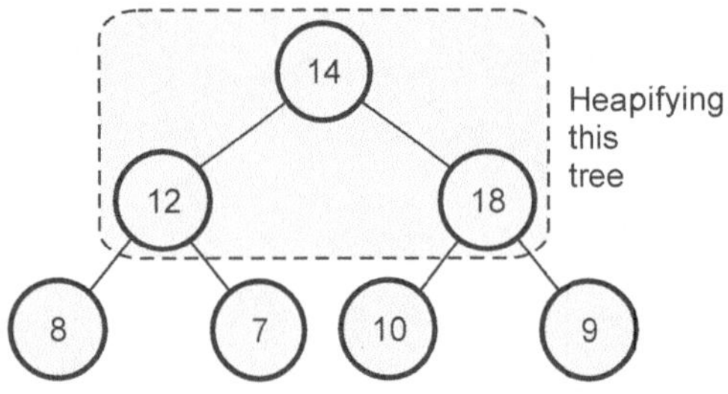

Heapifying this tree

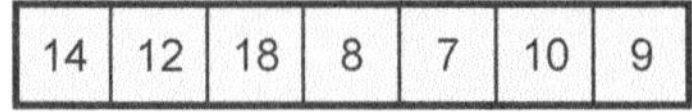

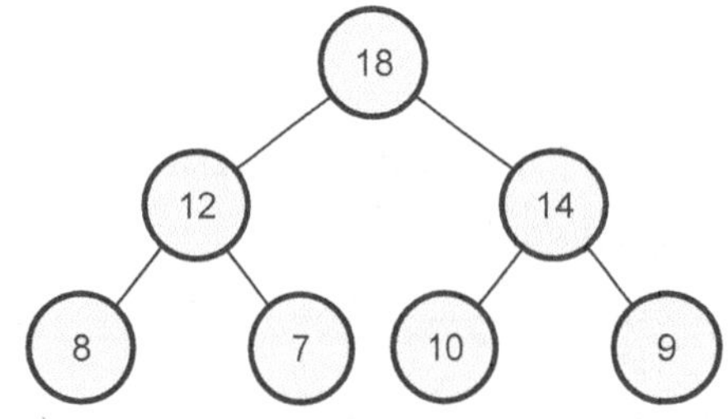

18	12	14	8	7	10	9

Stage II : **Maximum deletion**

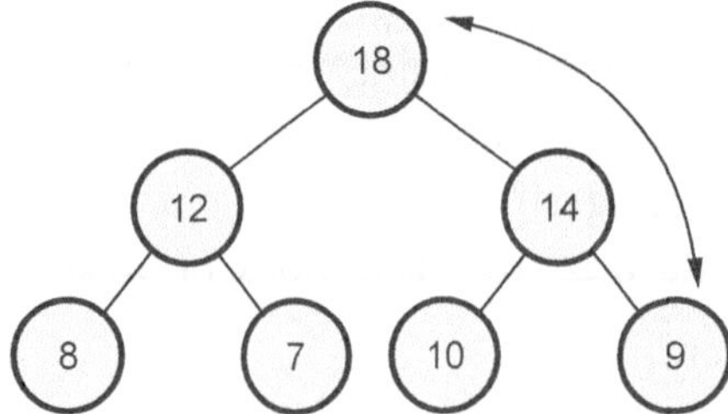

18	12	14	8	7	10	9

Swap with last node in heap

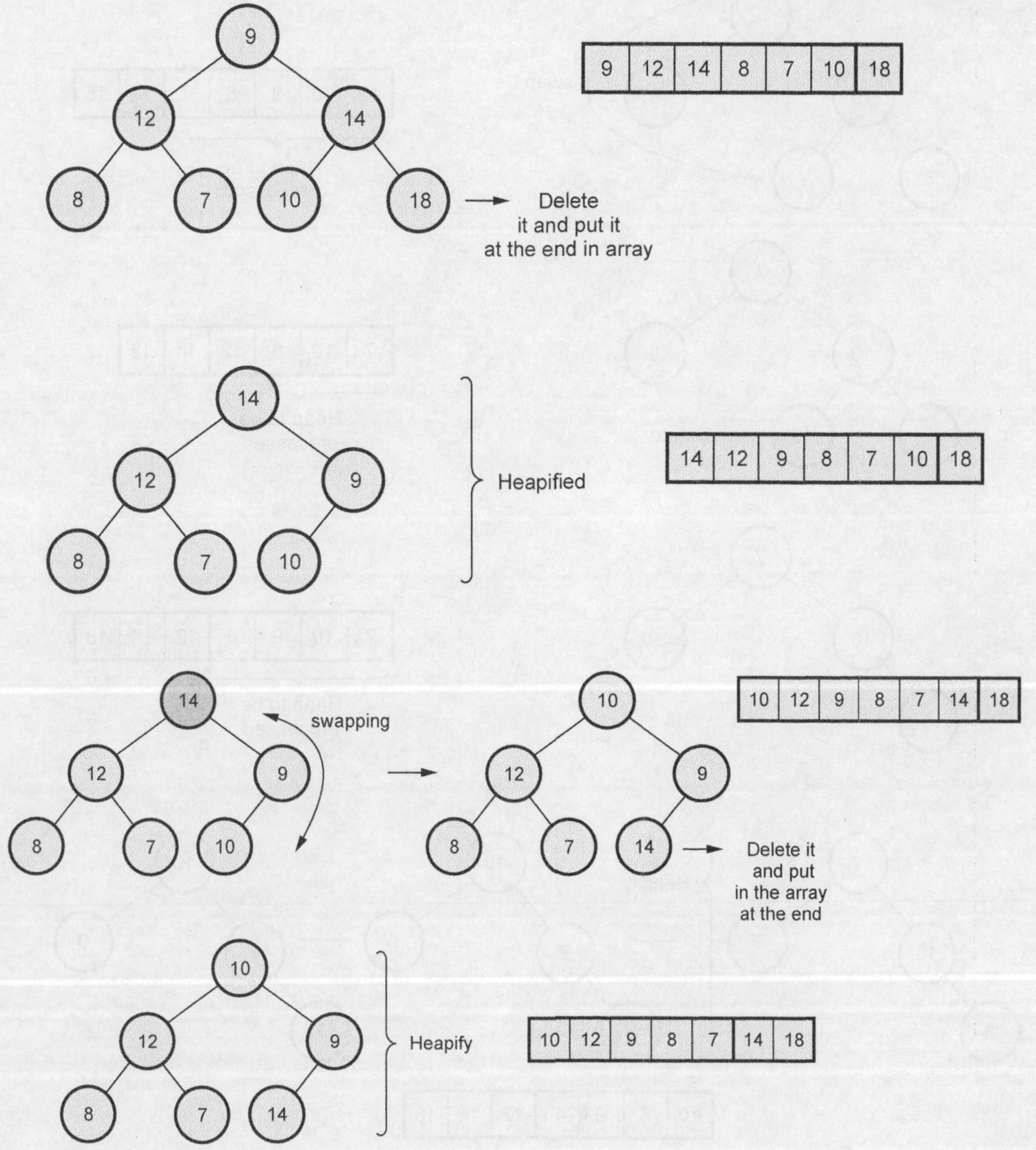

9
12
14
8
7
10
18
9 12 14 8 7 10 18
Delete it and put it at the end in array
14
12
9
8
7
10
Heapified
14 12 9 8 7 10 18
14
swapping
12
9
8
7
10
10
12
9
8
7
14
10 12 9 8 7 14 18
Delete it and put in the array at the end
10
12
9
8
7
14
Heapify
10 12 9 8 7 14 18

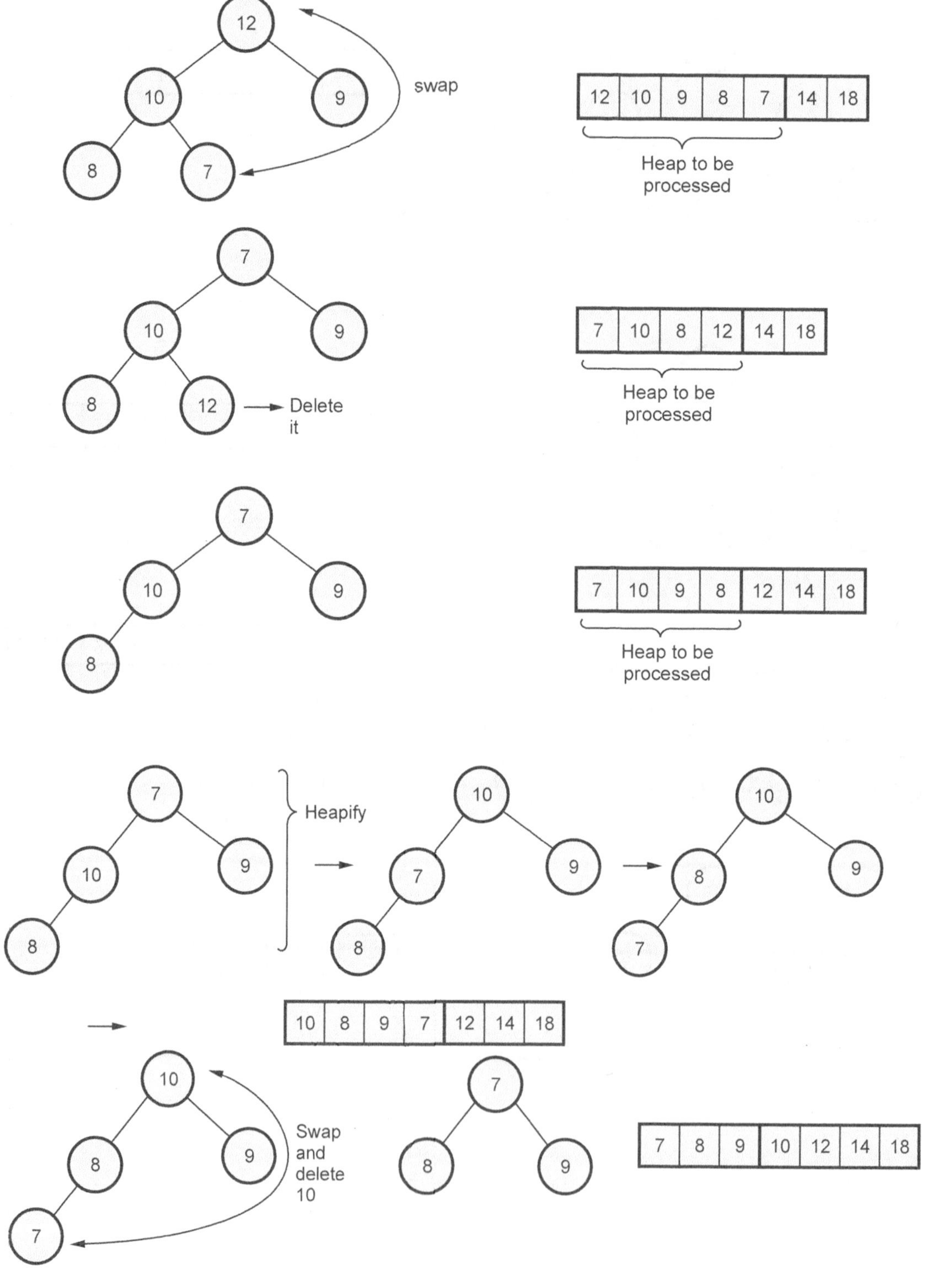
12
10
9
8
7
swap
12 10 9 8 7 14 18
Heap to be processed
7
10
9
8
12
Delete it
7 10 8 12 14 18
Heap to be processed
7
10
9
8
7 10 9 8 12 14 18
Heap to be processed
7
10
9
8
Heapify
10
7
9
8
10
8
9
7
10 8 9 7 12 14 18
10
8
9
7
Swap and delete 10
7
8
9
7 8 9 10 12 14 18

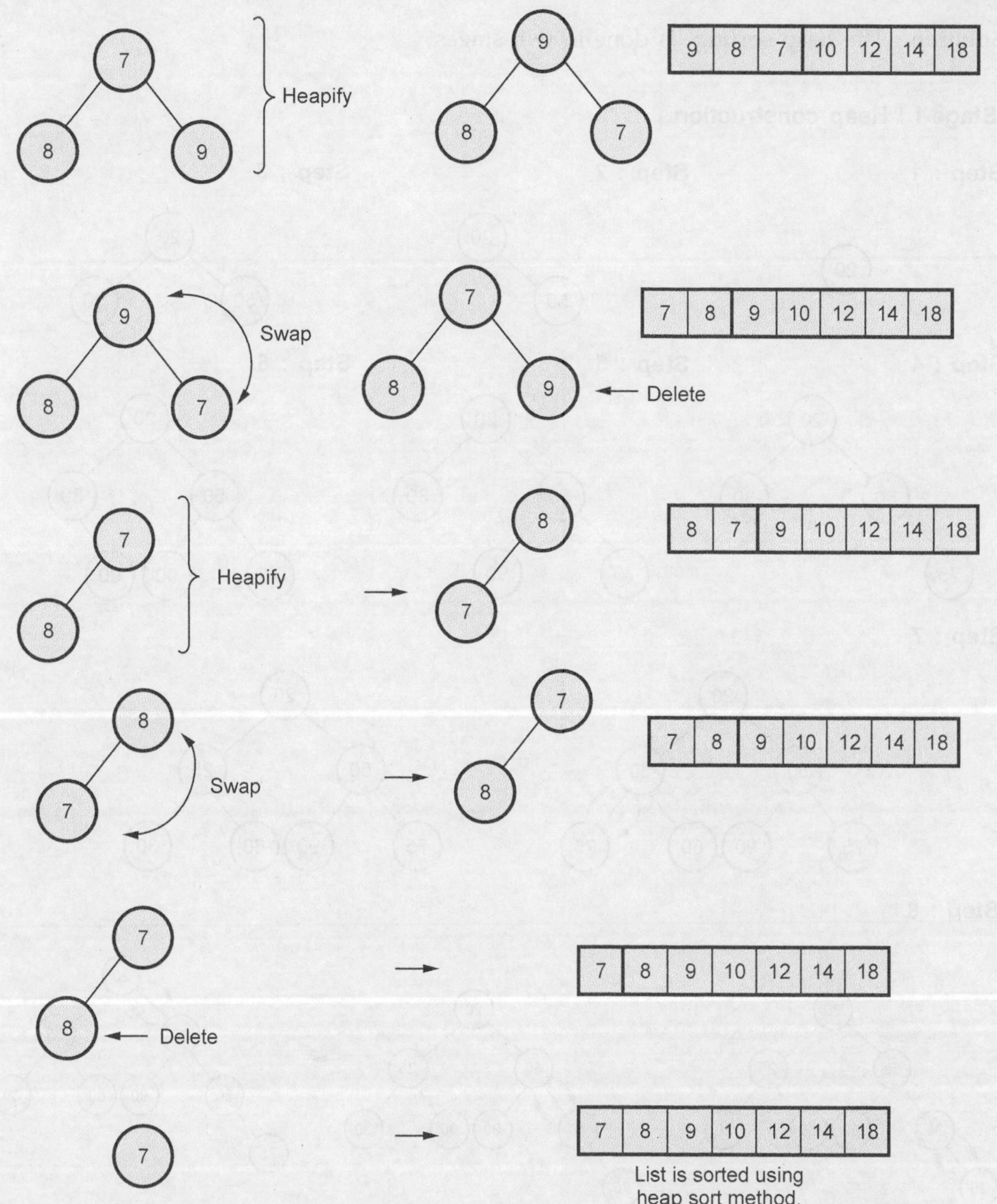

Example 2.8.3 *Sort the given elements with Heap Sort Method: 20, 50, 30, 75, 90, 60, 25, 10, 40.*

GTU : Winter-15, Marks 7

Solution : The heap sorting is done in two stages

Stage I : Heap construction

Step : 1

20

Step : 2

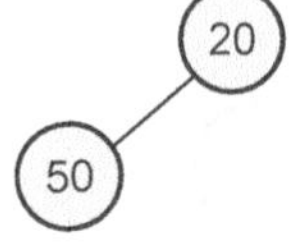

Step : 3

20
50 30

Step : 4

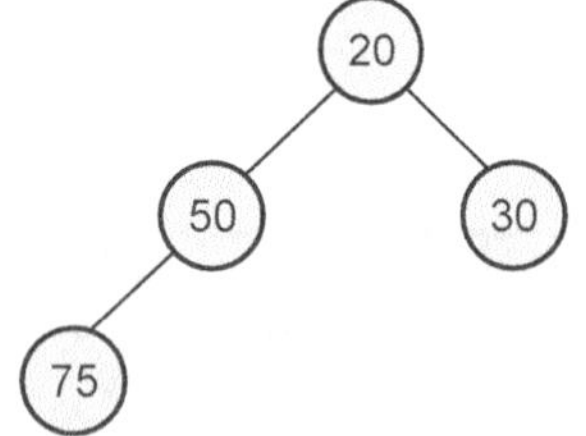

Step : 5

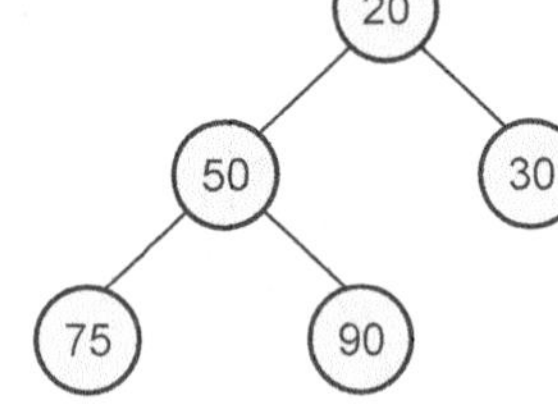

Step : 6

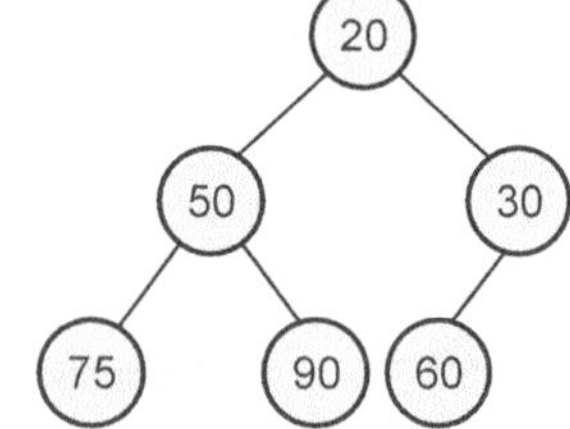

Step : 7

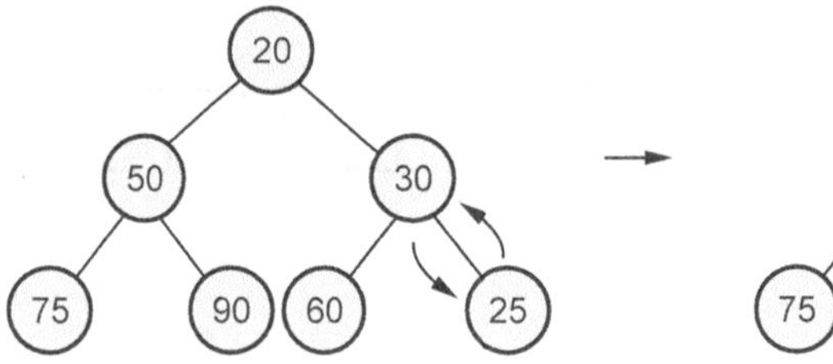

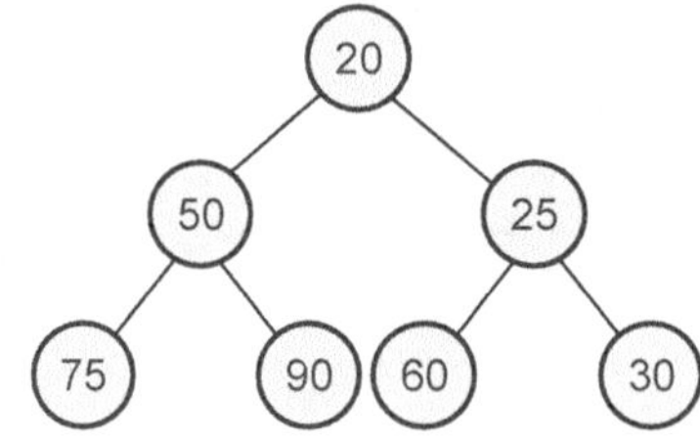

Step : 8

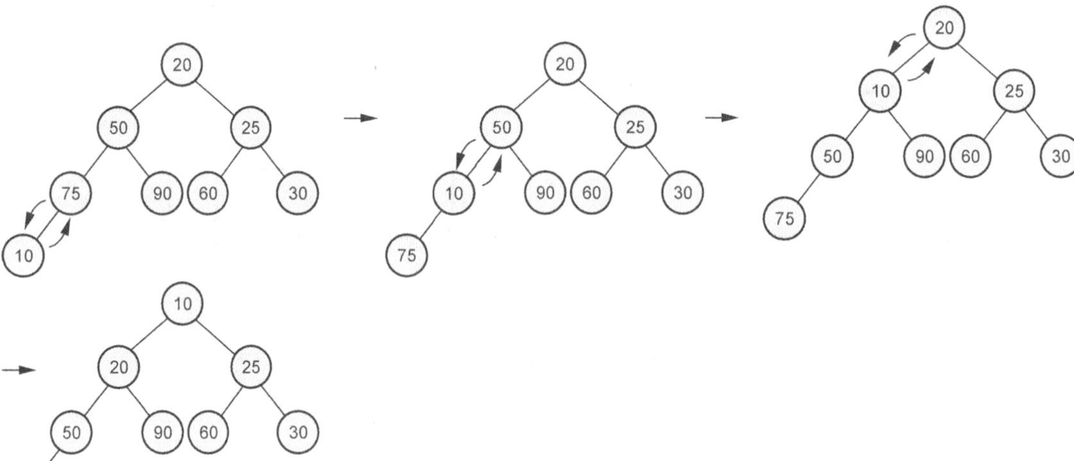

Stage II : Deletion of root

In this stage the root node is deleted and stored in priority queue. The min heap property is always maintained.

Step : 1 a : Deletion

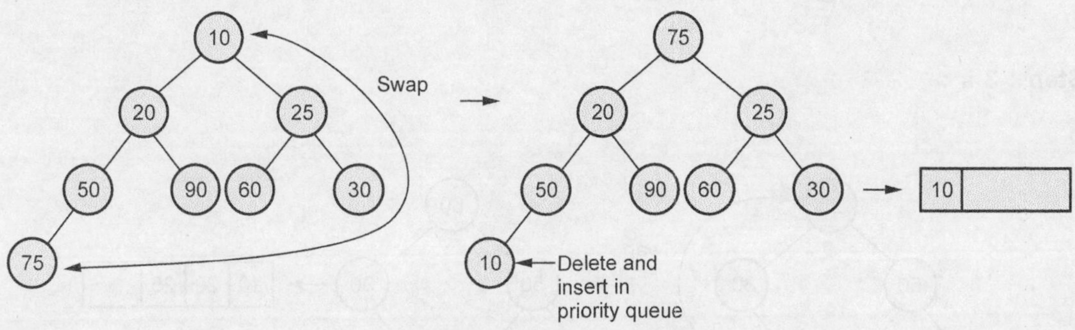

Step : 1 b : Adjusting heap property

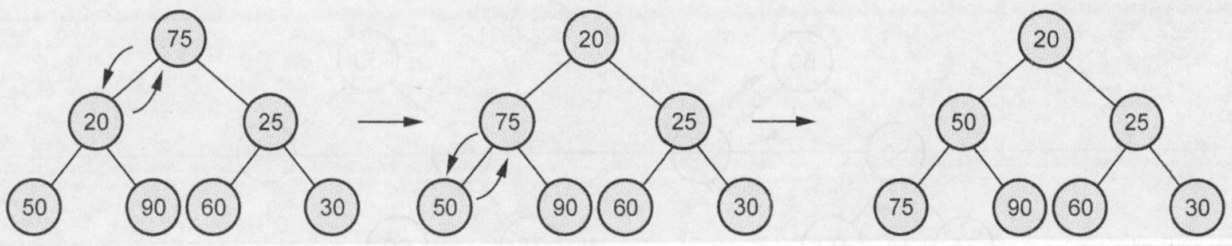

Step : 2 a :

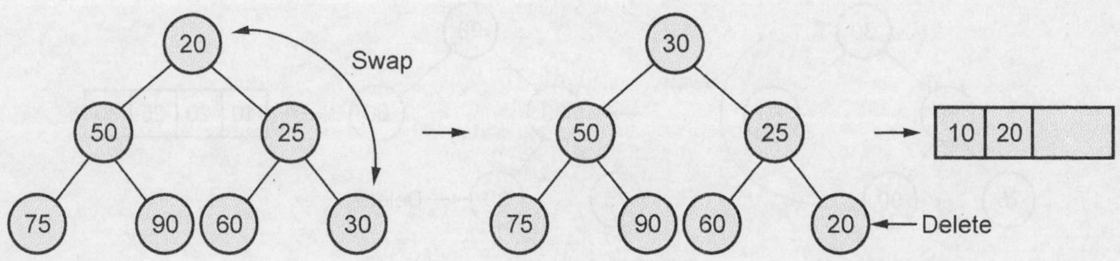

Step : 2 b :

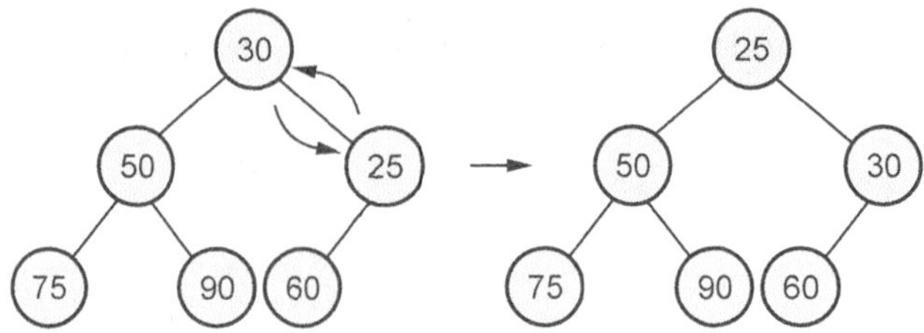

Step : 3 a :

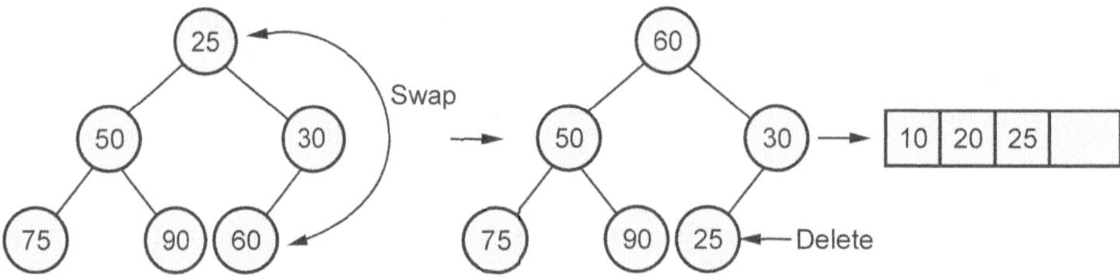

Step : 3 b :

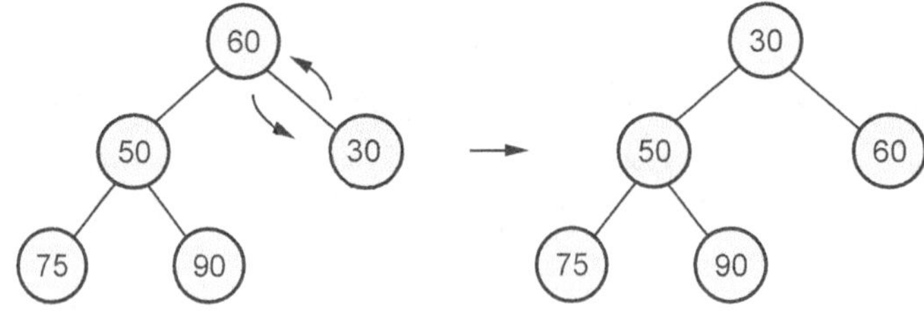

Step : 4 a :

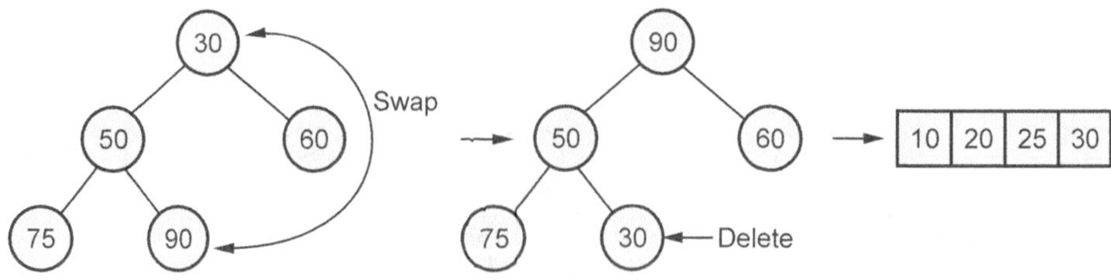

Step : 4 b :

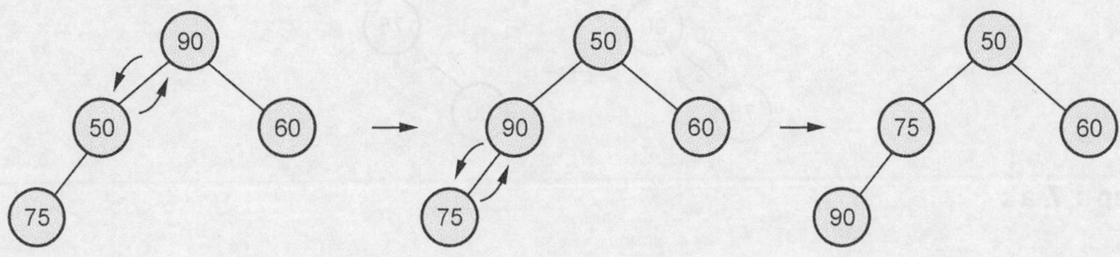

Step : 5 a :

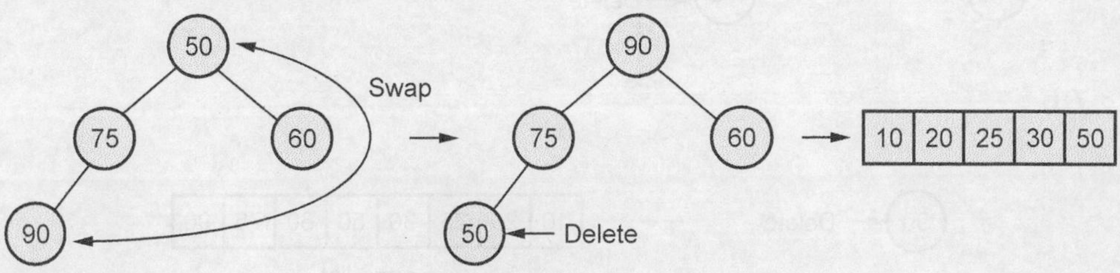

Step : 5 b :

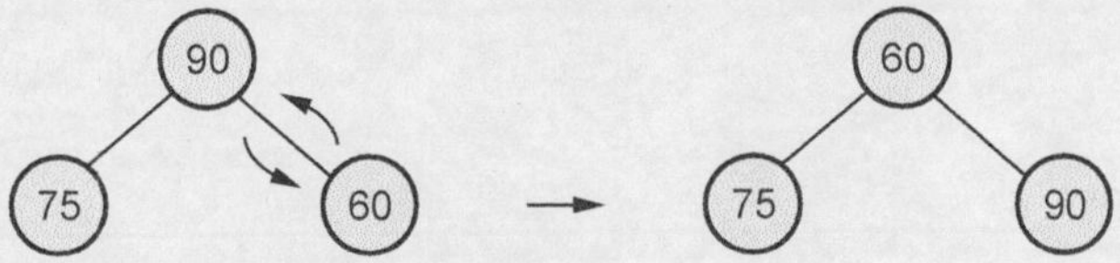

Step : 6 a :

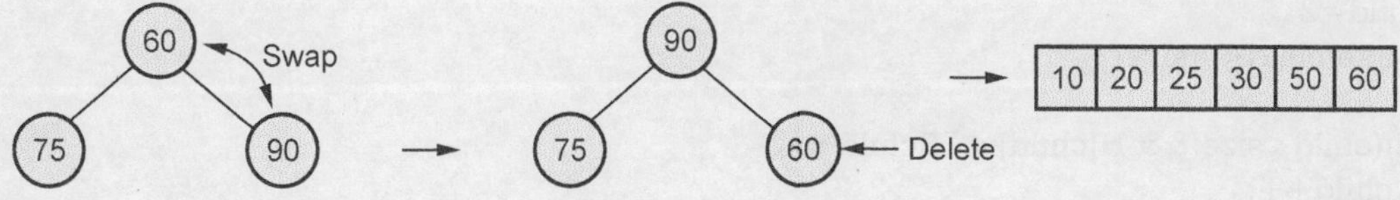

Step : 6 b :

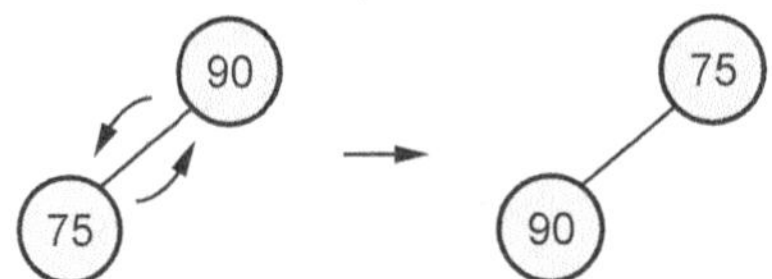

Step : 7 a :

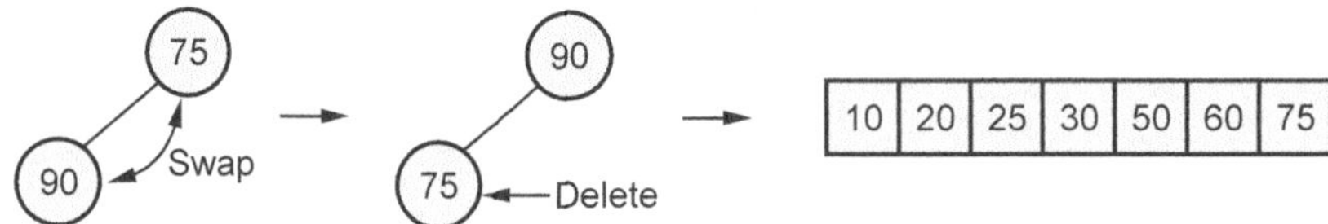

Step : 7 b :

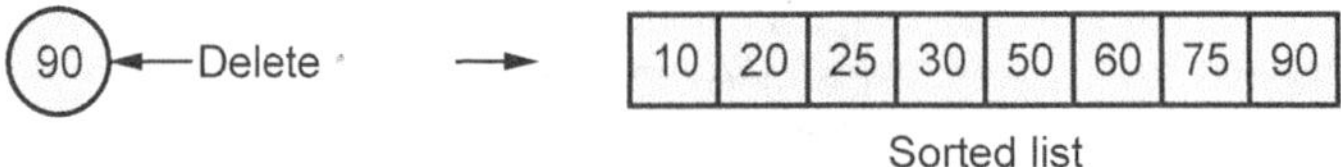

Pseudo code

```
void delet(int item)
{
 int item,temp;
 if(size==0)
  printf("Heap is empty");
 else
 {
  //remove the last element and reheapify
  item=H[size--];
 //item is placed at root
  temp=1;
  child=2
  while(child<=size)
  {
   if(child<size && H[child]< H[child+1]
    child++;
   if(item>=H[child])
    break;
   H[temp]=H[child]
   temp=child;
   child=child*2;
  }
```

```
 //place the largest item at root
 H[temp]=item;
 }
}
```

Analysis : Time complexity of heapsort is **O (log n)** in both worst and average case.

Features of heap sort

1. The time complexity of heap sort is Θ (n log n).
2. This is an in-place sorting algorithm. That means it does not require extra storage space while sorting the elements.
3. For random input it works slower than quick sort.
4. Heap sort is not a stable sorting method.
5. The space complexity of heap sort is O (1). As it does not require any extra storage to sort

'C' Program

```
/*******************************************************************
      This program is for implementing heap sort using heap construction
*******************************************************************/
#include<stdio.h>
#include<stdlib.h>
#include<conio.h>
#define MAX 10
void main()
{
      int i,n;
      int arr[MAX];
      void makeheap(int arr[MAX],int n);
      void heapsort(int arr[MAX],int n);
      void display(int arr[MAX],int n);
      clrscr();
       for(i=0;i<MAX;i++)
             arr[i]=0;
      printf("\n How many elements you want to insert?");
      scanf("%d",&n);
      printf("\n Enter the elements");
       for(i=0;i<n;i++)
            scanf("%d",&arr[i]);
      printf("\n The Elements are ...");
      display(arr,n);
      makeheap(arr,n);
      printf("\n Heapified");
      display(arr,n);
```

```
    heapsort(arr,n);
    printf("\nElements sorted by Heap sort... ");
    display(arr,n);
    getch();
}

void makeheap(int arr[MAX],int n)
{
    int i,val,j,father;
    for(i=1;i<n;i++)
    {
        val=arr[i];
        j=i;
        father=(j-1)/2;//finding the parent of node j
        while(j>0&&arr[father]<val)//creating a MAX heap
        {
            arr[j]=arr[father];//preserving parent dominance
            j=father;
            father=(j-1)/2;
        }
        arr[j]=val;
    }
}
void heapsort(int arr[MAX],int n)
{
        int i,k,temp,j;
        for(i=n-1;i>0;i--)
        {
            temp=arr[i];
            arr[i]=arr[0];
            k=0;
            if(i==1)
              j=-1;
            else
              j=1;
        if(i>2&&arr[2]>arr[1])
              j=2;
        while(j>=0&& temp <arr[j])
        {
            arr[k]=arr[j];
            k=j;
            j=2*k+1;
            if(j+1<=i-1&&arr[j]<arr[j+1])
                  j++;
            if(j>i-1)
                  j=-1;
        }
```

```
                    arr[k]=temp;
            }
}

void display(int arr[MAX],int n)
{
        int i;
        for(i=0;i<n;i++)
         printf("\n %d",arr[i]);

}
```

Output

```
        How many elements you want to insert?7

Enter the elements14
12
9
8
7
10
18

The Elements are ...
14
12
9
8
7
10
18
Heapified
18
12
14
8
7
9
10
Elements sorted by Heap sort...
  7
  8
  9
  10
  12
  14
  18
```

The tree can be

Heapified tree will be

sorted list will be

7	8	9	10	12	14	18

2.8.2 Sorting in Linear Time

2.8.2.1 Bucket Sort

Bucket sort is a sorting technique in which array is partitioned into buckets. Each bucket is then sorted individually, using some other sorting algorithm such as insertion sort.

Algorithm

1. Set up an array of initially empty buckets.
2. Put each element in corresponding bucket.
3. Sort each non empty bucket.
4. Visit the buckets in order and put all the elements into a sequence and print them.

Example 2.8.4 *Sort the elements using bucket sort. 56, 12, 84, 56, 28, 0, -13, 47, 94, 31, 12, -2.* **May-08**

Solution : We will set up an array as follows

	0	1	2	3	4	5	6	7	8	9	10
Range	−20 to −1	0 to 10	10 to 20	20 to 30	30 to 40	40 to 50	50 to 60	60 to 70	70 to 80	80 to 90	90 to 100

Now we will fill up each bucket by corresponding elements

0	1	2	3	4	5	6	7	8	9	10
−13	0	12	28	31	47	56			84	94
−2		12				56				

Now sort each bucket

0	1	2	3	4	5	6	7	8	9	10
−13	0	12	28	31	47	56			84	94
−2		12				56				

Print the array by visiting each bucket sequentially.

-13, -2, 0, 12, 12, 28, 31, 47, 56, 56, 84, 94.

This is the sorted list.

Example 2.8.5 *Sort the following elements in ascending order using bucket sort. Show all passes 121, 235, 55, 973, 327, 179* **Dec.-11**

Solution : We will set up an array as follows -

0 to 100	100 to 200	200 to 300	300 to 400	400 to 500	500 to 600	600 to 700	700 to 800	800 to 900	900 to 1000

Now we will fill up each bucket by corresponding element in the list

55	121, 179	235	237						973
0 to 100	100 to 200	200 to 300	300 to 400	400 to 500	500 to 600	600 to 700	700 to 800	800 to 900	900 to 1000

Now visit each bucket and sort it individually.

Finally read each element of the bucket and place in some array say b[]. The elements from array b are printed to display the sorted list

55	121	179	235	327	973

Pseudo Code

```
void bucketsort( int a[],int n,int max )
{
  int i,j=0;
//inialize each bucket 0 and thus indicates bucket to be empty
  int *buckets=calloc(max+1,sizeof(int));
//place Each element from unsorted array in each corresponding bucket
 for(int i=0;i<n;i++)
   buckets[a[i]]++;
//sort each bucket individually
// Sequentially empty each bucket in some array
for(i=0;i<max;i++)
   while(buckets[i]--)
     b[j++]=i;
//display the array b as sorted list of elements
```

Drawbacks

1. For bucket sort the maximum value of the element must be known.
2. We must have to create enough buckets in the memory for every element to place in the array.

Analysis

The best case, worst case and average case time complexity of this algorithm is O(n)

2.8.2.2 Radix Sort

In this mehod sorting can be done digit by digit and thus all the elements can be sorted.

Example for Radix sort

Consider the unsorted array of 8 elements.

45 37 05 09 06 11 18 27

Step 1 : Now sort the element according to the last digit.

Last digit	0	1	2	3	4	5	6	7	8	9
Elements		11				45, 05	06	37,27	18	09

Now sort this number

Last digit	Element
0	
1	11
2	
3	
4	
5	05,45
6	06
7	27,37
8	18
9	09

Step 2 : Now sort the above array with the help of second last digit.

Second last digit	Element
0	05,06,09
1	11,18
2	27
3	37
4	45
5	
6	
7	
8	
9	

Since the list of element is of two digit that is why, we will stop comparing. Now whatever list we have got (shown in above array) is of sorted elements. Thus finally the sorted list by radix sort method will be

05 06 09 11 18 27 37 45

Algorithm :

1. Read the total number of elements in the array.
2. Store the unsorted elements in the array.
3. Now the simple procedure is to sort the elements by digit by digit.
4. Sort the elements according to the last digit then second last digit and so on.
5. Thus the elements should be sorted for up to the most significant bit.
6. Store the sorted element in the array and print them.
7. Stop.

'C' Program

```
/**************************************************************
        Program for sorting the elements by radix sort.
**************************************************************/
/*Header Files*/
#include<stdio.h>
```

```
#include<conio.h>
#include<math.h>
void main()
  { int a[100][100],r=0,c=0,i,sz,b[50],temp;
    clrscr();
    printf("Size of array: ");
     scanf("%d",&sz);
    printf("\n");
    for(r=0;r<100;r++)
            { for(c=0;c<100;c++)
                a[r][c]=1000;
    }
    for(i=0;i<sz;i++)
    { printf("Enter element %d: ",i+1);
       scanf("%d",&b[i]);
      r=b[i]/100;
      c=b[i]%100;
      a[r][c]=b[i];
    }
    for(r=0;r<100;r++)
    { for(c=0;c<100;c++)
       { for(i=0;i<sz;i++)
         { if(a[r][c]==b[i])
           { printf("\n\t");
             printf("%d",a[r][c]);
           }
         }
       }
    }
    getch();
  }
/********************End of Program**************************/
```

Output

```
Size of array: 5

Enter element 1 : 7
Enter element 2 : 5
Enter element 3 : 37
Enter element 4 : 27
Enter element 5 : 29
      5
      7
      27
      29
      37
```

2.8.2.3 Counting Sort

In counting sort the elements are arranged at its proper position where position is determined by an integer m which is in the range 0 to n. In other words, if element p is at some location - say 5 then all the elements that are lesser than p will be at 0 to 4 positions and all the elements that are greater than p will be arranged from 6 to n-1 locations where n indicates the total number of elements.

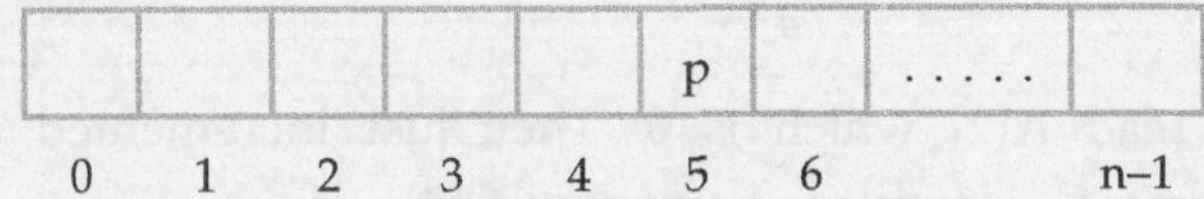

Let us first understand the counting sort method with the help of some example.

Example 2.8.6 *Sort the following elements using counting sort method.*
{6, 0, 2, 0, 1, 3, 4, 6, 1, 3, 2} **2008-09**

Solution : We will arrange all the elements in array A as follows.

1	2	3	4	5	6	7	8	9	10	11
6	0	2	0	1	3	4	6	1	3	2

We will maintain two more arrays : C[0...k] and B[1....n]. The array C will be for temporary purposes and array B will store the sorted list of elements. Now just observe the input elements. The input elements are with in the range 0 to 6. Hence we will have array C ranging from 0 to 6.

Step 1 :

	1	2	3	4	5	6	7	8	9	10	11
A	6	0	2	0	1	3	4	6	1	3	2

C	0	0	0	0	0	0	0	Initially
	0	1	2	3	4	5	6	

Read the first element from array A i.e. 6 Now look at array C which is initialized by 0. As we have read input 6 from array A just increment the value in 6th index of array C. Then we will get.

	1	2	3	4	5	6	7	8	9	10	11
A	6	0	2	0	1	3	4	6	1	3	2

C	0	0	0	0	0	0	1
	0	1	2	3	4	5	6

Step 2 :

	1	2	3	4	5	6	7	8	9	10	11
A	6	0	2	0	1	3	4	6	1	3	2

	0	1	2	3	4	5	6
C	1	0	0	0	0	0	1

Now we will read **A[2]** which is 0. Then just incremented the value at location 0 in array C. Hence we have now **C[0] = 1**

Step 3 :

	1	2	3	4	5	6	7	8	9	10	11
A	6	0	2	0	1	3	4	6	1	3	2

	0	1	2	3	4	5	6
C	1	0	1	0	0	0	1

Now read A[3] which 2. Hence increment C[2] by 1.

Step 4 :

	1	2	3	4	5	6	7	8	9	10	11
A	6	0	2	0	1	3	4	6	1	3	2

	0	1	2	3	4	5	6
C	2	0	1	0	0	0	1

Read A[4] which is 0. Hence increment C[0] by 1

Step 5 :

	1	2	3	4	5	6	7	8	9	10	11
A	6	0	2	0	1	3	4	6	1	3	2

	0	1	2	3	4	5	6
C	2	1	1	0	0	0	1

Read A[5] which is 1. Hence increment C[1] by 1.

Step 6 :

	1	2	3	4	5	6	7	8	9	10	11
A	6	0	2	0	1	3	4	6	1	3	2

	0	1	2	3	4	5	6
C	2	1	1	1	0	0	1

Read A[6] which is 3. Hence increment C[3] by 1.

Step 7 :

	1	2	3	4	5	6	7	8	9	10	11
A	6	0	2	0	1	3	4	6	1	3	2

	0	1	2	3	4	5	6
C	2	1	1	1	1	0	1

Read A[7] which is 4. Hence increment C[4] by 1.

Step 8 :

	1	2	3	4	5	6	7	8	9	10	11
A	6	0	2	0	1	3	4	6	1	3	2

	0	1	2	3	4	5	6
C	2	1	1	1	1	0	2

Read A[8] which is 8. Hence increment C[6] by 1.

Step 9 :

	1	2	3	4	5	6	7	8	9	10	11
A	6	0	2	0	1	3	4	6	1	3	2

	0	1	2	3	4	5	6
C	2	2	1	1	1	0	2

Read A[9] which 1. Hence increment C[6] by 1.

Step 10 :

	1	2	3	4	5	6	7	8	9	10	11
A	6	0	2	0	1	3	4	6	1	3	2

C	2	2	1	2	1	0	2
	0	1	2	3	4	5	6

Read A[10] which is 3. Hence increment C[3] by 1

Step 11 :

	1	2	3	4	5	6	7	8	9	10	11
A	6	0	2	0	1	3	4	6	1	3	2

C	2	2	2	2	1	0	2
	0	1	2	3	4	5	6

Read A[11] which is 2. Hence increment C[2] by 1.

Thus now we get array A and C ready for further processing. Now we will start reading C array from 1 to 6 and update the array elements by the following formula

$$C[i] = C[i] + C[i-1]$$

$$\therefore \quad C[1] = C[1] + C[0]$$

$$\therefore \quad C[1] = 2 + 2 = 4$$

Continuing in this fashion we can update the values in C array.

Step 12 : Following is a C array.

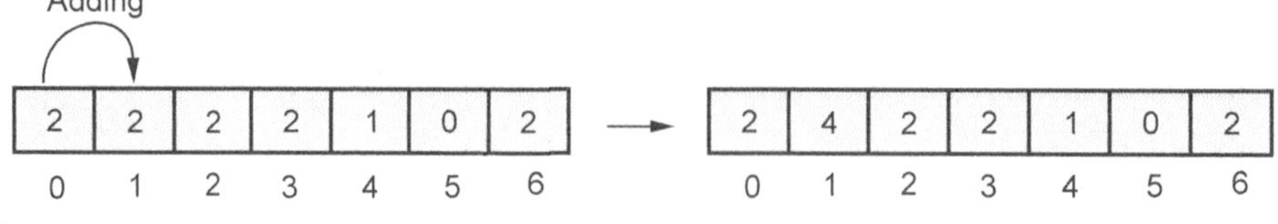

Step 13 :

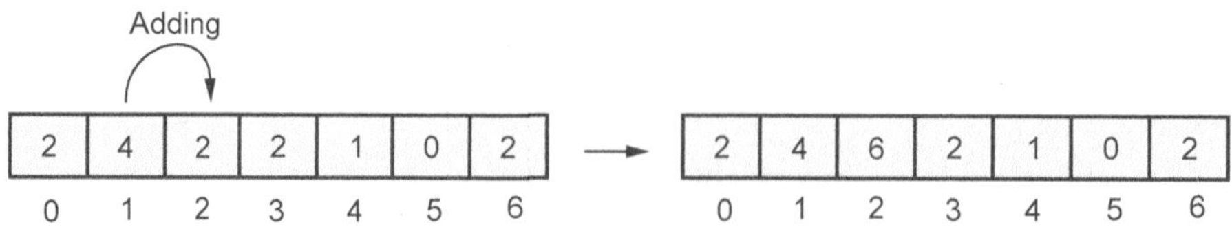

Step 14 :

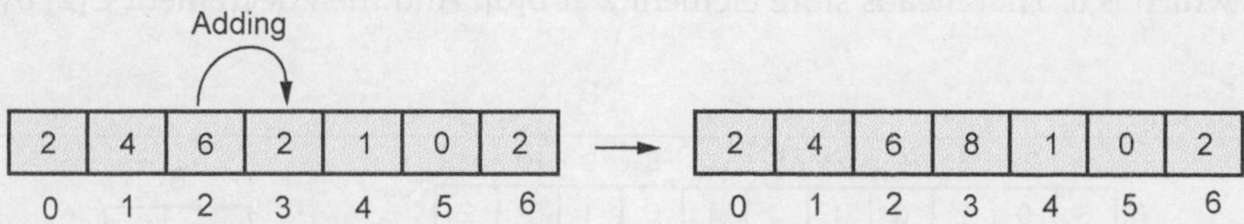

Step 15 :

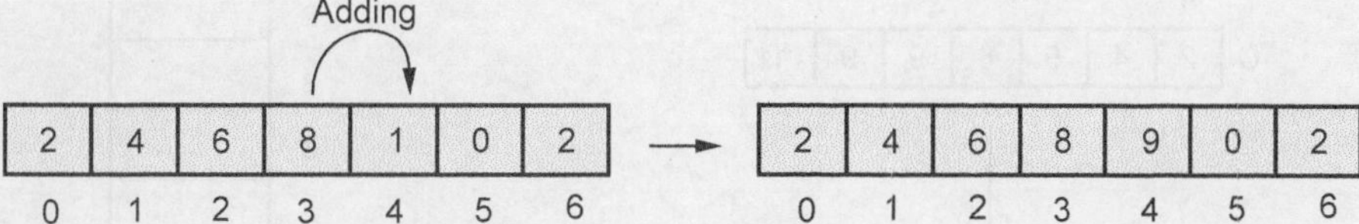

Step 16 :

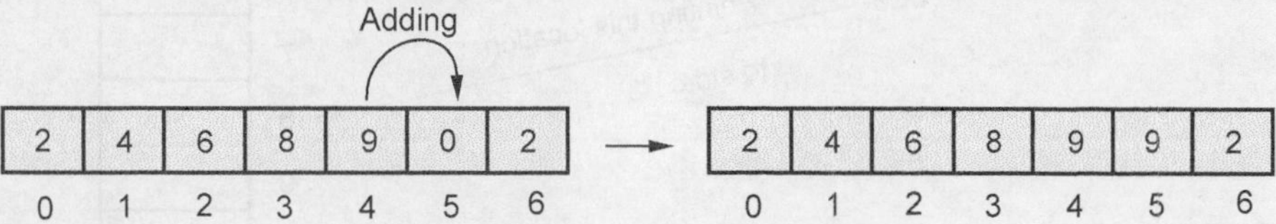

Step 17 :

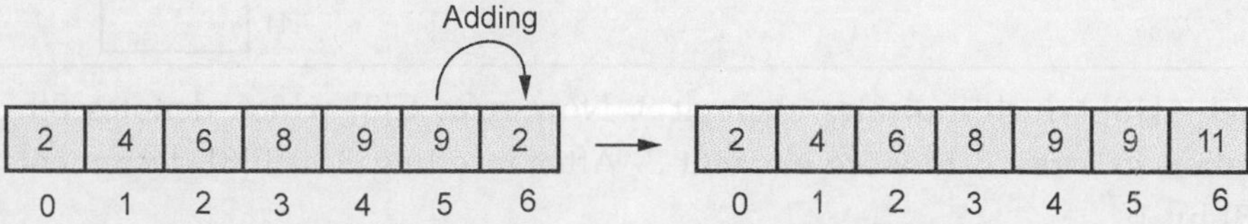

Now we have an array C which denotes the positions of elements in array B.

Now start reading array A from the end.

Step 18 :

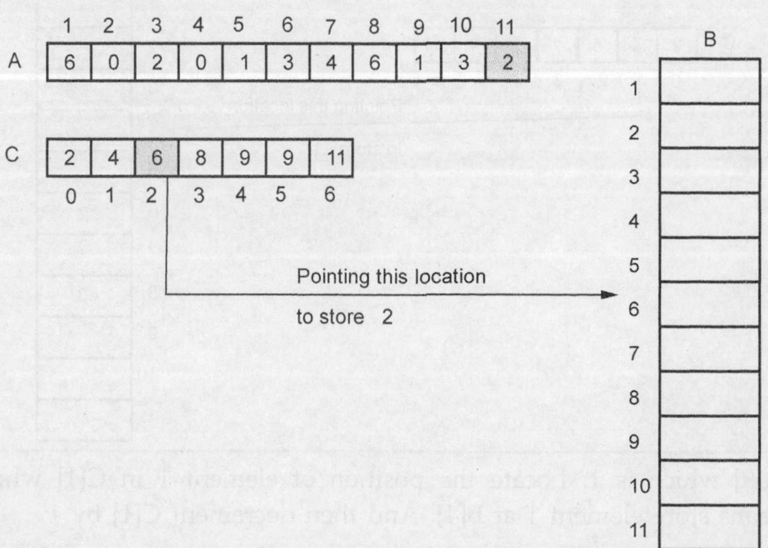

In step 18, we read array A[11]. The number is 2. Then located the position of element 2 in C[2] which is 6. That means store element 2 at B[6]. And then decrement C[2] by 1.

Step 19 :

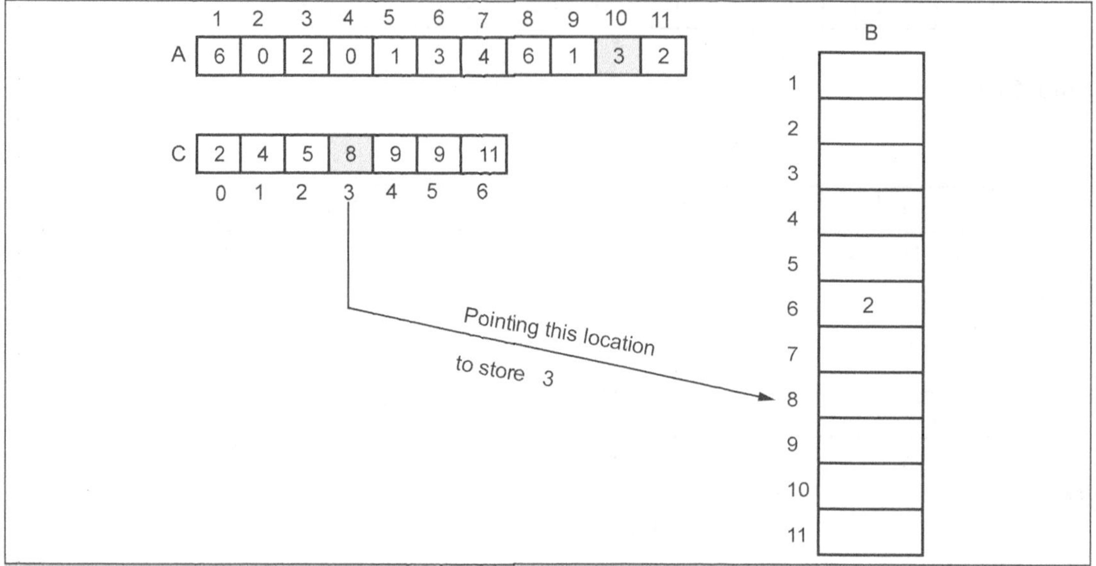

Read A[10] which indicates element 3. Now refer C[3] which denotes 8th location in array B to store element 3. After inserting 3 at B[8] decrement C[3] by 1

Step 20 :

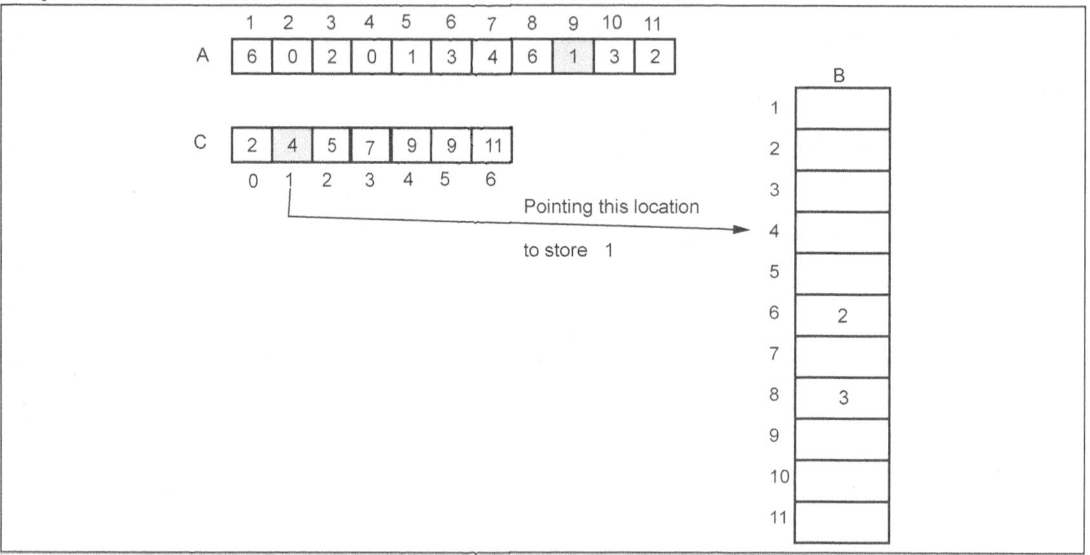

Read A[9] which is 1. Locate the position of element 1 in C[1] which is 4. That means store element 1 at B[4]. And then decrement C[1] by 1

Step 21 :

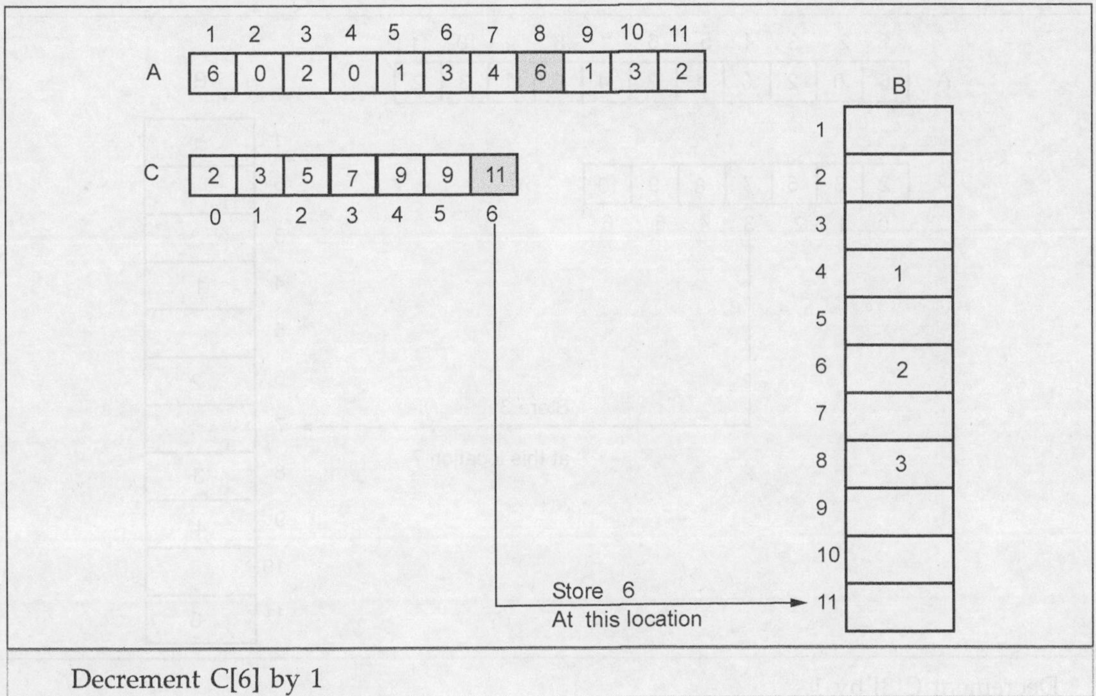

Decrement C[6] by 1

Step 22 :

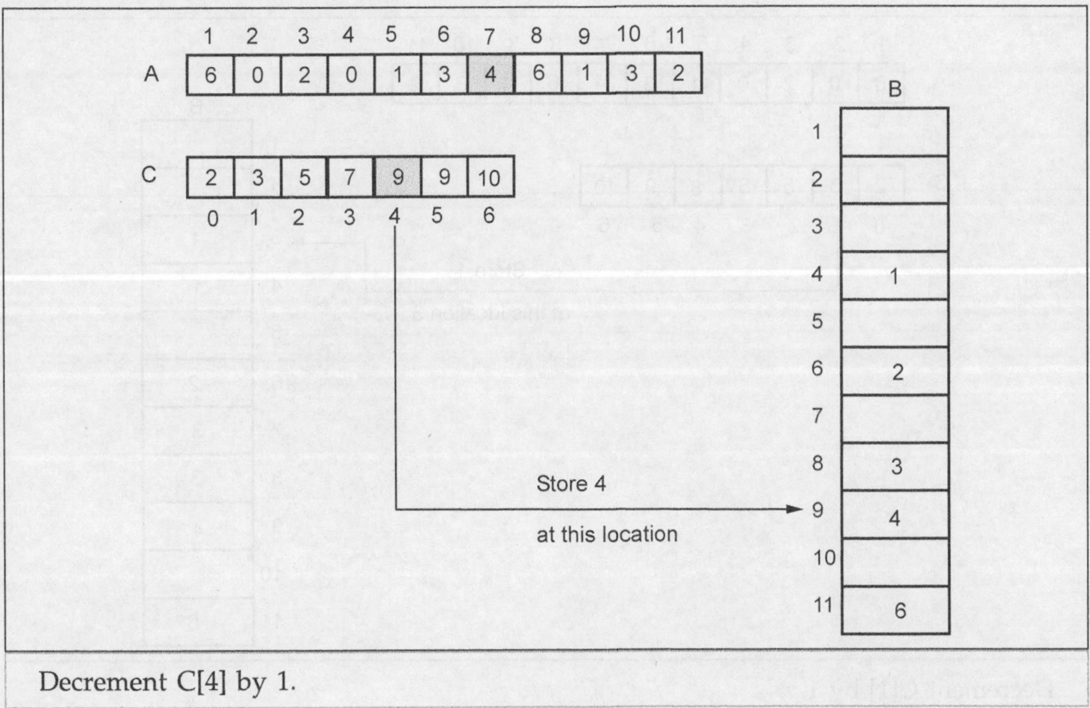

Decrement C[4] by 1.

Step 23 :

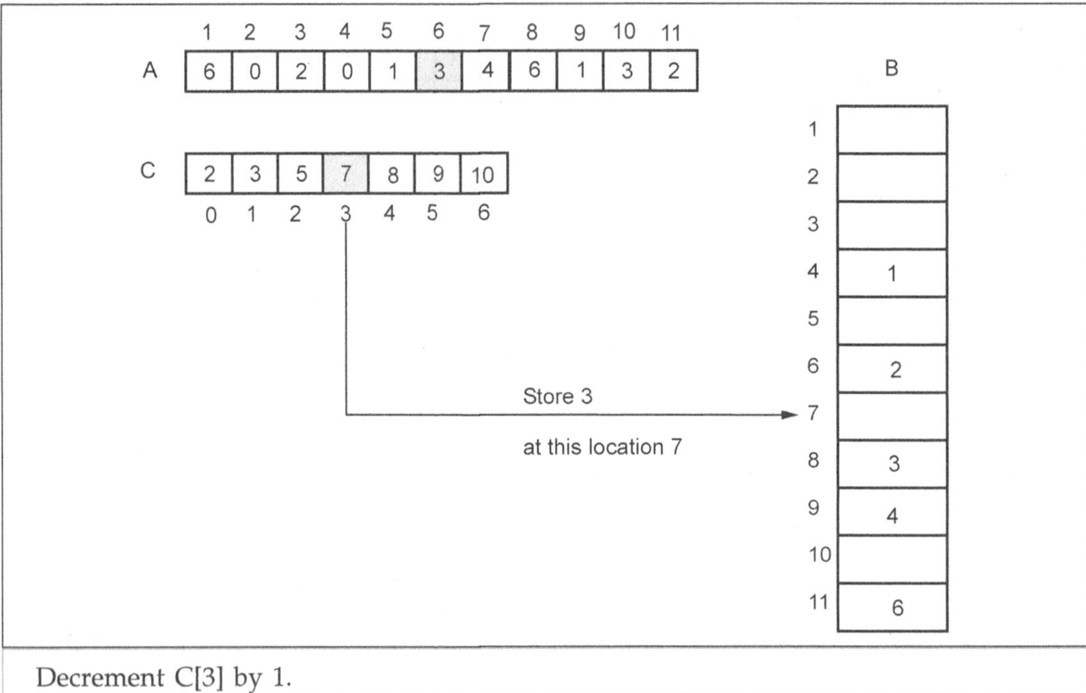

Decrement C[3] by 1.

Step 24 :

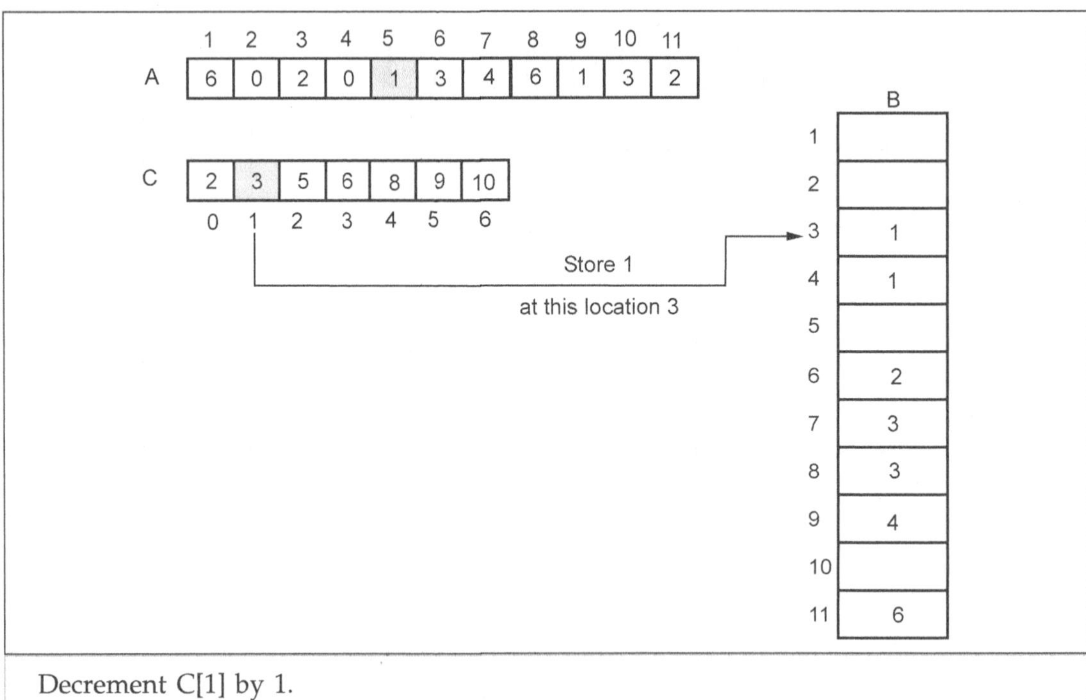

Decrement C[1] by 1.

Step 25 :

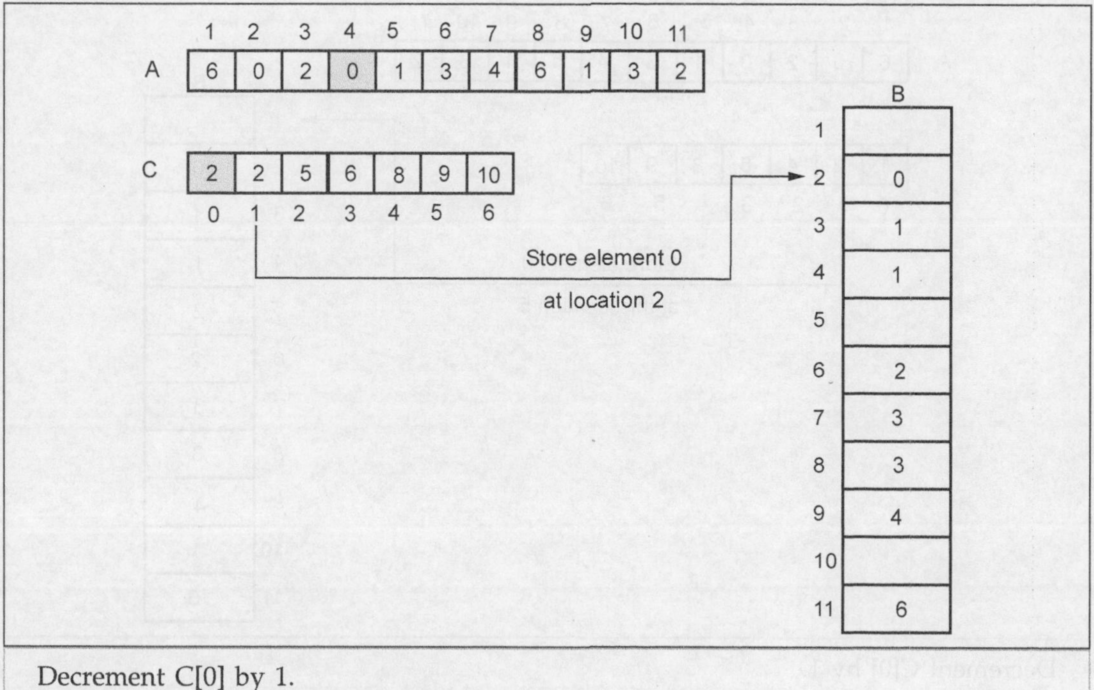

Decrement C[0] by 1.

Step 26 :

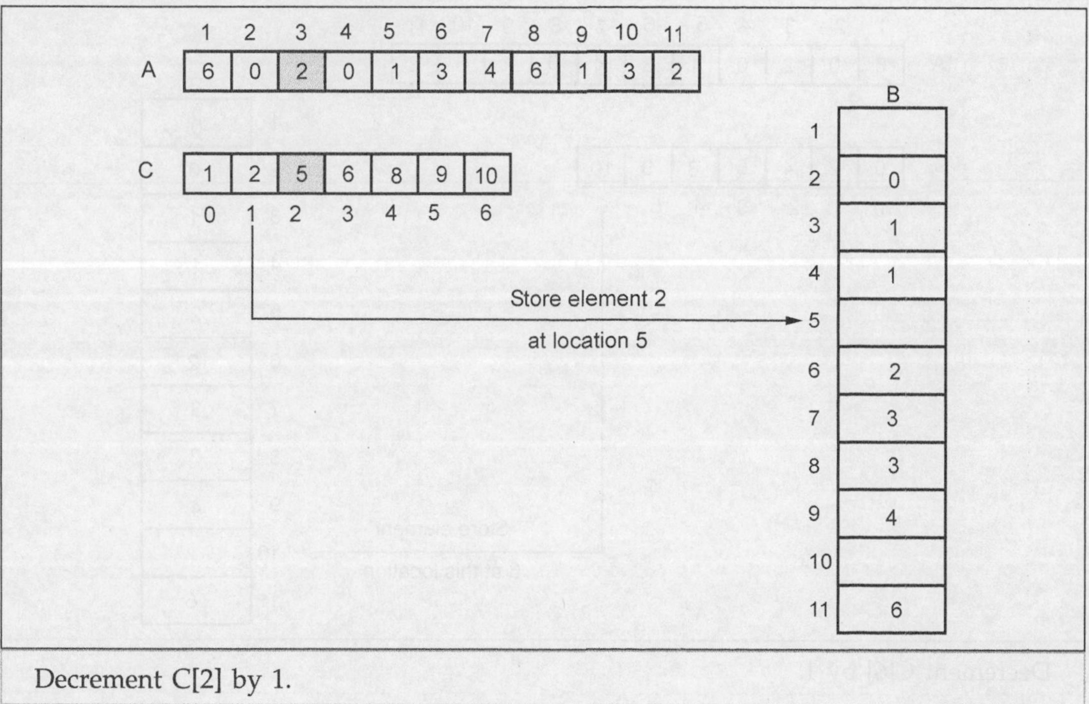

Decrement C[2] by 1.

Step 27 :

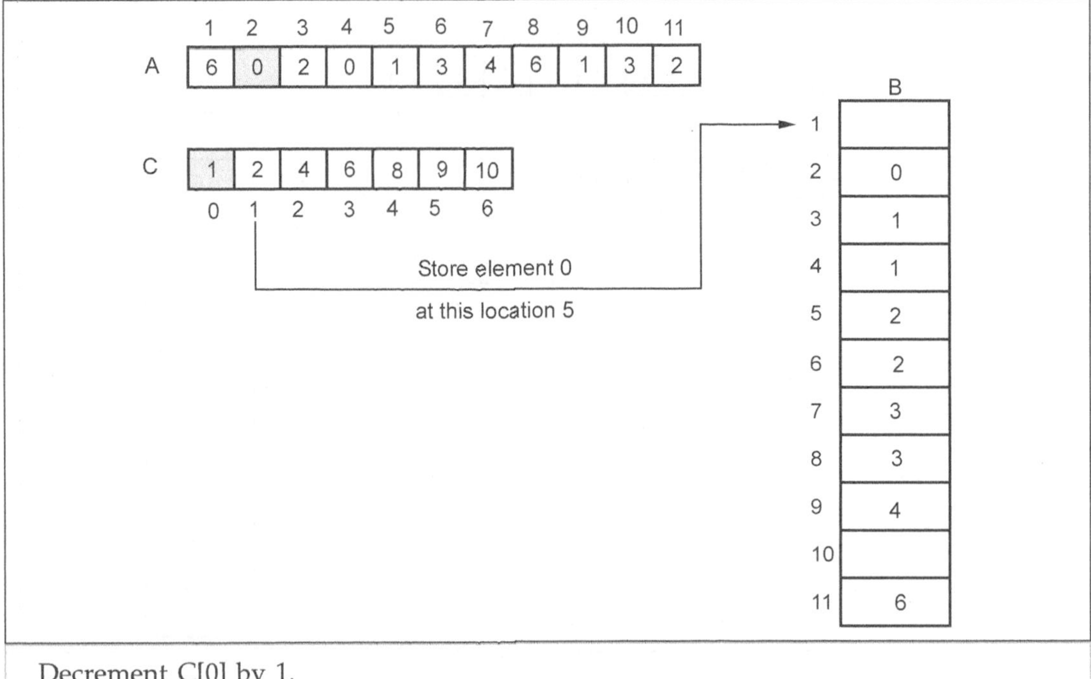

Decrement C[0] by 1.

Step 28 :

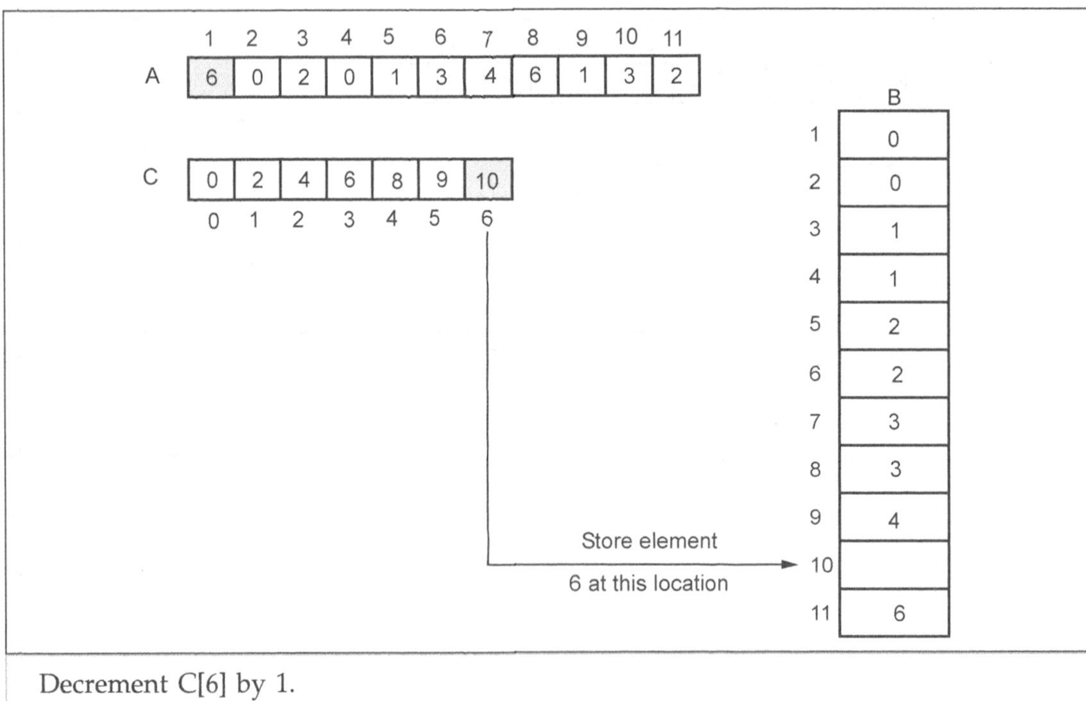

Decrement C[6] by 1.

Step 29 :

A

1	2	3	4	5	6	7	8	9	10	11
6	0	2	0	1	3	4	6	1	3	2

C

0	1	2	3	4	5	6
0	2	4	6	8	9	9

B

	B
1	0
2	0
3	1
4	1
5	2
6	2
7	3
8	3
9	4
10	6
11	6

Thus we get stored list in **B array.**

Algorithm

```
Algorithm counting _sort (A[1....n], B[1......n], k)
{
    // Problem Description: This algorithm sorts the
    // elements using counting sort method.
    // Input : Array A holds unsorted elements
    //  Array B will contain sorted elements
    // after applying sorting method
    //  Array K will be maximum range of input
    // Output: Array B will have sorted list of elements
        for i← 0 to k do
            C[i] ← 0
        for j ← 1 to length [A] do
            C[A[j]] ← C[A[j]]+1
        for i ← 1 to k do
            C[i] ← C[i] +C[i – 1] // C[i] will have positions
        for j← length [A] down to 1 do// reverse reading of A
            B[C[A[j]]] ← A[j]
            C[A[j]] ← C[A[j]] – 1 //decrementing current C value.
}
```

Analysis :

The time complexity of each important statement is as given below

1) **for** i← 0 **to** k **do**

   C[i] ← 0 Θ (k)

2) **for** j ← 1 **to** length [A] **do**

   C[A[j]] ← C[A[j]] + 1 Θ (n)

3) **for** i ← 1 to k **do**

   C[i] ← C[i] + C[i – 1] Θ (k)

4) **for** j ← length [A] **down to** 1 **do**

   B[C[A[j]]] ← A[j] Θ (n)

Hence total running time required by this algorithm is Θ (n).

Review Questions

1. *Write a program/algorithm of selection sort method. What is complexity of the method?* **GTU : Dec.-10, Marks 5; May-12, Marks 7**
2. *Explain bubble sort algorithm. Derive the algorithmic complexity in best case, worst case and average case analysis.* **GTU : Winter-14, Marks 7**
3. *Write an algorithm for insertion sort.*
   Analyze insertion sort algorithm for best case and worst case. **GTU : Summer-15, Marks 7**
4. *Explain an algorithm for selection sort algorithm. Derive its best case, worst case and average case time complexity.* **GTU : Winter-15, Marks 7**

2.9 University Questions with Answers

Regulation 2008

Dec. 2010

Q.1 *What is an algorithm ? Explain various properties of an algorithm.* **[Refer section 2.2]** [3]

Q.2 *What do you mean by asymptotic notations ? Explain.* **[Refer section 2.4]** [2]

Q.3 *Write a program/algorithm of selection sort method. What is complexity of the method ?* **[Refer section 2.8]** [7]

May 2011

Q.4 *Explain different asymptotic notations in brief.* **[Refer section 2.4]** [6]

Q.5 *What is an amortized analysis ? Explain aggregate method of amortized analysis using suitable example.* **[Refer section 2.7]** **[7]**

Dec. 2011

Q.6 *Answer the following : Explain asymptotic analysis of algorithm.* **[Refer section 2.4]** **[3]**

May 2012

Q.7 *Explain why analysis of algorithms is important ? Explain : Worst case best case and average case complexity* **[Refer section 2.2]** **[4]**

Q.8 *Define :Big Oh, Big Omega and Big Theta notation.* **[Refer section 2.4]** **[3]**

Q.9 *What is Recursion ? Give the implementation of Tower of Hanoi problem using recursion.* **[Refer section 2.6]** **[3]**

Q.10 *Write a program/algorithm of selection sort method. What is complexity of the method ?* **[Refer section 2.8]** **[3]**

Dec. 2012

Q.11 *Explain why analysis of algorithms is important ?* **[Refer section 2.1]** **[7]**

Q.12 *Explain : worst case, best case and average case complexity.* **[Refer section 2.2]** **[7]**

May 2013

Q.13 *Explain all asymptotic notations used in algorithm analysis.* **[Refer section 2.4]** **[6]**

May 2014

Q.14 *Why do we use asymptotic notations in the study of algorithms ? Briefly describe the commonly used asymptotic notations.* **[Refer section 2.4]** **[6]**

Dec. 2014

Q.15 *Explain all asymptotic notations used in algorithm analysis.* **[Refer section 2.4]** **[6]**

Q.16 *What is an amortized analysis ? Explain aggregate method of amortized analysis using suitable example.* **[Refer section 2.7]** **[7]**

Q.17 *What is an amortized analysis ? Explain potential method of amortized analysis using suitable example.* **[Refer section 2.7]** **[7]**

Q.18 *Explain bubble sort algorithm. Derive the algorithmic complexity in best case, worst case and average case analysis.* **[Refer section 2.8]** **[7]**

Summer 2015

Q.19 *Write an algorithm for insertion sort. Analyze insertion sort algorithm for best case and worst case.* **[Refer section 2.8]** [7]

Q.20 *Define an amortized analysis. Briefly explain its different techniques. Carry out aggregate analysis for the problem of implementing a k-bit binary counter that counts upward from 0.* **[Refer section 2.7]** [7]

Regulation 2013

Winter 2015

Q.21 *Explain an algorithm for selection sort algorithm. Derive its best case, worst case and average case time complexity.* **[Refer section 2.8]** [7]

2.10 Short Questions and Answers

Q.1 Mention the ways to specify the efficiency of algorithm.

Ans. : Time complexity and space complexity is used to specify the efficiency of algorithm.

Q.2 What is frequency count ?

Ans. : The frequency count is a count that denotes how many times particular statement is executed.

Q.3 What is best case time complexity ?

Ans. : If an algorithm takes minimum amount of time to run to completion for a specific set of input then it is called best case time complexity.

Q.4 What is worst case time complexity ?

Ans. : Worst case time complexity is a time complexity when algorithm runs for a longest time.

Q.5 What are elementary operations ?

Ans. : Elementary operations are those operations whose execution time is bounded by a constant which depends upon the type of implementation used. The elementary operations are addition, multiplication and assignment.

Q.6 What are asymptotic notations ?

Ans. : Asymptotic notation is a shorthand way to represent the time complexity. Various notations such as Ω, Θ, O.

Q.7 What does the omega notation represent ?

Ans. : The omega notation represents the lower bound of algorithm's running time.

Q.8 What does the big oh notation represent ?

Ans. : The big oh notation represents the upper bound of algorithm's running time.

Q.9 What is order of growth ?

Ans. : Measuring the performance of an algorithm in relation with the input size n is called order of growth.

Q.10 What is recurrence relation ?

Ans. : The recurrence relation is denoted by an equation in which the sequence is defined recursively.

For example

$$T(n) = T(n-1)+n \text{ for } n>0$$

$$T(0) = 0$$

Q.11 What are different methods used to solve the recurrence relation ?

Ans. : 1. Substitution method 2. Master's method

Q.12 If F(n) is $\Theta(n^d)$ where d >= 0 in the recurrence relation and if $a<bd$ then what is the value of T(n) ?

Ans. : $T(n) = \Theta(n^d)$

Q.13 Give the recurrence relation for Fibonacci sequence.

Ans. : $T(n)=2+T(n-1)+T(n-2)$

Q.14 What is amortized analysis ?

Ans. : An amortized analysis means finding average running time per operation over a worst case sequence of operations.

Q.15 List out the commonly used techniques for amortized analysis.

Ans. : The commonly used techniques for amortized analysis are

1. Aggregate analysis 2. Accounting method 3. Potential method.

Q.16 List out the problems that can be solved by algorithm.

Ans. : 1. Sorting 2. Searching 3. Numerical Problems 4. Combinatorial Problems 5. Graph Problems.

Q.17 What is in-place sorting algorithm ?

Ans. : The in-place sorting algorithm is an algorithm in which the input is overwritten by output and to execute the sorting method it does not require any more additional space.

Q.18 What is the time complexity of heap sort ?

Ans. : The time complexity of heap sort is O(logn).

❑❑❑

Notes

3 Divide and Conquer Algorithm

Syllabus

Introduction, Recurrence and different methods to solve recurrence, Multiplying large integers problem, Problem solving using divide and conquer algorithm - Binary search, Max-Min problem, Sorting (Merge sort, Quick sort), Matrix multiplication, Exponential.

Contents

3.1 Introduction

This chapter describes a very interesting algorithmic strategy called divide and conquer. As the name suggests in this strategy the big problem is broken down into **smaller sub problems** and solution to these sub problems is obtained. To understand this strategy we will discuss various applications such as binary search, merge sort, quick sort, matrix multiplication. The time complexities of these applications are also discussed along with the method.

3.2 General Method

- In divide and conquer method, a given problem is,
  - i) Divided into smaller sub problems.
  - ii) These sub problems are solved independently.
  - iii) Combining all the solutions of sub problems into a solution of the whole.
- If the sub problems are large enough then divide and conquer is reapplied.
- The generated sub problems are usually of same type as the original problem. Hence recursive algorithms are used in divided and conquer strategy.
- A **control abstraction** for divide and conquer is as given below - using control abstraction a flow of control of a procedure is given.

```
Algorithm DC(P)
{
    if P is too small then
    return solution of P.
    else
    {
        Divide (P) and obtain P1,P2,.......Pn
        where n ≥ 1
        Apply DC to each subproblem
        return combine (DC(P1),DC(P2)... (DC(Pn));
    }
}
```

- The computing time of above procedure of divide and conquer is given by the recurrence relation.

$$T(n) = \begin{cases} g(n) & \text{if n is small} \\ T(n_1)+T(n_2)+\ldots\ldots\ldots T(n_r)+F(n) & \text{when n is sufficiently large} \end{cases}$$

Where T(n) is the time for divide and conquer of size n. The g(n) is the computing time required to solve small inputs. The F(n) is the time required in dividing problem P and combining the solutions to sub problems. Let us now discuss some applications of this method.

The divide and conquer technique is as shown by Fig. 3.2.1.

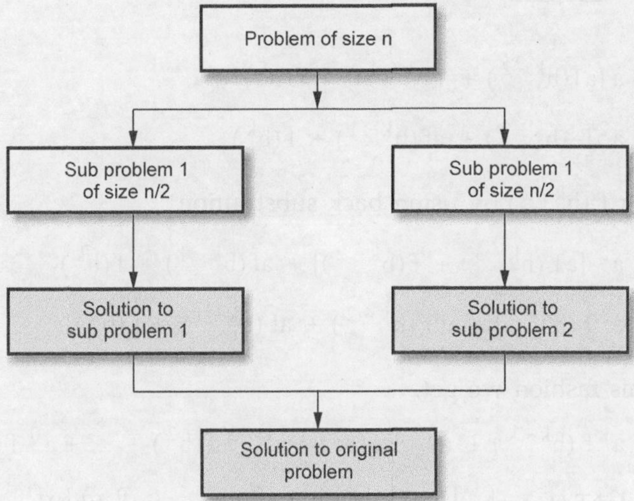

Fig. 3.2.1 Divide and conquer technique

The generated sub problems are usually of same type as the original problem. Hence sometimes recursive algorithms are used in divide and conquer strategy.

For example, if we want to compute sum of n numbers then by divide and conquer we can solve the problem as

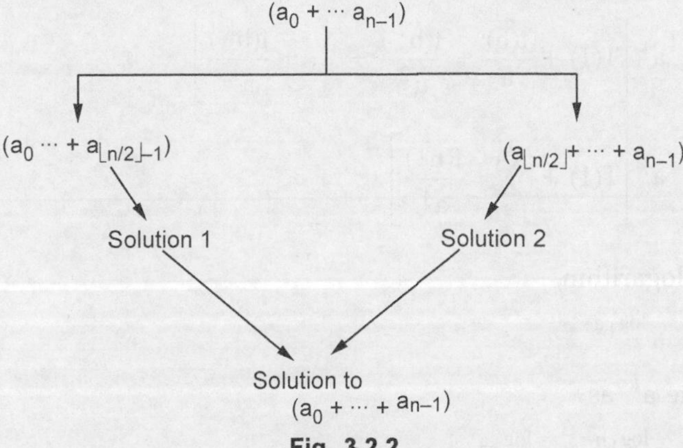

Fig. 3.2.2

3.2.1 Efficiency Analysis of Divide and Conquer

Let recurrence relation be

$$T(n) = aT(n/b) + f(n)$$

Consider $a \geq 1$ and $b \geq 2$. Assume $n = b^k$, where k = 1, 2, ...

$$T(b^k) = aT(b^k/b) + f(b^k)$$

$$= \underbrace{aT(b^{k-1})} + f(b^k)$$

$$= a[aT(b^{k-2}) + f(b^{k-1})] + f(b^k)$$

$$= a^2T(b^{k-2}) + af(b^{k-1}) + f(b^k)$$

Now substituting $T(b^{k-2})$ by using back substitution,

$$= a^2 [aT(b^{k-3}) + f(b^{k-2})] + af(b^{k-1}) + f(b^k)$$

$$= a^3T(b^{k-3}) + a^2f(b^{k-2}) + af(b^{k-1}) + f(b^k)$$

Continuing in this fashion we get,

$$= a^kT(b^{k-k}) + a^{k-1} f(b^1) + a^{k-2} f(b^2) + \ldots + a^0 f(b^k)$$

$$= [a^kT(1) + a^{k-1} f(b) + a^{k-2} f(b^2) + \ldots + a^0 f(b^k)]$$

This can also be written as,

$$= a^kT(1) + \frac{a^k}{a} f(b) + \frac{a^k}{a^2} f(b^2) + \ldots + \frac{a^k}{a^k} f(b^k)$$

Taking a^k as common factor

$$= a^k \left[T(1) + \frac{f(b)}{a} + \frac{f(b^2)}{a^2} + \ldots + \frac{f(b^k)}{a^k} \right]$$

$$= a^k \left[T(1) + \sum_{j=1}^{k} \frac{f(b^j)}{a^j} \right]$$

By property of logarithm,

$$a^{\log_b x} = x^{\log_b a}$$

Hence we can write a^k as

$$a^k = a^{\log_b n} = n^{\log_b a}$$

We can rewrite the equation

$$T(n) = a^k \left[T(1) + \sum_{j=1}^{k} f(b^j)/a^j \right]$$

$$T(n) = n^{\log_b a} \left[T(1) + \sum_{j=1}^{\log_b n} f(b^j)/a^j \right]$$

Thus order of growth of T(n) depends upon values of constants a and b and order of growth of function f(n).

3.3 Problem Solving using Divide and Conquer

Various problems that can be solved using divide and conquer strategy are -

1. Binary Search
2. Quick Sort
3. Merge Sort
4. Matrix Multiplication
5. Exponential.

Review Question

1. *Explain the general method for divide and conquer algorithm. Also give the efficiency analysis of it using the recurrence relation.*

3.4 Multiplying Large Integers Problems

GTU : June-11, Dec.-11, Winter-14, Marks 7

We are familiar with the multiplication performed using positional numeral system. This method of multiplying two numbers has taught us in schooling. In this method multiply the multiplicand by each digit of multiplier and then add up all the properly shifted results. This method is also called **grade-school multiplication.**

For example :

```
   42
 × 34
  168
+ 1260   ← padding 0 at units position
  1428
```

But this method is not convenient for performing multiplication of large integers. Hence let us discuss an interesting algorithm of multiplying large integers. **For example :** Consider multiplication of two integers 42 and 34. First let us represent these numbers according to positions.

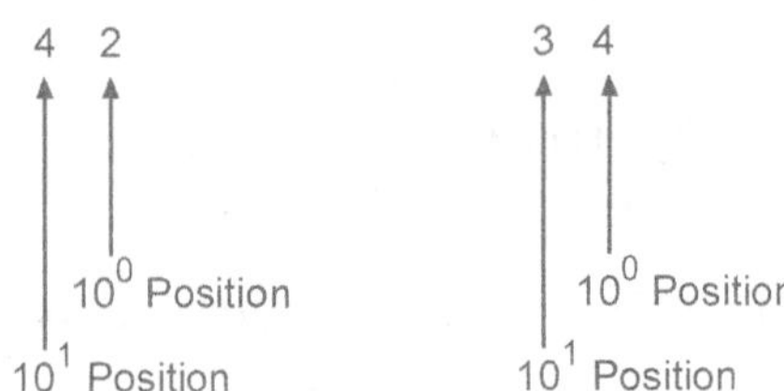

Fig. 3.4.1

i.e.
$$42 \times 34 = (4 \times 10^1 + 2 \times 10^0) * (3 \times 10^1 + 4 \times 10^0)$$
$$= (4 \times 3) 10^2 + (4 \times 4 + 2 \times 3) 10^1 + (2 \times 4) 10^0$$
$$= 1200 + 220 + 8$$
$$= 1428$$

Let us formulate this method -

Let,
$$c = a * b$$
$$c = c_2 \, 10^2 + c_1 \, 10^1 + c_0 \qquad \text{... (3.4.1)}$$

where
$$c_2 = a_1 * b_1$$
$$c_0 = a_0 * b_0$$
$$c_1 = (a_1 + a_0) * (b_1 + b_0) - (c_2 + c_0)$$

The 2 digit numbers are
$$a = a_1 \, a_0$$
$$b = b_1 \, b_0$$

Let perform multiplication operation with the help of formula given in equation (3.4.1).

$$c = a * b$$
$$= 42 \times 34 \qquad \text{where } a_1 = 4, \; a_0 = 2$$
$$b_1 = 3, \; b_0 = 4$$

Let us obtain c_0, c_1, c_2 values

$$c_2 = a_1 * b_1$$
$$= 4 * 3$$
$$\mathbf{c_2 = 12}$$
$$c_0 = a_0 * b_0$$
$$= 2 * 4$$
$$\mathbf{c_0 = 8}$$

$$c_1 = (a_1 + a_0) * (b_1 + b_0) - (c_2 + c_0)$$
$$= (4+2)*(3+4)-(12+8)$$
$$= 6*7-20$$
$$\mathbf{c_1 = 22}$$

$$\therefore \quad a * b = c_2\, 10^2 + c_1\, 10^1 + c_0$$
$$= 12*10^2 + 22*10^1 + 8$$
$$= 1200 + 220 + 8$$
$$a * b = \mathbf{1428}$$

Consider a multiplication of 981 * 1234, as 981 us a three digit number, we will make it four digit by padding a zero to it. Now 0981 * 1234 makes both the operands as 4 digit values.

We will write

$$c = a * b$$
$$= 0981 * 1234$$

Divide the numbers in equal halves.

$\therefore \quad a_1 = 09 \qquad a_0 = 81$

$b_1 = 12 \qquad b_0 = 34$

Let us obtain c_0, c_1, c_2 Values

$$c_2 = a_1 * b_1$$
$$= 09 * 12$$
$$\mathbf{c_2 = 108}$$
$$c_0 = a_0 * b_0$$
$$= 81 * 34$$
$$\mathbf{c_0 = 2754}$$
$$c_1 = (a_1 + a_0) * (b_1 + b_0) - (c_2 + c_0)$$
$$= (9+81)*(12+34)-(108+2754)$$
$$= 4140 - 2862$$
$$\mathbf{c_1 = 1278}$$

$$\therefore \quad a * b = c_2 10^4 + c_1 10^2 + c_0$$

$$= 108 * 10000 + 1278 * 100 + 2754$$

$$= 1080000 + 127800 + 2754$$

$$\mathbf{0981 * 1234 = 1210554}$$

We can generalize this formula as -

$c = a * b$
$c = c_2\ 10^n + c_1\ 10^{n/2} + c_0$
where, n is total number of digits in the integer
$c_2 = a_1 * b_1$
$c_0 = a_0 * b_0$
$c_1 = (a_1 + a_0) * (b_1 + b_0) - (c_2 + c_0)$

Clearly, this algorithm can be implemented using recursion. This recursion can be stopped when n reaches to 0.

Example 3.4.1 *What is divide and conquer technique ? Apply this method to find multiplication on integers 2101 and 1130.* **GTU : IT, Winter-14, Marks 7**

Solution : Refer section 3.2.

We will write

$$c = a * b$$

$$= 2101 * 1130$$

Divide the numbers in equal halves.

$$\therefore \quad a_1 = 21,\ a_0 = 01$$

$$b_1 = 11,\ b_0 = 30$$

Let us obtain c_0, c_1, c_2 values

$$c_2 = a_1 * b_1$$

$$= 21 * 11$$

$$\mathbf{c_2 = 231}$$

$$c_0 = a_0 * b_0$$

$$= 01 * 30$$

$$\mathbf{c_0 = 30}$$

$$c_1 = (a_1 + a_0) * (b_1 + b_0) - (c_2 + c_0)$$

$$= (21 + 01) * (11 + 30) - (231 + 30)$$

$$= (22*41) - 261$$

$$\mathbf{c_1 = 641}$$

$$a * b = c_2 10^4 + c_1 10^2 + c_0$$

$$= 231*10^4 + 641*10^2 + 30$$

$$= 2374130$$

Analysis

In this method there are 3 multiplication operations of 1 digit numbers.

i.e. $c_2 = a_1 * b_1$ → Multiplication 1

$c_0 = a_0 * b_0$ → Multiplication 2

$c_1 = (a_1 + a_0) * (b_1 + b_0) - (c_2 + c_0)$ → Multiplication 3

This is the case for two digit multiplication. Now if there are n digits to be multiplied then multiplication of n digits requires 3 multiplications of n/2 digit numbers. Hence recurrence relation can be given as -

$$C(n) = 3\,C(n/2) \quad \text{when } n > 1 \quad \text{... (3.4.2)}$$

And $$C(n) = 1 \quad \text{when } n = 1 \quad \text{... (3.4.3)}$$

Now put $n = 2^k$ in equation (3.4.2) we get,

$$C(2^k) = 3\,C(2^k/2)$$

$$C(2^k) = 3\,C(2^{k-1})$$

$$= 3[3\,C(2^{k-2})]$$

$$= 3[3(3\,C(2^{k-3}))]$$

$$\vdots$$

$$= 3^k(C(2^{k-k}))$$

$$= 3^k(C(2^0))$$

$$= 3^k\,C(1) \qquad \because 2^0 = 1$$

Using equation (3.4.3), C (1) = 1

$$\therefore \quad C(2^k) = 3^k \qquad \text{... (3.4.4)}$$

As $n = 2^k$ we get $k = \log_2 n$, equation (3.4.4) becomes

$$C(n) = 3^{\log_2 n}$$

$$= n^{\log_2 3} \qquad \because a^{\log_b c} = c^{\log_2 a}$$

$$C(n) \approx n^{1.58}$$

Review Questions

1. *Explain how multiplication of large integers can be done efficiently by using divide and conquer technique ?* **GTU : June-11, Marks 4**
2. *Explain how divide and conquer method help multiplying two large integers.* **GTU : Dec.-11, Marks 4**

3.5 Binary Search

GTU : Dec.-10,11, June-12, Winter-14, Marks 7

Binary search is an efficient searching method. While searching the elements using this method the most essential thing is that the elements in the array should be sorted one.

An element which is to be searched from the list of elements stored in array A[0…n – 1] is called KEY element.

Let A[m] be the mid element of array A. Then there are three conditions that needs to be tested while searching the array using this method

1. If KEY=A[m] then desired element is present in the list.
2. Otherwise if KEY<A[m] then search the left sub list
3. Otherwise if KEY>A[m] then search the right sub list.

This can be represented as

A[0] ... A[m–1] A[m] A[m+1] ... A[n–1]

Search here if KEY<A(m) | KEY ? | Search here if KEY>A(m)

Let us take one example to understand this method

Example 3.5.1 *Apply binary search method to search 60 from the list 10, 20, 30, 40, 50, 60, 70.*

Solution : Consider a list of elements stored in array A as

0	1	2	3	4	5	6
10	20	30	40	50	60	70
↑ Low						↑ High

The KEY element (i.e. the element to be searched) is 60.

Now to obtain middle element we will apply a formula :

$$m = (low + high)/2$$

$$m = (0 + 6)/2$$

$$m = 3$$

Then Check $A[m] \stackrel{?}{=} KEY$

i.e. $A[3] \stackrel{?}{=} 60$ NO $A[3] = 40$ and $40 < 60$

∴ Search the right sublist.

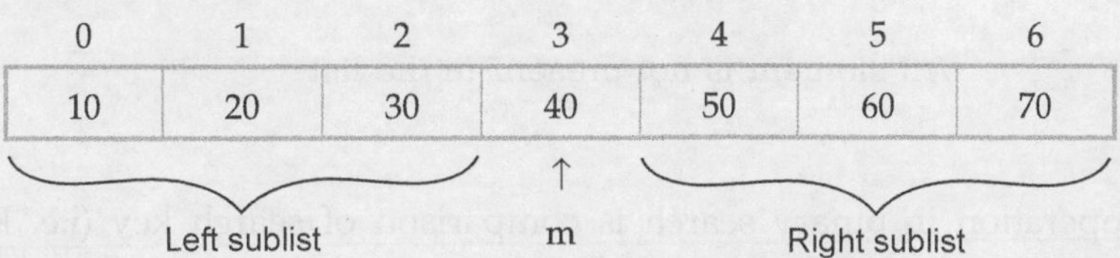

The right sublist is

...	50	60	70

Now we will again divide this list and check the mid element.

	4	5	6
...	50	60	70
	Left sublist	↑ m	Right sublist

$$m = (low + high)/2$$

$$m = (4 + 6)/2$$

$$\therefore m = 5$$

is $\quad A[m] \stackrel{?}{=} KEY$

i.e. $\quad A[5] \stackrel{?}{=} 60 \quad$ Yes, i.e. the number is present in the list.

Thus we can search the desired number from the list of elements.

Algorithm

```
Algorithm BinSearch(A[0...n−1],KEY)
//Problem Description: This algorithm is for searching the
//element using binary search method.
//Input: An array A from which the KEY element is to be
//searched.
//Output: It returns the index of an array element if it is
//equal to KEY otherwise it returns -1
low ← 0
high ← n−1
while (low<high) do
{
 m ← (low+high)/2       //mid of the array is obtained
      if (KEY=A[m])then
   return m
 else if(KEY<A[m])then
   high ← m−1           //search the left sub list
 else
   low ← m+1            //search the right sub list
}
return −1               //if element is not present in the list
```

Analysis

The basic operation in binary search is comparison of search key (i.e. KEY) with the array elements. To analyze efficiency of binary search we must count the number of times the search key gets compared with the array elements. The comparison is also called a three way comparison because algorithm makes the comparison to determine whether KEY is smaller, equal to or greater than A[m].

In the algorithm after one comparison the list of n elements is divided into n/2 sublists. The worst case efficiency is that the algorithm compares all the array elements for searching the desired element. In this method one comparison is made and based on this comparison array is divided each time in n/2 sub lists. Hence the worst case time complexity is given by

$$C_{worst}(n) = C_{worst}(n/2) + 1 \quad \text{for } n > 1$$

$C_{worst}(n/2)$: Time required to compare left sublist or right sublist

1: One comparison made with middle element

Also, $C_{worst}(1) = 1$

But as we consider the rounded down value when array gets divided the above equations can be written as

$$C_{worst}(n) = C_{worst}(\lfloor n/2 \rfloor) + 1 \quad \text{for } n > 1 \quad \ldots (3.5.1)$$

$$C_{worst}(1) = 1 \quad \ldots (3.5.2)$$

The above recurrence relation can be solved further. Assume $n = 2^k$ the equation (3.5.1) becomes,

$$C_{worst}(2^k) = C_{worst}(2^k/2) + 1$$

$$C_{worst}(2^k) = C_{worst}(2^{k-1}) + 1 \quad \ldots (3.5.3)$$

Using backward substitution method, we can substitute

$$C_{worst}(2^{k-1}) = C_{worst}(2^{k-2}) + 1$$

Then equation (3.5.3) becomes

$$C_{worst}(2^k) = \left[C_{worst}(2^{k-2}) + 1\right] + 1$$

$$= C_{worst}(2^{k-2}) + 2$$

$$\text{Then} C_{worst}(2^k) = \left[C_{worst}(2^{k-3}) + 1\right] + 2$$

$$\therefore \quad C_{worst}(2^k) = C_{worst}(2^{k-3}) + 3$$

...

...

...

$$C_{worst}(2^k) = C_{worst}(2^{k-k}) + k$$

$$= C_{worst}(2^0) + k$$

$$C_{worst}(2^k) = C_{worst}(1) + k \quad \ldots (3.5.4)$$

But as per equation (3.5.2),

$C_{worst}(1) = 1$ then we get equation (3.5.4),

$$C_{worst}(2^k) = 1 + k$$

$$\therefore \quad C_{worst}(n) = 1 + \log_2 n$$

$$\therefore \quad C_{worst}(n) \approx \log_2 n$$

for $n > 1$

> As we have assumed
>
> $n = 2^k$
>
> Taking logarithm (base 2) on both sides
>
> $$\log_2 n = \log_2 2^k$$
>
> $$\log_2 n = k \cdot \log_2 2$$
>
> $$\log_2 n = k(1) \qquad \because \log_2 2 = 1$$
>
> $$\therefore \quad k = \log_2 n$$

The worst case time complexity of binary search is $\Theta(\log_2 n)$.

As $C_{worst}(n) = \log_2 n + 1$ we can verify equation (3.5.1) with this value.

Consider equation (3.5.2),

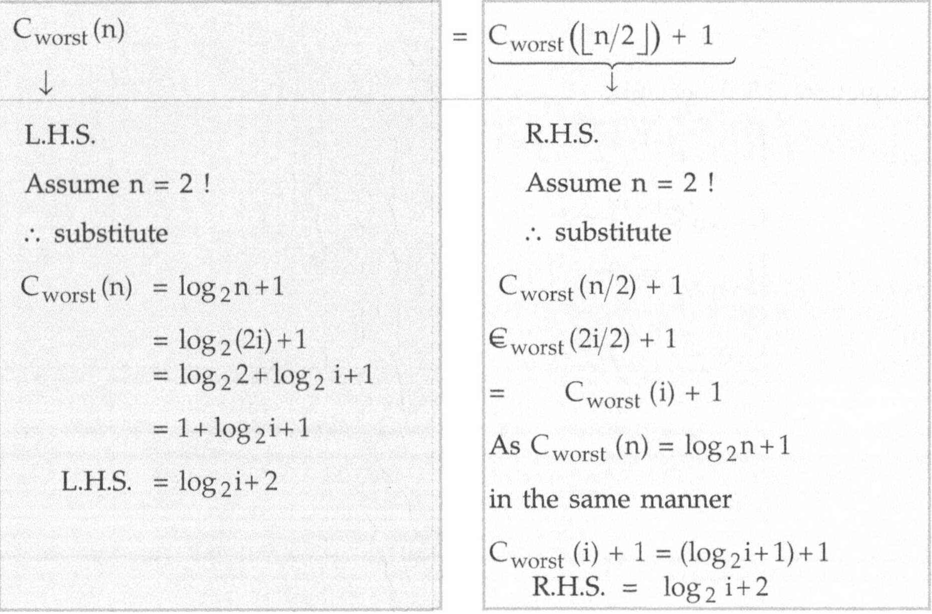

$C_{worst}(n)$ ↓	=	$C_{worst}(\lfloor n/2 \rfloor) + 1$ ↓
L.H.S. Assume n = 2 ! ∴ substitute $C_{worst}(n) = \log_2 n + 1$ $= \log_2(2i) + 1$ $= \log_2 2 + \log_2 i + 1$ $= 1 + \log_2 i + 1$ L.H.S. $= \log_2 i + 2$		R.H.S. Assume n = 2 ! ∴ substitute $C_{worst}(n/2) + 1$ $C_{worst}(2i/2) + 1$ $= C_{worst}(i) + 1$ As $C_{worst}(n) = \log_2 n + 1$ in the same manner $C_{worst}(i) + 1 = (\log_2 i + 1) + 1$ R.H.S. $= \log_2 i + 2$

Average case

To obtain average case efficiency of binary search we will consider some samples of input n.

If n = 1

i.e. only element 11 is there

$1 \rightarrow [11]$ Only 1 search is required to search some KEY.

If **n = 2** and search key = 22

Two comparisons are made to search 22.

	11	0
	22	1

If **n = 4** and search key = 44

m = (0 + 3)/2 = 1

As A[1] = 22 and 22 < 44

Search right sublist, again

m = (2 + 3)/2 = 2

	11	0
	22	1
	33	2
	44	3

Again A[2] = 33 and 33 < 44 we divide list. In right sublist A[4] = 44 and key is 44. Thus total 3 comparisons are made to search 44.

If **n = 8** and search key = 88

m = (0 + 7)/2 = 3

As A[3] = 44 and 44 < 88 search right sublist, again.

m = (4 + 7)/2 = 5

Again A[5] = 66 and 66 < 88 search right sublist, again,

m = (6 + 7)/2 = 6

But A[6] = 77 and 77 < 88.

Then search right sublist

m = (7 + 7)/2 = 7

A[m] = A[7] = 88. Is $A[7] \stackrel{?}{=} 88$.

Yes, the desired element is present.

Thus total 4 comparisons are made to search 88.

	11	0
	22	1
	33	2
	44	3
	55	4
	66	5
	77	6
	88	7

To summarize the above operations.

n	Total comparison (c)
1	1
2	2
4	3
8	4
16	5
⋮	⋮

Observing the above given table we can write

$$\log_2 n + 1 = c$$

For instance if n = 2 then

$$\log_2 2 = 1$$

Then, $c = 1 + 1$

$$c = 2$$

Similarly if n = 8, then

$$c = \log_2 n + 1$$

$$= \log_2 8 + 1$$

$$= 3 + 1$$

$\therefore$ $c = 4$

Thus we can write that

> Average case time complexity of binary search is Θ (log n).

Advantage of binary search :

1. Binary search is an optimal searching algorithm using which we can search the desired element very efficiently.

Disadvantage of binary search :

1. This algorithm requires the list to be sorted. Then only this method is applicable.

Applications of binary search :

1. The binary search is an efficient searching method and is used to search desired record from database.
2. For solving nonlinear equations with one unknown this method is used.

Time complexity of binary search

Best case	Average case	Worst case
$\Theta(1)$	$\Theta(\log_2 n)$	$\Theta(\log_2 n)$

C Program

There are two types of implementation possible

- Recursive Binary Search Program
- Non Recursive Binary Search Program

Let us understand both the implementations.

Recursive Binary Search Program

```
/******************************************************************
            Implementation of recursive Binary Search algorithm
******************************************************************/
#include<stdio.h>
#include<conio.h>
#define SIZE 10
int n;
void main()
{
        int A[SIZE],KEY,i,flag,low,high;
        int BinSearch(int A[SIZE],int KEY,int low,int high);
        clrscr();
        printf("\n How Many elements in an array?");
        scanf("%d",&n);
        printf("\n Enter The Elements");
        for(i=0;i<n;i++)
        scanf("%d",&A[i]);
        printf("\n Enter the element which is to be searched");
        scanf("%d",&KEY);
        low=0;
        high=n-1;
        flag=BinSearch(A,KEY,low,high);
        printf("\n The element is at A[%d] location",flag);
        getch();
}
int BinSearch(int A[SIZE],int KEY,int low,int high)
{
  int m;
  m=(low+high)/2;       //mid of the array is obtained
  if(KEY==A[m])
            return m;
  else if(KEY<A[m])
            BinSearch(A,KEY,low,m–1);//search the left sub list
  else
             BinSearch(A,KEY,m+1,high);//search the right sub list
}
```

Output

```
How Many elements in an array? 5

Enter The Elements 10 20 30 40 50

Enter the element which is to be searched 20

The element is at A[1] location
```

Non Recursive Binary Search Program

```
/*********************************************************************
Implementation of non recursive Binary Search algorithm
*********************************************************************/
#include<stdio.h>
#include<conio.h>
#define SIZE 10
int n;
void main()
{
 int A[SIZE],KEY,i,flag;
 int BinSearch(int A[SIZE],int KEY);
 clrscr();
 printf("\n How Many elements in an array?");
 scanf("%d",&n);
 printf("\n Enter The Elements");
 for(i=0;i<n;i++)
      scanf("%d",&A[i]);
 printf("\n Enter the element which is to be searched");
 scanf("%d",&KEY);
 flag=BinSearch(A,KEY);
 if(flag==-1)
      printf("\n The Element is not present");
 else
      printf("\n The element is at A[%d] location",flag);
 getch();
}
int BinSearch(int A[SIZE],int KEY)
{
 int low,high,m;
 low=0;
 high=n-1;
 while(low<=high)
 {
           m=(low+high)/2;//mid of the array is obtained
           if(KEY==A[m])
                  return m;
           else if(KEY<A[m])
                  high=m-1;        //search the left sub list
           else
                  low=m+1;         //search the right sub list
      }
      return-1; //if element is not present in the list
}
```

Output (Run 1)

```
How Many elements in an array? 6

Enter The Elements
10
20
30
40
50
60

    Enter the element which is to be searched 50

    The element is at A[4] location
```

(Run 2)

```
    How Many elements in an array? 5

    Enter The Elements
    10
    20
    30
    40
    50
    Enter the element which is to be searched 80

    The Element is not present
```

Sr. No.	Sequential technique	Binary search technique
1.	This is the simple technique of searching an element.	This is the efficient technique of searching an element.
2.	This technique does not require the list to be sorted.	This technique requires the list to be sorted. Then only this method is applicable.
3.	Every element of the list may get compared with the key element.	Only the mid element of the list is compared with key element.
4.	The worst case time complexity of this technique is O(n).	The worst case time complexity of this technique is O(log n).

Review Questions

1. *Explain the use of divide and conquer technique for binary search method. Give the algorithm for binary search method. What is the complexity of binary search method ?*

   GTU : IT, Dec.-10, Marks 7

2. *Explain binary search using divide and conquer method and compute its worst case running time.*

   GTU : IT ,Dec.-11, Marks 7

3. *What is divide and conquer technique? Give the use of it for binary searching method.*

   GTU : IT, June-12, Marks 7

4. *Explain Binary search algorithm with divide and conquer strategy and use the recurrence tree to show that the solution to the binary search recurrence $T(n) = T(n/2) + \Theta(1)$ is $T(n) = \Theta(lgn)$.*

   GTU : IT, Winter-14, Marks 7

3.6 Max-Min Problem

First of all we will discuss an algorithm of finding the minimum element from the set of n numbers.

```
Algorithm Minimum_val (A[1.....n])
{
// Problem Description : This algorithm is to
// find minimum value from array A of n
// elements
        min ← A[1] // Assuming first element as min.
for (i←2 to n) do
{
 if (min > A[i]) then
        min ← A[i] //set new min value
}
 return min
}
```

Thus we require total (n–1) comparison to obtain minimum value. Similarly we can obtain the maximum value from an array A in (n–1) comparison. Here is an algorithm for finding maximum element.

```
Algorithm Maximum_val (A[1.....n])
{
// Problem Description : This algorithm is to find maximum value from
// array A of n elements
        max ← A[1]
        for (i ← 2 to n) do
        {
                if [A[i] > max) then
                        max ← A[i]
        }
        return max
```

```
}
We can obtain maximum and minimum values from an array simultaneously using
following algorithm.
Algorithm Max_Min (A[1.....n], Max, Min)
{
// Problem Description : This algorithm obtains min and max values simultaneously.
          Max ← Min ← A[1]
for (i← 2 to n) do
 {
if (A[i] >Max) then
     Max ← A[i] // obtaining maximum value
if (A[i] < Min) then
     Min ← A[i] // obtaining minimum value.
 }
}
```

Thus we get maximum element in **max** and minimum element in **min** variable. Let us derive this algorithm for some example. Consider an array

1	2	3	4	5	6	7	8	9
50	40	– 5	– 9	45	90	65	25	75

Step 1 :

1	2	3	4	5	6	7	8	9
50	40	– 5	– 9	45	90	65	25	75

↑
Min
Max

Step 2 :

Now from index 2 to n we will compare an array element with Min and Max value.

1	2	3	4	5	6	7	8	9
50	40	– 5	– 9	45	90	65	25	75

Min = 40
Max = 50

Step 3 :

1	2	3	4	5	6	7	8	9
50	40	– 5	– 9	45	90	65	25	75

Min = – 5
Max = 50

Step 4 :

1	2	3	4	5	6	7	8	9
50	40	– 5	– 9	45	90	65	25	75

Min = – 9

Max = 50

Step 5 :

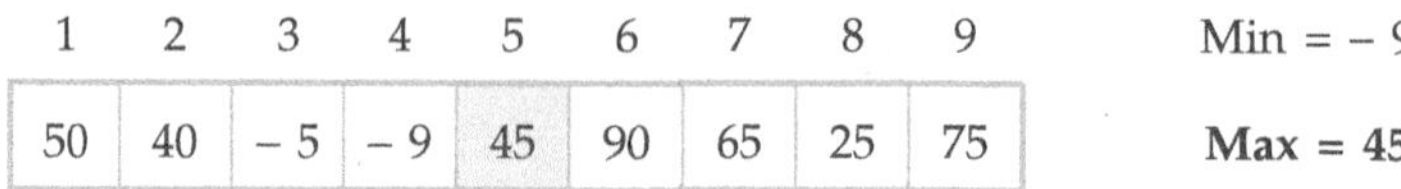

1	2	3	4	5	6	7	8	9
50	40	– 5	– 9	45	90	65	25	75

Min = – 9

Max = 45

Step 6 :

1	2	3	4	5	6	7	8	9
50	40	– 5	– 9	45	90	65	25	75

Min = – 9

Max = 90

Step 7 :

1	2	3	4	5	6	7	8	9
50	40	– 5	– 9	45	90	65	25	75

Min = – 9

Max = 90

Step 8 :

1	2	3	4	5	6	7	8	9
50	40	– 5	– 9	45	90	65	25	75

Min = – 9

Max = 90

Step 9 :

1	2	3	4	5	6	7	8	9
50	40	– 5	– 9	45	90	65	25	75

Min = – 9

Max = 90

Step 10 :

As we have reached at n^{th} location of the array we will terminate the procedure of finding minimum and maximum values and print minimum value as **– 9** and maximum value as **90**.

Analysis

The above algorithm takes $\Theta(n)$ run n time. This is because the basic operation of comparing array element with Min or Max value is done within a **for** loop.

The above algorithm is a straightforward algorithm of finding minimum and maximum. But we can obtain them using recursive method. This recursive algorithm makes use of divide and conquer strategy.

In this algorithm, the list of elements is divided at the mid in order to obtain two sublists. From both the sublist maximum and minimum elements are chosen. Two maxima and minima are compared and from them real maximum and minimum elements are determined. This process is carried out for entire list. The algorithm is as given below.

```
Algorithm Max_Min_Val (i, j, max, min)
//Problem Description : Finding min, max elements recursively.
//Input : i, j are integers used as index to an array A. The max and min will
//contain maximum and minimum value elements.
//Output : None
if (i = = j) then
{
    max ← A [i]
    min ← A [j]
}
else if (i = j–1) then
{
    if (A [i] < A [j]) then
    {
        max ← A [j]
        min ← A [i]
    }
    else
    {
        max ← A [i]
        min ← A [j]
    }           //end of else
}               //end of if
else
{
    mid ← (i+j) / 2                    //divide the list handling two lists separately
    Max Min Val (i, mid, max, min)
    Max Min val (mid + 1, j, max new, min new)
    if (max < max new) then
        max ← max new                  //combine solution
    if (min > min_new) then
        min ← min_new                  //combine solution
}
```

Example : Consider a list of some elements from which maximum and minimum element can be found out.

1	2	3	4	5	6	7	8	9
50	40	– 5	– 9	45	90	65	25	75

Step 1 :

1	2	3	4	5
50	40	– 5	– 9	45

Sublist 1

6	7	8	9
90	65	25	75

Sublist 2

We have divided the original list at mid and two sublists : Sublist 1 and sublist 2 are created. We will find min and max values respectively from each sublist.

Step 2 :

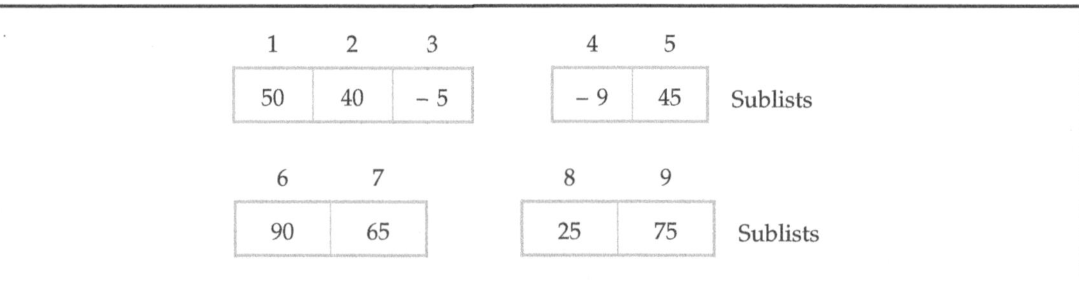

Again divide each sublist and create further sublists. Then from each sublist obtain min and max values.

Step 3 :

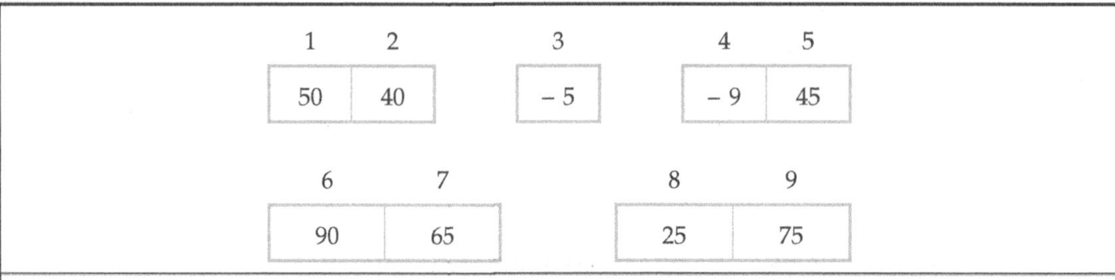

It is possible to divide the list (50, 40, – 5) further. Hence we have divided the list into sublists and min, max values are obtained.

Step 4 :

Now further division of the list is not possible. Hence we start combining the solutions of min and max values from each sublist.

1	2
50	40

3
– 5

Combine (1, 2) and (3) Min = – 5, Max = 50

1	2	3
50	40	– 5

4	5
– 9	45

Combine (1, ... 3) and (4, 5) Min = – 9, Max = 50

Now we will combine (1, ... 3) and (4, 5) and the min and max values among them are obtained. Hence,

min value = – 9

max value = 50

Step 5 :

6	7
90	65

8	9
25	75

Combine (6, 7) and (8, 9) Min = 25, Max = 90

Step 6 :

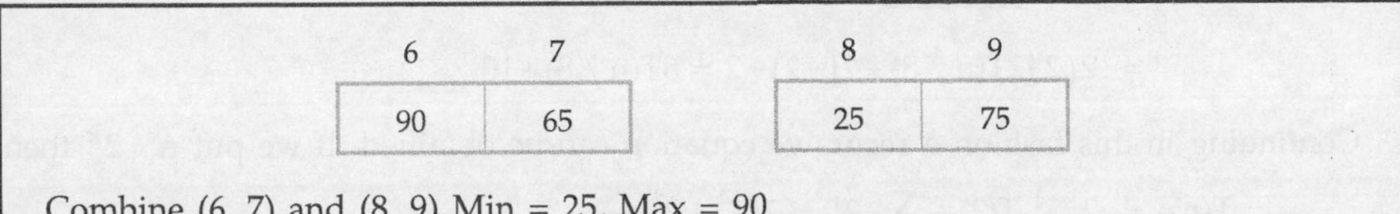

1	2	3	4	5
50	40	– 5	– 9	45

6	7	8	9
90	65	25	75

Combine the sublists (1, ... 5) and (6, ... 9). Find out min and max values which are

min = – 9 max = 90

Thus the complete list is formed from which the min and max values are obtained. Hence final min and max values are

min = – 9 and **max = 90**

The tree for recursive calls will be -

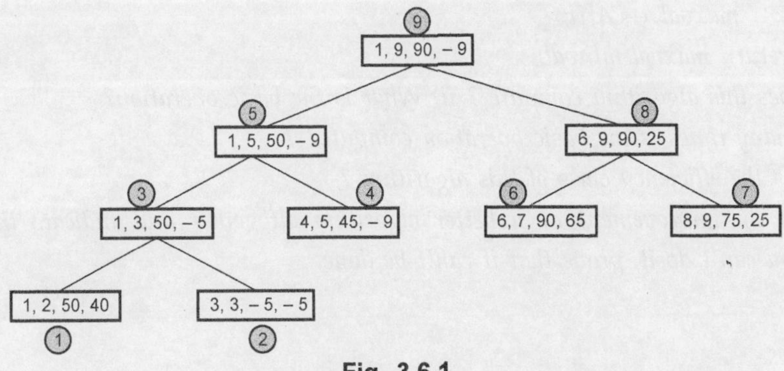

Fig. 3.6.1

Analysis

There are two recursive calls made in this algorithm, for each half divided sublist. Hence, time required for computing min and max will be

$$T(n) = T(\lceil n/2 \rceil) + T(\lceil n/2 \rceil) + 2 \text{ when } n > 2$$

$$T(n) = 1 \qquad \text{when } n = 2$$

If single element is present in the list then T(n) = 0.

Now time required for computing min and max will be -

$$T(n) = 2\,T\,(n / 2) + 2$$

$$= 2\,[2T\,(n / 4) + 2] + 2$$

$$= 2(2\,[2T(n / 8) + 2] + 2) + 2 = 8T(n / 8) + 10$$

Continuing in this fashion a recursive equation can be obtained. If we put $n = 2^k$ then

$$T(n) = 2^{k-1}\,T(2) + \sum_{i=1}^{k-1} 2^i = 2^{k-1} + 2^k - 2$$

$$T(n) = 3n / 2 - 2$$

Neglecting the order of magnitude, we can declare the time complexity is **O(n)**.

Example 3.6.1 *Consider the following algorithm :*

ALGORITHM Secret (A[0, ..., n−1])

//Input : An array A[0, ..., n−1] of n real numbers

```
    minval ← A[0];
    maxval ← A[0];
    for i ← 1 to n–1 do
        if A[i] < minval
            minval ← A[i];
        if A[i] > maxval
            maxval ← A[i];
        return maxval-minval;
```

i) What does this algorithm compute ? ii) What is the basic operation?

iii) How many times is the basic operation computed ?

iv) What is the efficiency class of this algorithm ?

v) Suggest an improvement or a better algorithm altogether and indicate the efficiency class. If you can't do it, prove that it can't be done.

AU : Dec.-08, Marks 16

Solution :

i) This algorithm finds the maximum and minimum element from given sequence of elements.

ii) The basic operation is to compare the array elements for finding minval and maxval.

iii) The basic operation is computed for n times inside a for loop.

iv) This algorithm has the time complexity of **O(n)**. The efficiency class for this algorithm is linear.

v) This algorithm can be improved by using divide an conquer the pseudo code for this is as given below -

```
Algorithm Max_Min_Val (i, j, max, min)
//Problem Description : Finding min, max elements recursively.
//Input : i, j are integers used as index to an array A. The max and min will
//contain maximum and minimum value elements.
//Output : None
if (i = = j) then
{
        max ← A [i]
        min ← A [j]
}
else if (i = j–1) then
{
        if (A [i] < A [j]) then
        {
        max ← A [j]
        min ← A [i]
    }
    else
    {
        max ← A [i]
        min ← A [j]
    }       //end of else
}           //end of if
else
{
        mid ← (i+j) / 2                //divide the list handling two lists separately
        Max_Min_Val (i, mid, max, min)
        Max_Min_val (mid + 1, j, max_new, min_new)
        if (max < max_new) then
        max ← max_new                  //combine solution
    if (min > min_new) then
                min ← min_new  //combine solution
}
```

The efficiency class for this algorithm is linear i.e. **O(n)**.

Example 3.6.2 *For the following list of elements trace the recursive algorithm for finding max and min and determine how many comparisons have been made.*

22, 13, – 5, – 8, 15, 60, 17, 31, 47. **AU : Dec.-10, Marks 8**

Solution : Let

0	1	2	3	4	5	6	7	8
22	13	– 5	– 8	15	60	17	31	47

Step 1 : Divide the list into sub-lists

0	1	2	3	4
22	13	– 5	– 8	15

5	6	7	8
60	17	31	47

Step 2 : Further divide the sublists

0	1	2
22	13	– 5

3	4
– 8	15

5	6
60	17

7	8
31	47

Step 3 : Divide the list (0 .... 2) further into sublists

0	1
22	13

2
– 5

3	4
– 8	15

5	6
60	17

7	8
31	47

Step 4 : We will combine list (0 ... 1) and (2).

The min = – 5, max = 22 Combine the list (0 .... 2) and (3, 4)

min = – 8 and max = 22

Step 5 : Combine (5, 6) and 7, 8)

min = 17, max = 60

Step 6 : Combine (0 ... 4) and (5 ... 8)

min = – 8, max = 60

Review Question

1. *Using the divide and conquer approach to find the maximum and minimum in a set of 'n' elements. Also find the recurrence relation for the number of elements compared and solve the same.*

3.7 Merge Sort

GTU : Winter-14, Marks 7

The merge sort is a sorting algorithm that uses the divide and conquer strategy. In this method division is dynamically carried out.

Merge sort on an input array with n elements consists of three steps:

Divide : Partition array into two sub lists s1 and s2 with n/2 elements each.

Conquer : Then sort sub list s1 and sub list s2.

Combine : Merge s1 and s2 into a unique sorted group.

Example : Consider the elements as
70, 20, 30, 40, 10, 50, 60

Now we will split this list into two sublists.

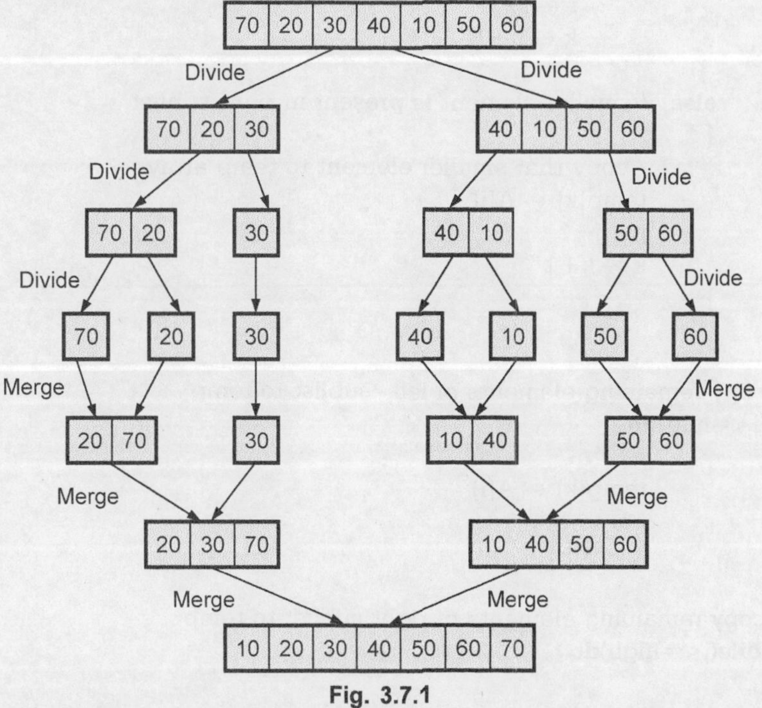

Fig. 3.7.1

Algorithm MergeSort(int A[0...n−1],low,high)
//Problem Description: This algorithm is for sorting the
//elements using merge sort
//Input: Array A of unsorted elements, low as beginning

```
//pointer of array A and high as end pointer of array A
//Output: Sorted array A[0...n - 1]
        if(low < high)then
        {
            mid ← (low+high)/2            // split the list at mid
            MergeSort(A,low,mid)          // first sublist
            MergeSort(A,mid+1,high) // second sublist
            Combine(A,low,mid,high) // merging of two sublists
        }
Algorithm Combine(A[0...n–1],low, mid, high)
{
        k ← low;   // k as index for array temp
        i ← low;        // i as index for left sublist of array A
        j ← mid+1 // j as index for right sublist of array A
        while(i <= mid and j <= high)do
        {
            if(A[i]<=A[j])then
        // if smaller element is present in left sublist
            {
                    // copy that smaller element to temp array
                    temp[k] ← A[i]
                    i ← i+1
                    k ← k+1
            }
            else //smaller element is present in right sublist
            {
                //copy that smaller element to temp array
                temp[k] ← A[j]
                j ← j+1
                k ← k+1
            }
        }

        //copy remaining elements of left  sublist to temp
    while(i<=mid)do
        {
                temp[k] ← A[i]
                i ← i+1
                k ← k+1
        }
        //copy remaining elements of right sublist to temp
        while(j<=high)do
        {
            temp[k] ← A[j]
            j ← j+1
            k ← k+1
        }
```

Logic Explanation

To understand above algorithm consider a list of elements as

70	20	30	40	10	50	60
0	1	2	3	4	5	6
↑			↑			↑
low			mid			high

Then we will first make two sublists as

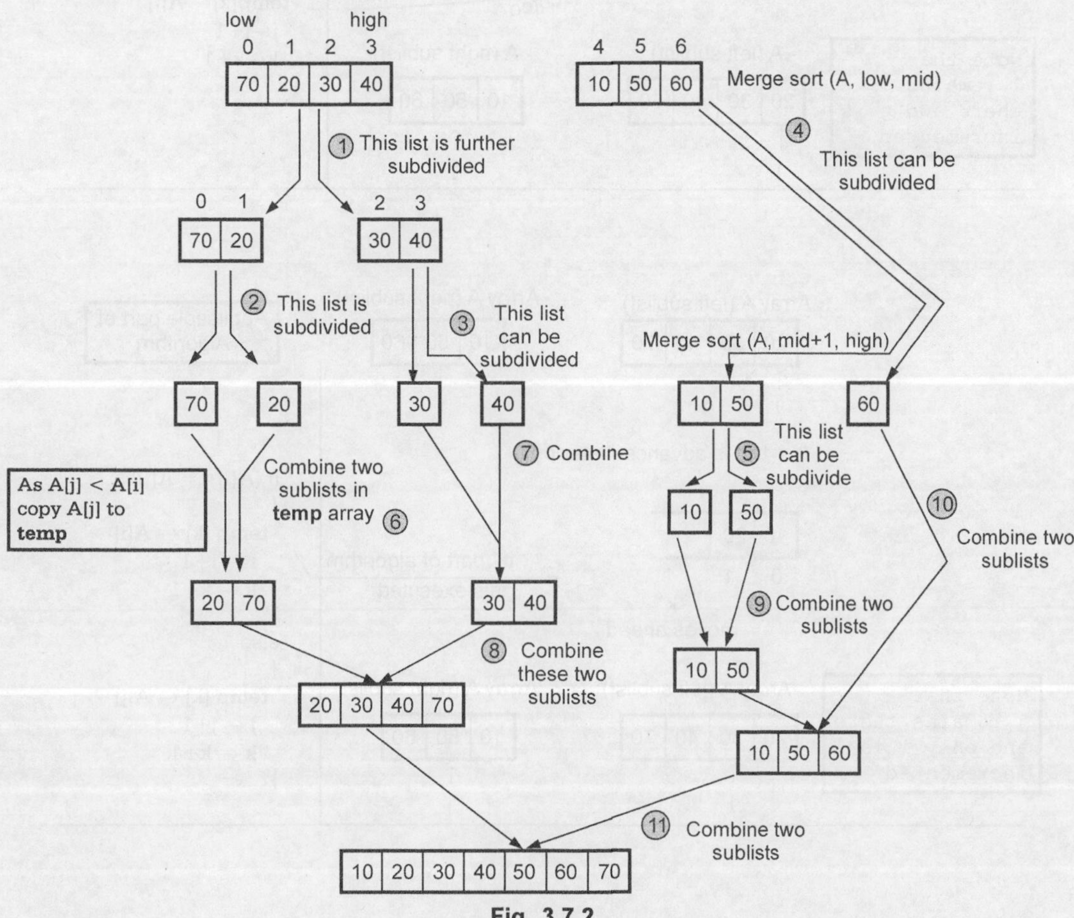

Fig. 3.7.2

Let us see the **combine** operation more closely with the help of some example.

Consider that at some instance we have got two sublist 20, 30, 40, 70 and 10, 50, 60, then

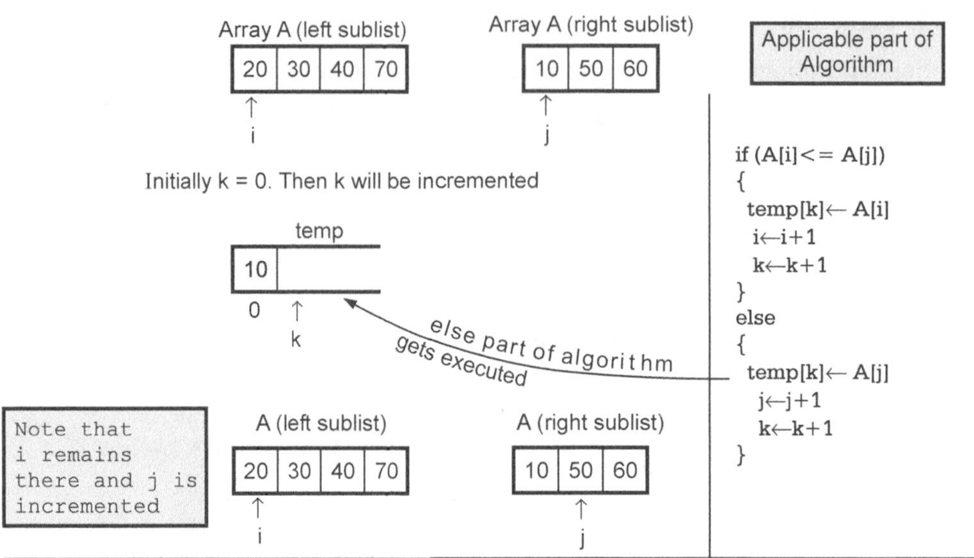
Array A (left sublist)
20 30 40 70
i
Array A (right sublist)
10 50 60
j
Applicable part of Algorithm
Initially k = 0. Then k will be incremented
temp
10
0
k
else part of algorithm gets executed
if (A[i]<= A[j])
{
temp[k]← A[i]
i←i+1
k←k+1
}
else
{
temp[k]← A[j]
j←j+1
k←k+1
}
Note that i remains there and j is incremented
A (left sublist)
20 30 40 70
i
A (right sublist)
10 50 60
j

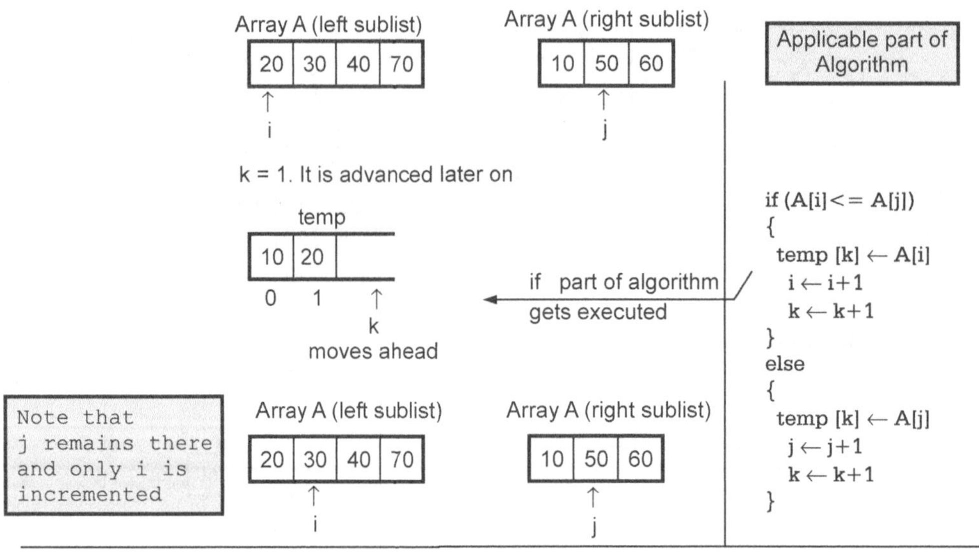
Array A (left sublist)
20 30 40 70
i
Array A (right sublist)
10 50 60
j
Applicable part of Algorithm
k = 1. It is advanced later on
temp
10 20
0 1
k
moves ahead
if part of algorithm gets executed
if (A[i]<= A[j])
{
temp [k] ← A[i]
i ← i+1
k ← k+1
}
else
{
temp [k] ← A[j]
j ← j+1
k ← k+1
}
Note that j remains there and only i is incremented
Array A (left sublist)
20 30 40 70
i
Array A (right sublist)
10 50 60
j

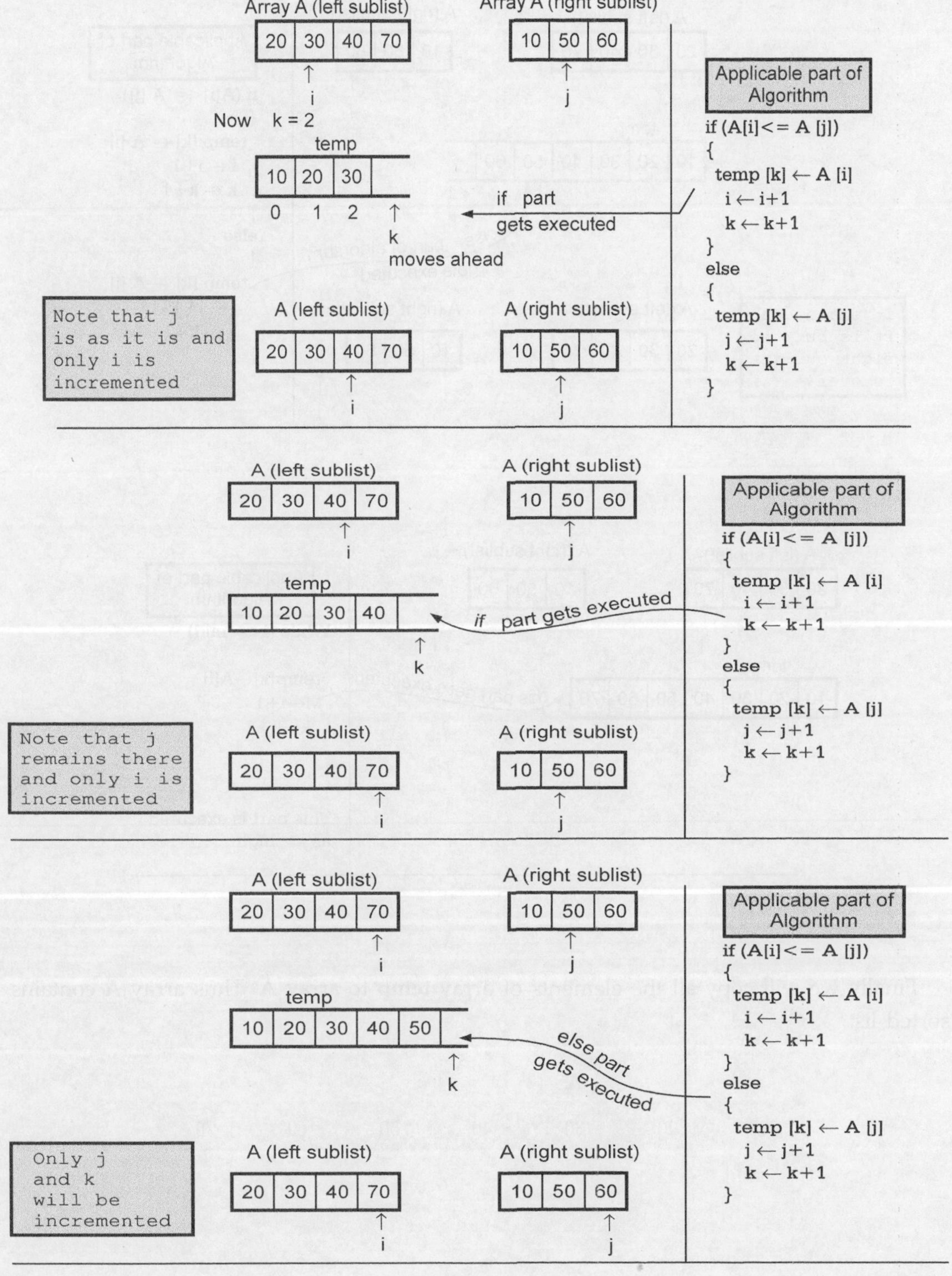
Array A (left sublist)
20 30 40 70
i
Array A (right sublist)
10 50 60
j
Applicable part of Algorithm
if (A[i]<= A [j])
{
temp [k] ← A [i]
i ← i+1
k ← k+1
}
else
{
temp [k] ← A [j]
j ← j+1
k ← k+1
}
Now k = 2
temp
10 20 30
0 1 2
k
moves ahead
if part gets executed
Note that j is as it is and only i is incremented
A (left sublist)
20 30 40 70
i
A (right sublist)
10 50 60
j
A (left sublist)
20 30 40 70
i
A (right sublist)
10 50 60
j
Applicable part of Algorithm
if (A[i]<= A [j])
{
temp [k] ← A [i]
i ← i+1
k ← k+1
}
else
{
temp [k] ← A [j]
j ← j+1
k ← k+1
}
temp
10 20 30 40
k
if part gets executed
Note that j remains there and only i is incremented
A (left sublist)
20 30 40 70
i
A (right sublist)
10 50 60
j
A (left sublist)
20 30 40 70
i
A (right sublist)
10 50 60
j
Applicable part of Algorithm
if (A[i]<= A [j])
{
temp [k] ← A [i]
i ← i+1
k ← k+1
}
else
{
temp [k] ← A [j]
j ← j+1
k ← k+1
}
temp
10 20 30 40 50
k
else part gets executed
Only j and k will be incremented
A (left sublist)
20 30 40 70
i
A (right sublist)
10 50 60
j

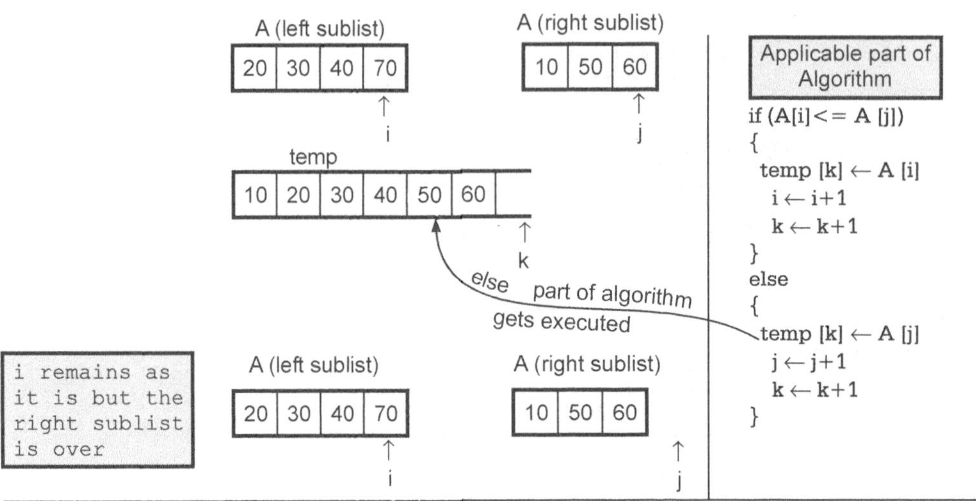

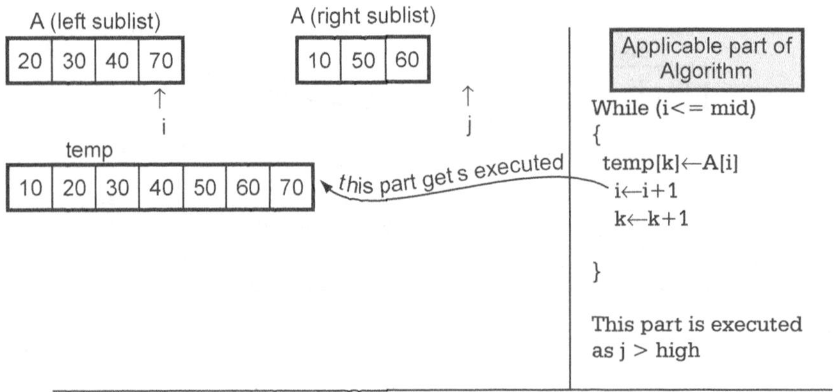

Finally we will copy all the elements of array **temp** to array **A.** Thus array **A** contains sorted list.

A

10	20	30	40	50	60	70

C Function

```
void MergeSort(int A[10], int low, int high)
{
        int mid;
        void Combine(int A[10]; int low, int mid, int high);
        if(low < high)
        {
            mid = (low+high)/2;             //split the list at mid
            MergeSort(A,low,mid);         //first sublist
            MergeSort(a,mid+1,high);      //second sublist
            Combine(A,low,mid,high);      //merging of two sublists
        }
}
void Combine(int A[10], int low, int mid, int high)
{
        int i,j,k;
        int temp[10];
        k=low;
        i=low;
        j=mid+1;
        while(i <= mid && j <= high)
        {
            if(A[i]<=A[j])
            {
                temp[k]=A[i];
                i++;

                k++;
}
            else
                {
                    temp[k]=A[j];
j++;
                    k++;
                }
            }
            while(i<=mid)
            {
                temp[k]=A[i];
                i++;
                k++;

            }
            while(j<=high)
            {
                temp[k]=A[j];
                j++;
                k++;
```

```
        }
            //copy the elements from temp array to A
            for(k=low;k<=high;k++)
                    A[k]=temp[k];
}
```

Analysis

In merge sort algorithm the two recursive calls are made. Each recursive call focuses on n/2 elements of the list. After two recursive calls one call is made to combine two sublists i.e. to merge all n elements. Hence we can write recurrence relation as

$$T(n) = T(n/2) + T(n/2) + cn$$

	Time taken by left sublist to get sorted	Time taken by right sublist to get sorted	Time taken for combining two sublists
$T(n) =$	$T(n/2)$	$T(n/2)$	cn

where n > 1 T (1) = 0

We can obtain the time complexity of Merge Sort using two methods

1. Master theorem 2. Substitution method

1. Using master theorem :

Let, the recurrence relation for merge sort is

$$T(n) = T(n/2) + T(n/2) + cn$$

i.e. $$T(n) = 2T(n/2) + cn \quad \text{... (3.7.1)}$$

$$T(1) = 0 \quad \text{... (3.7.2)}$$

As per Master theorem

$$T(n) = \Theta(n^d \log n) \quad \text{if } a = b$$

As in equation (3.6.1),

$$a = 2,\ b = 2 \text{ and } f(n) = cn \text{ i.e. } n^d \text{ with } d = 1.$$

and $$a = b^d$$

i.e. $$2 = 2^1$$

This case gives us

$$T(n) = \Theta(n \log_2 n)$$

Hence the average and worst case time complexity of merge sort is $\Theta(n \log_2 n)$.

2. Using substitution method :

Let, the recurrence relation for Merge Sort be

$$T(n) = T(n/2) + T(n/2) + cn \quad \text{for } n > 1$$

i.e. $$T(n) = 2T(n/2) + cn \quad \text{... (3.7.3)}$$

$$T(1) = 0 \quad \text{... (3.7.4)}$$

Let us apply substitution on equation (3.6.3). Assume $n = 2^k$.

$$T(n) = 2T(n/2) + cn$$

$$T(n) = 2T\left(\frac{2^k}{2}\right) + c \cdot 2^k \quad \text{...} \because n = 2^k$$

$$T(2^k) = 2T(2^{k-1}) + c \cdot 2^k$$

It we put k = k – 1 then,

$$T(2^k) = \underbrace{2T(2^{k-1}) + c \cdot 2^k}$$

$$\downarrow$$

$$= \overbrace{2\,[2T(2^{k-2}) + c \cdot 2^{k-1}] + c \cdot 2^k}$$

$$= 2^2\, T(2^{k-2}) + 2 \cdot c \cdot 2^{k-1} + c \cdot 2^k$$

$$= 2^2\, T(2^{k-2}) + 2 \cdot c \cdot \frac{2^k}{2} + c \cdot 2^k$$

$$= 2^2\, T(2^{k-2}) + c \cdot 2^k + c \cdot 2^k$$

$$T(2^k) = 2^2\, T(2^{k-2}) + 2c \cdot 2^k$$

Similarly we can write,

$$T(2^k) = 2^3 T(2^{k-3}) + 3c \cdot 2^k$$

$$= 2^4 T(2^{k-4}) + 4c \cdot 2^k$$

...

...

...

$$= 2^k T(2^{k-k}) + k \cdot c \cdot 2^k$$

$$= 2^k T(2^0) + k \cdot c \cdot 2^k$$

$$T(2^k) = 2^k T(1) + k \cdot c \cdot 2^k \quad \text{... (3.7.5)}$$

But as per equation (3.6.4), T(1) = 0,

∴ Equation (3.6.5) becomes,

$$T(2^k) = 2^k \cdot 0 + k \cdot c \cdot 2^k$$

$$T(2^k) = k \cdot c \cdot 2^k$$

But we assumed $n = 2^k$, taking logarithm on both sides.

i.e. $\log_2 n = k$

∴ $T(n) = \log_2 n \cdot cn$

∴ $T(n) = \Theta(n \cdot \log_2 n)$

Hence the average and worst case time complexity of merge sort is $\Theta(n \log_2 n)$.

Time complexity of merge sort

Best case	Average case	Worst case
$\Theta(n \log_2 n)$	$\Theta(n \log_2 n)$	$\Theta(n \log_2 n)$

Example 3.7.1 *Is merge sort stable sorting algorithm ?* **Dec.-10, Marks 2**

Solution : Yes, merge sort is the stable sorting algorithm. A sorting algorithm is said to be stable if it preserves the ordering of similar (equal) elements after applying sorting method. And merge sort is a method which preserves this kind of ordering. Hence merge sort is a stable sorting algorithm.

Example 3.7.2 *Give the time efficiency and drawback of merge sort algorithm.*

Solution : Time efficiency : The best, worst and average case time complexity of merge sort is O (n log n).

Drawbacks :

i) This algorithm requires extra storage to execute this method.

ii) This method is slower than the quick sort method.

iii) This method is complicated to code.

C Program

```
/***********************************************************************
This program is for Merge Sort using divide and conquer strategy.
***********************************************************************/
#include<conio.h>
```

```
#include<stdio.h>
#include<stdlib.h>
int n;
void main()
{
        int i,low,high;
        int A[10];
        void MergeSort(int A[10],int low,int high);
        void Display(int A[10]);
        clrscr();
        printf("\n\t\t Merge Sort \n");
        printf("\n Enter the length of list:");
        scanf("%d",&n);
        printf("\n Enter list elements:");
        for(i=0;i<n;i++)
        scanf("%d",&A[i]);
        low=0;
        high=n-1;
        MergeSort(A,low,high);
        Display(A);
        getch();
}
/*
 This function is to split the list into sublists
*/
void MergeSort(int A[10],int low,int high)
{
        int mid;
        void Combine(int A[10],int low,int mid,int high);
        if(low < high)
        {
            mid = (low+high)/2;//split the list at mid
            MergeSort(A,low,mid);//first sublist
            MergeSort(A,mid+1,high);//second sublist
            Combine(A,low,mid,high);//merging of two sublists
        }
}
/* This function is for merging the two sublists*/
void Combine(int A[10],int low,int mid,int high)
{
        int i,j,k;
        int temp[10];
        k=low;
        i=low;
```

```
        j=mid+1;
        while(i <= mid && j <= high)
        {
         if(A[i]<=A[j])
    {
                temp[k]=A[i];
                i++;
                k++;
         }
         else
          {
                    temp[k]=A[j];
                    j++;
                    k++;
             }
           }
           while(i<=mid)
           {
                    temp[k]=A[i];
                    i++;
                    k++;
           }
           while(j<=high)
           {
                    temp[k]=A[j];
                    j++;
                    k++;
           }
           //copy the elements from temp array to A
           for(k=low;k<=high;k++)
                    A[k]=temp[k];
}
/* function to display sorted array */
void Display(int A[10])
{
           int i;
           printf("\n\n The Sorted Array Is ...\n");
           for(i=0;i<n;i++)
                  printf("%d\t",A[i]);
}
```

We compare elements from left sublist and right sublist. If element in the left sublist is lesser than the element in the right sublist then copy that smaller element of left sublist to **temp** array

We compare elements from left sublist and right sublist. If element in the right sublist is lesser than the element in the left sublist then copy that smaller element of right sublist to **temp** array

Reached at the end of right sublist and elements of left sublist are remaining, then copy the remaining elements of left sublist to **temp**

Reached at the end of left sublist and elements of right sublist are remaining, then copy the remaining elements of right sublist to **temp**

Output

```
                         Merge Sort

Enter the length of list :7
```

```
Enter list elements :
70
20
30
40
10
50
60

The Sorted Array Is ...
10    20    30    40    50    60    70
```

Review Question

1. *Explain merge sort problem using divide and conquer technique. Give an example.*
GTU : Winter-14, Marks 7

3.8 Quick Sort **GTU : Dec.-10,11, June-11,12, Summer-13,14, Winter-14,15, Marks 7**

Quick sort is a sorting algorithm that uses the divide and conquer strategy. In this method division is dynamically carried out. The three steps of quick sort are as follows :

- **Divide :** Split the array into two sub arrays that each element in the left sub array is less than or equal the middle element and each element in the right sub array is greater than the middle element. The splitting of the array into two sub arrays is based on pivot element. All the elements that are less than pivot should be in left sub array and all the elements that are more than pivot should be in right sub array.

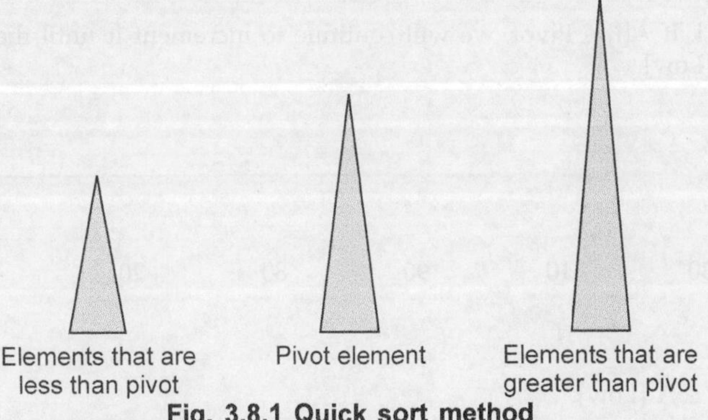

Fig. 3.8.1 Quick sort method

- **Conquer :** Recursively sort the two sub arrays.
- **Combine :** Combine all the sorted elements in a group to form a list of sorted elements.

In merge sort the division of array is based on the positions of array elements, but in quick sort this division is based on actual value of the element. Consider an array A[i] where i is ranging from 0 to n – 1 then we can formulate the division of array elements as

Let us understand this algorithm with the help of some example.

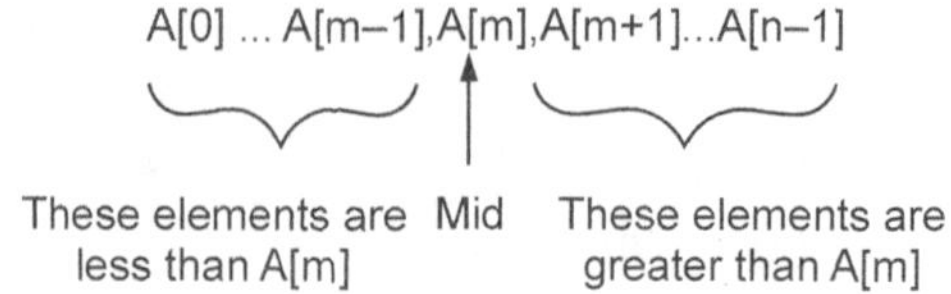

Example :

Step 1 :

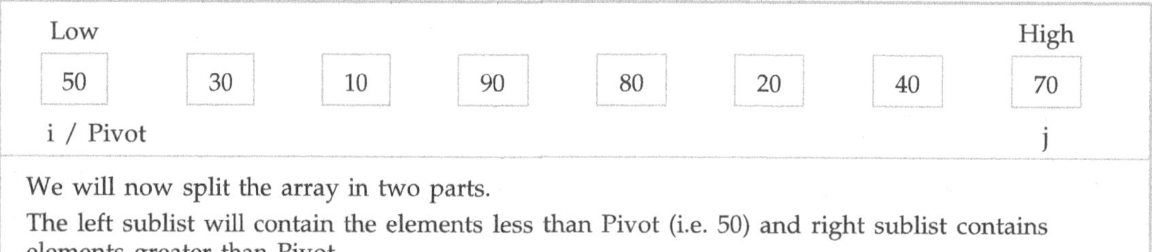

Step 2 :

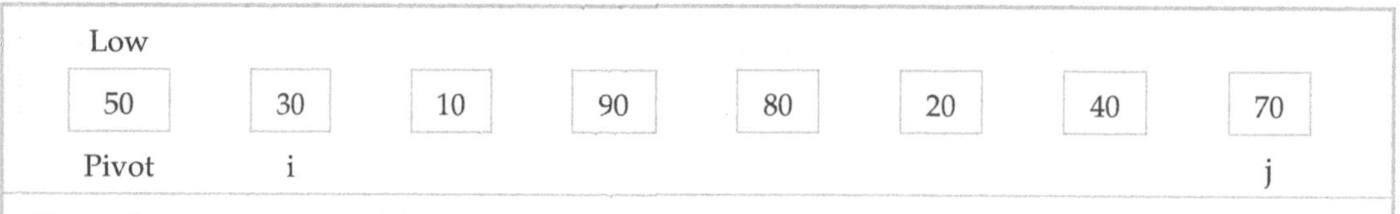

Step 3 :

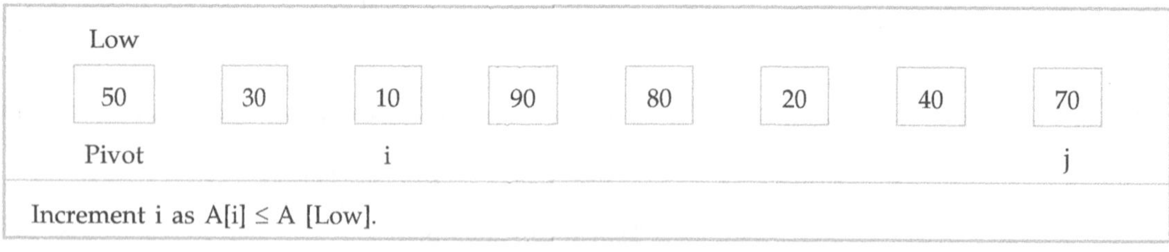

Step 4 :

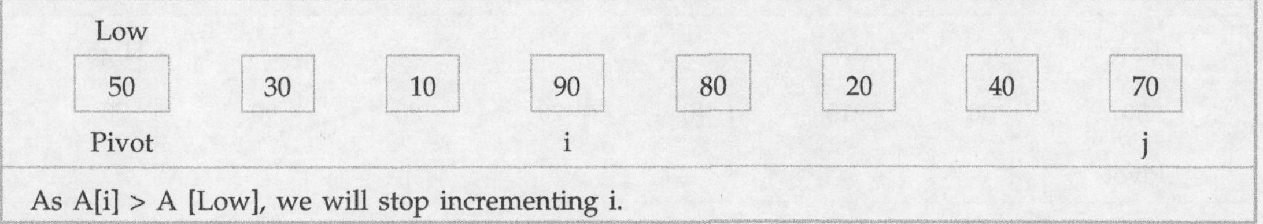

As A[i] > A [Low], we will stop incrementing i.

Step 5 :

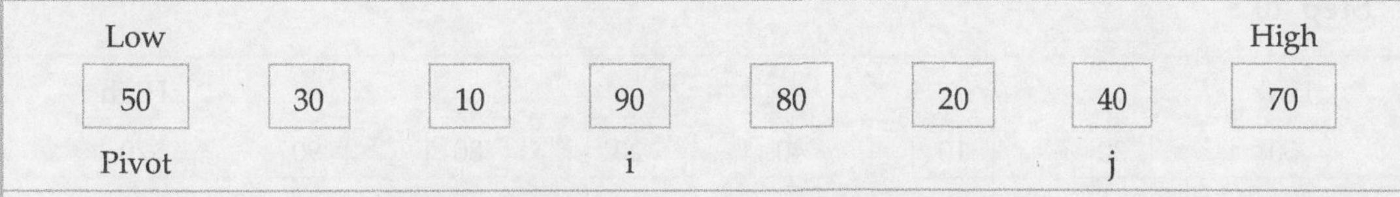

As A[j] > Pivot (i.e. 70 > 50). We will decrement j. We will continue to decrement j until the element pointed by j is less than A [Low].

Step 6 :

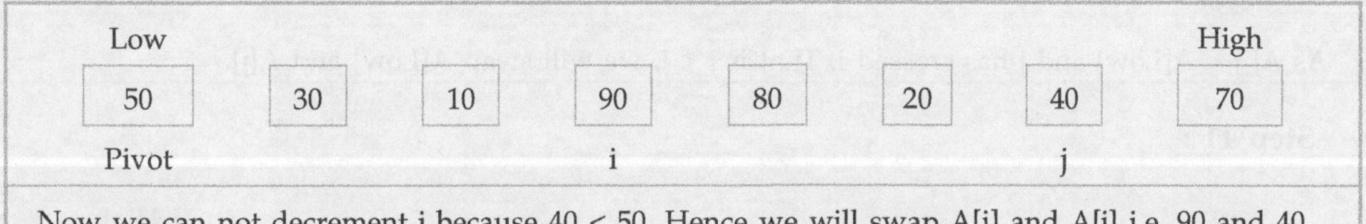

Now we can not decrement j because 40 < 50. Hence we will swap A[i] and A[j] i.e. 90 and 40.

Step 7 :

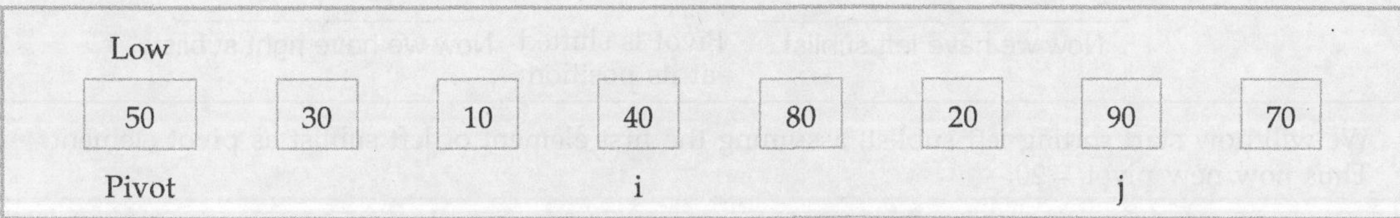

As A[i] is less than A[Low] and A[j] is greater than A[Low] we will continue incrementing i and decrementing j, until the false conditions are obtained.

Step 8 :

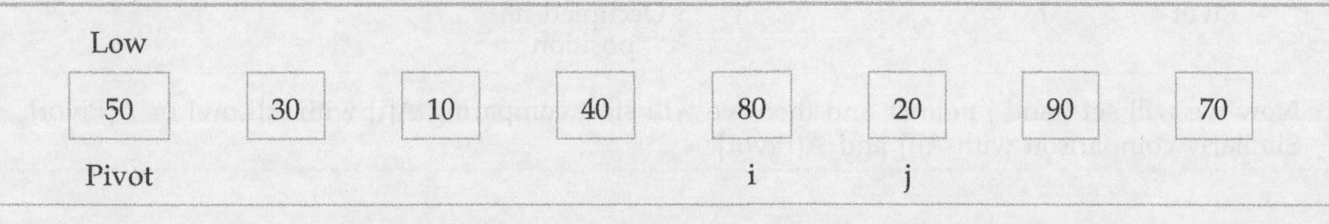

We will stop incrementing i and stop decrementing j. As i is smaller than j we will swap 80 and 20.

Step 9 :

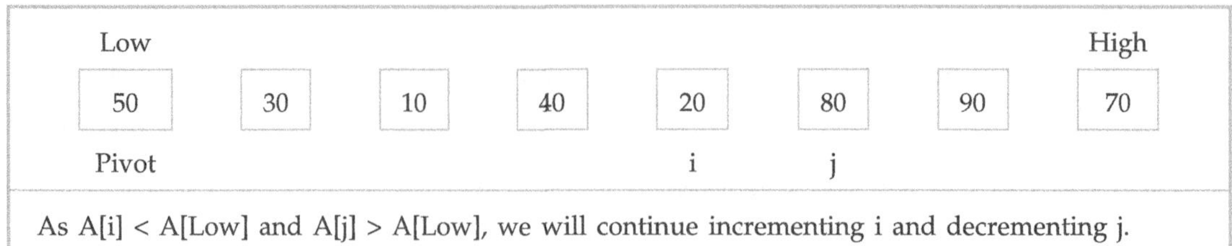

Step 10 :

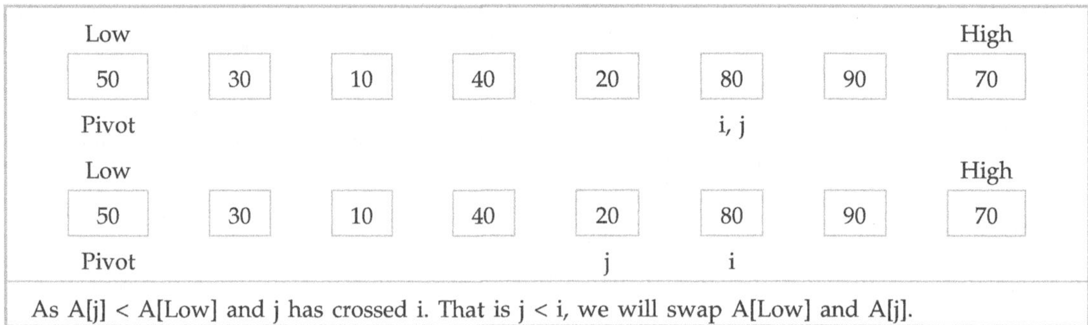

Step 11 :

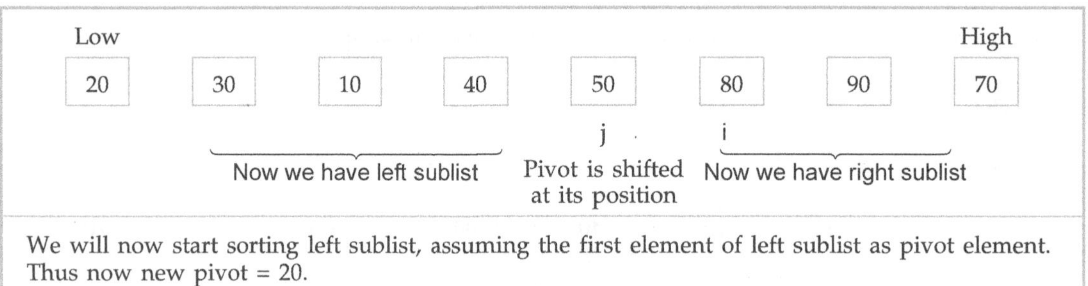

Step 12 :

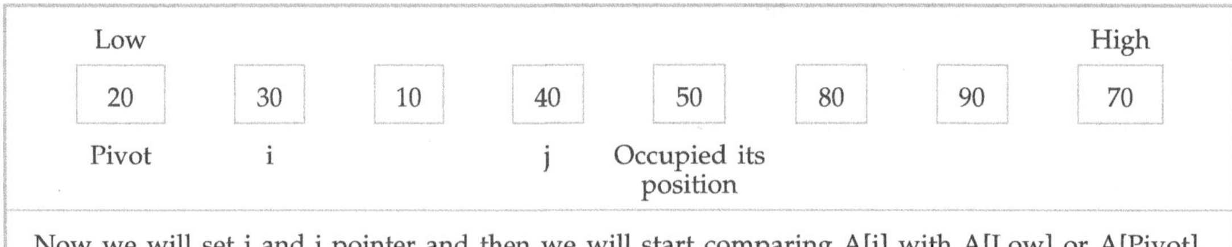

Step 13 :

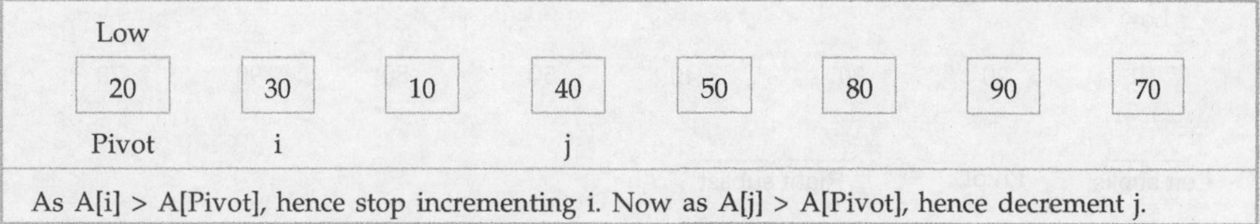

As A[i] > A[Pivot], hence stop incrementing i. Now as A[j] > A[Pivot], hence decrement j.

Step 14 :

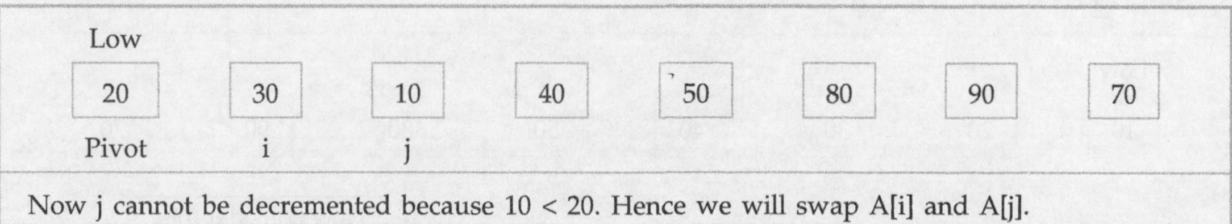

Now j cannot be decremented because 10 < 20. Hence we will swap A[i] and A[j].

Step 15 :

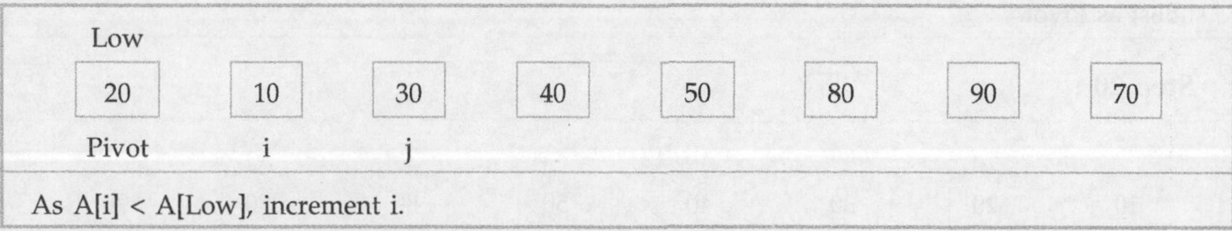

As A[i] < A[Low], increment i.

Step 16 :

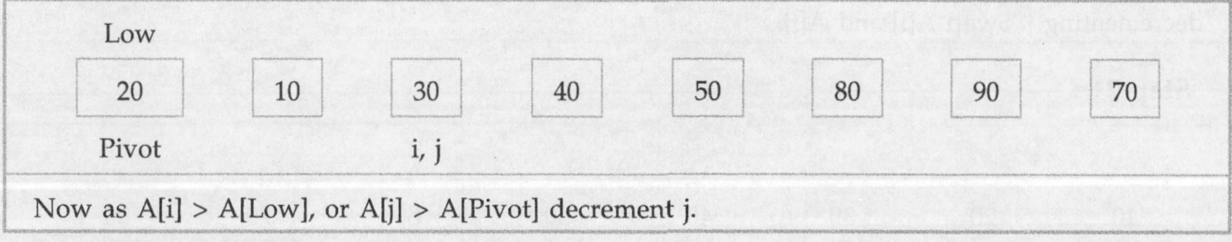

Now as A[i] > A[Low], or A[j] > A[Pivot] decrement j.

Step 17 :

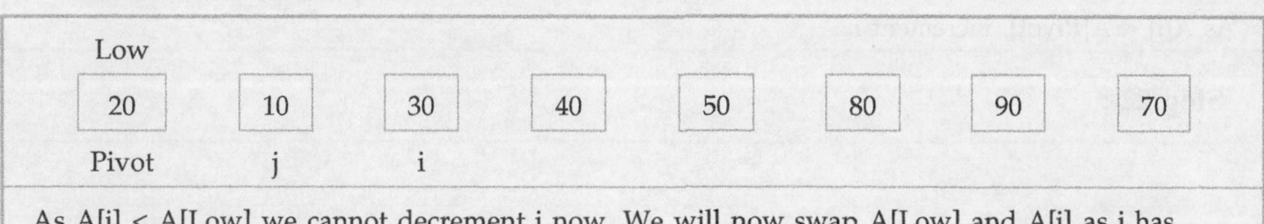

As A[j] < A[Low] we cannot decrement j now. We will now swap A[Low] and A[j] as j has crossed i and i > j.

Step 18 :

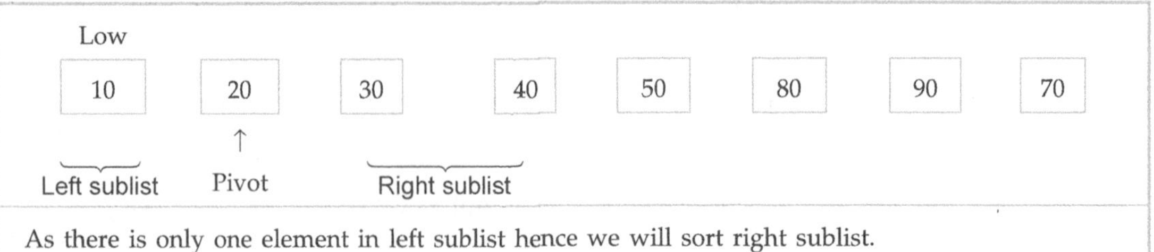

As there is only one element in left sublist hence we will sort right sublist.

Step 19 :

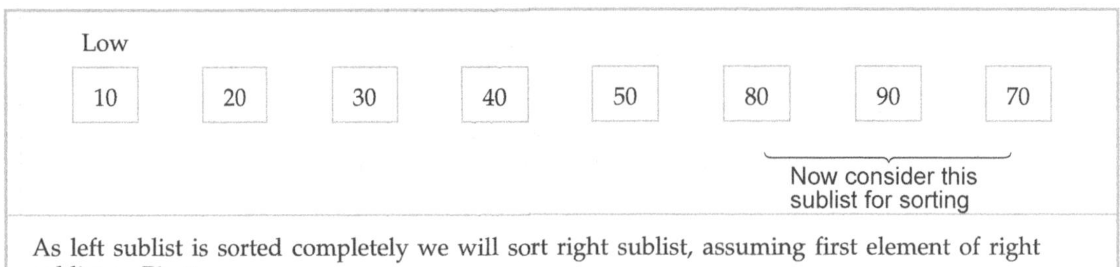

As left sublist is sorted completely we will sort right sublist, assuming first element of right sublist as Pivot.

Step 20 :

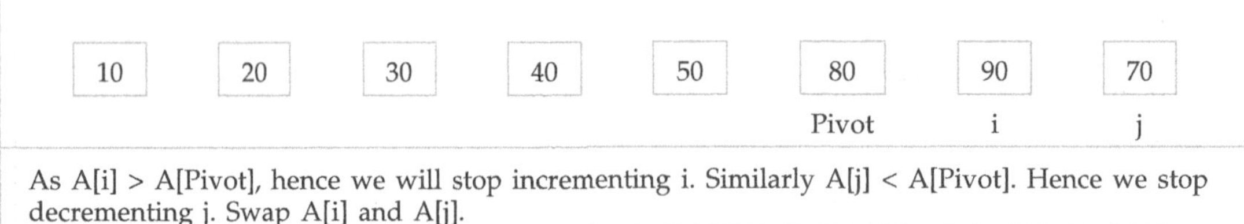

As A[i] > A[Pivot], hence we will stop incrementing i. Similarly A[j] < A[Pivot]. Hence we stop decrementing j. Swap A[i] and A[j].

Step 21 :

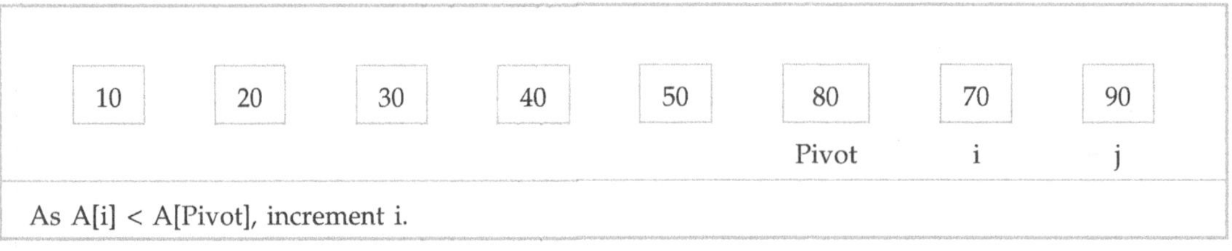

As A[i] < A[Pivot], increment i.

Step 22 :

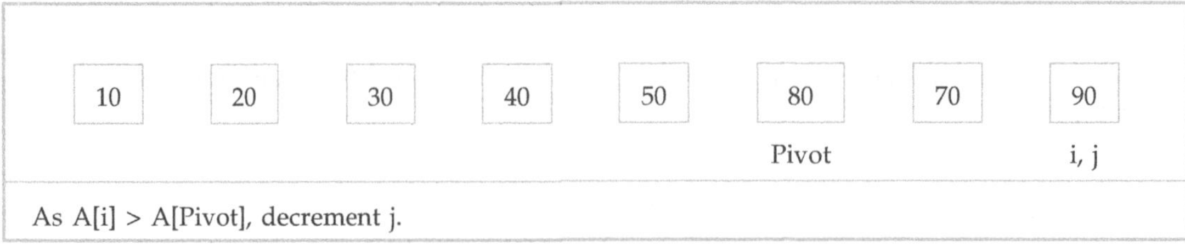

As A[i] > A[Pivot], decrement j.

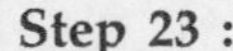

Step 23 :

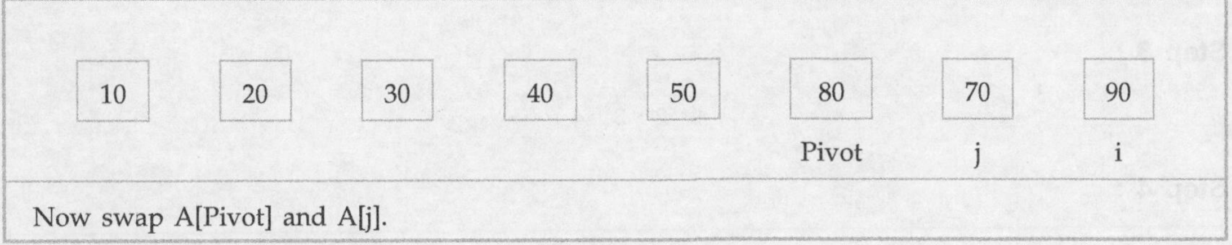

Now swap A[Pivot] and A[j].

Step 24 :

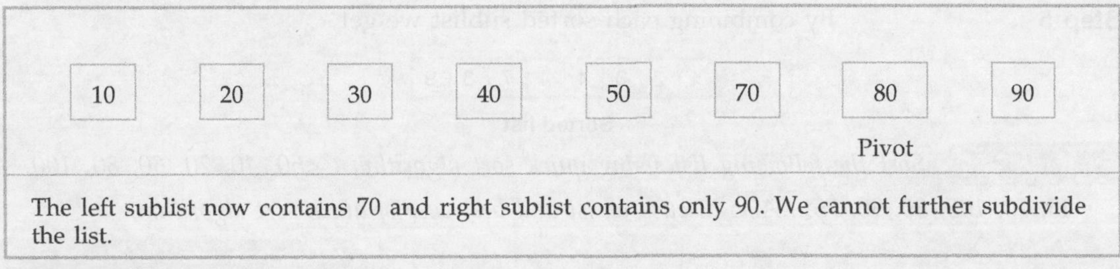

The left sublist now contains 70 and right sublist contains only 90. We cannot further subdivide the list.

Hence list is

This is a sorted list.

Example 3.8.1 *Write the quick sort algorithm. Trace the same on data set - 4, 3, 1, 9, 8, 2, 4, 7.* **GTU : Summer-13, Marks 8**

Solution : Consider the elements

Step 1 : We will assume first element as pivot. From second element onwards, we will compare all the elements with pivot value (i.e .4). All the elements less than pivot will occupy left sublist and all the elements greater than pivot will occupy right sublist.

Thus pivot will occupy its proper position

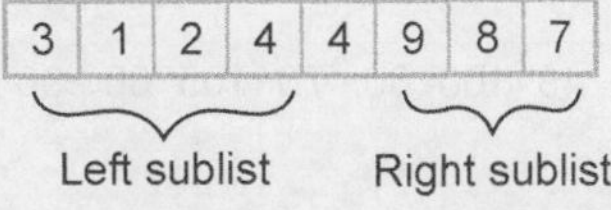

Step 2 : The above procedure will be repeated for each sublists recursively and newer sub-sub lists will be generated.

Step 3 :

1	2	3	4	...

Step 4 :

7	8	9

Step 5 : By combining each sorted sublist we get -

Sorted list

Example 3.8.2 *Sort the following list using quick sort algorithm : <50, 40, 20, 60, 80, 100, 45, 70, 105, 30, 90, 75>. Also discuss worst and best case of quick sort algorithm.*

GTU : Summer-14, Marks 7

Solution : Consider the list in an array

Array A[ ]

50	40	20	60	80	100	45	70	105	30	90	75

Step 1 :

We will assume first element as pivot element. Second element onwards we will compare the elements with pivot.

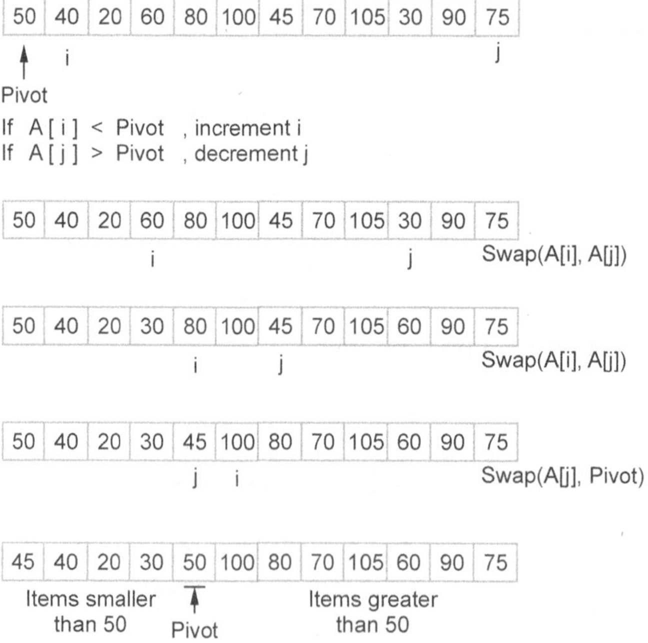

Pass 2a (left sublist)

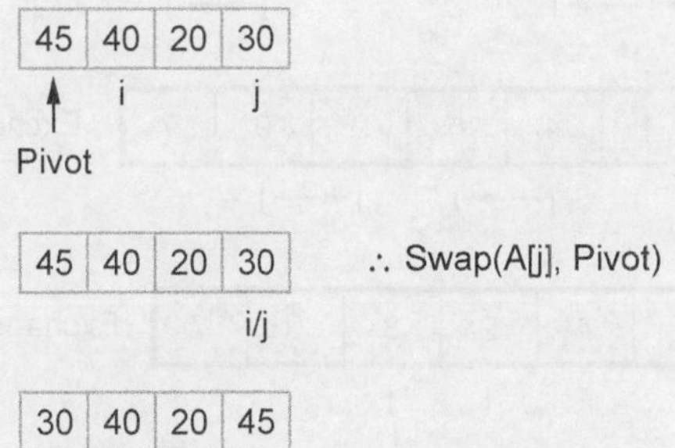

Pass 2b (Right sublist)

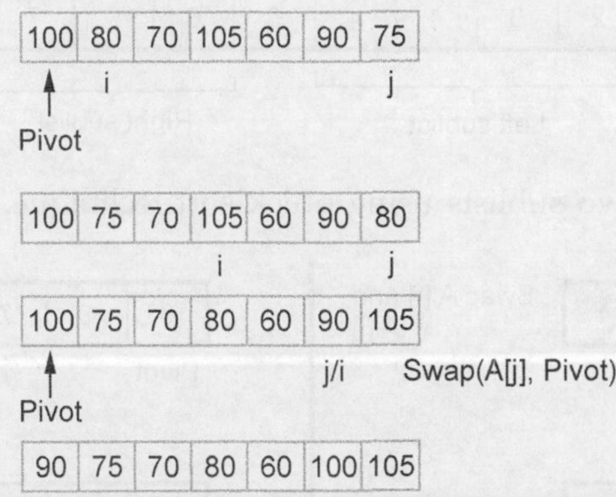

Thus continuing in this fashion, by sorting each sub-sublists finally we get the sorted list as

20	30	40	45	50	60	70	75	80	90	100	105

Example 3.8.3 *Write the Quick sort algorithm. Track the same on data set : 5, 3, 1, 9, 8, 2, 4, 7*

GTU : IT, Winter-14, Marks 7

Solution : Arrange the elements in an array.

Step 1 :

0	1	2	3	4	5	6	7
5	3	1	9	8	2	4	7
Pivot	i						j

If A [i] < A [pivot], increment i.

If A [j] > A[pivot], decrement j.

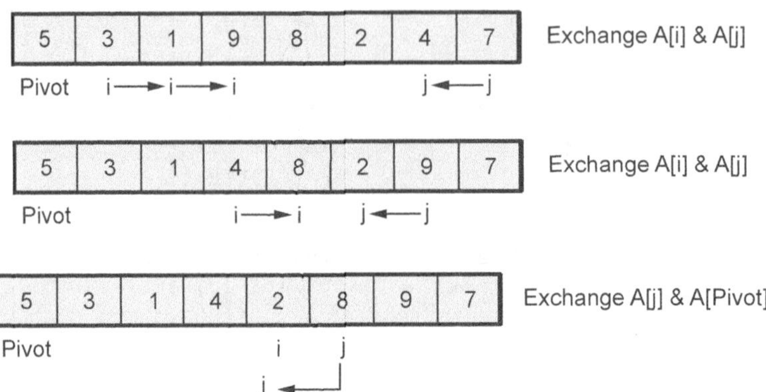

After pass 1

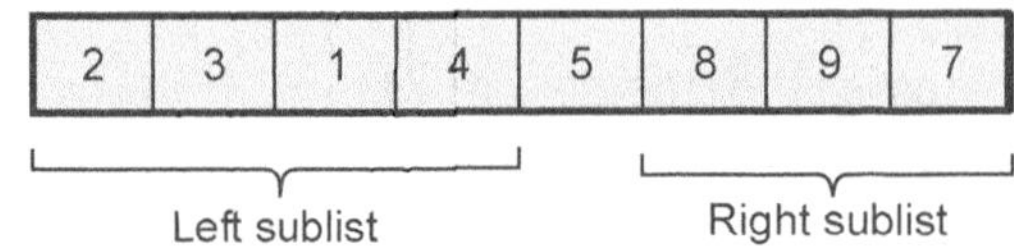

Step 2 : Now sorting two sublists using quick sort technique.

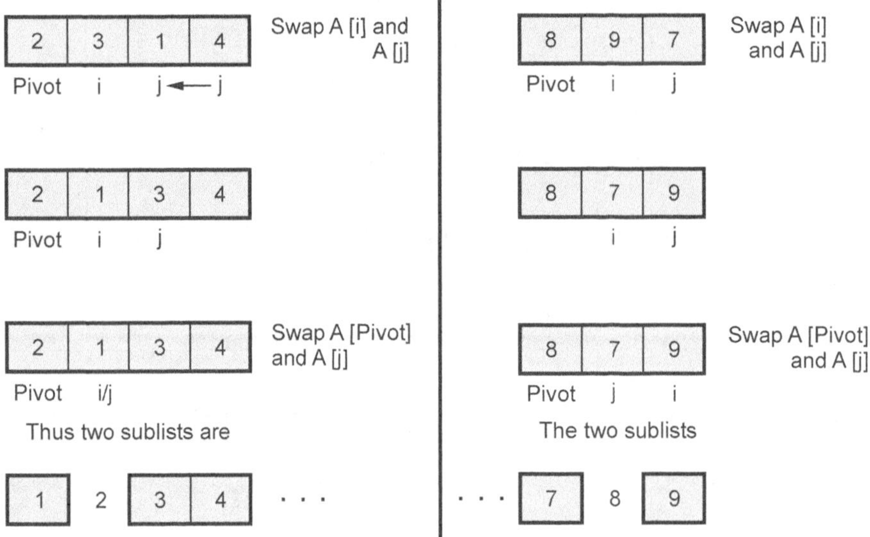

Step 3 : Now sorting sub-sublist

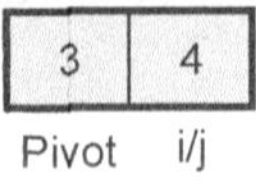

we will get

3	4

Step 4 : Finally the entire list will be

1	2	3	4	5	7	8	9

Example 3.8.4 *Write an algorithm for quick sort and derive best case, worst case using divide and conquer technique also trace given data (3, 1, 4, 5, 9, 2, 6, 5)*

GTU : Winter-15, Marks 7

Solution : Algorithm : Refer section 3.8.

Derivation for best, worst case : Refer section 3.8.

Step 1 : Consider the elements in an array

0	1	2	3	4	5	6	7
3	1	4	5	9	2	6	5
Pivot	i						j

If A[Pivot] > A[i] increment i

If A[Pivot] < A[j] increment j

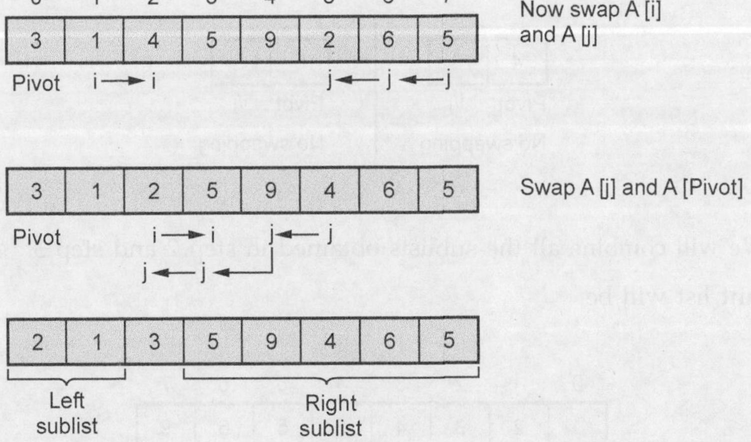

Step 2 : Now sorting two sublists using quick sort technique.

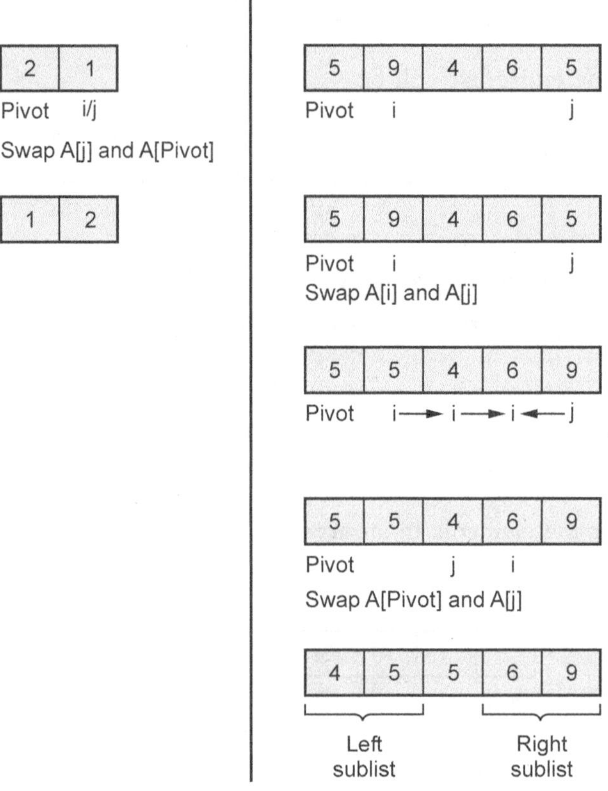

Step 3 : We will sort two sublists obtained in step 2.

4	5

Pivot i/j

No swapping

6	9

Pivot i/j

No swapping

Step 4 : We will combine all the sublists obtained in step 2 and step 3.

The resultant list will be

0	1	2	3	4	5	6	7
1	2	3	4	5	5	6	9

This is a sorted list

Algorithm

The quick sort algorithm is performed using following two important functions - *Quick* and *partition*. Let us see them-

```
Algorithm Quick(A[0...n–1], low,high)
//Problem Description : This algorithm performs sorting of
//the elements given in Array A[0...n–1]
//Input: An array A[0...n–1] in which unsorted elements are
//given. The low indicates the leftmost element in the list
//and high indicates the rightmost element in the list
//Output: Creates a sub array which is sorted in ascending
//order
if(low<high)then
//split the array into two sub arrays
m ← partition(A[low...high])// m is mid of the array
Quick(A[low...m–1])
Quick(A[mid+1...high])
```

In above algorithm call to partition algorithm is given. The *partition* performs arrangement of the elements in ascending order. The recursive *quick* routine is for dividing the list in two sub lists. The pseudo code for *Partition* is as given below -

```
Algorithm Partition (A[low...high])
//Problem Description: This algorithm partitions the
//subarray using the first element as pivot element
//Input: A subarray A with low as left most index of the
//array and high as the rightmost index of the array.
//Output: The partitioning of array A is done and pivot
//occupies its proper position. And the rightmost index of
//the list is returned
pivot ← A[low]
i ← low
j ← high+1
while(i<=j) do
{
 while(A[i]<=pivot) do
      i ← i+1
  while(A[j]>=pivot) do
      j ← j–1;
  if(i<=j) then
            swap(A[i],A[j])//swaps A[i] and A[j]
}
swap(A[low],A[j])//when i crosses j swap A[low] and A[j]
return j//rightmost index of the list
```

The Partition function is called to arrange the elements such that all the elements that are less than pivot are at the left side of pivot and all the elements that are greater than pivot are all at the right of pivot. In other words pivot is occupying its proper position and the partitioned list is obtained in an ordered manner.

Analysis

Best case (split in the middle)

If the array is always partitioned at the mid, then it brings the best case efficiency of an algorithm.

The recurrence relation for quick sort for obtaining best case time complexity is,

$$C(n) = C(n/2) + C(n/2) + n \quad \text{... equation (3.8.1)}$$

	$C(n/2)$	$C(n/2)$	n
	Time required to sort left sub array	Time required to sort right sub array	Time required for partitioning the sub array

and $C(1) = 0$

Method 1 : Using Master theorem

We will solve equation (3.7.1) using master theorem.

The master theorem is

If $f(n) \in \Theta(n^d)$ then

1. $T(n) = \Theta(n^d)$ if $a < b^d$
2. $T(n) = \Theta(n^d \log n)$ if $a = b^d$
3. $T(n) = \Theta(n^{\log_b a})$ if $a > b^d$

We get,

$$C(n) = 2\,C(n/2) + n$$

Here $f(n) \in n^1$ $\therefore d = 1$

Now, $a = 2$ and $b = 2$.

As from case 2 we get $a = b^d$ i.e. $2 = 2^1$, we get

$$T(n) \text{ i.e. } C(n) = \Theta(n^d \log n)$$

$$\therefore \quad C(n) = \Theta(n \log n)$$

Thus,

Best case time complexity of quick sort is $\Theta(n \log_2 n)$.

The best case of quick sort can be represented by Fig. 3.8.2.

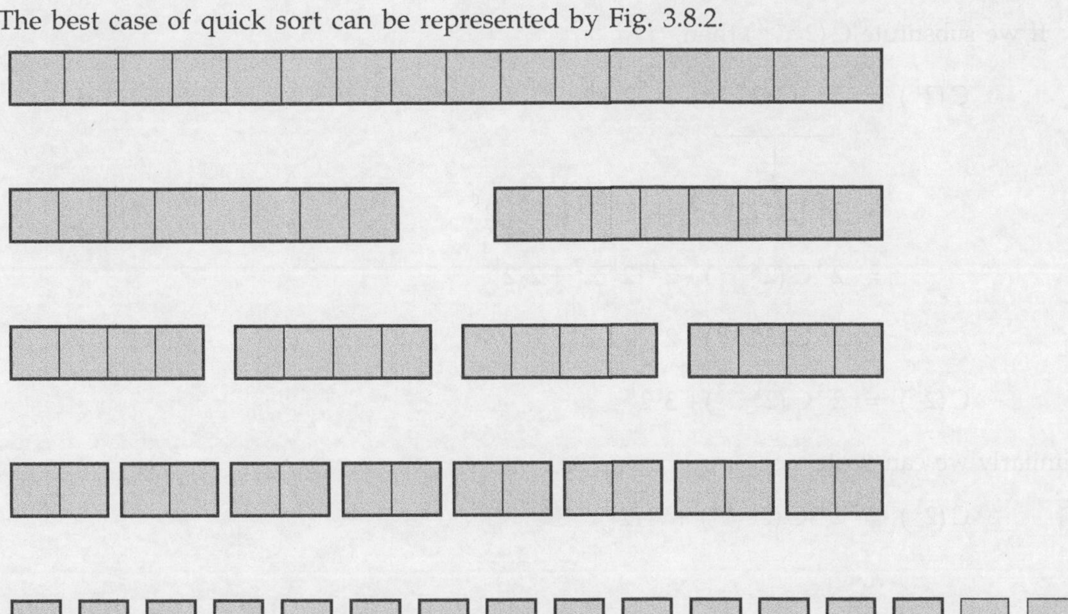

Fig. 3.8.2

Method 2 :

We can obtain the best case time complexity of quick sort using substitution method as well. Consider equation (1) once again

$$C(n) = C(n/2) + C(n/2) + n$$

$$C(n) = 2C(n/2) + n$$

We assume $n = 2^k$ since each time the list is divided into two equal halves. Then equation becomes,

$$C(2^k) = 2C(2^k/2) + 2^k$$

$$= 2C(2^{k-1}) + 2^k$$

Now substitute $C(2^{k-1}) = 2C(2^{k-2}) + 2^{k-1}$

We get $C(2^k) = 2[2C(2^{k-2}) + 2^{k-1}] + 2^k$

$$C(2^k) = 2^2 C(2^{k-2}) + 2 \cdot 2^{k-1} + 2^k$$

$$= 2^2 C(2^{k-2}) + 2^k + 2^k$$

$$C(2^k) = 2^2 C(2^{k-2}) + 2 \cdot 2^k$$

If we substitute $C(2^{k-2})$ then,

$$C(2^k) = 2^2 \, C(2^{k-2}) + 2 \cdot 2^k$$

$$= 2^2 [2C(2^{k-3}) + 2^{k-2}] + 2 \cdot 2^k$$

$$= 2^3 C(2^{k-3}) + 2^2 \cdot 2^{k-2} + 2 \cdot 2^k$$

$$= 2^3 C(2^{k-3}) + 2^k + 2 \cdot 2^k$$

$$C(2^k) = 2^3 C(2^{k-3}) + 3 \cdot 2^k$$

Similarly we can write

$$C(2^k) = 2^4 \, C(2^{k-4}) + 4 \cdot 2^k$$

$$\ldots$$

$$\ldots$$

$$\ldots$$

$$= 2^k \, C(2^{k-k}) + k \cdot 2^k$$

$$= 2^k \, C(2^0) + k \cdot 2^k$$

$$C(2^k) = 2^k \, C(1) + k \cdot 2^k$$

But $C(1) = 0$ Hence the above equation becomes

$$C(2^k) = 2^k \cdot 0 + k \cdot 2^k$$

Now as we assumed $n = 2^k$ we can also say

$$k = \log_2 n \quad \text{[By taking logarithm on both sides]}$$

$$C(n) = n \cdot 0 + \log_2 n \cdot n$$

$$C(n) = n \cdot 0 + \log_2 \cdot n$$

Thus it is proved that best case time complexity of quick sort is $\Theta(\mathbf{n} \log_2 \mathbf{n})$.

Worst case (sorted array)

The worst case for quick sort occurs when the pivot is a minimum or maximum of all the elements in the list. This can be graphically represented as

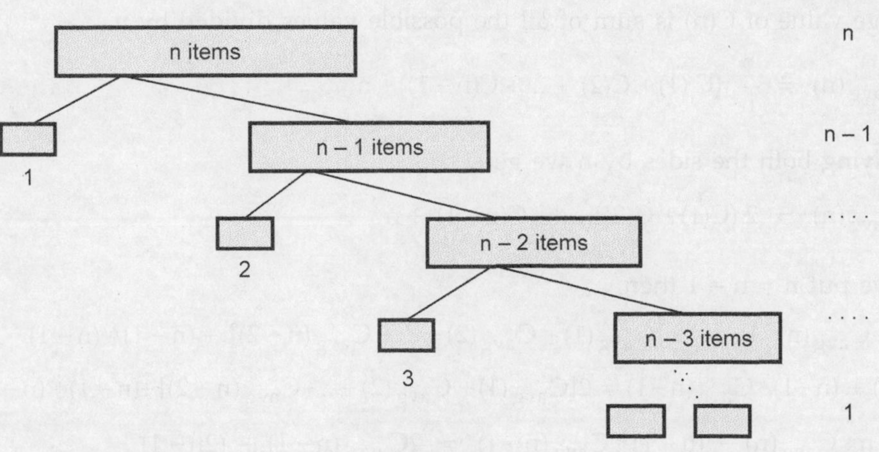

Fig. 3.8.3

We can write it as

$$C(n) = C(n-1) + n$$

or $$C(n) = n + (n-1) + (n-2) + \ldots + 2 + 1$$

But as we know

$$1 + 2 + 3 + \ldots + n = \frac{n(n+1)}{2} \approx \frac{1}{2} n^2.$$

$$\therefore \quad C(n) = \Theta(n^2)$$

> The time complexity of worst case of quick sort is $\Theta(n^2)$.

Average case (random array)

Let, $C_{avg}(n)$ denotes the average time of quick sort (A[1 ... n]).

The recurrence relation for random input array is

$$C(n) = C(0) + C(n-1) + n$$

or $$C(n) = C(1) + C(n-2) + n$$

or $$C(n) = C(2) + C(n-3) + n$$

or $$C(n) = C(3) + C(n-4) + n$$

...

...

...

$$C(n) = C(n-1) + C(0) + n$$

The average value of C(n) is sum of all the possible values divided by n.

$$\therefore \quad C_{avg}(n) = \frac{2}{n}(C(1) + C(2) + \ldots + C(n-1)) + n$$

Multiplying both the sides by n we get,

$$n * C_{avg}(n) = 2(C(1) + C(2) + \ldots + C(n-1)) + n^2$$

Now we put n = n – 1 then,

$$(n-1) * C_{avg}(n-1) = 2[C_{avg}(1) + C_{avg}(2) + \ldots + C_{avg}(n-2)] + (n-1) * (n-1)$$

$$n * C_{avg}(n) - (n-1) * C_{avg}(n-1) = 2[C_{avg}(1) + C_{avg}(2) + \ldots + C_{avg}(n-2)] + (n-1) * (n-1)$$

$$n * C_{avg}(n) - (n-1) * C_{avg}(n-1) = 2C_{avg}(n-1) + (2n-1)$$

$$n * C_{avg}(n) = (n+1) * C_{avg}(n-1) + (2n-1) < (n+1) * C_{avg}(n-1) + 2n$$

If we assume

$$(n+1) * C_{avg}(n-1) + 2n = (n+1) * C_{avg}(n-1) + C'n$$

Then,

$$(n+1) * C_{avg}(n-1) < (n+1) * C_{avg}(n-1) + C'n$$

Divide this equation by n (n + 1) then

$$n * C_{avg}(n) < (n+1) * C_{avg}(n-1) + C'n$$

$$\frac{C_{avg}(n)}{(n+1)} < \frac{C_{avg}(n-1)}{n} + \frac{C'}{(n+1)}$$

If we assume

$$A(n) = \frac{C_{avg}(n)}{(n+1)} \text{ then}$$

$$A(n) < A(n-1) + \frac{C'}{(n+1)}$$

$$A(n-1) < A(n-2) + \frac{C'}{n}$$

$$A(n-2) < A(n-3) + \frac{C'}{n-1}$$

...

...

...

$$A(1) < A(0) + \frac{C'}{2}$$

Adding and canceling these equations we get,

$$A(n) < C' * \left[\frac{1}{2} + \frac{1}{3} + \ldots + \frac{1}{n} + \frac{1}{n+1}\right]$$

$$\therefore C_{avg}(n) = (n+1) * A(n)$$

i.e. $(n+1) * A(n) < C''(n+1)\log n$

$$\therefore C_{avg}(n) = \Theta(n \log n)$$

Hence average case time complexity of quick sort is $\Theta(n \log n)$.

Time complexity of quick sort

Best case	Average case	Worst case
$\Theta(n \log_2 n)$	$\Theta(n \log_2 n)$	$\Theta(n^2)$

C Function

```
int partition(int A[SIZE],int low,int high)
{
        int pivot=A[low],i=low,j=high;
        while(i<=j)
        {
         while(A[i]<=pivot)
                i++;
         while(A[j]>pivot)
                j--;
         if(i<j)
                swap(A,&i,&j);
        }
        swap(A,&low,&j);
        return j;
}
```

C Program

```
/***********************************************************************************
Program to sort the elements in ascending order using Quick Sort.
***********************************************************************************/.
#include<stdio.h>
#include<conio.h>
#include<stdlib.h>
#define SIZE 10
void Quick(int A[SIZE],int,int);
int partition(int A[SIZE],int,int);
void swap(int A[SIZE],int *,int *);
int n;
int main()
{
        int i;
        int A[SIZE];
        clrscr();
        printf("\n\t\t Quick Sort Method \n");
        printf("\n Enter Total numbers to sort : ");
        scanf("%d",&n);
```

```
        for(i=0;i<n;i++)
        {
         printf("\nEnter %dth number : ",i+1);
         scanf("%d",&A[i]);
        }
        Quick(A,0,n-1);
        printf("\n\n\t Sorted Array Is: \n");
        for(i=0;i<n;i++)
         printf("\t%d ",A[i]);
        getch();
        return 0;
}

/*
This function is to sort the elements in a sublist
*/
void Quick(int A[SIZE],int low,int high)
{
        int m,i;
        if(low<high)
        {
                m=Partition(A,low,high);//setting pivot element
                Quick(A,low,m-1);//splitting of list
                Quick(A,m+1,high);//splitting  of list
        }

}
/*
This function is to partition a list and decide the pivot element
*/
int Partition(int A[SIZE],int low,int high)
{
        int pivot=A[low],i=low,j=high;
        while(i<=j)
        {
         while(A[i]<=pivot)
                i++;
         while(A[j]>pivot)
                j--;
         if(i<j)
                swap(A,&i,&j);
        }
        swap(A,&low,&j);
        return j;
}
```

```
void swap(int A[SIZE],int *i,int *j)
{
        int temp;

        temp=A[*i];
        A[*i]=A[*j];
        A[*j]=temp;
}
```

Output

```
                    Quick Sort Method

Enter Total numbers to sort : 8

Enter 1th number : 50

Enter 2th number : 30

Enter 3th number : 10

Enter 4th number : 90

Enter 5th number : 80

Enter 6th number : 20

Enter 7th number : 40

Enter 8th number : 70

    Sorted Array Is:
    10   20   30   40   50   70   80   90
```

Examples for Practice

Example 3.8.4 : *Trace the quick sort algorithm for the following data : 36, 37, 11, 10, 42, 72, 65, 98, 88, 78.*

Example 3.8.5 : *Is quick sort a stable sorting method ? Justify*

Example 3.8.6 : *Search the element 'r' from the list s, e, a, r, c, h. Show each step.*

Review Questions

1. *Explain how to apply the divide and conquer strategy for sorting the elements using quick sort with example.* **GTU : Winter-14, Dec.-10, Marks 7**
2. *Design and analyze quick sort algorithm using divide and conquer technique.* **GTU : June-11, Marks 7**
3. *Explain quick sort using divide and conquer method and computer it's worst case running time.* **GTU : Dec.-11, Marks 7**
4. *Explain quick sort method with example.* **GTU : June-12, Marks 7**

3.9 Matrix Multiplication

GTU : Dec.-11, Winter-14, Marks 4

Suppose we want to multiply two matrices A and B each of size N i.e.

$$C = A \times B \quad \text{then}$$

$$\begin{pmatrix} C_{11} & C_{12} \\ C_{21} & C_{22} \end{pmatrix} = \begin{pmatrix} A_{11} & A_{12} \\ A_{21} & A_{22} \end{pmatrix} \times \begin{pmatrix} B_{11} & B_{12} \\ B_{21} & B_{22} \end{pmatrix}$$

The multiplication gives

$$C_{11} = A_{11} \times B_{11} + A_{12} \times B_{21}$$

$$C_{12} = A_{11} \times B_{12} + A_{12} \times B_{22}$$

$$C_{21} = A_{21} \times B_{11} + A_{22} \times B_{21}$$

$$C_{22} = A_{21} \times B_{12} + A_{22} \times B_{22}$$

Thus to accomplish 2×2 matrix multiplication there are total 8 multiplications and 4 additions.

To accomplish this multiplication we can write the following algorithm for the same.

```
Algorithm Mat_Mul (A,B,C,n)
{
    for i:=1 to n do
        for j:=1 to n do
        C[i,j]:= 0;
            for k:=1 to n do
            C[i,j] := C[i,j] + A[i,j] × B[i,j] ;
}
```

The time complexity of above algorithm turns to be

$$O(n \times n \times n) = O(n^3)$$

Strassen showed that 2 × 2 matrix multiplication can be accomplished in 7 multiplication and 18 additions or subtractions.

The divide and conquer approach can be used for implementing Strassen's matrix multiplication.

- **Divide** : Divide matrices into sub-matrices : A0 , A1, A2 etc.
- **Conquer** : Use a group of matrix multiply equations.
- **Combine** : Recursively multiply sub-matrices and get the final result of multiplication after performing required additions or subtractions.

$$\begin{pmatrix} C_{11} & C_{12} \\ C_{21} & C_{22} \end{pmatrix} = \begin{pmatrix} A_{11} & A_{12} \\ A_{21} & A_{22} \end{pmatrix} \times \begin{pmatrix} B_{11} & B_{12} \\ B_{21} & B_{22} \end{pmatrix}$$

$$S1 = (A_{11}+ A_{22})(B_{11} + B_{22})$$

$$S2 = (A_{21} + A_{22}) \times B_{11}$$

$$S3 = A_{11} \times (B_{12} - B_{22})$$

$$S4 = A_{22} \times (B_{21} - B_{11})$$

$$S5 = (A_{11} + A_{12}) \times B_{22}$$

$$S6 = (A_{21} - A_{11}) \times (B_{11} + B_{12})$$

$$S7 = (A_{12} - A_{22}) \times (B_{21} + B_{22})$$

$$C_{11} = S1 + S4 - S5 + S7$$

$$C_{12} = S3 + S5$$

$$C_{21} = S2 + S4$$

$$C_{22} = S1 + S3 - S2 + S6$$

Now we will compare the actual our traditional matrix multiplication procedure with Strassen's procedure. In Strassen's multiplication

$$\begin{aligned} C_{11} &= S1 + S4 - S5 + S7 \\ &= (A_{11}+ A_{22})(B_{11}+B_{22}) + A_{22} \times (B_{21} - B_{11}) - (A_{11} + A_{12}) \times \\ &\qquad B_{22} + (A_{12} - A_{22}) \times (B_{21} + B_{22}) \\ &= A_{11} B_{11} + A_{11} B_{22} + A_{22} B_{11} + A_{22} B_{22} + A_{22} B_{21} - A_{22} B_{11} \\ &\quad - A_{11} B_{22} - A_{12} B_{22} + A_{12} B_{21} + A_{12} B_{22} - A_{22} B_{21} - A_{22} B_{22} \\ &= A_{11} B_{11} + A_{12} B_{21} \end{aligned}$$

Example 3.9.1

$$\text{If } A = \begin{bmatrix} 5 & 3 & 0 & 2 \\ 4 & 3 & 2 & 6 \\ 7 & 8 & 1 & 4 \\ 9 & 4 & 6 & 7 \end{bmatrix}, \quad B = \begin{bmatrix} 3 & 2 & 4 & 7 \\ 2 & 5 & 2 & 9 \\ 3 & 9 & 0 & 3 \\ 7 & 6 & 2 & 1 \end{bmatrix}$$

Implement Strassen's matrix multiplication on A and B.

Solution : The given matrix is of order 4×4. Hence we will subdivide it in 2×2 submatrices. Hence we will compute $S_1, S_2, S_3, S_4, S_5, S_6$ and S_7.

Let,

$$\begin{bmatrix} A_{11} & A_{12} \\ A_{21} & A_{22} \end{bmatrix} \times \begin{bmatrix} B_{11} & B_{12} \\ B_{21} & B_{22} \end{bmatrix}$$

$$A = \begin{bmatrix} \begin{bmatrix} 5 & 3 \\ 4 & 3 \end{bmatrix} & \begin{bmatrix} 0 & 2 \\ 2 & 6 \end{bmatrix} \\ \begin{bmatrix} 7 & 8 \\ 9 & 4 \end{bmatrix} & \begin{bmatrix} 1 & 4 \\ 6 & 7 \end{bmatrix} \end{bmatrix} \qquad B = \begin{bmatrix} \begin{bmatrix} 3 & 2 \\ 2 & 5 \end{bmatrix} & \begin{bmatrix} 4 & 7 \\ 2 & 9 \end{bmatrix} \\ \begin{bmatrix} 3 & 9 \\ 7 & 6 \end{bmatrix} & \begin{bmatrix} 0 & 3 \\ 2 & 1 \end{bmatrix} \end{bmatrix}$$

Now,

$$S_1 = (A_{11} + A_{22})(B_{11} + B_{22})$$

$$= \left[\begin{bmatrix} 5 & 3 \\ 4 & 3 \end{bmatrix} + \begin{bmatrix} 1 & 4 \\ 6 & 7 \end{bmatrix}\right]\left[\begin{bmatrix} 3 & 2 \\ 2 & 5 \end{bmatrix} \begin{bmatrix} 0 & 3 \\ 2 & 1 \end{bmatrix}\right] = \begin{bmatrix} 6 & 7 \\ 10 & 10 \end{bmatrix}\begin{bmatrix} 3 & 5 \\ 4 & 6 \end{bmatrix}$$

$$= \begin{bmatrix} 18+28 & 30+42 \\ 30+40 & 50+60 \end{bmatrix} = \begin{bmatrix} 46 & 72 \\ 70 & 110 \end{bmatrix}$$

$$S_2 = (A_{21} + A_{22}) B_{11}$$

$$= \left[\begin{bmatrix} 7 & 8 \\ 9 & 4 \end{bmatrix} + \begin{bmatrix} 1 & 4 \\ 6 & 7 \end{bmatrix}\right]\begin{bmatrix} 3 & 2 \\ 2 & 5 \end{bmatrix} = \begin{bmatrix} 8 & 12 \\ 15 & 11 \end{bmatrix}\begin{bmatrix} 3 & 2 \\ 2 & 5 \end{bmatrix}$$

$$= \begin{bmatrix} 24+24 & 16+60 \\ 45+22 & 30+55 \end{bmatrix}$$

$$S_2 = \begin{bmatrix} 48 & 76 \\ 67 & 85 \end{bmatrix}$$

$$S_3 = A_{11}(B_{12} - B_{22})$$

$$= \begin{bmatrix} 5 & 3 \\ 4 & 3 \end{bmatrix} \times \begin{bmatrix} 4 & 7 \\ 2 & 9 \end{bmatrix} - \begin{bmatrix} 0 & 3 \\ 2 & 1 \end{bmatrix} = \begin{bmatrix} 5 & 3 \\ 4 & 3 \end{bmatrix} \times \begin{bmatrix} 4 & 4 \\ 0 & 8 \end{bmatrix}$$

$$= \begin{bmatrix} 20+0 & 20+24 \\ 16+0 & 16+24 \end{bmatrix}$$

$$S_3 = \begin{bmatrix} 20 & 44 \\ 16 & 40 \end{bmatrix}$$

$$S_4 = A_{22} \times (B_{21} - B_{11})$$

$$= \begin{bmatrix} 1 & 4 \\ 6 & 7 \end{bmatrix} \times \begin{bmatrix} 3 & 9 \\ 7 & 6 \end{bmatrix} - \begin{bmatrix} 3 & 2 \\ 2 & 5 \end{bmatrix} = \begin{bmatrix} 1 & 4 \\ 6 & 7 \end{bmatrix} \times \begin{bmatrix} 0 & 7 \\ 5 & 1 \end{bmatrix}$$

$$= \begin{bmatrix} 0+20 & 7+4 \\ 0+35 & 42+7 \end{bmatrix}$$

$$S_4 = \begin{bmatrix} 20 & 11 \\ 35 & 49 \end{bmatrix}$$

$$S_5 = (A_{11} + A_{12}) \times B_{22}$$

$$= \begin{bmatrix} 5 & 3 \\ 4 & 3 \end{bmatrix} + \begin{bmatrix} 0 & 2 \\ 2 & 6 \end{bmatrix} \times \begin{bmatrix} 0 & 3 \\ 2 & 1 \end{bmatrix} = \begin{bmatrix} 5 & 5 \\ 6 & 9 \end{bmatrix} \times \begin{bmatrix} 0 & 3 \\ 2 & 1 \end{bmatrix}$$

$$= \begin{bmatrix} 0+10 & 15+5 \\ 0+18 & 18+9 \end{bmatrix} = \begin{bmatrix} 10 & 20 \\ 18 & 27 \end{bmatrix}$$

$$S_6 = (A_{21} - A_{11}) \times (B_{11} + B_{12})$$

$$= \begin{bmatrix} 7 & 8 \\ 9 & 4 \end{bmatrix} - \begin{bmatrix} 5 & 3 \\ 4 & 3 \end{bmatrix} \times \begin{bmatrix} 3 & 2 \\ 2 & 5 \end{bmatrix} + \begin{bmatrix} 4 & 7 \\ 2 & 9 \end{bmatrix}$$

$$= \begin{bmatrix} 2 & 5 \\ 5 & 1 \end{bmatrix} \times \begin{bmatrix} 7 & 9 \\ 4 & 14 \end{bmatrix} = \begin{bmatrix} 14+20 & 18+70 \\ 35+4 & 45+14 \end{bmatrix}$$

$$S_6 = \begin{bmatrix} 34 & 88 \\ 39 & 49 \end{bmatrix}$$

$$S_7 = (A_{12} - A_{22}) \times (B_{21} + B_{22})$$

$$= \begin{bmatrix} 0 & 2 \\ 2 & 6 \end{bmatrix} - \begin{bmatrix} 1 & 4 \\ 6 & 7 \end{bmatrix} \times \begin{bmatrix} 3 & 9 \\ 7 & 6 \end{bmatrix} + \begin{bmatrix} 0 & 3 \\ 2 & 1 \end{bmatrix}$$

$$= \begin{bmatrix} -1 & -2 \\ -4 & -1 \end{bmatrix} \times \begin{bmatrix} 3 & 12 \\ 9 & 7 \end{bmatrix}$$

$$S_7 = \begin{bmatrix} -21 & -26 \\ -21 & -55 \end{bmatrix}$$

$$C_{11} = S_1 + S_4 - S_5 + S_7$$

$$= \begin{bmatrix} 46 & 72 \\ 70 & 110 \end{bmatrix} + \begin{bmatrix} 20 & 11 \\ 35 & 49 \end{bmatrix} - \begin{bmatrix} 10 & 20 \\ 18 & 27 \end{bmatrix} + \begin{bmatrix} -21 & -26 \\ -21 & -55 \end{bmatrix}$$

$$C_{11} = \begin{bmatrix} 35 & 37 \\ 66 & 77 \end{bmatrix}$$

$$C_{12} = S_2 + S_4$$

$$= \begin{bmatrix} 20 & 44 \\ 16 & 40 \end{bmatrix} + \begin{bmatrix} 10 & 20 \\ 18 & 27 \end{bmatrix}$$

$$C_{12} = \begin{bmatrix} 30 & 64 \\ 34 & 67 \end{bmatrix}$$

$$C_{21} = S_2 + S_4$$

$$= \begin{bmatrix} 48 & 76 \\ 67 & 85 \end{bmatrix} + \begin{bmatrix} 20 & 11 \\ 35 & 49 \end{bmatrix} = \begin{bmatrix} 68 & 87 \\ 102 & 134 \end{bmatrix}$$

$$C_{22} = S_1 + S_3 - S_2 + S_6$$

$$\begin{bmatrix} 46 & 72 \\ 70 & 110 \end{bmatrix} + \begin{bmatrix} 20 & 44 \\ 16 & 40 \end{bmatrix} - \begin{bmatrix} 48 & 76 \\ 67 & 85 \end{bmatrix} + \begin{bmatrix} 34 & 88 \\ 39 & 49 \end{bmatrix}$$

$$= \begin{bmatrix} 66 & 116 \\ 86 & 150 \end{bmatrix} - \begin{bmatrix} 48 & 76 \\ 67 & 85 \end{bmatrix} - \begin{bmatrix} 34 & 88 \\ 39 & 49 \end{bmatrix}$$

$$= \begin{bmatrix} 52 & 128 \\ 58 & 124 \end{bmatrix}$$

Thus the final product matrix C will be -

$$\begin{bmatrix} C_{11} & C_{12} \\ C_{21} & C_{22} \end{bmatrix}$$

$$= \begin{bmatrix} \begin{bmatrix} 35 & 37 \\ 66 & 77 \end{bmatrix} & \begin{bmatrix} 30 & 64 \\ 34 & 67 \end{bmatrix} \\ \begin{bmatrix} 68 & 87 \\ 102 & 134 \end{bmatrix} & \begin{bmatrix} 52 & 128 \\ 58 & 124 \end{bmatrix} \end{bmatrix} = \begin{bmatrix} \mathbf{35} & \mathbf{37} & \mathbf{30} & \mathbf{64} \\ \mathbf{66} & \mathbf{77} & \mathbf{34} & \mathbf{67} \\ \mathbf{68} & \mathbf{87} & \mathbf{52} & \mathbf{128} \\ \mathbf{102} & \mathbf{134} & \mathbf{58} & \mathbf{124} \end{bmatrix}$$

3.9.1 Algorithm

Here we are dividing matrices in sub-matrices and recursively multiplying sub-matrices

```
Algorithm St_Mul(int *A, int *B, int *C, int n)
{
 if (n == 1)then
 {
      (*C) =(*C)+ (*A) * (*B);
 }
 else
 {
      St_Mul(A,B,C,n/4);
      St_Mul(A, B+(n/4), C+(n/4), n/4);
      St_Mul(A+2 *(n/4), B, C+2 *(n/4), n/4);
      St_Mul(A+2 *(n/4), B+(n/4), C+3 *(n/4), n/4);
      St_Mul(A+(n/4), B+2*(n/4), C, n/4);
      St_Mul(A+(n/4), B+3*(n/4), C+(n/4), n/4);
      St_Mul(A+3*(n/4), B+2*(n/4), C+2*(n/4), n/4);
      St_Mul(A+3*(n/4), B+3*(n/4), C+3*(n/4), n/4);
 }
}
```

3.9.2 Analysis of Algorithm

$$T(1) = 1 \qquad \text{assume } n = 2^k$$

$$T(n) = 7\,T(n/2)$$

$$T(n) = 7^k\,T(n/2^k)$$

$$T(n) = 7^{\log n}$$

$$T(n) = n^{\log 7} = n^{2.81}$$

Thus divide and conquer is an algorithmic strategy having with the principle idea of dividing the problem into subproblems. Then solution to these subproblems is obtained in order to get the final solution for the given problem.

Review Question

1. *Explain how divide and conquer method help multiplying two square matrices.*

GTU : Dec.-11, Marks 4

3.10 Exponential

While performing exponentiation operation we can make use of divide and conquer strategy.

Following algorithm shows how to perform exponentiation using divide and conquer

```
Algorithm    Exponentiation (x, n)
{
    if (n =0) then
        return 1 ;
    else
    r = Exponentiation (x, n/2);
    if (n % 2 = = 0) then
        return (r * r)     // when exponentiation value is even
    else
        return (r * r * x) // when expo. value is odd.
}
```

For example : suppose we wish to find 3^4 then $x = 3$ and $n = 4$. According to the divide and conquer algorithm, we divide n repeatedly.

When n is even	When n is odd
$(3)^4$	$(3)^5$
$= (3)^2 * (3)^2$	$= 3\,(3)^4$
$= (3 * 3) * (3 * 3)$	$= 3\left[(3)^2 * (3)^2\right]$
$= 9 * 9$	$= 3[9 * 9]$
$= 81$	$= 3 * 81$
	$= 243$

Analysis The algorithm takes **O(log n)** time to compute exponentiation.

Review Question

1. *Explain how the exponentiation operation can be performed using the divide and conquer method ?*

3.11 University Questions with Answers

Regulation 2008

Dec. 2010

Q.1 *Explain the use of divide and conquer technique for binary search method. Give the algorithm for binary search method. What is the complexity of binary search method ?* **[Refer section 3.5]** **[7]**

Q.2 *Explain how to apply the divide and conquer strategy for sorting the elements using quick sort with example.* **[Refer section 3.8]** **[7]**

May 2011

Q.3 *Explain how multiplication of large integers can be done efficiently by using divide and conquer technique ?* **[Refer section 3.4]** **[4]**

Q.4 *Design and analyze quick sort algorithm using divide and conquer technique.* **[Refer section 3.8]** **[7]**

Dec. 2011

Q.5 *Explain how divide and conquer method help multiplying two large integers.* **[Refer section 3.4]** **[4]**

Q.6 *Explain binary search using divide and conquer method and compute its worst case running time.* **[Refer section 3.5]** **[7]**

Q.7 *Explain quick sort using divide and conquer method and computer it's worst case running time.* **[Refer section 3.8]** **[7]**

Q.8 *Explain how divide and conquer method help multiplying two square matrices.* **[Refer section 3.9]** **[4]**

May 2012

Q.9 *What is divide and conquer technique? Give the use of it for binary searching method.* **[Refer section 3.5]** **[7]**

Q.10 *Explain quick sort method with example.* **[Refer section 3.8]** **[7]**

Dec. 2014

Q.11 *Explain Binary search algorithm with divide and conquer strategy and use the recurrence tree to show that the solution to the binary search recurrence* $T(n) = T(n/2) + \Theta(1)$ *is* $T(n) = \Theta(\lg n)$. **[Refer section 3.5]** **[7]**

Q.12 *Explain merge sort problem using divide and conquer technique. Give an example.* **[Refer section 3.7]** **[7]**

Q.13 *Explain how to apply the divide and conquer strategy for sorting the elements using quick sort with example.* **[Refer section 3.8]** **[7]**

Regulation 2013

Winter - 2015

Q.14 *Write an algorithm for quick sort and derive best case, worst case using divide and conquer technique also trace given data (3, 1, 4, 5, 9, 2, 6, 5).*
[Refer example 3.8.4] **[7]**

3.12 Short Questions and Answers

Q.1 What is the basic principle of divide and conquer algorithm?

Ans. : In divide and conquer method, a given problem is,

i) Divided into smaller sub problems. ii) These sub problems are solved independently. iii) Combining all the solutions of sub problems into a solution of the whole.

Q.2 Give the recurrence relation for divide and conquer.

Ans. : T(n)=aT(n/b)+f(n)

Q.3 Enlist various problems that can be solved using divide and conquer method

Ans. : 1. Binary Search 2. Merge Sort 3. Quick sort 4. Matrix Multiplication

Q.4 What is the recurrence relation for large number multiplication?

Ans. : T(n)=3 T (n/2)

Q.5 What is the precondition necessary for binary search?

Ans. : The list of numbers from which the key element is to be searched must be sorted.

Q.6 What is the time complexity of binary search?

Ans. : The time complexity of binary search algorithm is $O(\log_2 n)$

Q.7 What is the major advantage of binary search method?

Ans. : Binary search is an optimal searching algorithm using which we can search the desired element very efficiently.

Q.8 What is the application of binary search method?

Ans. : i) Binary search method is used to search the record from the database.

ii) Binary search method is used for solving nonlinear equations with one unknown.

Q.9 Give the difference between linear search and binary search method.

Ans. :

Sr. No.	Sequential technique	Binary search technique
1.	This is the simple technique of searching an element.	This is the efficient technique of searching an element.
2.	This technique does not require the list to be sorted.	This technique requires the list to be sorted. Then only this method is applicable.
3.	Every element of the list may get compared with the key element.	Only the mid element of the list is compared with key element.

Q.10 Name two sorting techniques that make use of divide and conquer technique.

Ans. : Merge sort and quick sort are two sorting methods that make use of divide and conquer technique.

Q.11 Write a C code that illustrates the use of recursive call for merge sort.

Ans. :

```
Algorithm MergeSort(int A[0...n-1],low,high)
{
    if(low < high)then
    {
        mid  (low+high)/2                // split the list at mid
        MergeSort(A,low,mid)   // first sublist
        MergeSort(A,mid+1,high) // second sublist
        Combine(A,low,mid,high) // merging of two sublists
    }
}
```

Q.12 Why merge sort is called stable sorting algorithm ?

Ans. : A sorting algorithm is said to be stable if it preserves the ordering of similar (equal) elements after applying sorting method. And merge sort is a method which preserves this kind of ordering. Hence merge sort is a stable sorting algorithm.

Q.13 Enlist two drawbacks of merge sort.

Ans. : i) This algorithm requires extra storage to execute this method.

ii) This method is slower than the quick sort method.

Q.14 Give time complexity of merge sort algorithm.

Ans. : The best, worst and average case time complexity of merge sort is O(n log n).

Q.15 What is the time complexity of Strassen's Matrix Multiplication?

Ans. : $T(n) = n^{\log 7}$

$= n^{2.81}$

❑❑❑

Notes

4 Dynamic Programming

Syllabus

Introduction, The principle of optimality, Problem solving using dynamic programming - Calculating the binomial coefficient, Making change problem, Assembly line-scheduling, Knapsack problem, All points shortest path, Matrix chain multiplication, Longest common subsequence.

Contents

4.1 Introduction

Dynamic programming is typically applied to optimization problem. This technique is invented by a U.S. Mathematician Richard Bellman in 1950. In the word dynamic programming the word **programming** stands for **planning** and it does not mean by computer programming.

- Dynamic programming is technique for solving problems with overlapping subproblems.
- In this method each subproblem is solved only once. The result of each subproblem is recorded in a table from which we can obtain a solution to the original problem.

4.1.1 General Method

Dynamic programming is typically applied to optimization problems.

For each given problem, we may get any number of solutions we seek for optimum solution (i.e. minimum value or maximum value solution). And such an optimal solution becomes the solution to the given problem.

4.2 Comparison of Dynamic Programming with Other Strategies

GTU : Dec.-10,11, May-12, Marks 4

4.2.1 Divide and Conquer and Dynamic Programming

Sr. No.	Divide and conquer	Dynamic programming
1.	The problem is divided into small subproblems. These subproblems are solved independently. Finally all the solutions of subproblems are collected together to get the solution to the given problem.	In dynamic programming many decision sequences are generated and all the overlapping subinstances are considered.
2.	In this method duplications in subsolutions are neglected. i.e., duplicate subsolutions may be obtained.	In dynamic computing duplications in solutions is avoided totally.
3.	Divide and conquer is less efficient because of rework on solutions.	Dynamic programming is efficient than divide and conquer strategy.
4.	The divide and conquer uses top down approach of problem solving (recursive methods).	Dynamic programming uses bottom up approach of problem solving (iterative method).
5.	Divide and conquer splits its input at specific deterministic points usually in the middle.	Dynamic programming splits its input at every possible split points rather than at a particular point. After trying all split points it determines which split point is optimal.

4.2.2 Steps of Dynamic Programming

Dynamic programming design involves 4 major steps :

1. Characterize the structure of optimal solution. That means develop a mathematical notation that can express any solution and subsolution for the given problem.
2. Recursively define the value of an optimal solution.
3. By using bottom up technique compute value of optimal solution. For that you have to develop a recurrence relation that relates a solution to its subsolutions, using the mathematical notation of step 1.
4. Compute an optimal solution from computed information.

4.2.3 Principle of Optimality

The dynamic programming algorithm obtains the solution using principle of optimality.

The principle of optimality states that "in an optimal sequence of decisions or choices, each subsequence must also be optimal."

When it is not possible to apply the principle of optimality it is almost impossible to obtain the solution using the dynamic programming approach.

For example : Finding of shortest path in a given graph uses the principle of optimality.

4.2.4 Problem Solving using Dynamic Programming

Various problems that can be solved using dynamic programming are -

1. Calculating the Binomial coefficient
2. Making change problem
3. Assembly line scheduling
4. Knapsack problem
5. Shortest path
6. Matrix chain Multiplication

Review Questions

1. *Define : Principle of optimality.* **GTU : Dec.-10, Marks 2**
2. *Explain the difference between divide and conquer and dynamic programming.* **GTU : Dec.-11, Marks 3**

> 3. *What is principle of optimality? Explain its use in dynamic programming method.*
>
> **GTU : May-12, Marks 4**

4.3 Calculating the Binomial Coefficient

Computing binomial coefficient is a typical example of applying dynamic programming.

In mathematics, particularly in **combinatorics**, binomial coefficient is a coefficient of any of the terms in the expansion of $(a+b)^n$. It is denoted by C(n, k) or $\binom{n}{k}$ where $(0 \leq k \leq n)$.

The **formula** for computing binomial coefficient is,

$$C(n, k) = C(n-1, k-1) + C(n-1, k)$$

and

$$C(n, 0) = 1$$

$$C(n, n) = 1$$

where $n > k > 0$

Example 4.3.1 *Compute C (4, 2) using Dynamic programming.*

Solution : $n = 4, k = 2$

$$C(4, 2) = C(n-1, k-1) + C(n-1, k)$$

$$C(4, 2) = C(3, 1) + C(3, 2) \qquad \text{... (4.3.1)}$$

As there are two unknowns : C(3, 1) and C(3, 2) in above equation we will compute these sub instances of C(4, 2).

$\therefore \quad n = 3, k = 1$

$$C(3, 1) = C(2, 0) + C(2, 1)$$

As $C(n, 0) = 1$ We can write

$$C(2, 0) = 1$$

$$\therefore \quad C(3, 1) = 1 + C(2, 1) \qquad \text{... (4.3.2)}$$

Hence let us compute C(2, 1).

$n = 2, k = 1$

$$\therefore \quad C(2, 1) = C(n-1, k-1) + C(n-1, k)$$

$$= C(1, 0) + C(1, 1)$$

But as $C(n, 0) = 1$ and $C(n, n) = 1$ we get

$$C(1, 0) = 1 \quad \text{and} \quad C(1, 1) = 1$$

$$\therefore \quad C(2, 1) = C(1, 0) + C(1, 1)$$

$$= 1 + 1$$

$$C(2, 1) = 2 \qquad \text{... (4.3.3)}$$

Put this value in equation (4.3.2) and we get

$$C(3, 1) = 1 + 2$$

$$C(3, 1) = 3 \qquad \text{... (4.3.4)}$$

Now to solve equation (4.3.1) we will first compute C(3, 2) with n = 3 and k = 2.

$$\therefore \quad C(3, 2) = C(n - 1, k - 1) + C(n - 1, k)$$

$$C(3, 2) = C(2, 1) + C(2, 2)$$

But as C(n, n) = C(2, 2) = 1, we will put values of C(2, 1) [obtained in equation (4.3.3) and C(2, 2) in C(3, 2) we get,

$$C(3, 2) = C(2, 1) + C(2, 2)$$

$$= 2 + 1$$

$$C(3, 2) = 3 \qquad \text{... (4.3.5)}$$

Put equation (4.3.4) and (4.3.5) in equation (4.3.1), then we get

$$C(4, 2) = C(3, 1) + C(3, 2)$$

$$= 3 + 3$$

$C(4, 2) = 6$ is the final answer.

How Dynamic Programming approach is used ?

While computing C(n,k) the smaller overlapping sequences get generated by C(n – 1, k – 1) and C(n – 1, k). These overlapping, smaller instances of problem need to be solved first. The solutions which we obtained by solving these instances will ultimately generate the final solution. Thus for computing binomial coefficient dynamic programming is used.

If we record binomial coefficients n and k values ranging from 0 to n and 0 to k then

	0	1	2	3	4	5	...	(k – 1)	k
0	1								
1	1	1							
2	1	2	1						
3	1	3	3	1					
4	1	4	6	4	1				
5									
⋮									
k	1								1
⋮									
(n – 1)	1							C(n – 1, k – 1)	C(n – 1, k)
n	1								C(n,k)

This basically is a structure known as Pascal's triangle.

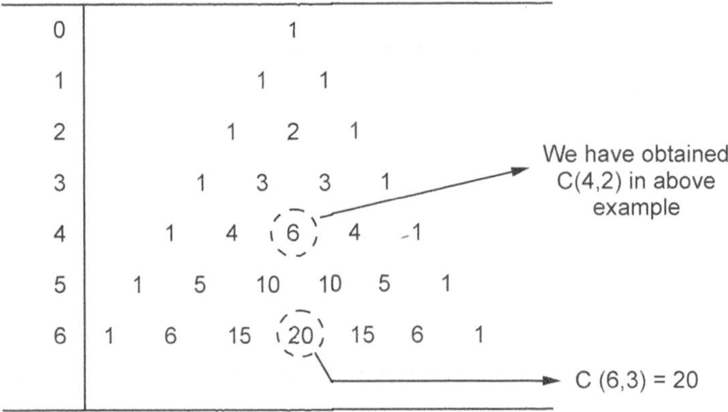

To compute C(n,k) we fill up the above given table row by row starting with C(n,0) = 1 and ending with C(n, n) = 1. The cell at current row is calculated by two adjacent cells of previous row. The algorithm for computing binomial coefficient is as given below,

Algorithm

```
Algorithm Binomial (n,k)
//Problem Description : This algorithm is for
//computing C(n,k) i.e., Binomial coefficient
//Input : A pair of non negative integers n and k.
//Output : The value of C(n,k)
    for i ← 0 to n do
    {
```

```
            for j←0 to k do
//k is computed as min(i,k)
                    if ((j=0 or (i=j)) then
                    C[i,j] ← 1
                    else //start filling the table
                            C[i,j] ← C[i–1,j–1] + C[i–1,j]
    }
    return C[n,k] //Computed value of C(n,k)
```

Analysis

The basic operation is addition i.e.,

$$C[i, j] \leftarrow C[i-1, j-1] + C[i-1, j]$$

Let A(n,k) denotes total additions made in computing C(n,k).

$$A(n,k) = \sum_{i=1}^{k} \sum_{j=1}^{i-1} 1 + \sum_{i=k+1}^{n} \sum_{j=1}^{k} 1$$

$$= \sum_{i=1}^{k} [(i-1)-1+1] + \sum_{i=k+1}^{n} (k-1+1)$$

$$\because \sum_{i=l}^{n} 1 = (n-l+1)$$

$$= \sum_{i=1}^{k} (i-1) + \sum_{i=k+1}^{n} k$$

$$= [1+2+3+\ldots(k-1)] + k \sum_{i=k+1}^{n} 1$$

$$= \frac{(k-1)k}{2} + k \sum_{i=k+1}^{n} 1$$

$$= \frac{(k-1)k}{2} + k(n-(k+1)+1)$$

$$= \frac{(k-1)k}{2} + k(n-k-1+1)$$

$$= \frac{(k-1)k}{2} + k(n-k)$$

$$= \frac{k^2}{2} - \frac{k}{2} + nk - k^2$$

$$\approx nk$$

Hence time complexity of binomial coefficient is Θ (nk).

C Program

```
/*****************************************************************
Program for computing binomial coefficient C(n,k)

*****************************************************************/
#include<stdio.h>
#include<conio.h>
#define MAX 10
void main()
{
 int n,k,result;
 int Binomial(int n,int k);
 clrscr();
 printf("\n Enter the value of n and k");
 scanf("%d%d",&n,&k);
 result= Binomial(n,k);
 printf("\n The Binomial Coefficient ");
         printf("C(%d,%d)= %d",n,k,result);
 getch();
}
int Binomial(int n,int k)
{
 int i,j;
 int C[MAX][MAX];
 for(i=0;i<MAX;i++)
 for(j=0;j<MAX;j++)
         C[i][j]=0;

 for(i=0;i<=n;i++)
 {
         for(j=0;j<=k;j++)
         {
         if((j==0)||(i==j))
              C[i][j]=1;
          else
              C[i][j]=C[i-1][j-1]+C[i-1][j];
         }
 }
 return C[n][k];
}

int min(int a,int b)
{
 if(a<b)
         return a;
     else
         return b;
```

```
}
```

Output

```
Enter the value of n and k = 4,2

The Binomial Coefficient? C(4,2) = 6
```

4.4 Making Change Problem

GTU : June-11, May-12, Summer-13, Winter-15, Marks 7

Suppose there are some coins available. The values of these coins are as follows.

1 dollar = 100 cents

1 quarter = 25 cents

1 dimes = 10 cents

1 nickels = 5 cents

1 pennies = 1 cent

Now the making change problem is to pay the desired amount of money by using as few coins as possible.

For example : If a customer wants to pay 3.37 $ then he should pay 3 dollars (= 300 cents) + 1 quarter (= 25 cents) + 1 dime (= 10 cents) + 2 pennies (= 2 cents) = 3.37 $.

This method uses **Greedy** approach because at every step it chooses the largest coin it can. Furthermore, once the coin is selected then that is the final. This approach does not allow to change the decision. Unfortunately although **Greedy** approach is very efficient, it works only for limited number of instances. For example if there exists coins of 1, 4 and 6 units and we have to make change for 9 units. Then there are two ways :

1. **Greedy Method :** Select one coin of 6 unit and 3 coins of 1 unit = **4 coins.**
2. **Better Method :** Select two coins of 4 units and 1 coin of 1 unit = **3 coins.**

This better method is devised by dynamic programming approach.

For solving this problem using dynamic programming approach we need to build a table, in which rows correspond to denomination and column corresponds to 0 to N units.

Example 4.4.1 *Solve making change problem for* $d_1 = 1$, $d_2 = 4$, $d_3 = 6$, $n = 3$, *and* $N = 8$ *units.* GTU : June-11, May-12, Marks 7

Solution : Given that :

$$d_1 = 1,\ d_2 = 4,\ d_3 = 6,\ n = 3,\ N = 8 \text{ units.}$$

Hence we will create a table with rows ranging from 1 to 3 and columns ranging from 0 to 8.

Initially c [i, 0] = 0 ∴ c [1, 0] = c [2, 0] = c [3, 0] = 0

j →

		0	1	2	3	4	5	6	7	8
i = 1	$d_1 = 1$	0								
i = 2	$d_2 = 4$	0								
i = 3	$d_3 = 6$	0								

We can perform computations row-by-row from left to right, or column-by-column from top to bottom or diagonally.

Here we will perform computation **column-by-column** and fill up the table accordingly. We will use following formula for computations.

1. If i = 1 then $c[i, j] = 1 + c[1, j - d_1]$
2. If $j < d_i$ then $c[i, j] = c[i-1, j]$
3. Otherwise $c[i][j] = \min(c[i-1, j], 1 + c[i, j - d_i])$

c [1, 1] with $i = 1,\ j = 1,\ d_1 = 1$.

As i = 1

Formula used : $1 + c[1, j - d_1]$

$= 1 + c[1, 1-1]$

$= 1 + c[1, 0]$

$= 1 + 0$

$= 1$

∴ **c[1, 1] = 1**

c [2, 1] with $i = 2,\ j = 1,\ d_2 = 4$.

As $j < d_2$ i.e. 1 < 4

Formula used : $c[i-1, j]$

$= c[1, 1]$

$= 1$

∴ **c[2, 1] = 1**

c [3, 1] with $i = 3,\ j = 1,\ d_3 = 6$

As $j < d_3$ i.e. 1 < 6

Formula used : $c[i-1, j]$

$= c[3-1, 1]$

$= c[2, 1]$

$= 1$

$\therefore$ **$c[3, 1] = 1$**

$c[1, 2]$ with $i = 1$, $j = 2$, $d_1 = 1$

As $i = 1$

Formula used : $1 + c[1, j - d_1]$

$= 1 + c[1, 2-1]$

$= 1 + c[1, 1]$

$= 1 + 1$

$= 2$

$\therefore$ **$c[1, 2] = 2$**

$c[2, 2]$ with $i = 2$, $j = 2$, $d_2 = 4$

As $j < d_2$ i.e. $2 < 4$

Formula used : $c[i-1, j]$

$= c[1, 2]$

$= 2$

$\therefore$ **$c[2, 2] = 2$**

$c[3, 2]$ with $i = 3$, $j = 2$, $d_3 = 6$

As $j < d_3$ i.e. $2 < 6$

Formula used : $c[i-1, j]$

$= c[2, 2]$

$= 2$

$\therefore$ **$c[2, 2] = 2$**

$c[1, 3]$ with $i = 1$, $j = 3$, $d_1 = 1$

As $i = 1$

Formula used : $1 + c[1, j - d_1]$

$= 1 + c[1, 3-1]$

$= 1 + c[1, 2]$

$= 1 + 2$

$= 3$

$\therefore \quad c[1, 3] = \mathbf{3}$

c [2, 3] with $i = 2, \; j = 3, \; d_2 = 4$

As $j < d_3$ i.e. $3 < 4$

Formula used : $c[i-1, j]$

$= c[1, 3]$

$= 3$

$\therefore \quad c[2, 3] = \mathbf{3}$

c [3, 3] with $i = 3, \; j = 3, \; d_3 = 6$

As $j < d_3$ i.e. $3 < 6$

Formula used : $c[i-1, j]$

$= c[2, 3]$

$= 3$

$\therefore \quad c[3, 3] = \mathbf{3}$

c [1, 4] with $i = 1, \; j = 4, \; d_1 = 1$

As $i = 1$

Formula used : $1 + c[1, j-d_1]$

$= 1 + c[1, 4-1]$

$= 1 + c[1, 3]$

$= 1 + 3$

$= 4$

$\therefore \quad c[1, 4] = \mathbf{4}$

c [2, 4] with $i = 2, \; j = 4, \; d_2 = 4$

As $i \neq 1$ and $j > d_2$

Formula used : $\min\left(c\,[i-1,j],1+c\left[i,j-d[i]\,\right]\right)$

$= \min\left(c\,[2-1,4\,],\ 1+c[2,4-4\,]\right)$

$= \min\left(c\,[1,4\,]\ 1+c[2,0\,]\right)$

$= \min\ (\ 4,\ 1\ +\ 0\ )$

$= 1$

$\therefore$ **c[2, 4] = 1**

c [3, 4] with $i=3,\ \ j=4,\ \ d_3 = 6$

As $j < d_3$ i.e. $4 < 6$

Formula used : $c\,[\,i-1,j\,]$

$= c\,[\,2,4\,]$

$= 1$

$\therefore$ **c[3, 4] = 1**

c [1, 5] with $i=1,\ \ j=5,\ \ d_1 = 1$

As i = 1

Formula used : $1 + c\,[1,j-d_1]$

$= 1 + c\,[1,5\text{-}1]$

$= 1 + c\,[1,4]$

$= 1 + 4$

$= 5$

$\therefore$ **c[1, 5] = 5**

c [2, 5] with $i=2,\ \ j=5,\ \ d_2 = 4$

As $i \neq 1$ and $j > d_2$

Formula used : $\min\left(c\,[i-1,j],\ 1+c\left[i,j-d_2\,\right]\right)$

$= \min\left(c\,[1,5\,],1+c[2,5-4]\right)$

$= \min\left(c\,[1,5\,],1+c[2,1\,]\right)$

$= \min(5,1+1)$

$= 2$

$\therefore$ **c[2, 5] = 2**

c [3, 5] with $i=3,\ \ j=5,\ \ d_3 = 6$

As $j < d_3$ i.e. $5 < 6$

Formula used : $c[i-1,j]$

$= c[3-1,5]$

$= c[2,5]$

$\therefore$ **c[3, 5] = 2**

c [1, 6] with $i=1,\ j=6,\ d_1=1$

As i = 1

Formula used : $1 + c[1, j-d_1]$

$= 1 + c[1, 6-1]$

$= 1 + c[1,5]$

$= 6$

$\therefore$ **c[1, 6] = 6**

c [2, 6] with $i=2,\ j=6,\ d_2=4$

As $i \neq 2$ and $j > d_2$

Formula used : $\min(c[i-1,j], 1+c[i, j-d_2])$

$= \min(c[1,6], 1+c[2,2])$

$= \min(6, 1+2)$

$= 3$

$\therefore$ **c[2, 6] = 3**

c [3, 6] with $i=3,\ j=6,\ d_3=6$

As $i \neq 3$ and $j > d_3$

Formula used : $\min(c[i-1,j], 1+c[i, j-d_3])$

$= \min(c[2,6], 1+c[3,0])$

$= \min(3, 1+0)$

$= 1$

$\therefore$ **c[3, 6] = 1**

c [1, 7] with $i=1,\ j=7,\ d_1=1$

As i = 1

Formula used : $1 + c[1, j-d_1]$

$= 1 + c[1, 6]$

$= 1 + 6$

$\therefore \quad c[1, 7] = 7$

c [2, 7] with $i = 2$, $j = 7$, $d_2 = 4$

As $i \neq 1$ and $j > d_2$

Formula used : $\min(c[i-1, j], 1 + c[i, j-d_2])$

$= \min(c[1, 7], 1 + c[2, 3])$

$= \min(7, 1 + 3)$

$= 4$

$\therefore \quad c[2, 7] = 4$

c [3, 7] with $i = 3$, $j = 7$, $d_3 = 6$

As $i \neq 1$ and $j > d_3$

Formula used : $\min(c[i-1, j], 1 + c[i, j-d_3])$

$= \min(c[2, 7], 1 + c[3, 1])$

$= \min(4, 1 + 1)$

$= 2$

$\therefore \quad c[3, 7] = 2$

c [1, 8] with $i = 1$, $j = 8$, $d_1 = 1$

As i = 1

Formula used : $1 + c[1, j-d_1]$

$= 1 + c[1, 7]$

$= 1 + 7$

$= 8$

$\therefore \quad c[1, 8] = 8$

c [2,8] with $i = 2$, $j = 8$, $d_2 = 4$

As $i \neq 1$ and $j > d_2$

Formula used : $\min(c[i-1, j], 1 + c[i, j-d_2])$

$$= \min(c[1,8],\ 1+c[2,4\ ])$$
$$= \min\ (\ 8,\ 1 + 1\ )$$
$$= 2$$

$\therefore$ $\qquad c[2, 8] = \mathbf{2}$

c [3, 8] with $i=3,\ j=8,\ d_3 = 6$

As $i \neq 1$ and $j > d_3$

Formula used : $\min(c\ [i-1,j],1+c[i,j-d_3])$

$$= \min(c[2,8],\ 1+c[3,2])$$
$$= \min\ (\ 2,\ 1 + 2\ )$$
$$= 2$$

$\therefore$ $\qquad c[3, 8] = \mathbf{2}$

Thus we can represent the table filled up by above computations will be

		0	1	2	3	4	5	6	7	8
i = 1	$d_1 = 1$	0	1	2	3	4	5	6	7	8
i = 2	$d_2 = 4$	0	1	2	3	1	2	3	4	2
i = 3	$d_3 = 6$	0	1	2	3	1	2	1	2	2

↑ Total number of coins

The value c [n, N] i.e. c [3, 8] = 2 represents the minimum number of coins required to get the sum for 8 units. Hence we require 2 coins for getting 8 units. The coins are :

	4 units	=	1coin
+	4 units	=	1coin
	8 units	=	2 coins

Example 4.4.2 *Given coins of denominations 2, 4 and 5 with amount to be pay is 7. Find optimal number of coins and sequence of coins used to pay given amount using dynamic method.*

GTU : Summer-13, Marks 7

Solution : $d_1 = 2,\ d_2 = 4,\ d_3 = 5.\ \ N = 7$

We will create a table with rows ranging from 1 to 3 and column ranging from 0 to 7.

Initially C [i, 0] = 0

∴ C[1, 0] = C [2, 0] = C [3, 0] = 0

		0	1	2	3	4	5	6	7	8
i = 1	$d_1 = 2$	0								
i = 2	$d_2 = 4$	0								
i = 3	$d_3 = 5$	0								

Computations can be performed column by column; and fill up the table accordingly.

C [1, 1] with i = 1, j = 1, $d_1 = 2$

As i = 1

C [1,1] = 1+C[1,j-d1]

C [1,1] = 1+C[1,-1]

C [1, 1] = ∞

C [2, 1] with i = 2, j = 1, $d_2 = 4$

C [2, 1] = C [i – 1, j]

C [2, 1] = C [1, 1]

C [2, 1] = ∞

C [3, 1] with i = 3, j = 1, $d_3 = 5$

As $j < d_3$

C [i, j] = C [i – 1, j]

C [3, 1] = C [2, 1]

∴ **C [3, 1] = ∞**

C [1, 2] with i = 1, j = 2, $d_1 = 2$

As i = 1

C [i, j] = 1+ C [1, j – d_1]

C [1, 2] = 1 + C [1, 0] = 1 + 0

∴ **C [1, 2] = 1**

C [2, 2] with i = 2, j = 2, $d_2 = 4$

As $j < d_2$

C [i, j] = C [i – 1, j]

C [2, 2] = C [1, 2]

C [2, 2] = 1

C[3, 2] with i = 3, j = 2, $d_3 = 5$

As $j < d_3$

$$C[i, j] = C[i-1, j]$$

$$\therefore \quad C[3, 2] = C[2, 2]$$

$$\therefore \quad \mathbf{C[3, 2] = 1}$$

C [1, 3] with i = 1, j = 3 $d_1 = 2$

As i = 1

$$C[i, j] = 1 + C[1, j - d_1]$$

$$= 1 + C[1, 3 - 2] = 1 + C[1, 1]$$

$$\mathbf{C[1, 3] = \infty}$$

C [2, 3] with i = 2, j = 3, $d_2 = 4$

As $j < d_2$

$$C[i, j] = C[i - 1, j]$$

$$C[2, 3] = C[1, 3]$$

$$\therefore \quad \mathbf{C[2, 3] = \infty}$$

C [3, 3] with i = 3, j = 3, $d_3 = 5$

As $j < d_3$

$$C[i, j] = C[i-1, j]$$

$$\therefore \quad C[3, 3] = C[2, 3]$$

$$\therefore \quad \mathbf{C[3, 3] = \infty}$$

C [1, 4] with i = 1, j = 4, $d_1 = 2$

As i = 1

$$C[i, j] = 1 + C[1, j - d_1]$$

$$C[1, 4] = 1 + C[1, 2] = 1 + 1$$

$$\therefore \quad \mathbf{C[1, 4] = 2}$$

C [2, 4] with i = 2, j = 4, $d_2 = 4$

As $d_2 = j$ and $i \neq 1$

$$C[i, j] = \min\left(C[i-1, j], 1 + C[i, j - d[i]]\right)$$

$$= \min\left(C[1,4], 1 + C[2, 4 - 4]\right)$$

$= \min(C[1,4],\ 1+0)$

C [2, 4] = min (2, 1)

C [3, 4] with i = 3, j = 4 and $d_3 = 5$

As $j < d_3$

C [i, j] = C [i – 1, j]

C [3, 4] = C [2, 4]

∴ **C [3, 4] = 1**

C [1, 5] with i = 1, j = 5 and $d_1 = 2$

As i = 1

C [i , j] = 1 + C [i, j – d_1]

= 1+ C [1, 3]

C [1, 5] = ∞

C [2, 5] with i = 2, j = 5 and $d_2 = 4$

$C[i, j] = \min(C[i-1,j],\ 1+C[i,j-d[i]])$

$= \min(C[1,5],\ 1+C[2,1])$

$C[2, 5] = \min(\infty,\ 1+\infty)$

C [2, 5] = ∞

C[3, 5] with i = 3, j = 5 and $d_3 = 5$

$C[i, j] = \min(C[i-1,j],\ 1+C[i,j-d[i]])$

$= \min(C[2,5],\ 1+C[3,0])$

$C[3, 5] = \min(\infty, 1+0)$

C [3, 5] = 1

C[1, 6] with i = 1, j = 6, $d_1 = 2$

As i = 1

C [i, j] = 1 + C [i, j – d_1]

C [1, 6] = 1 + C [1, 4] = 1 + 2

C[1, 6] = 3

C [2, 6] with i = 2, j = 6, $d_2 = 4$

$C[i, j] = \min(C[i-1,j],\ 1+C[i,j-d[i]])$

$= \min(C[1,6],\ 1+C[2,2])$

$C[2, 6] = \min(3, 1+1)$

$\mathbf{C[2, 6] = 2}$

C [3, 6] with $i = 3, j = 6, d_3 = 5$

$C[i, j] = \min(C[i-1,j],\ 1+C[i,j-d[i]])$

$= \min(C[2,6],\ 1+C[3,1])$

$= \min(2,\ 1+\infty)$

$\mathbf{C[3, 6] = 2}$

C [1, 7] with $i = 1, j = 7$ and $d_1 = 2$

As i = 1

$C[i, j] = 1 + C[i, j - d_1]$

$= 1 + C[1, 5] = 1+\infty$

$\mathbf{C[1, 7]} = \infty$

C [2,7] with $i = 2, j = 7$ and $d_2 = 4$

$C[i, j] = \min(C[i-1,j],\ 1+C[i,j-d[i]])$

$= \min(C[1,7],\ 1+C[2,3])$

$= \min(\infty, 1+\infty)$

$\mathbf{C[2, 7]} = \infty$

C [3, 7] with $i = 3, j = 7$ and $d_3 = 5$

$C[i, j] = \min(C[i-1,j],\ 1+C[i,j-d[i]])$

$= \min(C[2,7],\ 1+C[3,2])$

$= \min(\infty,\ 1+1)$

$\mathbf{C[3, 7] = 2}$

The table can be

		0	1	2	3	4	5	6	7
i = 1	$d_1 = 2$	0	∞	1	∞	2	∞	3	∞
i = 2	$d_2 = 4$	0	∞	1	∞	1	∞	2	∞
i = 3	$d_3 = 5$	0	∞	1	∞	1	1	2	2

↑ Total number of coins

That means 2 coins are required for sum as 7. The coins are,

$$d_1 = 2 \rightarrow 1 \text{ coin}$$

$$d_3 = 5 \rightarrow 1 \text{ coin}$$

Total 7 with 2 coins

Example 4.4.3 *Solve making change problem using Dynamic Programming. (Denominations : d1 = 1, d2 = 4, d3 = 6). Give your answer for making change of Rs. 9.*

GTU : Winter-15, Marks 7

Solution : $d_1 = 1$, $d_2 = 4$, d3 = 6, N = 9 ₹, n = 3. Hence we will create a table with rows ranging from 1 to 3 and columns ranging from 0 to 9.

Initially C[i, 0] = 0 ∴ C[1, 0] = C [2, 0] = C [3, 0] = 0

j →

	0	1	2	3	4	5	6	7	8	9
$d_1 = 1$	0									
$d_2 = 4$	0									
$d_3 = 6$	0									

We will complete the table **column-by-column :** Refer example 4.4.1.

	0	1	2	3	4	5	6	7	8	9
$d_1 = 1$	0	1	2	3	4	5	6	7	8	
$d_2 = 4$	0	1	2	3	1	2	3	4	2	
$d_3 = 6$	0	1	2	3	1	2	1	2	2	

c[1, 9] with i = 1, j = 9, $d_1 = 1$

As i = 1

Formula used : $1 + c\,[1, j - d_1]$

$= 1 + c\,[1, 8]$

$= 1 + 8$

$= 9$

∴ **c[1, 9] = 9**

c[2, 9] with i = 2, j = 9, $d_2 = 4$

As $i \neq 1$ and $j > d_2$

Formula used : $\min(c[i-1, j], 1 + c[i, j - d_2])$

$= \min(c[1, 9], 1 + c[2, 5])$

$= \min(9, 1 + 2)$

$= 3$

$\therefore$ **c[2, 9] = 3**

c [3, 9] with i = 3, j = 9, d_3 = 6

As $i \neq 1$ and $j > d_3$

Formula used : $\min(c[i-1, j], 1 + c[i, j - d_3])$

$= \min(c[2, 9], 1 + c[3, 3])$

$= \min(3, 1 + 3)$

$= 3$

$\therefore$ **c[3, 9] = 3**

Thus the complete table filled up by all the computations will be

	0	1	2	3	4	5	6	7	8	9
$d_1 = 1$	0	1	2	3	4	5	6	7	8	9
$d_2 = 4$	0	1	2	3	1	2	3	4	2	3
$d_3 = 6$	0	1	2	3	1	2	1	2	2	3

Total number of coins

The value c[n, N] i.e. c [3, 9] = 3 represents the minimum number of coins required to get the sum for 9 units. Hence coins will be

$d_2 = 4$	1 coin
$d_2 = +4$	1 coin
$d_1 = +1$	1 coin

₹ 9 = 3 coins

Algorithm Number_of_Coins (N)

{

// **Problem Description** : This algorithm computes

```
//minimum number of coins required to make
// change for N units.
        for ( i ← 1 to n) do
        initialize array d[i] with the values of coins.
for ( i ← 1 to n ) do
            c [i, 0] ← 0          Initialising first column by 0
For ( i ← 1 to n ) do
{
        For ( i ← 1 to N ) do     Using this nested for loops the table values are computed
        {
            if (i = 1 & & j < d [ i] ) then
                c [ i ] [ j ] = infinity ;
            else if ( i = 1 ) then
                c [ i ] [ j ] = 1+c[1, j-d[1]];
            else if ( j <d [ i ] ) then
                c [ i ] [ j ] = c[j-1, j];
            else
                c [ i ] [ j ] = min(c[i-1, j],  1 + c [i, j - d[i]]) ;
            }
}
return c [ n, N]     Total number of coins in the change
```

Analysis - As the basic operation in above algorithms is to fill up the table, which is performed within nested for loops. Hence the time complexity of this algorithm is $\Theta(nN)$.

4.5 Assembly Line Scheduling

GTU : June-11, Winter-14, Summer-15, Marks 7

This example of manufacturing problem is based on dynamic programming. The problem of assembly line scheduling can be described as follows -

In an automobile factory, the automobiles are produced using assembly lines. The chassis enters each assembly line and along this line path there are various stations at which the parts are added. Then a finished auto exits at the end of the line. The problem is to determine which stations to choose from line 1 and which to choose from line 2 in order to minimize the total time through the factory for one auto. The structure of assembly lines along with the stations is as shown in Fig. 4.5.1.

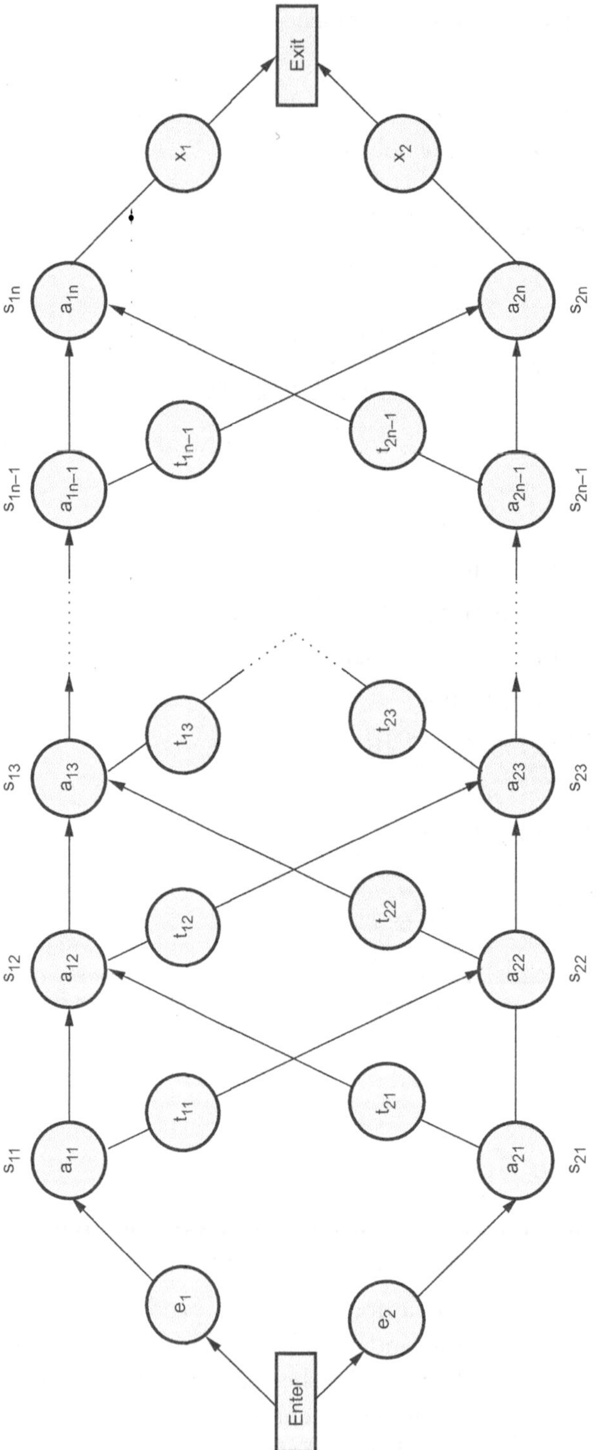

Fig. 4.5.1 Assembly line scheduling

In this Fig. 4.5.1, e_i denotes the entry time of the chassis. The assembly time at line 1 is denoted by a_{1j} and that of at line 2 is denoted by a_{2j}. There is no cost required to stay on the same line. But if it is required to change the assembly line the time required is denoted by t_{ij}. Using dynamic programming approach we have to determine which stations to choose from line 1 and from line 2 so that within minimum amount of time the auto gets produced. This problem can be solved by applying the steps of dynamic programming.

Step 1 : Characterizing the structure of optimal solution

The goal of this problem is to compute the fastest assembly time. Hence we need to know, the fastest time from entry to S_{1n} and from entry to S_{2n} for assembly line 1 and assembly line 2 respectively. Then we have to consider two exiting points x_1 and x_2.

Step 2 : Recursively define the value of an optimal solution

In this step we have to compute fastest possible time to get station s_{ij}. This fastest possible time is denoted by f_i [j] where i is either 1 or 2 and j, is

$i \leq j \leq n$

The fastest possible time can be obtained using following formula -

$$f_1[j] = \min(f_1[j-1] + a_{1j}, f_2[j-1] + t_{2j-1} + a_{1j})$$

$$f_2[j] = \min(f_1[j-1] + t_{1j-1} + a_{2j}, f_2[j-1] + a_{2j})$$

Let, f^* be the fastest time for entire assembling. It can be computed as :

$$f^* = \min(f_1[n] + x_1, f_2[n] + x_2)$$

Step 3 : Compute the fastest time for assembly

Using the formula defined in step 2, we can compute the fastest time for assembly. Let us compute the fastest assembly time with the help of some example -

See Fig. 4.5.2 on next page.

$$f_1[1] = e_1 + a_{11}$$
$$= 4 + 2$$
$$\boxed{f_1[1] = 6}$$
$$f_2[1] = e_2 + a_{21}$$
$$= 2 + 6$$
$$\boxed{f_2[1] = 8}$$

Initially $f_1[1] = e_i + a_{i1}$

$$f_1[2] = \min(f_1[j-1] + a_{1j}, f_2[j-1] + t_{2j-1} + a_{1j}$$
$$= \min(f_1[1] + a_{12}, f_2[1] + t_{21} + a_{12})$$
$$= \min(6 + 8, 8 + 3 + 8)$$

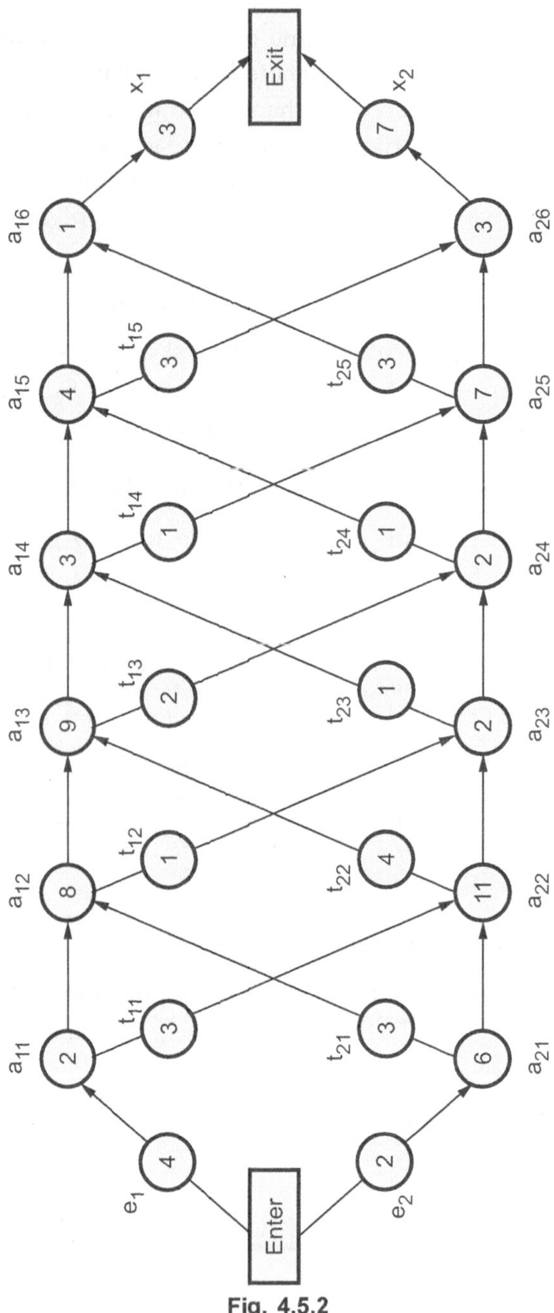

Fig. 4.5.2

$$= \min(14, 19)$$

$$\boxed{f_1[2] = 14}$$

$$f_2[2] = \min(f_1[j-1] + t_{1j-1} + a_{2j},\ f_2[j-1] + a_{2j})$$

$$= \min(f_1[1] + t_{11} + a_{22},\ f_2[1] + a_{22})$$

$= \min(6 + 3 + 11, 8 + 11)$

$= \min(20, 19)$

$f_2[2] = 19$

$f_1[3] = \min(f_1[j-1] + a_{ij}, f_2[j-1] + t_{2j-1} + a_{1j})$

$= \min(F_1[2] + a_{13}, f_2[2] + t_{22} + a_{13})$

$= \min(14 + 9, 19 + 4 + 9)$

$= \min(23, 32)$

$f_1[3] = 23$

$f_2[3] = \min(f_1[j-1] + t_{1j-1} + a_{2j}, f_2(j-1) + a_{2j})$

$= \min(f_1[2] + t_{12} + a_{23}, f_2[2] + a_{23})$

$= \min(14 + 1 + 2, 19 + 2)$

$= \min(17, 21)$

$f_2[3] = 17$

$f_1[4] = \min(f_1[j-1] + a_{1j}, f_2(j-1) + t_{2j-1} + a_{1j})$

$= \min(f_1[3] + a_{14}, f_2[3] + t_{23} + a_{14}$

$= \min(23 + 3, 17 + 1 + 3)$

$= \min(26, 21)$

$f_1[4] = 21$

$f_2(4) = \min(f_1[j-1] + t_{1j-1} + a_{2j}, f_2[j-1] + a_{2j})$

$= \min(f_1[3] + t_{13} + a_{24}, f_2[3] + a_{24})$

$= \min(23 + 2 + 2, 17 + 2)$

$= \min(27, 19)$

$f_2[4] = 19$

$f_1[5] = \min(f_1[j-1] + a_{1j}, f_2[j-1] + t_{2j-1} + a_{1j})$

$= \min(f_1[4] + a_{15}, f_2[4] + t_{24} + a_{15})$

$= \min(21 + 4, 19 + 1 + 4)$

$= \min(25, 24)$

$f_1[5] = 24$

$f_2[5] = \min(f_1[j-1] + t_{1j-1} + a_{2j}, f_2[j-1] + a_{2j})$

$= \min (f_1[4] + t_{14} + a_{25} , f_2[4] + a_{25})$

$= \min (21 + 1 + 7, 19 + 7)$

$= \min (29 , 26)$

$\boxed{f_2[5] = 26}$

$f_1[6] = \min (f_1 [j - 1] + a_{1j} , f_2[j - 1] + t_{2j-1} + a_{1j})$

$= \min (f_1[5] + a_{16}, f_2[5] + t_{25} + a_{16})$

$= \min (24 + 1 , 26 + 3 + 1)$

$= \min (25 , 30)$

$\boxed{f_1[6] = 25}$

$f_2[6] = \min (f_1[j - 1] + t_{1j-1} + a_{2j} , f_2 [j - 1] + a_{2j})$

$= \min (f_1[5] + t_{15} + a_{26} , f_2[5] + a_{26})$

$= \min (24 + 3 + 3 , 26 + 3)$

$f_2[6] = \min (30, 29)$

$\boxed{f_2 [6] = 29}$

Hence we can summerize $f_1(j)$ and $f_2(j)$ values as follows.

	j = 1	j = 2	j = 3	j = 4	j = 5	j = 6
$f_1[j]$	6	14	23	21	24	25
$f_2[j]$	8	19	17	19	26	29

Now we can compute f* as

$f^* = \min (f_1[n] + x_1 , f_2[n] + x_2)$

$= \min (25 + 3, 29 + 7)$

$= \min (28 , 36)$

$\therefore \quad \boxed{f^* = 28}$

Step 4 : Computing fastest path from computed information

For each i = 1 or i = 2 and for each j varying from 2 to n we can compute *l*[j]. The *l*[j] will be either 1 or 2 depending upon : whether $f_1[j]$ or $f_2[j]$ value is selected.

For example :

$l_1[2] = 1$ because while computing $f_1[2]$ we have obtained min value from $f_1[1]$ and not from $f_2[1]$.

$l_2[2] = 2$

$l_1[3] = 1$

$l_2[3] = 1$

$l_1[4] = 2$

$l_2[4] = 2$

$l_1[5] = 2$

$l_2[5] = 2$

$l_1[6] = 1$

$l_2[6] = 2$

We can put it together as :

	2	3	4	5	6
$l_1[j]$	1	1	2	2	1
$l_2[j]$	2	1	2	2	2

As we get f^* value from $f_1[n] + x_1$ l^* **= 1** i.e. f^* value is derived from $f_1[n]$. Hence, $l^* = 1$

Now to obtain the path which gives fastest time in producing auto we will use all the $l_i[j]$ values.

Let

$$i = l^*$$

Hence print " line " i " station" n

As i = 1 we will get first message as **line 1 station 6 .**

Then

```
for ( j = n ; j >= 2 ; j – –)
{
        i = l_i[j]
        print " line " i " station " j – 1
}
```

Let, j = 6 then i = $l_1[6]$ = 1. Hence message will be **line 1 station 5.**

Let, j = 5 then i = $l_1[5]$ = 2. Hence message will be **line 2 station 4.**

Let, j = 4 then i = $l_2[4]$ = 2. Hence message will be **line 2 station 3.**

Let j = 3 then i = $l_2[3]$ = 1. Hence message will be **line 1 station 2.**

Thus the optimal path in assembly line scheduling will be

line 1 station 6

line 1 station 5

line 2 station 4

line 2 station 3

line 1 station 2

line 1 station 1

It can be as shown below -

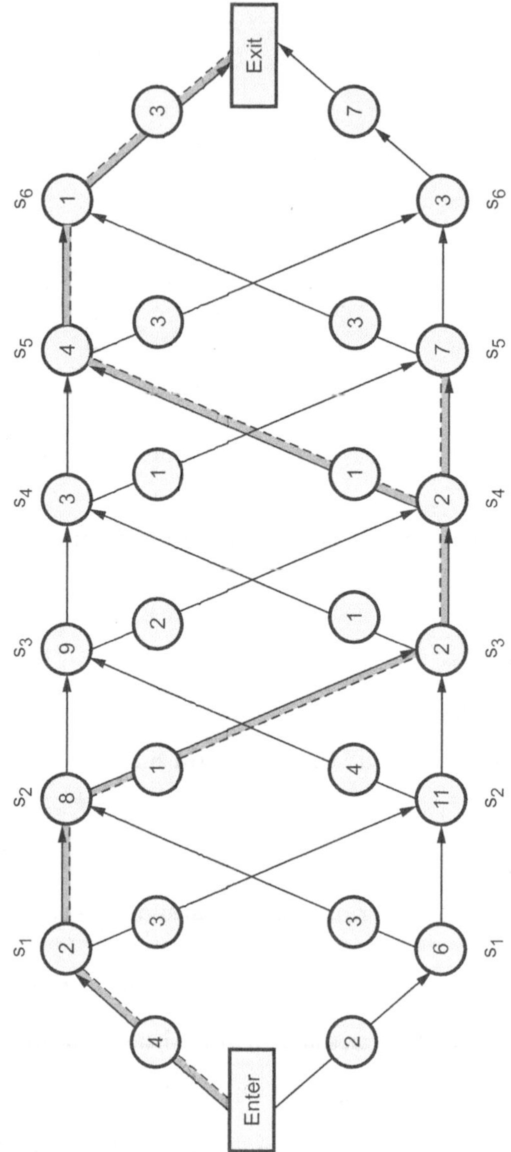

Fig. 4.5.3 Optimal path in assembly line scheduling

The algorithm for finding fastest path is as given below -

4.5.1 Algorithm

```
Algorithm Fastest_time_computation(a[ ][ ], t[ ][ ], e[ ], x[ ],n)
{
//Problem Description: This algorithm is for computing f_i[j] and l_i[j] values
f_1[1]← e[1]+a[1][1]
f_2[1]← e[2]+a[1][2]
```

```
for(j ← 2 to n) do
{
 if(f1[j – 1]+a[1][j]<=f2[j – 1]+t[2][j – 1]+a[1][j]) then
 {
     f1[j] ← f1[j – 1]+a[1][j]
   l1[j] ← 1
 }
 else
 {
       f1[j] ← f2[j – 1]+t[2][j – 1]+a[1][j]
             l1[j] ← 2
 }
 if(f2[j – 1]+a[2][j]<=f1[j –1]+t[1][j – 1]+a[2][j]) then
 {
           f2[j] ← f2[j –1]+a[2][j]
     l2[j] ← 2
 }
 else
 {
           f2[j] ← f1[j – 1]+t[1][j – 1]+a[2][j]
                 l2[j] ← 1
 }
}//end of for loo
if (f1[n]+x[1]<=f2[n]+x[2]) then
{
 f_star ← f1[n]+x[1]
 l_star ← 1
}
else
{
 f_star ← f2[n]+x[2]
 l_star ← 2
}
}//end of algorithm
```

Computing **f_1[j]** and **l_1[j]**

Computing **f_2[j]** and **l_2[j]**

Computing **f*** and **l***

Analysis

The basic operation in assembly line problem is computing of $f_i[j]$ and $l_i[j]$ values. This is done within a **for loop**. Hence the total running time required by this algorithm will be Θ **(n).**

Review Questions

1. *Describe an assembly line scheduling problem and give dynamic programming algorithm to solve it.* **GTU : June-11, Marks 6, Winter-14, Marks 7**
2. *Discuss Assembly line scheduling problem using dynamic programming with example.* **GTU : Summer-15, Marks 7**

4.6 Knapsack Problem

GTU : Dec.-10, May-12, Summer-13,14,15, Winter-14, Marks 8

As we know that dynamic programming is a technique for solving problems with overlapping subproblems. These subproblems are typically based on recurrence relation. In this section we will discuss the method of solving **knapsack problem** using dynamic programming approach. The knapsack problem can be defined as follows : If there are n items with the weights $w_1, w_2, \ldots w_n$ and values (profit associated with each item) $v_1, v_2, \ldots v_n$ and capacity of knapsack to be W, then find the most valuable subset of the items that fit into the knapsack.

To solve this problem using dynamic programming we will write the recurrence relation as :

$$\textbf{table [i, j]} = \textbf{maximum} \{\text{table}[i-1, j], v_i + \text{table}[i-1, j-w_i]\} \textbf{ if } j \geq w_i$$

or

$$\textbf{table [i - 1, j] if } j < w_i$$

That means, a table is constructed using above given formula. Initially,

table [0, j] = 0 as well as table [i, 0] = 0 when $j \geq 0$ and $i \geq 0$.

The initial stage of the table can be

	0	1		$j-w_i$		j		W
0	0	0	...	0	...	0	...	0
	:			table $[i-1, j-w_i]$				
i – 1	0					table $[i-1, j]$		
i	0					table $[i, j]$		
	:							
n	0							table [n, W]

Goal i.e., maximum value of items

The table [n, W] is a goal i.e., it gives the total items sum of all the selected items for the knapsack.

From this goal value the selected items can be traced out. Let us solve the knapsack problem using the above mentioned formula -

Example 4.6.1 *For the given instance of problem obtain the optimal solution for the knapsack problem.*

Item	Weight	Value
1	2	3
2	3	4
3	4	5
4	5	6

The capacity of knapsack is W = 5.

Solution : Initially, table [0, j] = 0 and table [i, 0] = 0. There are 0 to n rows and 0 to W columns in the table.

	0	1	2	3	4	5
0	0	0	0	0	0	0
1	0					
2	0					
3	0					
4	0					

Now we will fill up the table either row by row or column by column. Let us start filling the table **row by row** using following formula :

$$\text{table}[i, j] = \begin{cases} \text{maximum}\{\text{table}[i-1, j], v_i + \text{table}[i-1, j-w_i]\} \text{ when } j \geq w_i \\ \text{or} \\ \text{table}[i-1, j] \quad \text{if } j < w_i \end{cases}$$

table [1, 1] With i = 1, j = 1, $w_i = 2$ and $v_i = 3$.

As $j < w_i$ we will obtain table [1, 1] as

table [1, 1] = table [i – 1, j]

= table [0, 1]

∴ table [1, 1] = 0

table [1, 2] With i = 1, j = 2, $w_i = 2$ and $v_i = 3$

As $j \geq w_i$ we will obtain table [1, 2] as

$$\text{table }[1, 2] = \text{maximum}\{\text{table}[i-1, j], v_i + \text{table}[i-1, j-w_i]\}$$
$$= \text{maximum}\{(\text{table}[0, 2]), (3 + \text{table}[0, 0])\}$$
$$= \text{maximum }\{0, 3 + 0\}$$

$\therefore$ table [1, 2] = 3

table [1, 3] With i = 1, j = 3, w_i = 2 and v_i = 3

As $j \geq w_i$ we will obtain table [1, 3] as

$$\text{table }[1, 3] = \text{maximum}\{\text{table}[i-1, j], v_i + \text{table}[i-1, j-w_i]\}$$
$$= \text{maximum}\{\text{table }[0, 3], 3 + \text{table }[0, 1]\}$$
$$= \text{maximum }\{0, 3 + 0\}$$

$\therefore$ table [1, 3] = 3

table [1, 4] With i = 1, j = 4, w_i = 2 and v_i = 3

As $j \geq w_i$, we will obtain table [1, 4] as

$$\text{table }[1, 4] = \text{maximum}\{\text{table}[i-1, j], v_i + \text{table}[i-1, j-w_i]\}$$
$$= \text{maximum}\{\text{table}[0, 4], 3 + \text{table}[0, 2]\}$$
$$= \text{maximum }\{0, 3 + 0\}$$

$\therefore$ table [1, 4] = 3

table [1, 5] With i = 1, j = 5, w_i = 2 and v_i = 3

As $j \geq w_i$ we will obtain table [1, 5] as

$$\text{table }[1, 5] = \text{maximum}\{\text{table}[i-1, j], v_i + \text{table}[i-1, j-w_i]\}$$
$$= \text{maximum }\{\text{table }[0, 5], 3 + \text{table }[0, 3]\}$$
$$= \text{maximum }\{0, 3 + 0\}$$

$\therefore$ table [1, 5] = 3

The table with these values can be

	0	1	2	3	4	5
0	0	0	0	0	0	0
1	0	0	3	3	3	3
2	0					
3	0					
4	0					

Now let us fill up next row of the table.

table [2, 1] With i = 2, j = 1, $w_i = 3$ and $v_i = 4$

As $j < w_i$, we will obtain table [2, 1] as

table [2, 1] = table [i – 1, j]

= table [1, 1]

∴ table [2, 1] = 0

table [2, 2] With i = 2, j = 2, $w_i = 3$ and $v_i = 4$

As $j < w_i$, we will obtain table [2, 2] as

table [2, 2] = table [i – 1, j]

= table [1, 2]

∴ table [2, 2] = 3

table [2, 3] With i = 2, j = 3, $w_i = 3$ and $v_i = 4$

As $j \geq w_i$, we will obtain table [2, 3] as

table [2, 3] = maximum $\{\text{table}[i-1, j], v_i + \text{table}[i-1, j-w_i]\}$

= maximum {table [1, 3], 4 + table [1, 0]}

= maximum {3, 4 + 0}

∴ table [2, 3] = 4

table [2, 4] With i = 2, j = 4, $w_i = 3$ and $v_i = 4$

As $j \geq w_i$, we will obtain table [2, 4] as

table [2, 4] = maximum $\{\text{table}[i-1, j], v_i + \text{table}[i-1, j-w_i]\}$

= maximum {table [1, 4], 4 + table [1, 1]}

$= \text{maximum } \{3, 4 + 0\}$

$\therefore$ table [2, 4] = 4

table [2, 5] With i = 2, j = 5, $w_i = 3$ and $v_i = 4$

As $j \geq w_i$, we will obtain table [2, 5] as

$$\text{table } [2, 5] = \text{maximum } \{\text{table}[i-1, j], v_i + \text{table}[i-1, j-w_i]\}$$

$$= \text{maximum } \{\text{table } [1, 5], 4 + \text{table } [1, 2]\}$$

$$= \text{maximum } \{3, 4 + 3\}$$

$\therefore$ table [2, 5] = 7

The table with these computed values will be

	0	1	2	3	4	5
0	0	0	0	0	0	0
1	0	0	3	3	3	3
2	0	0	3	4	4	7
3	0					
4	0					

table [3, 1] With i = 3, j = 1, $w_i = 4$ and $v_i = 5$

As $j < w_i$, we will obtain table [3, 1] as

$$\text{table } [3, 1] = \text{table } [i-1, j]$$

$$= \text{table } [2, 1]$$

$\therefore$ table [3, 1] = 0

table [3, 2] With i = 3, j = 2, $w_i = 4$ and $v_i = 5$

As $j < w_i$, we will obtain table [3, 2] as

$$\text{table } [3, 2] = \text{table } [i-1, j]$$

$$= \text{table } [2, 2]$$

$\therefore$ table [3, 2] = 3

table [3, 3] with i = 3, j = 3, w_i = 4 and v_i = 5

As j < w_i, we will obtain table [3, 3] as

table [3, 3] = table [i – 1, j]

= table [2, 3]

∴ table [3, 3] = 4

table [3, 4] With i = 3, j = 4, w_i = 4 and v_i = 5

As j≤ w_i, we will obtain table [3, 4] as

$$\text{table } [3, 4] = \text{maximum}\{\text{table}[i-1, j], v_i + \text{table}[i-1, j-w_i]\}$$

= maximum {table [2, 4], 5 + table [2, 0]}

= maximum {4, 5 + 0}

∴ table [3, 4] = 5

table [3, 5] With i = 3, j = 5, w_i = 4 and v_i = 5

As j≥ w_i, we will obtain table [3, 5] as

$$\text{table } [3, 5] = \text{maximum}\{\text{table}[i-1, j], v_i + \text{table}[i-1, j-w_i]\}$$

= maximum {table [2, 5], 5 + table [2, 1]}

= maximum {7, 5 + 0}

∴ table [3, 5] = 7

The table with these values can be

	0	1	2	3	4	5
0	0	0	0	0	0	0
1	0	0	3	3	3	3
2	0	0	3	4	4	7
3	0	0	3	4	5	7
4	0					

table [4, 1] With $i = 4, j = 1, w_i = 5, v_i = 6$

As $j < w_i$, we will obtain table [4, 1] as

$$\text{table } [4, 1] = \text{table } [i - 1, j] = \text{table } [3, 1]$$

∴ table [4, 1] = 0

table [4, 2] With $i = 4, j = 2, w_i = 5$ and $v_i = 6$

As $j < w_i$, we will obtain table [4, 2] as

$$\text{table } [4, 2] = \text{table } [i - 1, j] = \text{table } [3, 2]$$

∴ table [4, 2] = 3

table [4, 3] With $i = 4, j = 3, w_i = 5$ and $v_i = 6$

As $j < w_i$, we will obtain table [4, 3] as

$$\text{table } [4, 3] = \text{table } [i - 1, j] = \text{table } [3, 3]$$

∴ table [4, 3] = 4

table [4, 4] with $i = 4, j = 4, w_i = 5$ and $v_i = 6$

As $j < w_i$, we will obtain table [4, 4] as

$$\text{table } [4, 4] = \text{table } [i - 1, j] = \text{table } [3, 4]$$

∴ table [4, 4] = 5

table [4, 5] With $i = 4, j = 5, w_i = 5$ and $v_i = 6$

As $j \geq w_i$, we will obtain table [4, 5] as

$$\text{table } [4, 5] = \text{maximum } \{\text{table } [i-1, j], v_i + \text{table}[i-1, j-w_i]\}$$

$$= \text{maximum } \{\text{table } [3, 5] , 6 + \text{table } [3, 0]\}$$

$$= \text{maximum } \{7, 6 + 0\}$$

∴ table [4, 5] = 7

Thus the table can be finally as given below

	0	1	2	3	4	5
0	0	0	0	0	0	0
1	0	0	3	3	3	3
2	0	0	3	4	4	7
3	0	0	3	4	5	7
4	0	0	3	4	5	7

This is the total value of selected items (table [4, 5] = 7)

How to find actual knapsack items ?

Now, as we know that table [n, W] is the total value of selected items, that can be placed in the knapsack. Following steps are used repeatedly to select actual knapsack item

```
Let, i = n and k = W then
while (i>0 and k>0)
{
        if(table [i,k] ≠ table[i – 1,k])then
        mark i^th item as in knapsack
        i = i–1 and k=k – w_i          //selection of i^th item
    else
        i = i–1 //do not select i^th item
}
```

Let us apply these steps to the above given problem. As we have obtained the final table as.

	0	1	2	3	4	5
0	0	0	0	0	0	0
1	0	0	3	3	3	3
2	0	0	3	4	4	7
3	0	0	3	4	5	7
4	0	0	3	4	5	7

Start from here (table [4, 5] = 7)

i = 4 and k = 5

i.e., table [4, 5] = table [3, 5]

$\therefore$ Do not select i^{th} i.e., 4th item.

	0	1	2	3	4	5
0	0	0	0	0	0	0
1	0	0	3	3	3	3
2	0	0	3	4	4	7
3	0	0	3	4	5	7
4	0	0	3	4	5	7

Now set $i = i - 1$

$i = 3$

Capacity →

items ↓	0	1	2	3	4	5
0	0	0	0	0	0	0
1	0	0	3	3	3	3
2	0	0	3	4	4	7
3	0	0	3	4	5	7
4	0	0	3	4	5	7

As table [i, k] = table [i – 1, k]

i.e., table [3, 5] = table [2, 5]

∴ Do not select i^{th} item i.e., 3rd item.

	0	1	2	3	4	5
0	0	0	0	0	0	0
1	0	0	3	3	3	3
✓2	0	0	3	4	4	7
3	0	0	3	4	5	7
4	0	0	3	4	5	7

Now set $i = i - 1 = 2$

As table [i, k] ≠ table [i – 1, k]

i.e. table [2, 5] ≠ table [1, 5]

Select i^{th} item.

That is, select 2nd item.

Set $i = i - 1$ and $k = k - w_i$

i.e. $i = 1$ and $k = 5 - 3 = 2$

	0	1	2	3	4	5
0	0	0	0	0	0	0
✓1	0	0	3	3	3	3
✓2	0	0	3	4	4	7
3	0	0	3	4	5	7
4	0	0	3	4	5	7

As table $[i, k] \neq$ table $[i - 1, k]$

i.e. table $[1, 2] \neq$ table $[0, 2]$

Select i^{th} item.

That is select 1st item.

Set $i = i - 1$ and $k = k - w_i$

i.e. $i = 0$ and $k = 2 - 2 = 0$

Thus we have selected **item 1** and **item 2** for the knapsack. This solution can also be represented by solution vector **(1, 1, 0, 0).**

Example 4.6.2 *Solve the following 0/1 Knapsack problem using dynamic programming. There are five items whose weights and values are given in following arrays.*

Weight w[] = { 1, 2, 5, 6, 7 }

Value v [] = { 1, 6, 18, 22, 28 }

Show your equation and find out the optimal Knapsack items for weight capacity of 11 units. **GTU : Dec.-10, Marks 8**

Solution :

Let,

Item	Weight	Value
1	1	1
2	2	6

3	5	18
4	6	22
5	7	28

The capacity W = 11.

Initially table , table [0, j] = 0 and table [i, 0] = 0.

There are 0 to n rows and 0 to W columns.

	0	1	2	3	4	5	6	7	8	9	10	11
0	0	0	0	0	0	0	0	0	0	0	0	0
1	0											
2	0											
3	0											
4	0											
5	0											

Now we will fill up table **row by row** using following formula -

$$\text{table}[i, j] = \begin{cases} \max\{\text{table}[i-1, j], \; v_i + \text{table}[i-1, j-w_i] \text{ when } j \geq w_i\} \\ \text{or} \\ \text{table}[i-1, j] \text{ if } j < w_i \end{cases}$$

i = 1, j = 1, w_i = 1, v_i = 1

$$\text{table}[i, j] = \max\begin{Bmatrix} \text{table}[i-1, j], \\ v_i + \text{table}[i-1, j-w_i] \end{Bmatrix} \qquad \because j \geq w_i$$

$$= \max\{0, 1+0\}$$

table [1, 1] = 1

i = 1, j = 2, w_i = 1, v_i = 1

$$\text{table}[i, j] = \max\begin{Bmatrix} \text{table}[i-1, j], \\ v_i + \text{table}[i-1, j-w_i] \end{Bmatrix} \qquad \because j \geq w_i$$

$$= \max\{0, 1+0\}$$

table [1, 2] = 1

i = 1, j = 3 , w_i = 1, v_i = 1

$$\text{table}[i, j] = \max\begin{cases}\text{table}[i-1,\ j],\\ v_i + \text{table}[i-1,\ j-w_i]\end{cases} \quad \because\ j \geq w_i$$

$$= \max\{0,\ 1+0\}$$

table [1, 3] = 1

i = 1, j = 4, w_i = 1, v_i = 1

$$\text{table}[i, j] = \max\begin{cases}\text{table}[i-1,\ j],\\ v_i + \text{table}[i-1,\ j-w_i]\end{cases} \quad \because\ j \geq w_i$$

$$= \max\{0,\ 1+0\}$$

table [1, 4] = 1

Continuing in this fashion we can compute all the values of table.The table will be -

	0	1	2	3	4	5	6	7	8	9	10	11
0	0	0	0	0	0	0	0	0	0	0	0	0
1	0	1	1	1	1	1	1	1	1	1	1	1
2	0	1	6	7	7	7	7	7	7	7	7	7
3	0	1	6	7	7	18	19	24	25	25	25	25
4	0	1	6	7	7	18	22	24	28	29	29	40
5	0	1	6	7	7	18	22	28	29	34	35	40

This is the total value of selected items

Now we will find the actual Knapsack items.

	0	1	2	3	4	5	6	7	8	9	10	11
0	0	0	0	0	0	0	0	0	0	0	0	0
1	0	1	1	1	1	1	1	1	1	1	1	1
2	0	1	6	7	7	7	7	7	7	7	7	7
3	0	1	6	7	7	18	19	24	25	25	25	25
4	0	1	6	7	7	18	22	24	28	29	29	40
5	0	1	6	7	7	18	22	28	29	34	35	40

table [4, 11] = table [5, 11]

∴ Do not select i^{th} i.e. 5th item.

Now set $i = i - 1$

∴ $i = 4$

	0	1	2	3	4	5	6	7	8	9	10	11
0	0	0	0	0	0	0	0	0	0	0	0	0
1	0	1	1	1	1	1	1	1	1	1	1	1
2	0	1	6	7	7	7	7	7	7	7	7	7
3	0	1	6	7	7	18	19	24	25	25	25	25
(4)	0	1	6	7	7	18	22	24	28	29	29	40
5	0	1	6	7	7	18	22	28	29	34	35	40

table [4, 11] ≠ table [3, 11]

∴ Select 4th item. (i.e. i^{th} item.)

Set $i = i-1, \quad k = k - w_i$

$i = 4-1, \quad k = 11-6$

$i = 3, \quad k = 5$

	0	1	2	3	4	5	6	7	8	9	10	11
0	0	0	0	0	0	0	0	0	0	0	0	0
1	0	1	1	1	1	1	1	1	1	1	1	1
2	0	1	6	7	7	7	7	7	7	7	7	7
(3)	0	1	6	7	7	18	19	24	25	25	25	25
(4)	0	1	6	7	7	18	22	24	28	29	29	40
5	0	1	6	7	7	18	22	28	29	34	35	40

table [3, 5] ≠ table [2, 5]

∴ Select 3rd item. (i.e. i^{th} item.)

$i = i-1, \quad k = k - w_i$

$= 5 - 5$

i.e. $i = \mathbf{2}, \quad k = 0$

table [2, 0] = 0.

Thus we have selected **item 3** and **item 4,** for the Knapsack.

The total profit $= 18 + 22 = \mathbf{40}.$

Example 4.6.3 *Solve the following problem using dynamic method. Write the equation for solving above problem.* **GTU : May-12, Marks 8**

n = 5 , W = 100					
Object →	1	2	3	4	5
Weight (w) →	10	20	30	40	50
Value (v)→	20	30	66	40	60

Solution : We have to build a table for 0 to n rows and with 0 to W columns. i.e. For 0 to 5 rows and for 0 to 100 columns. But practically designing a table of 0 to 100 column is complicated.

Hence we will divide each weight by 10 and capacity (W) by 10. Hence new data that can be considered for processing will be

w[i]	v[i]
1	20
2	30
3	66
4	40
5	60

Now we will fill up the table row by row, using following formula :

$$\text{table}[i, j] = \begin{cases} \text{maximum } \{\text{table}[i-1, j], \ v_i + \text{table}[i-1, j-w_i] \text{ when } j \geq w_i\} \\ \text{or} \\ \text{table}[i-1, j] \ \text{ if } j < w_i \end{cases}$$

The table can be computed as follows -

	0	1	2	3	4	5	6	7	8	9	10
0	0	0	0	0	0	0	0	0	0	0	0
1	0	20	20	20	20	20	20	20	20	20	20
2	0	20	30	50	50	50	50	50	50	50	50
3	0	20	30	66	86	96	116	116	116	116	116
4	0	20	30	66	86	96	116	116	126	136	156
5	0	20	30	66	86	96	116	116	126	146	156

The items that can be selected as item 1, item 2, item 3 and item 4. Hence solution for this knapsack problem is (1, 1, 1, 0) with profit **156**.

Example 4.6.4 *Solve following Knapsack problem using dynamic programming algorithm with given capacity W=5, weight and value are as follows :*
(2, 12), (1, 10), (3, 20), (2, 15). **GTU : Summer-13, Marks 7**

Solution : We will create a table using following formula -

$$\text{table }[i, j] = \begin{cases} \text{maximum }\{\text{table }[i-1, j], v_i + \\ \text{table }[i-1, j-w_i] \text{ where } j \geq w_i\} \\ \text{or} \\ \quad \text{table }[i-1, j] \quad \text{if } j < w_i \end{cases}$$

The table will be

Max items allowed	Max weight					
	0	1	2	3	4	5
0	0	0	0	0	0	0
1	0	0	12	12	12	12
2	0	10	12	22	22	22
3	0	10	12	22	30	32
4	0	10	15	25	30	37

The maximum profit is table [4, 5] = $ 37

As table [4, 5] ≠ table [3, 5]. Item 4 is included.

Total capacity 5–2 = 3 .

Now table [3, 3] = table [2, 3]. Item 3 is not included.

Now table [2, 3] ≠ table [1, 3]. Item 2 is included.

Remaining weight 3 – 1 = 2

This specifies to select item 1.

∴ Solution = {item 1, item 2, item 4}

Example 4.6.5 *Given a Knapsack having maximum weight capacity W = 4, and number of items available are three, such that*

$S = 3$

$w_i = <1, 3, 4>$

$v_i = <3, 4, 5>$

Fill the Knapsack using dynamic programming such that Knapsack should not exceed its maximum capacity and it should have maximum profit value. Is dynamic programming a top-down or a bottom-up technique ? Why ?

Write the recurrence for solving Tower of Hanoi problem having n rings and 3 rods.

GTU : Summer-14, Marks 5

Ans. :

Let, W = 4

w_i	v_i
1	3
3	4
4	5

Initially table [0, j] = 0 and table [i, 0] = 0.

There are 0 to n rows and 0 to W columns in the table.

	0	1	2	3	4
0	0	0	0	0	0
1	0				
2	0				
3	0				

We will fill up the table row by row by using following formula.

$$\text{table } [i, j] = \begin{cases} \text{maximum } \{ \text{table}[i-1, j], v_i + \text{table}[i-i, j-w_i] \\ \qquad\qquad\qquad\qquad \text{when } j \geq w_i \\ \text{or} \\ \text{table } [i-1, j] \text{ if } \qquad j < w_i \end{cases}$$

table [1, 1] with i = 1, j = 1, w_i = 1, v_i = 3

As $j \geq w_i$

$$\text{table } [1, 1] = \max\{ \text{table } [i-1, j], v_i + \text{table } [i-1, j-w_i]\}$$

$$= \max\{ \text{table } [0, 1], 3 + \text{table } [0, 0]\}$$

table [1, 1] = 3

table [1, 2] with i = 1, j = 2, w_i = 1, v_i = 3

As $j \geq w_i$

$$\text{table } [1, 2] = \max\{ \text{table } [i-1, j], v_i + \text{table } [i-1, j-w_i]\}$$

$$= \max\{ \text{table } [0, 2], 3 + \text{table } [0, 1]\}$$

$$= \max\{0, 3+0\}$$

table [1, 2] = 3

table [1, 3] with i = 1, j = 3, $w_i = 1$, $v_i = 3$

As $j > w_i$

$$\text{table } [1, 3] = \max\{\text{table } [i-1, j], v_i + \text{table } [i-1, j-w_i]\}$$

$$= \max\{\text{table } [0, 3], 3 + \text{table } [0, 2]\}$$

table [1, 3] = 3

table [1, 4] with i = 1, j = 4, $w_i = 1$, $v_i = 3$

As $j > w_i$

$$\text{table } [1, 4] = \max\{\text{table } [i-1, j], v_i + \text{table } [i-1, j-w_i]\}$$

$$= \max\{\text{table } [0, 4], 3 + \text{table } [0, 3]\}$$

$$= \max\{0, 3+0\}$$

table [1, 4] = 3

The table can be represented as

	0	1	2	3	4
0	0	0	0	0	0
1	0	3	3	3	3
2	0				
3	0				

table [2, 1] with i = 2, j = 1, $w_i = 3$, $v_i = 4$

As $j < w_i$

$$\text{table } [2, 1] = \text{table } [i-1, j]$$

$$= \text{table } [1, 1]$$

table [2, 1] = 0

table [2, 2] with i = 2, j = 2, $w_i = 3$, $v_i = 4$

As $j < w_i$

$$\text{table } [2, 2] = \text{table } [i-1, j]$$

$$= \text{table } [1, 2]$$

table [2, 2] = 3

table [2, 3] with i = 2, j = 3, $w_i = 3$, $v_i = 4$

As $j = w_i$

$$\text{table }[2, 3] = \max\{\text{table }[i-1,\ j],\ v_i + \text{table }[i-1,\ j-w_i]\}$$
$$= \max\{[1,\ 3],\ 4 + \text{table }[1,\ 0]\}$$
$$= \max\{3, 4+0\}$$

table [2, 3] = 4

table [2, 4] with i = 2, j = 4, $w_i = 3$, $v_i = 4$

As $j > w_i$

$$\text{table }[2, 4] = \max\{\text{table}[i-1, j], v_i + \text{table}[i-1, j-w_i]\}$$
$$= \max\{\text{table }[1, 4], 4 + \text{table }[1, 1]\}$$
$$= \max\{3,\ 4+3\}$$

table [2, 4] = 7

The table now is -

	0	1	2	3	4
0	0	0	0	0	0
1	0	3	3	3	3
2	0	0	3	4	7
3	0				

table [3, 1] with i = 3, j = 1, $w_i = 4$, $v_i = 5$

As $j < w_i$

$$\text{table }[3, 1] = \text{table }[i-1, j]$$
$$= \text{table }[2,\ 1]$$

table [3, 1] = 0

table [3, 2] with i = 3, j = 2, $w_i = 4$, $v_i = 5$

As $j < w_i$

$$\text{table }[3, 2] = \text{table }[i-1, j]$$
$$= \text{table }[2,\ 2]$$

table [3, 2] = 3

table [3, 3] with i = 3, j = 3, $w_i = 4$, $v_i = 5$

As $j < w_i$

$$\text{table }[3, 3] = \text{table }[i-1, j]$$
$$= \text{table }[2,\ 3]$$

table [3, 3] = 4

table [3, 4] with i = 3, j = 4, $w_i = 4$, $v_i = 5$

As $j = w_i$

$$\text{table }[3, 4] = \max\{\text{table}[i-1, j], v_i + \text{table}[i-1, j-W_i]\}$$
$$= \max\{\text{table}[2, 4], 5 + \text{table}[2, 0]\}$$
$$= \max\{7, 5+0\}$$

table [3, 4] = 7

Now the complete table is -

	0	1	2	3	4
0	0	0	0	0	0
1	0	3	3	3	3
2	0	0	3	4	7
3	0	0	3	4	7

Now we will find the actual items of Knapsack

Step 1 :

table [2, 4] = table [3, 4]

∴ Do not select $i^{th} = 3^{rd}$ item

	0	1	2	3	4
0	0	0	0	0	0
1	0	3	3	3	3
2	0	0	3	4	7
3	0	0	3	4	7

Step 2 :

Set $i = i-1$

∴ $i = 2$

table [2, 4] ≠ table [1, 4]

∴ Select i^{th} i.e. 2nd item

	0	1	2	3	4
0	0	0	0	0	0
1	0	3	3	3	3
②	0	0	3	4	7
3	0	0	3	4	7

Step 3 :

$$i = i-1 = 1$$
$$j = j - w_i = 4 - 3 = 1$$

table [1, 1] $\neq$ table [0, 1]

$\therefore$ Select i^{th} i.e. 1st item

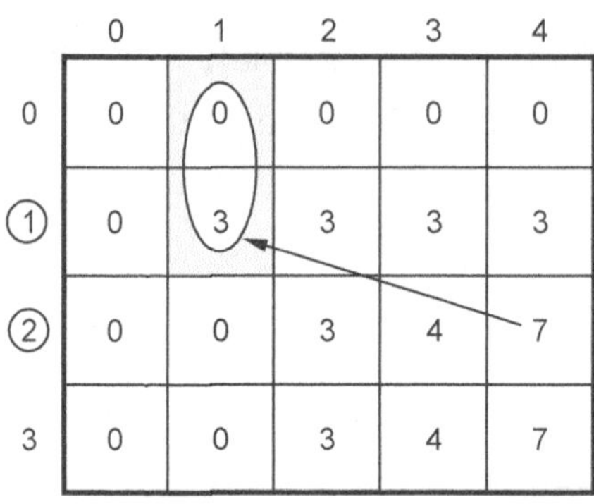

Step 4 :

$$i = i - 1 = 0$$

$$j = j - w_i = 1 - 1 = 0$$

Thus we have selected **item 1** and **item 2**

Total maximum profit = 3 + 4 = 7

Dynamic programming uses both top down and bottom up approaches. The top down method uses memorization technique while bottom up method uses tabulation technique.

Example 4.6.6 *Solve the following knapsack problem with the given capacity W = 5 using dynamic programming.* **GTU : Winter-14, Marks 7**

Item	Weight	Value
1	2	$12
2	1	$10
3	3	$20
4	2	$15

Solution : Initially, table [0, j] and table [i, 0] = 0. There are 0 to n rows and 0 to W columns in the table.

	0	1	2	3	4	5
0	0	0	0	0	0	0
1	0					
2	0					
3	0					
4	0					

Now we will fill up the table row by row. Let us start filling the table row by row using following formula :

$$\text{table }[i, j] = \begin{cases} \text{maximum } \{\text{table}[i-1, j],\ v_i + \text{table }[i-1,\ j-w_i] & \text{when } j \geq w_i \\ \text{or} & \\ \text{table }[i-1, j] \text{ if } j < w_i & \end{cases}$$

table [1, 1] with $i = 1, j = 1$, and $w_i = 2, v_i = 12$

As $j < w_i$

table [1, 1] = table [i−1, j]

= table [0, 1]

table [1, 1] = 0

table [1, 2] with $i = 1, j = 2, w_i = 2, v_i = 12$

As $j \geq w_i$

$$\text{table }[1, 2] = \max\{\text{table}[i-1, j], v_i + \text{table}[i-1, j-w_i]\}$$

$$= \max\{0, 12+0\}$$

∴ **table [1, 2] = 12**

table [1, 3] with $i = 1, j = 3, w_i = 2, v_i = 12$

As $j \geq w_i$

$$\text{table }[1, 3] = \max\{\text{table}[i-1, j], v_i + \text{table}[i-1, j-w_i]\}$$

$$= \max\{0, 12 + 0\}$$

∴ **table [1, 3] = 12**

table [1, 4] with $i = 1, j = 4, w_i = 2$ and $v_i = 12$

As $j \geq w_i$

$$\text{table }[1, 4] = \max\{\text{table}[i-1, j], v_i + \text{table}[i-1, j-w_i]\}$$

$$= \max\{0, 12+0\}$$

∴ **table [1, 4] = 12**

table [1, 5] with $i = 1, \; j = 5, \; w_i = 2$ and $v_i = 12$

As $j \geq w_i$

$$\text{table } [1, 5] = \max \{\text{table}[i-1, j], v_i + \text{table}[i-1, j-w_i]\}$$

$$= \max \{0, 12+0\}$$

∴ **table [1, 5] = 12**

The table with these values will be.

	0	1	2	3	4	5
0	0	0	0	0	0	0
1	0	0	12	12	12	12
2	0					
3	0					
4	0					

table [2, 1] with $i = 2, j = 1, w_i = 1, v_i = 10$

As $j \geq w_i$

$$\text{table } [2, 1] = \max \{\text{table}[i-1, j], v_i + \text{table}[i-1, j-w_i]\}$$

$$= \max \{0, 10+0\}$$

∴ **table [2, 1] = 10**

table [2, 2] with $i = 2, j = 2, w_i = 1, v_i = 10$

As $j \geq w_i$

$$\text{table } [2, 2] = \max \{\text{table}[i-1, j], v_i + \text{table}[i-1, j-w_i]\}$$

$$= \max \{\text{table } [1, 2], 10 + \text{table } [1, 1]\}$$

$$= \max \{12, 10+0\}$$

table [2, 2] = 12

table [2, 3] with $i = 2, j = 3, w_i = 1, v_i = 10$

As $j \geq w_i$

$$\text{table } [2, 3] = \max \{\text{table}[i-1, j], v_i + \text{table}[i-1, j-w_i]\}$$

$$= \max \{\text{table } [1, 3], 10 + \text{table } [1, 2]\}$$

$$= \max \{12, 10+12\}$$

∴ **table [2, 3] = 22**

table [2, 4] with $i = 2, j = 4, w_i = 1, v_i = 10$

As $j \geq w_i$

$$\text{table } [2, 4] = \max\{\text{table}[i-1, j], v_i + \text{table}[i-1, j-w_i]\}$$

$$= \max\{\text{table } [1, 4], 10 + \text{table } [1, 3]\}$$

table [2, 4] = 22

table [2, 5] with $i = 2, j = 5, w_i = 1, v_i = 10$

As $j \geq w_i$

$$\text{table } [2, 5] = \max\{\text{table}[i-1, j], v_i + \text{table}[i-1, j-w_i]\}$$

$$= \max\{\text{table } [1, 5], 10 + \text{table } [1, 4]\}$$

table [2, 5] = 22 . The partial table will be -

	0	1	2	3	4	5
0	0	0	0	0	0	0
1	0	0	12	12	12	12
2	0	10	12	22	22	22
3	0					
4	0					

table [3, 1] with $i = 3, j = 1, w_i = 3, v_i = 20$

As $j \geq w_i$

$$\text{table } [3, 1] = \text{table } [i-1, j]$$

$$= \text{table } [2, 1]$$

∴ **table [3, 1] = 10**

table [3, 2] with $i = 3, j = 2, w_i = 3, v_i = 20$

As $j < w_i$

$$\text{table } [3, 2] = \text{table } [i-1, j]$$

$$= \text{table } [2, 2]$$

∴ **table [3, 2] = 12**

table [3, 3] with $i = 3, j = 3, w_i = 3, v_i = 20$

As $j \geq w_i$

$$\text{table } [3, 3] = \max\{\text{table}[i-1, j], v_i + \text{table}[i-1, j-w_i]\}$$

$$= \max\{\text{table } [2, 3], 20 + \text{table } [2, 0]\}$$

$$= \max \{22, 20+0\}$$

$\therefore$ **table [3, 3] = 22**

table [3, 4] with $i = 3, j = 4, w_i = 3, v_i = 20$

As $j \geq w_i$

$$\text{table [3, 4]} = \max \{\text{table}[i-1, j], v_i + \text{table}[i-1, j-w_i]\}$$
$$= \max \{\text{table [2, 4]}, 20 + \text{table [2, 1]}\}$$
$$= \max \{22, 20+10\}$$

$\therefore$ **table [3, 4] = 30**

table [3, 5] with $i = 3, j = 5, w_i = 3, v_i = 20$

As $j \geq w_i$

$$\text{table [3, 5]} = \max \{\text{table}[i-1, j], v_i + \text{table}[i-1, j-w_i]\}$$
$$= \max \{\text{table [2, 5]}, 20 + \text{table [2, 2]}\}$$
$$= \max \{22, 20+12\}$$

$\therefore$ **table [3, 5] = 32**

The partially filled up table is as follows -

	0	1	2	3	4	5
0	0	0	0	0	0	0
1	0	0	12	12	12	12
2	0	10	12	22	22	22
3	0	10	12	22	30	32
4	0					

table [4, 1] with $i = 4, j = 1, w_i = 2, v_i = 15$

As $j < w_i$

$$\text{table [4, 1]} = \text{table } [i-1, j]$$
$$= \text{table [3, 1]}$$

$\therefore$ **table [4, 1] = 10**

table [4, 2] with $i = 4, j = 2, w_i = 2, v_i = 15$

As $j \geq w_i$

$$\text{table [4, 2]} = \max \{\text{table}[i-1, j], v_i + \text{table}[i-1, j-w_i]\}$$
$$= \max \{\text{table [3, 2]}, 15 + \text{table [3, 0]}\}$$

$= \max\{12, 15+0\}$

$\therefore$ **table [4, 2] = 15**

table [4, 3] with $i = 4, j = 3, w_i = 2, v_i = 15$

As $j \geq w_i$

$$\text{table}[4, 3] = \max\{\text{table}[i-1, j], v_i + \text{table}[i-1, j-w_i]\}$$
$$= \max\{\text{table}[3, 3], 15 + \text{table}[3, 1]\}$$
$$= \max\{22, 15+10\}$$

$\therefore$ **table [4, 3] = 25**

table [4, 4] with $i = 4, j = 4, w_i = 2, v_i = 15$

As $j \geq w_i$

$$\text{table}[4, 4] = \max\{\text{table}[i-1, j], v_i + \text{table}[i-1, j-w_i]\}$$
$$= \max\{\text{table}[3, 4], 15 + \text{table}[3, 2]\}$$
$$= \max\{30, 15+12\}$$

$\therefore$ **table [4, 4] = 30**

table [4, 5] with $i = 4, j = 5, w_i = 2, v_i = 15$

As $j \geq w_i$

$$\text{table}[4, 5] = \max\{\text{table}[i-1, j], v_i + \text{table}[i-1, j-w_i]\}$$
$$= \max\{\text{table}[3, 5], 15 + \text{table}[3, 3]\}$$
$$= \max\{32, 15+22\}$$

$\therefore$ **table [4, 5] = 37**

	0	1	2	3	4	5
0	0	0	0	0	0	0
1	0	0	12	12	12	12
2	0	10	12	22	22	22
3	0	10	12	22	30	32
4	0	10	15	25	30	37

Now we will trace for the solution using above table -

$i = 4, k = 4$

As table [i, j] $\neq$ table [i−1, k]

i.e. table [4, 5] $\neq$ table [3, 5]

Select i^{th} i.e. **4th item.**

Now $i = i - 1$ and $k = k - w_i$

$\therefore$ $i = 4 - 1 = 3$ and $k = 5 - 2 = 3$

As table [i, k] = table [i−1, k]

i.e. table [3, 3] = table [2, 3]

$\therefore$ Do not select i^{th} i.e. 3rd item.

Now set $i = i - 1$

$\therefore$ $i = 2$ and $k = 3$.

As table [2, 3] $\neq$ table [1, 3]

$\therefore$ Select i^{th} i.e **2nd item.**

Set $i = i - 1$ and $k = k - w_i$

$\therefore$ $i = 1$ and $k = 3 - 1 = 2$.

As table [1, 2] $\neq$ table [0, 2]

Select i^{th} i.e. **1st item.**

Now set $i = i - 1$ and $k = k - w_i$

$\therefore$ $i = 0$ and $k = 0$

Thus solution to this Knapsack problem is **(item 1, item 2, item 4)** with total **profit = 37.**

Examples for Practice

Example 4.6.7 *Consider 0/1 knapsack problem N = 3, w = (4, 6, 8), p = (10, 12, 15) using dynamic programming devise the recurrence relations for the problem and solve the same. Determine the optimal profit for the knapsack of capacity 10.*

GTU : Dec.-11, 12

[Ans. : table [1, 1]=0, table [1, 2]= 0, table [1, 4]= 10, table [2, 1]= 0, table [2, 6]= 12, table [3, 10]= 22]

Example 4.6.8 *Using dynamic programming solve the following Knapsack instance :*

$n = 3, [w_1, w_2, w_3] = [1,2,2]$ and $[P_1, P_2, P_3] = [18,16,6]$ and $M = 4$

Let us now discuss the algorithm for the knapsack problem using dynamic programming.

Algorithm

```
Algorithm Dynamic_Knapsack(n,W,w[ ],v[ ])
//Problem Description : This algorithm is for obtaining knapsack
//solution using dynamic programming
//Input: n is total number of items, W is the capacity of
//knapsack, w[ ] stores weights of each item and v[ ] stores
//the values of each item.
//Output: Returns the total value of selected items for the
//knapsack.
for (i ← 0 to n) do
{
 for (j ← 0 to W) do
 {
   table[i,0]=0   // table initialization
   table[0,j]=0
 }
}
for (i ← 0 to n) do
{
 for (j ← 0 to W) do
 {
  if(j<w[i]) then
   table[i,j]← table[i – 1, j]
  else if(j>=w[i]) then
   table[i,j]← max (table[i-1 ,j],(v[i]+table[i – 1,j – w[i]]) )
 }
}
return table[n,W]
```

Analysis

In this algorithm the basic operation is **if ... else if** statement within two nested for loops.

Hence

$$c(n) = \sum_{i=0}^{n} \sum_{j=0}^{W} 1 = \sum_{i=0}^{n} W - 0 + 1$$

$$= \sum_{i=0}^{n} (W + 1)$$

$$= \sum_{i=0}^{n} W + \sum_{i=0}^{n} 1$$

$$= W \cdot \sum_{i=0}^{n} 1 + \sum_{i=0}^{n} 1$$

$$= W(n - 0 + 1) + (n - 0 + 1)$$

$$= W_n + W + n + 1$$

Thus $c(n) \approx W_n$

The time complexity of this algorithm is $\Theta(\mathbf{nW})$.

4.6.1 Memory Functions

While solving recurrence relation using dynamic programming approach common subproblems may be solved more than once and this makes inefficient solving of the problem. Hence memory function is a method that solves only necessary subproblems. Hence we can define the goal of memory function as : solve only subproblems that are **necessary** and solve these subproblems **only once.**

Memorization is a way to deal with overlapping subproblems in dynamic programming. During memorization -

1. After computing the solution to a subproblem, store it in a table.
2. Make use of recursive calls.

The 0-1 Knapsack Memory Function Algorithm is as given below -

Globally some values are to be set before the actual memory function algorithm

```
for (i←1 to n) do
 for (j←1 to W) do
  table[i,j]←-1
 for (j←0 to W) do
  table[0,j]← 0  //making 0th row 0
for i←1 to n do
  table[i,0]←0  //making 0th column 0
 Algorithm Mem_Fun_knapsack(i,j)
//Problem Description : Implementation of memory function method
//for the knapsack problem
//Input: i is the number of items and j denotes the knapsack's capacity
//Output : optimal solution subset
if (table[i,j] < 0) then
{
 if (j < w[i]) then
   value ← Mem_Fun_knapsack(i – 1, j)
 else
  value ← max(Mem_Fun_knapsack(i – 1, j),
    v[i] + Mem_Fun_knapsack(i – 1, j – w[i]))
  table[i,j]← value
}
return table[i, j]
```

Review Question

1. *Discuss and derive an equation for solving the 0/1 Knapsack problem using dynamic programming method. Design and analyze the algorithm for the same.* **GTU : Summer-15, Marks 7**

4.7 Shortest Path

GTU : Summer-13, Marks 7

The all pair shortest path is the problem of determining shortest path distances between every pair of vertices in a given graph. The use of this algorithm is in routing problems. Following are the algorithms used for finding all - pair shortest path-

1. Matrix multiplication and shortest path
2. Floyd-Warshall's algorithm

Let us discuss these algorithms with suitable examples.

4.7.1 Shortest Path and Matrix Multiplication

The shortest path for all pair can be obtained using dynamic programming approach. This operation of finding shortest path is similar to matrix multiplication. Hence the algorithm of finding shortest path between all pairs will look like repeated matrix multiplication. Let us apply following steps to obtain all pair shortest path using matrix multiplication approach.

Step 1 : Deciding Structure of a Shortest Path

The structure of optimal solution has to characterized. For that matter, the graph is represented by adjacency matrix. In this representation if there is an edge between i to j then the M[i][j] = Wij, where Wij represents the weight of edge between i and j. The shortest path between all i and j pairs is obtained by the path p which is denoted by m number of edges. This can be denoted as

$i \overset{p'}{\leadsto} k \rightarrow j$ means the path from vertex i to k comprised of path p' containing at the most m–1. Then the weight wkj should be then added to reach to j.

Step 2 : Recursive Definition

Let,

$l_{ij}^{(m)}$ be the minimum weight from vertex i to j made up of m edges.

$$l_{ij}^{(0)} = \begin{cases} 0 & \text{if } i = j \\ \infty & \text{if } i \neq j \end{cases}$$

and

$$l_{ij}^{(m)} = \min\left\{ l_{ij}^{(m-1)}, \min_{1 \le k \le n} \left\{ l_{ik}^{(m-1)} + w_{kj} \right\} \right\}$$ ← Finding intermediate edge with minimum weight.

$$= \min_{i \le k \le n} \left\{ l_{ik}^{(m-1)} + W_{kj} \right\}$$

Where $m \geq 1$

Step 3 : Computing the Shortest Path

The algorithm for shortest path are

```
Algorithm shortest_path()
{
// probelm Description : This algorithm finds the
// Shortest path using matrix multiplication approach
for i← 1 to n
    {
        for j ← 1 to n
        l_ij ← min (l_ij, l_ik + W_kj====

    }
}
    return
} // end of algorithm
```

As there are three nested for loops the running time is Θ **(n^3).**

Example 4.7.1 *Consider following graph for finding all pair of shortest path.*

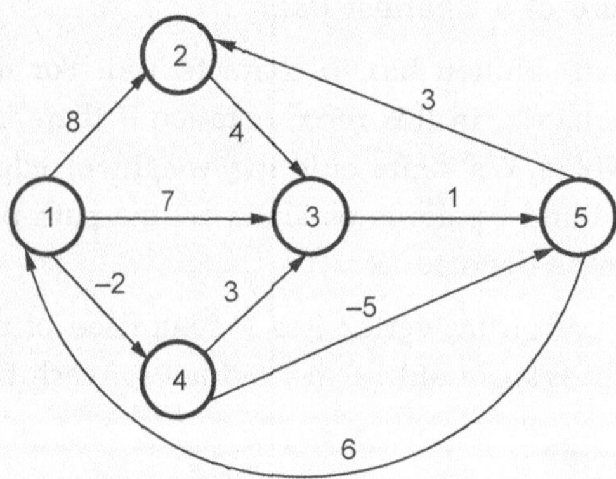

Solution : Here only one edge is allowed between any i and j vertices. In other words, only direct edges are allowed M[i, i] = 0. If there is no direct edge between i and j the M[i, j] = ∞

$$M[1, 3] = M[1, 4] + M[4, 3]$$
$$= -2 + 3$$
$$\mathbf{M[1,3] = 1}$$

Thus two edges are allowed between i to j.

similarly M[1, 5] = M[1, 4]+M[4, 5]

$L^{(1)}$=

	1	2	3	4	5
1	0	8	7	−2	∞
2	∞	0	4	∞	∞
3	∞	∞	0	∞	1
4	∞	∞	3	0	−5
5	6	3	∞	∞	0

M[1,5] = –7

M[3, 1] = M[3, 5] + M[5, 1]

= 1 + 6

M [3,1] = 7

M[3, 2] = M[3, 5] + M[5,2]

= 1 + 3

M[3, 2] = 4

M[4, 1] = M[4, 5] + M[5, 1]

= – 5 + 6

M[4, 1] = 1

M[4, 2] = M[4, 5] + M [5, 2]

= – 5 + 3

M[4, 2] = –2

M[5, 3] = M[5, 2] + M [2, 3]

= 3 + 4

M[5, 3] = 7

M[5, 4] = M[5, 1] + M[1, 4]

= 6 + -2

M[5, 4] = 4

$L^{(2)}$ =

	1	2	3	4	5
1	0	8	1	–2	–7
2	∞	0	4	∞	5
3	7	4	0	∞	1
4	1	–2	3	0	–5
5	6	3	7	4	0

Now,

Here at the most three edges are allowed from i to j vertices. For example :

M[1, 2] = M[1, 4] + M[4, 5] + M[5, 2]

= –2 + –5 + 3

M[1, 2] = – 4

Here at the most 4 edges are allowed between i to j. Hence

M[2, 4] = M[2, 3] + M[3, 5]

+M[5, 1]+ M[1, 4]

= 4 + 1 + 6 + –2

M [2, 4] = **9**

$L^{(3)}$ =

	1	2	3	4	5
1	0	–4	1	–2	–7
2	11	0	4	∞	5
3	7	4	0	5	1
4	1	–2	3	0	–5
5	6	3	7	4	0

Since $L^{(4)}$ is = $L^{(5)}$, We declare $L^{(5)}$ denotes all pair shortest paths.

$$L^{(1)} = W$$

$$L^{(2)} = W \cdot W = W^2$$

$$L^{(3)} = W^2 \cdot W^2 = W^4$$

Thus shortest path can be obtained as matrix multiplication procedure.

$L^{(4)}$ =

	1	2	3	4	5
1	0	–4	0	–2	–7
2	11	0	4	9	5
3	7	4	0	5	1
4	1	–2	3	0	–5
5	6	3	7	4	0

$L^{(5)}$ =

	1	2	3	4	5
1	0	–4	0	–2	–7
2	11	0	4	9	5
3	7	4	0	5	1
4	1	–2	3	0	–5
5	6	3	7	4	0

4.7.2 The Floyd-Warshall Algorithm

Floyd's algorithm is for finding the shortest path between every pair of vertices of a graph. The algorithm works for both directed and undirected graphs. This algorithm is invented by **R. Floyd** and hence is the name. Before getting introduced with this algorithm, let us revise few concepts related with graph.

Weighted graph : The weighted graph is a graph in which weights or distances are given along the edges. The weighted graph can be represented by weighted matrix as follows,

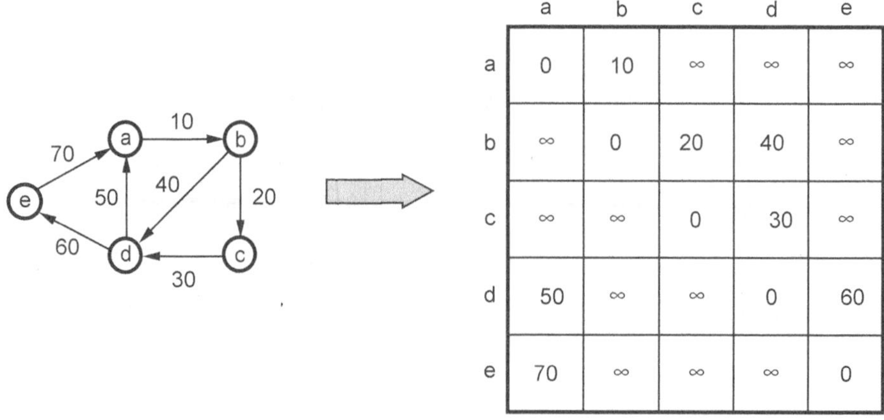

	a	b	c	d	e
a	0	10	∞	∞	∞
b	∞	0	20	40	∞
c	∞	∞	0	30	∞
d	50	∞	∞	0	60
e	70	∞	∞	∞	0

Here W[i][j] = 0 if i = j

W[i][j] = ∞ if there is no edge (direct edge) between i and j.

W[i][j] = Weight of edge.

Basic concept of Floyd's Algorithm

- The Floyd's algorithm is for computing shortest path between every pair of vertices of graph.
- The graph may contain negative edges but it should not contain negative cycles.
- The Floyd's algorithm requires a weighted graph.
- Floyd's algorithm computes the distance matrix of a weighted graph with n vertices through a series of n by n matrices :

$$D^{(0)}, D^{(1)}, \ldots D^{(k-1)}, \ldots D^{(n)}$$

- In each matrix $D^{(k)}$ the shortest distance "d_{ij}" has to be computed between vertex v_i and v_j.
- In particular the series starts with $D^{(0)}$ with no intermediate vertex. That means $D^{(0)}$ is a matrix in which v_i and v_j i.e. i^{th} row and j^{th} column contains the weights given by direct edges. In $D^{(1)}$ matrix - the shortest distance going through one intermediate vertex (starting vertex as intermediate) with maximum path length of 2 edges is given continuing in this fashion we will compute $D^{(n)}$, containing the lengths of shortest paths among all paths that can use all n vertices as intermediate. Thus we get all pair shortest paths from matrix $D^{(n)}$.

Let us first understand this algorithm with the help of some example.

Example 4.7.2 *Obtain the all pair-shortest path using Floyd's algorithm for the following weighted graph,*

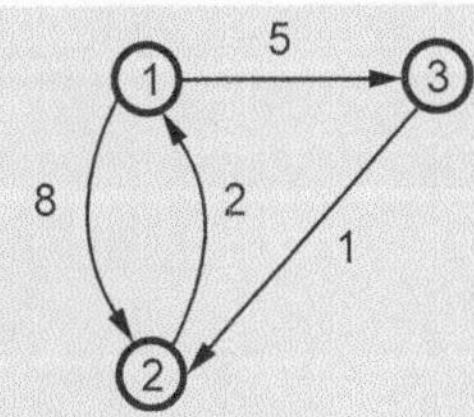

Solution : First we will compute weighted matrix with no intermediate vertex. i.e., $D^{(0)}$.

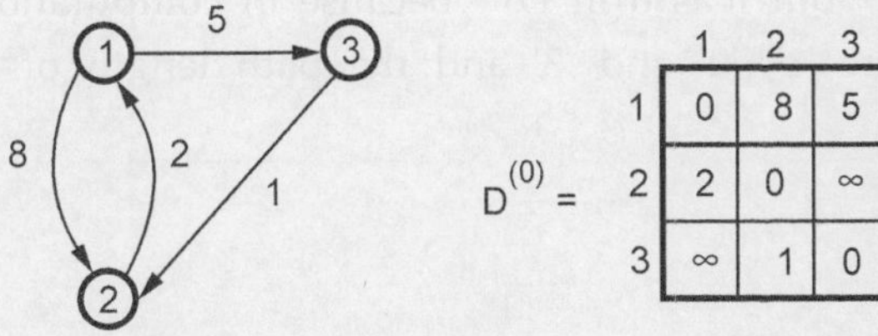

	1	2	3
1	0	8	5
2	2	0	∞
3	∞	1	0

The matrix $D^{(0)}$ is simply a weighted matrix. If i = j then D[i][j] = 0, if there is no direct edge present in vertex v_i and v_j set i^{th} row and j^{th} column of matrix D as ∞. Otherwise put the weight given along the edge between v_i and v_j.

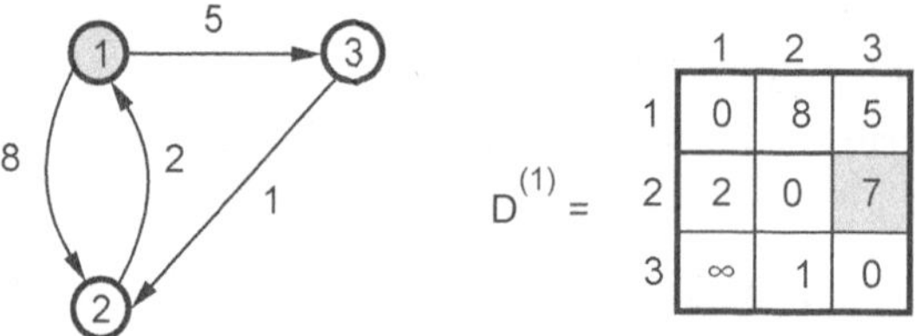

	1	2	3
1	0	8	5
2	2	0	7
3	∞	1	0

While computing $D^{(1)}$ we have considered '1' as intermediate vertex and path containing maximum two edges is taken. For instance : 2-1-3 path gives total weight 2 + 5 = 7. And 7 < ∞. Hence the previous entry of ∞ for 2nd row and 3rd column is replaced by 7.

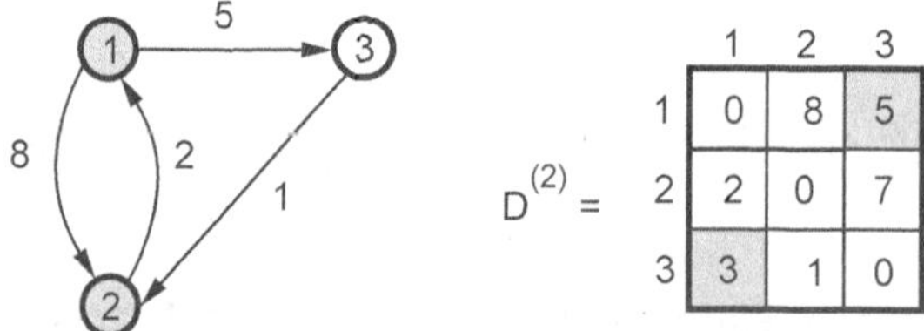

	1	2	3
1	0	8	5
2	2	0	7
3	3	1	0

While computing $D^{(2)}$, we have considered '1' and '2' as intermediate vertices path length of maximum three edges.

For instance : In $D^{(1)}$ we have got ∞ in 3rd row and 1st column as distance between vertex 3 and 1. But we get another distance 3 – 2 – 1 with weight 1 + 2 = 3. As 3 < ∞. Put 3 in 3rd row and 1st column. Note that this distance is going through intermediate vertices '1' and '2'.

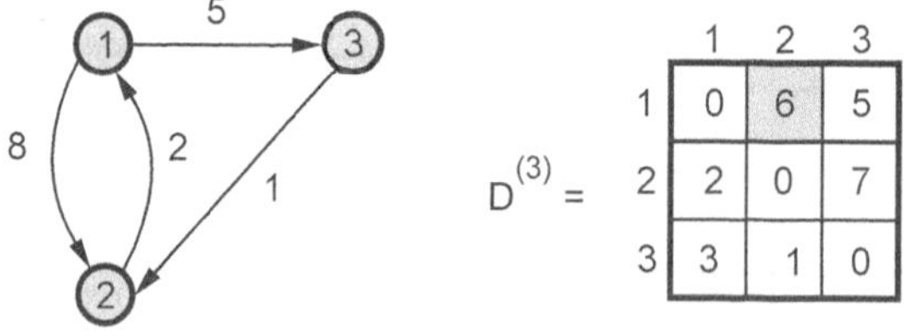

	1	2	3
1	0	6	5
2	2	0	7
3	3	1	0

D[1][2] was 8 in $D^{(2)}$ but it is 6 in $D^{(3)}$ because in computation of $D^{(3)}$ the allowed intermediate vertices are '1', '2' and '3' and the path length of maximum 4 edges is allowed.

Thus we have computed $D^{(3)}$. As n = total number of vertices = 3, we will stop computing series of $D^{(k)}$. The matrix $D^{(3)}$ is representing shortest paths from all pairs of vertices.

Let us now formulate this procedure.

Formulation

Let, $D^k[i, j]$ denotes the weight of shortest path from v_i to v_j using $\{v_1, v_2, v_3 \dots v_k\}$ as intermediate vertices.

Initially $D^{(0)}$ is computed as weighted matrix.

There exists two cases -

1. A shortest path from v_i to v_j with intermediate vertices from $\{v_1, v_2, \dots v_k\}$ that does not use v_k. In this case,

$$D^k[i, j] = D^{(k-1)}[i, j]$$

2. A shortest path from v_i to v_j restricted to using intermediate vertices $\{v_1, v_2, \dots v_k\}$ which uses v_k. In this case -

$$D^k[i, j] = D^{(k-1)}[i, k] + D^{(k-1)}[k, j]$$

The graphical representation of these two cases is

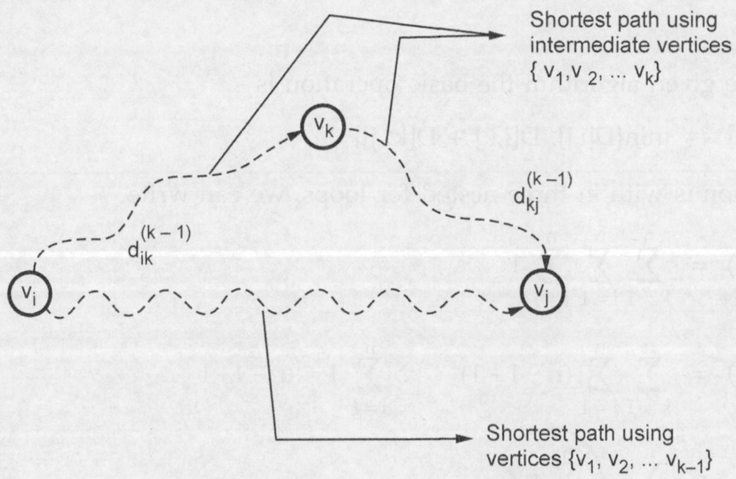

Fig. 4.7.1 Formulation of Floyd's algorithm

As these cases give us

1. $D^{(k)}[i, j] = D^{(k-1)}[i, j]$

2. $D^{(k)}[i, j] = D^{(k-1)}[i, k] + D^{(k-1)}[k, j]$

We can now write,

$$D^{(k)}[i, j] = \min\left\{D^{(k-1)}[i, j], D^{(k-1)}[i, k] + D^{(k-1)}[k, j]\right\}$$

Algorithm

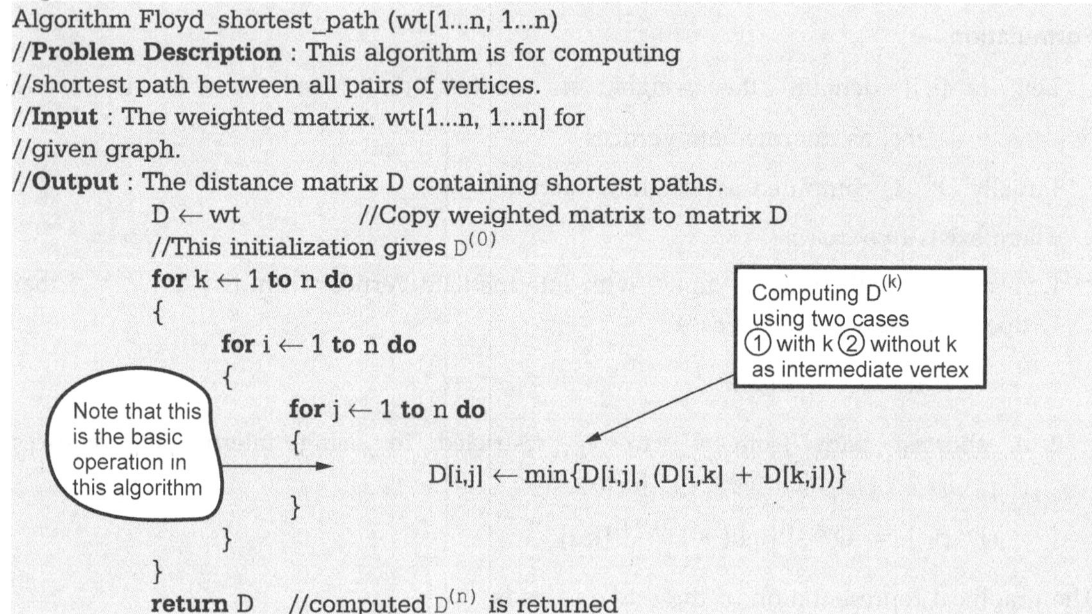

```
Algorithm Floyd_shortest_path (wt[1...n, 1...n)
//Problem Description : This algorithm is for computing
//shortest path between all pairs of vertices.
//Input : The weighted matrix. wt[1...n, 1...n] for
//given graph.
//Output : The distance matrix D containing shortest paths.
    D ← wt          //Copy weighted matrix to matrix D
    //This initialization gives D(0)
    for k ← 1 to n do
    {
        for i ← 1 to n do
        {
            for j ← 1 to n do
            {
                D[i,j] ← min{D[i,j], (D[i,k] + D[k,j])}
            }
        }
    }
    return D    //computed D(n) is returned
```


Analysis

In the above given algorithm the basic operation is -

$$D[i, j] \leftarrow \min\{D[i,j], D[i,k] + D[k, j]\}$$

This operation is with in three nested for loops, we can write

$$C(n) = \sum_{k=1}^{n} \sum_{i=1}^{n} \sum_{j=1}^{n} 1$$

$$C(n) = \sum_{k=1}^{n} \sum_{i=1}^{n} (n-1+1) \quad \because \sum_{i=l}^{u} 1 = u - l + 1$$

$$= \sum_{k=1}^{n} \sum_{i=1}^{n} n$$

$\sum_{i=1}^{n} i \approx \frac{1}{2} n^2$, we can neglect constants and write it as n^2

$$= \sum_{k=1}^{n} n^2$$

$$C(n) = n^3 \qquad \because \sum_{i=1}^{n} n^2 \approx \frac{1}{3} n^3 \text{, we neglect constants.}$$

The time complexity of finding all pair shortest path is $\Theta(n^3)$.

Let us compute $D^{(0)}, D^{(1)}, \ldots D^{(n)}$ using the formula for Floyd's algorithm.

Consider,

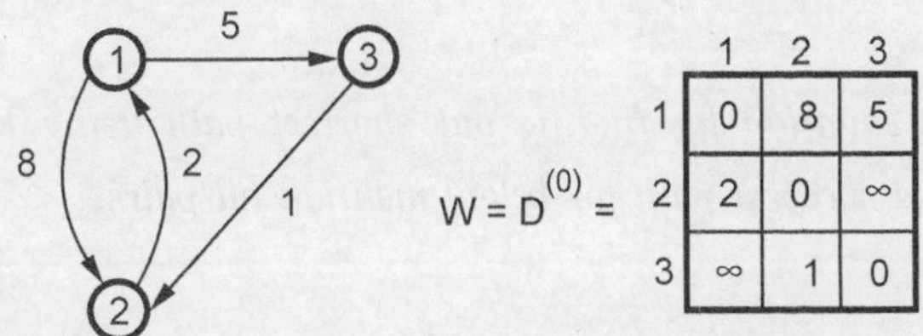

For $D^{(1)}$, k = 1 i.e. vertex 1 can be an intermediate vertex.

$\therefore$ $D^{(1)}$ =

	1	2	3
1	0	8	5
2	2	0	7
3	∞	1	0

$$D^1[2, 3] = \min\{D^0[2, 3], D^0[2, 1] + D^0[1, 3]\}$$

$$= \min\{\infty, 7\}$$

$$D^1[2, 3] = 7$$

$\therefore$ $D^{(2)}$ =

	1	2	3
1	0	8	5
2	2	0	7
3	3	1	0

For $D^{(2)}$, k = 2 i.e., vertices 1 and 2 can be intermediate vertices.

$$\therefore \quad D^2[1, 3] = \min\{D^1[1, 3], D^1[1, 2] + D^1[2, 3]\}$$

$$= \min\{5, (8 + 7)\}$$

$D^2[1, 3] = 5$ i.e., remains unchanged.

Similarly we will compute $D^2[3, 1]$.

$$D^2[1, 3] = D^2[3, 1] = \min\{D^1[3, 1], D^1[3, 2] + D^1[2, 1]\}$$

$$= \min\{\infty, 1 + 2\}$$

$$\therefore \quad D^2[3, 1] = 3$$

For $D^{(3)}$ computation, k = 3 i.e. intermediate vertices can be 1, 2 and 3.

$D^{(3)} =$

	1	2	3
1	0	6	5
2	2	0	7
3	3	1	0

$$\therefore \quad D^3[1,2] = \min\{D^2[1,2], D^2[1,3] + D^2[3,2]\}$$

$$= \min\{8, 5+1\}$$

$$D^3[1,2] = 6$$

Continuing in this fashion we can find all the shortest path distances from all the vertices.

Example 4.7.3 *Write the equation for finding out shortest path using Floyd's algorithm. Use Floyd's method to find shortest path for below mention all pairs.*

GTU : Summer-13, Marks 7

$$\begin{pmatrix} 0 & \infty & 3 & \infty \\ 2 & 0 & \infty & \infty \\ \infty & 7 & 0 & 1 \\ 6 & \infty & \infty & 0 \end{pmatrix}$$

Solution : Consider the matrix, we will compute $D^{(0)}$, $D^{(1)}$, $D^{(2)}$,.......

$D^{(0)} =$

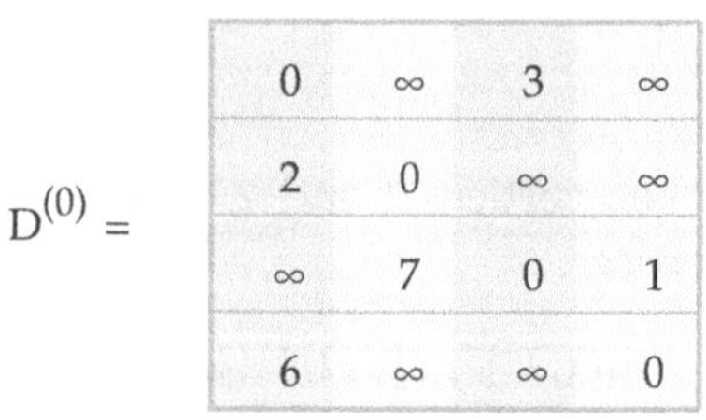

0	∞	3	∞
2	0	∞	∞
∞	7	0	1
6	∞	∞	0

For i = j We will assign 0 to Matrix [i] [j]

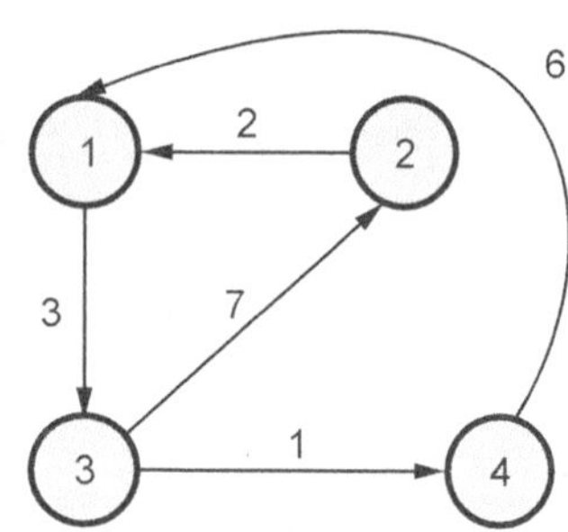

We will apply formula,

$$D^{(k)}[i,j] = \min\left\{D^{(k-1)}[i,j], D^{(k-1)}[i,k] + D^{(k-1)}[k,j]\right\}$$

k = 1, i = 0, j = 0

$$D[0,0] = \min\left\{D^0[0,0], D^0[0,1] + D^0[1,0]\right\}$$

$$= \min\{0, \infty + 2\}$$

$$D^1[0,0] = 0$$

k = 1, i = 0, j = 1

$$D^1[0, 1] = \min\left\{D^1[0,1], D^0[0,1]+D^0[1,1]\right\}$$

$$= \min\{\infty, \infty+0\}$$

$$D^1[0, 1] = \infty$$

In this way all the computations are carried out. The values of $D^{(1)}$, $D^{(2)}$, ... are

$D^{(1)} =$

0	∞	3	∞
2	0	5	∞
∞	7	0	1
6	∞	9	0

$D^{(2)} =$

0	∞	3	∞
2	0	5	∞
9	7	0	1
6	∞	9	0

$D^{(3)} =$

0	10	3	4
2	0	5	6
9	7	0	1
6	16	9	0

$D^{(4)} =$

0	10	3	4
2	0	5	6
7	7	0	1
6	16	9	0

'C' Program

```
/*******************************************************************
This program is for computing shortest path using
Floyd's Algorithm
*******************************************************************/
#include<stdio.h>
#include<conio.h>
void main()
{
 int wt[10][10],n,i,j;
 void Floyd_shortest_path(int matrix[10][10],int n);
 clrscr();
 printf("\n create a graph using adjacency matrix");
 printf("\n\n How many vertices are there ?");
 scanf("%d",&n);
 printf("\n Enter the elements");
 printf("[Enter 999 as infinity value]");
```

```
for(i=1;i<=n;i++)
{
        for(j=1;j<=n;j++)
        {
         printf("\nwt[%d][%d]",i,j);
         scanf("%d",&wt[i][j]);
        }
    }
printf("\n\t Computing All pair shortest path ...\n");
Floyd_shortest_path(wt,n);
getch();
}
void Floyd_shortest_path(int wt[10][10],int n)
{
 int D[5][10][10],i,j,k;
 int min(int,int);
 for(i=1;i<=n;i++)
 {
        for(j=1;j<=n;j++)
        {
         D[0][i][j]=wt[i][j];//computing D(0)
        }
    }
 for(k=1;k<=n;k++)
 {
        for(i=1;i<=n;i++)
        {
         for(j=1;j<=n;j++)
         {
             D[k][i][j]= min(D[k-1][i][j],(D[k-1][i][k]+D[k-1][k][j]));
        }
 }
}
/*
printing D(k)
*/
for(k=0;k<=n;k++)
```

```
{
        printf(" R(%d)=\n",k);
        for(i=1;i<=n;i++)

        {
        for(j=1;j<=n;j++)
        {
         printf("%d",D[k][i][j]);
        }
        printf("\n");
 }
}
}
int min(int a,int b)
{
if(a<b)
 return a;
else
 return b;
}
```

Output

```
create a graph using adjacency matrix

How many vertices are there? 3

Enter the elements[Enter 999 as infinity value]
wt[1][1] 0

wt[1][2] 8

wt[1][3] 5

wt[2][1] 2

wt[2][2] 0

wt[2][3] 999

wt[3][1] 999

wt[3][2] 1
```

The input graph is

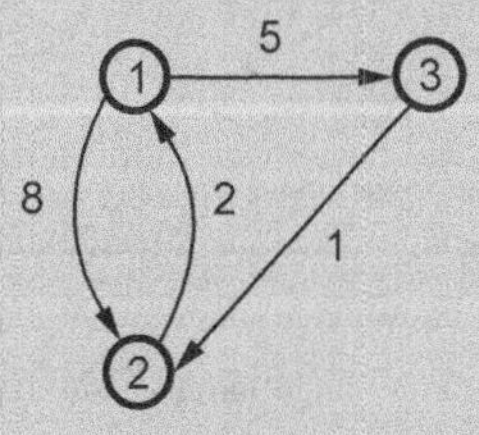

```
wt[3][3] 0

  Computing All pair shortest path ...
D(0) =
 0          8          5
 2          0          999
 999        1          0
D(1) =
       0       8   5
       2       0   7
       999     1   0
D(2) =
         0     8   5
         2     0   7
         3     1   0
D(3) =
         0     6   5
         2     0   7
         3     1   0
```

Examples for Practice

Example 4.7.4 *Find the shortest path between all pairs of nodes in the following graph. (Refer Fig. 4.7.2)*

Example 4.7.5 *Find the shortest path using Floyd Warshall algorithm. (Refer Fig. 4.7.3)*

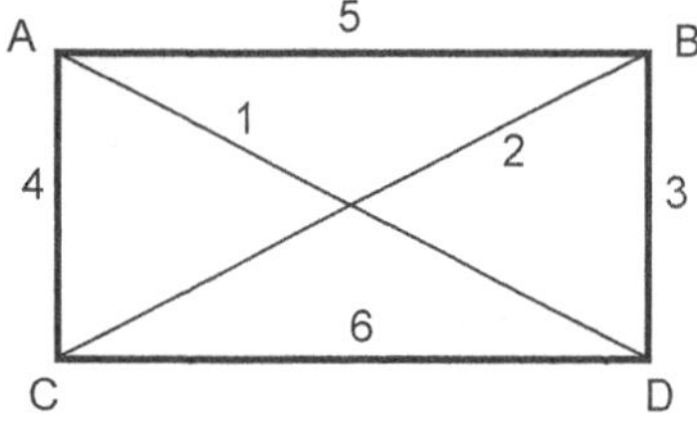

Fig. 4.7.2

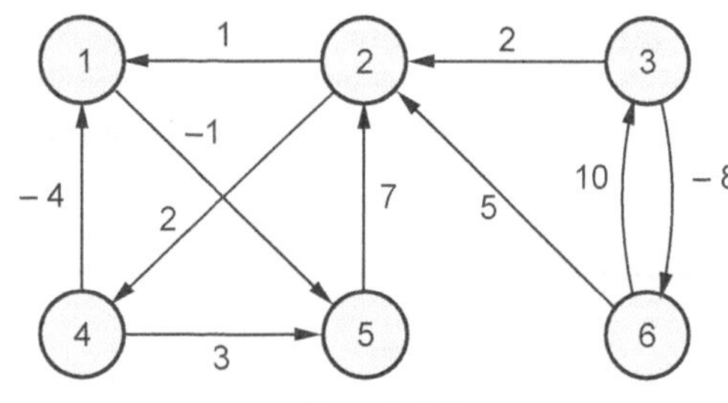

Fig. 4.7.3

4.8 Matrix Chain Multiplication

GTU : June-11,12, Dec.-11, Summer-15, Winter-14,15, Marks 8

- **Input :** n matrices A_1, A_2,..., A_n of dimensions $P_1 \times P_2$, $P_2 \times P_3$, ... , $P_n \times P_{n+1}$, respectively.
- **Goal :** To compute the matrix product $A_1A_2...A_n$

- **Problem :** In what order should $A_1A_2...A_n$ be multiplied so that it would take the minimum number of computations to derive the product.

For performing Matrix multiplication the cost is :

Let A and B be two matrices of dimensions $p \times q$ and $q \times r$.

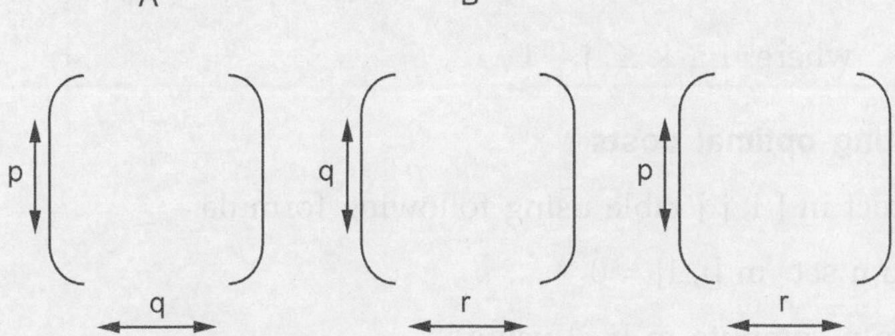

Then $C = AB \cdot C$ is of dimensions $p \times r$.

Thus C_{ij} takes n scalar multiplications and (n – 1) scalar additions.

Consider an example of the best way of multiplying 3 matrices:

Let A_1 of dimensions 5×4, A_2 of dimensions 4×6, and A_3 of dimensions 6×2.

$(A_1A_2)A_3$ takes $(5 \times 4 \times 6) + (5 \times 6 \times 2) = 180$

$A_1(A_2A_3)$ takes $(5 \times 4 \times 2) + (4 \times 6 \times 2) = 88$

Thus, $A_1(A_2A_3)$ is much cheaper to compute than $(A_1A_2)A_3$, although both lead to the same final answer. Hence optimal cost is 88.

To solve this problem using dynamic programming method we will perform following steps.

Step 1 : Decide the structure of optimal parenthsization

In this step we have to find the optimal substructure. This substructure is used to construct an optimal solution to the problem. Suppose that there is a production sequence of matrix $A_i\ A_{i+1}\ ...\ A_j$ such that i < j. Then in optimal parenthsization we have to split this sequence into $A_1\ ....\ A_k$ and $A_{k+1}\ ...\ A_j$. The cost of parenthsization is obtained so that total computing cost can be decided. Here k is some integer value ranging from $i \le k < j$. Hence **optimal substructure problem** can be described as follow - " Consider that there is sequence $A_i\ A_{i+1}\ ...\ A_j$ which can be split into two products A_k and A_{k+1}. Then the parenthsization should produce subchain $A_i\ A_{i+1}....\ A_k$which is 1 of optimal cost. Thus optimal substructure is important for producing optimal solution. This suggests **bottom up** approach for computing optimal cost.

Step 2 : A recursive solution

For each i , which is within a range of 1 to n and for each j which is within a range of 1 to n the optimal cost m [i, j] is computed using following formula :

For all i, $1 \leq i \leq n$, m [i, i] = 0

and for all i and j such that

$1 \leq i < j \leq n$

$$m[i, j] = \min \{ m[i, k] + m[k+1, j] + P_{i-1} P_k P_j \}$$

where $i \leq k \leq j - 1$

Step 3 : Computing optimal costs

We will construct m [i, j] table using following formula -

i) For i = 1 to n set m [i, i] = 0

ii) For $l \leftarrow 2$ to n compute m [i, j] using

$$m[i, j] = \min \{ m[i,k] + m[k+1, j] + P_{i-1} P_k P_j \}$$

with $i \leq k \leq j - 1$

Let us understand the procedure of computing optimal cost with some example -

Example 4.8.1 *Consider*

Matrix	Dimension
A_1	5×4
A_2	4×6
A_3	6×2
A_4	2×7

Compute matrix chain order. **GTU : Winter-2015, Marks 7**

Solution : Here $P_0 = 5$, $P_1 = 4$, $P_2 = 6$, $P_3 = 2$, $P_4 = 7$

For all i, $1 \leq i \leq n$

$$m[i, i] = 0$$

Hence m [1, 1] = 0

m [2, 2] = 0

m [3, 3] = 0

m [4, 4] = 0

Hence

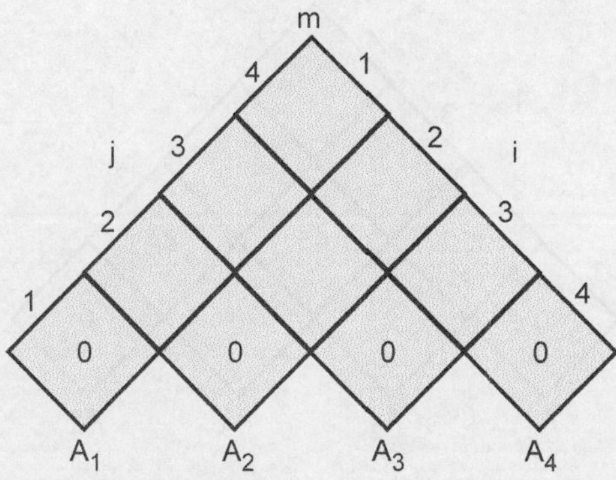

Now we will fill up the table horizontally from left to right, assuming $i \le k \le j - 1$

Let i = 1, j = 2, k = 1

$\therefore \quad m[1, 2] = m[i, k] + m[k+1, j] + P_{i-1} P_k P_j$

$= m[1,1] + m[2, 2] + P_0 P_1 P_2$

$= 0 + 0 + 5 \times 4 \times 6$

m [1, 2] = 120

Let, i = 2, j = 3, k =2.

$\therefore \quad m[2, 3] = m[i, k] + m[k + 1, j] + P_{i-1} P_k P_j$

$= m[2, 2] + m[3, 3] P_1 P_2 P_3$

$= 0 + 0 + 4 \times 6 \times 2$

m [2, 3] = 48

Let , i = 3, j = 4, k = 3

$m[3, 4] = m[i, k] + m[k+1, j] + P_{i-1} P_k P_j$

$= m[3, 3] + m[4, 4] + P_2 P_3 P_4$

$= 0 + 0 + 6 \times 2 \times 7$

m [3, 4] = 84

The table will be partially

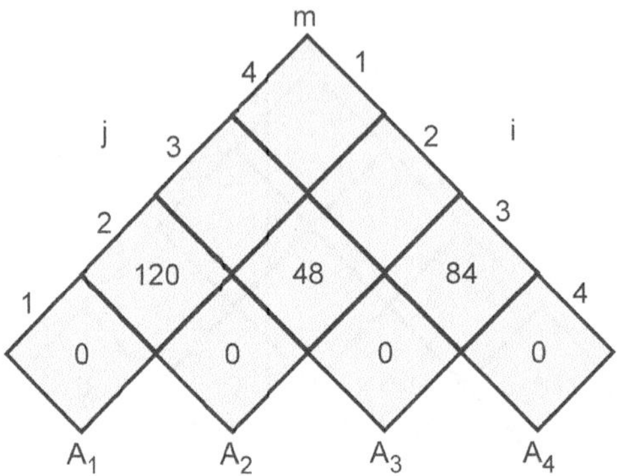

Let i = 1 , j = 3 k = 1 or k = 2

$$m[1,3] = \min \begin{cases} (m[1,1]+m[2,3]+P_0\ P_1\ P_3) & \rightarrow\ k=1 \\ (m[1,2]+m[3,3]+P_0\ P_2\ P_3) & \rightarrow\ k=2 \end{cases}$$

$$= \min \begin{cases} (0+48+5\times 4\times 2) \\ (120+0+5\times 6\times 2) \end{cases}$$

$$= \min \begin{cases} 48+40=88 & \textbf{when } \mathbf{k=1} \\ 120+60=180 \end{cases}$$

$$m[1,3] = 88$$

Let i = 2 , j = 4, k = 2, or k = 3

$$m[2,4] = \min \begin{Bmatrix} (m[2,2]+m[3,4]+P_1\ P_2\ P_4 & \rightarrow & k=2 \\ (m[2,3]+m[4,4]+P_1\ P_3\ P_4 & \rightarrow & k=3 \end{Bmatrix}$$

$$= \min \begin{Bmatrix} 0+84+4\times 6\times 7 \\ 48+0+4\times 2\times 7 \end{Bmatrix}$$

$$\min[2,4] = \min \begin{Bmatrix} 84+168 \\ 48+56 \end{Bmatrix}$$

$$= \min \begin{cases} 252 \\ 104 & \rightarrow \textbf{when } \mathbf{k=3} \end{cases}$$

$$\min[2,4] = 104$$

The table can be partially shown as :

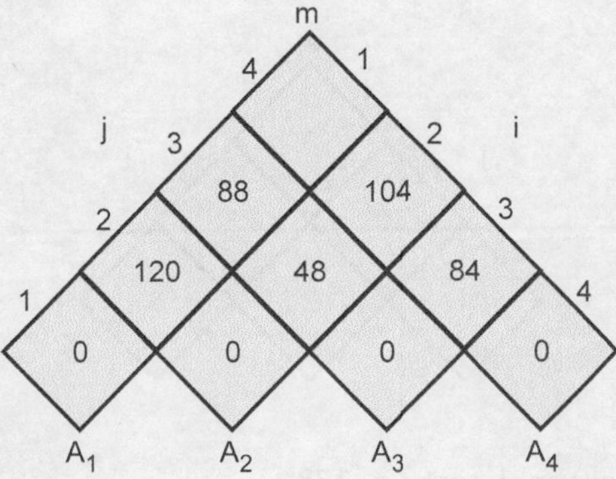

Now, Let i = 1, j = 4 then k = 1 or 2 or 3

$$m[1,4] = \min \begin{cases} m[1,1] + m[2,4] + P_0\,P_1\,P_4 & \rightarrow\ k = 1 \\ m[1,2] + m[3,4] + P_0\,P_2\,P_4 & \rightarrow\ k = 2 \\ m[1,3] + m[4,4] + P_0\,P_3\,P_4 & \rightarrow\ k = 3 \end{cases}$$

$$= \min \begin{cases} 0 + 104 + 5 \times 4 \times 7 \\ 120 + 84 + 5 \times 6 \times 7 \\ 88 + 0 + 5 \times 2 \times 7 \end{cases}$$

$$= \min \begin{cases} 244 \\ 414 \\ 158 & \rightarrow \textbf{when } k = 3 \end{cases}$$

Hence the matrix table will be -

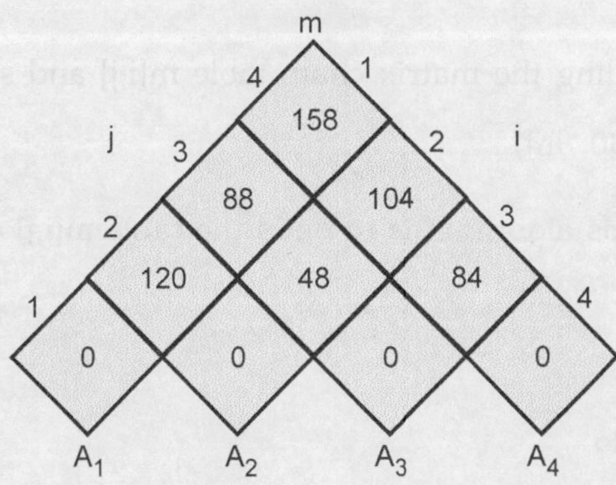

We will build the s table using s [i, j] = k

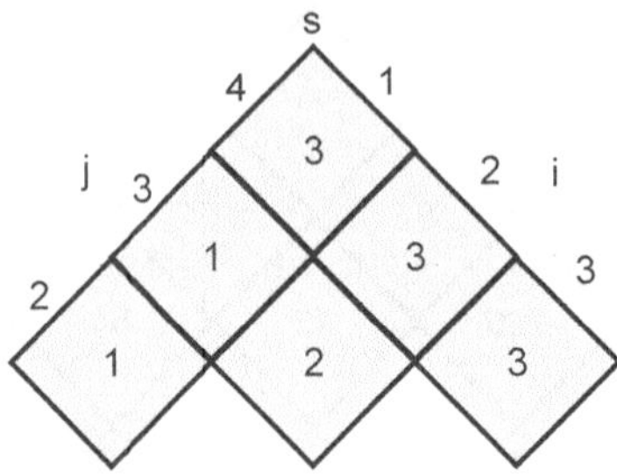

m [1, 4] determines the optimal cost i.e. **158**

Step 4 : Printing optimal parenthesization

The sequence of optimal parenthesization which gives the optimum cost is obtained using following algorithm.

```
Algorithm display_matrix_order ( s, i, j )
// Problem Description : This algorithm prints
// the optimal parenthsization of matrix
if ( i = j ) then
      print ( " A "_i )
else
{ print " ( "
      display_matrix_order ( s, i, s [ i, j ] )
      display_matrix_order ( s, s [ i, j ] + 1 , j )
      print " ) "
} // end of else
} // end of algorithm
```

Using above algorithm we get the matrix chain order as (A_1 (A_2 A_3)) A_4

4.8.1 Algorithm

The algorithm for building the matrix chain table m[i,j] and s[i,j] is as follows -

```
Algorithm Matrix_chain(p[0...n])
{
//Problem Description: This algorithm is to build the table m[i,j] and s[i,j]
 for (i ← 1 to n) do
   m[i,i] ← 0
for(len ← 2 to n) do
{
 for (i←2 to (n – len+1) ) do
 {
   j ← i+len – 1
```

```
    m[i,j]=infinity
    for (k ← i to j – 1) do
    {
     q ← m [i,k] +m[k+1,j]+p[i–1]*p[k]*p[j]
      if (q<m[i,j]) then
      {
        m[i,j]← q
        s[i,j] ← k
      }//end of if
    }//end of k's for loop
  }//end of i's for loop
 }//end of len's for loop
 return m[1,n]
}//end of algorithm
```

Computing **m[i, j]** and **s[i,j]**

Analysis

The basic operation in this algorithm is computation of m[i,j] and s[i,j] which is within three nested for loops. Hence the time complexity of the above algorithm is Θ **(n^3)**.

Example 4.8.2 *Consider the chain of matrices A1, A2, ... A6 with the dimensions given below. Give the optimal parenthsization to get the product A2 ... A5.* **GTU : June-11, Marks 7**

Matrix	Dimension
A1	30 × 35
A2	35 × 15
A3	15 × 5
A4	5 × 10
A5	10 × 20
A6	20 × 25

Solution : We will compute matrix chain order.

Here $P_0 = 30$, $P_1 = 35$, $P_2 = 15$, $P_3 = 5$, $P_4 = 10$, $P_5 = 20$, $P_6 = 25$

For all $1 \le i \le n$

$$m[i, i] = 0 \quad \therefore m[1, 1] = m[2, 2] = m[3, 3] = m[4, 4] = m[5, 5] = m[6, 6] = 0$$

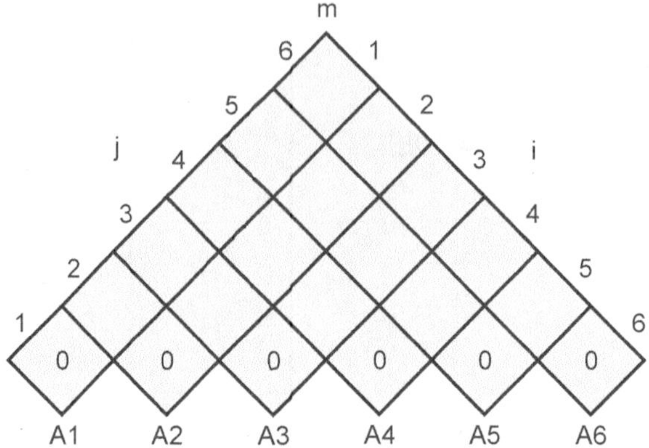

Now, we will fill up the table horizontally from left to right, assuming $i \le k \le j - 1$

Let i = 1, j = 2, k = 1

$$\therefore \quad m[1, 2] = m[i, k] + m[k+1, j] + P_{i-1} P_k P_j$$

$$= m[1, 1] + m[2,2] + P_0 P_1 P_2$$

$$= 0 + 0 + 30 * 35 * 15$$

$$= 15750. \quad \textbf{with k = 2}$$

Similarly

$$m[2, 3] = m[2, 2] + m[3, 3] + P_1 P_2 P_3$$

$$= 0 + 0 + 35 * 15 * 5$$

$$\mathbf{m[2, 3] = 2625 \quad with\ k = 2}$$

$$m[3, 4] = m[3, 3] + m[4, 4] + P_2 P_3 P_4$$

$$= 0 + 15 * 5 * 10$$

$$\mathbf{m[3, 4] = 750 \quad with\ k = 3}$$

$$m[4, 5] = m[4, 4] + m[5, 5] + P_3 P_4 P_5$$

$$\mathbf{m[4, 5] = 1000 \quad with\ k = 4}$$

$$m[5, 6] = m[5, 5] + m[6, 6] + P_4 P_5 P_6$$

$$\mathbf{m[5, 6] = 5000 \quad with\ k = 5}$$

The table will be.

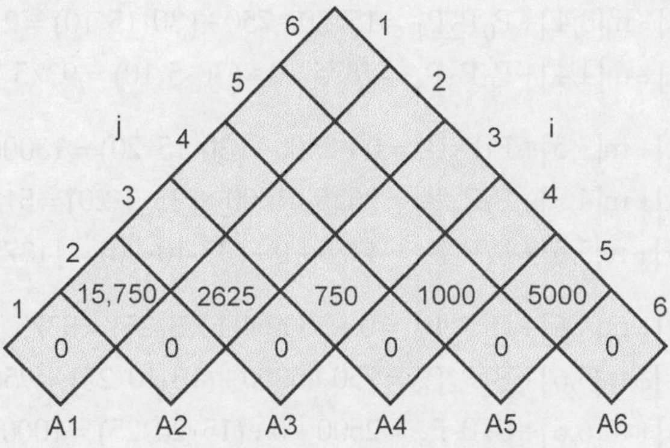

Now

i = 1, j = 3 k = 1 or 2.

$$m[1, 3] = \min \begin{cases} m[1, 1] + m[2, 3] + P_0 P_1 P_2 = 0 + 2625 + (30 \cdot 35 \cdot 5) = 7875 \\ m[1, 2] + m[3, 3] + P_0 P_2 P_3 = 15750 + 0 + (30 \cdot 15 \cdot 5) = 18000 \end{cases}$$

m[1, 3] = 7875 with k = 1

$$m[2, 4] = \min \begin{cases} m[2, 2] + m[3, 4] + P_1 P_2 P_4 = 0 + 750 + (35 \cdot 15 \cdot 10) = 6000 \\ m[2, 3] + m[4, 4] + P_1 P_3 P_4 = 2625 + 0 + (35 \cdot 5 \cdot 10) = 4375 \end{cases}$$

m[2, 4] = 4375 with k = 3

$$m[3, 5] = \min \begin{cases} m[3, 3] + m[4, 5] + P_2 P_3 P_5 = 0 + 1000 + (15 \cdot 5 \cdot 20) = 2500 & \textbf{min = 2500} \\ m[3, 4] + m[5, 5] + P_2 P_4 P_5 = 750 + 0 + (15 \cdot 10 \cdot 20) = 3750 & \textbf{k = 3} \end{cases}$$

$$m[4, 6] = \min \begin{cases} m[4, 4] + m[5, 6] + P_3 P_4 P_6 = 0 + 5000 + (5 \cdot 10 \cdot 25) = 6250 & \textbf{min = 3500} \\ m[4, 5] + m[6, 6] + P_3 P_5 P_6 = 1000 + 0 + (5 \cdot 20 \cdot 25) = 3500 & \textbf{k = 5} \end{cases}$$

The table will then be -

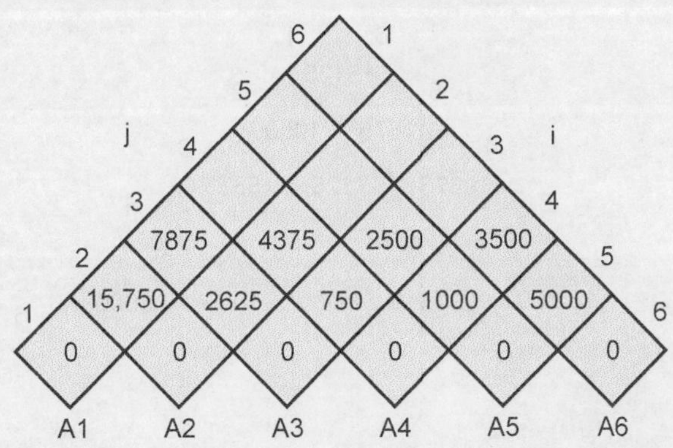

$$m[1,4] = \min\begin{cases} m[1,1]+m[2,4]+P_0P_1P_4 = 0+4375+(30\cdot 35\cdot 10) = 14875 \\ m[1,2]+m[3,4]+P_0P_2P_4 = 15750+750+(30\cdot 15\cdot 10) = 21000 & \textbf{min} = \textbf{9375} \\ m[1,3]+m[4,4]+P_0P_3P_4 = 7875+0+(30\cdot 5\cdot 10) = 9375 & \textbf{k} = \textbf{3} \end{cases}$$

$$m[2,5] = \min\begin{cases} m[2,2]+m[3,5]+P_1P_2P_5 = 0+2500+(30\cdot 15\cdot 20) = 13000 \\ m[2,3]+m[4,5]+P_1P_3P_5 = 2625+1000+(35\cdot 5\cdot 20) = 5125 & \textbf{min} = \textbf{7125} \\ m[2,4]+m[5,5]+P_1P_4P_5 = 4375+0+(35\cdot 10\cdot 20) = 11375 & \textbf{k} = \textbf{3} \end{cases}$$

$$m[3,6] = \min\begin{cases} m[3,3]+m[4,6]+P_2P_3P_6 = 0+3500+(15\cdot 5\cdot 25) = 5375 \\ m[3,4]+m[5,6]+P_2P_4P_6 = 750+5000+(15\cdot 10\cdot 25) = 9500 & \textbf{min} = \textbf{5375} \\ m[3,5]+m[6,6]+P_2P_5P_6 = 2500+0+(15\cdot 20\cdot 25) = 10000 & \textbf{k} = \textbf{3} \end{cases}$$

$$m[1,5] = \min\begin{cases} m[1,1]+m[2,5]+P_0P_1P_5 = 0+7125+(30\cdot 35\cdot 20) = 25125 \\ m[1,2]+m[3,5]+P_0P_2P_5 = 15750+2500+(30\cdot 15\cdot 20) = 27250 & \textbf{min} = \textbf{11875} \\ m[1,3]+m[4,5]+P_0P_3P_5 = 7875+1000+(30\cdot 5\cdot 20) = 11875 & \textbf{k} = \textbf{3} \\ m[1,4]+m[5,5]+P_0P_4P_5 = 9375+0+(30\cdot 10\cdot 20) = 15375 \end{cases}$$

$$m[2,6] = \min\begin{cases} m[2,2]+m[3,6]+P_1P_2P_6 = 0+9375+(35\cdot 15\cdot 25) = 22500 \\ m[2,3]+m[4,6]+P_1P_3P_6 = 2625+3500+(35\cdot 5\cdot 25) = 10500 & \textbf{min} = \textbf{10500} \\ m[2,4]+m[5,6]+P_1P_4P_6 = 4375+5000+(35\cdot 10\cdot 25) = 18125 & \textbf{k} = \textbf{3} \\ m[2,5]+m[6,6]+P_1P_5P_6 = 7125+0+(35\cdot 20\cdot 25) = 24625 \end{cases}$$

$$m[1,6] = \min\begin{cases} m[1,1]+m[2,6]+P_0P_1P_6 = 0+10500+(30\cdot 35\cdot 25) = 36750 \\ m[1,2]+m[3,6]+P_0P_2P_6 = 15750+9375+(30\cdot 15\cdot 25) = 36375 & \textbf{min} = \textbf{15125} \\ m[1,3]+m[4,6]+P_0P_3P_6 = 7875+3500+(30\cdot 5\cdot 25) = 15125 & \textbf{k} = \textbf{3} \\ m[1,4]+m[5,6]+P_0P_4P_6 = 9375+5000+(30\cdot 10\cdot 25) = 21875 \\ m[1,5]+m[6,6]+P_0P_5P_6 = 11875+0+(30\cdot 20\cdot 25) = 26875 \end{cases}$$

The table will then be -

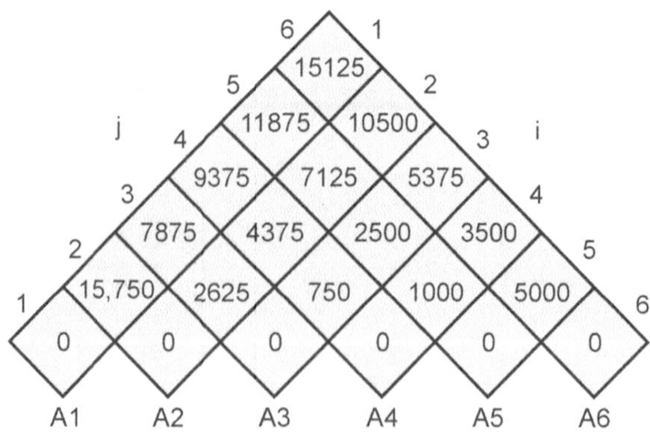

The table s [i, j] for k will be

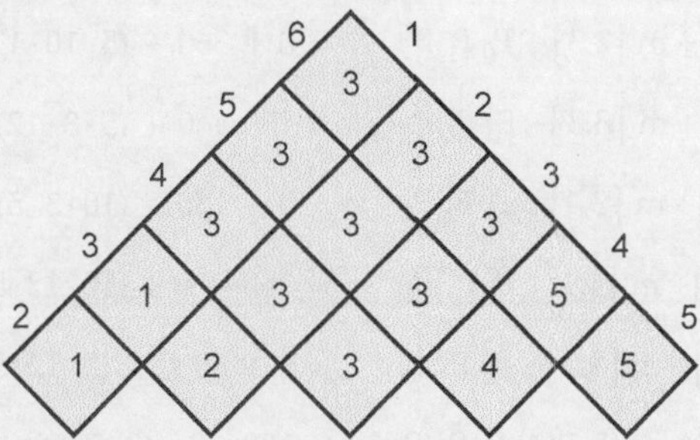

The matrix chain order will be

$((A_1(A_2A_3))\ ((A_4A_5)A_6))$

Example 4.8.3 *Using algorithm find an optimal parenthsization of matrix chain product whose sequence of dimension is (5, 10, 3, 12, 5, 50, 6) (use dynamic programming).*

GTU : Dec.-11, Marks 7

Solution : We will compute matrix chain order.

Here $P_0 = 5, P_1 = 10, P_2 = 3, P_3 = 12, P_4 = 5, P_5 = 50, P_6 = 6$.

Our first step is to set m[i, i] = 0. for $1 \le i \le 5$

Hence m[1, 1] = m [2, 2] = m [3, 3] = m [4, 4] = 0.

Now

$$m[1, 2] = P_0 * P_1 * P_2 = 5 * 10 * 3 = 150$$

$$m[2, 3] = P_1 * P_2 * P_3 = 10 * 3 * 12 = 360$$

$$m[3, 4] = P_2 * P_3 * P_4 = 3 * 12 * 5 = 180$$

$$m[4, 5] = P_3 * P_4 * P_5 = 12 * 5 * 50 = 3000$$

$$m[5, 6] = P_4 * P_5 * P_6 = 5 * 50 * 6 = 1500$$

The table will then be

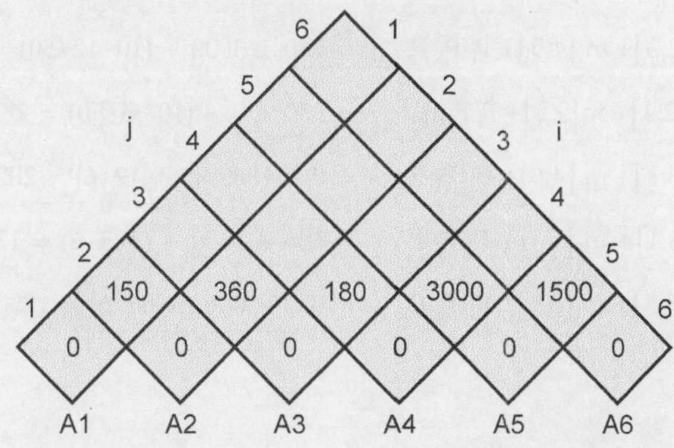

Now we will fill up the table for the values m[1, 3], m[2, 4], m[3, 5] and m[4, 6].

m[1, 3] = **min**	m [1,1]+ m [2,3]+ $P_0 P_1 P_3$	= 0 + 360 + (5 · 10 · 12) = 960	min = 330 with k = 2
	m [1,2]+ m [3,3]+ $P_0 P_2 P_3$	= 150 + 0 + (5 · 3 · 12) = 330	
m[2, 4] = **min**	m [2,2]+ m [3,4]+ $P_1 P_2 P_4$	= 0 + 180 + (10 · 3 · 5) = 330	min = 330 k = 2
	m [2,3]+ m [4,4]+ $P_1 P_3 P_4$	= 360 + 0 + (10 · 12 · 50) = 6360	
m[3,5] = **min**	m [3,3]+ m [4,5]+ $P_2 P_3 P_5$	= 0 + 3000 + (3 · 12 · 50) = 4800	min = 930 k = 4
	m [3,4]+ m [5,5]+ $P_2 P_4 P_5$	= 180+ 0+ (3 · 5 · 50) = 930	
m[4, 6] = **min**	m [4,4]+ m [5,6]+ $P_3 P_4 P_6$	= 0 + 1500 + (12 · 5 · 6) = 1860	min = 1860 k = 4
	m [4,5]+ m [6,6]+ $P_3 P_5 P_6$	= 3000 + 0 + (12 · 50 · 6) = 6600	

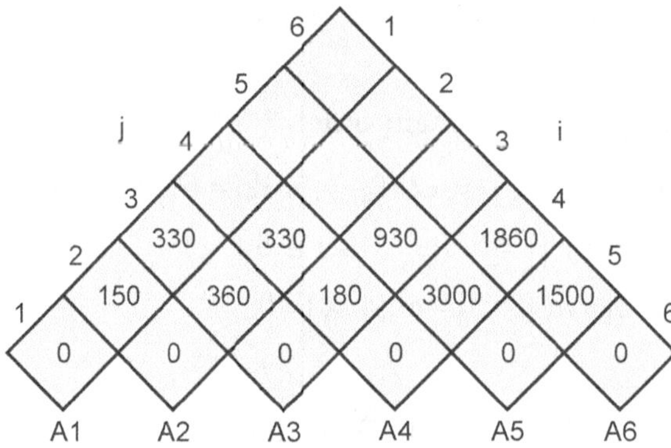

Now we will compute m[1, 4], m[2, 5] and m[3, 6]

	m [1,1]+ m [2,4]+ $P_0 P_1 P_4$	= 0 + 330 + (5 · 10 · 5) = 580	min = 405 k = 2
m[1, 4] = **min**	m [1,2]+ m [3,4]+ $P_0 P_2 P_4$	= 150 + 180 + (5 · 3 · 5) = 405	
	m[1,3]+ m[4,4]+ $P_0 P_3 P_4$	= 330 + 0 + (5 · 12 · 5) = 630	
	m [2,2]+ m [3,5]+ $P_1 P_2 P_5$	= 0 + 930 + (10 · 3 · 50) = 2430	min = 2430 k = 2
m[2, 5] = **min**	m [2,3]+ m [4,5]+ $P_1 P_3 P_5$	= 360 + 3000 + (10 · 12 · 50)= 9360	
	m[2,4]+ m[5,5]+ $P_1 P_4 P_5$	= 330 + 0 + (10 · 5 · 50) = 2830	
	m [3,3]+ m [4,6]+ $P_2 P_3 P_6$	= 0 + 1860 + (3 · 12 · 6) = 2076	min = 1770 k = 4
m[3, 6] = **min**	m [3,4]+ m [5,6]+ $P_2 P_4 P_6$	= 180 + 1500 + (3 · 5 · 6) = 1770	
	m [3,5]+ m [6,6]+ $P_2 P_5 P_6$	= 930 + 0 + (3 · 50 · 6) = 1830	

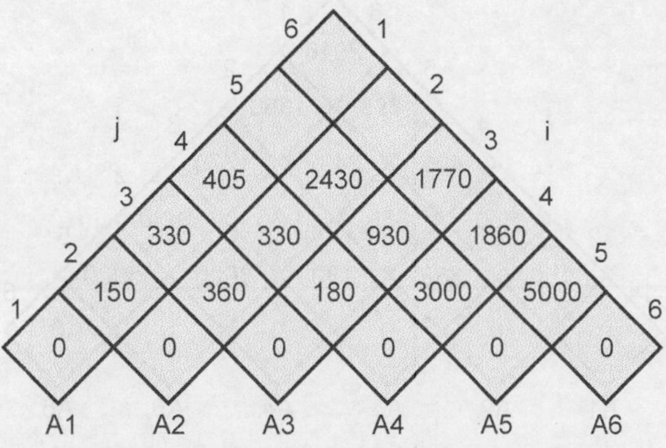

m[1, 5] = min	$m[1, 1] + m[2, 5] + P_0 P_1 P_5$	$= 0 + 2430 + (5 \cdot 10 \cdot 50) = 4930$	min = 1655 k = 4
	$m[1, 2] + m[3, 5] + P_0 P_2 P_5$	$= 150 + 930 + (5 \cdot 3 \cdot 50) = 1830$	
	$m[1, 3] + m[4, 5] + P_0 P_3 P_5$	$= 330 + 3000 + (5 \cdot 12 \cdot 50) = 6330$	
	$m[1, 4] + m[5, 5] + P_0 P_4 P_5$	$= 405 + 0 + (5 \cdot 5 \cdot 50) = 1655$	
m[2, 6] = min	$m[2, 2] + m[3, 6] + P_1 P_2 P_6$	$= 0 + 1770 + (10 \cdot 3 \cdot 6) = 1950$	min = 1950 k = 2
	$m[2, 3] + m[4, 6] + P_1 P_3 P_6$	$= 360 + 1860 + (10 \cdot 12 \cdot 6) = 2940$	
	$m[2, 4] + m[5, 6] + P_1 P_4 P_6$	$= 330 + 1500 + (10 \cdot 5 \cdot 6) = 2130$	
	$m[2, 5] + m[6, 6] + P_1 P_5 P_6$	$= 2430 + 0 + (10 \cdot 50 \cdot 6) = 5430$	

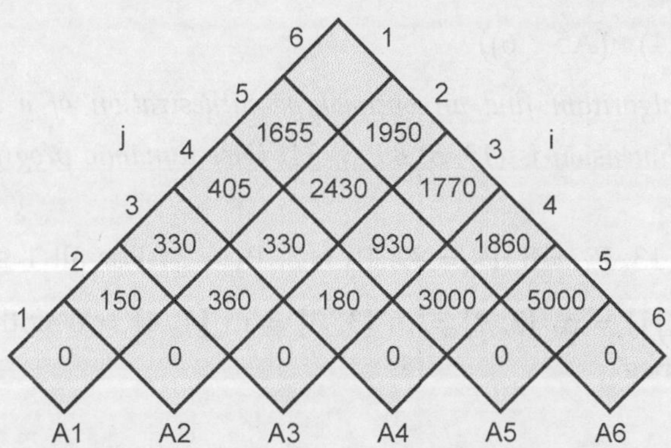

m[1,6] = min	$m[1, 1] + m[2, 6] + P_0 P_1 P_6$	$= 0 + 1950 + (5 \cdot 10 \cdot 6) = 2250$	min = 2010 k = 2
	$m[1, 2] + m[3, 6] + P_0 P_2 P_6$	$= 150 + 1770 + (5 \cdot 3 \cdot 6) = 2010$	
	$m[1, 3] + m[4, 6] + P_0 P_3 P_6$	$= 330 + 1860 + (5 \cdot 12 \cdot 6) = 2550$	
	$m[1, 4] + m[5, 6] + P_0 P_4 P_6$	$= 405 + 1500 + (5 \cdot 5 \cdot 6) = 2055$	
	$m[1, 5] + m[6, 6] + P_0 P_5 P_6$	$= 1655 + 0 + (5 \cdot 50 \cdot 6) = 3155$	

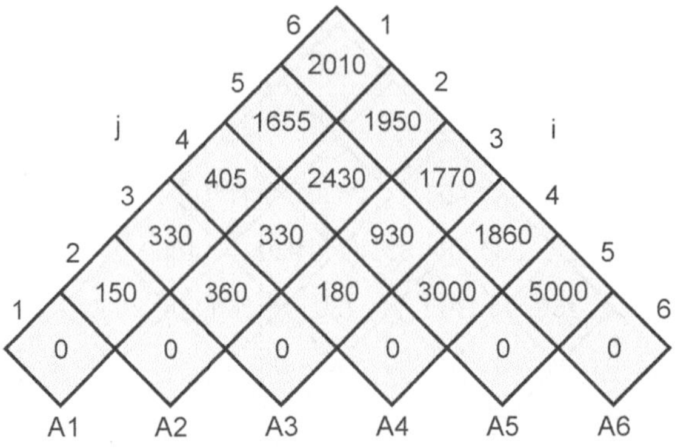

The s [i, j] table for the values of k will be

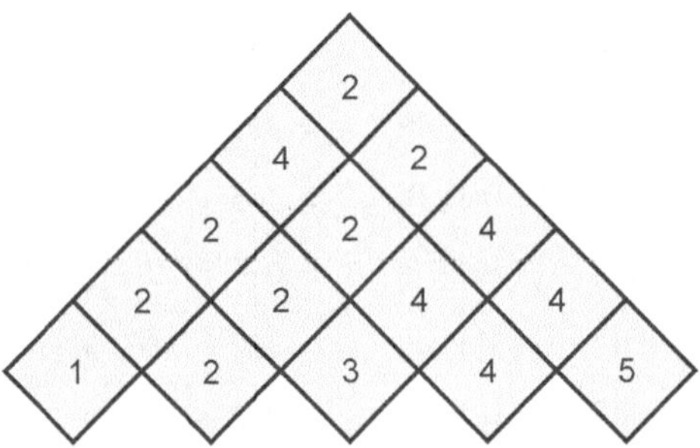

The optimal parenthesization will be

(A1 $*$ A2)$*$((A3 $*$ A4) $*$(A5 $*$ 6))

Example 4.8.4 *Using algorithm find an optimal parenthesization of a matrix chain product whose sequence of dimension is (13, 5, 89, 3, 34) (Use dynamic programming) .*

GTU : Winter-14, Marks 7,CSE

Solution : Here $P_0 = 13$, $P_1 = 5$, $P_2 = 89$, $P_3 = 3$, $P_4 = 34$ For all $1 \le i \le n$

m [i, i] = 0 $\therefore$ m [1, 1] = m [2, 2] = m [3, 3] = m [4, 4] = 0 with value of k = 1, 2, 3 and 4 respectively Hence

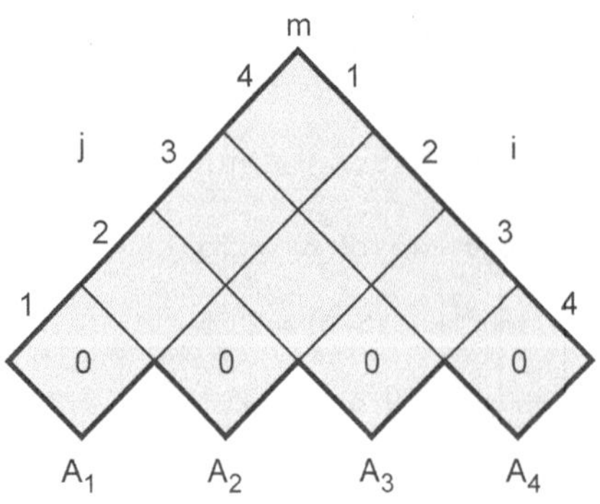

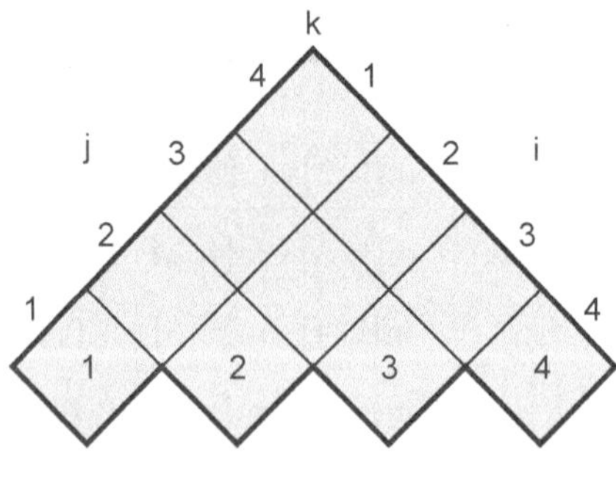

m[1, 2] = $P_0*P_1*P_2$ = 13 * 5 * 89 = 5785 with k = 1

m[2, 3] = $P_1*P_2*P_3$ = 5 * 89 * 3 = 1335 with k = 2

m[3, 4] = $P_2*P_3*P_4$ = 89 * 3 * 34 = 9078 with k = 3

The table will be partially filled up as -

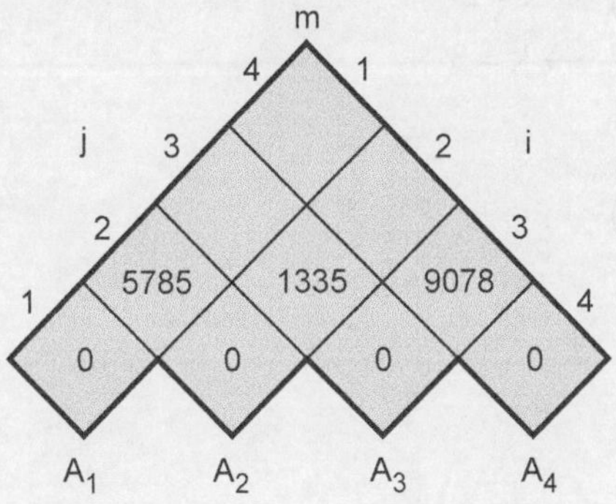

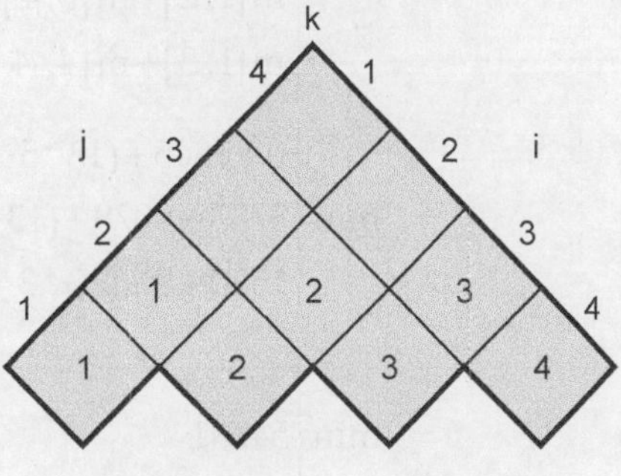

Now we will compute m[1, 3], m[2, 4]

m[1,3] Here value of k = 1 or k = 2	$\min\left\{m[i,k]+m[k+1,j]+P_{i-1}+P_kP_j\right\}$ where $i \le k \le j-1$	0 + 1335+(13 * 5 * 3) = 1530	∴ [1, 3] = 1530 with k = 1
	$m[1,1]+m[2,3]+P_0*P_1*P_3$		
	$m[1,2]+m[3,3]+P_0*P_2*P_3$	5785 + 0 + (13 * 89 *3) = 9256	
		$\therefore \min\{1530, 9256\}$ = 1530	
m[2, 4] Here value of k = 2 or k = 3	$m[2,2]+m[3,4]+P_1\,P_2\,P_4$	0+9078+(5*89*34) = 24208	∴ m [2, 4] = 1845 with k = 3
	$m[2,3]+m[4,4]+P_1\,P_3\,P_4$	1335 + 0 + (5*3*34) = 1845	

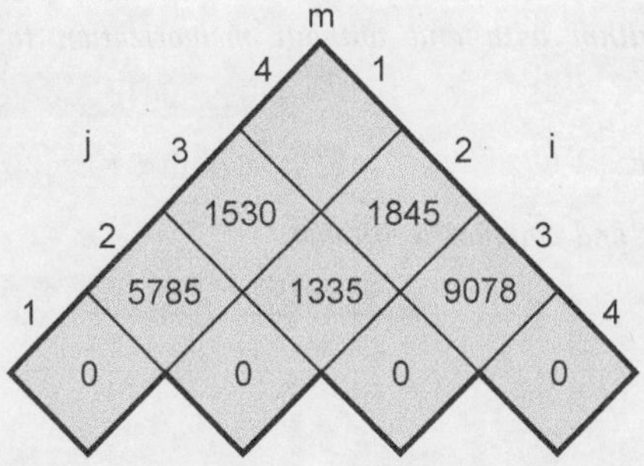

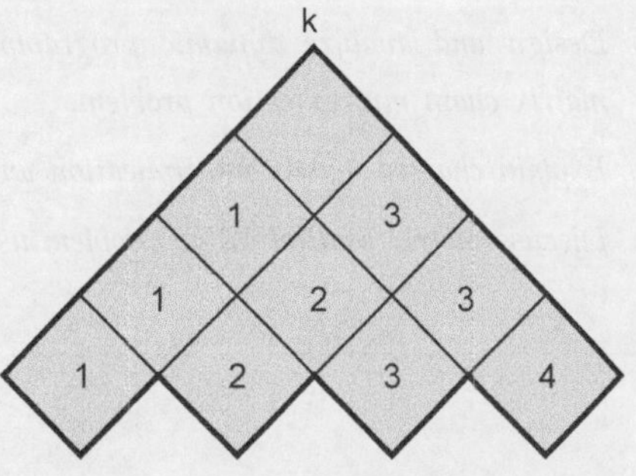

Now we will compute m [1, 4]

i = 1, j = 4 then k = 1, 2 or 3.

$$\therefore \quad m[1,4] = \min \begin{cases} m[i,k] + m[k+1, j] + P_{i-1}P_kP_j \\ m[1,1] + m[2,4] + P_0P_1P_4 \to k = 1 \\ m[1,2] + m[3,4] + P_0P_2P_4 \to k = 2 \\ m[1,3] + m[4, 4] + P_0P_3P_4 \to k = 3 \end{cases}$$

$$= \min \begin{cases} 0 + 1845 + (13 * 5 * 34) \\ 5785 + 9078 + (13 * 89 * 34) \\ 1530 + 0 + (13 * 3 * 34) \end{cases}$$

$$= \min \begin{cases} 4055 \\ 54201 \\ 2856 \end{cases}$$

$$m[1,4] = 2856 \text{ with } k = 3$$

Hence m-table and k table will be -

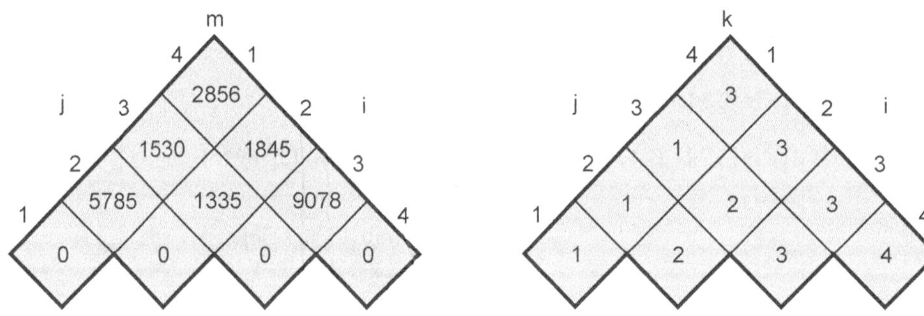

The matrix chain order will be $((A_1(A_2A_3))A_4)$.

Review Questions

1. *Design and analyze dynamic programming algorithm with and without memorization to solve matrix chain multiplication problem.* **GTU : June-11, Marks 8**
2. *Explain chained matrix multiplication with example.* **GTU : June-12, Marks 7**
3. *Discuss matrix multiplication problem using divide and conquer technique.* **GTU : Summer-15, Marks 7**

4.9 Longest Common Subsequence

GTU : Dec.-10,11, June-11, Summer-13,14, Winter-14,15, Marks 8

Let , B = < b_1, b_2 ...... b_n > and A = < a_1, a_2 ... a_m > be strings over an alphabet. Then B is a subsequence of A if B can be generated by striking out some elements from A .

For example

< x, z, y, x > is a subsequence of < x, **y** , x, **z**, **y**, z, y, **x**, z >

The **longest Common Subsequence** problem (LCS) is the problem of finding given two sequences A = < a_1, a_2 ... a_m > and B = < b_1, b_2, b_3, ... b_n > a maximum length common subsequence of A and B. Let us apply the steps of dynamic programming for obtaining Longest Common Subsequence (LCS)

Step 1 : Characterizing the longest common subsequence

If we apply the straightforward approach of obtaining common subsequence then for the sequence A = < a_1, a_2 ... a_m > and B = < b_1, b_2, ...b_n > , all the sequences of A has to be checked against all the subsequences of B. But this approach will not useful for long sequences. Hence to solve the problem of LCS we need to define **optimal substructure** of LCS. Let us discuss one theorem based on optimal substructure of LCS.

Theorem : Let, A = < a_1, a_2, ... a_m > and B = < b_1, b_2, ... b_n > then,

i) If a_m = b_n, then longest common subsequence of A_{m-1} and B_{n-1} can be constructed by appending a_m (= b_n)to LCS of A and B.

ii) If $a_m \neq b_n$ then it implies

a) LCS of A_{m-1} and B or

b) LCS of A and $B_{n-1.}$

Proof : Consider C = < c_1, c_2, c_3 ... c_k > be the LCS of A and B. Then if c_k = a_m then we could append a_m = b_n to C for getting the longest common subsequence. If necessary modify the production of C from either A or from B, so that its last element could be A_m or B_n. Then C becomes a common subsequence of string of A_{m-1} and B_{n-1}. Hence C with maximum length becomes the longest common subsequence.

If $c_k \neq a_m$, then for any LCS of C of A and B, generation of C cannot use both a_m and b_n. So C is either a_n LCS of A and B_{n-1} or it can be LCS of A_{m-1} and B.

Step 2 : A recursive definition

If a_m = b_n then we should find LCS of A_{m-1} and B_{n-1} otherwise, compare LCS of A and B_{n-1} and LCS of A_{m-1} and B. Then from these sequences pick up the longer sequence.

Let,

c [i, j] be the length of an LCS of A_i and B_j then we get a recursive definition :

$$c[i,j] = \begin{cases} 0 \text{ if } i=0 \text{ or } j=0 \\ c[i-1,j-1]+1 \text{ if } i,j>0 \text{ and } a_i = b_j \\ \max(c[i,j-1], c[i-1,j]) \text{ if } i,j>0 \text{ and } a_i \neq b_j. \end{cases}$$

From this definition we could build c [i, j] table and d-table in which directions are mentioned.

Step 3 : Computing length of an LCS

Let us construct an algorithm using which the LCS can be computed.

```
Algorithm compute_LCS ( A, B )
// Problem Description : This algorithm builds c [ i, j ] and d [ i , j ] table.
m ← length ( A )
n ← length ( B )
for ( i ← 1 to m ) do
      c [ i, 0 ] ← 0 }
for  ( j ← 0 to n ) do
      c [ 0, j ] ← 0          } making first column zero
for ( i ← 1 to m ) do
{
      for ( i ← 1 to n ) do   } making first row zero.
      {
      if ( a_i = b_i ) then
      {
      c [ i, j ] ← c [ i - 1, j - 1 ] + 1

            d [ i , j ] ← " ↖ " // Putting direction
      } else if ( c [ i - 1 , j ] ≥ c [ i, j - 1 ] then
      {
      c [ i, j ] ← c [ i - 1, j ]
      d [ i, j ] ← " ↑ "
      }
      else
      {
      c [ i, j ] ← c [ i, j - 1]
      d [ i, j ] ← " ← "
      }
}// end of inner for loop
}// end of outer for loop.
      return c and d
}
```

From the above algorithm let us solve some problem of computing longest common subsequence.

Example 4.9.1 *Given two sequences of characters*

A=< X, Y, Z, Y, T, X, Y > and

B=< Y, T, Z, X, Y, X >

obtain longest common subsequence. **GTU : Winter-14, Marks 7**

Solution : We have to obtain longest common subsequence. Arrange elements of A and B in the arrays as -

	1	2	3	4	5	6	7
A[i]	X	Y	Z	Y	T	X	Y
B [j]	Y	T	Z	X	Y	X	

Step 1 : We will build c [i, j] and d [i, j]. Initially c [i , 0] ← 0 where i represents row and c [0, j] ← 0 where j represents the column. Note that c table will store values and d table will store directions.

	0	1	2	3	4	5	6
0	0	0	0	0	0	0	0
1	0						
2	0						
3	0						
4	0						
5	0						
6	0						
7	0						

Then

for (i ← 1 to m) and

for (j ← 1 to n)

We go on filling up c [i, j] and d [i, j] horizontally

∴ Let i = 1, j = 1

	1	2	3	4	5	6	7
A[i]	X	Y	Z	Y	T	X	Y
B[j]	Y	T	Z	X	Y	X	

j →

		0	1	2	3	4	5	6
	0	0	0	0	0	0	0	0
	1	0	0 ↑					
	2	0						
	3	0						
i ↑	4	0						
	5	0						
	6	0						
	7	0						

As $A[i] \neq B[j]$

If ($c[0, 1] \geq c[1, 0]$) is true

$\therefore \quad 0 \geq 0$

$c[1,1] \leftarrow c[i-1, j]$

$\therefore \quad c[1,1] \leftarrow c[0,1]$

$\therefore \quad c[1,1] \leftarrow 0$

and $d[1, 1] \leftarrow \uparrow$

Step 2 :

Let $i = 1, j = 2$ then

	1	2	3	4	5	6	7
A [i]	X	Y	Z	Y	T	X	y
B [j]	Y	T	Z	X	Y	X	

As $A[i] \neq B[j]$

then if ($c[i-1, j] \geq c[i, j-1]$) $\rightarrow$ is true

$\therefore \quad c[0, 2] \geq c[1, 1]$

i.e. $0 \geq 0$

Hence $c[i, j] \leftarrow c[i-1, j]$

$d[i, j] \leftarrow$ " $\uparrow$ "

We get $c[1, 2] \leftarrow c[0, 2]$ i.e. 0

and d [i, j] ← " ↑ "

	0	1	2	3	4	5	6
0	0	0	0	0	0	0	0
1	0	↑ 0	↑ 0				
2	0						
3	0						
4	0						
5	0						
6	0						
7	0						

Continuing in this fashion we can fill up the table as follows -

	0	1	2	3	4	5	6
0	0	0	0	0	0	0	0
1	0	0 ↑	0 ↑	0 ↑	1 ↖	1 ←	1 ↖
2	0	1 ↖	1 ←	1 ←	1 ↑	2 ↖	2 ←
3	0	1 ↑	1 ↑	2 ↖	2 ←	2 ↑	2 ↑
4	0	1 ↖	1 ↑	2 ↑	2 ↑	3 ↖	3 ←
5	0	1 ↑	2 ↖	2 ↑	2 ↑	3 ↑	3 ↑
6	0	1 ↑	2 ↑	2 ↑	3 ↖	3 ↑	4 ↖
7	0	1 ↖	2 ↑	2 ↑	3 ↑	4 ↖	4 ↑

Now we can construct a longest common subsequence using c [i, j] and d [i , j].

Step 3 : Constructing LCS

To decide the LCS We have to make use of d - table. The algorithm for this task is as shown below -

```
Algorithm display_ LCS ( d, A [ ], i , j )
{
// Problem Description : This algorithm
// points the longest common subsequence
    if (i = 0 || j = 0) then
        return
if ( d [ i, j ] = "↖ " then
    {
        display LCS ( d, A, i – 1, j – 1 )
        print ( a_i )
}
    else if ( d [ i, j ] = " ↑ ") then
    {   display_ LCS ( d, A, i – 1, j )
    }
else
    display_LCS ( d, A, i, j – 1 )
}// end of algorithm
```

Let us apply this algorithm for obtaining LCS. Initially a call is given as :

```
display_LCS ( d, A [ ] ,7, 6 )
```

Here 7 is upper bound of i and 6 is the upper bound of j.

As d [7, 6] = ↑ we get recursive call display_ LCS (d, A, 6, 6). Then [d[6 ,6] = ↖] a recursive call display_LCS (d, A, 5, 5) is encountered. Then the algorithm tells us to print value of a_i which is a_6 . Thus if we follow the complete algorithm we get YZYX as LCS.

Example 4.9.2 *Explain how to find out longest common subsequence of two strings using dynamic programming method. Find any one Longest Common Subsequence of given two strings using dynamic programming.*

S1 = abbacdcba

S2 = bcdbbaac **GTU : Dec.-10, Marks 8,Winter-14,15, Marks 7**

Solution : Longest common subsequence - Refer section 4.9.

Let, S1 = abbacdcba

S2 = bcdbbcaac

We will arrange these strings in arrays

	1	2	3	4	5	6	7	8	9
S1 [i]	a	b	b	a	c	d	c	b	a
S2 [j]	b	c	d	b	b	c	a	a	c

Step 1 : We will build c [i, j] and d [i, j]. Initially c [i, 0] ← 0 where i represents columns and c [0, j] ← 0 where j represents the rows.

The c table stores the values and d table stores the directions. The table will be

i →

			a	b	b	a	c	d	c	b	a
		0	1	2	3	4	5	6	7	8	9
	0	0	0	0	0	0	0	0	0	0	0
b	1	0									
c	2	0									
d	3	0									
b	4	0									
b	5	0									
c	6	0									
a	7	0									
a	8	0									
c	9	0									

j ↓

for (i ← 1 to m) and

for (j ← 1 to n)

We go on filling up c [i, j] and d [i, j] vertically

∴ Let i = 1, j = 1

	1	2	3	4	5	6	7	8	9
S1 [i]	a	b	b	a	c	d	c	b	a
S2 [j]	b	c	d	b	b	c	a	a	c

S1 [i] ≠ S2 [j]

if (c [i - 1, j] ≥ c [i, j - 1]) true

i.e. if (c [0, 1] ≥ c [1, 0]) true

∴ 0 ≥ 0

c [1, 1] ← c [i - 1, j]

c [1, 1] ← c [0, 1]

c [1, 1] ← 0

d [1, 1] ← ↑

Step 2 :

Let i = 1, j = 2

S1 [i] = a and S2 [j] = c

i.e. S1 [i] ≠ S2 [j]

if (c [i - 1, j] ≥ c [i, j - 1]

i.e. if (c [0,2] ≥ c [1, 1]

0 ≥ 0 → is true

∴ c [1,2] ← c [i-1, j]

c [1,2] ← c [0,2]

∴c [1, 2] ← 0

d [1,2] ← ↑

Step 3 :

Let i = 1, j = 3

S1 [1] = a and S2 [3] = d

i.e. S1 [1] ≠ S2 [3]

if (c [i - 1, j] ≥ c [i, j - 1])

i.e. if (c [0, 3] ≥ c [1,2])

i.e. if (0 ≥ 0) → is true.

∴ c [1, 3] = c [i - 1, j]

= c [0, 3]

c [1, 3] = 0

d [1, 3] = ↑

Step 4 :

Let i = 1, j = 4

S1 [1] = a, S2 [4] = b

i.e. S1 [i] $\neq$ S2 [j]

if (c [i - 1, j] $\geq$ c [i, j - 1])

i.e. if (c[0, 4] : $\geq$ c[1, 3])

i.e. if (0 $\geq$ 0) $\rightarrow$ is true.

$\therefore$ c [1,4] = c [i-1, j]

= c [0, 4]

$\therefore$ **c [1, 4] = 0**

d [1, 4] = ↑

We will start filling up the table in this manner finally we will get.

		0	a 1	b 2	(b) 3	a 4	(c) 5	(d) 6	c 7	(b) 8	(a) 9
0		0	0	0	0	0	0	0	0	0	0
1	(b)	0	↑0	↖1	↖1	←1	←1	←1	←1	↖1	←1
2	(c)	0	↑0	↑1	↑1	↑1	↖2	←2	↖2	←2	←2
3	(d)	0	↑0	↑1	↑1	↑1	↑2	↖3	←3	←3	←3
4	b	0	↑0	↖1	↖2	←2	↑2	↑3	↑3	↖4	←4
5	(b)	0	↑0	↖1	↖2	↑2	↑2	↑3	↑3	↖4	↑4
6	c	0	↑0	↑1	↑2	↑2	↖3	↑3	↖4	↑4	↑4
7	a	0	↖1	↑1	↑2	↖3	↑3	↑3	↑4	↑4	↖5
8	(a)	0	↖1	↑1	↑2	↖3	↑3	↑3	↑4	↑4	↖5
9	c	0	↑1	↑1	↑2	↑3	↖4	←4	↖4	↑4	↑5

Thus the matching longest sub sequence is **bcdba**.

Example 4.9.3 *Using algorithm determine longest sequence of (A, B, C, D, B, A, C, D, F) and (C, B, A, F) (use dynamic programming).* **GTU : Dec.-11, Marks 7**

Solution : Let,

	1	2	3	4	5	6	7	8	9
A[i]	A	B	C	D	B	A	C	D	F
B [j]	C	B	A	F					

We will build c [i, j] and d [i, j]. Initially c [i , 0] ← 0 where i represents row and c [0, j] ← 0 where j represents the column. The c table will store some values and d table will store directions.

Step 1 :

	0	1 C	2 B	3 A	4 F
0		0	0	0	0
A 1	0				
B 2	0				
C 3	0				
D 4	0				
B 5	0				
A 6	0				
C 7	0				
D 8	0				
F 9	0				

Step 2 :

	1	2	3	4	5	6	7	8	9
A[i]	A	B	C	D	B	A	C	D	F
B [j]	C	B	A	F					

As $A[i] \neq B[j]$

If ($c[0, 1] \geq c[1, 0]$) is true

i.e. $0 \geq 0$

$c[1, 1] = c[i - 1, j]$

$c[1, 1] = c[0,1]$

$c[1, 1] = 0$

d [1, 1] = ↑

Step 3 :

Let i = 1, j = 2 then

	1	2	3	4	5	6	7	8	9
A[i]	A	B	C	D	B	A	C	D	F
B [j]	C	B	A	F					

As A [i] ≠ B [j]

If (c [i – 1, j] ≥ c [i , j – 1])

i.e. c [0, 2] ≥ c [1, 1] is true i.e. 0 ≥ 0.

c [i, j] = c [i – 1, j]

c [1, 2] = c [0, 2] = 0

d [i, j] = ↑

The table will be

	0	1	2	3	4
0		0	0	0	0
1	0	0 ↑	0 ↑		
2	0				
3	0				
4	0				
5	0				
6	0				
7	0				
8	0				
9	0				

Continuing in this fashion we can fill up the table as follows -

		0	Ⓒ 1	Ⓑ 2	Ⓐ 3	Ⓕ 4
	0		0	0	0	0
A	1	0	0 ↑	0 ↑	1 ↖	← 1
B	2	0	0 ↑	1 ↖	1 ↑	1 ↑
Ⓒ	3	0	1 ↖	1 ↑	1 ↑	1 ↑
D	4	0	1 ↑	1 ↑	1 ↑	1 ↑
Ⓑ	5	0	1 ↑	2 ↖	2 ←	2 ←
Ⓐ	6	0	1 ↑	2 ↑	3 ↖	3 ←
C	7	0	1 ↖	2 ↑	3 ↑	3 ↑
D	8	0	1 ↑	2 ↑	3 ↑	3 ↑
Ⓕ	9	0	1 ↑	2 ↑	3 ↑	4 ↖

Example 4.9.4 *Given two sequences of characters, P = <MLNOM> Q = <MNOM>, Obtain the longest common subsequence.* **GTU : Summer-13, 14, Marks 7**

Solution :

Let

	1	2	3	4	5
P[i]	M	L	N	O	M
Q[i]	M	N	O	M	

We will build the c [i,j] and d [i, j] table as follows

		0	Ⓜ 1	Ⓝ 2	Ⓞ 3	Ⓜ 4
	0		0	0	0	0
Ⓜ	1	0	↖1	←1	←1	↖1
L	2	0	↑1	↑1	↑1	↑1
Ⓝ	3	0	↑1	↖2	←2	←2
Ⓞ	4	0	↑1	↑2	↖3	←3
Ⓜ	5	0	↖1	↑2	↑3	↖4

Review Question

1. *Describe LCS problem with example and obtain optimal substructure required to solve it using dynamic programming.* **GTU : June-11, Marks 4**

4.10 University Questions with Answers

Regulation 2008

Dec. 2010

Q.1 *Define : Principle of optimality.* **[Refer section 4.2]** [2]

May 2011

Q.2 *Describe an assembly line scheduling problem and give dynamic programming algorithm to solve it.* **[Refer section 4.5]** [6]

Q.3 *Design and analyze dynamic programming algorithm with and without memorization to solve matrix chain multiplication problem.* **[Refer section 4.8]** [8]

Q.4 *Describe LCS problem with example and obtain optimal substructure required to solve it using dynamic programming.* **[Refer section 4.9]** [4]

Dec. 2011

Q.5 *Explain the difference between divide and conquer and dynamic programming.* **[Refer section 4.2]** [3]

May 2012

Q.6 *What is principle of optimality? Explain its use in dynamic programming method.* **[Refer section 4.2]** [4]

Q.7 *Explain chained matrix multiplication with example.* **[Refer section 4.8]** [7]

Dec. 2014

Q.8 *Describe an assembly line scheduling problem and give dynamic programming algorithm to solve it.* **[Refer section 4.5]** [7]

Summer 2015

Q.9 *Discuss matrix multiplication problem using divide and conquer technique.* **[Refer section 4.8]** [7]

Q.10 *Discuss and derive an equation for solving the 0/1 Knapsack problem using dynamic programming method. Design and analyze the algorithm for the same.* **[Refer section 4.6]** [7]

Q.11 *Discuss Assembly line scheduling problem using dynamic programming with example.* **[Refer section 4.5]** [7]

4.11 Short Questions and Answers

Q.1 Which type of problems can be solved using dynamic programming ?

Ans. : Dynamic programming is technique for solving problems with overlapping subproblems. Dynamic programming is typically applied to optimization problems.

Q.2 Write the general procedure of dynamic programming.

Ans. : Dynamic programming is typically applied to optimization problems. For each given problem, we may get any number of solutions from which we seek for optimum solution (i.e. minimum value or maximum value solution). And such an optimal solution becomes the solution to the given problem.

Q.3 State how dynamic programming solves the complex problems.

Ans. : In dynamic programming method, each subproblem is solved only once. The result of each subproblem is recorded in a table from which we can obtain a solution to original problem. This method is based on principle of optimality.

Q.4 What is the difference between divide conquer and dynamic programming method?

Ans. :

Sr. No.	Divide and conquer	Dynamic programming
1.	The problem is divided into small subproblems. These subproblems are solved independently. Finally all the solutions of subproblems are collected together to get the solution to the given problem.	In dynamic programming many decision sequences are generated and all the overlapping subinstances are considered.
2.	Divide and conquer is less efficient because of rework on solutions.	Dynamic programming is efficient than divide and conquer strategy.

Q.5 What does dynamic programming have in common with divide and conquer ?

Ans. : Both the divide and conquer and dynamic programming solve the problem by breaking it into number of subproblems. In both these methods solutions from subproblems are collected together to form a solution to given problem.

Q.6 What is principle of optimality ?

Ans. : The principle of optimality states that "in an optimal sequence of decisions or choices, each subsequence must also be optimal."

Q.7 State the applications of dynamic programming.

Ans. : 1. Calculating the Binomial coefficient 2. Making change problem

3. Assembly line scheduling 4. Knapsack problem 5. Shortest path

Q.8 What is the formula for computing Binomial coefficient ?

Ans. :

$$C(n, k) = C(n-1, k-1) + C(n-1, k)$$

and

$$C(n, 0) = 1$$

$$C(n, n) = 1 \quad \text{where } n > k > 0$$

Q.9 What is the time complexity of binomial coefficient?

Ans. : The time complexity of binomial coefficient is $\Theta(nk)$.

Q.10 Which algorithmic strategy is applied to solve the coin change problem?

Ans. : Using dynamic programming the making coin change problem can be solved.

Q.11 Which formula is used to compute the number of changing coins?

Ans. : 1. If i = 1 then c[i,j]=1+c[1,j-d1]

2. If j < di then c[i,j]=c[i-1,j]

3. Otherwise c[i,j] = min (c[i-1,j],1+ c[i,j-di]

Q.12 What is Knapsack problem ?

Ans. : The knapsack problem can be defined as follows : If there are n items with the weights w1,w2,…,wn and values (profit associated with each item) v1,v2,v3,…vn and capacity of knapsack to be W, then find the most valuable subset of the items that fit into the knapsack.

Q.13 Give at least two variations of knapsack problem.

Ans. : 1. The 0-1 knapsack problem (Using dynamic programming approach)

2. Fractional knapsack problem (Using Greedy method)

Q.14 What is the recurrence relation used to solve knapsack problem using dynamic programming ?

Ans. : The table is created and filled up using following formula while solving knapsack problem

table[i,j] = maximum(table[i-1,j],vi+table[i-1,j-wi]) if j>=wi

or

= table[i-1,j] if j<wi

Q.15 What is memory function?

Ans. : While solving recurrence relation using dynamic programming approach common subproblems may be solved more than once and this makes inefficient solving of the problem. Hence memory function is a method that solves only necessary subproblems. Hence we can define the goal of memory function as : solve only subproblems that are necessary and solve these subproblems only once.

Q.16 List out the methods used for finding out the all pair shortest path.

Ans. : 1. Matrix multiplication and shortest path

2. Floyd-Warshall's algorithm

Q.17 What is transitive closure ?

Ans. : The transitive closure is basically a Boolean matrix in which the existence of directed paths of arbitrarily lengths between vertices is mentioned.

Q.18 What is the purpose of Floyd and Warshall's algorithm ?

Ans. : The Floyd - Warshall algorithm is used to construct transitive closure of a given diagraph.

Q.19 What is matrix chain problem ?

Ans. : The problem can be stated as - In what order should A1A2...An be multiplied so that it would take the minimum number of computations to derive the product.

Q.20 What is the time complexity of matrix chain multiplication method ?

Ans. : The time complexity of matrix chain multiplication method is $O(n^3)$.

Q.21 State the longest common subsequence problem.

Ans. : The longest Common Subsequence problem (LCS) is the problem of finding given two sequences A = < a1, a2 ... am > and B = < b1, b2, b3, ... bn > a maximum length common subsequence of A and B.

❑❑❑

5 Greedy Algorithm

Syllabus

General characteristics of greedy algorithms, Problem solving using - greedy algorithm- Activity selection problem, Elements of greedy strategy, Minimum spanning trees (Kruskal's algorithm, Prim's algorithm), Graphs : Shortest paths, The knapsack problem, Job scheduling problem, Huffman code.

Contents

5.1 Introduction

In an algorithmic strategy like Greedy, the decision of solution is taken based on the information available. The Greedy method is a straightforward method. This method is popular for obtaining the **optimized solutions**. In Greedy technique, the solution is constructed through a sequence of steps, each expanding a partially constructed solution obtained so far, until a complete solution to the problem is reached. At each step the choice made should be,

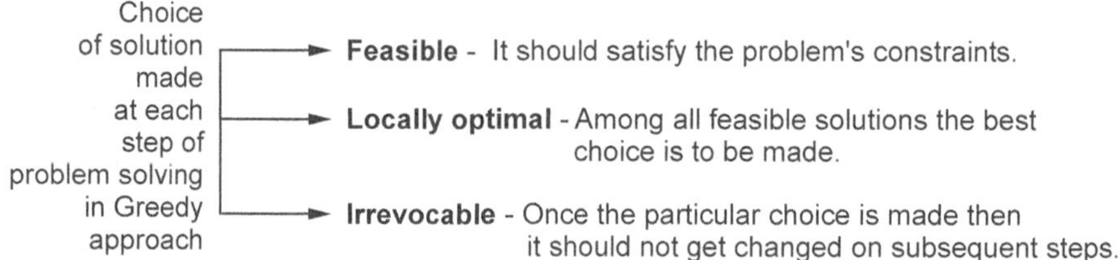

In short, while making a choice there should be a Greed for the optimum solution.

In this chapter we will first understand the concept of Greedy method. Then we will discuss various examples for which Greedy method is applied.

5.2 General Characteristics of Greedy Algorithm

GTU : Dec.-10, June-11,12, Marks 3

In this section we will understand *"What is Greedy method ?"*.

Algorithm

```
Greedy (D, n)
//In Greedy approach D is a domain
//from which solution is to be obtained of size n
//Initially assume
        Solution ← 0
        for i ← 1 to n do
                {
                s ← select (D) // section of solution from D
                if (Feasible (solution, s)) then
                   solution ← Union (solution, s);
                }
                return solution
```

Check if the selected solution is feasible or not. → if (Feasible (solution, s)) then

solution ← Union (solution, s); → Make a feasible choices and select optimum solution.

In Greedy method following **activities** are performed.

1. First we select some solution from input domain.
2. Then we check whether the solution is feasible or not.

3. From the set of feasible solutions, particular solution that satisfies or nearly satisfies the objective of the function. Such a solution is called optimal solution.
4. As Greedy method works in stages. At each stage only one input is considered at each time. Based on this input it is decided whether particular input gives the optimal solution or not.

5.3 Comparison between Greedy and Dynamic Program

GTU : Dec.-10, June-11,12,Summer-15, Marks 3

In this section we will discuss *"What are the differences and similarities between Greedy algorithm and dynamic programming?"*

Sr. No.	Greedy method	Dynamic programming
1.	Greedy method is used for obtaining **optimum solution.**	Dynamic programming is also for obtaining **optimum solution.**
2.	In Greedy method a set of **feasible solutions** and the picks up the optimum solution.	There is **no** special set of **feasible solutions** in this method.
3.	In Greedy method the optimum selection is **without revising previously** generated solutions.	Dynamic programming considers **all possible sequences** in order to obtain the optimum solution.
4.	In Greedy method there is **no** as such **guarantee** of getting **optimum solution.**	It is guaranteed that the dynamic programming will generate optimal solution using **principle of optimality.**

Review Questions

1. *Give the characteristics of greedy algorithms.* **GTU : Dec.-10, June-11, 12, Marks 3**
2. *What are the differences between greedy approach and dynamic programming ?* **GTU : Summer-15, Marks 3**

5.4 Problem Solving using Greedy Algorithm

In this section we will discuss various problems that can be solved Greedy approach -

i) Knapsack problem
ii) Prim's algorithm for minimum spanning tree.
iii) Kruskal's algorithm for minimum spanning tree.
iv) Finding shortest path.
v) Job sequencing with deadlines.
vi) Activity selection problem

For solving all above problems a set of feasible solutions is obtained. From these solution optimum solution is selected. This optimum solution then becomes the final solution for given problem.

With these fundamental issues of Greedy method, let us now discuss various applications of Greedy algorithm.

5.5 Elements of Greedy Strategy

GTU : June-11, Marks 2

Following are the **elements** of Greedy strategy -

1. Greedy choice property :

By this property, a globally optimal solution can be arrived at by making a locally optimal choice. That means, for finding the solution to the problem. We solve the subproblems, and whichever choice. We find the best possible solution for the subproblem. Then solve the subproblem is considered. Then solve the subproblem arising after the choice is made. This choice may depend upon the previously made choices but it does not depend on any future choice. Thus in greedy method, greedy choices are made one after the another, reducing each given problem instance to smaller one. The greedy choice property brings efficiency in solving the problem with the help of subproblems.

2. Optimal substructure :

A problem shows optimal substructure if an optimal solution to the problem contains optimal solution to the sub-problems. In other words a problem has optimal substructure if the best next choice always leads to the optimal solution.

Review Questions

1. *Explain the elements of the greedy strategy.*
2. *Explain the term - optimal substructure property.* GTU : June-11, Marks 2

5.6 Activity Selection Problem

Activity selection problem is defined as follows :

Given a **resource** such as a CPU or a **lecture** hall and n set of **activities**, such as task or lectures that want to utilize the resource. The activity i have the **starting** and **finishing time** which can be denoted by S_i and F_i. Then activity selection problem is to find max_size subset A of **mutually compatible** activities. [i.e. maximize the number of lecture all in the lecture hall or maximize number of tasks assigned to the CPU].

Example 5.6.1 *Consider the following set of activities denoted by S. select the compatible set of activities.*

i	1	2	3	4	5	6	7	8	9	10	11
S_i	1	3	0	5	3	5	6	8	8	2	14
F_i	4	5	6	7	8	9	10	11	12	15	16

Solution :

Step 1 : Sort F_i i.e. finishing time into non-decreasing order. After sorting $F_1 \le F_2 \le F_3 \le \ldots\ldots \le F_n$

Step 2 : Select the next activity i to the solution set if i is compatible with each activity in the solution set.

Step 3 : Repeat step 2, until all the activities get examined.

From above set first of all we will select a_1, the finish time of a_1 is 4, Hence we will search for the activity with $S_i \ge 4$. We will select a_4 (because $S_4 = 5$ which ≥ 4). The F_4 is 7. Hence select next activity such that $S_i \ge 7$. We will get S_8. The $F_8 = 11$. Hence select next activity such that $S_i \ge 11$. We obtain a_{11} activity. We select a_{11}. Hence the solution set = **{1, 4, 8, 11}**.

The algorithm for activity selection problem is as given below.

Algorithm

```
Algorithm Greedy_Act_sel (S, F)
// Problem Description : This algorithm selects the activities
// that are compatible to each other
// Input : The set of starting time and finish time.
// Output : Set of selected activities.
    n ← length [S] // n represents total number of activities.
    A ← {a} // selection of first activity.
    i ← 1 // current activity is denoted by a_i .
    for m ← 2 to n
    {                       F_i is maximum finish
    if (S_m ≥ F_i) then     time of any activity in A

        A ← A ∪ {a_m}  }    Selection of next
        i ← m              feasible activity
    }
        return A
```

Analysis : The algorithm using greedy approach for activity selection works in θ **(n)** time.

The activity selection problem can be solved using two approaches -

1. Greedy-choice property.
2. Optimal substructure.

1. Greedy choice property :

- In this approach of problem solution a globally optimal solution can be obtained by making a **locally optimal choice.**
- Select a **choice** whichever seems to be **best at the moment** and then solve the subproblem arising after the choice is made.
- The choice made by a greedy algorithm depends upon the **choices made so far** but it does not depend upon the future choices.

2 Optimal substructure

A problem shows **optimal substructure** if an optimal solution to the problem contains within it optimal solutions to sub-problems.

The optimal solution is denoted by A. The selection process starts by selecting activity 1 and then $A' = A - \{1\}$ where $i \in s$ and $S_i \geq f_1$.

Review Question

1. *Explain the two approaches that can be used for solving activity selection problem using greedy strategy.*

5.7 Minimum Spanning Tree

GTU : Dec.-10,11, June-11, 12, May-12, Winter-15, Summer-14,15, Marks 8

Spanning tree

A spanning tree of a graph G is a subgraph which is basically a tree and it contains **all the vertices** of G containing **no circuit.**

Minimum spanning tree

A minimum spanning tree of a weighted connected graph G is a spanning tree with minimum or smallest weight.

Weight of the tree

A weight of the tree is defined as the sum of weights of all its edges.

For example :

Consider a graph G as given below. This graph is called weighted connected graph because some weights are given along every edge and the graph is a connected graph.

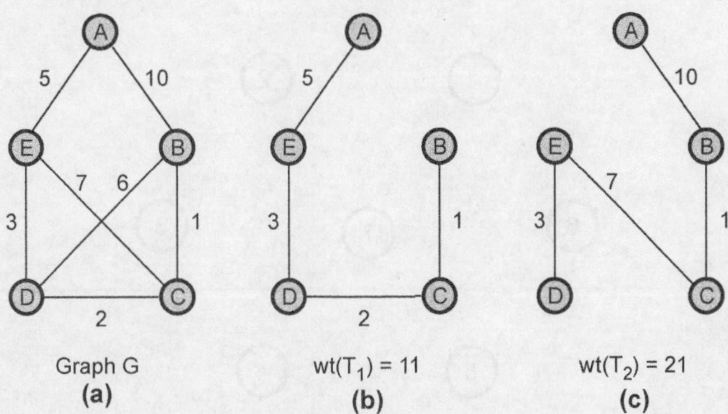

Fig. 5.7.1 Graph and two spanning trees out of which (b) is a minimum spanning tree

Applications of spanning trees :

1. Spanning trees are very important in designing efficient routing algorithms.
2. Spanning trees have wide applications in many areas such as network design.

5.7.1 Prim's Algorithm

Let us understand the prim's algorithm with the help of example.

Example 5.7.1 *Consider the graph given below. Obtain minimum spanning tree using prims algorithm.*

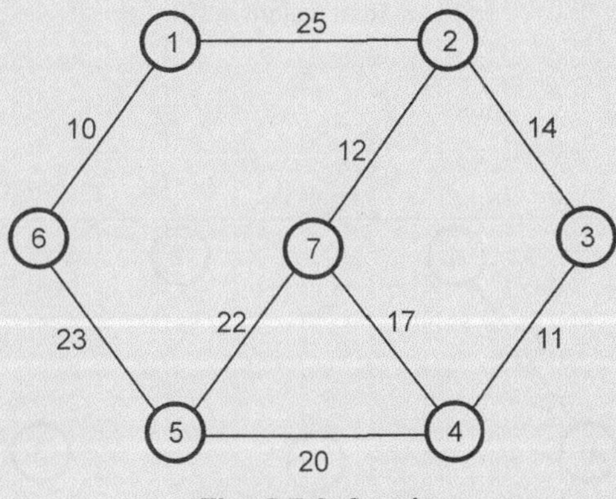

Fig. 5.7.2 Graph

Solution : Now, we will consider all the vertices first. Then we will select an edge with minimum weight. The algorithm proceeds by selecting adjacent edges with minimum weight. Care should be taken for **not forming circuit**.

Step 1 :

Total weight = 0

Step 2 :

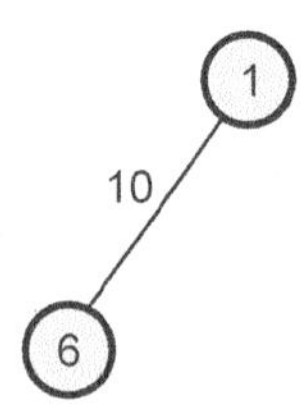

Total weight = 10

Step 3 :

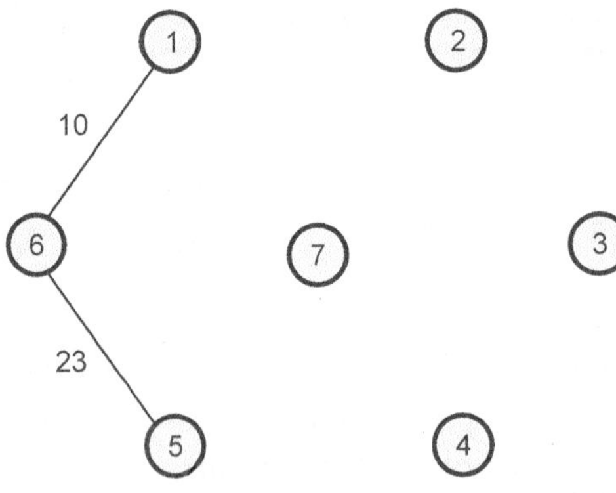

Total weight = 33

Step 4 :

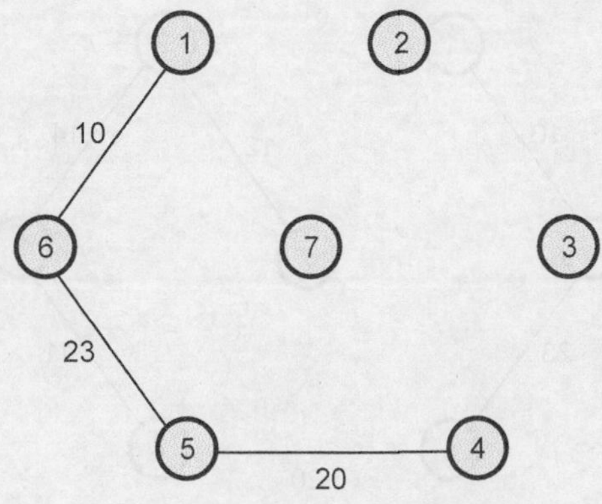

Total weight = 53

Step 5 :

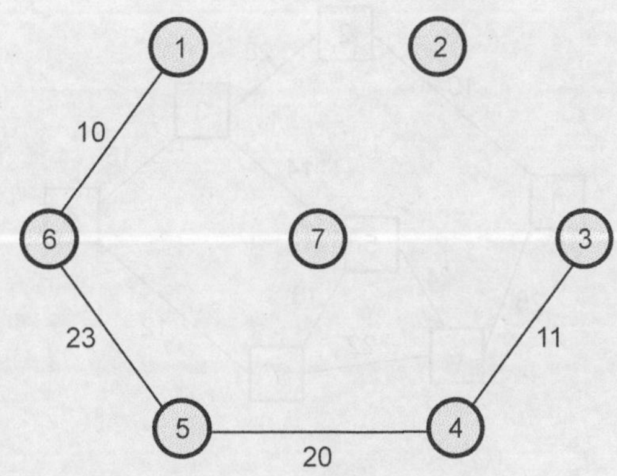

Total weight = 64

Step 6 :

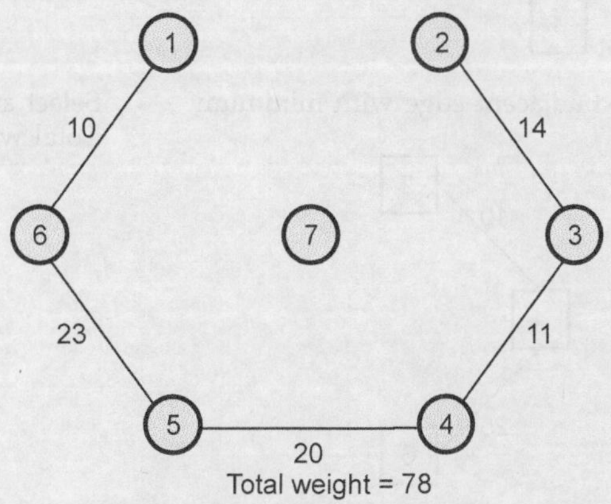

Total weight = 78

Step 7 :

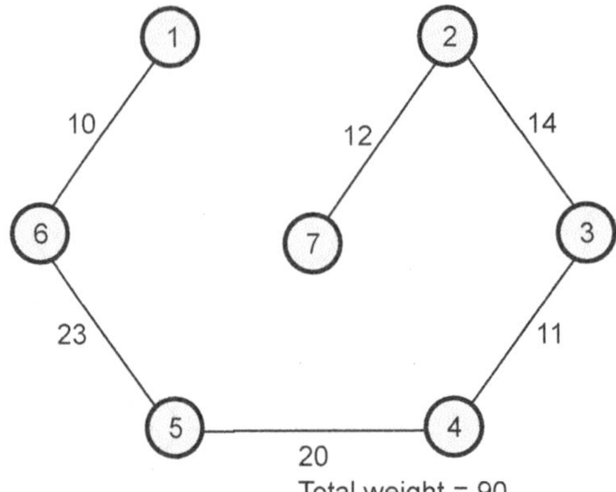

Example 5.7.2 *Generate minimum spanning tree of following figure using Prim's algorithm.*

GTU : Dec.-11, Marks 7

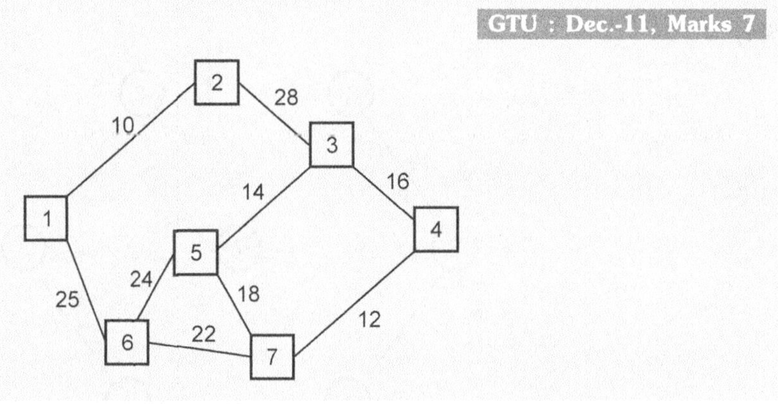

Solution :

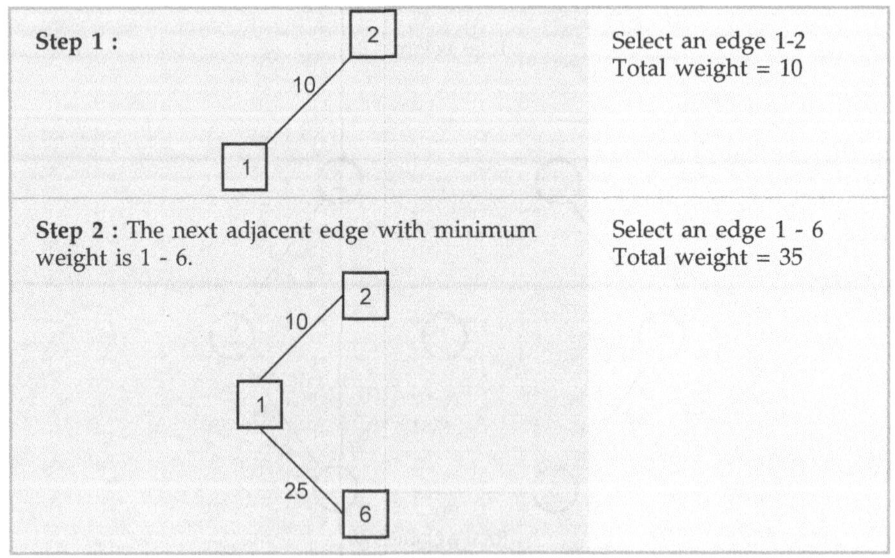

Step 1 :	Select an edge 1-2 Total weight = 10
Step 2 : The next adjacent edge with minimum weight is 1 - 6.	Select an edge 1 - 6 Total weight = 35

Step 3 : Select next adjacent edge with minimum weight. 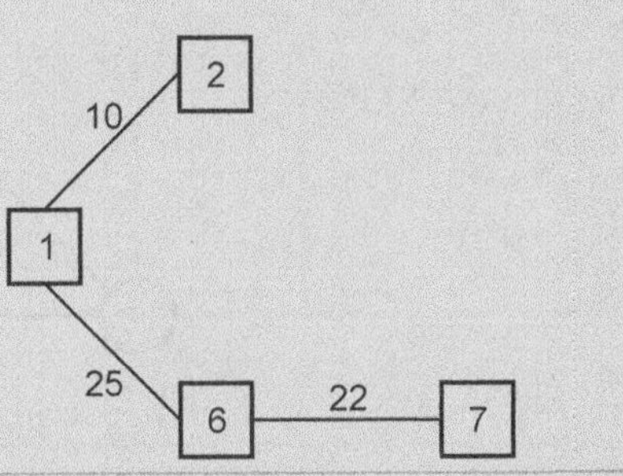	Select an edge 6 - 7. Total weight = 57
Step 4 : Select next adjacent edge with minimum weight. 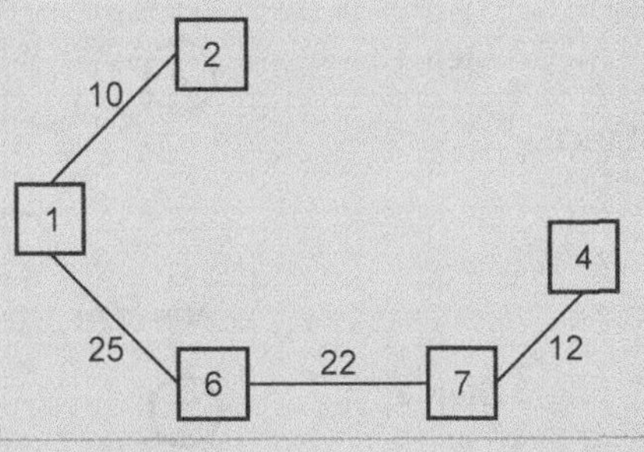	Select an edge 7 - 4 Total weight = 69
Step 5 : Select next adjacent edge with minimum weight. 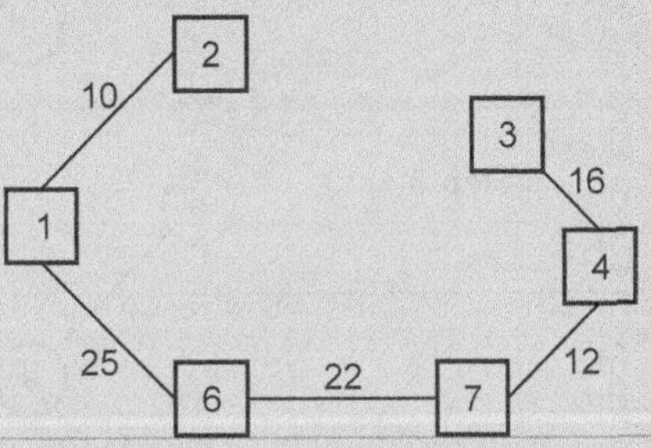	Select an edge 3 - 4 Total weight = 85
Step 6 : Select next adjacent edge with minimum weight. 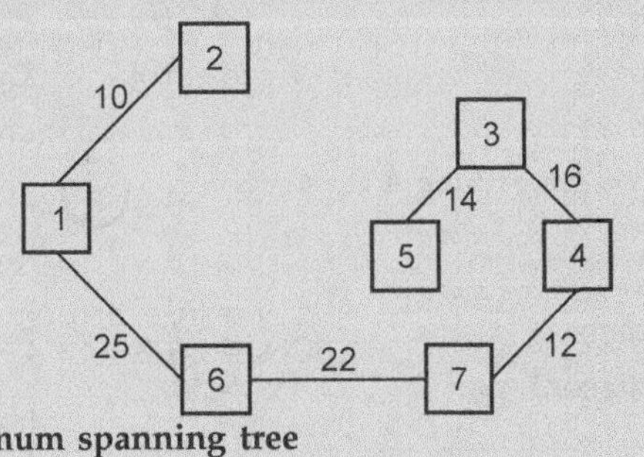 **Minimum spanning tree**	Select an edge 3 - 5 **Total weight = 99**

Example 5.7.3 *Apply Prim's algorithm to the following graph and obtain minimum spanning tree.*

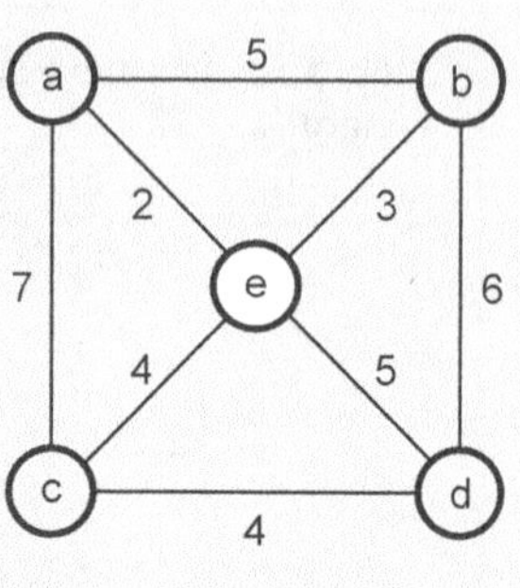

Fig. 5.7.3

Solution :

We will first select a minimum distance edge from given graph.	**Step 1 :** V = {a,e} Cost = 2
The next minimum distance edge is b-e. This edge is adjacent to previously selected vertex e.	**Step 2 :** V = {a,e,b} Cost = 2 + 3 = 5
The next minimum distance edge is c-e which is adjacent to already selected edge b-e.	**Step 3 :** V = {a,e,b,c} Cost = 2 + 3 + 4 = 9
Then next select an edge c-d which is with minimum distance and it is adjacent to already selected edge c-e.	**Step 4 :** V = {a, e, b, c, d} Cost = 2 + 3 + 4 + 4 = 13

Since all the vertices are visited and we get a connected tree as minimum spanning tree.

Step 5 : V{a, e ,b, c, d} and

Cost = 2 + 3 + 4 + 4 = 13.

The final minimum spanning tree will be -

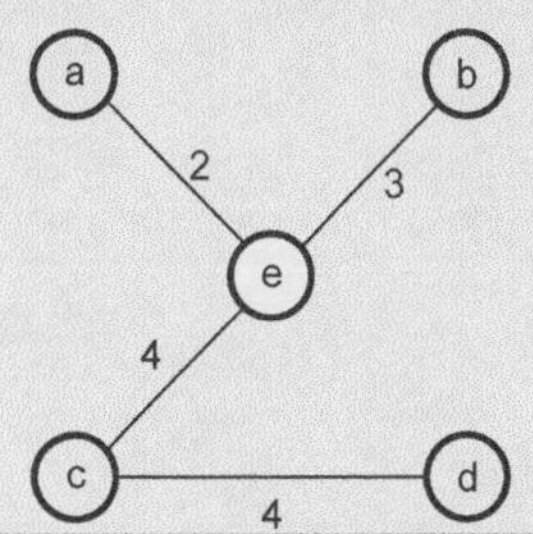

Example 5.7.4 *Find minimum spanning tree for the given graph using Prim's Algo. (initialization from node A).*

GTU : Winter-14

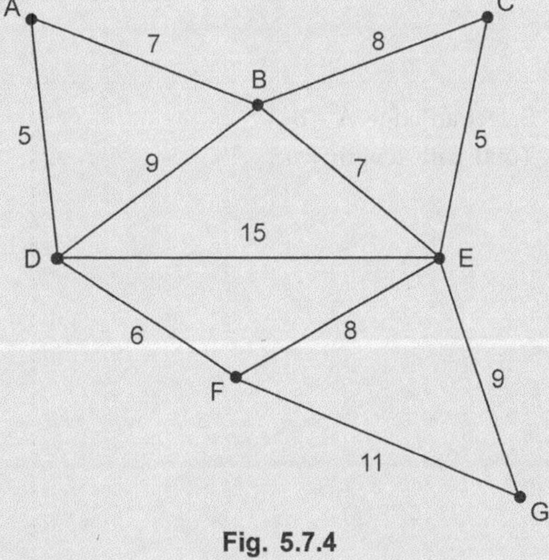

Fig. 5.7.4

Solution :

Select an edge A - D

Total path length = 5

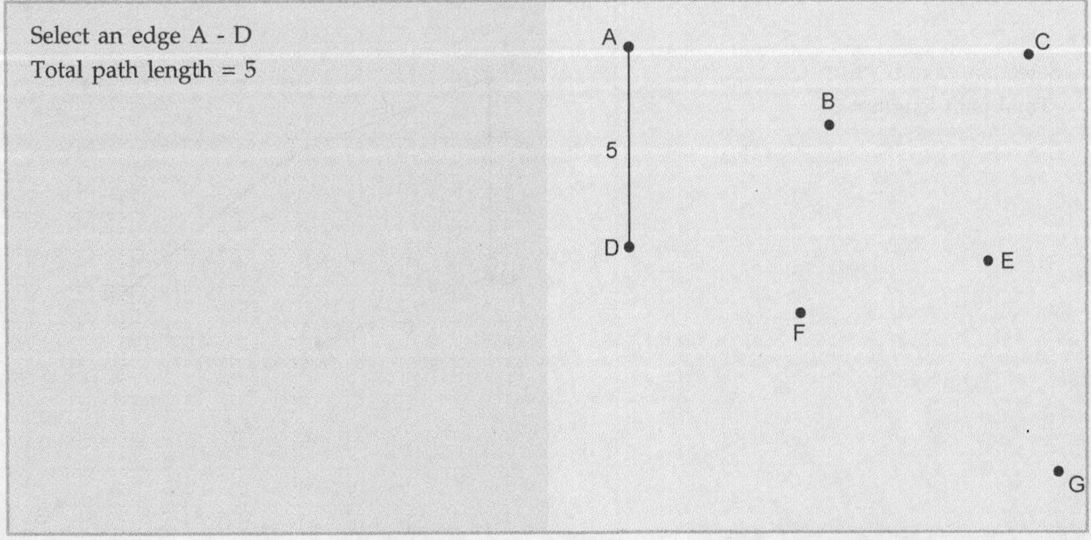

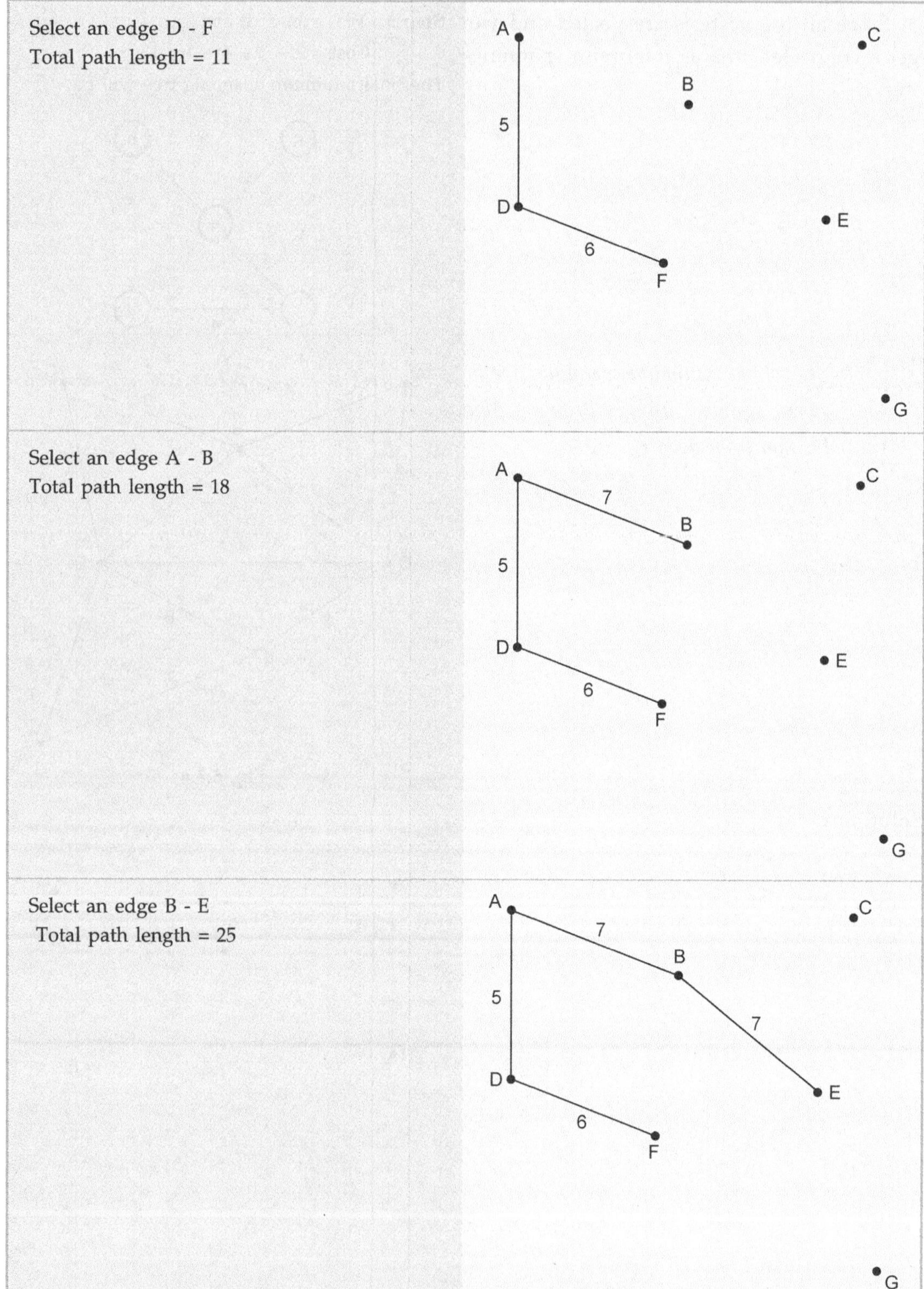
Select an edge D - F
Total path length = 11
A
C
B
5
D
E
6
F
G
Select an edge A - B
Total path length = 18
A
C
7
B
5
D
E
6
F
G
Select an edge B - E
Total path length = 25
A
C
7
B
5
7
D
E
6
F
G

Select an edge C - E
Total path length = 30

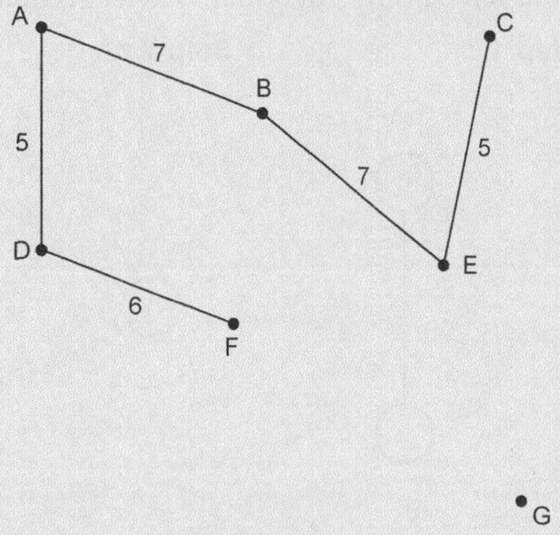

Select an edge E - G
Total path length = 39
This is required minimum spanning tree

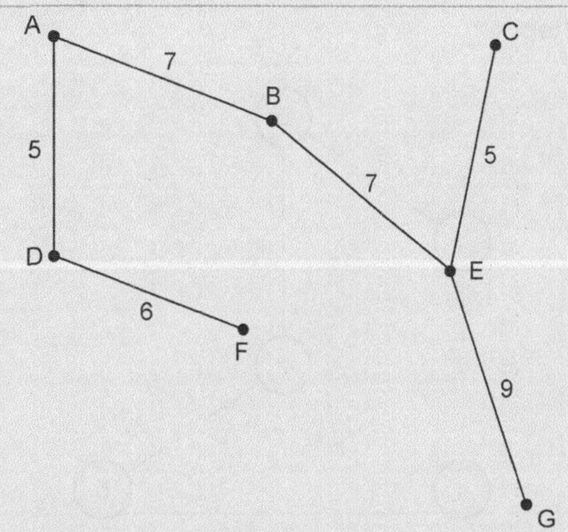

Example 5.7.5 *Write the Prim's Algorithm to find out Minimum Spanning Tree. Apply the same and find MST for the graph given below.* **GTU : Winter-15, Marks 7**

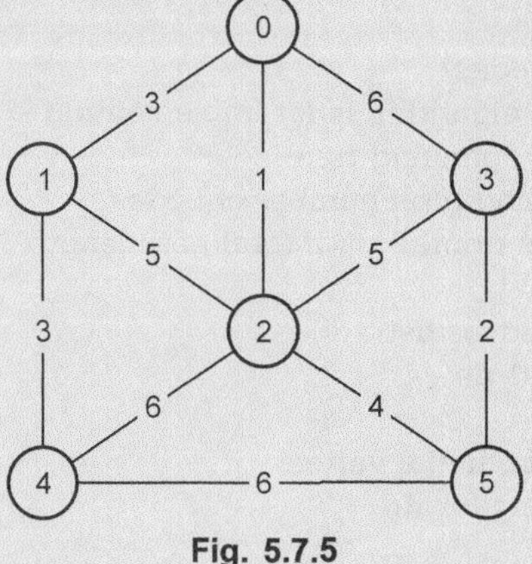

Fig. 5.7.5

Solution : Prim's Algorithm - Refer section 5.7.1.

Step 1 :

Step 2 : 

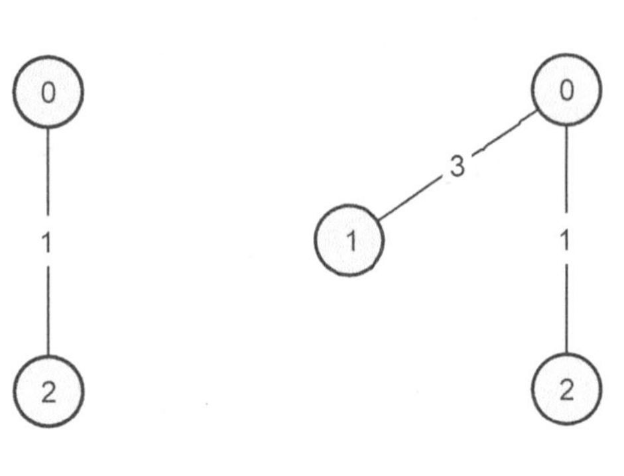

Step 3 :

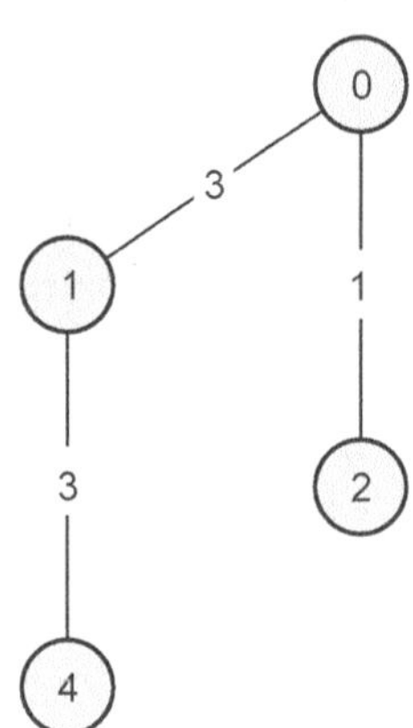

Step 4 :

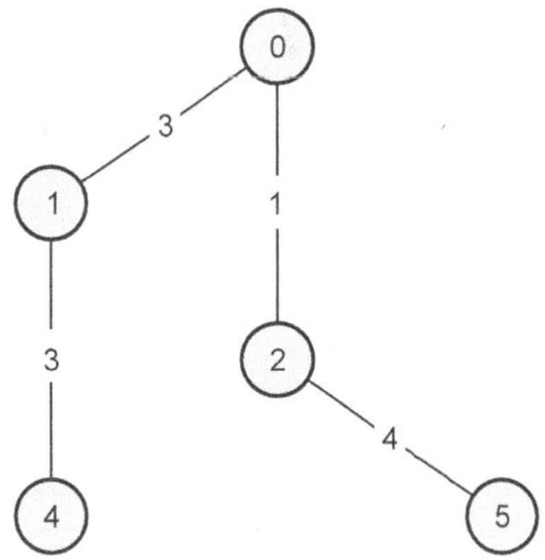

Step 5 :

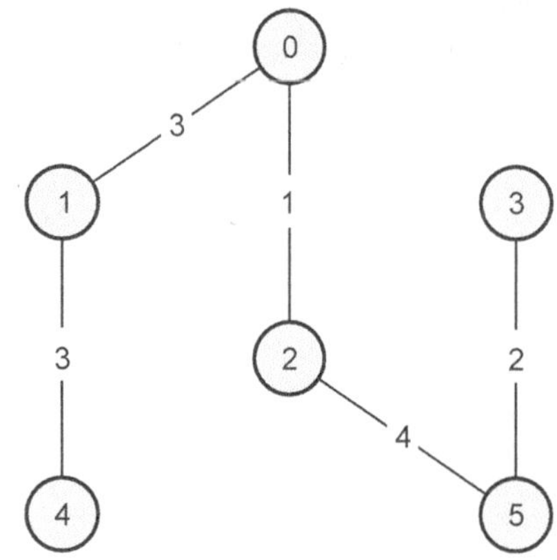

Total path length = 13

Prim's Algorithm

Algorithm

```
Prim(G[0...Size-1,0...Size-1],nodes)
//Problem Description : This algorithm is for implementing
//Prim's algorithm for finding spanning tree
//Input : Weighted Graph G and total number of nodes
//Output : Spanning tree gets printed with total path length
      total=0;
  //Initialize the selected vertices list
          for i←0 to nodes–1 do
            tree[i] ← 0
            tree[0] = 1;//take initial vertex
              for k←1 to nodes do
              {
```

```
            min_dist ← ∞
        //initially assign minimum dist as infinity
        for i←0 to nodes–1 do
        {
            for j←0 to nodes–1 do
                {
                if (G [i,j]AND ((tree[i]AND !tree[j])OR(!tree[i]AND
                tree[j])))then
                 {
                    if(G[i,j] < min_dist)then
                    {
                        min_dist←G[ij]
                        v1←i
                        v2←j
                    }
                 }
            }
        }
    Write(v1,v2,min_dist);
    tree[v1] ← tree[v2] ← 1
    total ← total+min_dist
 }
 Write("Total Path Length Is",total)
```

Select an edge such that one vertex is selected and other is not and the edge has the least weight.

Obtained edge with minimum wt.

Picking up those vertices yielding minimum edge.

C function

```
void Prim(int G[][SIZE], int nodes)
{
        int tree[SIZE], i, j, k;
        int min_dist, v1, v2,total=0;
        //Initialize the selected vertices list
        for (i=0 ; i<nodes ; i++)
             tree[i] = 0;
        printf("\n\n The Minimal Spanning Tree Is : \n");
        tree[0] = 1;
        for (k=1 ; k<=nodes-1 ; k++)
        {
            min_dist = INFINITY;
        //initially assign minimum dist as infinity
        for (i=0 ; i<=nodes–1 ; i++)
        {
            for (j=0 ; j<=nodes–1 ; j++)
             {
                if (G[i][j] && ((tree[i] && !tree[j])||
                (!tree[i] && tree[j])))
                {
                    if (G[i][j] < min_dist)
```

```
                {
                        min_dist = G[i][j];
                        v1 = i;
                        v2 = j;
                }
            }
        }
    }

    printf("\n Edge (%d %d )and weight = %d",v1,v2,min_dist);
    tree[v1] = tree[v2] = 1;
    total =total+min_dist;
    }
    printf("\n\n\t Total Path Length Is = %d",total);
}
```

Analysis

The algorithm spends most of the time in selecting the edge with minimum length. Hence the **basic operation** of this algorithm is to find the edge with **minimum path length.** This can be given by following formula.

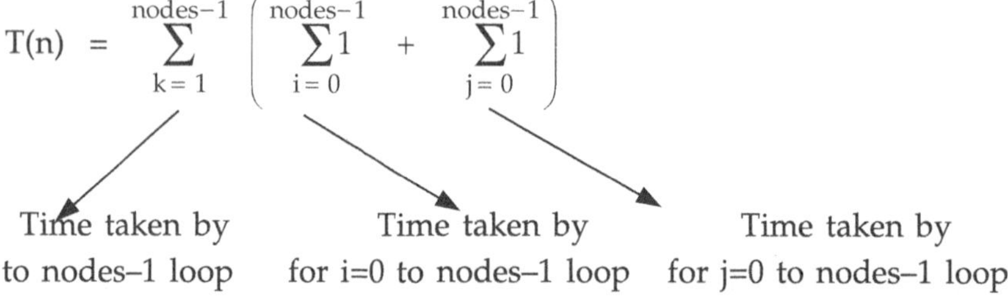

We take variable n for 'nodes' for the sake of simplicity of solving the equation then

$$T(n) = \sum_{k=1}^{n-1} \left(\sum_{i=0}^{n-1} 1 + \sum_{j=0}^{n-1} 1 \right)$$

$$= \sum_{k=1}^{n-1} [((n-1)+0+1)+((n-1)+0+1)]$$

$$= \sum_{k=1}^{n-1} (2n)$$

$$= 2n \sum_{k=1}^{n-1} 1$$

$$= 2n[(n-1)-1+1] = 2n(n-1)$$

$$= 2n^2 - 2n$$

$\therefore \quad T(n) \approx n^2$

$\therefore \quad T(n) = \Theta(n^2)$

But n stands for total number of nodes or vertices in the tree. Hence we can also state

Time complexity of Prim's Algorithm is $\Theta(|V^2|)$.

But if the Prim's algorithm is implemented using binary heap with the creation of graph using adjacency list then its time complexity becomes $\Theta(E \log_2 V)$ where E stands for total number of edges and V stands for total number of vertices.

C Program

```
/*******************************************************************
This program is to implement Prim's Algorithm using Greedy Method
*******************************************************************/
#include<stdio.h>
#include<conio.h>
#define SIZE 20
#define INFINITY 32767

/*This function finds the minimal spanning tree by Prim's Algorithm */

void Prim(int G[][SIZE],int nodes)
{
        int tree[SIZE],i,j,k;
        int min_dist,v1,v2,total=0;
    //Initialize the selected vertices list
    for (i=0; i<nodes; i++)
      tree[i] = 0;
    printf("\n\n The Minimal Spanning Tree Is :\n");
    tree[0] = 1;
    for (k=1; k<=nodes-1; k++)
    {


        min_dist = INFINITY;
        //initially assign minimum dist as infinity
          for (i=0; i<=nodes-1; i++)
            {
                    for (j=0; j<=nodes-1; j++)
                {
                    if (G[i][j]&&((tree[i]&&!tree[j])||
                            (!tree[i]&&tree[j])))
                    {
                    if (G[i][j]<min_dist)
                    {
                        min_dist=G[i][j];
```

```
                                v1 = i;
                                v2 = j;
                        }
                        }
                }
        }

        printf("\n Edge (%d %d )and weight = %d",v1,v2,min_dist);
                tree[v1] = tree[v2] = 1;
        total =total+min_dist;
        }
        printf("\n\n\t Total Path Length Is = %d",total);
}
void main()
{
        int G[SIZE][SIZE],nodes;
        int v1,v2,length,i,j,n;

        clrscr();
        printf("\n\t Prim'S Algorithm\n");

        printf("\n Enter Number of Nodes in The Graph");

        scanf("%d",&nodes);
        printf("\n Enter Number of Edges in The Graph");
        scanf("%d",&n);

        for (i=0 ; i<nodes ; i++)// Initialize the graph
                for (j=0 ; j<nodes ; j++)
                        G[i][j] = 0;
        //entering weighted graph
        printf("\n Enter edges and weights \n");
        for (i=0 ; i<n; i++)
        {
                printf("\n Enter Edge by V1 and V2:");
                printf("[Read the graph from starting node 0]");
                scanf("%d %d",&v1,&v2);
                printf("\n Enter corresponding weight:");
                scanf("%d",&length);
                G[v1][v2] = G[v2][v1] = length;
        }
        getch();
        printf("\n\t");
        clrscr();
        Prim(G,nodes);
        getch();
}
```

Output

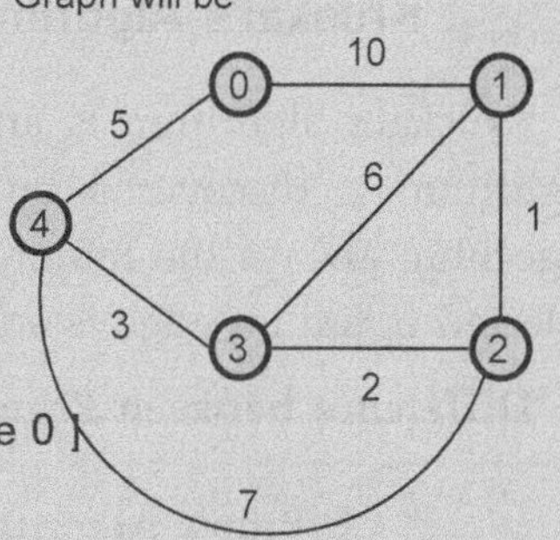

Fig. 5.7.6

```
    Prim'S Algorithm
 Enter Number of Nodes in The Graph  5

 Enter Number of Edges in The Graph  7

 Enter edges and weights

Enter Edge by V1 and V2 : [Read the graph from starting node 0 ]
0 1

Enter corresponding weight : 10

Enter Edge by V1 and V2 : [Read the graph from starting node 0]
    1 2

Enter corresponding weight : 1

Enter Edge by V1 and V2 :[Read the graph from starting node 0]
    2 3

Enter corresponding weight :2

Enter Edge by V1 and V2 : [Read the graph from starting node 0]
    3 4

Enter corresponding weight : 3

Enter Edge by V1 and V2 : [Read the graph from starting node 0]
    4 0

Enter corresponding weight :5

Enter Edge by V1 and V2 : [Read the graph from starting node 0]
    1 3

Enter corresponding weight : 6

Enter Edge by V1 and V2 : [Read the graph from starting node 0]
    4 2

Enter corresponding weight : 7

The Minimal Spanning Tree Is :
Edge (0 4)and weight = 5
Edge (3 4)and weight = 3
Edge (2 3)and weight = 2

   Total Path Length Is = 11
```

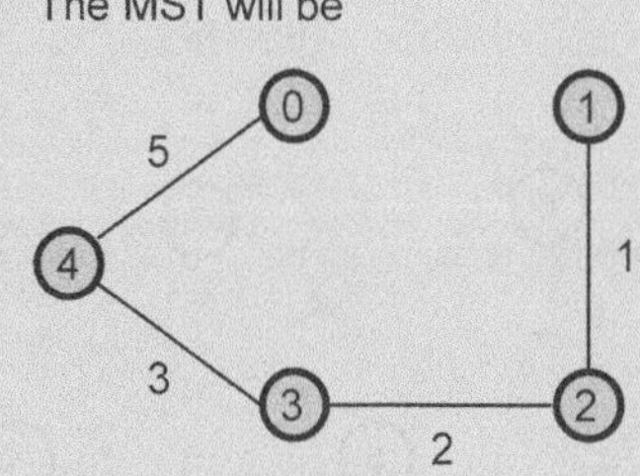

5.7.2 Kruskal's Algorithm

Kruskal's algorithm is another algorithm of obtaining minimum spanning tree. This algorithm is discovered by a second year graduate student **Joseph Kruskal**. In this algorithm always the minimum cost edge has to be selected. But it is not necessary that selected optimum edge is adjacent.

Difference between Prim's and Kruskal's Algorithm

Prim's Algorithm	Kruskal's Algorithm
This algorithm is for obtaining minimum spanning tree by selecting the adjacent vertices of already selected vertices.	This algorithm is for obtaining minimum spanning tree but it is not necessary to choose adjacent vertices of already selected vertices.

Let us understand this algorithm with the help of some example.

Example 5.7.6 *Consider the graph given below and obtain MST using kruskal's algorithm*

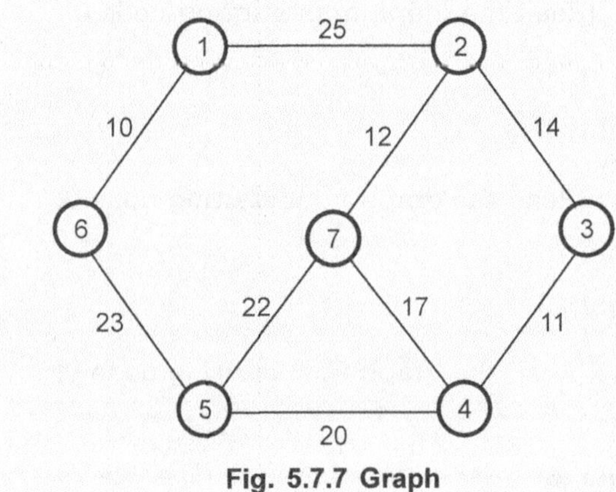

Fig. 5.7.7 Graph

Solution : First we will select all the vertices. Then an edge with optimum weight is selected from heap, even though it is not adjacent to previously selected edge. Care should be taken for **not forming circuit**.

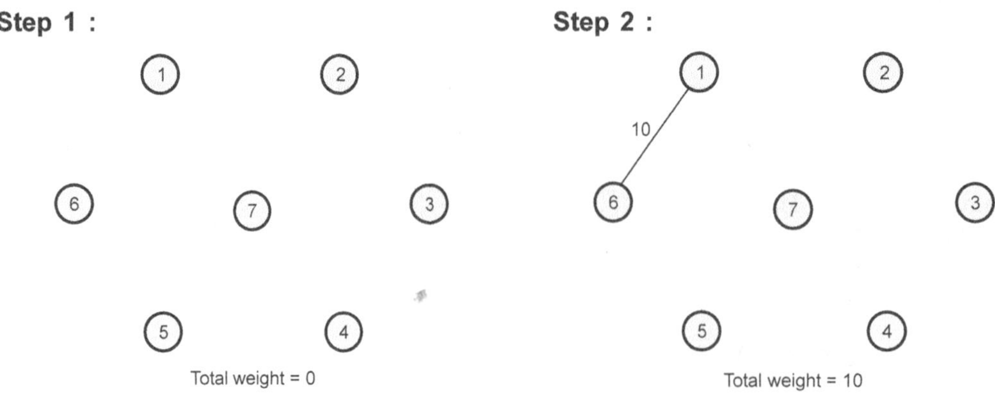

Step 3 :

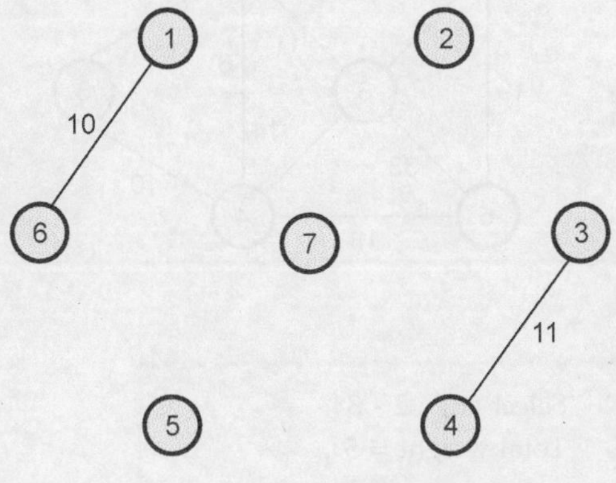

Total weight = 21

Step 4 :

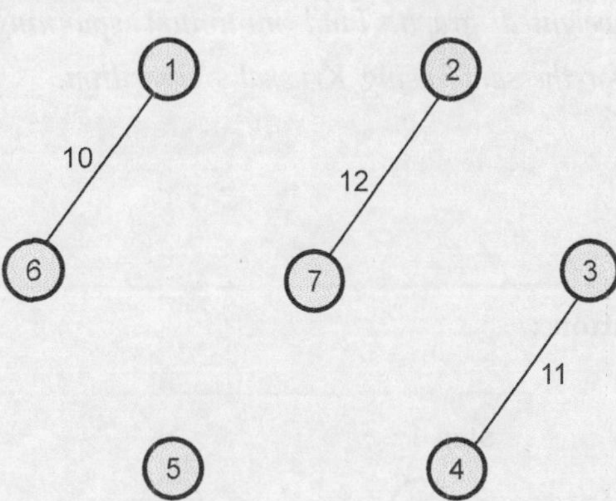

Total weight = 33

Step 5 :

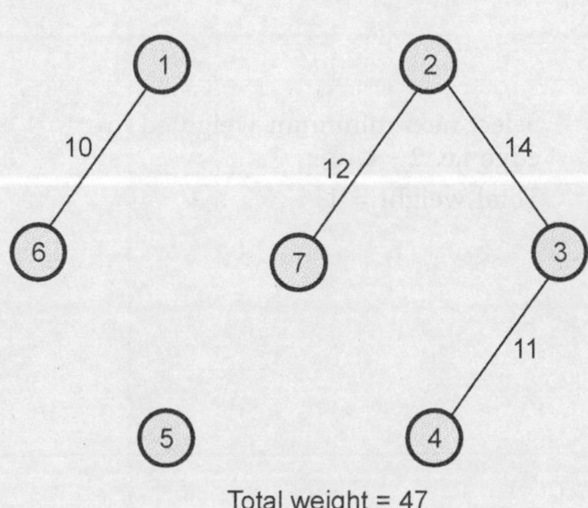

Total weight = 47

Step 6 :

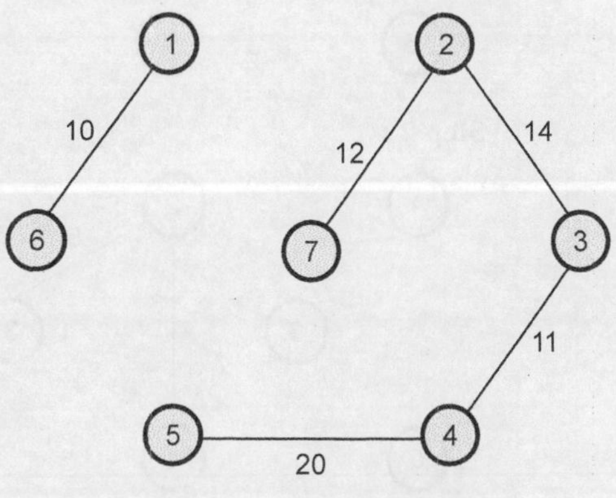

Total weight = 67

Step 7 :

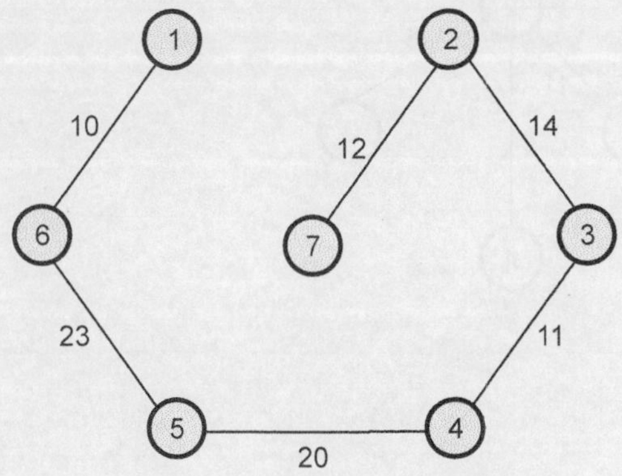

Total weight = 90

Example 5.7.7 *Consider the following undirected weighted graph. Find minimum spanning tree for the same using Kruskal's algorithm.*

GTU : June-11, Marks 4

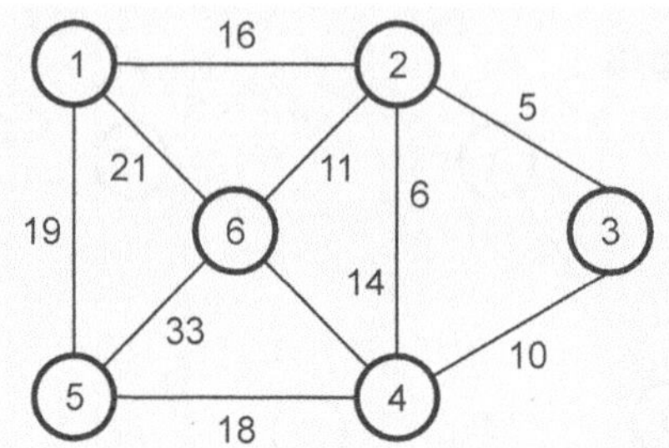

Solution :

Step 1 :	Select edge 2 - 3 Total weight = 5
Step 2 :	Select next minimum weighted edge i.e. 2 - 4. Total weight = 11
Step 3 : If we select edge 3 - 4, then a cycle will be formed which is not desired.	Select an edge 2 - 6. Total weight = 22

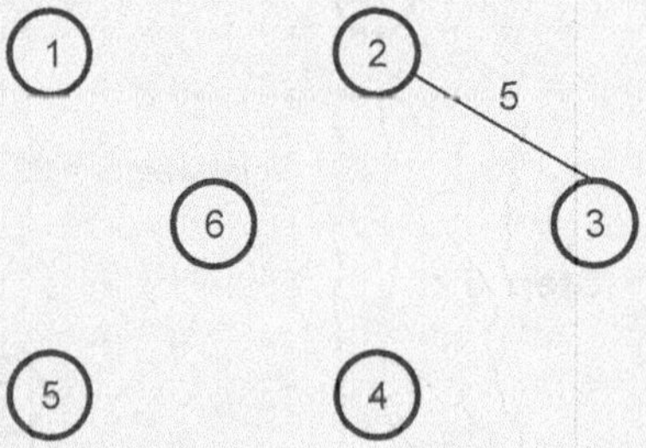

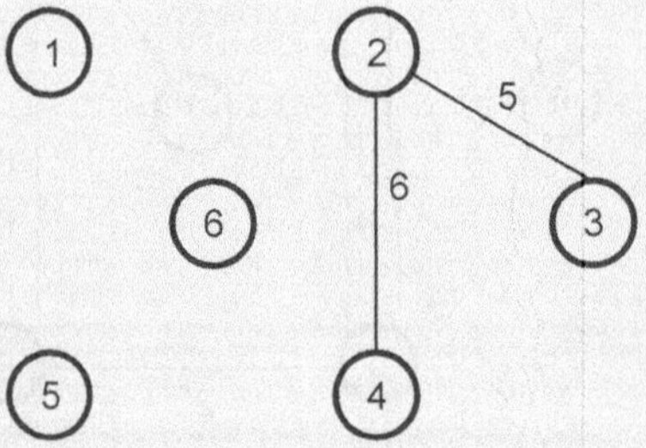

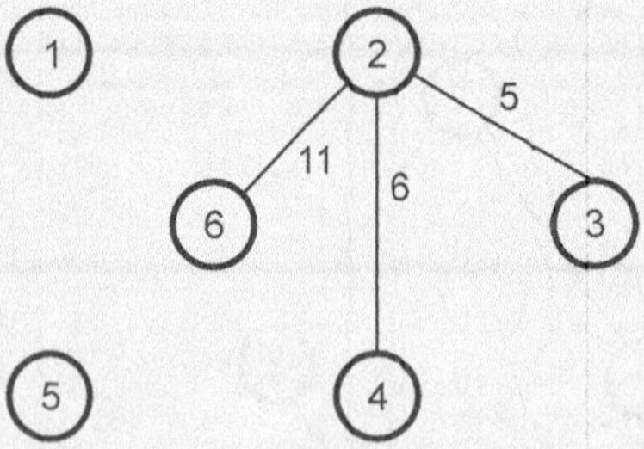

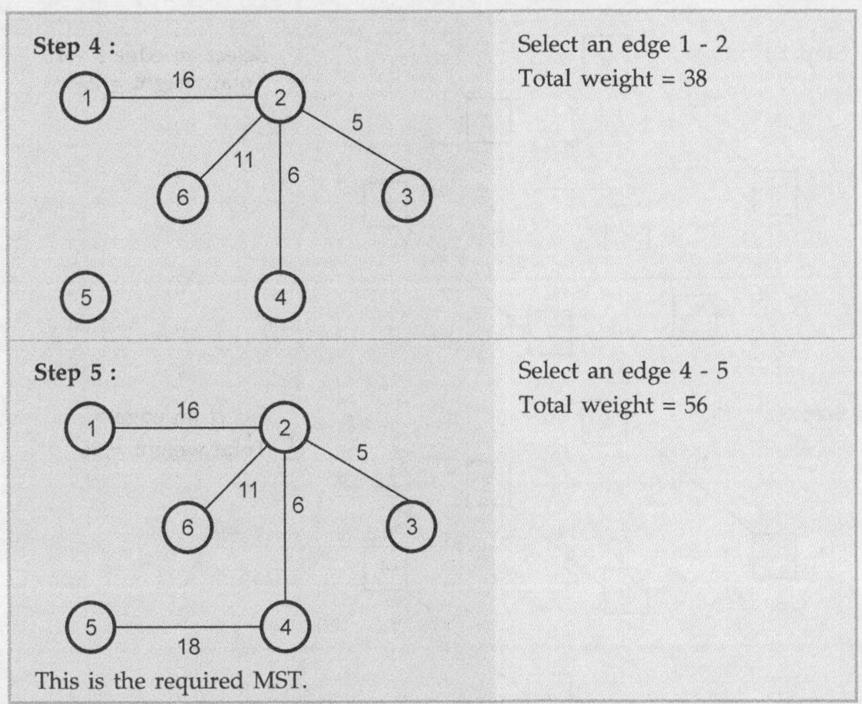

Example 5.7.8 *Generate minimum spanning tree of following figure using Kruskal's algorithm.*

GTU : Dec.-11, Marks 3

Solution :

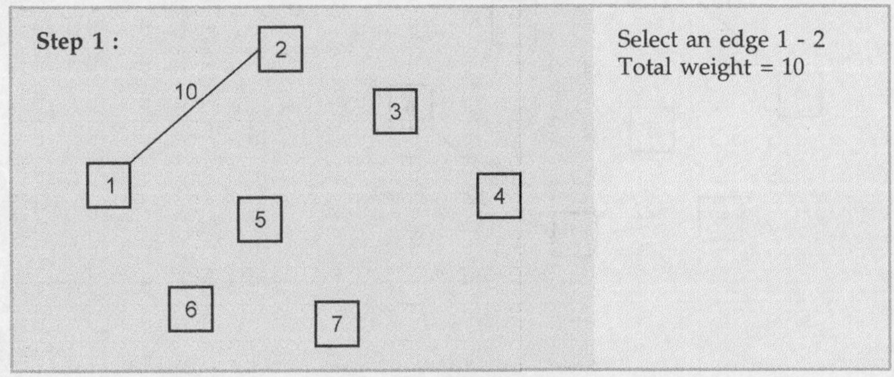

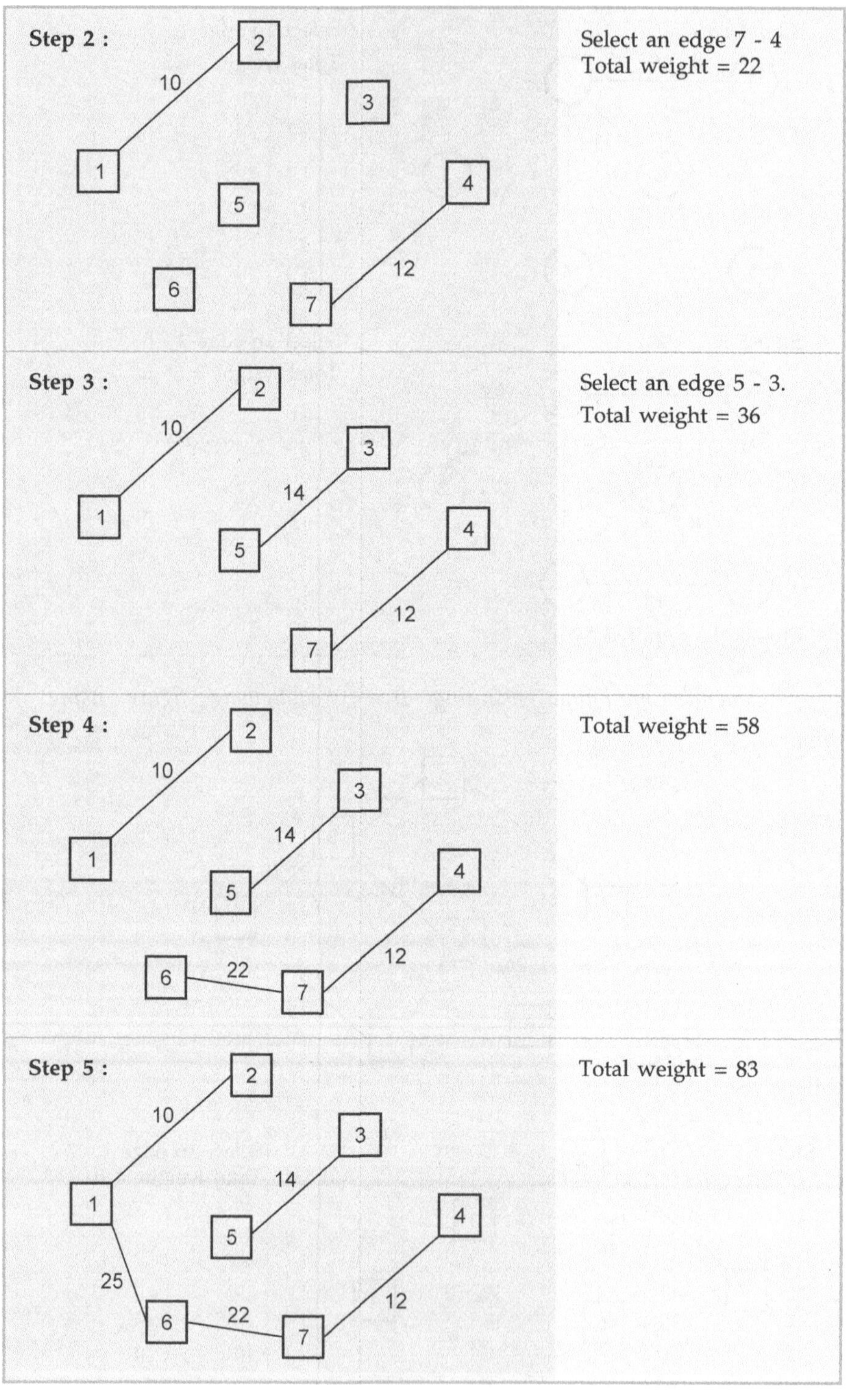
Step 2 :
10
12
1
2
3
4
5
6
7
Select an edge 7 - 4
Total weight = 22
Step 3 :
10
14
12
1
2
3
4
5
7
Select an edge 5 - 3.
Total weight = 36
Step 4 :
10
14
12
22
1
2
3
4
5
6
7
Total weight = 58
Step 5 :
10
14
12
22
25
1
2
3
4
5
6
7
Total weight = 83

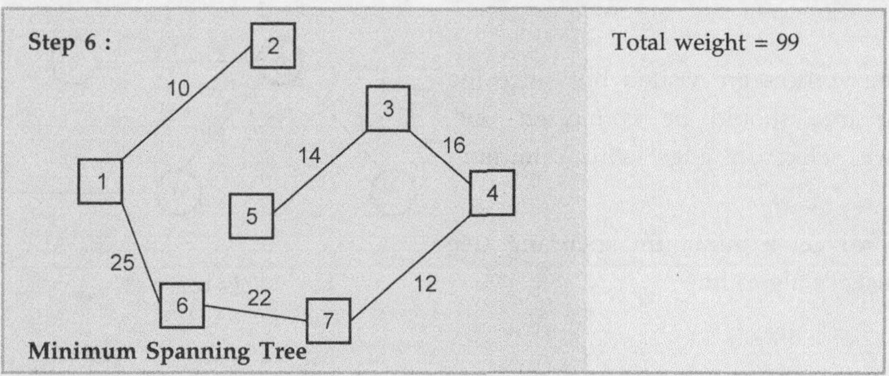

Minimum Spanning Tree

Example 5.7.9 *Apply Kruskal's algorithm to find a minimum spanning tree of a given graph.*

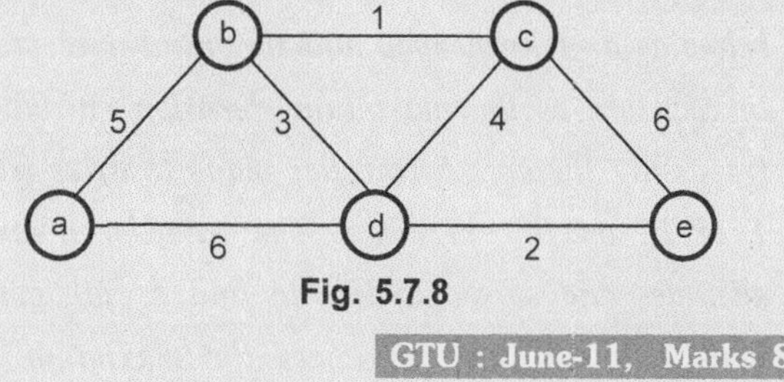

Fig. 5.7.8

GTU : June-11, Marks 8

Solution :

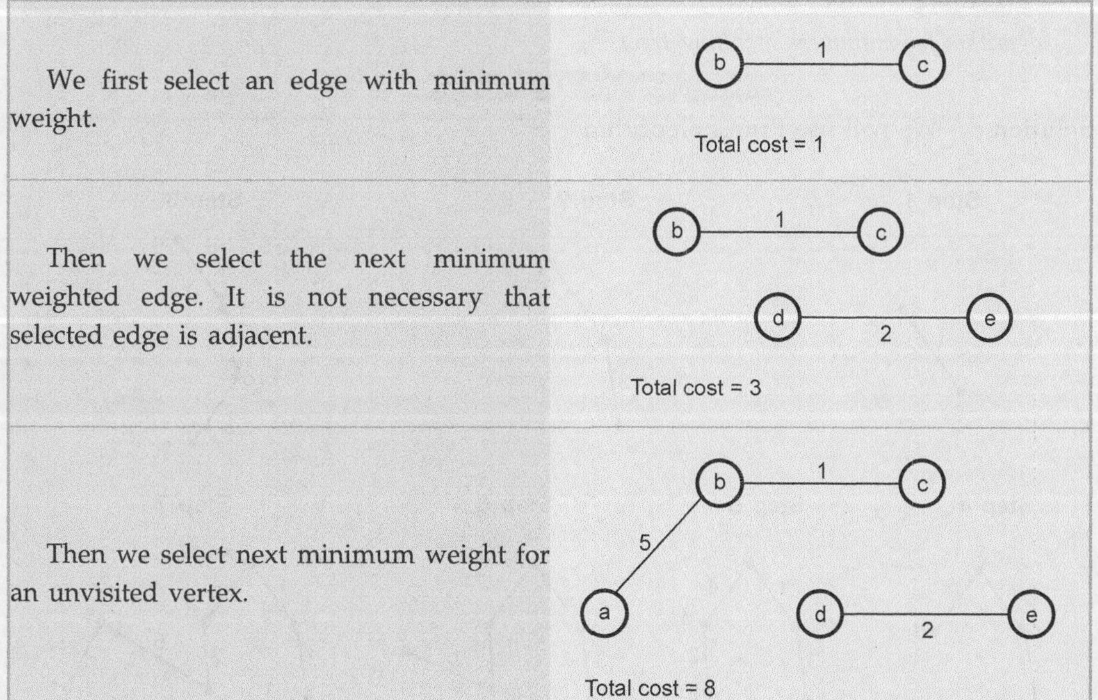

We first select an edge with minimum weight.

Then we select the next minimum weighted edge. It is not necessary that selected edge is adjacent.

Then we select next minimum weight for an unvisited vertex.

All the vertices are visited but since the spanning tree should be connected one. Hence we select an edge with minimum weight.

Thus we get a minimum spanning tree with Kruskal's algorithm.

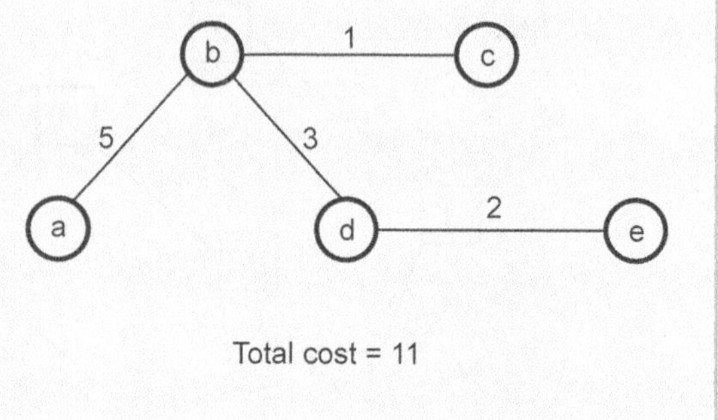

Example 5.7.10 *There is a network given in the figure below as a highway map and the number recorded next to each arc as the maximum elevation encountered in traversing the arc. A traveller plans to drive from node 1 to 12 on this highway. The traveller dislikes high altitudes and so would like to find a path connecting node 1 to 12 that minimizes the maximum altitude. Find the best path for the traveller using a MST.(Graph to be drawn for Kruskal or Prims algorithm for minimum spanning tree)*

GTU : Summer-14, Marks 7

Solution : We will use Prim's algorithm.

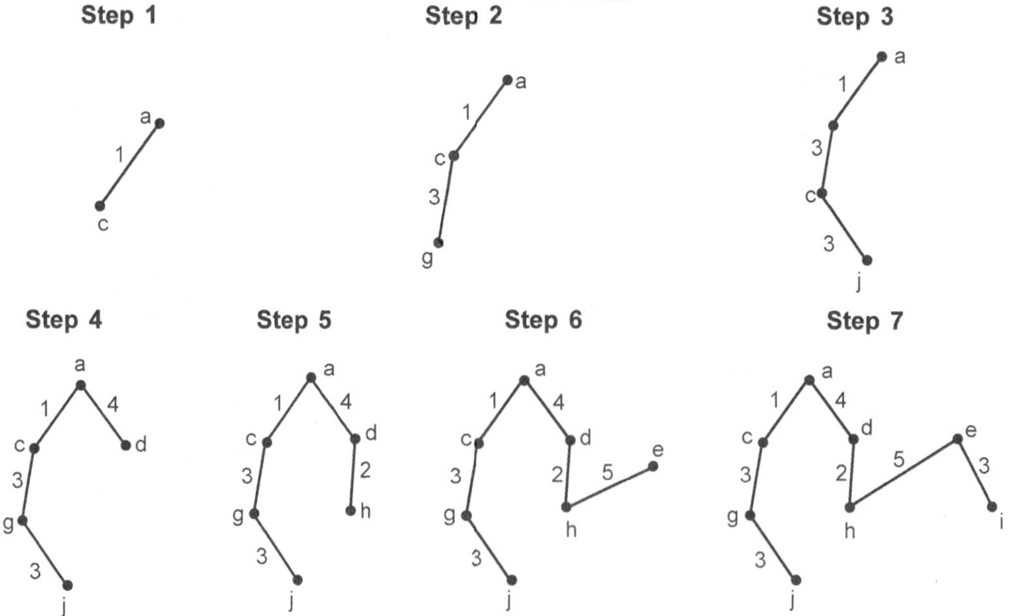

Step 8

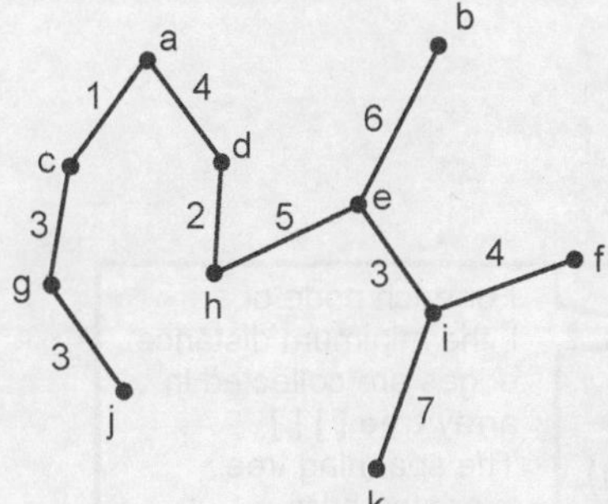

Step 9

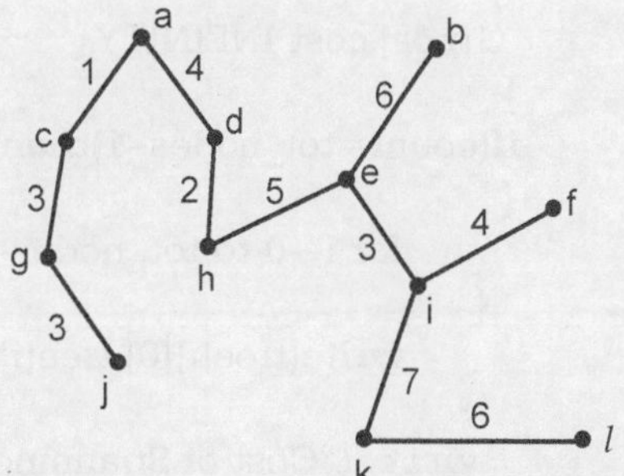

This is the best path for the traveller.

5.7.3 Algorithm

```
Algorithm spanning_tree()
//Problem Description : This algorithm finds the minimum
//spanning tree using Kruskal's algorithm
//Input : The adjacency matrix graph G containing cost
//Output : prints the spanning tree with the total cost of
//spanning tree
 count←0
 k←0
 sum←0
      for i←0 to tot_nodes do
            parent[i]←i
while(count!=tot_nodes-1)do
 {
      pos←Minimum(tot_edges);//finding the minimum cost edge
            if(pos=-1)then//Perhaps no node in the graph
                  break
             v1←G[pos].v1
             v2←G[pos].v2
             i←Find(v1,parent)
             j←Find(v2,parent)
             if(i!=j)then
             {
              tree[k][0] ←v1
             //storing the minimum edge in array tree[]
              tree[k][1] ←v2
              k++
              count++;
              sum+←G[pos].cost
             //accumulating the total cost of MST
```

tree [ ] [ ] is an array in which the spanning tree edges are stored.

Computing total cost of all the minimum distances.

```
            Union(i,j,parent);
            }
            G[pos].cost INFINITY
          }
          if(count=tot_nodes-1)then
          {
                for i←0 to tot_nodes-1
            {
                write(tree[i][0],tree[i][1])
            }
            write("Cost of Spanning Tree is ",sum)
          }
```

For each node of i, the minimum distance edges are collected in array **tree [ ] [ ]**. The spanning tree is printed here.

C function

```
void spanning_tree()
{
 int count,k,v1,v2,i,j,tree[10][10],pos,parent[10];
 int sum;
 int Find(int v2,int parent[]);
 void Union(int i,int j,int parent[]);
 count=0;
 k=0;
 sum=0;
 for(i=0 ; i<tot_nodes ; i++)
          parent[i]=i ;
 while(count!=tot_nodes-1)
 {
          pos = Minimum(tot_edges);//finding the minimum cost edge
          if(pos==-1)//Perhaps no node in the graph break;
          v1 = G[pos].v1;
          v2 = G[pos].v2;
          i = Find(v1,parent);
          j=Find(v2,parent);
          if(i! = j)
          {
               tree[k][0] = v1;//storing the minimum edge in array tree[]
               tree[k][1] = v2;
               k++;
               count++;
               sum+=G[pos].cost;//accumulating the total cost of MST
               Union(i,j,parent);
          }
          G[pos].cost = INFINITY;
         }
         if(count==tot_nodes-1)
         {
```

```
        printf("\n Spanning tree is...");
        printf("\n-------------------------\n");
        for(i=0 ; i<tot_nodes-1 ; i++)
        {
                printf("[%d",tree[i][0]);
                printf(" - ");
                printf("%d",tree[i][1]);
                printf("]");
        }
        printf("\n-------------------------");
        printf("\nCost of Spanning Tree is = %d",sum);
       }
       else
       {
            printf("There is no Spanning Tree");
       }
}
```

Analysis

The efficiency of Kruskal's algorithm is $\Theta(|E| \log |E|)$ where E is total number of edges in the graph.

C Program

```
/*****************************************************************
     Implementation of Kruskal's Algorithm
*****************************************************************/
#include<stdio.h>
#define INFINITY 999
typedef struct Graph
{
 int v1;
 int v2;
 int cost;
}GR;
GR G[20];
int tot_edges,tot_nodes;
void create();
void spanning_tree();
int Minimum(int);

void main()
{
 printf("\n\t Graph Creation by adjacency matrix ");
 create();
 spanning_tree();
}
```

```
void create()
{
 int k;
 printf("\n Enter Total number of nodes: ");
 scanf("%d",&tot_nodes);
 printf("\n Enter Total number of edges: ");
 scanf("%d",&tot_edges);
 for(k=0;k<tot_edges;k++)
 {
       printf("\n Enter Edge in (V1 V2)form ");
       scanf("%d%d",&G[k].v1,&G[k].v2);
       printf("\n Enter Corresponding Cost ");
       scanf("%d",&G[k].cost);
 }
}
void spanning_tree()
{
 int count,k,v1,v2,i,j,tree[10][10],pos,parent[10];
 int sum;
 int Find(int v2,int parent[]);
 void Union(int i,int j,int parent[]);
 count=0;
 k=0;
 sum=0;
 for(i=0;i<tot_nodes;i++)
                 parent[i] = i ;
 while(count!=tot_nodes-1)
 {
           pos=Minimum(tot_edges);//finding the minimum cost edge
           if(pos==-1)//Perhaps no node in the graph break;
           v1 =G[pos].v1;
           v2 = G[pos].v2;
           i=Find(v1,parent);
           j=Find(v2,parent);
           if(i!=j)
           {
                  tree[k][0]=v1;//storing the minimum edge in array tree[ ] [ ]
                  tree[k][1]=v2;
                  k++;
                  count++;
                  sum+= G[pos].cost;//accumulating the total cost of MST
                  Union(i,j,parent);
           }
           G[pos].cost = INFINITY;
      }
           if(count==tot_nodes-1)
           {
```

```
            printf("\n Spanning tree is...");
            printf("\n--------------------------\n");
            for(i=0 ; i<tot_nodes-1;i++)
            {
                  printf("[%d",tree[i][0]);
                  printf(" – ");
                  printf("%d",tree[i][1]);
                  printf("]");
            }
            printf("\n--------------------------");
            printf("\nCost of Spanning Tree is = %d",sum);
           }
           else
            {
                  printf("There is no Spanning Tree");
            }
}
int Minimum(int n)
{
 int i,small,pos;
 small = INFINITY;
 pos=-1;
 for(i=0 ; i<n;i++)
 {
           if(G[i].cost<small)
           {
                 small=G[i].cost;
                 pos=i ;
           }
 }
 return pos;
}
int Find(int v2,int parent[])
{
  while(parent[v2]! = v2)
{
           v2=parent[v2];
       }
       return v2;
}
void Union(int i,int j,int parent[])
{
 if(i<j)
            parent[j]=i ;
 else
            parent[i]=j ;
}
```

Output

```
        Graph Creation by adjacency matrix
Enter Total number of nodes: 4

Enter Total number of edges: 5

Enter Edge in (V1 V2)form 1 2

Enter Corresponding Cost 2

Enter Edge in (V1 V2)form 1 4

Enter Corresponding Cost 1

Enter Edge in (V1 V2)form 1 3

Enter Corresponding Cost 3

Enter Edge in (V1 V2)form 2 3

Enter Corresponding Cost 3

Enter Edge in (V1 V2)form 4 3

Enter Corresponding Cost 5

Spanning tree is...
---------------------------
    [1 - 4][1 - 2][1 - 3]
---------------------------
    Cost of Spanning Tree is = 6
```

Graph to be taken as input

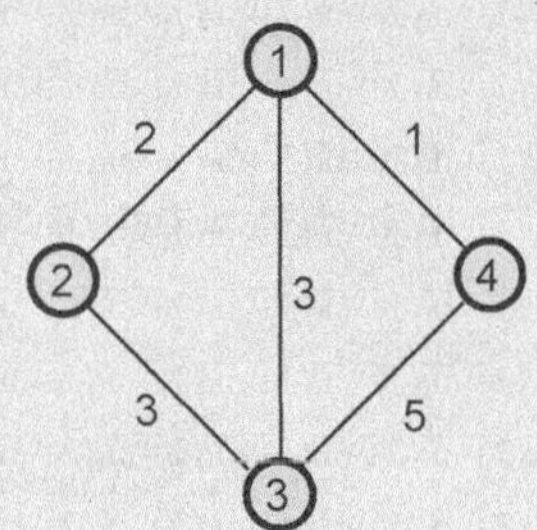

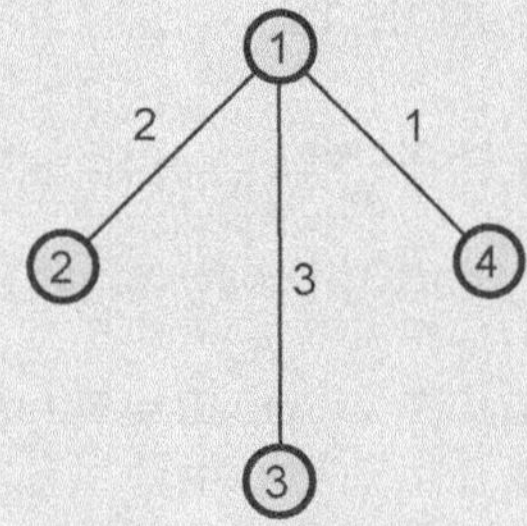

Fig. 5.7.9 Spanning tree

Examples For Practice

Example 5.7.11 *Find out minimum cost spanning tree using KRUSKAL algorithm.*

Edge	Cost	Edge	Cost
(V_1, V_7)	1	(V_4, V_5)	7
(V_3, V_4)	3	(V_1, V_2)	20
(V_2, V_7)	4	(V_1, V_6)	23
(V_3, V_7)	9	(V_5, V_7)	25
(V_2, V_3)	15	(V_5, V_6)	28
(V_4, V_7)	16	(V_6, V_7)	36

Example 5.7.12 *Find MST using Prim's algorithm.*

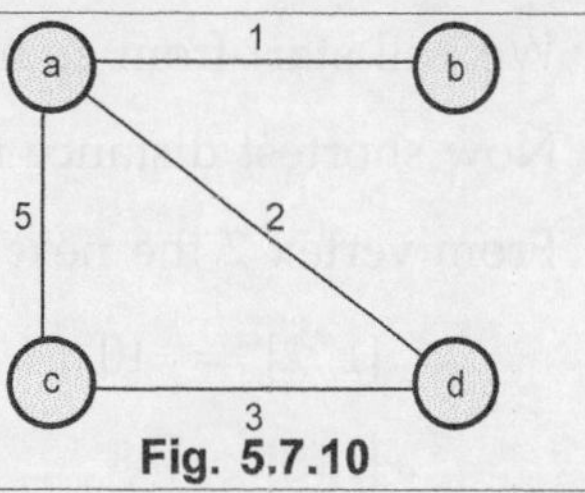

Fig. 5.7.10

Review Questions

1. *Give and explain the Prim's algorithm to find out minimum spanning tree with illustration.*
GTU : Dec.-10, Marks 7

2. *Give and explain the Kruskal's algorithm to find out minimum spanning tree with illustration.*
GTU : Dec.-10, Marks 7

3. *Write and analyze Prim's algorithm to generate minimum spanning tree.*
GTU : June-11, Marks 4

4. *Define Minimal Spanning Tree (MST). Explain Krushkal's Algorithm to find MST with example.*
GTU : June-12, Marks 7

5. *Mention applications of minimum spanning tree.* **GTU : Summer-15, Marks 2**

5.8 Graphs : Shortest Path

GTU : June-11, May-12, Winter-14, Marks 7

Many times, Graph is used to represent the distances between the two cities. Everybody is often interested in moving from one city to other as quickly as possible. The single source shortest path is based on this interest.

In single source shortest path problem the shortest distance from a single vertex called source is obtained. This shortest path algorithm is called Dijkstra's shortest path algorithm.

Let G(V, E) be a graph, then in single source shortest path the shortest paths from vertex v_0 to all remaining vertex is determined. The vertex v_0 is then called as source and the last vertex is called destination.

It is assumed that all the distances **are positive**. This algorithm does not work for negative distances.

Example : Consider a graph G as given below.

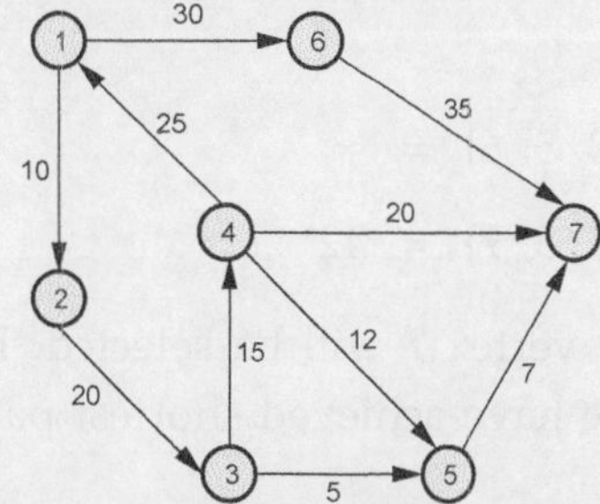

Fig. 5.8.1 Directed graph for single source shortest path

We will start from source vertex 1. Hence set S[1] = 1.

Now shortest distance from vertex 1 is 10. i.e. $1 \rightarrow 2 = 10$. Hence {1, 2} and min = 10.

From vertex 2 the next vertex chosen is 3.

$$\{1, 2\} = 10$$
$$\{1, 3\} = \infty$$
$$\{1, 5\} = \infty$$
$$\{1, 6\} = \infty$$
$$\{1, 7\} = \infty$$

Now

$$\{1, 2, 3\} = 30$$
$$\{1, 2, 4\} = \infty$$
$$\{1, 2, 7\} = \infty$$
$$\{1, 2, 5\} = \infty$$
$$\{1, 2, 6\} = \infty$$

Hence select 3.

$$\therefore \quad S[3] = 1$$

Now

$$\{1, 2, 3, 4\} = 45$$
$$\{1, 2, 3, 5\} = 35$$
$$\{1, 2, 3, 6\} = \infty$$
$$\{1, 2, 3, 7\} = \infty$$

Hence select next vertex as 5.

$$\therefore \quad S[5] = 1$$

Now

$$\{1, 2, 3, 5, 6\} = \infty$$
$$\{1, 2, 3, 5, 7\} = 42$$

Hence vertex 7 will be selected. In single source shortest path if destination vertex is 7 then we have achieved shortest path 1 - 2 - 3 - 5 - 7 with path length 42.

The single source shortest path from each vertex is summerised below -

1, 2	10
1, 2, 3	30
1, 2, 3, 4	45
1, 2, 3, 5	35
1, 2, 3, 4, 7	65
1, 2, 3, 5, 7	42
1, 6	30
1, 6, 7	65

Example 5.8.1 *Solve the following instances of single-source shortest path problem with vertex a as source.* **GTU : Winter-14, Marks 7**

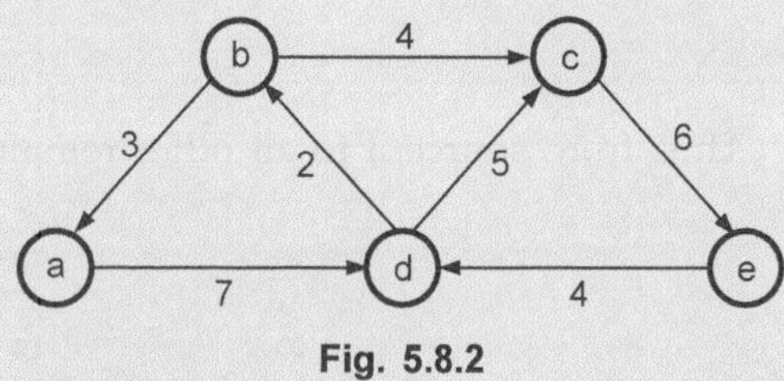

Fig. 5.8.2

Solution : We will find the distances from source a to every other vertices. We write the distances in **destination (source minimum distance)** form.

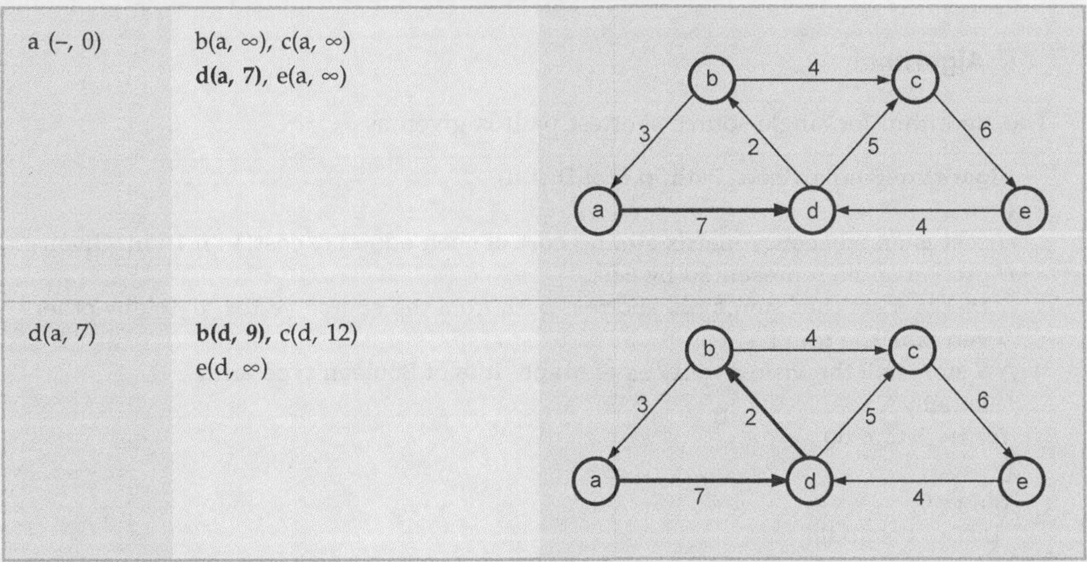

a (–, 0)	b(a, ∞), c(a, ∞) **d(a, 7)**, e(a, ∞)	
d(a, 7)	**b(d, 9)**, c(d, 12) e(d, ∞)	

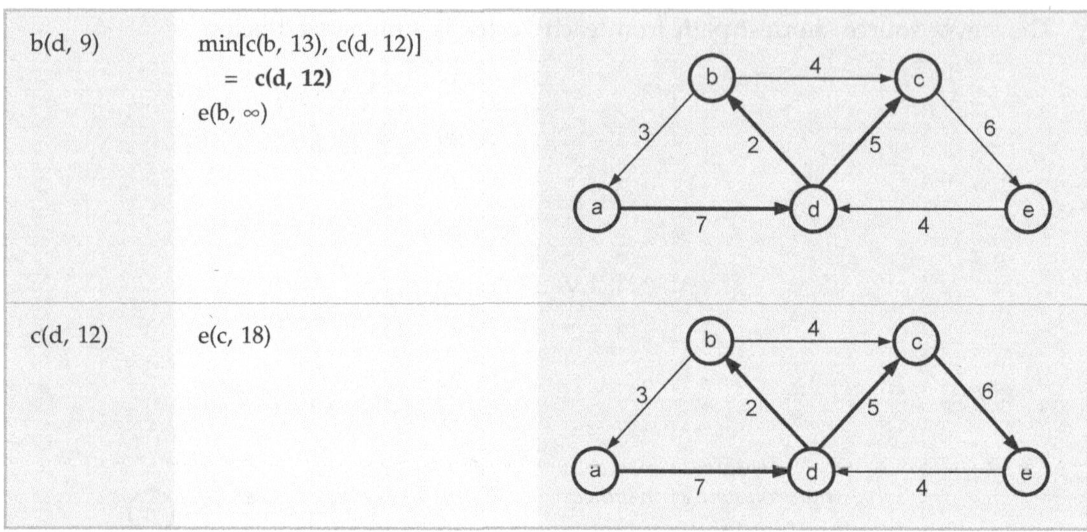

b(d, 9)	min[c(b, 13), c(d, 12)] = **c(d, 12)** e(b, ∞)	
c(d, 12)	e(c, 18)	

Thus from source a to all other remaining vertices the shortest paths are -

a to b	(a-d-b)	Path = 9
a to c	(a-d-c)	Path = 12
a to d	(a-d)	Path = 7
a to e	(a-d-c-e)	Path = 18

5.8.1 Algorithm

The algorithm for single source shortest path is given as

```
Algorithm Single_Short_Path( p,cost,Dist,n)
{
// cost is an adjacency matrix storing cost of each edge i.e. cost[1 : n,1 : n]. Given
// graph can be represented by cost.
// Dist is a set that stores the shortest path from the source vertex 'p' to any other
// vertex in the graph.
// S stores all the visited vertices of graph. It is of Boolean type array.
// initially
 for i ←1 to n do
 {
 S[i] ← 0;
  Dist ← cost[p,i];
 }
S[p] ←1 // set pth vertex to true in array S and i.e. put p in S
Dist[p] ← 0.0;
for val ← 2 to n–2 do
{
```

```
    // obtain n–1 paths from p
   Choose q from the vertices that are not visited (not in S) and with minimum
  distance.
  Dist[q] = min{Dist[i]};
   S[q] ← 1// put q in S
   /*update the Distance values of the other nodes*/
    for (all node r adjacent to q with S[r] = 0) do
      if( Dist[r]>(Dist[q]+cost[p,q])) then
           Dist[r] ← Dist[q]+Dist[p,q];
   }
  }
```

5.8.2 Analysis

Time Complexity of the algorithm:

- The 1st for-loop clearly takes O(n) time
- Choosing q takes O(n) time, because it involves finding a minimum in an array.
- The innermost for-loop for updating Dist iterates at most n times, thus takes O(n) time.
- Therefore, the for-loop iterating over val takes O(n*n) time

Thus, single source shortest path takes $\mathbf{O(n^2)}$ time.

5.8.3 C Program

```
/*****************************************************************
This program is for implementing Dijkstra's single source shortest
path Algorithm
*****************************************************************/
#include<stdio.h>
#include<conio.h>
#define infinity 999
int path[10];
void main()
{
 int tot_nodes,i,j,cost[10][10],dist[10],s[10];
 void create(int tot_nodes,int cost[][10]);
 void Dijkstra(int tot_nodes,int cost[][10],int i,int dist[10]);
 void display(int i,int j,int dist[10]);
 clrscr();
 printf("\n\t\t Creation of graph ");
 printf("\n Enter total number of nodes ");
 scanf("%d",&tot_nodes);
 create(tot_nodes,cost);
 for(i=0;i<tot_nodes ; i++)
 {
```

```
                printf("\n\t\t\t Press any key to continue...");
                printf("\n\t\t\t When Source = % d\n",i);
     or(j=0 ; j<tot_nodes ; j++)
            {
            Dijkstra(tot_nodes,cost,i,dist);
            if(dist[j] == infinity)
                printf("\n There is no path to %d\n",j);
            else
            {

                display(i,j,dist);
            }
            }
        }
}
void create(int tot nodes,int cost[][10])
{
 int i,j,val,tot edges,count=0;
 for(i=0 ; i<tot nodes; i++)
 {
            for(j=0 ; j<tot nodes ; j++)
            {
            if(i==j)
                cost[i][j]=0 ; //diagonal elements are 0
            else
                cost[i][j] = infinity;
            }
 }
 printf("\n Total number of edges ");
 scanf("%d",&tot_edges);
 while(count<tot_edges)
            {
            printf("\n Enter Vi and Vj");
            scanf("%d%d",&i,&j);
            printf("\n Enter the cost along this edge ");
            scanf("%d",&val);
            cost[j][i] = val;
            cost[i][j] = val;
            count++;
            }
}
void Dijkstra(int tot_nodes,int cost[10][10],int source,int
dist[])
{
 int i,j,v1,v2,min_dist;
 int s[10];
 for(i=0;i<tot_nodes;i++)
 {
```

```
            dist[i] =cost[source][i];//initially put the
            s[i]=0; //distance from source vertex to i
            //i is varied for each vertex
            path[i] = source;//all the sources are put in path
}
s[source] = 1;
for(i=1;i<tot_nodes;i++)
{
            min_dist = infinity;
            v1=-1 ; //reset previous value of v1
            for(j=0 ; j<tot_nodes ; j++)
            {
             if(s[j]==0)
             {
                   if(dist[j]<min_dist)
                   {
                    min_dist = dist[j] ; //finding minimum distance
                    v1=j;
                   }
             }
            }
            s[v1]=1;
            for(v2=0 ; v2<tot_nodes ; v2++)
            {
             if(s[v2]==0)
             {
                   if(dist[v1]+cost[v1][v2]<dist[v2])
                   {
                          dist[v2] = dist[v1]+cost[v1][v2];
                          path[v2] = v1;
                   }
             }
            }
      }
}
void display(int source,int destination,int dist[])
{
 int i;
 getch();
 printf("\n Step by Step shortest path is...\n");
 for(i=destination ; i! = source ; i = path[i])
 {
            printf("%d<-",i);
 }
 printf("%d",i);
 printf("  The length = %d",dist[destination]);
}
```

Output

The input graph is

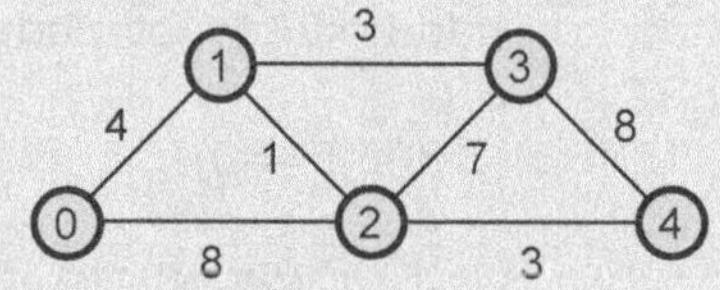


```
 Creation of graph
Enter total number of nodes 5

Total number of edges 7

Enter Vi and Vj 0 1

Enter the cost along this edge 4

Enter Vi and Vj 0 2

Enter the cost along this edge 8

Enter Vi and Vj 1 2

Enter the cost along this edge 1

Enter Vi and Vj 1 3

Enter the cost along this edge 3

Enter Vi and Vj 2 3

Enter the cost along this edge 7

Enter Vi and Vj 2 4

Enter the cost along this edge 3

Enter Vi and Vj 3 4

Enter the cost along this edge 8

                Press any key to continue...
            When Source = 0
Step by Step shortest path is...
0  The length=0
Step by Step shortest path is...
1<- 0  The length=4
Step by Step shortest path is...
2<-1<- 0  The length=5
Step by Step shortest path is...
3<-1<- 0  The length=7
Step by Step shortest path is...
4<-2<-1<- 0  The length=8
```

```
                    Press any key to continue...
          When Source =1

 Step by Step shortest path is...
0<-1  The length = 4
 Step by Step shortest path is...
1  The length = 0
 Step by Step shortest path is...
2<-1  The length = 1
 Step by Step shortest path is...
3<-1  The length = 3
 Step by Step shortest path is...
4<-2<-1  The length = 4
                    Press any key to continue...
          When Source =2

 Step by Step shortest path is...
0<-1<- 2  The length = 5
 Step by Step shortest path is...
1<- 2  The length = 1
 Step by Step shortest path is...
2  The length = 0
 Step by Step shortest path is...
3<-1<- 2  The length = 4
 Step by Step shortest path is...
4<- 2  The length = 3
                    Press any key to continue...
          When Source =3

 Step by Step shortest path is...
0<-1<- 3  The length = 7
 Step by Step shortest path is...
1<- 3  The length = 3
 Step by Step shortest path is...
2<-1<- 3  The length = 4
 Step by Step shortest path is...
3  The length = 0
 Step by Step shortest path is...
4<- 2<- 1<- 3  The length = 7
                    Press any key to continue...
          When Source = 4

 Step by Step shortest path is...
0<-1<- 2<- 4  The length = 8
 Step by Step shortest path is...
1<- 2<- 4  The length = 4
```

```
Step by Step shortest path is...
2<- 4 The length = 3
Step by Step shortest path is...
3<-1<-2<- 4 The length = 7
Step by Step shortest path is...
4 The length = 0
```

Review Questions

1. *Design and explain Dijkstra's shortest path algorithm.* **GTU : June-11, Marks 5**
2. *Explain Dijkstra's algorithm to find minimum distance of all nodes from a given node. (Greedy algorithm)]* **GTU : May-12, Marks 6**

5.9 Knapsack Problem

GTU : June-11, Dec.-11, Marks 7

The Knapsack problem can be stated as follows.

Suppose there are n objects from i = 1, 2,...n. Each object i has some positive weight w_i and some profit value is associated with each object which is denoted as p_i. This Knapsack carry at the most weight W.

While solving above mentioned Knapsack problem we have the capacity constraint. When we try to solve this problem using Greedy approach our goal is,

1. Choose only those objects that give maximum profit.
2. The total weight of selected objects should be $\leq$ W.

And then we can obtain the set of feasible solutions. In other words,

$$\text{maximized} \sum_{n}^{1} p_i x_i \text{ subject to } \sum_{n}^{1} w_i x_i \leq W$$

Where the Knapsack can carry the fraction x_i of an object i such that $0 \leq x_i \leq 1$ and $1 \leq i \leq n$.

Example 5.9.1 *Consider that there are three items. Weight and profit value of each item is as given below,*

i	W_i	P_i
1	18	30
2	15	21
3	10	18

Also W=20. Obtain the solution for the above given Knapsack problem.

Solution : The feasible solutions are as given below.

x_1	x_2	x_3
1/2	1/3	1/4
1	2/15	0
0	2/3	1
0	1	1/2

Let us compute $\sum W_i X_i$

1. 1/2 *18 + 1/3 *15 + 1/4 *10

   = **16.5**

2. 1 * 18 + 2/15 * 15 + 0*8

   = **20**

3. 0 * 18 +2/3 * 15 +10

   = **20**

4. 0 * 18 +1 * 15 +1/2 * 10

   = **20**

Let us compute $\sum P_i X_i$

1. 1/2 * 30 + 1/3 * 21 + 1/4 * 18

   = **26.5**

2. 1*30 + 2/15 * 21 + 0 * 18

   = **32.8**

3. 0 * 30 +2/3 * 21 +18

   = **32**

4. 0 * 30 +1 * 21 +1/2 * 18

   = **30**

To summarize this

$\sum W_i X_i$	$\sum P_i X_i$
16.5	26.5
20	32.8
20	32
20	30

The solution 2 gives the maximum profit and hence it turns out to be optimum solution.

Example 5.9.2 *Find the optimal solution of the Knapsack instance* $n = 7$, $M = 15$, $(P_1, P_2, \ldots P_7) = (10, 5, 15, 7, 6, 18, 3)$ *and* $(w_1, w_2, w_3, \ldots w_7) = (2, 3, 5, 7, 1, 4, 1)$

GTU : Dec.-11, Marks 7

Solution : For solving this problem, we will find out the fraction of weight that can be used to fill up the Knapsack satisfying the given capacity with maximum weight. We will try various solutions for the same.

Feasible solutions can be

Solution	x_1	x_2	x_3	x_4	x_5	x_6	x_7
1	1/2	1/3	1/4	1/7	1	3/4	1
2	1/2	1/3	1	1/7	0	1	1/2
3	1	1/3	1	1/7	1	1	1
4	1	1/3	1	1/7	0	1	1
5	1	2/3	1	0	1	1	1

Solution 1 :

$$\sum w_i x_i = \left(2*\frac{1}{2}\right)+\left(3*\frac{1}{3}\right)+\left(5*\frac{1}{4}\right)+\left(7*\frac{1}{7}\right)+(1*1)+\left(4*\frac{3}{4}\right)+1$$

$$= 1 + 1 + 1.25 + 1 + 1 + 3 + 1$$

$$\sum w_i x_i = \mathbf{9.25}$$

$$\sum p_i x_i = \left(10*\frac{1}{2}\right)+\left(5*\frac{1}{3}\right)+\left(15*\frac{1}{4}\right)+\left(7*\frac{1}{7}\right)+(6*1)+\left(18*\frac{3}{4}\right)+3$$

$$= 5 + 1.67 + 3.75 + 1 + 6 + 13.5 + 3$$

$$\sum p_i x_i = \mathbf{33.92}$$

Solution 2 :

$$\sum w_i x_i = \left(2*\frac{1}{2}\right)+\left(3*\frac{1}{3}\right)+(5*1)+\left(7*\frac{1}{7}\right)+(1*0)+(4*1)+\left(1*\frac{1}{2}\right)$$

$$= 1 + 1 + 5 + 1 + 0 + 4 + 0.5$$

$$\sum w_i x_i = \mathbf{12.5}$$

$$\sum p_i x_i = \left(10*\frac{1}{2}\right)+\left(5*\frac{1}{3}\right)+(15*1)+\left(7*\frac{1}{7}\right)+(6*0)+(18*1)+\left(3*\frac{1}{2}\right)$$

$$= 5 + 1.67 + 15 + 0 + 18 + 1.5$$

$$\sum p_i x_i = \mathbf{42.17}$$

Solution 3 :

$$\sum w_i x_i = (2*1)+\left(3*\frac{1}{3}\right)+(5*1)+\left(7*\frac{1}{7}\right)+(1*1)+(4*1)+(1*1)$$

$$= 2 + 1 + 5 + 1 + 1 + 4 + 1$$

$$\sum w_i x_i = \mathbf{15}$$

$$\sum p_i x_i = (10*1)+\left(5*\frac{1}{3}\right)+(15*1)+\left(7*\frac{1}{7}\right)+(6*1)+(18*1)+(3*1)$$

$$= 10 + 1.67 + 15 + 1 + 6 + 18 + 3$$

$$\sum p_i x_i = \mathbf{54.67}$$

Solution 4 :

$$\sum w_i x_i = (2*1)+\left(3*\frac{1}{3}\right)+(5*1)+\left(7*\frac{1}{7}\right)+(1*0)+(4*1)+(1*1)$$

$$\sum w_i x_i = \mathbf{14}$$

$$\sum p_i x_i = (10*1)+\left(5*\frac{1}{3}\right)+(15*1)+\left(7*\frac{1}{7}\right)+(6*0)+(18*1)+(3*1)$$

$$\sum p_i x_i = \mathbf{48.67}$$

Solution 5 :

$$\sum w_i x_i = (2*1)+\left(3*\frac{2}{3}\right)+(5*1)+(7*0)+(1*1)+(4*1)+(1*1)$$

$$= 2 + 2 + 5 + 1 + 4 + 1$$

$$\sum w_i x_i = \mathbf{15}$$

$$\sum p_i x_i = (10*1)+\left(5*\frac{2}{3}\right)+(15*1)+(7*0)+(6*1)+(18*1)+(3*1)$$

$$= 10 + 3.33 + 15 + 0 + 6 + 18 + 3$$

$$\sum p_i x_i = \mathbf{55.33}$$

From above computations, clearly solution 5 gives maximum profit. Hence solution 5 is considered as optimum solution.

5.9.1 Algorithm

The algorithm for solving Knapsack problem with Greedy approach is as given below.

```
Algorithm Knapsack_Greedy(W,n)
{
//p[i] contains the profits of i items such that 1 ≤ i ≤ n
//w[i] contains weights of I items.
//x[i] is the solution vector.
//W is the total size of Knapsack.
        for i : =1 to n do
{
if[w[i]<W) then//capacity of knapsack is a constraint
{
 x[i] : =1.0;
 W=W - w[i];
}
}
if(i<=n) then x[i] : =W/w[i];
}
```

This is the basic operation of selecting x[i] lies within for loop.
∴ Time complexity = $\Theta(n)$.

Review Question

1. *What is a fractional knapsack problem ? Design and analyze greedy algorithm to solve it.*
GTU : June-11, Marks 5

5.10 Job Scheduling Problem

GTU : Dec.-11, Winter-14,15, Marks 7

Consider that there are n jobs that are to be executed. At any time t = 1,2,3,.. only exactly one job is to be executed. The profits pi are given. These profits are gained by corresponding jobs. For obtaining feasible solution we should take care that the jobs get completed within their given deadlines.

Let n = 4

n	pi	di
1	70	2
2	12	1
3	18	2
4	35	1

We will follow following rules to obtain the feasible solution

- Each job takes one unit of time.

- If job starts **before or at its deadline**, profit is obtained, otherwise no profit.
- Goal is to schedule jobs to maximize the total profit.
- Consider all possible schedules and compute the minimum total time in the system.

Consider the Time line as

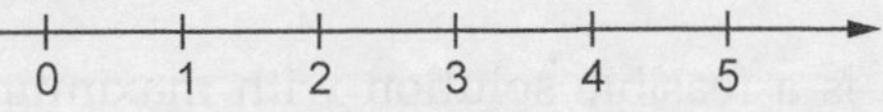

The feasible solutions are obtained by various permutations and combinations of jobs.

n	pi
1	70
2	12
3	18
4	35
1,3	88
2,1	82
2,3	30
3,1	88
4,1	105
4,3	53

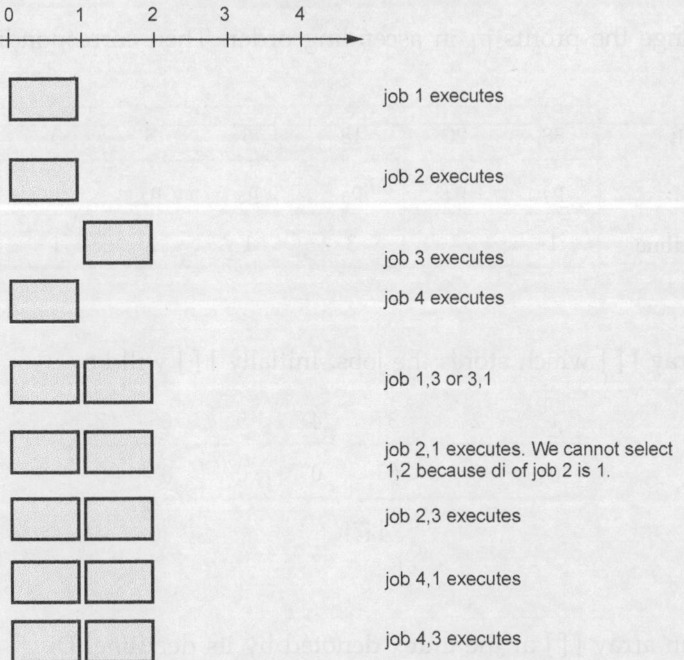

Fig. 5.10.1 Job sequencing with deadline

Each job takes only one unit of time. Deadline of job means a time **on which or before which the job has to be executed.** The sequence {2,4} is not allowed because both have deadline 1. If job 2 is started at 0 it will be completed on 1 but we cannot start job 4 on 1 since deadline of job 4 is 1. The feasible sequence is a sequence that allows all jobs in a sequence to be executed within their deadlines and highest profit can be gained.

- The optimal solution is a feasible solution with maximum profit.
- In above example sequence 3,2 is not considered as $d_3>d_2$ but we have considered the sequence 2,3 as feasible solution because $d_2<d_3$.
- We have chosen job 1 first then we have chosen job 4. The solution 4,1 is feasible as the order of execution is 4 then 1. Also $d_4<d_1$. If we try {1,3,4} then it is not a feasible solution, hence reject 3 from the set. Similarly if we add job 2 in the sequence then the sequence becomes {1,2,4}. This is also not a feasible solution hence reject it. Finally the feasible sequence is 4,1. This sequence is optimum solution as well.

Example 5.10.1 *Using greedy algorithm find an optimal schedule for following jobs with n = 7 profits: (P1,P2,P3,P4,P5,P6,P7) = (3,5,18,20,6,1,38) and deadline (d1,d2,d3,d4,d5,d6,d7) = (1,3,3,4,1,2,1)* **GTU : Dec.-11, Marks 7**

Solution :

Step 1 :

We will arrange the profits p_i in ascending order. Then corresponding deadlines will appear.

Profit	38	20	18	6	5	3	1
Job	p_7	p_4	p_3	p_5	p_2	p_1	p_6
Deadline	1	4	3	1	3	1	2

Step 2 :

Create an array J [ ] which stores the jobs. Initially J [ ] will be

1	2	3	4	5	6	7
0	0	0	0	0	0	0

J [7]

Step 3 :

Add i^{th} job in array J [ ] at the index denoted by its deadline. Di.

First job is p_7. The deadline for this job is 1. Hence insert p_7 in the array j [ ] at 1st index.

1	2	3	4	5	6	7
p_7						

Step 4 :

Next job is p_4. Insert it in array J [ ] at index 4.

1	2	3	4	5	6	7
p_7			p_4			

Step 5 :

Next job is p_3. Its has a deadline 3. Therefore insert it at index 3

1	2	3	4	5	6	7
p_7		p_3	p_4			

Step 6 : Next job is p_5, it has deadline 1. But as 1 is already occupied and there is no empty slot at index < J [1] . Hence just discard job p_5. Similarly job p_5 will get discarded.

Step 7 : Next job is p_2. Its has a deadline 3. There is an empty slot at index < J [3] Therefore insert it at index 2

1	2	3	4	5	6	7
p_7	p_2	p_3	p_4			

Step 8 : Thus we now obtain the job sequence as **7-2-3-4** with the profit of **81.**

Example 5.10.2 *Using greedy algorithm find an optimal schedule for following jobs with n = 5 profits : (P1, P2, P3,P4,P5) = (3,5,18,20,38) and deadline : (d1,d2,d3,d4,d5) = (1,3,3,4,1)*

GTU : Winter -14, Marks 7

Solution : Step 1 : We will arrange profits Pi in descending order. The corresponding deadlines are also mentioned.

Profit	38	20	18	5	3
Job	P5	P4	P3	P2	P1
Deadline	1	3	3	4	1

Step 2 : Create an array J[ ] which stores the job. Initially J [ ] will be.

1	2	3	4	5
0	0	0	0	0

J[5]

Step 3 : Add i^{th} job in array J [ ] at index denoted by its deadline Di. First job is P5 in array J[ ] at 1st index, because its deadline is 1.

1	2	3	4	5
P5				

Step 4 : Next job is P_4. Insert it at index 3.

1	2	3	4	5
P5		P4		

Step 5 : Next job is P3, but its deadline is 3 and it is not possible to insert P3 at 3. Hence just discard it.

Step 6 : Insert P_2 at 4th index as deadline of P_2 is 4.

1	2	3	4	5
P5		P4	P2	

Step 7 : Just discard P1 whose deadline is 1.

Step 8 : Thus we now obtain the job sequence as **5-4-2** with profit of **63.**

Example 5.10.3 *Using greedy algorithm find an optimal schedule for following jobs with n = 6.*

Profits : (Pl, P2, P3, P4, P5, P6) = (20, 15, 10, 7, 5, 3)

Deadline : (d1, d2, d3, d4, d5, d6) = (3 , 1, 1, 3, 1, 3) **GTU : Winter -15, Marks 7**

Solution :

Step 1 : We will arrange the profits P_i in descending order. Then corresponding deadlines will appear.

Profit	20	15	10	7	5	3
Job	P1	P2	P3	P4	P5	P6
Deadline	3	1	1	3	1	3

Step 2 : Create an array J [ ] which stores the jobs. Initially J [ ] will be

1	2	3	4	5	6
0	0	0	0	0	0

J[6]

Step 3 : Add i^{th} job in array J [ ] at index denoted by its deadline d_i. First job is P1. The deadline for this job is 3. Hence insert P1 at index 3 in J [ ] array.

1	2	3	4	5	6
		P1			

Step 4 : Next job is P2. Insert it at index 1 in J [ ] array.

1	2	3	4	5	6
P2		P1			

Step 5 : Next job is P3 having deadline 1. There is no empty slot at index 1 in J [ ] array. Hence discard P3.

Step 6 : Next job is P4 having deadline 3. The index 3 in J [ ] array is already occupied but there is empty slot at index 2 in J [ ] array. Hence insert P4 at index 2.

1	2	3	4	5	6
P2	P4	P1			

Step 7 : Next job is P5 whose deadline is 1. Discard it. Similarly discard the next job i.e. P6 as its deadline is 3.

Step 8 : Thus we now obtain the job sequence as **2 – 4 – 1** with profit 15 + 7 + 20 = **42**.

5.10.1 Algorithm

The algorithm for job sequencing is as given below

```
Algorithm Job_seq(D,J,n)
{
//Problem description : This algorithm is for job sequencing using Greedy method.
//D[i] denotes ith deadline where 1 ≤ i ≤ n
//J[i] denotes ith job
// D[J[i]] ≤ D[J[i+1]]
//Initially
D[0]←0;
J[0]←0;
J[1]←1;
count←1;
for ←2 to n do
{
 t←count;
 while(D[J[t]] > D[i]) AND D[J[t]]!=t)) do t←t-1;
 if((D[J[t]] ≤ D[i])AND(D[i] > t)) then
```

```
{
    //insertion of ith feasible sequence into J array
    for s←count to (t+1) step -1 do
    J[s+1] ← J[s];
    J[t+1]←I;
    count←count+1;
}//end of if
}//end of while
return count;
}
```

The sequence of J will be inserted if and only if D[J[t]]!=t. This also means that the job J will be processed if it is in within the deadline.

The computing time taken by above Job_seq algorithm is $O(n^2)$, because the basic operation of computing sequence in array J is within two nested for loops.

5.11 Huffman Code

GTU : Winter-15, Marks 7

The Huffman's algorithm was developed by David. Huffman when he was a Ph.D. student at MIT. This algorithm is basically a coding technique for encoding data. Such an encoded data is used in data compression techniques.

- In Huffman's coding method, the data is inputted as a sequence of characters. Then a table of frequency of occurence of each character in the data is built.
- From the table of Frequencies **Huffman's tree** is constructed.
- The Huffman's tree is further used for encoding each character, so that binary encoding is obtained for given data.
- In Huffman's tre is further is a specific method of representing each symbol. This method produces a code in such a manner that no code word is **Prefix** of some other code word. Such codes are called **Prefix codes** or **Prefix Free** codes. Thus this method is useful for obtaining optimal data compression.

Let us understand the technique of Huffman's coding with the help of some example.

Example 5.11.1 *Obtain Huffman's encoding for following data*

a : 39 b : 10 c : 9 d : 25 e : 7 f : 3

Solution : Basically there are two types of coding **fixed length coding** and **varible length coding**. If we use fixed length coding we will need fixed number of bits to represent any character from a to h : We use 3 bits to represent any character. Hence we will arrange given symbols along with their frequencies as follows -

Step 1 : The symbols are arranged in ascending order of frequencies

Step 2 :

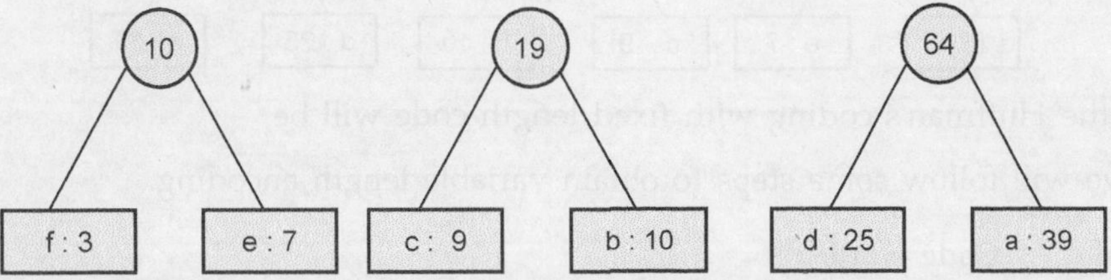

We will encode each of the above branch. The encoding should start from top to down. If we follow the **left branch** then we should encode it as **" 0 "** and if we follow the **right branch** then we should encode it as "1". Hence we get

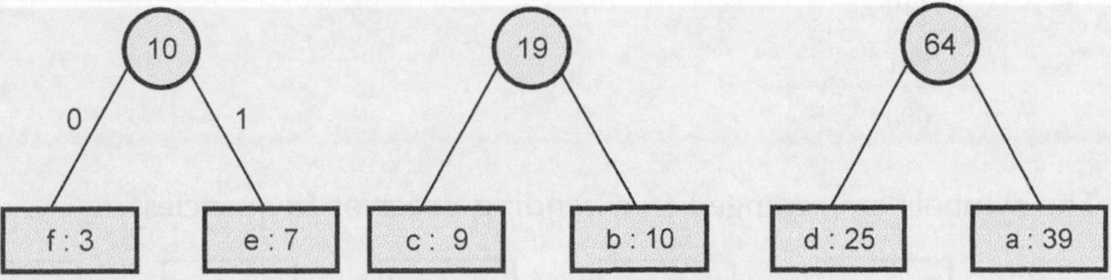

Step 3 :

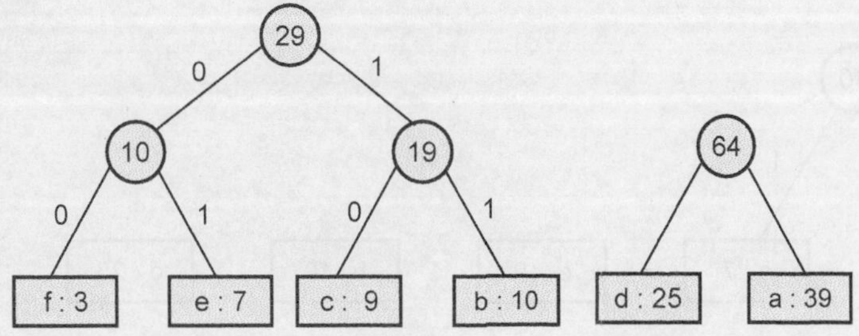

Step 4 :

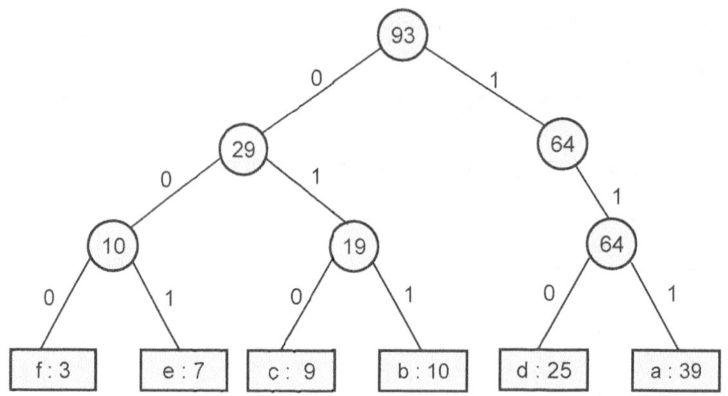

Hence the Huffman's coding with fixed length code will be

Now we will follow some steps to obtain variable length encoding.

Symbol	Code word
a	111
b	011
c	010
d	110
e	001
f	000

If we want to encode a string "aeed" then we get **111001001110** as a code word.

Step 1 : The symbols are arranged in ascending order of frequencies.

f : 3	e : 7	c : 9	b : 10	d : 25	a : 39

Step 2 :

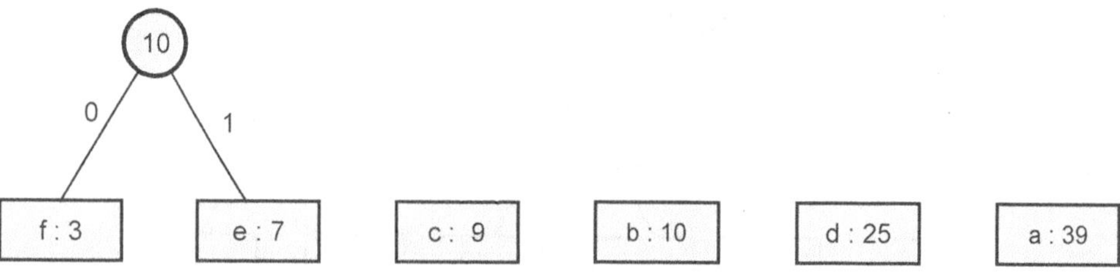

Step 3 :

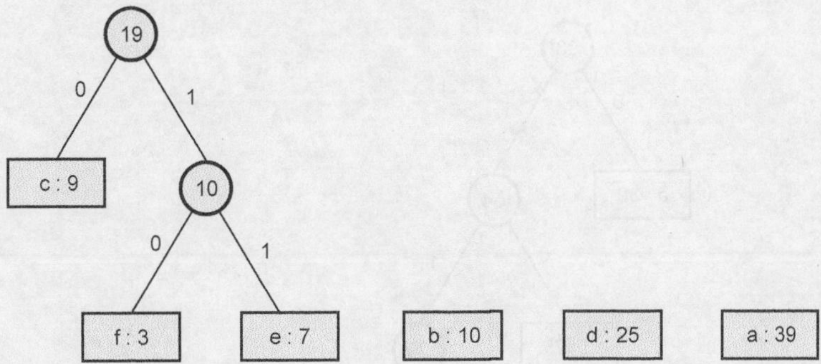

Step 4 :

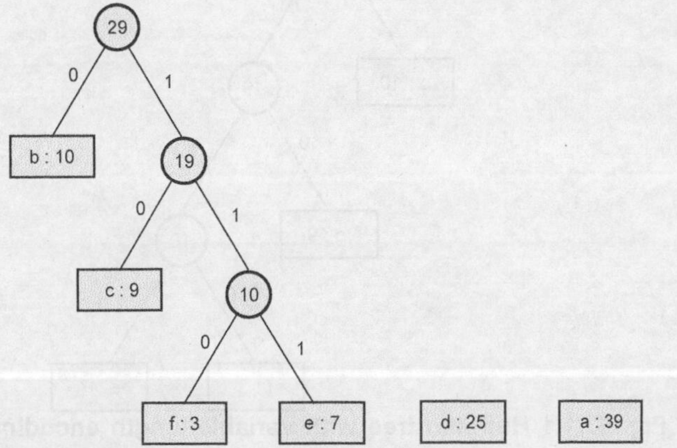

Step 5 :

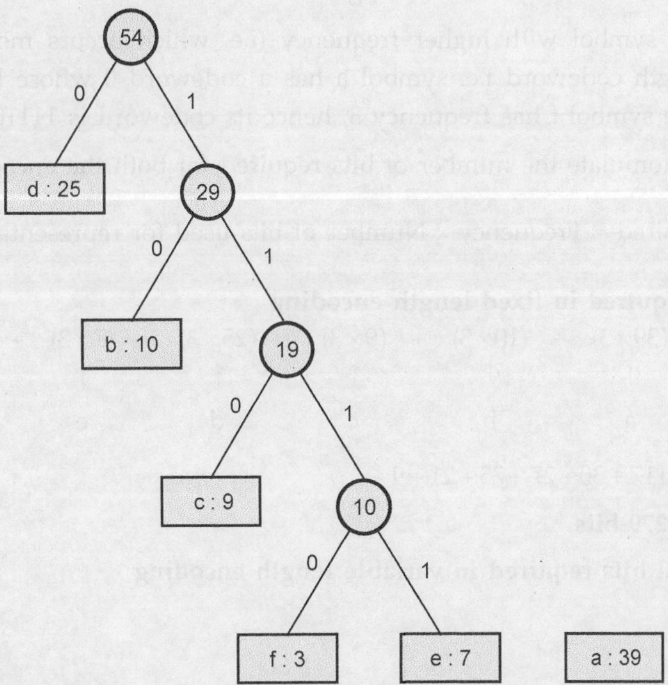

Step 6 :

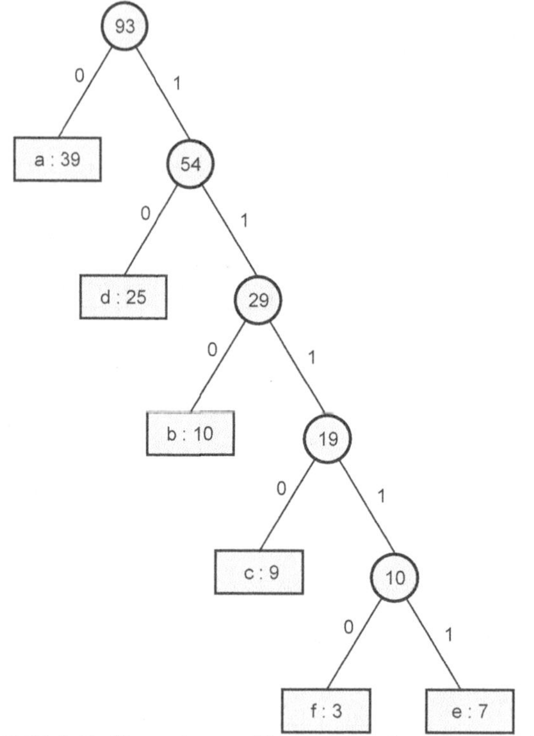

Fig. 5.11.1 Huffman tree with variable length encoding

The codewords for each symbol are as given below

Note that the symbol with higher frequency (i.e. which occurs more than often) is having small length codeword i.e. symbol a has a codeword 0 whose length is one. On the contarary, the symbol f has frequency 3, hence its codeword is 11110 i.e. of length 5.

Now we will fomulate the number of bits required for both the encoding technique -

> Total bits required = Frequency × Number of bits used for representation

$\therefore$**Total bits required in fixed length encoding**

$$= \underset{a}{\underset{\uparrow}{(39\times 3)}} + \underset{b}{\underset{\uparrow}{(10\times 3)}} + \underset{c}{\underset{\uparrow}{(9\times 3)}} + \underset{d}{\underset{\uparrow}{(25\times 3)}} + \underset{e}{\underset{\uparrow}{(7\times 3)}} + \underset{f}{\underset{\uparrow}{(3\times 3)}}$$

$= 117 + 30 + 27 + 75 + 21 + 9$

$=$ **279-bits**

similarly, **Total bits required in variable length encoding**

$$= \underset{\substack{\uparrow \\ a}}{(39\times1)} + \underset{\substack{\uparrow \\ d}}{(25\times2)} + \underset{\substack{\uparrow \\ b}}{(10\times3)} + \underset{\substack{\uparrow \\ c}}{(9\times4)} + \underset{\substack{\uparrow \\ f}}{(3\times5)} + \underset{\substack{\uparrow \\ e}}{(7\times5)}$$

$$= 39+50+30+36+15+35$$

$$= \textbf{205-bits}$$

Clearly variable length encoding requires less number of bits than fixed length encoding .

Merits of variable length encoding

1. The variable length encoding method, assigns short code word for more frequently used characters and long code word for in frequent characters.
2. This method is more efficient than fixed length encoding.

Decoding

Decoding is an exact reverse procedure of encoding. In a constructed Huffman's tree the leaves represent the character and from given code word we can find out the original characters.

Example 5.11.2 *Construct the Huffman tree for the following data and obtain its Huffman code.* **May-12**

Character	A	B	C	D	E	-
Probability	0.5	0.35	0.5	0.1	0.4	0.2

Encode text DAD-BE using the above code.

Decode the text 1100110110 using above information.

Solution : Step 1 :

We will arrange the characters by ascending order of their probabilities.

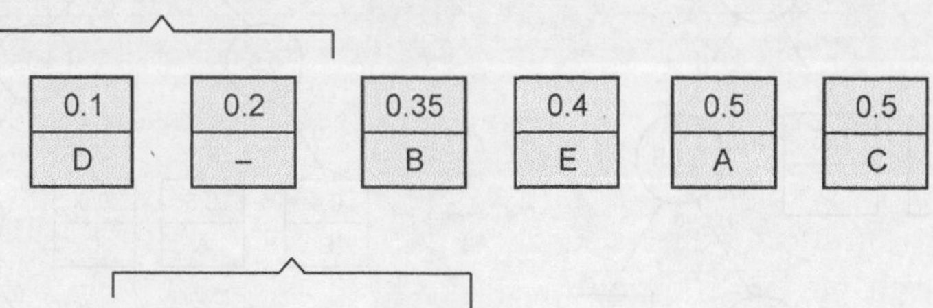

Step 2 :

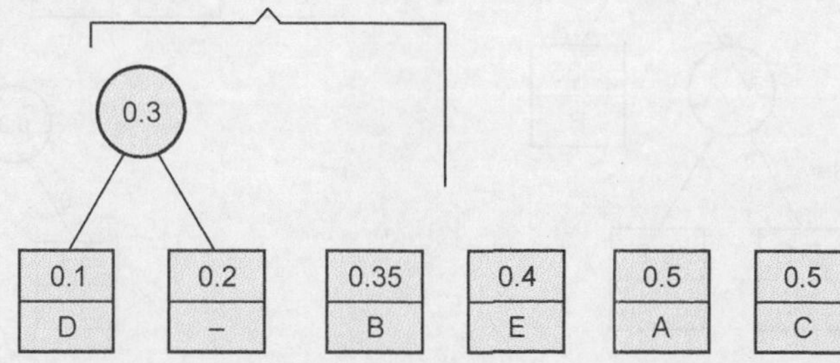

Step 3 :

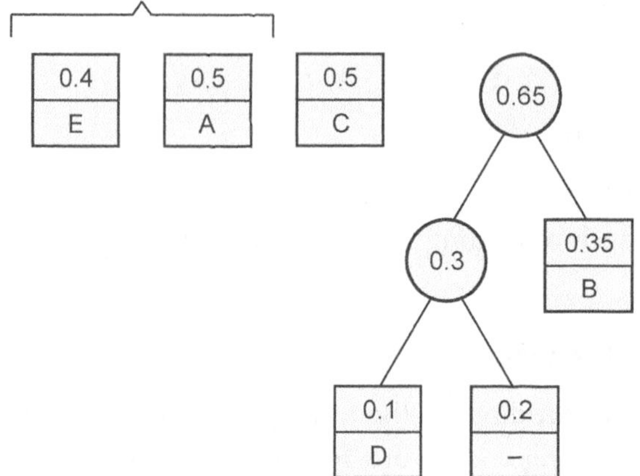

Step 4 :

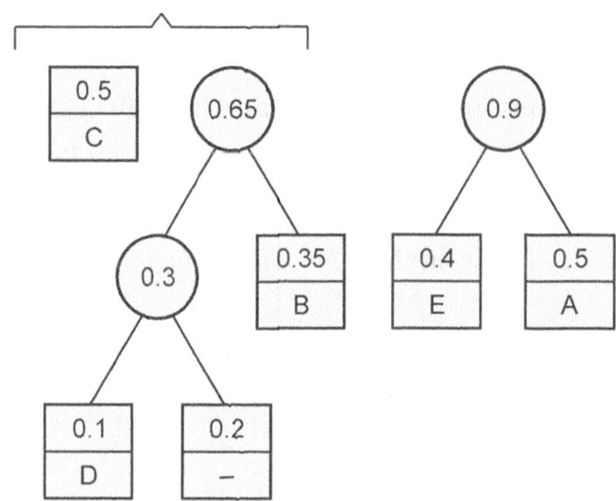

Step 5 :

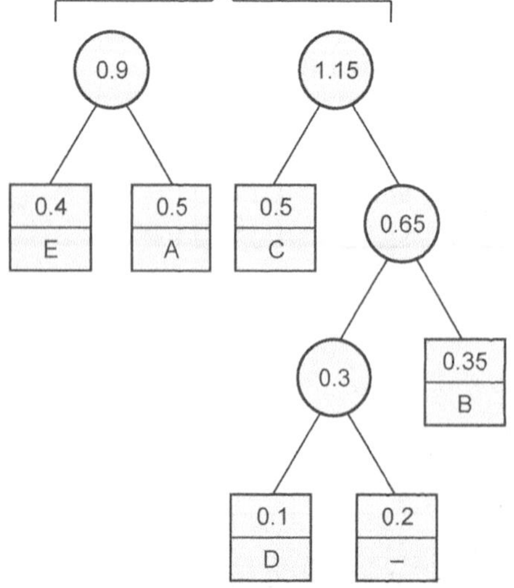

Step 6 :

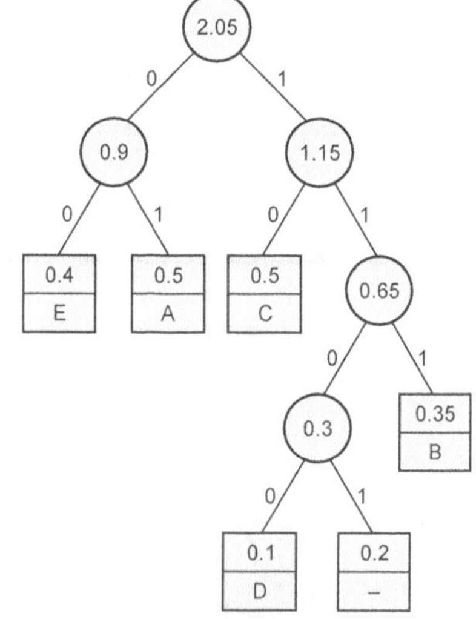

The encoding for each character will be

Character	Code
A	01
B	111
C	10
D	1100
E	00
-	1101

The encoding of DAD - BE is 1100011100 110111100

Decoding of **1100110110 is** D - C

Example 5.11.3 *Why Huffman code is called prefix free code ? Construct a Huffman tree for the following data :*

Character	A	B	C	D	'–'
Probability	0.35	0.1	0.2	0.2	0.15

Find codes of A, B, C, D and '–' **Dec.-13**

Solution :

Step 1 : We will arrange the characters by ascending order of probabilities.

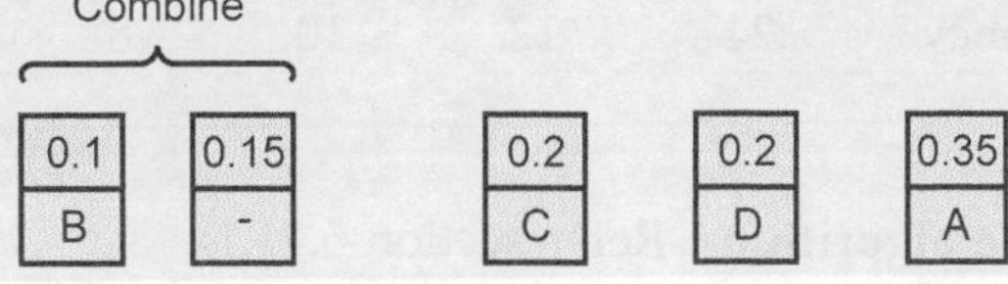

Step 2 : **Step 3 :**

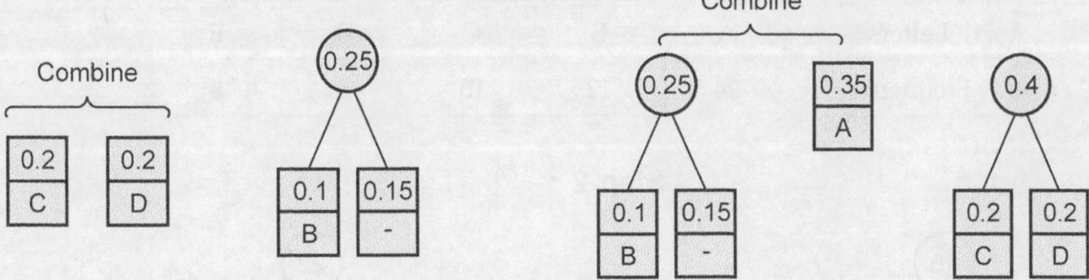

Step 4 :

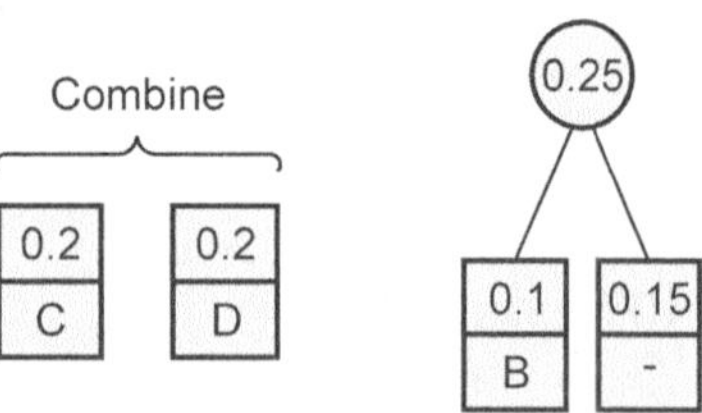

Step 5 :

Combine

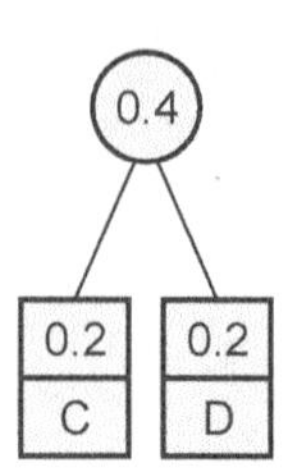

Step 6 : We will encode the Huffman's tree created in step 5. The encoding for each character is summerized in the table.

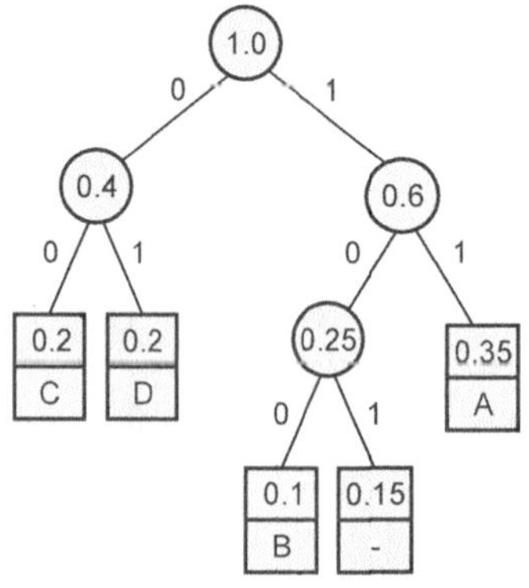

Character	Code
A	11
B	100
C	00
D	01
'-'	101

Example 5.11.4 *Write Huffman code algorithm and Generate Huffman code for following*

Letters	A	B	C	D	E
Frequency	24	12	10	8	8

GTU : Winter-15, Marks 7

Solution : Huffman code algorithm : Refer section 5.11.1.

Example

Letters	A	B	C	D	E
Frequency	24	12	10	8	8

Step 1 :

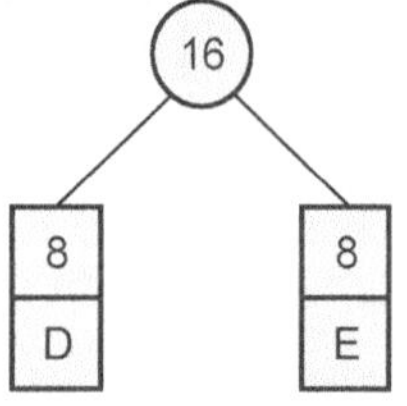

Step 2 :

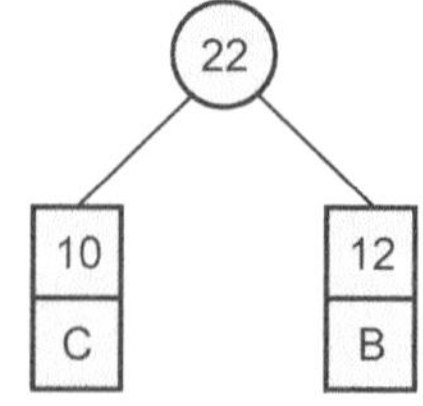

Step 3 :

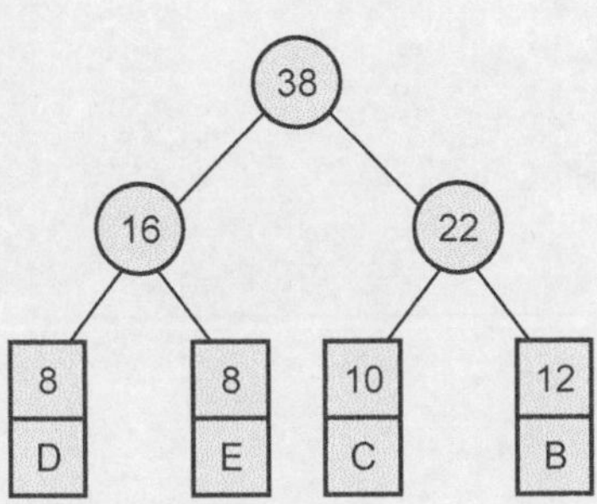

Step 4 :

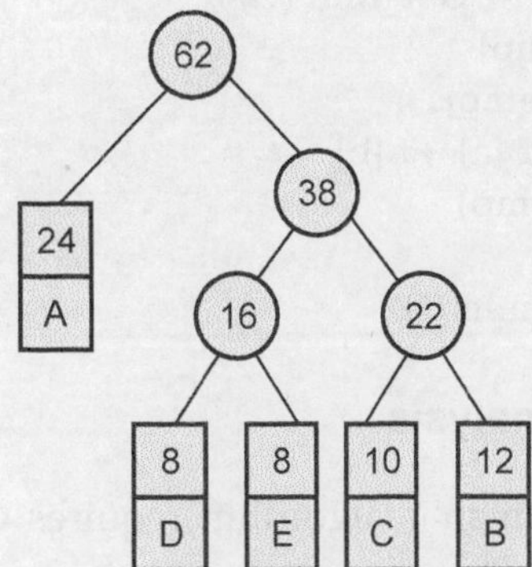

Step 5 : Apply codes. The left branch is coded to be 0 and right branch is coded to be 1.

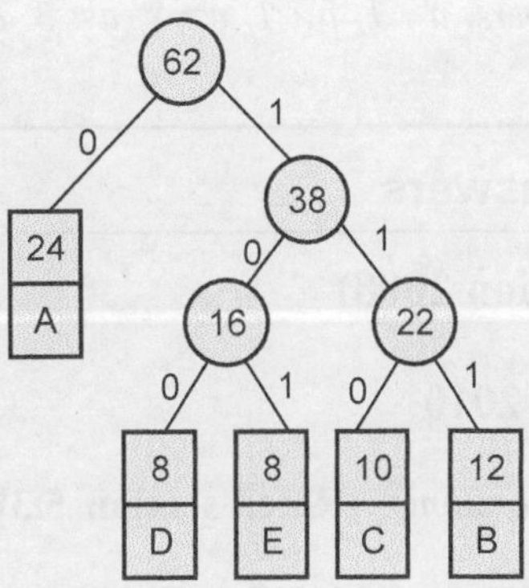

Letter	Code
A	0
B	111
C	110
D	100
E	101

5.11.1 Algorithm

The method which is used to construct optimal prefix code is called **Huffman coding.** This algorithm builds a tree in bottom up manner. We can denote this tree by T.

Let, $|c|$ be number of leaves

$|c|-1$ are number of operations required to merge the nodes.

Q be the priority queue which can be used while constructing binary heap.

```
Algorithm Huffman (c )
{
n = |c|
Q = c
for i ← 1 to n – 1
do
{
temp ← get _ node ()
```

```
left [temp] Get_min (Q)
right [temp] = Get_Min (Q)
a = left [temp]
b = right [temp]
F [temp] ← f [a] +f [b]
insert (Q, temp)
}
return Get_min (Q)
```

5.11.2 Analysis

The Huffman' s algorithm requires **O(log n)** time.

Example for Practice

Example 5.11.5 : *What is the optimal Huffman code for the following set of frequencies based on first 8 Fibonacci numbers. a : 1, b : 1, c : 2, d : 3, e : 5, f : 8, g : 13, h : 21*

5.12 University Questions with Answers

(Regulation 2008)

Dec. 2010

Q.1 *Give the characteristics of greedy algorithms.* **[Refer section 5.3]** [3]

Q.2 *Give and explain the Prim's algorithm to find out minimum spanning tree with illustration.* **[Refer section 5.7]** [7]

Q.3 *Give and explain the Kruskal's algorithm to find out minimum spanning tree with illustration.* **[Refer section 5.7]** [7]

May 2011

Q.4 *Give the characteristics of greedy algorithms.* **[Refer section 5.3]** [3]

Q.5 *Explain the term - optimal substructure property.* **[Refer section 5.5]** [2]

Q.6 *Write and analyze Prim's algorithm to generate minimum spanning tree.* **[Refer section 5.7]** [4]

Q.7 *Design and explain Dijkstra's shortest path algorithm.* **[Refer section 5.8]** [5]

Q.8 *What is a fractional knapsack problem ? Design and analyze greedy algorithm to solve it.* **[Refer section 5.9]** [5]

May 2012

Q.9 *Give the characteristics of greedy algorithms.* **[Refer section 5.3]** [3]

Q.10 *Define Minimal Spanning Tree (MST). Explain Krushkal's Algorithm to find MST with example.* **[Refer section 5.7]** [7]

Q.11 *Explain Dijkstra's algorithm to find minimum distance of all nodes from a given node. (Greedy algorithm)* **[Refer section 5.7]** [6]

5.13 Short Questions and Answers

Q.1 State the general principle of Greedy algorithm.

Ans. : In Greedy technique, the solution is constructed through a sequence of steps, each expanding partially constructed solution obtained so far, until a complete solution to a problem is reached. At each step the choice of feasible solutions is made. From the set of feasible solutions the optimal solution is selected as the solution to the problem.

Q.2 State the general characteristics of Greedy algorithm.

Ans. : There are two general characteristics of Greedy algorithm -

a) Greedy choice property b) Optimal substructure property .

Q.3 Why is the name Greedy method ?

Ans. : The name greedy suggests that for solving the given problem, on each step, the choice made must be feasible, locally optimal and irrevocable. Thus there is always a greed for obtaining optimum solution. This method provides optimal solution directly.

Q.4 What is feasible solution ?

Ans. : For solving the particular problem there exists n inputs and we need to obtain a subset that satisfies some constraints. Then any subset that satisfies these constraints is called feasible solution.

Q.5 What is an optimal solution ?

Ans. : Optimal solution is the best choice selected from the set of feasible solutions. This solution can be minimum or the maximum value of the solution.

Q.6 Compare feasible and optimal solution.

Ans. : While solving the problem using Greedy approach solutions are obtained in number of stages. These solutions satisfy problem's constraints. Such solutions are called feasible solutions. Among the feasible solutions if the best solution (either with minimum or with maximum value) is chosen then that solution is called optimal solution.

Q.7 How to get optimal solution ?

Ans. : Following are the activities that are performed in Greedy algorithm for getting the optimal solution -

a) Select some solutions from input domain.

b) Then check whether the solution is feasible or not.

c) From the set of feasible solutions there exists particular solution that satisfies or nearly satisfies the objective of the function. Select such solution as an optimal solution.

Q.8 What is objective function ?

Ans. : A feasible solution that either minimizes or maximizes a given objective function is called objective function.

Q.9 What is the drawback of Greedy algorithm ?

Ans. : Following are the demerits of greedy method :

1. Greedy method is comparatively efficient than divide and conquer but there is no as such guarantee of getting optimum solution.
2. In greedy method, the optimum selection is without revising previously generated solutions.

Q.10 What is minimum spanning tree ?

Ans. : A minimum spanning tree of a weighted connected graph G is a spanning tree with minimum or smallest weight.

Q.11 What is spanning tree ?

Ans. : A spanning tree of a graph G is a subgraph which is basically a tree and it contains all the vertices of G containing no circuit.

Q.12 What are the applications of spanning trees ?

Ans. : 1. Spanning trees are very important in designing efficient routing algorithms.

2. Spanning trees have wide applications in many areas such as network design.

Q.13 List the algorithms used for minimum spanning tree

Ans. : 1. Prim's algorithm 2. Kruskal's algorithm

Q.14 What is the difference between Prim's and Kruskal's algorithm?

Ans. : Prim's algorithm is for obtaining minimum spanning tree by selecting the adjacent vertices of already selected vertices.

Kruskal's algorithm is for obtaining minimum spanning tree but it is not necessary to choose adjacent vertices of already selected vertices.

Q.15 State the time complexity of Prim's algorithm.

Ans. : The time complexity of Prim's algorithm is O(|V2|).

Q.16 What is the purpose of Dijkstra's algorithm?

Ans. : The Dijkstra's algorithm is to find the shortest path from a single source vertex. This algorithm works for non negative weights only.

Q.17 Does Dijkstra's algorithm work for negative weight ?

Ans. : No, Dijkstra's algorithm does not work for negative weights.

Q.18 Is it possible to solve the 0/1 knapsack problem using greedy approach ?

Ans. : The greedy method is not suitable for solving the 0/1 knapsack problem. This problem can be solved using the dynamic programming method.

Q.19 What is Job sequencing problem?

Ans. : Consider that there are n jobs that are to be executed. At any time t = 1,2,3,.. only exactly one job is to be executed. The profits pi are given. These profits are gained by corresponding jobs. For obtaining feasible solution we should take care that the jobs get completed within their given deadlines.

Q.20 What is the purpose of Huffman's tree ?

Ans. : The Huffman trees are constructed for encoding a given text of n characters. While encoding a given text, each character is associated with some bit sequence. Such a bit sequence is called code word.

Q.21 What is prefix code ?

Ans. : In Huffman's tree is further is a specific method of representing each symbol. This method produces a code in such a manner that no code word is Prefix of some other code word. Such codes are called Prefix codes or Prefix Free codes.

Q.22 State the applications of Huffman's tree.

Ans. : 1. Huffman encoding is used in file compression algorithm.

2. Huffman's code is used in transmission of data in an encoded form.

3. This encoding is used in game playing method in which decision trees need to be formed.

❑❑❑

Notes

6 Exploring Graphs

Syllabus

An introduction using graphs and games, Undirected graph, Directed graph, Traversing graphs, Depth first search, Breadth first search, Topological sort, Connected components.

Contents

6.1 An Introduction using Graphs and Games

GTU : June-11, Marks 4

Various problems can be formulated using graphs. Graph is a non linear data structure. Game playing applications can be represented using graphs. Consider a game named **Mgrienbad** which is variant of **Nim** (Nim is a popular game which is originated in China). To understand the strategy for this game consider following rules -

1. Initially there is a heap of objects between two players.
2. Each player can pick up the objects alternatively.
3. Each player can pick up at the most twice the number of objects than its opponent and not more than that.
4. Any object is removed from one row at a time.
5. The person who picks up lastly looses. And the opponent wins.
6. There is no draw between two players.

To illustrate this game consider that there are two Players : I and you. The heap of objects is arranged in two rows namely A and B. Following are some instances which shows winning and loosing of two players.

Instance 1 :

A	B	Moves
3	2	I take 1 from B.
3	1	You take 2 from A.
1	1	I take 1 from A.
0	1	You take 1 from B. ∴ I win and you loose.

Because you have picked up lastly.

Instance 2 :

A	B	Moves
3	2	I take 2 from B.
3	0	You take 3 from A. ∴ I win and you loose.

Instance 3 :

A	B	Moves
3	2	I take 2 from B.
3	0	You take 2 from A.
1	0	I take 1 from A. ∴ I loose and you win.

Instance 4 :

A	B	Moves
3	2	I take 1 from A.
2	2	You take 1 from B.
2	1	I take 1 from A.
1	1	You take 1 from B.
1	0	I take 1 from A. ∴ I loose and you win.

Instance 5 :

A	B	Moves
3	2	I take 1 from A.
2	2	You take 1 from B.
2	1	I take 2 from A.
0	1	You take 1 from B. ∴ I win and you loose.

These moves can be represented by the graph as follows -

Fig. 6.1.1 graph showing moves in the game - Marienbad. If we assume that I always play first, then the shaded nodes in graph shows that "**I win**".

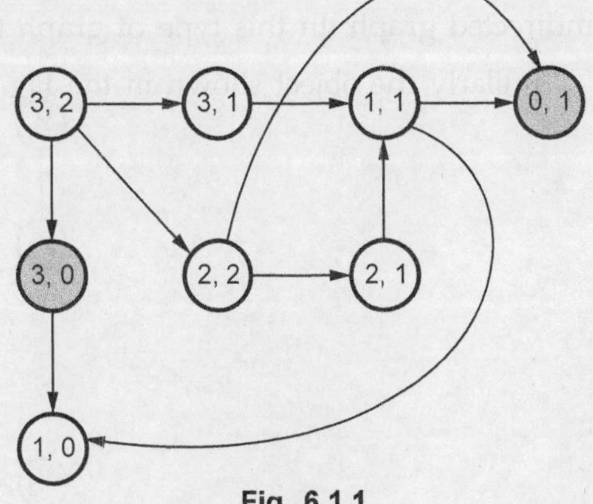

Fig. 6.1.1

Review Question

1. *Explain with example how games can be formulated using graphs ?* **GTU : June-11, Marks 4**

6.2 Concept of Graph

Definition of Graph

A graph is a collection of two sets V and E where V is a finite non empty set of vertices and E is a finite non empty set of edges.

Vertices are nothing but the nodes in the graph and the two adjacent vertices are joined by edges. The graph is thus a set of two sets. Any graph G is denoted by

G = {V,E}.

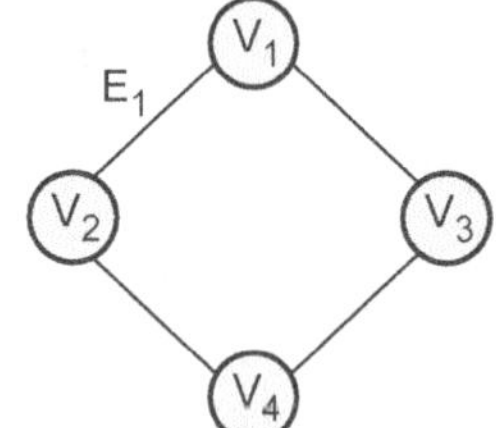

Fig. 6.2.1 Undirected graph

6.3 Directed and Undirected Graph

Basically graphs are of two types

1. Directed graphs
2. Undirected graphs.

In the directed graph the directions are shown on the edges. As shown in the Fig. 6.3.1 the edges between the vertices are ordered. In this type of graph, the edge E_1 is in between the vertices V_1 and V_2. The V_1 is called head and the V_2 is called the tail. Similarly for V_1 head the tail is V_3 and so on.

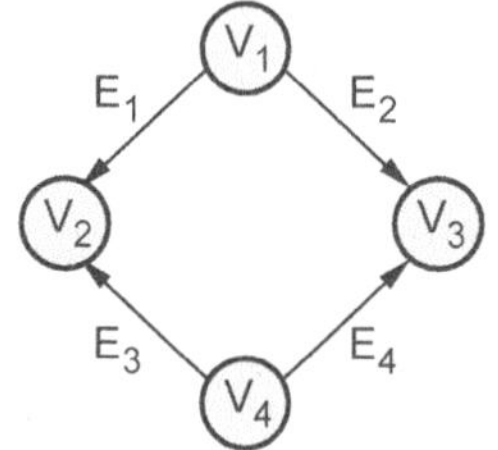

Fig. 6.3.1 Directed graph

We can say E_1 is the set of (V_1, V_2) and not of (V_2, V_1).

Similarly, in an undirected graph, the edges are not ordered. See the Fig. 6.3.2 for clear understanding of undirected graph. In this type of graph the edge E_1 is set of (V_1 , V_2) or (V_2 , V_1).

Similarly the object shown in the Fig. 6.3.2 is a multigraph .

Fig. 6.3.2 A multigraph

Directed Acyclic Graph (DAG)

A directed acyclic graph is a directed graph that contains no cycle. This type of graph is used in compilers for identifying the common subexpressions.

For example

Consider an expression

(a – b)*c + (a – b) *d

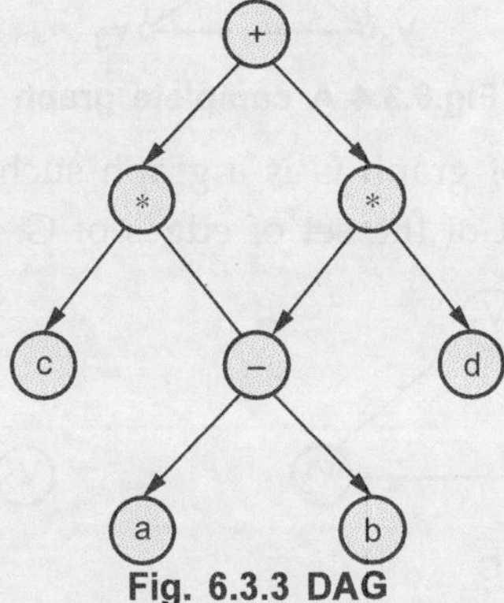

Fig. 6.3.3 DAG

Dense graph : The graph which contains maximum number of edges for connecting vertices of a graph is called the dense graph.

For example : Following graph is a sense graph.

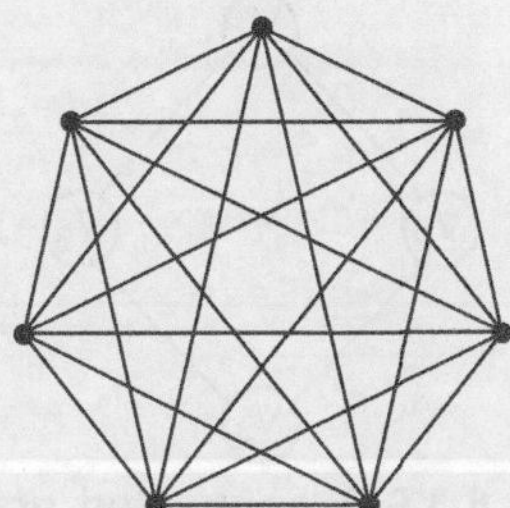

Sparse graph : The sparse graph is a kind of graph having minimum number of edges within it.

For example : Following graph is a sparse graph.

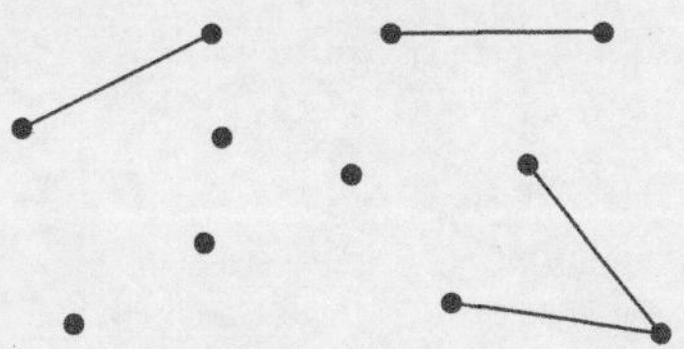

Properties of Graph

Complete graph : If an undirected graph of n vertices consists of n(n − 1)/2 number of edges then it is called as complete graph.

The graph shown in Fig. 6.3.4 is a complete graph.

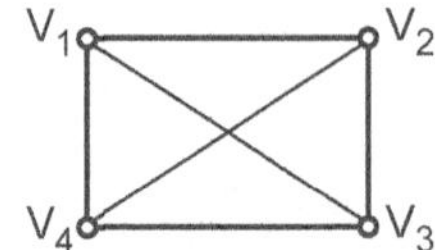

Fig.6.3.4 A complete graph

Subgraph : A subgraph G′ of graph G is a graph such that the set of vertices and set of edges of G′ are proper subset of the set of edges of G.

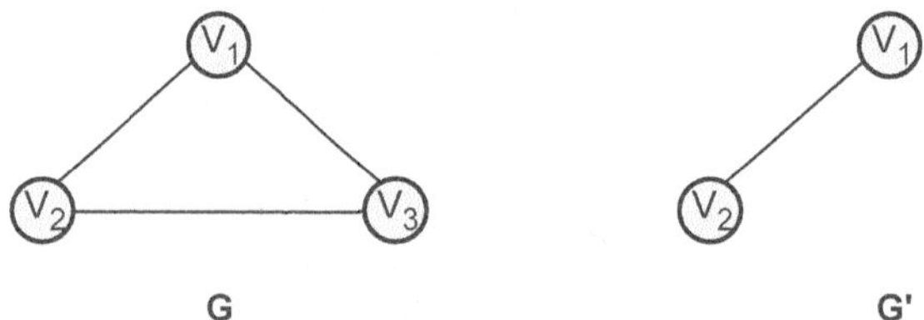

Fig. 6.3.5 A subgraph

Connected graph : An undirected graph is said to be connected if for every pair of distinct vertices V_i and V_j in V(G) there is a graph from V_i to V_j in G.

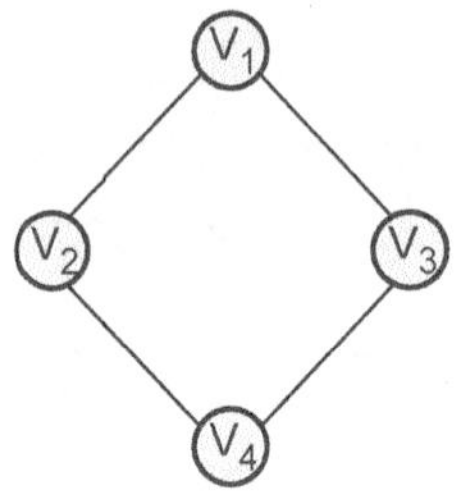

Fig. 6.3.6 A connected graph

6.4 Representation of Graphs

GTU : Dec.-10, June-12, Summer-13, Marks 7

There are several representations of graphs, but we will discuss the two commonly used representations called

- **Adjacency matrix**
- **Adjacency lists**

Let us see each one by one.

Adjacency Matrix

Consider a graph G of n vertices and the matrix M. If there is an edge present between vertices V_i and V_j then M[i][j] = 1 else M[i][j] = 0. Note that for an undirected graph if M[i][j] = 1 then for M[j][i] is also 1. Here are some graphs shown by adjacency matrix.

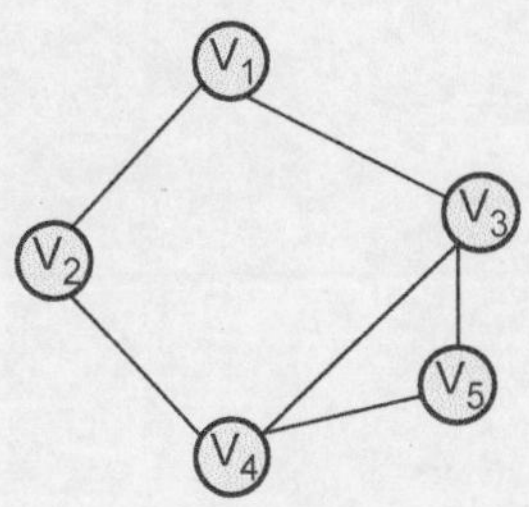

	1	2	3	4	5
1	0	1	1	0	0
2	1	0	0	1	0
3	1	0	0	1	1
4	0	1	1	0	1
5	0	0	1	1	0

Adjacency List

In the previous sections we have seen how a graph can be represented using adjacency matrix. Mainly we have used array data structure over there. But the problems associated with array are still there in the adjacency matrix. So somewhere we feel that there should be some flexible data structure and so we go for a linked data structure for creation of a graph. The type in which a graph is created with the linked list is called adjacency list. So all the advantages of linked list can be obtained in this type of graph. We need not have a prior knowledge of maximum number of nodes. Actually there are many ways to create a adjacency matrix but we will discuss the two methods of adjacency list.

Method 1 : As we know the graph is a set of vertices and edges, we will maintain the two structures, for vertices and edges respectively.

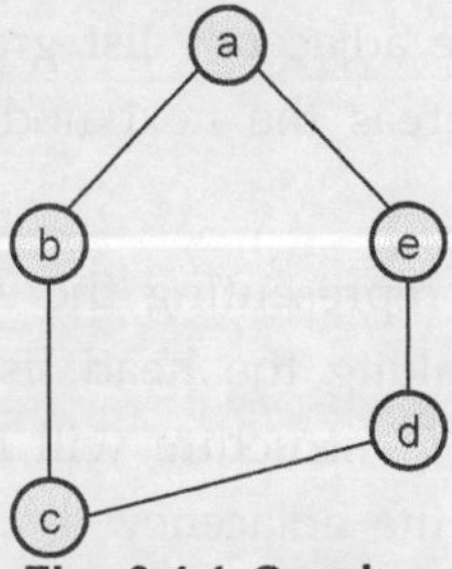

Fig. 6.4.1 Graph g

For example

Now the above graph have the nodes as a, b, c, d, e so we will maintain the linked list of these head nodes as well as the adjacent nodes. The 'C' structure will be

```
typedef struct head
{
   char data;
```

```
        struct head *down;
        struct head *next;
    }
    typedef struct node
    {
     int ver;
    struct node *link;
    }
```

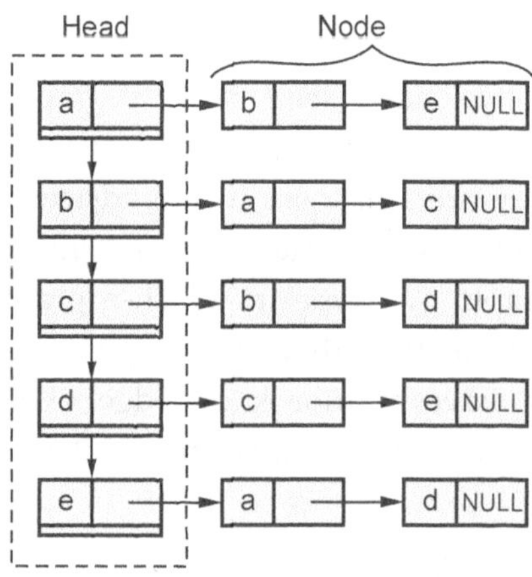

Fig. 6.4.2 Adjacency list

Explanation : This is purely the adjacency list graph. The down pointer helps us to go to each node in the graph whereas the next node is for going to adjacent node of each of the head node.

Method 2 : In this method of representing the adjacency list, We take mixed data structure. That means instead of taking the head list as a linked list we will take an array of head nodes. So only one 'C' structure will be there representing the adjacent nodes. See the figure representing the adjacency list for the above graph. First, let us see the 'C' structure.

```
typedef struct node1
{
      char vertex;
      struct node1*next
}node
node * head [10]
```

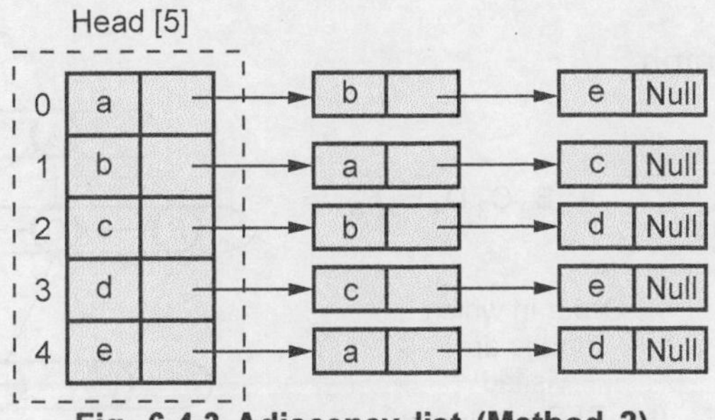

Fig. 6.4.3 Adjacency list (Method 2)

Explanation : This is the graph which can be represented with the array and linked list data structures. Array is used to store the head nodes. The node structure will be the same throughout.

Review Questions

1. *Define the terms : Directed acyclic graph, dense graph, sparse graph.*

   GTU : Dec.-10, June-12, Marks 3

2. *Define graph. Explain types of graph and different ways of graph representation.*

   GTU : Summer-13, Marks 7

6.5 Traversing a Graph

GTU : June-12, Winter-15, Marks 7

Searching a graph means traversing a graph from given vertex. There are two commonly used graph searching algorithms.

- Breadth first search
- Depth first search

Let us discuss these algorithms with the help of suitable examples.

6.5.1 Breadth First Search (BFS)

Let us define some terminologies in BFS formally.

Breadth First Forest

The breadth first forest is a collection of trees in which the traversal's starting vertex serves as the root of the first tree in such a forest. Whenever a new unvisited vertex is visited then it is attached as a child to the vertex from which it is being reached.

Consider following graph

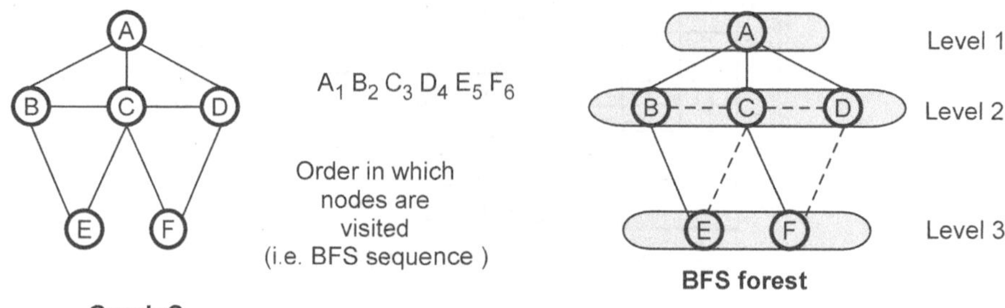

Tree Edge

In a graph G containing an edge (u, v), if a new unvisited vertex v is reached from the current vertex then edge (u, v) is called **tree edge.**

The edges between these vertices are tree edges.

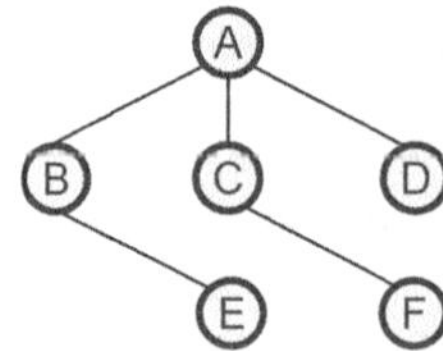

Cross Edge

If an edge leading to its previously visited vertex other than its immediate predecessor is encountered then that edge is called **cross edge**.

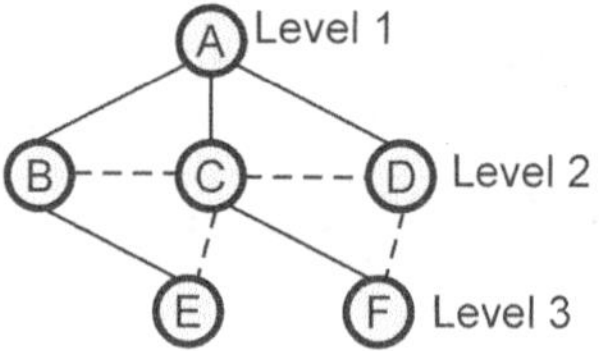

The cross edges are shown by dotted line and tree edges are shown by solid edges. The cross edges connect either siblings or cousins on the same level.

BFS follows the following rules :

1. Select an unvisited node v, visit it, have it be the root in a BFS tree being formed. Its level is called the current level.
2. From each node x in the current level, in the order in which the level nodes were visited, visit all the unvisited neighbours of x. The newly visited nodes from this level form a new level. This new level becomes the next current level.
3. Repeat step 2 for all the unvisited vertices.
4. Repeat from Step 1 until no more vertices are remaining.

Algorithm

```
Algorithm BFS(G)
{
//Problem Description : This algorithm is for finding BFS.
  Queue Q; //create a que for storing the adjacent vertices
 // visit[ ] is an array that keeps track of all the visited nodes.
 //Initially,the visit[ ] is initialized to 0
  while (G has an unvisited node) do
  {
    v ← an unvisited node;
    visit[v] ← 1;
    en que(v,Q);//add element to the queue
    while (Q is not empty) do
    {
     x ← del que(Q);//delete element from the queue
      for (unvisited neighbour y of x) do
      {
       visit[y] ← 1;
        en que(v,Q); //add adjacent vertices of x to que
      }//end of for loop
    }// end of inner while
  }//end of outer while
}
```

Example : Consider the graph given below :

Step 1 :

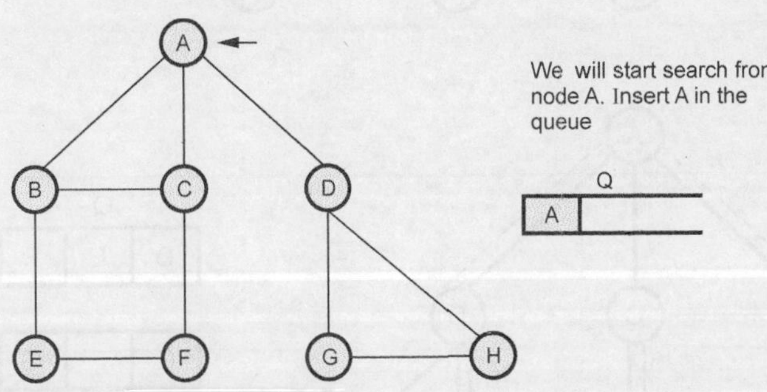

Step 2 :

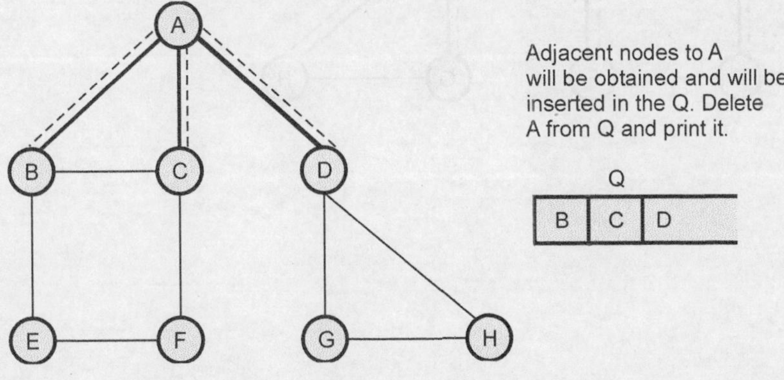

Step 3 :

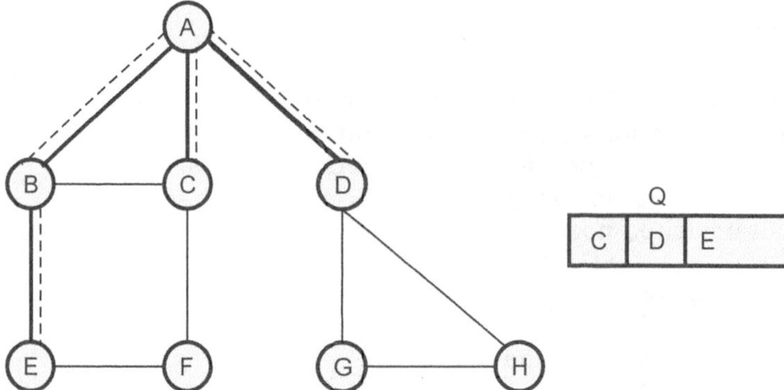

Step 4 :

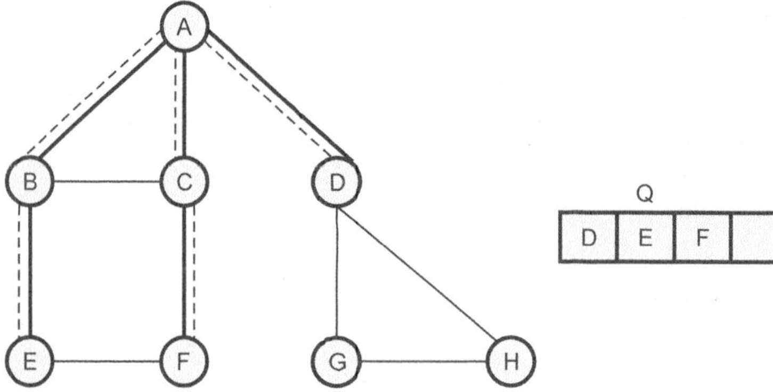

Step 5 :

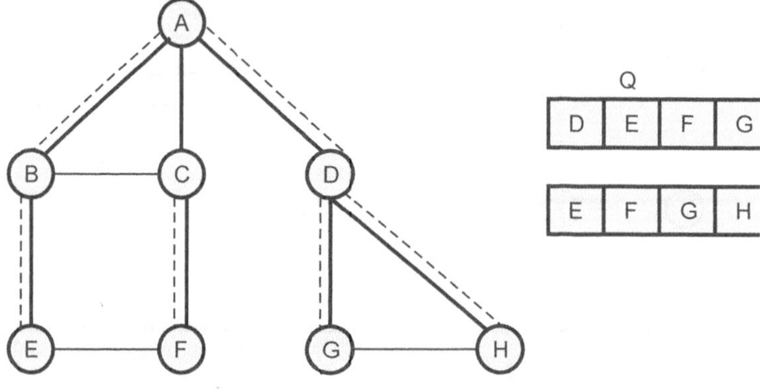

Step 6 :

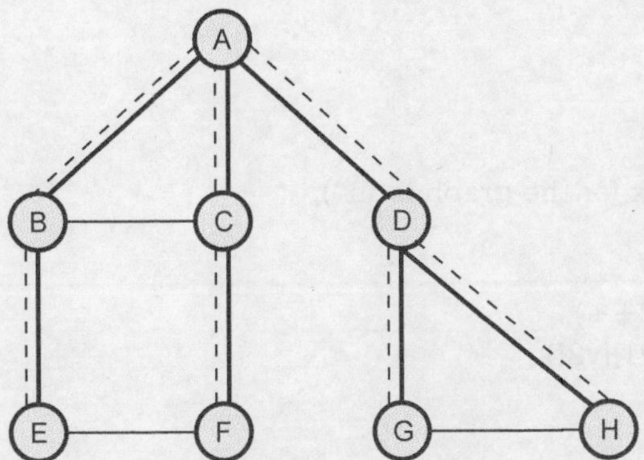

As there is no unvisited node remaining we will delete the vertices from queue and print.

Hence we get a sequence as A, B, C, D, E, F, G, H.

'C' Program

```
/***************************************************************
     Program to create a Graph. The graph is represented using
     Adjacency Matrix.
***************************************************************/

#include <stdio.h>
#include <conio.h>
#include <stdlib.h>


#define    size      20
#define    TRUE      1
#define    FALSE     0

int   g[size][size];
int   visit[size];

int   Q[size];
int   front, rear;
int n;
/*
_____________________________________________________________
 The main Function
 Calls:create,bfs
 Called By:O.S.
_____________________________________________________________
*/
void main ( )
{
     int v1, v2;
```

```
    char ans ='y';
    void create(),bfs();
    clrscr();
    create();
    clrscr();
    printf("The Adjacency Matrix for the graph is \n");
    for ( v1 = 0; v1 < n; v1++)
    {
        for ( v2 = 0; v2 < n; v2++)
            printf(" %d ", g[v1][v2]);
        printf("\n");
    }
    getch();
    do
    {
        for ( v1 = 0; v1 < n; v1++)
             visit[v1] = FALSE;
        clrscr();
        printf("Enter the Vertex from which you want to traverse ");
        scanf("%d", &v1);
        if ( v1 >= n )
            printf("Invalid Vertex\n");
        else
        {
        printf("The Breadth First Search of the Graph is \n");
        bfs(v1);
        getch();
        }
        printf("\nDo you want to traverse from any other node?");
        ans=getche();
    }while(ans=='y');
    exit(0);
}

/*
------------------------------------------------------------------
    The create function
    g :None
    Output:None, creates graph and stores in Adj. Matrix
    Parameter Passing Method :None
    Called By : main()
------------------------------------------------------------------
*/
void create()
{
    int   v1, v2
```

```
    char ans='y';
    printf("\n\t\t This is a Program To Create a Graph");
    printf("\n\t\t The Display Is In Breadth First Manner");
    printf("\nEnter no. of nodes");
    scanf("%d",&n);
    for ( v1 = 0; v1 < n; v1++)
        for ( v2 = 0; v2 < n; v2++)
            g[v1][v2] = FALSE;
    printf("\nEnter the vertices no. starting from 0");
    do
    {
        printf("\nEnter the vertices v1 & v2");
        scanf("%d%d", &v1, &v2);
        if ( v1 >= n || v2 >= n)
            printf("Invalid Vertex Value\n" );
        else
        {
            g[v1][v2] = TRUE;
            g[v2][v1] = TRUE;
        }
        printf("\n\nAdd more edges??(y/n)");
        ans=getche();
    }while(ans=='y');
}

/*
-----------------------------------------------------------------
    The bfs function
    g :Pointer to a vertex of a graph
    Output: Displays data in breadth First Search order
    Parameter Passing Method : By Value
    Called By : main()
    Calls : None
-----------------------------------------------------------------
*/
void bfs(int v1)
{
    int v2;

    visit[v1] = TRUE;
    front = rear = -1;
    Q[++rear] = v1;
    while ( front != rear )
    {
        v1 = Q[++front];
        printf("%d\n", v1);
        for ( v2 = 0; v2 < n; v2++)
```

```
            {
                if ( g[v1][v2] == TRUE && visit[v2] == FALSE )
                {
                    Q[++rear] = v2;
                    visit[v2] = TRUE;
                }
            }
        }
}
```

Output

```
        This is a Program To Create a Graph
        The Display Is In Breadth First Manner
Enter no. of nodes 4
Enter the vertices no. starting from 0
Enter the vertices v1 & v2
0 1
Add more edges??(y/n)y
Enter the vertices v1 & v2
0 2
Add more edges??(y/n)y
Enter the vertices v1 & v2
1 3
Add more edges??(y/n)y
Enter the vertices v1 & v2
2 3
Add more edges??(y/n)
The Adjacency Matrix for the graph is
 0      1      1      0
 1      0      0      1
 1      0      0      1
 0      1      1      0

Enter the Vertex from which you want to traverse 0
The Breadth First Search of the Graph is
0
1
2
3
Do you want to traverse from any other node?
Enter the Vertex from which you want to traverse 1
The Breadth First Search of the Graph is
1
0
3
2
Do you want to traverse from any other node?
```

Explanation of Logic of BFS

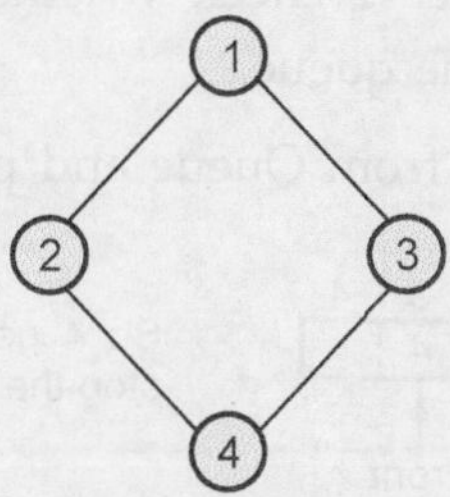

In BFS the queue is maintained for storing the adjacent nodes and an array 'visited' is maintained for keeping the track of visited nodes. i.e., once a particular node is visited it should not be revisited again. Let us see how our program works :

Step 1 : Start with vertex 1

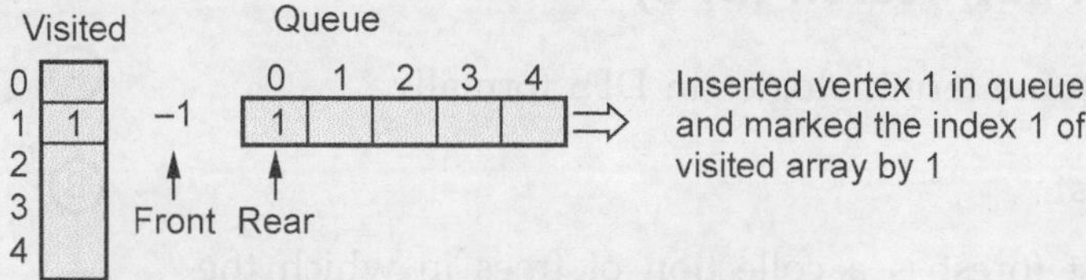

Step 2 :

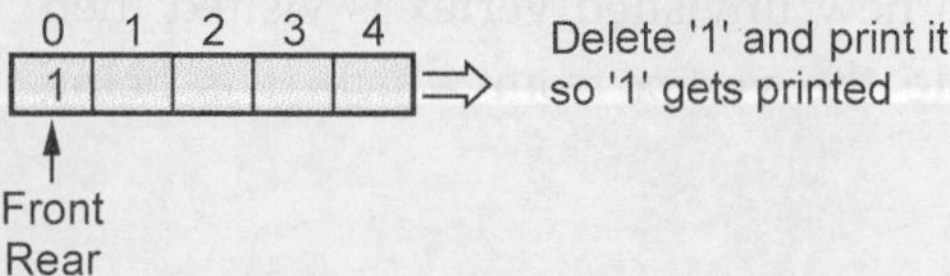

Step 3 : Find adjacent vertices of vertex 1 and mark them as visited, insert those in Queue.

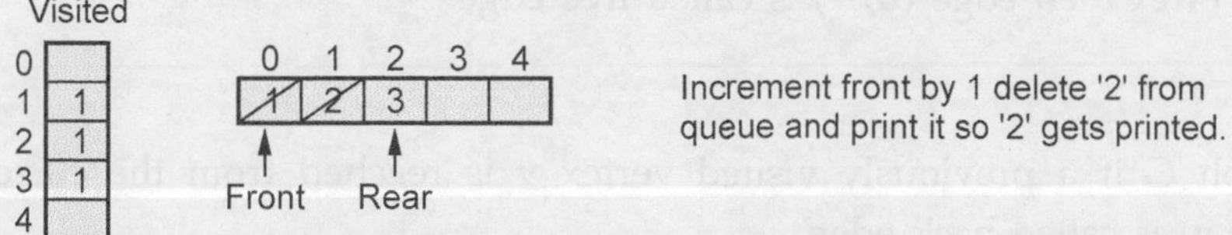

Step 4 : Find adjacent to '2' and insert those nodes in queue as well as mark them as visited.

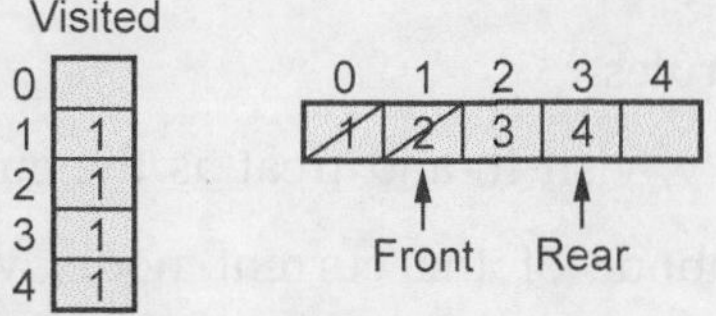

Step 5 : Increment front and delete the node print it.

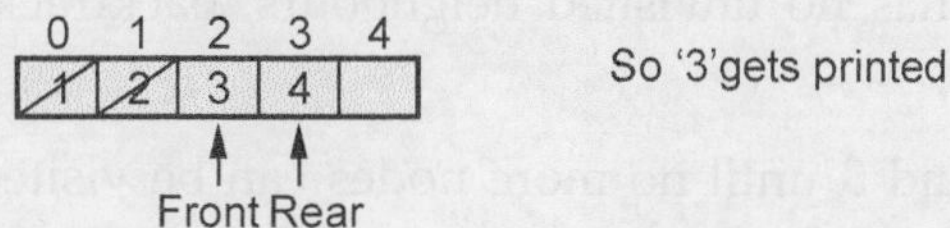

Step 6 : Find adjacent to '3' i.e. 4 check whether it is marked as visited. If it is marked as visited donot insert in the queue.

Increment front, delete the node from Queue and print it.

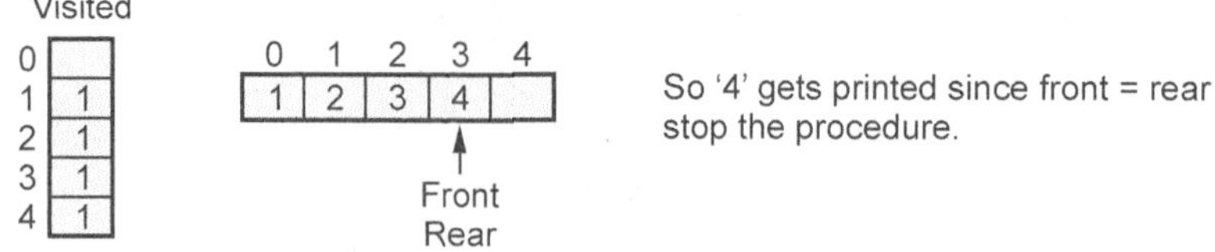

So output will be - BFS for above graph as

1 2 3 4

6.5.2 Depth First Search (DFS)

Let us define some terminologies in DFS formally.

Depth First Forest

The depth first forest is a collection of trees in which the traversal's starting vertex serves as the root of the first tree in such a forest. Whenever a new unvisited vertex is visited then it is attached as a child to the vertex from which it is being reached.

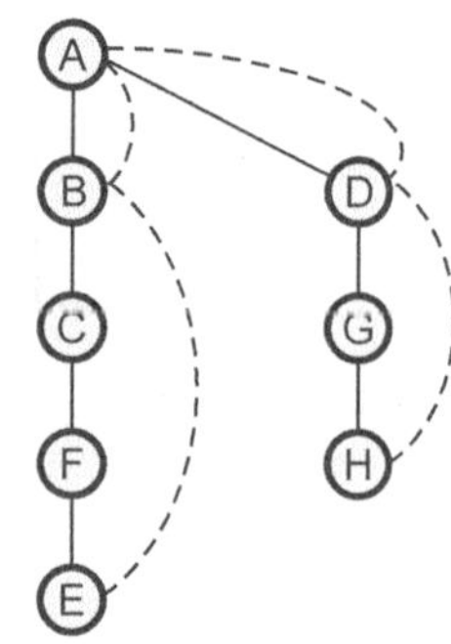

Fig. 6.5.1 DFS forest

Tree Edge

In a graph G containing an edge (u, v) if a new unvisited vertex v is reached from the current vertex then edge (u, v) is called tree edge.

Back Edge

In a graph G if a previously visited vertex v is reached from the current vertex u then edge (u,v) is called back edge.

In Fig. 6.5.1 the tree edge and back edges are shown. The solid edges are tree edges and dotted lines show back edges.

DFS follows the following rules :

1. Select an unvisited node v, visit it, and treat as the current node.
2. Find an unvisited neighbour of the current node, visit it, and make it the new current node.
3. If the current node has no unvisited neighbours, backtrack to its parent, and make it new current node;
4. Repeat the steps 2 and 3 until no more nodes can be visited.
5. Repeat from step 1 for the remaining nodes.

Algorithm

The recursive algorithm for implementing the depth first traversal is as given below

```
Algorithm DFS(v)
{
 visit[v]=1;
 for (each vertex x adjacent from v)
  {
   if ( visit[x]=0) then
     DFS(x);
  }
}
```

Analysis

Every node is visited once. Also, every edge (v,x) is crossed while performing DFS. Therefore, the time of DFS is O(n+|E|).

Example :

Step 1 :

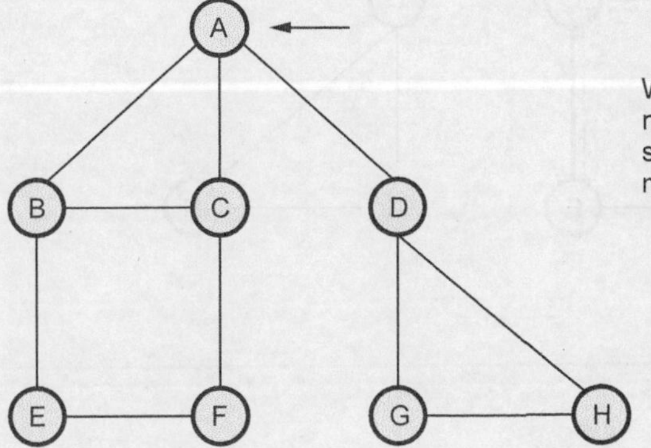

We will start search from node A. We will start searching in depth first manner.

Step 2 :

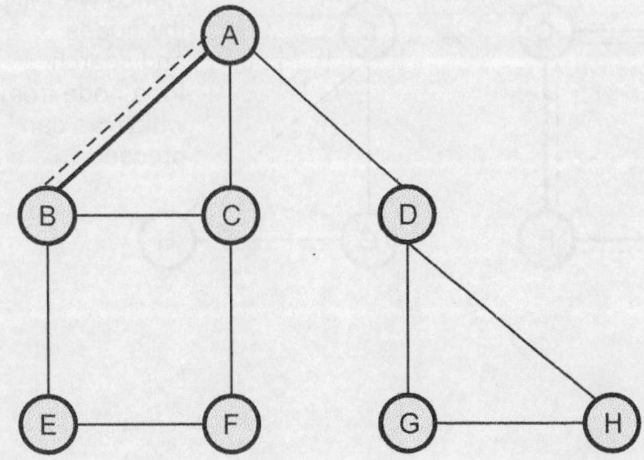

Step 3 :

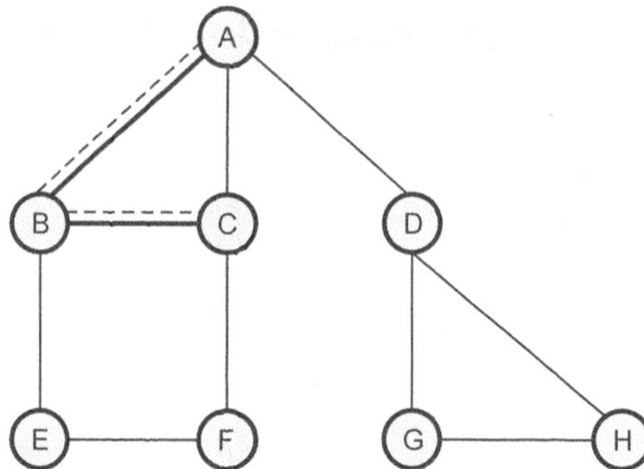

Step 4 :

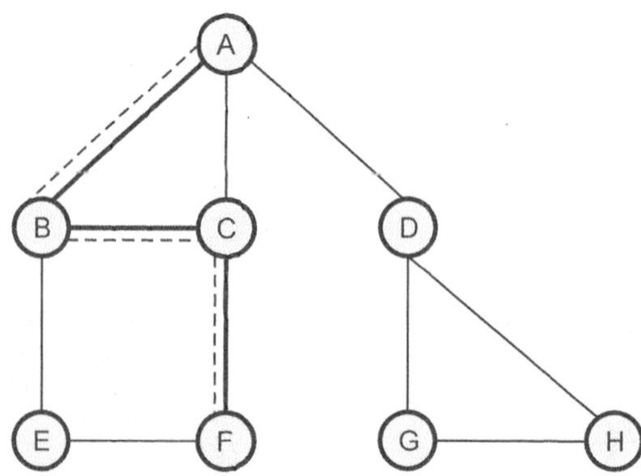

Step 5 :

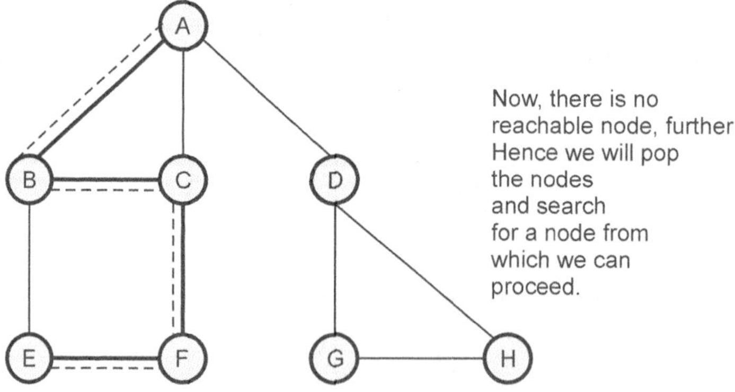

Step 6 :

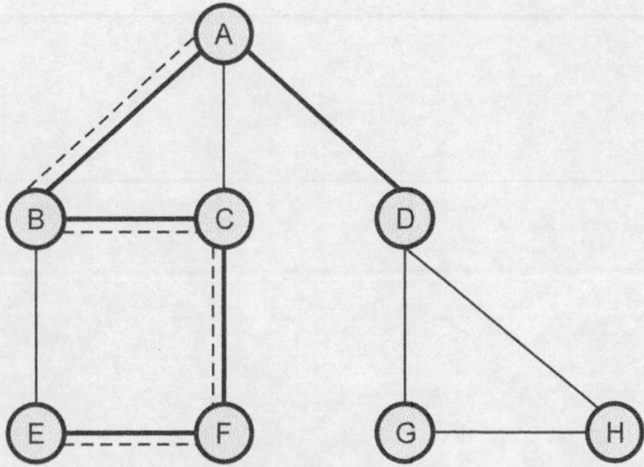

Step 7 :

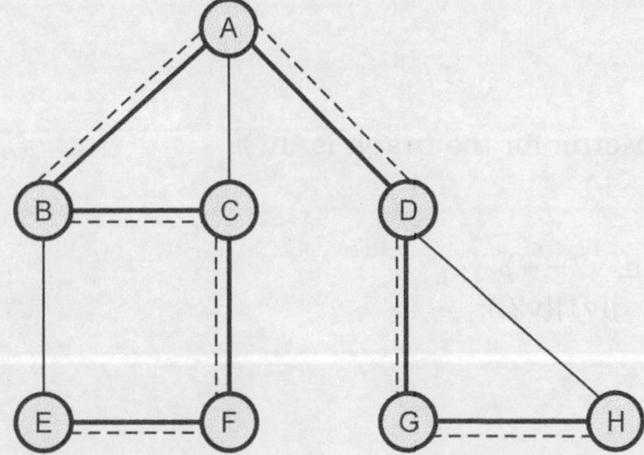

Hence we obtain DFS sequence as A, B, C, F, E, D, G, H.

'C' Program

```
/***************************************************************
Program to create a Graph. The graph is represented using
Adjacency Matrix.
***************************************************************/
#include <stdio.h>
#include <conio.h>
#include <stdlib.h>

/* List of defined constants */
#define MAX 20
#define TRUE 1
#define  FALSE 0

/* Declare an adjacency matrix for storing the graph */

int   g[MAX][MAX];
int   v[MAX];
int n;
```

```
/*
________________________________________________

The main function
Called By : The O.S.
Calls : create(), Dfs()
________________________________________________
*/
void main ( )
{
 /* Local declarations */
  int v1, v2;
  char ans;
  void create();
  void Dfs(int);
  clrscr();
  create();
  clrscr();
  printf("The Adjacency Matrix for the graph is \n");
  for ( v1 = 0; v1 < n; v1++)
  {
        for ( v2 = 0; v2 < n; v2++)
              printf(" %d ", g[v1][v2]);
        printf("\n");
}
getch();
do
{
  for ( v1 = 0; v1 < n; v1++)
        v[v1] = FALSE;
  clrscr();
  printf("Enter the Vertex from which you want to traverse :");
  scanf("%d", &v1);
  if ( v1 >= MAX )
  printf("Invalid Vertex\n");
  else
  {
       printf("The Depth First Search of the Graph is \n");
       Dfs(v1);
  }
  printf("\n Do U want To Traverse By any Other Node?");
  ans=getch();
 }while(ans=='y');
}
/*
________________________________________________
The create function
Output:None, creates graph and stores in Adj. Matrix
```

```
Parameter Passing Method :None
Called By : main()
_______________________________________________________________
*/

void  create()
{
        int ch, v1, v2, flag;
        char ans='y';
        printf("\n\t\t This is a Progrm To Create a Graph");
        printf("\n\t\t The Display Is In Depth First Manner");
        getch();
        clrscr();
        flushall();
        for ( v1 = 0; v1 < n; v1++)
                for ( v2 = 0; v2 < n; v2++)
                        g[v1][v2] = FALSE;
        printf("\nEnter no. of nodes");
        scanf("%d",&n);
        printf("\nEnter the vertices no. starting from 0");
        do
        {
                printf("\nEnter the vertices v1 & v2");
                scanf("%d%d", &v1, &v2);
                if ( v1 >= n || v2 >= n)
                        printf("Invalid Vertex Value\n" );
                else
                {
                        g[v1][v2] = TRUE;
                        g[v2][v1] = TRUE;
                }
                printf("\n\nAdd more edges??(y/n)");
                ans=getche();
        }while(ans=='y');
}
/*
_______________________________________________________________
The Dfs function
Input :Pointer to a vertex of a graph
Output: Displays data in Depth First Search order
Parameter Passing Method : By Value
Called By : main()
Calls : Dfs() itself(recursive call)
_______________________________________________________________
*/
void Dfs(int v1)
```

```
{
  int v2;
  printf("%d\n", v1);
  v[v1] = TRUE;
  for ( v2 = 0; v2 < MAX; v2++)
    if ( g[v1][v2] == TRUE && v[v2] == FALSE )
      Dfs(v2);
}
```

Output

```
This is a Progrm To Create a Graph
The Display Is In Depth First Manner
Enter no. of nodes 4
Enter the vertices no. starting from 0
Enter the vertices v1 & v2 0 1
Add more edges??(y/n)y
Enter the vertices v1 & v2 0 2
Add more edges??(y/n)y
Enter the vertices v1 & v2 1 3
Add more edges??(y/n)y
Enter the vertices v1 & v2 2 3
Add more edges??(y/n)
The Adjacency Matrix for the graph is
0       1       1       0
1       0       0       1
1       0       0       1
0       1       1       0
Enter the Vertex from which you want to traverse :1
The Depth First Search of the Graph is
1
0
2
3
 Do U want To Taverse By any Other Node?
```

Explanation of Logic for Depth First Traversal

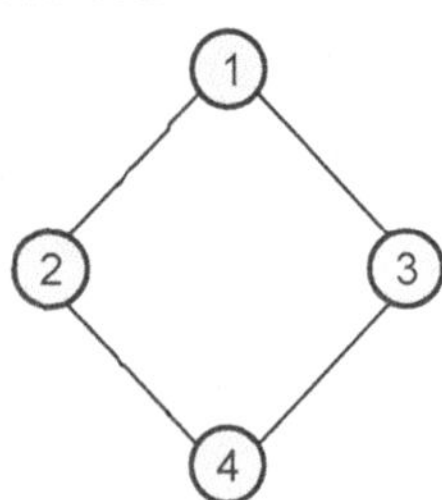

In DFS the basic data structure for storing the adjacent nodes is stack. In our program we have used a recursive call to DFS function. When a recursive call is invoked actually push operation gets performed. When we exit from the loop pop operation will be performed. Let us see how our program works.

Step 1 : Start with vertex 1, print it so '1' gets printed. Mark 1 as visited.

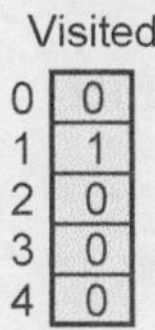

Step 2 : Find adjacent vertex to 1, say i.e. 2 if it is not visited, call DFS(2) i.e. 2 will get inserted in the stack, mark it as visited.

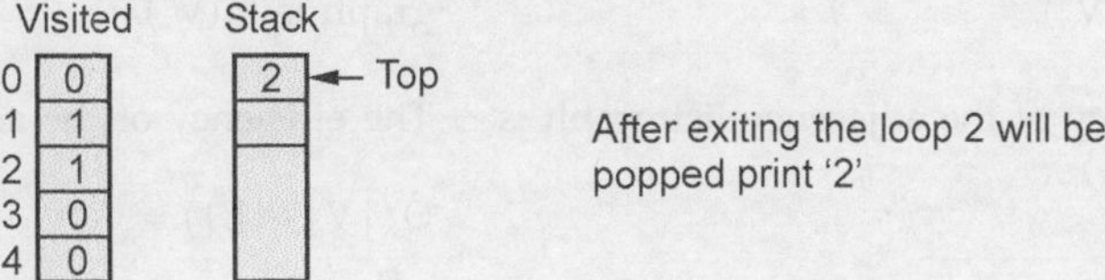

Step 3 : Find adjacent to '2' i.e. vertex 4 if it is not visited call DFS(4) i.e., 4 will get pushed on to the stack mark it as visited.

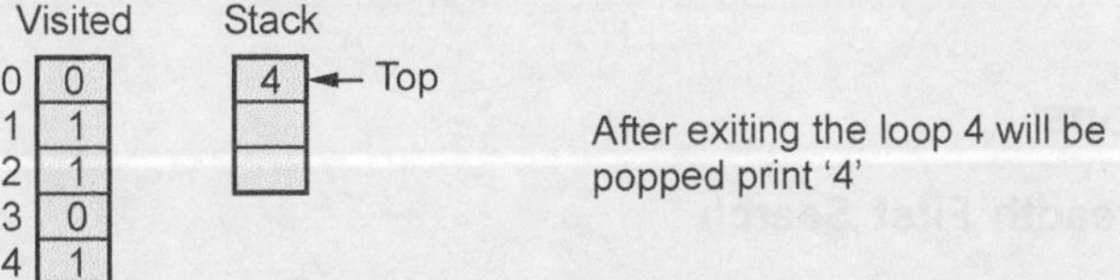

Step 4 : Find adjacent to '4' i.e. vertex 3 if it is not visited call DFS(3) i.e. 3 will be pushed onto the stack mark it visited.

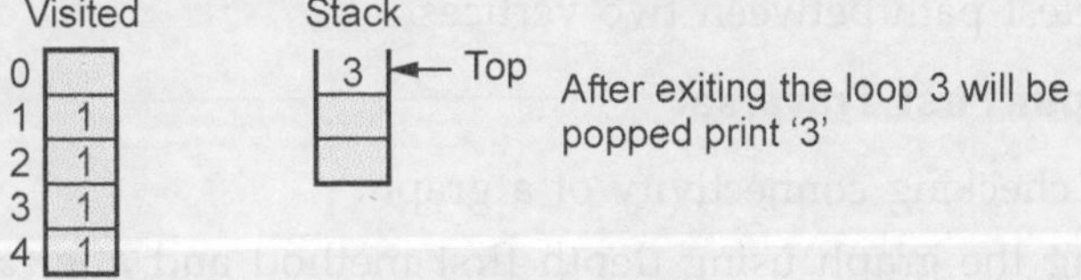

Since all the nodes are covered stop the procedure.

So output of DFS is

1 2 4 3

Difference between BFS and DFS

Sr. No.	Depth First Traversal (DFS)	Breadth First Traversal (BFS)
1.	This traversal is done with the help of **stack** data structure.	This traversal is done with the help of **queue** data structure.

2.	It works using **two ordering**. The first order is the order in which the vertices are reached for the first time (i.e. the visited vertices are pushed onto the stack) and the second order in which the vertices become dead end (the vertices are popped off the stack).	It works using **one ordering**. The order in which the vertices are reached in the same order they get removed from the queue.
3.	The DFS sequence is composed of tree edges and **back edges**.	The DFS sequence is composed of tree edges and **cross edges**.
4.	The efficiency of the adjacency matrix graph is $\Theta(V^2)$.	The efficiency of the adjacency matrix graph is $\Theta(V^2)$.
5.	The efficiency of the adjacency list graph is $\Theta(\|V\|+\|E\|)$.	The efficiency of the adjacency list graph is $\Theta(\|V\|+\|E\|)$.
6.	**Application :** To check connectivity, acyclicity of a graph and to find articulation point DFS is used.	**Application :** To check connectivity, acyclicity of a graph and to find shortest path between two vertices BFS is used.

6.5.3 Applications

Applications of Breadth First Search

1. For finding the connected components in the graph.
2. For checking if any cycle exits in the given graph.
3. To obtain shortest path between two vertices.

Applications of Depth First Traversal

1. DFS is used for checking connectivity of a graph.
   - Start traversing the graph using depth first method and after an algorithm halts if all the vertices of graph are visited then the graph is said to be a connected graph.

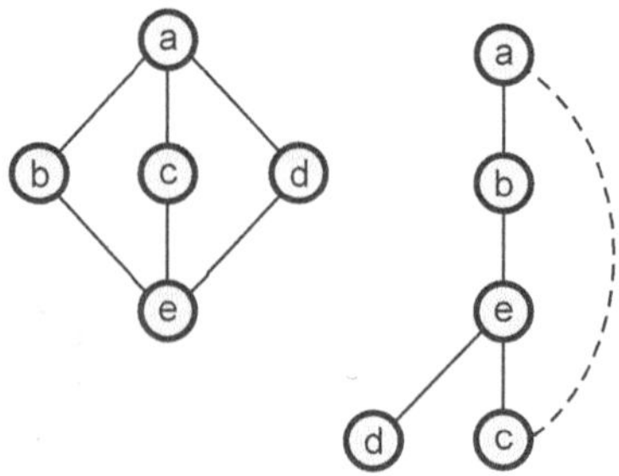

2. DFS is used for checking acyclicity of graph. If the DFS forest does not have back edge then the graph is said to be acyclic.

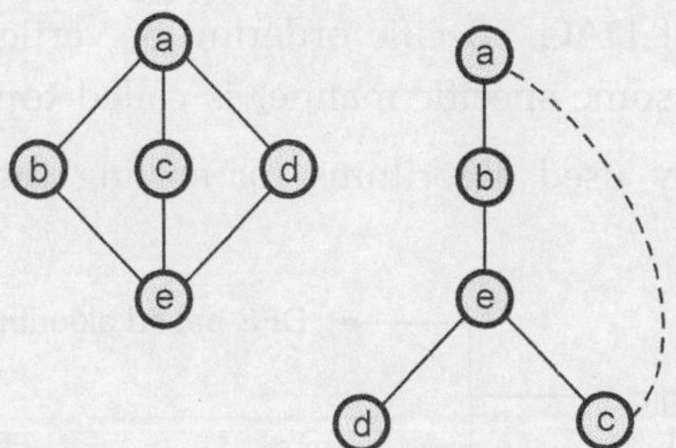

This graph contains cycle, because it contains back edge (shown by dotted lines in above graph).

3. DFS is used to find articulation point.

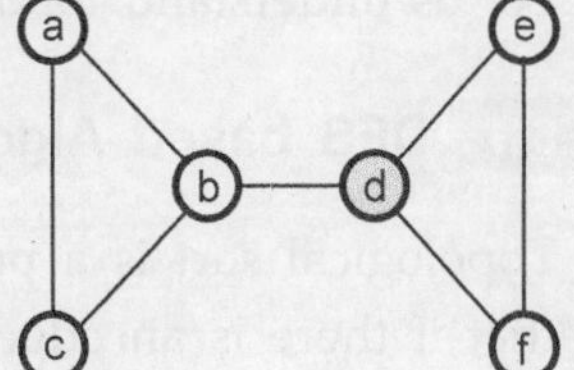

A vertex of connected graph is said to be its articulation point if its removal with all its incident edges breaks the graph into disjoint pieces.

The vertex d is an articulation point.

Review Questions

1. *Explain breadth first traversal method for graph with algorithm.* **GTU : June-12, Marks 7**
2. *Explain Depth First Traversal Method for Graph with algorithm with example.* **GTU : Winter-15, Marks 7**

6.6 Topological Sort

We have discussed two principle traversal algorithms and those are DFS and BFS. One of the application of DFS is that it helps us to find whether a cycle exists in the graph or not. Let us define one commonly used terminology in Depth First search of a digraph i.e. **DAG.**

Definition of DAG

A **directed acyclic graph** is a directed graph with no cycles.

For example :

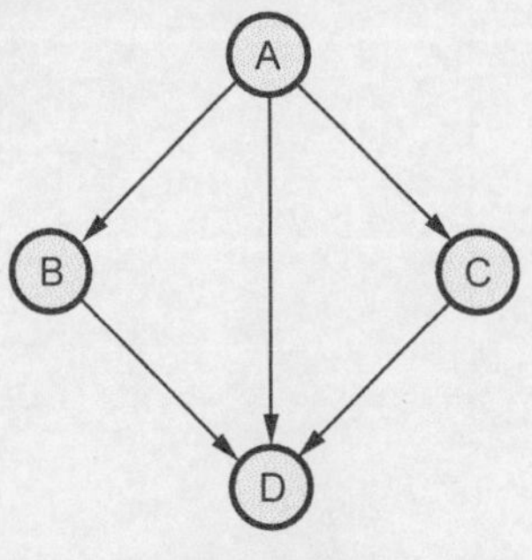

It is a DAG

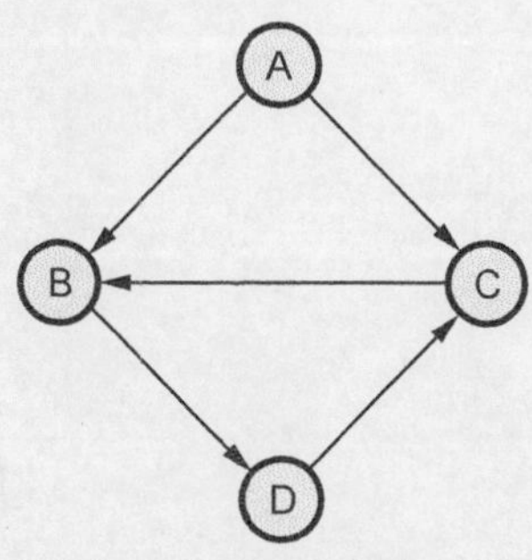

It is not a DAG

Based on the principle of DAG, specific ordering of vertices is possible. This method of arranging the vertices in some specific manner is called **topological sort.**

There are two commonly used algorithms for sorting the vertices using topological sort method.

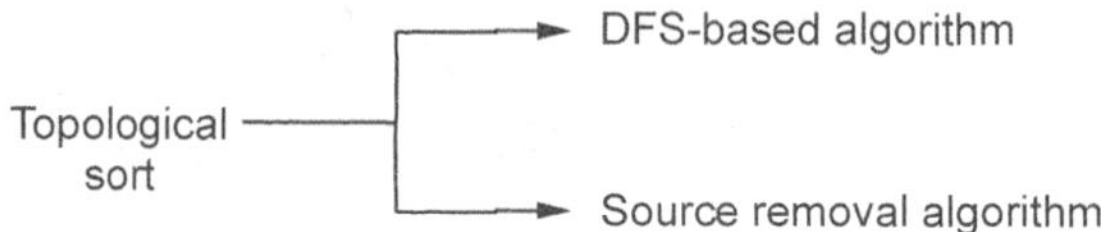

Let us understand topological sorting with the help of these two algorithms.

6.6.1 DFS based Algorithm

Topological sort is a process of assigning a linear ordering to the vertices of a DAG, so that if there is an edge from vertex i to vertex j then i appears before j in the linear ordering.

In this method the depth first search is done. Then note the order in which vertices become dead ends. The dead end vertices are popped off the stack. Then reverse the contents that are popped off the stack.

Example 6.6.1 *Sort the digraph for topological sort using DFS based algorithm.*

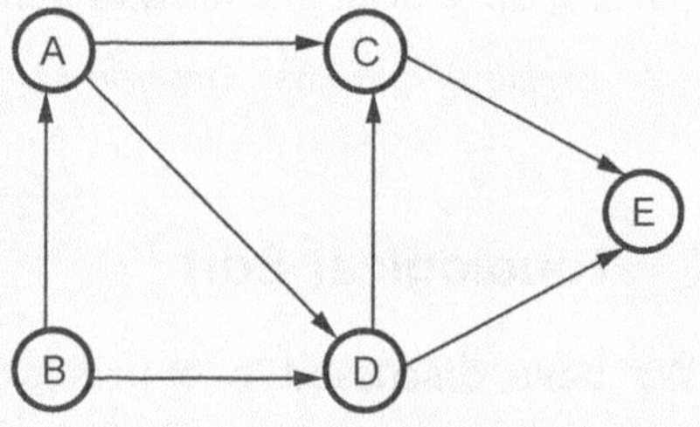

Solution : As the graph contains no cycle i.e. the graph is a DAG, the topological sorting is possible.

Step 1 : First find the Depth First Search and push the visited vertices in the stack. Thus create a DFS traversal stack.

DFS stack
E_1
C_2
D_3
A_4
B_5

DFS stack

Step 2 : Now pop-off the contents of the stack E, C, D, A, B.

Step 3 : Reverse the popped contents. The list which are getting is a topologically sorted list.

∴ B, A, D, C, E.

Example 6.6.2 *Sort the given digraph using topological sort using DFS based algorithm .*

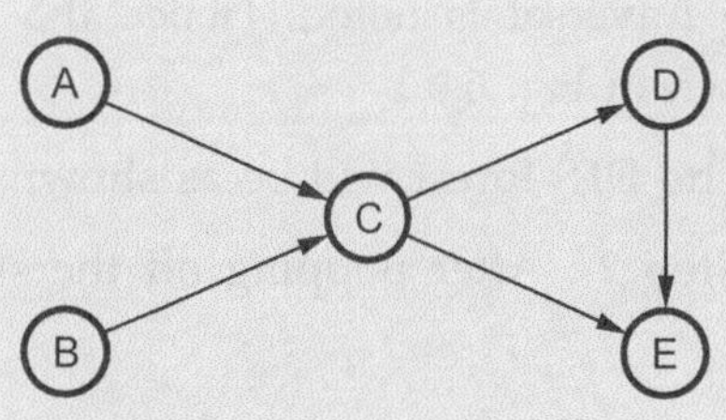

Solution : The graph is a acyclic graph, hence topological sorting is possible.

Step 1 : Create a DFS traversal stack by finding vertices in depth first search.

E_1
D_2
C_3
A_4 B_5

DFS stack

Step 2 :

Now pop-off the contents of the stack.

E, D, C, A, B

Step 3 :

Reverse the popped contents. Thus the list which we are getting is a topologically sorted list.

∴ B, A, C, D, E.

Example 6.6.3 *Apply the DFS based algorithm to solve the topological sorting problem for following digraphs.*

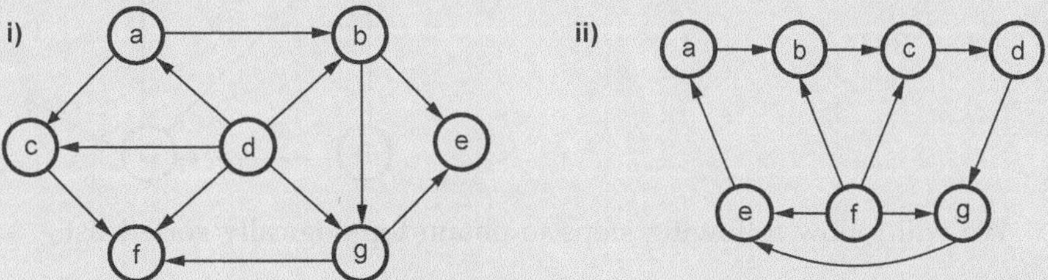

Solution : **i)** As the graph contains no cycle, topological sorting is possible.

Step 1 :

The order in which the vertices are visited in DFS traversal is noted. Hence the stack will be as shown in Fig. 6.6.1

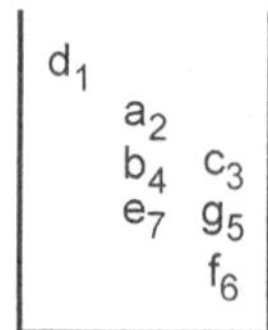

Fig. 6.6.1 DFS stack

The DFS forest will be as shown in Fig. 6.6.2

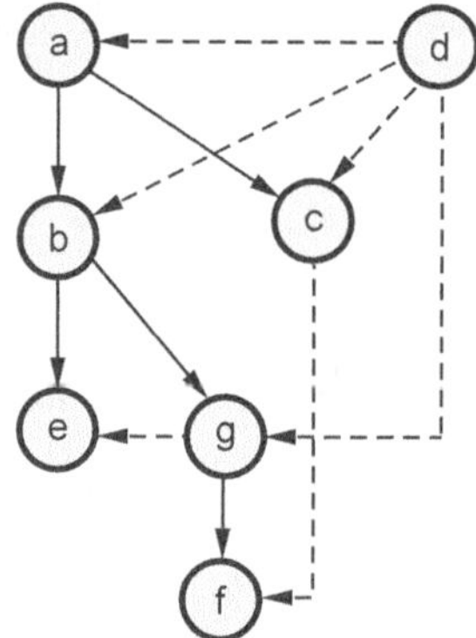

Step 2 : After popping off the stack contents we get

e, f, g, b, c, a, d

Step 3 : Reversing the stack contents we get topologically sorted list as

d, a, c, b, g, f, e

ii) As the graph contains cycle topological ordering is not possible.

6.6.2 Source Removal Algorithm

This is a direct implementation of decrease and conquer method. Following are the steps to be followed in this algorithm -

1. From a given graph find a vertex with no incoming edges. Delete it along with all the edges outgoing from it. If there are more than one such vertices then break the tie randomly.
2. Note the vertices that are deleted.
3. All these recorded vertices give topologically sorted list.

Let us understand this algorithm with some examples -

Example 6.6.4 *Sort the digraph for topological sort using source removal algorithm.*

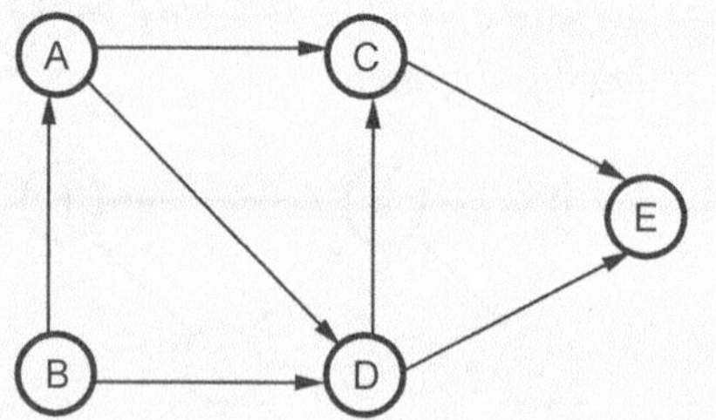

Solution : We will follow following steps to obtain topologically sorted list.

Choose vertex B, because it has no incoming edge, delete it along with its adjacent edges.

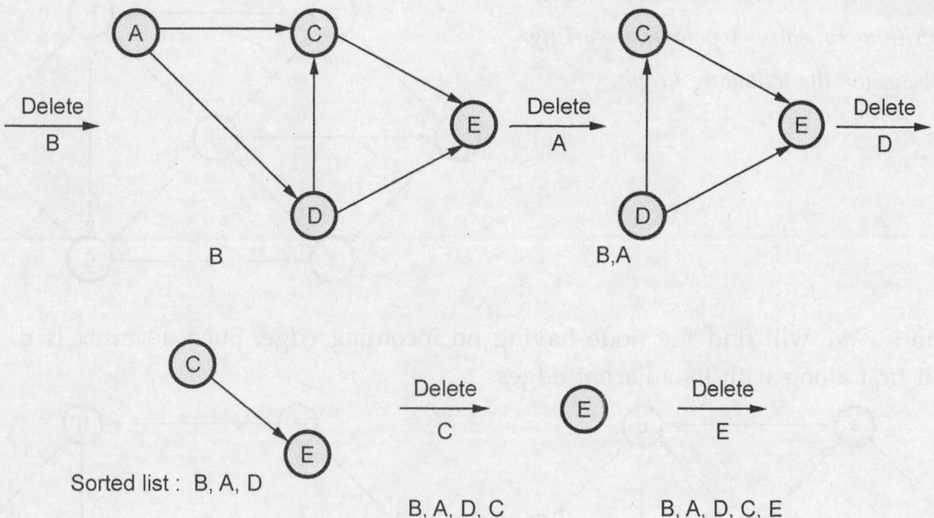

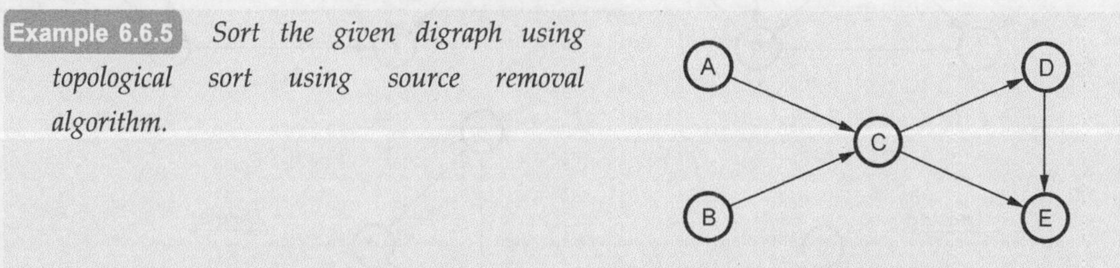

Hence the list after topological sorting will be B, A, D, C, E.

Example 6.6.5 *Sort the given digraph using topological sort using source removal algorithm.*

Solution : Let us start with the vertex with no incoming edge. There are two such vertices A and B. The tie can be broken arbitrarily. Let us first delete vertex B.

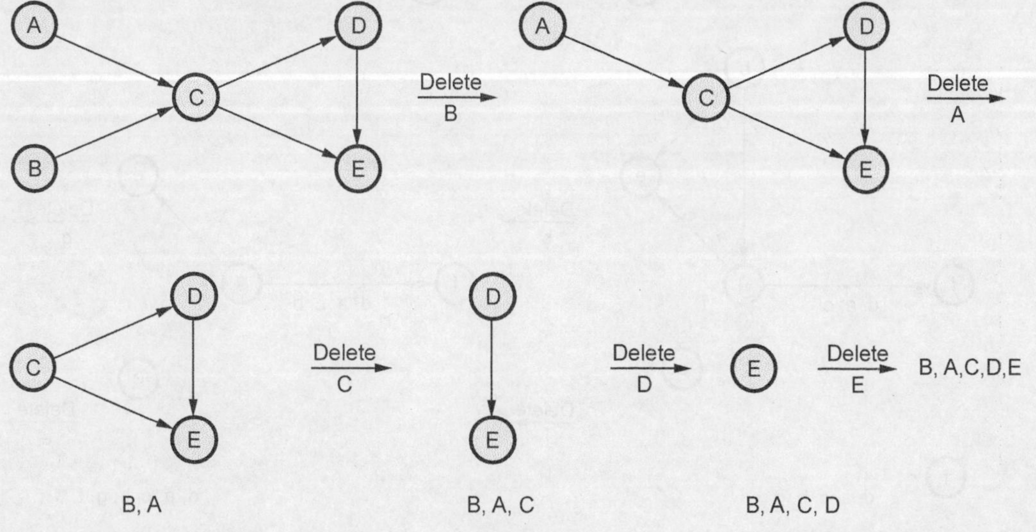

Thus the topologically sorted list is B, A, C, D, E.

Example 6.6.6 *Apply source removal algorithm to solve topological sorting problem for the following graph.*

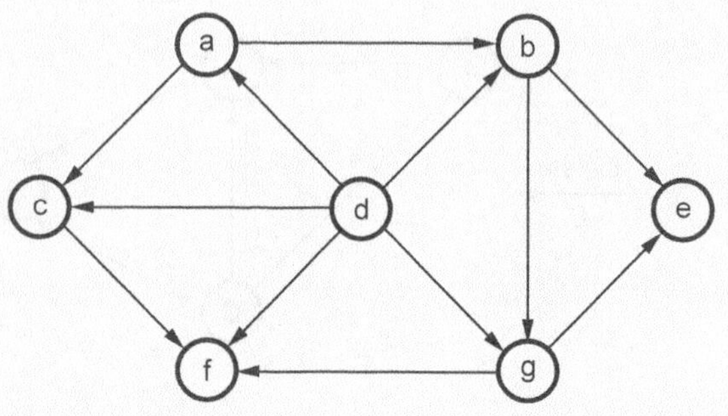

Solution : We will find the node having no incoming edge. Such a vertex is d. Hence delete it first along with its adjacent edges.

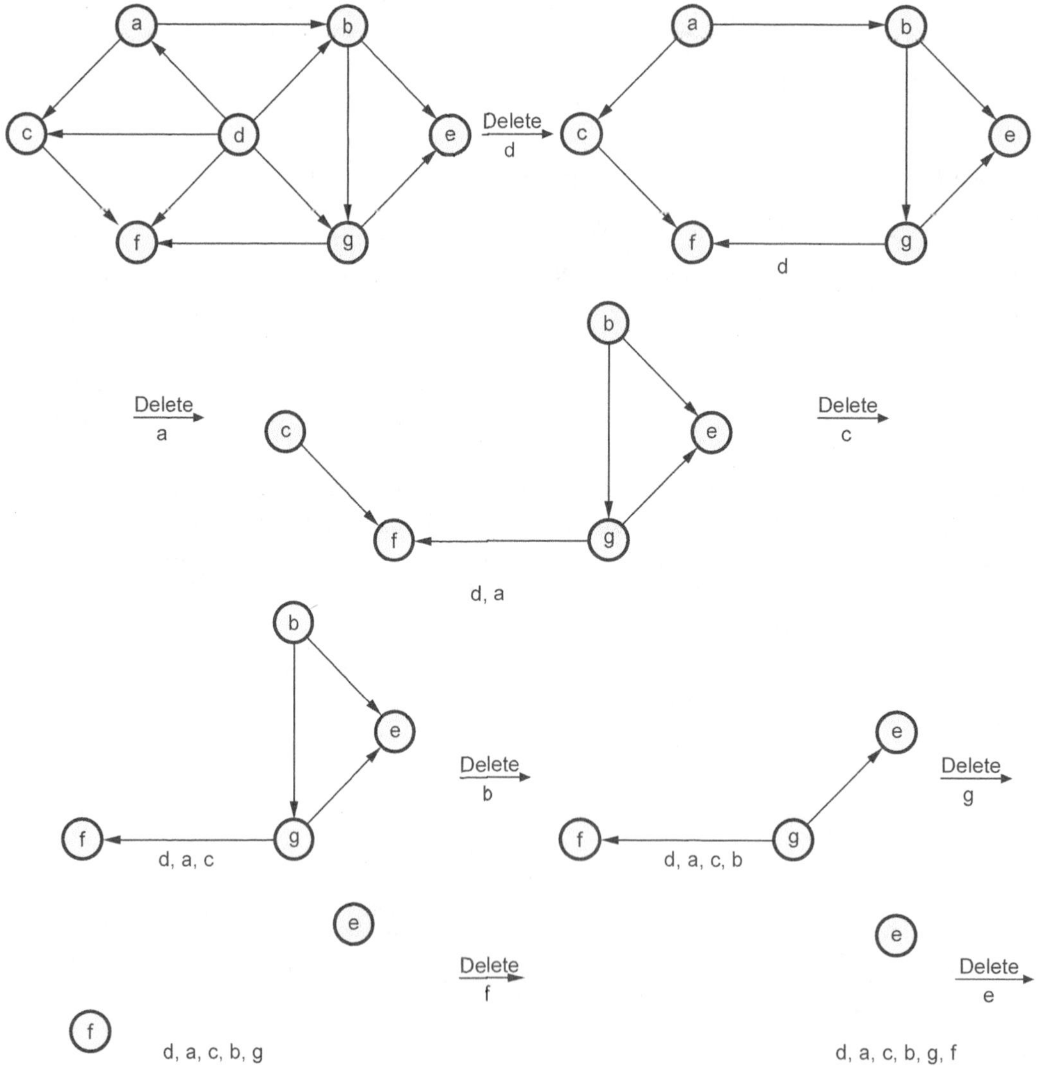

Delete d

d

Delete a

d, a

Delete c

d, a, c

Delete b

d, a, c, b

Delete g

d, a, c, b, g

Delete f

d, a, c, b, g, f

Delete e

Hence topologically sorted list is d, a, c, b, g, f and e.

6.7 Bi - Connected Components

GTU : June-11, Winter-14, Dec.-10, Marks 7

Let us now discuss strongly connected components for undirected graph.

In this section we will understand two important concepts those are articulation point and bi-connected components. We will also learn how depth first search helps in finding an articulation point and bi-connected components.

> **Definition of articulation point :** Let G = (V, E_0) be a connected undirected graph, then an articulation point of graph G is a vertex whose removal disconnects graph G. This articulation point is a kind of cut-vertex.

For example :

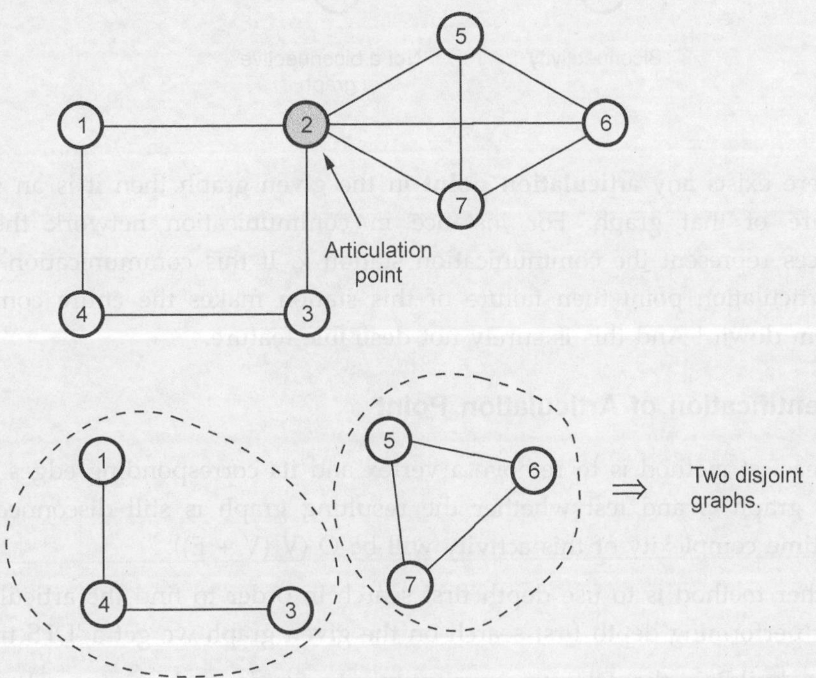

- A graph G is said to be bi-connected if it contains no articulation points.

For example :

Even through we remove any single vertex we do not get disjoint graphs. Let us remove vertex 2 and we will get

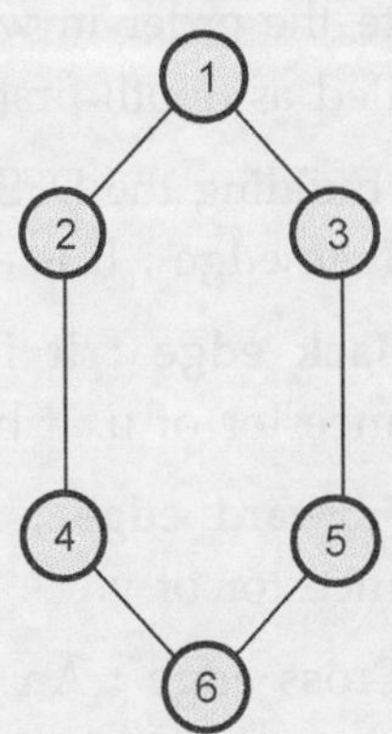

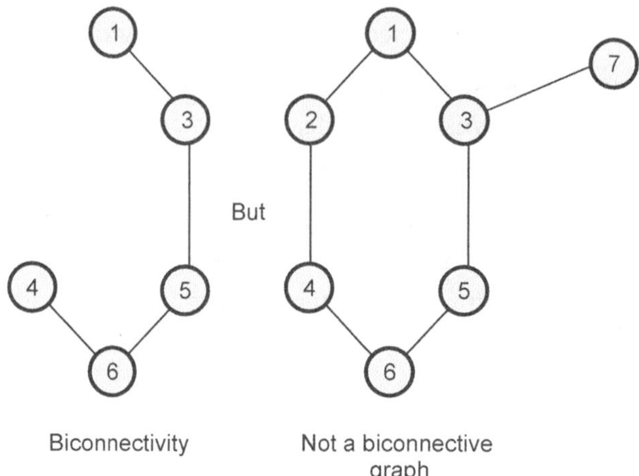

Biconnectivity Not a biconnective graph

- If there exists any **articulation point** in the given graph then it is an **undesirable feature** of that graph. For instance in communication network the nodes or vertices represent the communication station x. If this communication station x is an articulation point then failure of this station makes the entire communication system down ! And this is surely not desirable feature.

6.7.1 Identification of Articulation Point

- The easiest method is to remove a vertex and its corresponding edges one by one from graph G and test whether the resulting graph is still disconnected or not. The time complexity of this activity will be O (V (V + E)).
- Another method is to use depth first search in order to find the articulation point. After performing depth first search on the given graph we get a 'DFS tree'.
- While building the DFS tree we number outside each vertex. These numbers indicate the order in which a depth first search visits the vertices. These numbers are called as depth first search numbers (dfn) of the corresponding vertex.
- While building the DFS tree we can classify the graph into four categories :
  - i) **Tree edge :** It is an edge in depth first search tree.
  - ii) **Back edge :** It is an edge (u,v) which is not in DFS tree and v is an ancestor of u. It basically indicates a loop.
  - iii) **Forward edge :** An edge (u,v) which is not in search tree and u is an ancestor of v.
  - iv) **Cross edge :** An edge (u,v) not in search tree and v is neither an ancestor nor a descendant of u.

- To identify articulation points following observations can be made.
  i) The root of the DFS tree is an articulation if it has two or more children.
  ii) A leaf node of DFS tree is not an articulation point.
  iii) If u is any internal node then it is not an articulation point if and only if from every child w of u it is possible to reach an ancestor of u using only a path made up of descendant of w and back edge.

  This observation leads to a simple rule as,

Low [u] = min { dfn [u], min {Low [w]/w is a child of u}, min {dfn [w]/ (u,w) is a back edge}}

Where Low [u] is the lowest depth first number that can be reached from u using a path of descendant followed by at most one back edge. The vertex u is an articulation point if u is child of w such that

$L[w] \geq dfn[u]$.

Example 6.7.1 *Obtain the articulation point for following graph.*

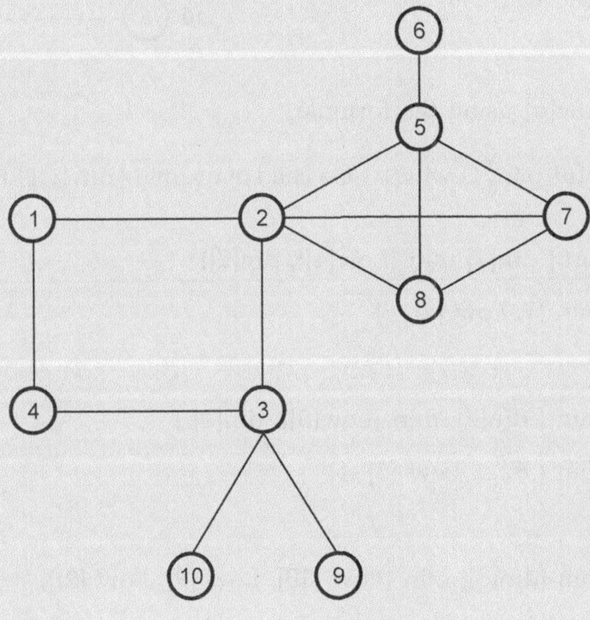

Solution : The DFS tree can be drawn as follows

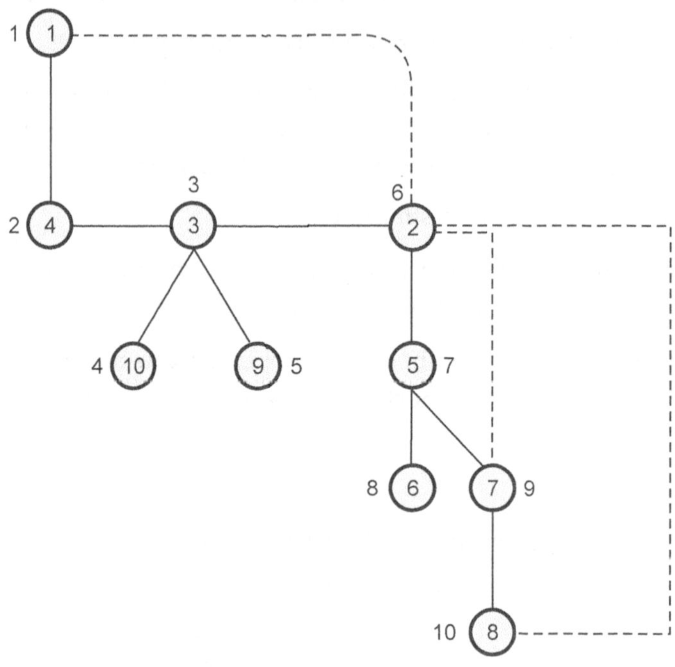

Let us compute Low[u] using the formula

$$\text{Low}[u] = \min\left\{ \text{dfn}[u], \min\{\text{Low}[w] \mid w \text{ is a child of } u\}, \min\{\text{dfn}[w] \mid (u, w) \text{ is backedge}\} \right\}$$

Low [1] = min { dfn[1] min {Low[4]}, dfn[2]}

= min {1, Low [4], 6}

∴ Low [1] = 1 ∵ nothing is less than 1

Low [2] = min { dfn[2], min {Low[5]}, dfn[1] }

= min { 6, ... Low [5], 1}

∴ Low [2] = 1

Low [3] = min {dfn[3], min {Low [10], Low [9], Low [2]}, no backedge}

= min {3, min {Low[10], Low[9], 1} – }

= min {3, 1, –}

∴ Low [3] = 1

Low [4] = min {dfn [4], min {Low [3]} – }

= min {2, 1, – }

∴ Low [4] = 1

Low [5] = min {dfn [5], min {Low [6], Low [7], – } }

= min {7, min{Low [6], Low [7] – } }

∴ Low [5] = Keep it as it is after getting value of Low[6] and Low [7] we will decide Low [5]

Low [6] = min {dfn [6], – , – } ∵ leaf mode

∴ Low [6] = 8

Low [7] = min {dfn[8], – ,dfn [2]}

= min {10, –, 6}

∴ Low [7] = 6

As we have got Low [6] = 8 and Low [7] = 6. We will compute our incomplete computation Low [5].

∴ Low [5] = min {7, min {8, 6}, – }

= min {7, 6, – }

∴ Low [5] = 6

Now Low [8] = min {dfn [8], – , dfn [2] }

= min {10, 6}

∴ Low [8] = 6

Low [9] = min {dfn [9], – , – }

∴ Low [9] = 5

Low [10] = min {dfn [10], – , – }

= min {4, –, –}

∴ Low [10] = 4

Hence Low values are Low [1 : 10] = {1, 1, 1, 1, 6, 8, 6, 6, 5, 4}. Here vertex 3 is articulation point because child of 3 is 10 and Low [10] = 4. dfn[3] = 3. That is Low [w] ≥ dfn [u].

Similarly vertex 2 is an articulation point. Because child of 2 is 5 and

Low [5] = 6

dfn [2] = 6

i.e. Low [w] ≥ dfn[u]

Vertex 5 is articulation point because child of 5 is 6.

Low [6] = 8

dfn [5] = 7

i.e. Low [w] ≥ dfn [u]

Hence in above given graph vertex 2, 3 and 5 are articulation points.

Algorithm for Articulation Points

The algorithm for obtaining the articulation point is as given below

```
Algorithm DFS_Art(u,v)
// the vertex u is a starting vertex for depth first traversal.
//In depth first tree v is a parent(ancestor) of u.
//Initially an array dfn[ ] is initialized to 0.The def[ ] stores the depth first search
//numbers
//Array Low[ ] is used to gives the lowest depth first number that can be reached
//from u
{
//put the dfn number for u in dfn array
dfn[u]:=dfn_num;
Low[u]:=dfn_num;
def_num := dfn_num +1;
for ( each vertex w adjacent to u ) do
{
 // w is child of u and if w is not visited
 if(dfn[w]=0) then
 {
  DFS_Art(w,u);//finding the dfn of w
  Low[u]:=min(Low[u],Low[w]);
}
else if(w!=u) then //the edge u w can be a back edge then update //Low[u]
 Low[u]:=min(Low[u],dfn[w]);
}
}
```

Analysis

The DFS_Art has a complexity O (n + E) where E is number of edges in graph G and n is total number of nodes. Thus the articulation point can be determined in O(n+E) time.

6.7.2 Identification of Bi-Connected Components

- A bi-connected graph G = (V, E) is a connected graph which has no articulation points.
- A bi-connected component of a graph G is maximal biconnected subgraph. That means it is not contained in any larger bi-connected subgraph of G.
- Some key observations can be made in regard to bi-connected components of graph.
  1. Two different bi-connected components should not have any common edges.
  2. Two different bi-connected components can have common vertex.
  3. The common vertex which is attaching two (or more) bi-connected components must be an articulation point of G.

For example : In following graph,

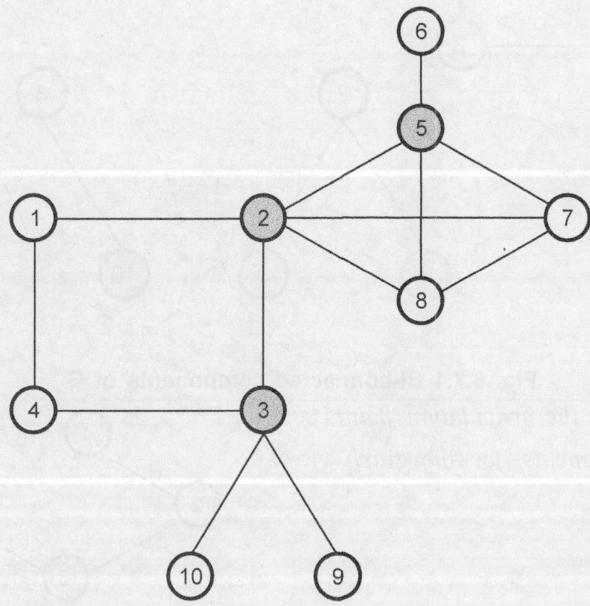

The articulation points are 2, 3, 5. Hence bi-connected components are

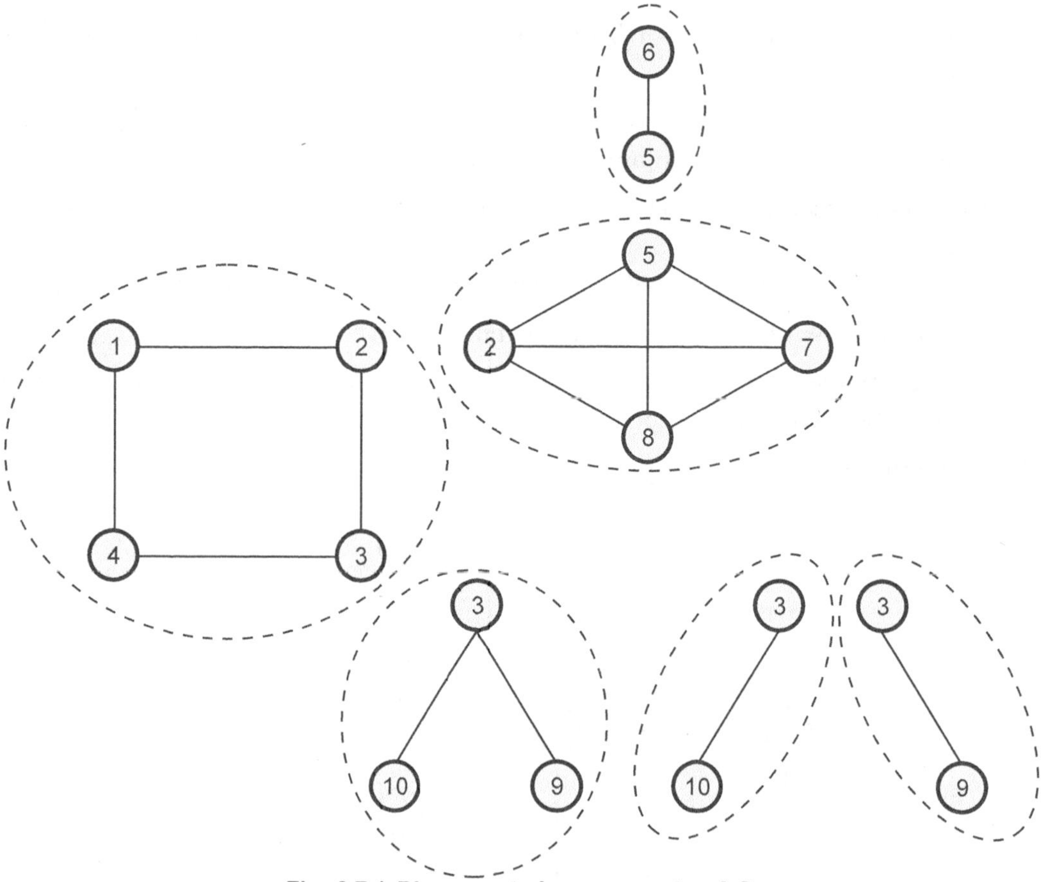

Fig. 6.7.1 Bi-connected components of G

Example 6.7.2 *Decide the articulation points and bi-connected components, for the graph given below in Fig. 6.7.2.*

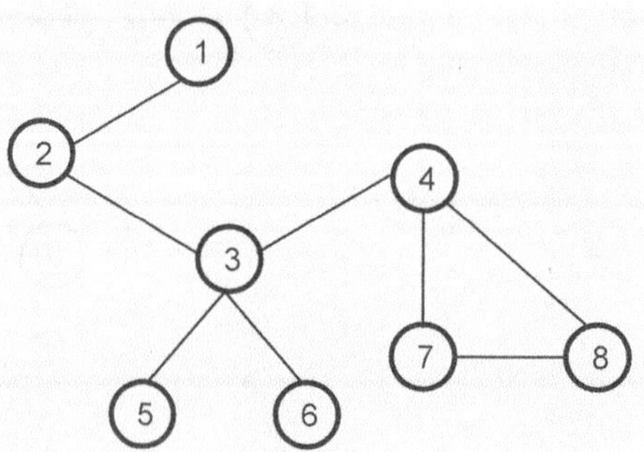

Fig. 6.7.2

Solution : The articulation point can be calculated as follows -

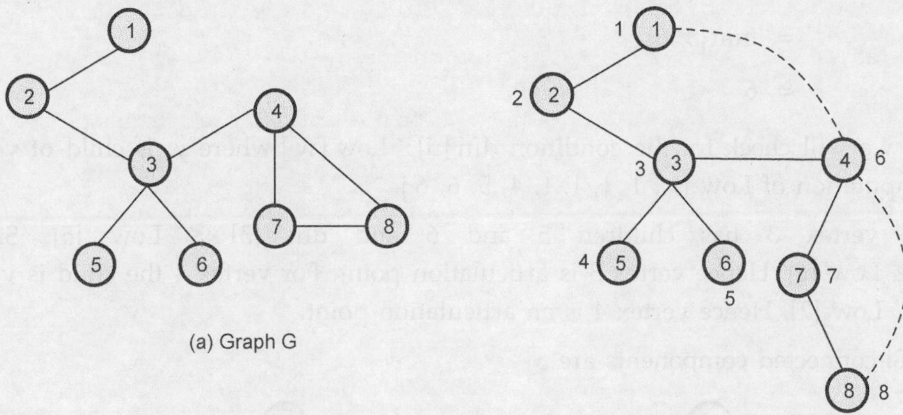

Fig. 6.7.3

Consider the given graph G and let us draw a depth first tree for the same.

Now let us compute Low[u] for each vertex u using following formula.

$$\text{Low}[u] = \min \left\{ \begin{array}{l} \text{dfn}[u], \min\{\text{Low }[w] \mid w \text{ is child of } u\}, \\ \min\{\text{dfn}[w] \mid (u, w) \text{ is backedge}\} \end{array} \right\}$$

$$\text{Low }[1] = \min \{\text{dfn}[1], \min\{ \text{Low }[2]\}, \text{dfn }[4] \}$$

$$\text{Low }[1] = \min \{ 1, \min\{ \text{Low }[2]\}, 6 \}$$

$$\text{Low }[1] = 1$$

$$\text{Low }[2] = \min \{ \text{dfn}[2] , \min \{\text{Low }[3] \}\}$$

$$\text{Low }[2] = 1$$

$$\text{Low }[3] = \min \{ \text{dfn}[3] , \min\{\text{Low }[4], \text{Low }[5], \text{Low }[6]\} \}$$

$$\text{Low }[3] = 1$$

$$\text{Low }[4] = \min \{ \text{dfn}[4] , \text{Low }[7], \text{dfn}[1] \} = 1$$

$$\text{Low }[5] = \min \{ \text{dfn}[5] , -, -\} = 4$$

$$\text{Low }[6] = \min \{ \text{dfn}[6] , -, -\} = 5$$

$$\text{Low }[7] = \min \{ \text{dfn}[7] , \text{Low }[8] \} = \min\{7, 6\} = 6$$

$$\text{Low }[8] = \min \{ \text{dfn}[8], -, \text{dfn}[4] \}$$
$$= \min\{8, 6\}$$
$$= 6$$

Now we will check for the condition dfn [u] ≤ Low [w] where w is child of vertex u. The computation of Low is { 1, 1, 1, 1, 4, 5, 6, 6}.

Now vertex 3 has children 5 and 6 and dfn [3] ≤ Low [5]. Similarly dfn [3] ≤ Low [6]. Hence vertex 3 is articulation point. For vertex 4 the child is vertex 7. dfn [4] ≤ Low [7]. Hence vertex 4 is an articulation point.

The Bi-connected components are

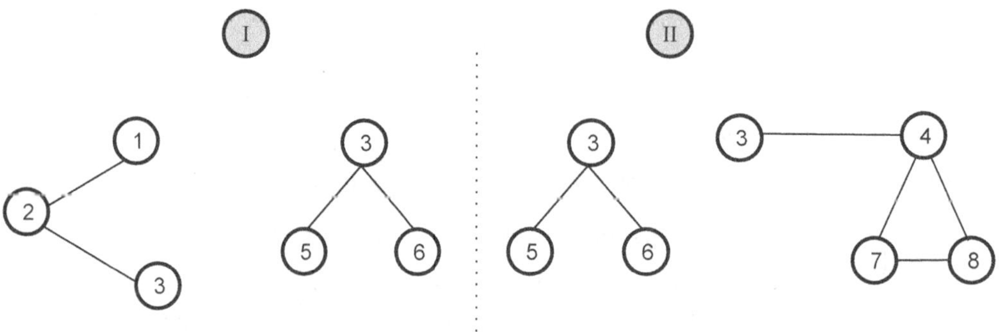

Fig. 6.7.4 Bi-connected components

Algorithm for Bi-connected Components

The algorithm for obtaining bi-connected components is as given below

```
Algorithm Bi_connect(u,v)
// the vertex u is a starting vertex for depth first traversal.
//In depth first tree v is a parent(ancestor) of u.
//Initially an array dfn[ ] is initialized to 0.The def[ ] stores the depth first search
// numbers
//Array Low[ ] is used to gives the lowest depth first number that can be reached
//from u
{
//put the dfn number for u in dfn array
dfn[u]←dfn_num;
Low[u]←dfn_num;
def_num ← dfn_num +1;
for ( each vertex w adjacent to u ) do
{
 // w is child of u and if w is not visited
if((v!=w) and (dfn[w]<dfn[u])) then
  push(u,w) onto the stack st;
 if(dfn[w]=0) then
{
```

```
 if(Low[w]>=dfn[u]) then
 {
   write ("Obtained Articulation Point");
   write("The new bi-connected component :");
   repeat
   {
    edge(x,y)← pop edge from the top of the stack;
    write(x,y);
   }until(((x,y)=(u,w)) OR ((x,y) = (w,u)));
}
 // if w is unvisited then
 Bi_connect(w,u)
 // update Low[u]
 Low[u]←min(Low[u],Low[w]);
}
else if(w!=u) then //the edge u w can be a back edge then update Low[u]
 Low[u]←min(Low[u],dfn[w]);
}
}
```

For the above given algorithm the time complexity remains O (n + E).

University Questions

1. *Explain the term : (Give example wherever necessary)*
   Articulation point **GTU : June-11, Marks 2**
2. *Write down the algorithm to determine articulation points in a given undirected graph. Give any application where it is applicable.* **GTU : June-11, Marks 4**
3. *Give the algorithm for depth first search of a graph. Also define " articulation point" of the graph and explain how to find it.* **GTU : Winter-14, Marks 7, Dec.-10, Marks 6**
4. *How you can identify articulation points explain with example. Describe use of articulation point.* **GTU : Winter-14, Marks 7**

6.8 University Questions with Answers

Regulation 2008

Dec. 2010

Q.1 *Define the terms : Directed acyclic graph, dense graph, sparse graph.* **[Refer section 6.4]** [3]

Q.2 *Give the algorithm for depth first search of a graph. Also define " articulation point" of the graph and explain how to find it.* **[Refer section 6.7]** [4]

May 2011

Q.3 *Explain with example how games can be formulated using graphs ?* **[Refer section 6.1]** **[4]**

Q.4 *Explain the term : (Give example wherever necessary)*
Articulation point **[Refer section 6.7]** **[2]**

Q.5 *Write down the algorithm to determine articulation points in a given undirected graph. Give any application where it is applicable.* **[Refer section 6.7]** **[4]**

May 2012

Q.6 *Define the terms : Directed acyclic graph, dense graph, sparse graph.* **[Refer section 6.4]** **[3]**

Q.7 *Explain breadth first traversal method for graph with algorithm.* **[Refer section 6.5]** **[7]**

May 2013

Q.8 *Define graph. Explain types of graph and different ways of graph representation* **[Refer section 6.4]** **[7]**

Winter- 2014

Q.9 *Give the algorithm for depth first search of a graph. Also define " articulation point" of the graph and explain how to find it.* **[Refer section 6.7]** **[4]**

Q.10 *How you can identify articulation points explain with example. Describe use of articulation point.* **[Refer section 6.7]** **[7]**

Regulation 2013

Winter- 2015

Q.11 *Explain Depth First Traversal Method for Graph with algorithm with example.* **[Refer section 6.5]** **[7]**

6.9 Short Questions and Answers

Q.1 Name the two components of a graph.

Ans. : The graph contains vertices and edges.

Q.2 What are the two different types of graph ?

Ans. : Two types of graph are directed and undirected graphs.

Q.3 What is DAG ?

Ans. : A directed acyclic graph is a directed graph that contains no cycle.

Q.4 Where is the DAG used ?

Ans. : DAG is used in compilers for optimization of code.

Q.5 What is complete graph ?

Ans. : If an undirected graph of n vertices consists of $n(n - 1)/2$ number of edges then it is called as complete graph.

Q.6 What is connected graph ?

Ans. : An undirected graph is said to be connected if for every pair of distinct vertices V_i and V_j in V(G) there is a graph from V_i to V_j in G.

Q.7 List out different method of representation of graph.

Ans. : Two commonly used method for representation of graph are

1. Adjacency matrix 2. Adjacency list

Q.8 Name the method of representation of graph in which matrix is used.

Ans. : Adjacency matrix.

Q.9 Name the method of representation of graph in which linked list is used.

Ans. : Adjacency list.

Q.10 Which data structure is used for breadth first search?

Ans. : The queue is used for breadth first search.

Q.11 Which data structure is used for depth first search?

Ans. : The stack data structure is used for depth first search.

Q.12 Specify two applications of BFS.

Ans. : 1. For finding the connected components in the graph.

2. To obtain shortest path between two vertices.

Q.13 List out two applications of DFS.

Ans. : 1. For checking the connectivity of graph 2. In topological sorting

Q.14 What is articulation point?

Ans. : Let G = (V, E) be a connected undirected graph, then an articulation point of graph G is a vertex whose removal disconnects graph G. This articulation point is a kind of cut-vertex.

❑❑❑

Notes

7 Backtracking and Branch and Bound

Syllabus

Introduction, The eight queens problem , Knapsack problem, Travelling salesman problem, Minimax principle.

Contents

7.1 Introduction

GTU : Winter-14, Marks 7

- In the backtracking method
  1. The desired solution is expressible as an n tuple $(x_1, x_2, \ldots x_n)$ where x_i is chosen from some finite set S_i.
  2. The solution maximizes or minimizes or satisfies a criterion function C $(x_1, x_2, \ldots x_n)$.
- The problem can be categorized into **three categories.**
  Finding whether there is any feasible solution?- Is the **decision problem.**
  What is the best solution ? - Is the **optimization problem.**
  Listing of all the feasible solution - Is the **enumeration problem.**
- The basic idea of backtracking is to build up a **vector,** one component at a time and to test whether the vector being formed has any chance of success.
- The major **advantage** of backtracking algorithm is that we can realize the fact that the partial vector generated does not lead to an optimal solution. In such a situation that vector can be ignored.
- Backtracking algorithm determines the solution by systematically searching the solution space (i.e. set of all feasible solutions) for the given problem.
- Backtracking is a **depth first search** with some **bounding function**.
- Backtracking algorithm solves the problem using **two types of constraints** - **Explicit constraint** and **Implicit constraints.**
- **Definition : Explicit constraints** are the rules that restrict each element x_i has to be chosen from given set only. Explicit constraints depends on particular instance I of the problem. All the tuples from solution set must satisfy the explicit constraints.
- **Definition : Implicit constraints** are the rules that decide which tuples in the solution space of I satisfy the criterion function. Thus the implicit constraints represent by which x_i in the solution set must be related with each other.

For example

Example 1 : 8-Queen's problem - The 8-queen's problem can be stated as follows. " Consider a chessboard of order 8×8. The problem is to place 8 queens on this board such that no two queens can attack each other. That means no two queens can be placed on the same row, column or diagonal. "

The solution to 8-queens problem can be obtained using backtracking method.

The solution can be given as below -

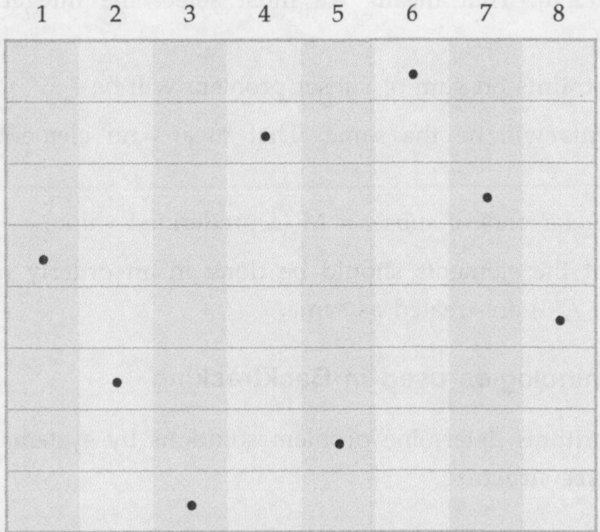

This 8 Queen's problem is solved by applying implicit and explicit constraints.

The **explicit constraints** show that the solution space S_i must be = {1, 2, 3, 4, 5, 6, 7, 8} with $1 \leq i \leq 8$. Hence solution space consists of 8^8 8-tuples.

The **implicit constraint** will be -

1) No two x_i will be same. That means all the queens must lie in different columns.

2) No two queens can be on the same row, column or diagonal.

Hence the above solution can be represented as an 8-tuple {4, 6, 8, 2, 7, 1, 3, 5}.

Example 2 : Sum of subsets -

"There are n positive numbers given in a set. The desire is to find all possible subsets of this set, the contents of which add onto a predefined value M."

In other words,

Let there be n elements given by the set w = $(w_1, w_2, w_3, \ldots, w_n)$ then find out all the subsets from whose sum is M.

For example

Consider n = 6 and $(w_1, w_2, w_3, w_4, w_5, w_6)$ = (25, 8, 16, 32, 26, 52) and M = 59 then we will get desired sum of subset as (25, 8, 26).

We can also represent the sum of subset as (1, 1, 0, 0, 1, 0). If solution subset is represented by an n-tuple $(x_1, x_2, \ldots x_n)$ such that x_i could be either 0 or 1. The $x_i = 1$ means the weight w_i is to be chosen and $x_i = 0$ means that weight w_i is not to be chosen.

The **explicit constraint** on sum of subset problem will be that any element $x_i \in \{i \mid i$ is an integer and $1 \le i \le n\}$. That means we must select the integer from given set of elements.

The **implicit constraints** on sum of subset problem will be -

1) No two elements will be the same. That means no element can be repeatedly selected.
2) The sum of the elements of subset = M (a predefined value).
3) The selection of the elements should be done in an orderly manner. That means (1, 3, 7) and (1, 7, 3) are treated as same.

7.1.1 Some Terminologies used in Backtracking

Backtracking algorithms determine problem solutions by systematically searching for the solutions using **tree structure.**

For example -

Consider a 4-queen's problem. It could be stated as "there are 4 queens that can be placed on 4 × 4 chessboard. Then no two queens can attack each other".

Following Fig. 7.1.1 shows tree organization for this problem.

(See Fig. 7.1.1 on next page)

- Each node in the tree is called **a problem state.**
- All paths from the root to other nodes define the **state space of** the problem.
- The solution states are those problem states s for which the path from root to s defines a **tuple** in the solution space.
  In some trees the leaves define the **solution states.**
- **Answer states :** These are the leaf nodes which correspond to an element in the set of solutions, these are the states which satisfy the implicit constraints.

For example

(See Fig. 7.1.2 on Page 7-6)

- A node which is been generated and all whose children have not yet been generated is called **live node.**
- The live node whose children are currently being expanded is called **E-node.**
- A **dead node** is a generated node which is not to be expanded further or all of whose children have been generated.
- There are two methods of generating state search tree -

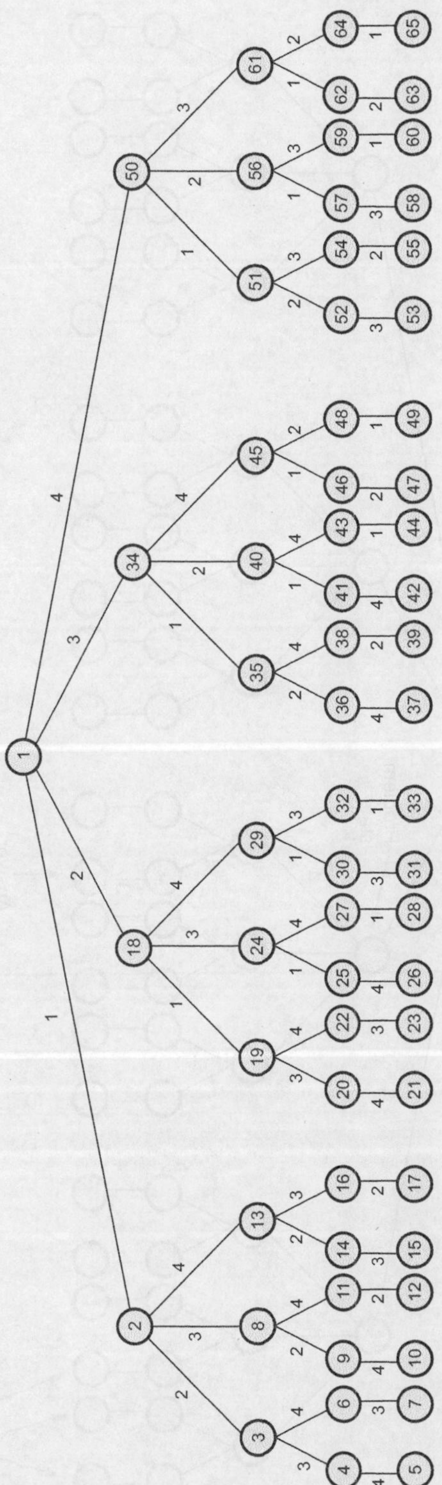

Fig. 7.1.1 State-space tree for 4-queen's problem

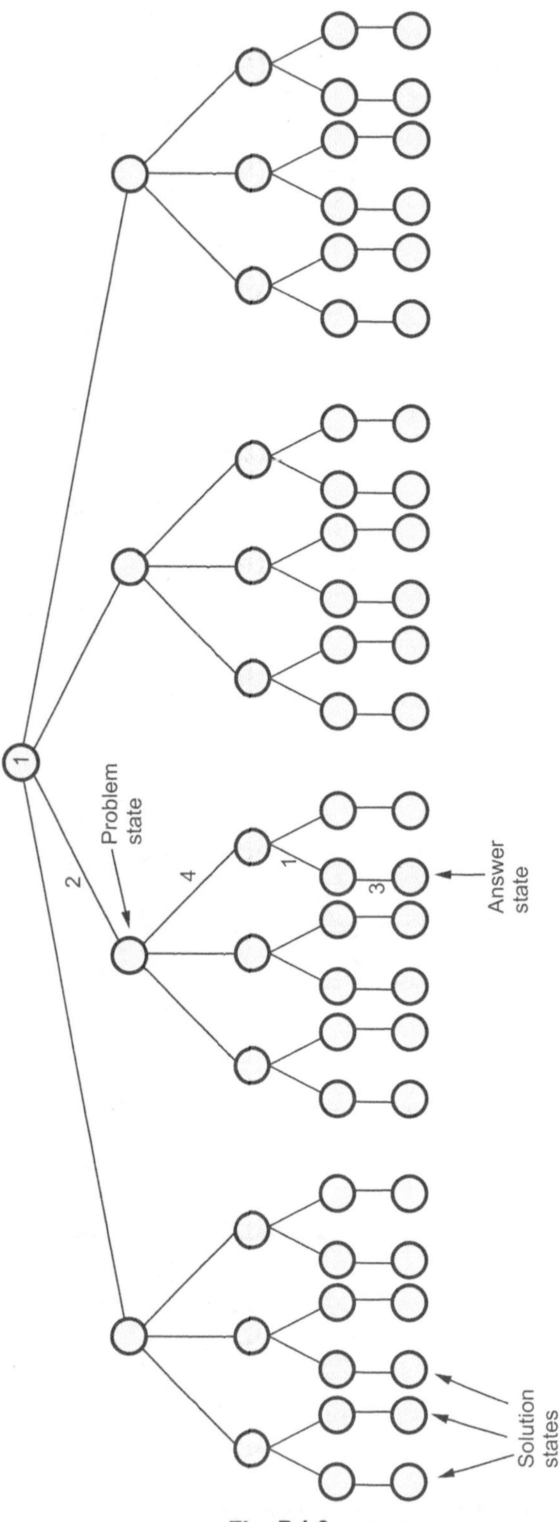

Fig. 7.1.2

i) **Backtracking -** In this method, as soon as new child C of the current E-node N is generated, this child will be the new E-node.

The N will become the E-node again when the subtree C has been fully explored.

ii) **Branch and Bound -** E-node will remain as E-node until it is dead.

- Both bracktracking and branch and bound methods use bounding functions. The bounding functions are used to kill live nodes without generating all their children. The care has to be taken while killing live nodes so that at least one answer node or all answer nodes are obtained.

Example 7.1.1 *Define following terms : State space, explicit constraints, implicit constraints, problem state, solution states, answer states, live node, E-node, dead node, bounding functions.* **May-11, Dec.-11,12**

Solution :

State space : All paths from root to other nodes define the state space of the problem.

Explicit constraints : Explicit constraints are rules, which restrict, each vector element to be chosen from given set.

Implicit constraints : Implicit constraints are rules which determine which of the tuples in the solution space satisfy the criterion function.

Problem states : Each node in the state space tree is called problem state.

Solution states : The solution states are those problem states s for which the path from root to s defines a tuple in the solution space. In some trees the leaves define solution states.

Answer states : These are the leaf nodes which correspond to an element in the set of solutions. These are the states which satisfy the implicit constraints.

Live node : A node which is generated and whose children have not yet been generated is called live node.

E-node : The live node whose children are currently being expanded is called E-node.

Dead node : A dead node is a generated node which is not to be expanded further or all of whose children have been generated.

Bounding functions : Bounding functions will be used to kill live nodes without generating all their children. A care should be taken while doing so, because atleast one answer node should be produced or even all the answer nodes be generated if problem needs to find all possible solutions.

7.1.2 Algorithms for Backtracking

Recursive Algorithm

```
Algorithm Backtrack()
//This is recursive backtracking algorithm
//a[k] is a solution vector. On entering (k-1) remaining next
//values can be computed.
//T(a1,a2,...ak) be the set of all values for a(i+1), such that
//(a1,a2,...ai+1) is a path to problem state.
// Bi+1 is a bounding function such that if Bi+1(a1,a2,...ai+1) is false
//for a path (a1,a2,...ai+1) from root node to a problem state then
//path can not be extended to reach an answer node
{
 for ( each ak that belongs to T(a1,a2,...ak-1)) do
 {
  if(Bk(a1,a2,...ak) = true) then // feasible sequence
  {
    if ((a1,a2,...ak) is a path to answer node then
      print(a[1],a[2],...a[k]);
    if (k<n) then
       Backtrack(k+1); //find the next set.
  }
 }
}
```

Iterative Algorithm

The non recursive backtracking algorithm can be given as -

```
Algorithm Non_Rec_Back(n)
// This is a non recursive version of backtracking
//a[1,...,n] is a solution vector and each a1,a2,...ak will be used to print solution.
{
 k:=1;
 while(k ≠ 0) do
 {
     if(any a[k] that belongs to T(a[1],a[2],...a[k-1])remains untried)
     AND (Bk (a[1],a[2]...,a[k] is true) then
  {
   if((a[1],a[2]...a[k]) is a path to answer node) then
    write(a[1],a[2],..a[k]); // solution printed
```

```
    //consider next element of the set
    k:=k+1;
    else
     k : =k–1; //backtrack to most recent value
   }
  }
}
```

Efficiency of Backtracking Algorithm

The efficiency of both the backtracking algorithm depends upon four factors -

1) The time required to generate a[k].
2) The number of a[k] elements which satisfy the explicit constraints.
3) The time required by bounding functions B_k to generate a feasible sequence.
4) The number of elements a[k] that satisfy the bounding functions B_k for all the values of k.

The first three factors are **independant** on the given **problem instance**. And the time complexity of these three factors is polynomial time. But the fourth factor varies according to the size of problem instance. That means, if there are n! nodes which satisfy the bounding function then the worst case time complexity of backtracking

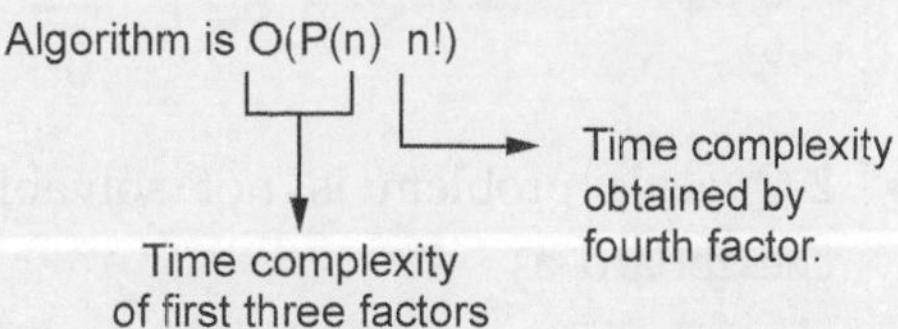

Review Question

1. *What is the central principle of backtracking taking n queens problem as an example, explain the solution process ?* **GTU : Winter-14, Marks 7**

7.2 Applications of Backtracking

Various applications that are based on backtracking method are -

1. 8 Queen's problem : This is a problem based on chess games. By this problem, it is stated that arrange the queens on chessboard in such a way that no two queens can attack each other.
2. Sub of subset problem.
3. Graph coloring problem.
4. Finding Hamiltonian cycle.
5. Knapsack problem.

7.3 The Eight Queens Problem

GTU : Dec.-10,11, June-11,12, Summer-13, Winter-15, Marks 7

The n-queen's problem can be stated as follows.

Consider a $n \times n$ chessboard on which we have to place n queens so that no two queens attack each other by being in the same row or in the same column or on the same diagonal.

For example

Consider 4×4 board

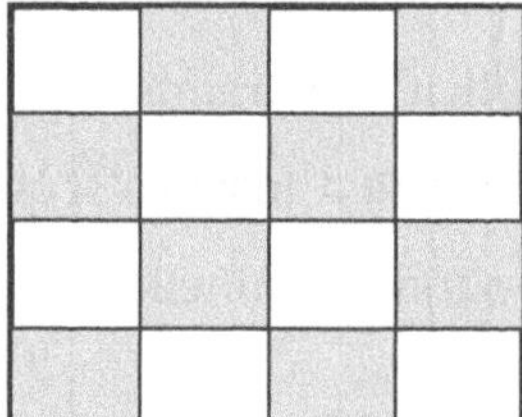

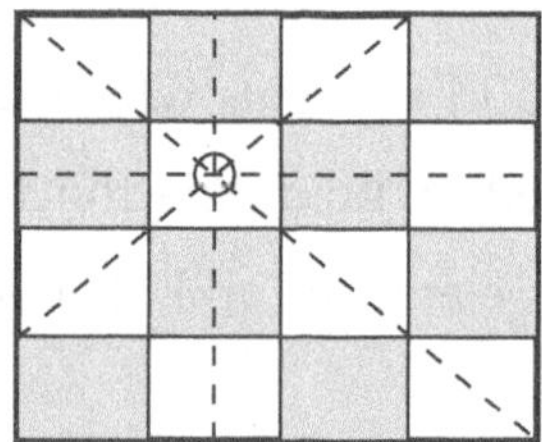

The next queen - if is placed on the paths marked by dotted lines then they can attack each other

- 2-Queen's problem is not solvable - Because 2-queens can be placed on 2×2 chessboard as

Illegal

Illegal

Illegal

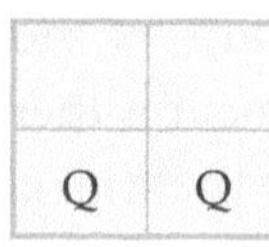

Illegal

Illegal

- But 4-queen's problem is solvable.

⇐ Note that no two queens can attack each other.

7.3.1 How to Solve n-Queen's Problem ?

Let us take 4-queens and 4×4 chessboard.

- Now we start with empty chessboard.
- Place queen 1 in the first possible position of its row i.e. on 1st row and 1st column.

- Then place queen 2 after trying unsuccessful place - 1(1, 2), (2, 1), (2, 2) at (2, 3) i.e. 2nd row and 3rd column.

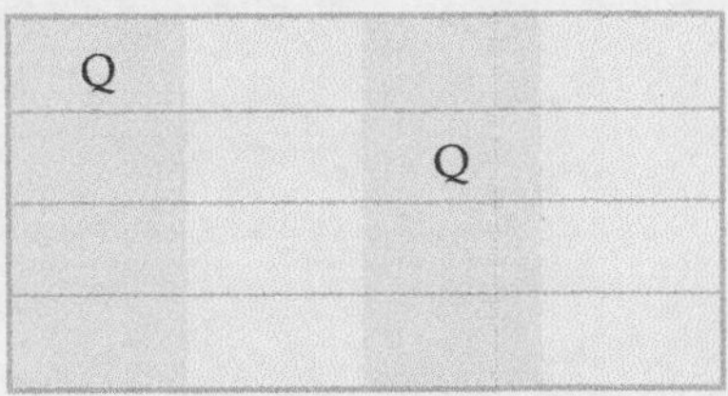

- This is the dead end because a 3rd queen cannot be placed in next column, as there is no acceptable position for queen 3. Hence algorithm **backtracks** and places the 2nd queen at (2, 4) position.

- The place 3rd queen at (3, 2) but it is again another dead end as next queen (4th queen) cannot be placed at permissible position.

- Hence we need to backtrack all the way upto queen 1 and move it to (1, 2).

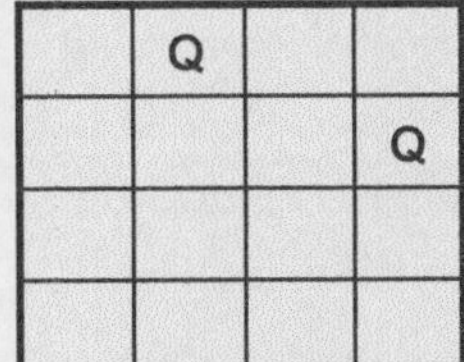

Thus solution is obtained.
(2, 4, 1, 3) in rowwise manner.

- Place queen 1 at (1, 2), queen 2 at (2, 4), queen 3 at (3, 1) and queen 4 at (4, 3). The state space tree of 4-queen's problem is shown in Fig. 7.3.1 (See on next page)

Now we will consider how to place **8-Queen's** on the chessboard.
Initially the chessboard is empty.

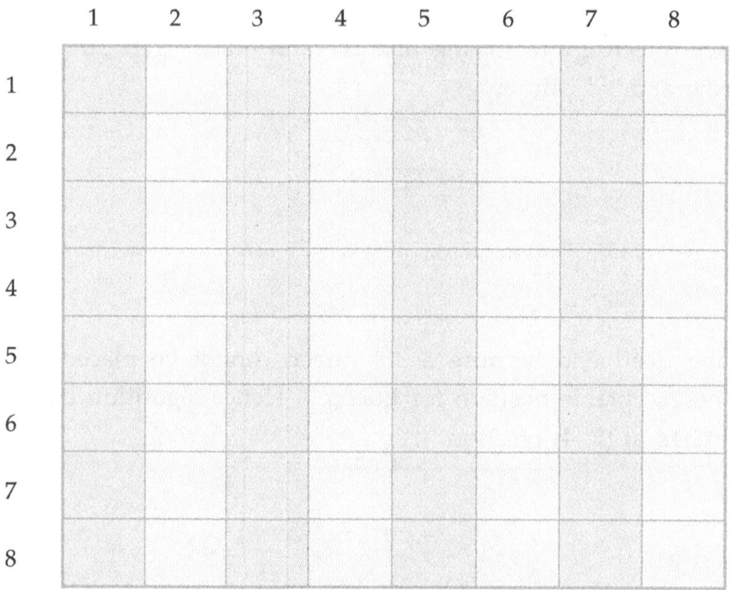

Now we will start placing the queens on the chessboard.

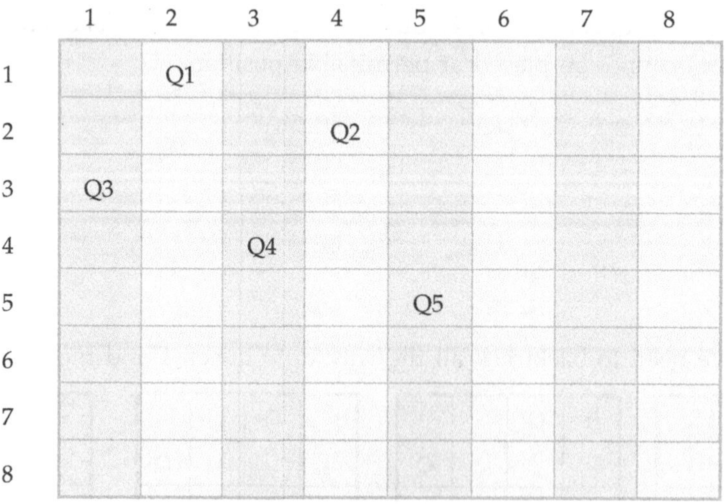

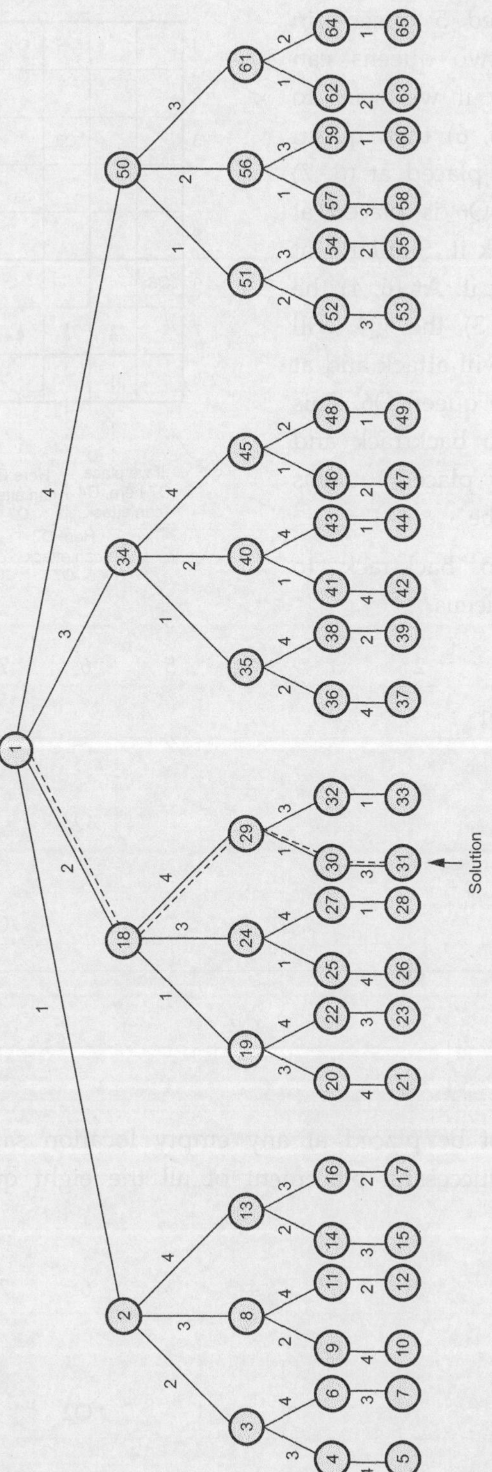

Fig. 7.3.1 State space tree for 4-queen's problem

Thus we have placed 5 queens in such a way that no two queens can attack each other. Now if we want to place Q6 at location (6, 6) then queen Q5 can attack, if Q6 is placed at (6, 7) then Q1 can attack, if Q6 is placed at (6, 8) then Q2 can attack it. Similarly at (6, 5) the Q5 will attack it. At (6, 4) the Q2 will attack, at (6, 3) the Q4 will attack, at (6, 2) the Q1 will attack and at (6, 1) Q3 will attack the queen Q6. This shows that we need to backtrack and change the previously placed queens positions. It could then be -

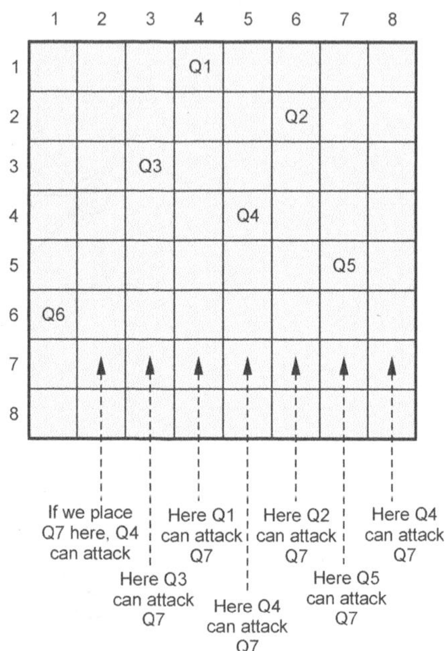

Hence we have to backtrack to adjust already placed queens.

	1	2	3	4	5	6	7	8
1	Q1							
2								Q2
3						Q3		
4			Q4					
5							Q5	
6		Q6						
7				Q7				
8								

But again Q8 cannot be placed at any empty location safely. Hence we need to backtrack. Finally the successful placement of all the eight queens can be shown by following figure.

	1	2	3	4	5	6	7	8
1			Q1					
2						Q2		
3		Q3						

4							Q4	
5	Q5							
6				Q6				
7								Q7
8					Q8			

7.3.2 Algorithm

```
Algorithm Queen(n)
//Problem description : This algorithm is for implementing n
//queen's problem
//Input : total number of queen's n.
        for column ←1 to n do
        {
            if(place(row,column))then
            {
             board[row]column//no conflict so place queen
            if(row=n)then//dead end
   print_board(n)
            //printing the board configuration
            else//try next queen with next position
                Queen(row+1,n)
            }
        }
Algorithm place(row,column)
//Problem Description : This algorithm is for placing the
//queen at appropriate position
//Input : row and column of the chessboard
//output : returns 0 for the conflicting row and column
//position and 1 for no conflict.
        for i ← 1 to row-1 do
        { //checking for column and diagonal conflicts
         if(board[i] = column)then
           return 0
        else if(abs(board[i]- column) = abs(i - row))then
            return 0
        }
        //no conflicts hence Queen can be placed
    return 1
```

This function checks if two queens are on the same diagonal or not.

Row by row each queen is placed by satisfying constraints.

Same column by 2 queen's

This formula gives that 2 queens are on same diagonal

C Functions

```
/* By this function we try the next free slot
and check for proper positioning of queen
```

```
*/
void Queen(int row,int n)
{
        int column;
        for(column=1;column<=n;column++)
        {
            if(place(row,column))

            {
             board[row] = column;//no conflict so place queen
             if(row==n)//dead end
                print_board(n);
                 //printing the board configuration
            else //try next queen with next position
                Queen(row+1,n);
            }
        }
}
int place(int row,int column)
{
        int i;
        for(i=1;i<=row - 1;i++)
        { //checking for column and diagonal conflicts
            if(board[i] == column)
                return 0;
            else
                if(abs(board[i] - column) == abs(i - row))
                    return 0;
        }
        //no conflicts hence Queen can be placed
        return 1;
}
```

Example 7.3.1 *Solve 8-queen's problem for a feasible sequence (6, 4, 7, 1).*

Solution : As the feasible sequence is given, we will place the queens accordingly and then try out the other remaining places.

	1	2	3	4	5	6	7	8
1						Q		
2				Q				
3							Q	
4	Q							
5								

6								
7								
8								

The diagonal conflicts can be checked by following formula -

Let, $P_1 = (i, j)$ and $P_2 = (k, l)$ are two positions. Then P_1 and P_2 are the positions that are on the same diagonal, if

$$i + j = k + l \quad \text{or}$$

$$i - j = k - l$$

Now if next queen is placed on (5, 2) then

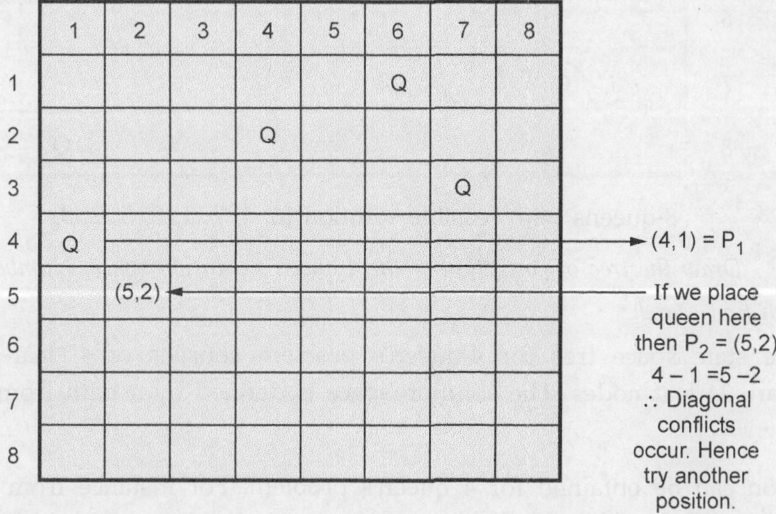

It can be summarized below.

Queen Positions								Action
1	2	3	4	5	6	7	8	
6	4	7	1					Start
6	4	7	1	2				As 4 – 1 = 5 – 2 conflict occurs.
6	4	7	1	3				5 – 3 ≠ 4 –1 or 5 + 3 ≠ 4 + 1 ∴ Feasible
6	4	7	1	3	2			As 5 + 3 = 6 + 2. It is not feasible.
6	4	7	1	3	5			Feasible
6	4	7	1	3	5	2		Feasible
6	4	7	1	3	5	2	8	List ends and we have got feasible sequence.

The 8-queens on 8×8 board with this sequence is -

	1	2	3	4	5	6	7	8
1						Q		
2				Q				
3							Q	
4	Q							
5			Q					
6					Q			
7		Q						
8								Q

8-queens with feasible solution (6, 4, 7, 1, 3, 5, 2, 8)

Example 7.3.2 *Draw the tree organization of the 4-queen's solution space. Number the nodes using depth first search.*

Solution : The state space tree for 4-queen's problem consists of 4! leaf nodes. That means there are 24 leaf nodes. The solution space is defined by a path from root to leaf node.

The solution can be obtained for 4 queen's problem. For instance from 1 to leaf 31 represents one possible solution.

Example 7.3.3 *For a feasible sequence (7, 5, 3, 1) solve 8 queen's problem using backtracking.* **May-14**

Solution : While placing the queen at next position we have to check whether the current position chosen is on the same diagonal of previous queen's position.

If $P_1 = (i, j)$ and $P_2 = (k, l)$ are two positions then P_1 and P_2 lie on the same diagonal if $i + j = k + l$ or $i - j = k - l$. Let us put the given feasible sequence and try out remaining positions.

(1), 2, (3), 4, (5), 6, (7), 8 → Already occupied position.

j → 1	2	3	4	5	6	7	8	
7	5	3	1					
7	5	3	1	2				The remaining vacant position is 2. But 4 – 1 = 5 – 2. Not feasible.
7	5	3	1	4				No conflict.
7	5	3	1	4	6			(3, 3) = (6, 6) ∴ Conflict occurs.
7	5	3	1	4	8			List ends and we can not place further queen's.
7	5	3	1	4				Hence backtrack.
7	5	3	1	6				The next free slot 6 is tried.
7	5	3	1	6	2			Not feasible because (7, 1) = (2, 6) 1 + 7 = 6 + 2. That is on same diagonal.
7	5	3	1	6	4			Occupied are circled.
7	5	3	1	6	4	2		
7	5	3	1	6	4	2	8	Conflict because (3, 3) = (8, 8)
7	5	3	1	6	4	2		Hence backtrack.
7	5	3	1	6	4	8		(6, 5) = (8, 7). Not feasible.
7	5	3	1	6	4			Backtrack.
7	5	3	1	6	8			
7	5	3	1	6	8	2		
7	5	3	1	6	8	2	4	List ends with solution of 8 queen's.

(i values i.e. row values)

Example 7.3.4 *Obtain any two solutions to 4-queen's problem. Establish the relationship between them.*

Solution : The solutions to 4-queen's problem are as given below.

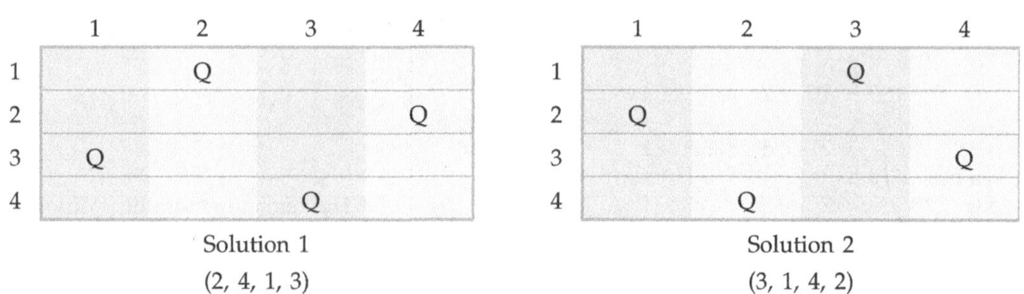

Solution 1 (2, 4, 1, 3) Solution 2 (3, 1, 4, 2)

If these two solutions are observed then we can say that second solution can be simply obtained by reversing the first solution.

Example 7.3.5 *Generate at least 3 solutions for 5-queen's problem.* **May-12**

Solution : The solutions are as given below.

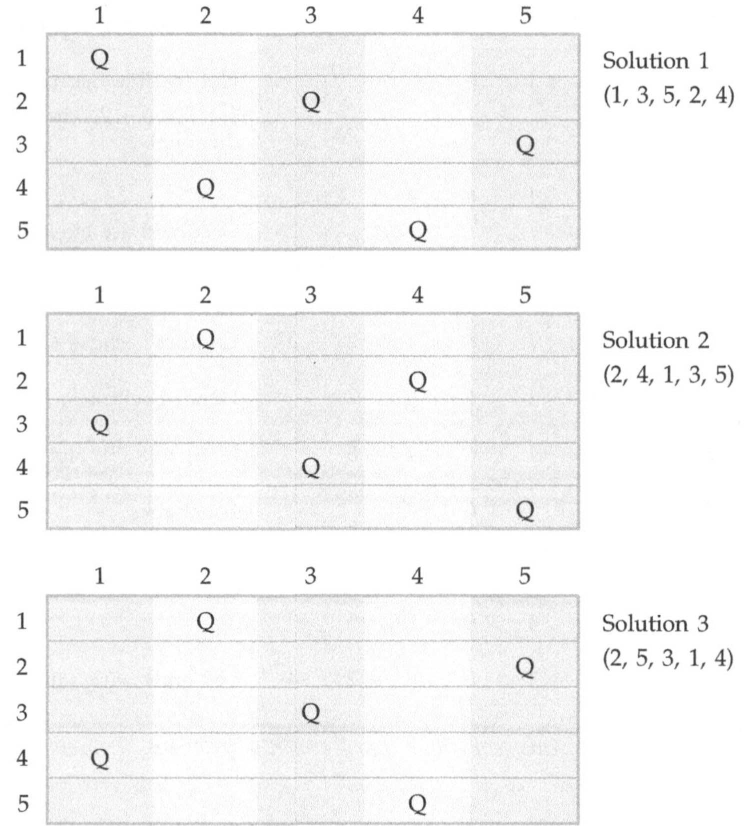

Solution 1 (1, 3, 5, 2, 4)

Solution 2 (2, 4, 1, 3, 5)

Solution 3 (2, 5, 3, 1, 4)

Review Questions

1. *Explain the use of backtracking method for solving eight queens problem giving its algorithm.* **GTU : Dec.-10, Marks 7**

2. *Discuss how 8-queen problem can be solved using backtracking.* **GTU : June-11, Marks 4**
3. *Find all possible solution for the 4 * 4 chessboard, 4 queen's problem using backtracking.* **GTU : Summer-13, Marks 7, Dec.-11, Marks 3**
4. *Explain backtracking method. What is n-queens problem ? Give solution of 4-queens problem using backtracking method.* **GTU : June-12, Winter-15, Marks 7**

7.4 Knapsack Problem

GTU : June-11, Winter-14, Marks 7

In this section we will discuss "How Knapsack problem be solved using backtracking". The Knapsack problem can be stated as follows.

Problem statement : "If we are given n objects and a Knapsack or a bag in which the object i with weight w_i is to be placed. The Knapsack has a capacity **m**. Then the profit value that can be earned is p_i. Then **objective** is to obtain filling up of Knapsack with maximum profit earned, but it should not exceed the capacity m of Knapsack.

To fill the given Knapsack we select the object with some weight and having some profit. This selected object is put in the Knapsack. Thus Knapsack is filled up with selected objects. Note that the Knapsack's capacity m should not be exceeded. Hence the first item gives best pay off per weight unit and last one gives the worst pay off per weight unit.

Hence we must arrange the given data in non-increasing order i.e.

$$p_i / w_i \geq p_{i+1} / w_{i+1}$$

- First of all we compute upper bound of the tree.
- We design a state space tree by inclusion or exclusion of some items.

The upper bound can be computed using following formula.

$$ub + (1-(c-m) / w_i) * p_i$$

The algorithm for computing an upper bound is as given below -

```
Algorithm Bound_Calculation (cp,cw,k)
//Problem description : This algorithm
//calculates the upper bound, for each item
//Input : cp is the current profit, cw is the
//current weight and k is the index of just
//removed item
//Output : The upper bound value can be returned
  ub ← cp
  c ← cw
  for (i ← k+1 to n) do
{
```

```
        c ← c+w[i]
        if (c < m) then            //m is capacity of knapsack
            ub ← ub + p[i]
        else
            {
                    ub ← ub + (1–(c–m)/w[i])*p[i]
                    return ub
            }
        return ub
    }
```

This function is invoked by a Knapsack function **Bk (k, cp, cw)**. The algorithm for the same is as given below.

```
    Algorithm Bk (k,cp,cw)
    //Problem description : This algorithm is to obtain
    //solution for knapsack problem. Using this algorithm
    //a state space tree can be generated.
    //Input : Initially k=1, cp=0 and cw=0. The
    //k represents the index of currently referred
    //item. The cp and cw represent the profit and
    //weights of items, so far selected.
    //Output : The set of selected items that are
    //satisfying the objective of knapsack problem.

    if (cw+w[i]<= m) then          Generates left child
    {
       temp[k] ← 1     //temp array                        stores currently
selected object
       if (k<n) then
   Bk(k+1,cp+p[k],cw+w[k])        //recursive call
   if ((cp+p[k] > final_profit) AND (k==n)) then
   { //final_profit is initially –1, it represents final profit
   final_profit ← cp + p[k]
      final_wt ← cw + w[k]         Finally get the solution
      for (j ← 1 to k) then
          x[j] ← temp[j]
    }                                           Generates right child
}
    if (Bound_calculation (cp,cw,k) ≥ final_profit) then
    {
          temp[k] ← 0
          if (k < n) then                 Invoke this function in order to
                Bk(k+1, cp, cw)           obtain upper bound.
          if((cp > final_profit) AND (k=n)) then
          {
```

```
30              final_profit ← cp
31              final_wt ← cw
32              for(j ← 1 to k)
33                    x[j] ← temp [j]
34        }
35}
```

Finally get the solution

Example 7.4.1 *Obtain the optimal solution to the Knapsack problem* $n = 3, m = 20$ $(p_1, p_2, p_3) = (25, 24, 15)$ *and* $(w_1, w_2, w_3) = (18, 15, 10)$. **May-14**

Solution : Given that n = 3 and m = Capacity of Knapsack = 20.

We have

i	p [i]	w [i]	p [i] / w [i]
1	25	18	1.3
2	24	15	1.6
3	15	10	1.5

As we want p[i] / w[i] ≥ p[i+1] / w [i+1], let us rearrange the items as

i	p [i]	w [i]	p [i] / w [i]
1	24	15	1.6
2	15	10	1.5
3	25	18	1.3

Step 1 : Here we will trace knapsack backtracking algorithm using above values.

Initially set **final_profit = – 1**

Bk (1, 0, 0)

∴ k = 1

cp = 0

cw = 0

Check if (cw + w [k] < = m)

i.e. if (0 + w [1] = 0 + 15 <= 20) → yes

∴ set temp [1] = 1

if (k < n) i.e. if (1 < 3) ? → yes

∴ Bk (k + 1, cp + p [k], cw + w [k]) is called

Hence Bk (2, 0 + 24, 0 + 15) will be called. Refer line 14 of **Algorithm Bk ( ).**

Step 2 :

$$k = 2$$
$$cp = 24$$
$$cw = 15$$

Check if (cw + w [k] <= m)

i.e. if (15 + w [2] i.e. 15 + 10 <= 20) → no

Hence we will calculate ub i.e. upper bound.

Step 3 : For calculating upper bound, initially set

ub = cp = 24

c = cw = 15 Refer line 8 and 9 of Algorithm Bound_calculation

for (i = k+1 to n) we will update upper bound value.

Consider i = k+1 = 3

$$c = c + w[i]$$
$$c = 15 + w[3]$$
$$\therefore \quad c = 15 + 18 = 33$$

As 33 > 20 i.e. exceeding the Knapsack capacity, we will compute ub as

$$ub = ub + (1-(c-m) / w[i]) * p[i]$$

← See line 17 of Bound_calculation

$$\therefore \quad ub = 24 + (1-(15-20) / w[3]) * p[3]$$
$$= 24 + (1-5/18) * 25$$
$$\mathbf{ub = 30.94 \approx 31}$$

As (ub > final_profit) i.e. 30.94 > – 1

Set temp [2] = 0

Now refer line 27 of **Bk** algorithm, a recursive call with k = 3 is made.

Step 4 :

$$k = 3$$
$$cp = 24 + p[2] = 24 + 15 = 39$$
$$cw = 15 + w[2] = 15 + 10 = 25$$

Check if (cw + w [k] <= m)

i.e. if (25 + w [3] = 25 + 18 < = 20) → no

Hence we will calculate upper bound.

Step 5 : For calculating upper bound, initially set

ub = cp = 39
c = cw = 25 } Refer line 8 and 9 of algorithm **Bound_ calculation**

Set i = k + 1 i.e. 3 + 1 = 4 But i = 4 > n

Hence we will keep ub as it is

∴ ub = 39

As (39 > final_profit) i.e. 39 > – 1

Set temp [k] = temp [3] = 0

Now k = n = 3 and cp = 39 > final_profit (i.e. – 1)

final_profit = cp = 39
final_wt = cw = 25 } Refer line 30 and 31 of algorithm **Bk**

Now copy all the contents of temp array to an array x [ ]. Refer line 32, 33 of **Algorithm Bk.**

Hence **x = {1, 0, 0}** i.e. item 1 with **weight = 15** and **profit = 24** is selected.

The state space tree can be drawn as

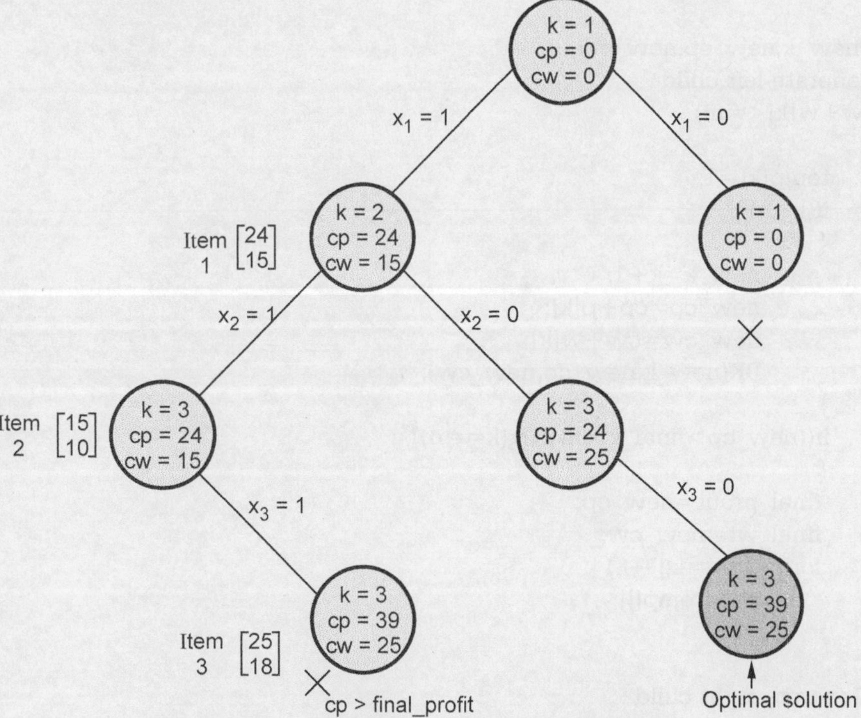

Fig. 7.4.1 State space tree for Knapsack

Here the left branch indicates inclusion of item and right branch indicates exclusion of items. Hence $x_1 = 1$ means 1st item selected and $x_2 = 0$, $x_3 = 0$ means 2nd and 3rd items are not selected. The state space tree can be created in DFS manner.

C Function

```
float Bound_Calculation(int cp,int cw,int k)
{
        int ub,c,i;
        ub=cp;c=cw;
        for(i=k+1;i<=n;i++)
        {
                c=c+w[i];
                if(c<m)
                        ub=ub+p[i];

                else
                        return(ub+(1-(c-m)/w[i])*p[i]);
        }
        return ub;
}
void BK(int k,int cp,int cw)
{
        int new_k,new_cp,new_cw,j;
        //Generate left child
        if(cw+w[k]<=m)
        {
                temp[k]=1;
                if(k<n)
                {
                        new_k=k+1;
                        new_cp=cp+p[k];
                        new_cw=cw+w[k];
                        BK(new_k,new_cp,new_cw);
                }
                if((new_cp>final_profit)&&(k==n))
                {
                 final_profit=new_cp;
                 final_wt=new_cw;
                 for(j=1;j<=k;j++)
                        x[j]=temp[j];
                }
        }
        //Generate right child
        if(Bound_Calculation(cp,cw,k)>=final_profit)
        {
```

```
            temp[k]=0;
            if(k<n)
                  BK(k+1,cp,cw);
            if((cp>final_profit)&&(k==n))
            {
                  final_profit=cp;
                  final_wt=cw;
                  for(j=1;j<=n;j++)
                  x[j]=temp[j];
            }
      }
}
```

Example 7.4.2 *Consider the following instance for knapsack problem using backtracking*

n = 8

P = (11, 21, 31, 33, 43, 53, 55, 65) W = (1, 11, 21, 23, 33, 43, 45, 55) M = 110.

Dec.-11, May-12

Solution : We will arrange all the items in $\frac{P_i}{W_i} > \frac{P_{i+1}}{W_{i+1}} > \frac{P_{i+2}}{W_{i+3}} \ldots$

The instance will be

Item	P_i	W_i	P_i / W_i
1	11	1	11
2	21	11	1.90
3	31	21	1.47
4	33	23	1.43
5	43	33	1.30
6	53	43	1.23
7	55	45	1.22
8	65	55	1.18

Let M = 110

Initially total-profit = – 1

cp = 0, cw = 0 Let k = 0

$$cp = cp + 11 = 0 + 11 = 11$$

$$cw = cw + 1 = 0 + 1 = 1 < m \qquad \therefore \text{select item1}$$

$$k = 1, \quad p[i] = 21$$

$$w[i] = 11$$

$$\therefore \quad cp = 11 + 21 = 32$$

$$cw = 1 + 11 = 12 < 110 \qquad \therefore \text{select item 2}$$

k = 2 $\quad p[3] = 31$

$w[3] = 21$

$\therefore \quad cp = 32 + 31 = 63$

$$cw = 12 + 21 = 33 < 110 \qquad \therefore \text{select item 3}$$

k = 3 $\quad p[4] = 33$

$w[4] = 23$

$\therefore \quad cp = 63 + 33 = 96$

$$cw = 33 + 23 = 56 < 110 \qquad \therefore \text{select item 4}$$

k = 4 $\quad p[5] = 43$

$w[5] = 33$

$\therefore \quad cp = 96 + 43 = 139$

$$cw = 33 + 56 = 89 < 110 \qquad \therefore \text{select item 5}$$

k = 5 $\quad p[6] = 53$

$w[6] = 43$

$\therefore \quad cp = 139 + 53 = 192$

$$cw = 99 + 43 = 142 > 110 \qquad \therefore \text{not to select item 6}$$

Thus upper bound will be, $11+21+31+33+43+\left(\frac{110-89}{43}\right)*53 = 164.88$ on selecting item 6, 7, 8 the total weight will exceed the capacity hence we will back track at item 4.

That means item 1, item 2, item 3, item 4 are selected. Thus upper bound will be calculated and a space tree is constructed, as follows. (See Fig. 7.4.2 on next page).

Computation at node I

$$ub = cp + \left(\frac{m - cw}{W_{i+1}}\right) * P_{i+1}$$

$$ub = 11+21+31+33+43+\left(\frac{110-89}{43}\right)*53$$

$$ub = 164.88$$

Computation at node II

$$ub = 11+21+31+33+\left(\frac{110-56}{33}\right)*43$$

$$= 166.09$$

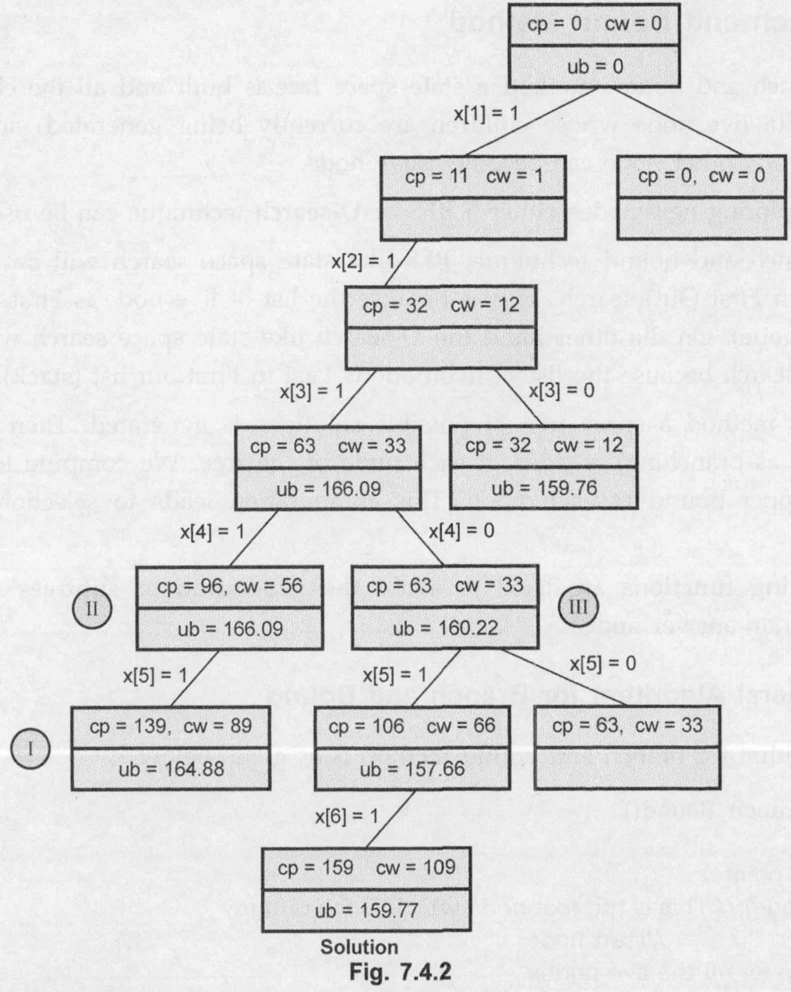

Fig. 7.4.2

Computation at node III

$$ub = 11+21+31+43+53+\left(\frac{110-109}{45}\right)*55$$

$$ub = 160.22$$

The solution giving maximum profit will be by selection of **item 1, item 2, item 3, item 5** and **item 6.**

Review Questions

1. *Construct an implicit tree for 0-1 knapsack problem. Give backtracking algorithm to solve it.* **GTU : June-11, Marks 6**
2. *Explain backtracking with knapsack problem.* **GTU : Winter-14, Marks 7**

7.5 Branch and Bound Method

- In branch and bound method a state space tree is built and all the children of E nodes (a live node whose children are currently being generated) are generated before any other node can become a live node.
- For exploring new nodes either a **BFS** or **D-search** technique can be used.
- In Branch and bound technique, **BFS-like** state space search will be called **FIFO** (First In First Out) search. This is because the list of live node is First In First Out list (**queue**). On the other hand the **D-search** like state space search will be called **LIFO** search because the list of live node is Last in First out list (**stack**).
- In this method a space tree of possible solutions is generated. Then partitioning (called as branching) is done at each node of the tree. We compute lower bound and upper bound at each node. This computation leads to selection of answer node.
- **Bounding functions** are used to **avoid the generation of subtrees** that do not contain an answer node.

7.5.1 General Algorithm for Branch and Bound

The algorithm for branch and bound method is as given below.

```
Algorithm Branch_Bound()
{
//E is a node pointer;
  E←new(node);// This is the root node which is the dummy
                              //start node
  //H is  heap for all the live nodes.
  // H is a min-heap for minimization problems,
  //H is a max-heap for maximization problems.
  while (true)
  {
   if (E is a final leaf) then
     {
           //E is an optimal solution
     write( path from E to the root);
     return;
     }
    Expand(E);
    if (H is empty) then //if no element is present in heap
           {
                 write(" there is no solution");
                 return;
     }
    E ←delete_top(H);
```

```
  }
}
```

Following is an algorithm named Expand is for generating state space tree -

```
Algorithm Expand(E)
{
  Generate all the children of E;
  Compute the approximate cost value of each child;
  Insert each child into the heap H;
}
```

For Example

Consider the 4-queens problem using branch and bound method. In branch and bound method a bounding function is associated with each node. The node with-optimum bounding function becomes an E-node. And children of such node get expanded. The state space tree for the same is as given below -

In Fig. 6.3.1 based on bounding function the nodes will be selected and answer node can be obtained. The numbers that are written outside the node indicates the order in which evaluation of tree takes place. (Refer Fig. 7.5.1 on next page)

Review Question

1. *Explain in brief : Branch and bound method.*

7.6 Traveling Salesman Problem

Problem Statement

If there are n cities and cost of travelling from any city to any other city is given. Then we have to obtain the cheapest round-trip such that each city is visited exactly once and then returning to starting city, completes the tour.

Typically travelling salesperson problem is represented by weighted graph.

For example : Consider an instance for TSP is given by G as,

$$G = \begin{bmatrix} \infty & 20 & 30 & 10 & 11 \\ 15 & \infty & 16 & 4 & 2 \\ 3 & 5 & \infty & 2 & 4 \\ 19 & 6 & 18 & \infty & 3 \\ 16 & 4 & 7 & 16 & \infty \end{bmatrix}$$

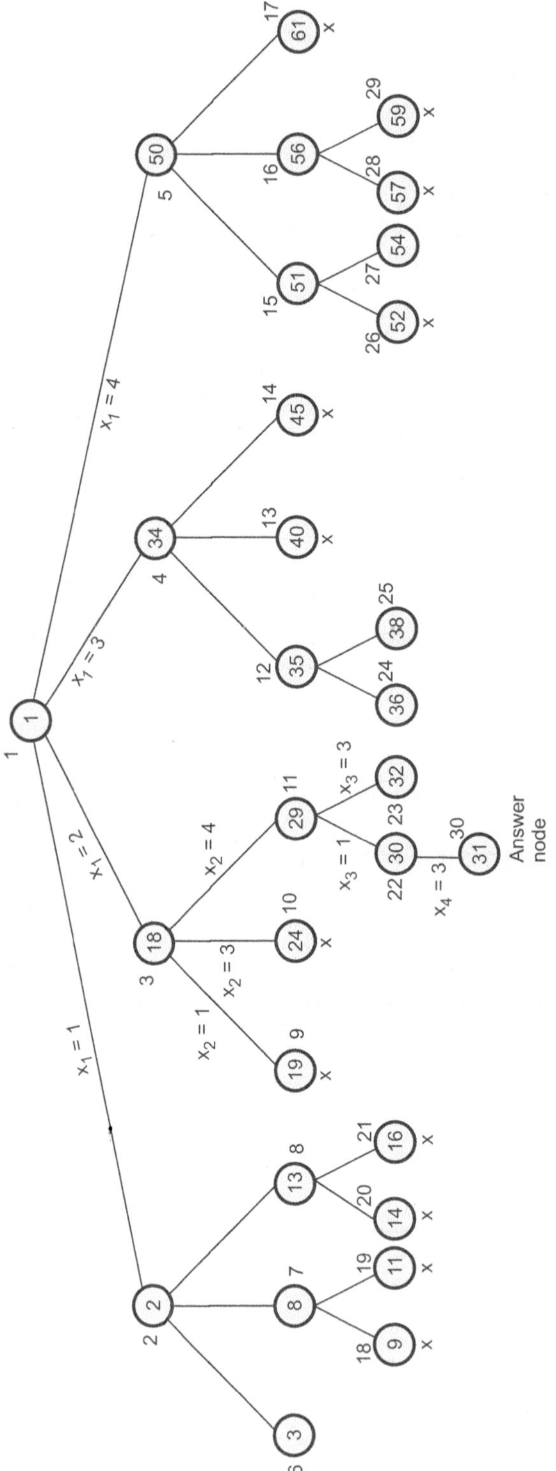

Fig. 7.5.1 Portion of state space tree using 4-queens

There n = 5 nodes. Hence we can draw a state space tree with 5 nodes as shown in Fig. 7.6.1.

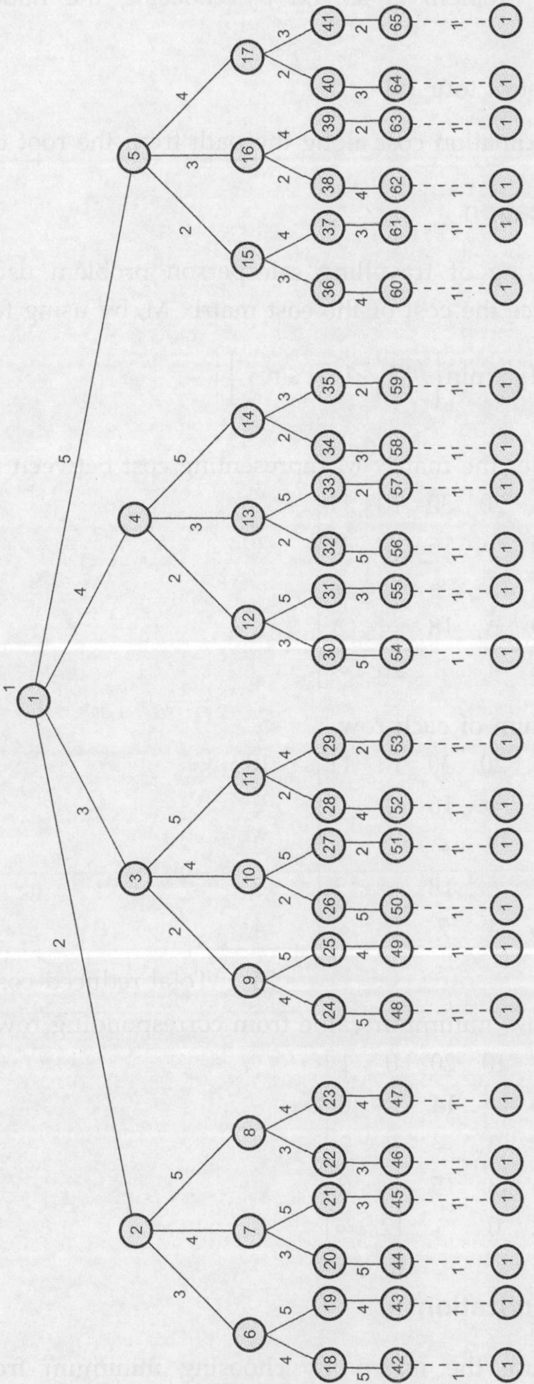

Fig. 7.6.1 State space tree for TSP

Tour(x) is the path that begins at root and reaching to node x in a state space tree and returns to root. In branch and bound strategy cost of each node x is computed. The travelling salesperson problem is solved by choosing the node with optimum cost. Hence,

$$c(x) = \text{cost of tour } (x) \qquad \text{where x is a leaf node.}$$

The c^(x) is the approximation cost along the path from the root to x.

7.6.1 Row Minimization

To understand solving of travelling salesperson problem using branch and bound approach we will reduce the cost of the cost matrix M, by using following formula.

$$\text{Red\_Row (M)} = \left[M_{ij} - \min\left\{ M_{ij} \middle| 1 \le j \le n \right\} \right] \qquad \text{where } M_{ij} < \infty$$

For example : Consider the matrix M representing cost between any two cities.

$$M = \begin{bmatrix} \infty & 20 & 30 & 10 & 11 \\ 15 & \infty & 16 & 4 & 2 \\ 3 & 5 & \infty & 2 & 4 \\ 19 & 6 & 18 & \infty & 3 \\ 16 & 4 & 7 & 16 & \infty \end{bmatrix}$$

We will find minimum of each row.

$$\begin{bmatrix} \infty & 20 & 30 & 10 & 11 \\ 15 & \infty & 16 & 4 & 2 \\ 3 & 5 & \infty & 2 & 4 \\ 19 & 6 & 18 & \infty & 3 \\ 16 & 4 & 7 & 16 & \infty \end{bmatrix} \quad \begin{matrix} 10 \\ 2 \\ 2 \\ 3 \\ 4 \\ \hline 21 \end{matrix} \quad \text{Total reduced cost.}$$

We will subtract the row_minimum value from corresponding row. Hence,

$$\text{Red\_Row(M)} = \begin{bmatrix} \infty & 10 & 20 & 0 & 1 \\ 13 & \infty & 14 & 2 & 0 \\ 1 & 3 & \infty & 0 & 2 \\ 16 & 3 & 15 & \infty & 0 \\ 12 & 0 & 3 & 12 & \infty \end{bmatrix}$$

7.6.2 Column Minimization

Now we will reduce the matrix by choosing minimum from each column. The formula for column reduction of matrix is

$$\text{Red\_Col(M)} = M_{ji} - \min\left\{ M_{ji} \,\middle|\, 1 \le j \le n \right\} \text{ where } M_{ji} < \infty$$

7.6.3 Full Reduction

Let M be the cost matrix for travelling salesperson problem for n vertices then M is called reduced if each row and each column consists of either entirely ∞ entries or else contain at least one zero. The full reduction can be achieved by applying both row_reduction and column reduction.

For example : Consider, the matrix M as given below and reduce it fully.

$$M = \begin{bmatrix} \infty & 20 & 30 & 10 & 11 \\ 15 & \infty & 16 & 4 & 2 \\ 3 & 5 & \infty & 2 & 4 \\ 19 & 6 & 18 & \infty & 3 \\ 16 & 4 & 7 & 16 & \infty \end{bmatrix}$$

Red_Row (M) can be obtained as,

$$\begin{bmatrix} \infty & 20 & 30 & 10 & 11 \\ 15 & \infty & 16 & 4 & 2 \\ 3 & 5 & \infty & 2 & 4 \\ 19 & 6 & 18 & \infty & 3 \\ 16 & 4 & 7 & 16 & \infty \end{bmatrix} \quad \begin{array}{c} 10 \\ 2 \\ 2 \\ 3 \\ 4 \\ \hline 21 \end{array}$$

$$\text{Red\_Row (M)} = \begin{bmatrix} \infty & 10 & 20 & 0 & 1 \\ 13 & \infty & 14 & 2 & 0 \\ 1 & 3 & \infty & 0 & 2 \\ 16 & 3 & 15 & \infty & 0 \\ 12 & 0 & 3 & 12 & \infty \end{bmatrix}$$

Red_Col(M) be obtained as,

$$\begin{bmatrix} \infty & 10 & 20 & 0 & 1 \\ 13 & \infty & 14 & 2 & 0 \\ 1 & 3 & \infty & 0 & 2 \\ 16 & 3 & 15 & \infty & 0 \\ 12 & 0 & 3 & 12 & \infty \end{bmatrix}$$

total = 4

If row or column contains at least one zero ignore corresponding row or column.

$$\text{Red\_Col(M)} = \begin{bmatrix} \infty & 10 & 17 & 0 & 1 \\ 12 & \infty & 11 & 2 & 0 \\ 0 & 3 & \infty & 0 & 2 \\ 15 & 3 & 12 & \infty & 0 \\ 11 & 0 & 0 & 12 & \infty \end{bmatrix}$$

Thus total reduced cost will be

$$= \text{cost (Red\_Row (M))} + \text{cost (Red\_Col(M))}$$

$$= \quad 21 \quad + \quad 4$$

$$= 25$$

$$\text{Thus} \begin{bmatrix} \infty & 20 & 30 & 10 & 11 \\ 15 & \infty & 16 & 4 & 2 \\ 1 & 5 & \infty & 2 & 4 \\ 19 & 6 & 18 & \infty & 3 \\ 16 & 4 & 7 & 16 & \infty \end{bmatrix} \xRightarrow[\text{reduced matrix}]{\text{fully}} \begin{bmatrix} \infty & 10 & 17 & 0 & 1 \\ 12 & \infty & 11 & 2 & 0 \\ 0 & 3 & \infty & 0 & 2 \\ 15 & 3 & 12 & \infty & 0 \\ 11 & 0 & 0 & 12 & \infty \end{bmatrix}$$

7.6.4 Dynamic Reduction

We obtained the total reduced cost as 25. That means all tours in the original graph have a length at least 25.

Using dynamic reduction we can make the choice of edge $i \rightarrow j$ with optimum cost.

Steps in dynamic reduction technique

1. Draw a state space tree with optimum cost at root node.
2. Obtain the cost of matrix for path $i \rightarrow j$ by making i^{th} row and j^{th} column entries as ∞. Also set $M[i][j] = \infty$.
3. Cost of corresponding node x with path i, j is optimum cost + reduced cost + M[i][j].
4. Set node with minimum cost as E-node and generate its children. Repeat step 1 to 4 for completing tour with optimum cost.

For example :

$$M = \begin{bmatrix} \infty & 20 & 30 & 10 & 11 \\ 15 & \infty & 16 & 4 & 2 \\ 3 & 5 & \infty & 2 & 4 \\ 19 & 6 & 18 & \infty & 3 \\ 16 & 4 & 7 & 16 & \infty \end{bmatrix}$$

Fully reduced matrix is,

$$\begin{bmatrix} \infty & 10 & 17 & 0 & 1 \\ 12 & \infty & 11 & 2 & 0 \\ 0 & 3 & \infty & 0 & 2 \\ 15 & 3 & 12 & \infty & 0 \\ 11 & 0 & 0 & 12 & \infty \end{bmatrix}$$

Optimum cost = 21 + 4 = 25.

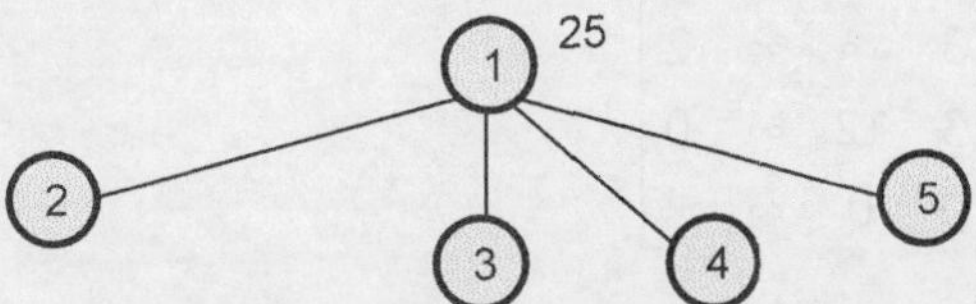

Fig. 7.6.2 Portion of state space tree

Consider path 1, 2. Make 1st row and 2nd column ∞. And set M [2] [1] = ∞.

∞	∞	∞	∞	∞	→ ignore
∞	∞	11	2	0	→ ignore
0	∞	∞	0	2	→ ignore
15	∞	12	∞	0	→ ignore
11	∞	0	12	∞	→ ignore
↓	↓	↓	↓	↓	
ignore	ignore	ignore	ignore	ignore	

Cost of node 2 is

25 + 0 + 10

↑ optimum cost, ↑ reduced cost, ↑ old value of M[1] [2]

= 35

Consider path 1, 3. Make 1st row = ∞. 3rd column = ∞ and M[3] [1] = ∞.

$$\begin{bmatrix} \infty & \infty & \infty & \infty & \infty \\ 12 & \infty & \infty & 2 & 0 \\ \infty & 3 & \infty & 0 & 2 \\ 15 & 3 & \infty & \infty & 0 \\ 11 & 0 & \infty & 12 & \infty \end{bmatrix}$$

↓ (first column)

11

Cost of node 3 is

$$= \underset{\text{optimum cost}}{\underset{\uparrow}{25}} + \underset{\text{reduced cost}}{\underset{\uparrow}{11}} + \underset{M[1][3]}{\underset{\uparrow}{17}}$$

$$= 53$$

Consider path 1, 4.

$$\begin{bmatrix} \infty & \infty & \infty & \infty & \infty \\ 12 & \infty & 11 & \infty & 0 \\ 0 & 3 & \infty & \infty & 2 \\ \infty & 3 & 12 & \infty & 0 \\ 11 & 0 & 0 & \infty & \infty \end{bmatrix}$$

Cost of node 4 is $= 25 + 0 + 0$

$= 25$

Consider path 1, 5.

$$\begin{bmatrix} \infty & \infty & \infty & \infty & \infty \\ 12 & \infty & 11 & 2 & \infty \\ 0 & 3 & \infty & 0 & \infty \\ 15 & 3 & 12 & \infty & \infty \\ \infty & 0 & 0 & 12 & \infty \end{bmatrix} \begin{matrix} \\ \rightarrow 2 \\ \\ \rightarrow 3 \\ \\ \end{matrix}$$

Cost of node 5 is $= 25 + 5 + 1$

$= 31$

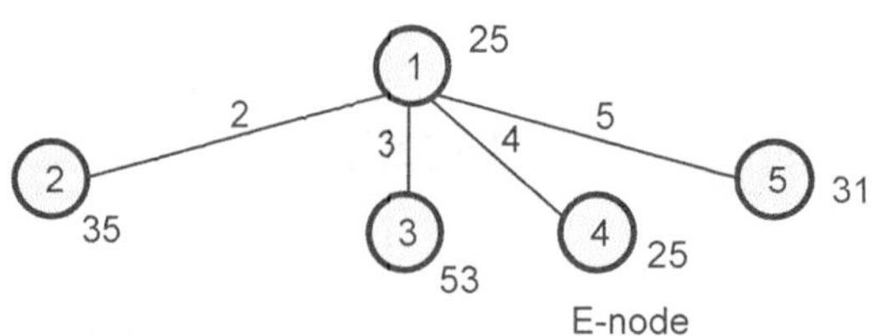

Fig. 7.6.3 Portion of state space tree

Now, as cost of node 4 is optimum, we will set node 4 as E-node and generate its children nodes 6, 7, 8.

Consider path 1, 4, 2 for node 6. Set 1st row, 4th row to ∞. Set 2nd column to ∞. Also $M[4]\ [1] = \infty$, $M[2]\ [1] = \infty$.

$$\begin{bmatrix} \infty & \infty & \infty & \infty & \infty \\ \infty & \infty & 11 & \infty & 0 \\ 0 & \infty & \infty & \infty & 2 \\ \infty & \infty & \infty & \infty & \infty \\ 11 & \infty & 0 & \infty & \infty \end{bmatrix}$$

Cost of node 6 = 25 + M [4, 2]

= 25 + 3

= 28

Consider path 1, 4, 3 for node 7. Set 1st row, 4th row to ∞. Set 4th column, 3rd column to ∞. Set M [4] [1] = M[3] [1] = ∞.

$$\begin{bmatrix} \infty & \infty & \infty & \infty & \infty \\ 12 & \infty & \infty & \infty & 0 \\ \infty & 3 & \infty & \infty & 2 \\ \infty & \infty & \infty & \infty & \infty \\ 11 & 0 & \infty & \infty & \infty \end{bmatrix} \begin{matrix} \\ \rightarrow 2 \\ \\ \\ \\ \end{matrix}$$

$$\begin{matrix} \uparrow \\ 11 \end{matrix}$$

Cost of node 7 = 25 + 13 + M [4] [3]

= 25 + 13 + 12

= 50

Consider path 1, 4, 5 for node 8.

$$\begin{bmatrix} \infty & \infty & \infty & \infty & \infty \\ 12 & \infty & 11 & \infty & \infty \\ 0 & 3 & \infty & \infty & \infty \\ \infty & \infty & \infty & \infty & \infty \\ \infty & 0 & 0 & \infty & \infty \end{bmatrix} \begin{matrix} \\ \rightarrow 11 \\ \\ \\ \\ \end{matrix}$$

Cost of node 8 = 25 + 11

= 36

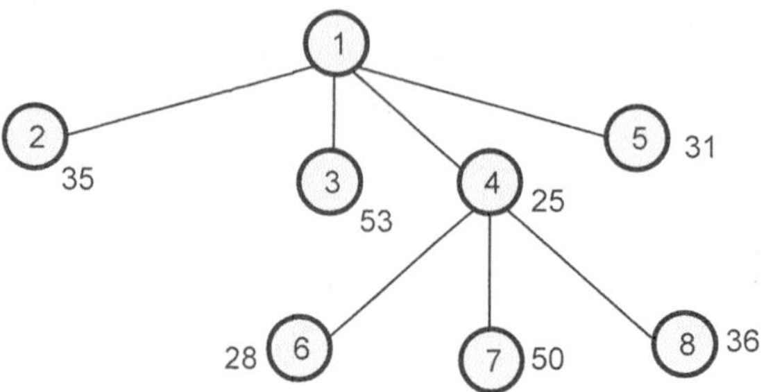

Fig. 7.6.4 Portion of state space tree

Now as cost of node 6 is minimum, node 6 becomes an E-node. Hence generate children for node 6. Node 9 and 10 are children nodes of node 6.

Consider path 1, 4, 2, 3 for node 9. Set 1st row, 4th row, 2nd row to ∞. Set 4th column, 2nd column and 3rd column to ∞.

Set M[4, 1] = M[2, 1] = M[3, 1] = ∞.

$$\begin{bmatrix} \infty & \infty & \infty & \infty & \infty \\ \infty & \infty & \infty & \infty & \infty \\ \infty & \infty & \infty & \infty & 2 \\ \infty & \infty & \infty & \infty & \infty \\ 11 & \infty & \infty & \infty & \infty \end{bmatrix} \begin{matrix} \\ \\ \rightarrow 2 \\ \\ \\ \end{matrix}$$

$$\begin{matrix} \downarrow \\ 11 \end{matrix}$$

Cost of node 9

$$= \underset{\text{optimum cost}}{\underset{\uparrow}{28}} + \underset{\text{reduced cost}}{\underset{\uparrow}{13}} + \underset{M[2][3]}{\underset{\uparrow}{11}}$$

$$= 52$$

Consider path 1, 4, 2, 5 for node 10. Set 1 st row, 4th row , 2nd row to ∞. Set 4th column, 2nd column and 5th column to ∞. Set M [4, 1] = M[2, 1] = M [5, 1] = ∞.

$$\begin{bmatrix} \infty & \infty & \infty & \infty & \infty \\ \infty & \infty & \infty & \infty & \infty \\ 0 & \infty & \infty & \infty & \infty \\ \infty & \infty & \infty & \infty & \infty \\ \infty & \infty & 0 & \infty & \infty \end{bmatrix}$$

$$\begin{aligned} \text{Cost of node 10} &= 28 + M[2]\,[5] \\ &= 28 + 0 \\ &= 28 \end{aligned}$$

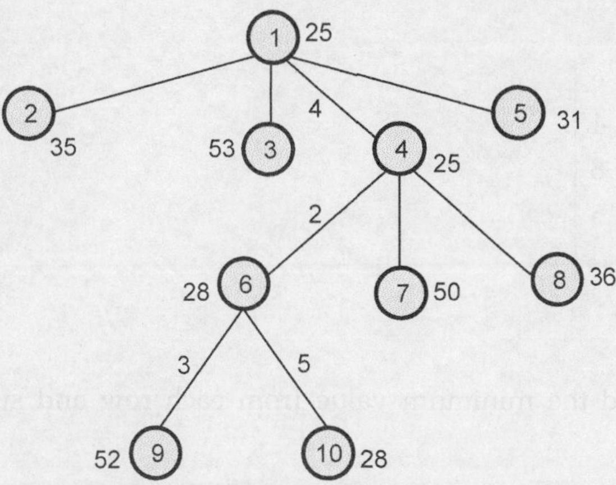

Fig. 7.6.5 Portion of state space tree

Node 10 becomes E-node now.

As for node 10 only child being generated is node 11. We set path as 1, 4, 2, 5, 3. To complete the tour we return to 1. Hence the state space tree is,

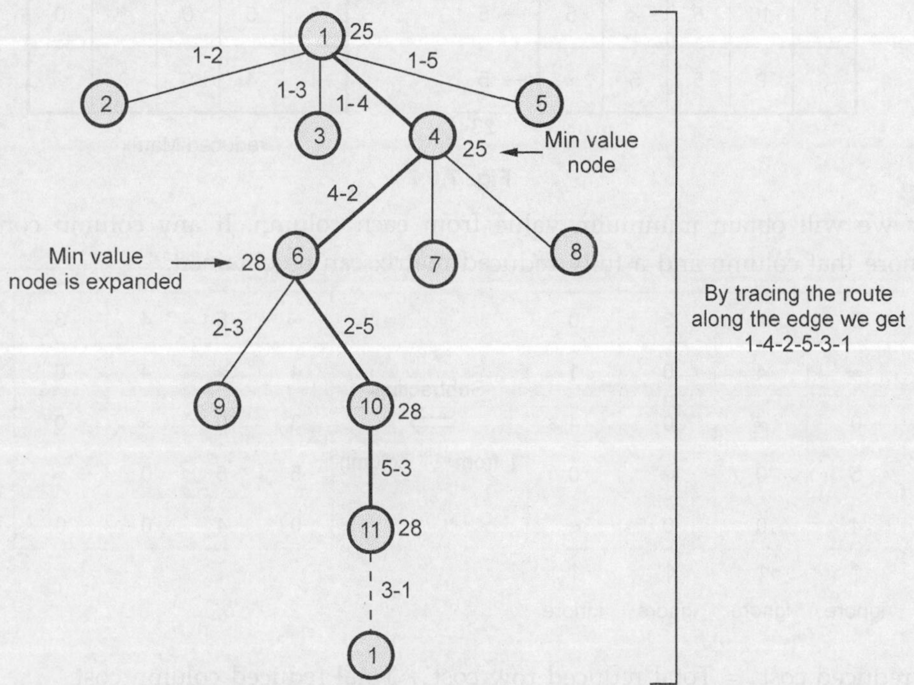

Fig. 7.6.6 State space tree

Hence the optimum cost of the tour is 28.

Example 7.6.1 *Apply the branch and bound algorithm to solve the TSP for the following cost matrix.*

$$\begin{bmatrix} \infty & 11 & 10 & 9 & 6 \\ 8 & \infty & 7 & 3 & 4 \\ 8 & 4 & \infty & 4 & 8 \\ 11 & 10 & 5 & \infty & 5 \\ 6 & 9 & 5 & 5 & \infty \end{bmatrix}$$

Solution :

Step 1 : We will find the minimum value from each row and subtract the value from corresponding row.

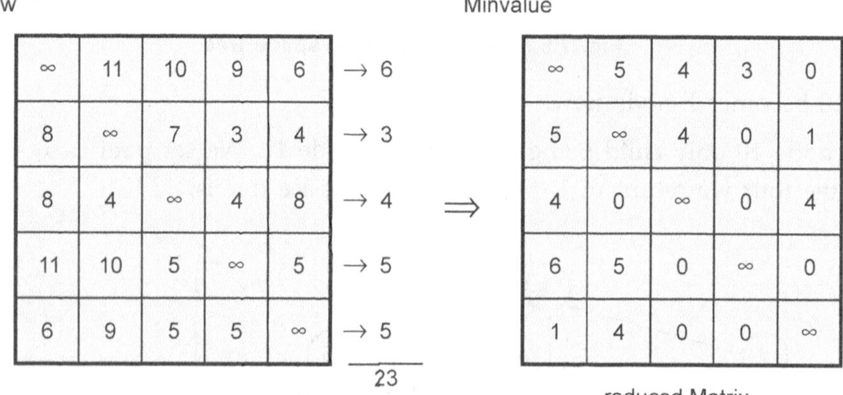

Fig. 7.6.7

Now we will obtain minimuim value from each column. If any column contains 0 then ignore that column and a fully reduced matrix can be obtained.

∞	5	4	3	0
5	∞	4	0	1
4	0	∞	0	4
6	5	0	∞	0
1	4	0	0	∞
↑	↑	↑	↑	↑
1	ignore	ignore	ignore	ignore

Subtracting ⇒ 1 from 1st column

∞	5	4	3	0
4	∞	4	0	1
3	0	∞	0	4
5	5	0	∞	0
0	4	0	0	∞

$$\begin{aligned} \text{Total reduced cost} &= \text{Total reduced row cost} + \text{Total reduced column cost} \\ &= 23 + 1 \\ &= 24 \end{aligned}$$

Now we will set 24 as the optimum cost.

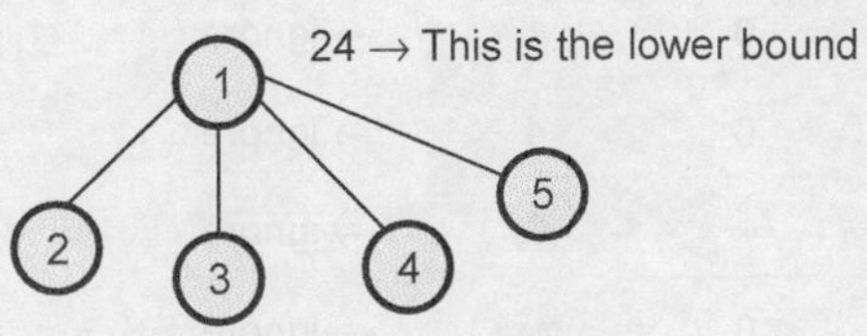

Fig. 7.6.8

Step 2 : Now we will consider the paths [1, 2], [1, 3], [1, 4] and [1, 5] of state space tree as given above consider path [1, 2] make 1st row, 2nd column to ∞. Set M [2] [1] = ∞.

∞	∞	∞	∞	∞	→ ignore
∞	∞	4	0	1	→ ignore
3	∞	∞	0	4	→ ignore
5	∞	0	∞	0	→ ignore
0	∞	0	0	∞	→ ignore

Now we will find min value from each corresponding column.

∞	∞	∞	∞	∞	
∞	∞	4	0	1	
3	∞	∞	0	4	
5	∞	0	∞	0	There is no minimum value from any column
0	∞	0	0	∞	
↑ ignore	↑ ignore	↑ ignore	↑ ignore	↑ ignore	

Hence total reduced cost for node 2 is -

= Optimum cost + old value of M [1] [2]

= 24 + 5

= **29**

Consider path (1, 3). Make 1st row, 3rd column to be ∞.

Set M [3] [1] = ∞.

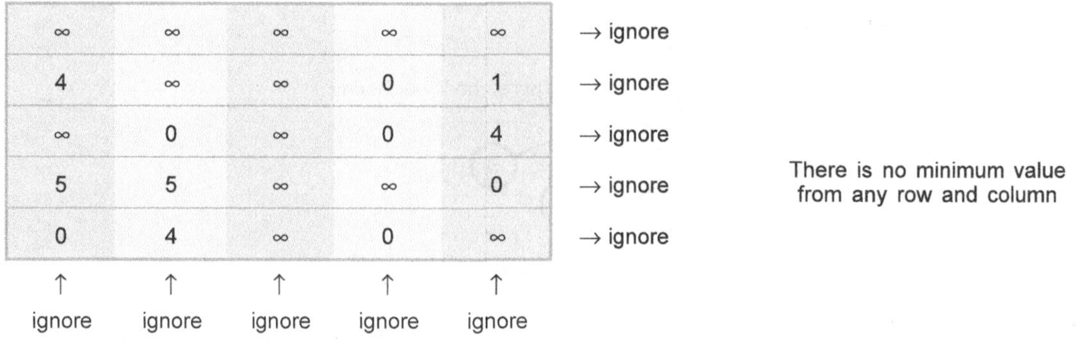

∞	∞	∞	∞	∞	→ ignore
4	∞	∞	0	1	→ ignore
∞	0	∞	0	4	→ ignore
5	5	∞	∞	0	→ ignore
0	4	∞	0	∞	→ ignore
↑ ignore	↑ ignore	↑ ignore	↑ ignore	↑ ignore	

There is no minimum value from any row and column

Hence total cost for node 3 is

= Optimum cost + M [1] [3]

= 24 + 4

= **28**

Consider path (1, 4). Make 1st row, 4th column to be ∞. Set M [4] [1] = ∞.

∞	∞	∞	∞	∞	→ ignore
4	∞	4	∞	1	→ 1
3	0	∞	∞	4	→ ignore
∞	5	0	∞	0	→ ignore
0	4	0	∞	∞	→ ignore

Subtracting ⇒ 1 from 2nd row

∞	∞	∞	∞	∞
4	∞	3	∞	0
3	0	∞	∞	4
∞	5	0	∞	0
0	4	0	∞	∞
↑ ignore	↑ ignore	↑ ignore	↑ ignore	↑ ignore

The total cost for node 4 is

= Optimum cost + M [1] [4] + Minimum row cost

= 24 + 3 + 1

= **28**

Consider the path (1, 5). Make 1st row, 5th column to be ∞. Set M [5] [1] = ∞.

∞	∞	∞	∞	∞	→ ignore
4	∞	4	0	∞	→ ignore
3	0	∞	0	∞	→ ignore
5	5	0	∞	∞	→ ignore
∞	4	0	0	∞	→ ignore
↑	↑	↑	↑	↑	
3	ignore	ignore	ignore	ignore	

Subtracting 3 from 1st column.

∞	∞	∞	∞	∞
1	∞	4	0	∞
0	0	∞	0	∞
2	5	0	∞	∞
∞	4	0	0	∞

The total cost at node 5 is

= Optimum cost + Reduced column cost + Old value M [1] [5]

= 24 + 3 + 0

= 27

The partial state space tree will be -

The node 5 shows minimum cost. Hence node 5 will be an E node. That means we will select node 5 for expansion.

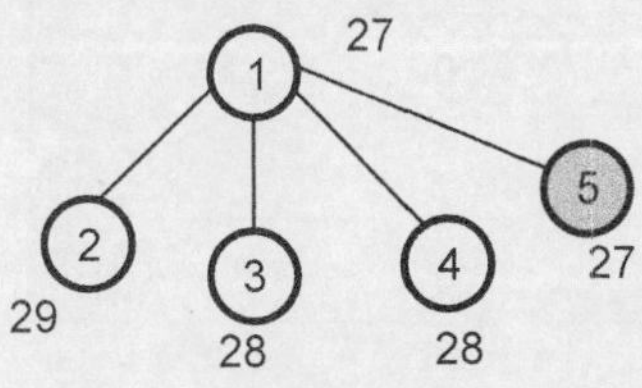

Fig. 7.6.9

Step 3 : Now we will consider the paths [1, 5, 2], [1, 5, 3] and [1, 5, 4], of above state space tree do the further computations. Consider path 1, 5, 2. Make 1st row, 5th row and second column as ∞. Set M [5] [1] and M [2] [1] = ∞.

∞	∞	∞	∞	∞	→ ignore
∞	∞	4	0	1	→ ignore
3	∞	∞	0	4	→ ignore
5	∞	0	∞	0	→ ignore
∞	∞	∞	∞	∞	→ ignore
↑	↑	↑	↑	↑	
3	ignore	ignore	ignore	ignore	

Now subtracting 3 from 1st column, we get -

∞	∞	∞	∞	∞
∞	∞	4	0	1
0	∞	∞	0	4
2	∞	0	∞	0
∞	∞	∞	∞	∞

Hence total cost for node 6 will be -

= Optimum cost at node 5 + Column-reduced cost + M [5] [2]

= 27 + 3 + 4

= 34

Consider path [1, 5, 3]. Make 1st row, 5th row and 3rd column as ∞.

Set M [5] [1] = M [3] [1] = ∞.

∞	∞	∞	∞	∞	→ ignore
4	∞	∞	0	∞	→ ignore
∞	0	∞	0	∞	→ ignore
5	5	∞	∞	∞	→ 5
∞	4	∞	0	∞	→ ignore

Subtracting ⇒ 5 from 4th row

∞	∞	∞	∞	∞
4	∞	∞	0	∞
∞	0	∞	0	∞
1	1	∞	∞	∞
∞	4	∞	0	∞
↑	↑	↑	↑	↑
1	ignore	ignore	ignore	ignore

Subtract 1 from 1st column

∞	∞	∞	∞	∞
3	∞	∞	0	∞
∞	0	∞	0	∞
0	1	∞	∞	∞
∞	4	∞	0	∞

The total cost for node 7 will be -

= Optimum cost at node 5 + Column reduced cost + M [5] [3]

= 27 + 1 + 0

= 28.

Consider the path [1, 5, 4]. Make first row, fifth row and forth column to be ∞. Set M [5] [1] = M [4] [1] = ∞.

∞	∞	∞	∞	∞	→ ignore
4	∞	4	∞	1	→ 1
3	0	∞	∞	4	→ ignore
∞	5	0	∞	0	→ ignore
∞	∞	∞	∞	∞	→ ignore

Subtracting 1 from ⇒ 2nd row

∞	∞	∞	∞	∞
3	∞	3	∞	0
3	0	∞	∞	4
∞	5	0	∞	0
∞	∞	∞	∞	∞
↑	↑	↑	↑	↑
3	ignore	ignore	ignore	ignore

Subtract 3 from ⇒ 1st column

∞	∞	∞	∞	∞
0	∞	3	∞	0
0	0	∞	∞	4
∞	5	0	∞	0
∞	∞	∞	∞	∞

The total cost for node 8 will be

= Optimum cost at node 5 + Column-reduced + Row-reduced cost + M [5] [4]

= 27 + (1 + 3) + 0

= 31

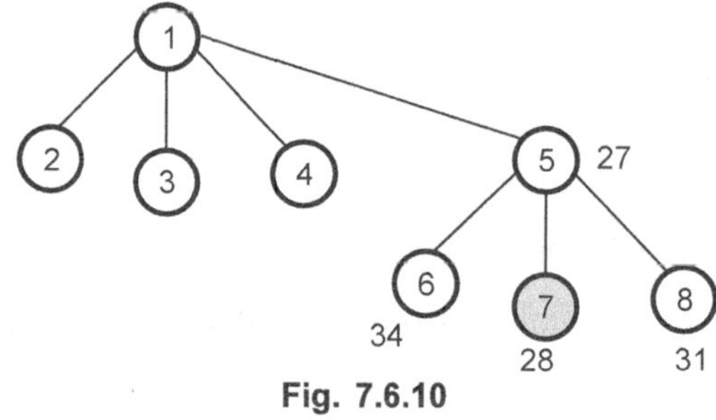

Fig. 7.6.10

The partial state space tree will be -

The node 7 has optimum cost. Hence 7 becomes an E node and it will be expanded further.

Step 4 : Now we will consider paths [1, 5, 3, 2] and [1, 5, 3, 4] for further computations. Consider path 1, 5, 3, 2 and make 1st, 5th, 3rd row as ∞ and 2nd column as ∞.
Set M [2] [1] = M [3] [1] = M[5][1] = ∞.

The matrix becomes -

∞	∞	∞	∞	∞	→ ignore
∞	∞	4	0	1	→ ignore
∞	∞	∞	∞	∞	→ ignore
5	∞	0	∞	0	→ ignore
∞	∞	∞	∞	∞	→ ignore
↑	↑	↑	↑	↑	
5	ignore	ignore	ignore	ignore	

Subtract 5 from 1st column.

∞	∞	∞	∞	∞
∞	∞	4	0	1
∞	∞	∞	∞	∞
0	∞	0	∞	0
∞	∞	∞	∞	∞

The reduced cost at node 9 [i.e. path [1, 5, 3, 2]] will be

= Optimum cost at node 7 + Column-reduced cost + M [3] [2]

= 28 + 5 + 0

= 33

Consider the path [1, 5, 3, 4]. Make 1st row, 5th row, 3rd row and 4th column as ∞.
Set M [5] [1] = M [3] [1] = M [4] [1] = ∞.

∞	∞	∞	∞	∞	→ ignore
4	∞	4	∞	1	→ 1
∞	∞	∞	∞	∞	→ ignore
∞	5	0	∞	0	→ ignore
∞	∞	∞	∞	∞	→ ignore

Subtracting 1 from second row,

∞	∞	∞	∞	∞
3	∞	3	∞	0
∞	∞	∞	∞	∞
∞	5	0	∞	0
∞	∞	∞	∞	∞
↑	↑			
3	5			

Subtracting 3 from 1st column and 5 from 2nd column

∞	∞	∞	∞	∞
0	∞	3	∞	0
∞	∞	∞	∞	∞
∞	0	0	∞	0
∞	∞	∞	∞	∞

The total reduced cost at node 10 [i.e. path 1, 5, 3, 4] is

= Optimum cost at node 7 + Row-reduced cost + M [3] [4]

= 28 + (3 + 5) + 0

= 36

The partial state space tree will be -

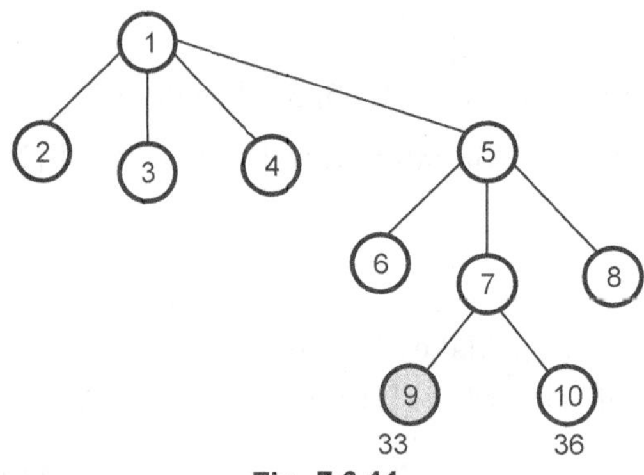

Fig. 7.6.11

Step 5 : Now consider path [1, 5, 3, 2, 4]

∞	∞	∞	∞	∞
∞	∞	∞	∞	∞
∞	∞	∞	∞	∞
∞	5	0	∞	0
∞	∞	∞	∞	∞

↓

5 minvalue

Now subtract 5 from 2nd column

∞	∞	∞	∞	∞
∞	∞	∞	∞	∞
∞	∞	∞	∞	∞
∞	0	0	∞	0
∞	∞	∞	∞	∞

The reduced cost at node 11 will be -

= Optimum cost at node 9 + column reduced cost + M [2] [4]

= 33 + 5 + 0

= 38

The final state space tree will be -

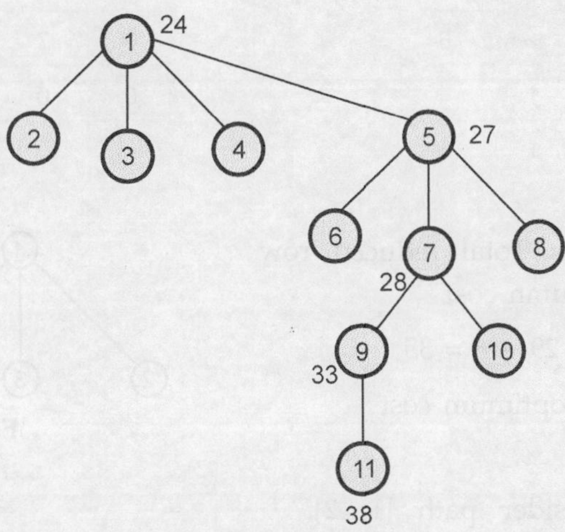

Fig. 7.6.12

The tour with minimum cost is 29. The path will be **1, 5, 3, 2, 4, 1.**

Example 7.6.2 *What is travelling salesperson problem ? Find the solution of the following travelling salesperson problem using dynamic approach and branch and bound approach.*

May-12

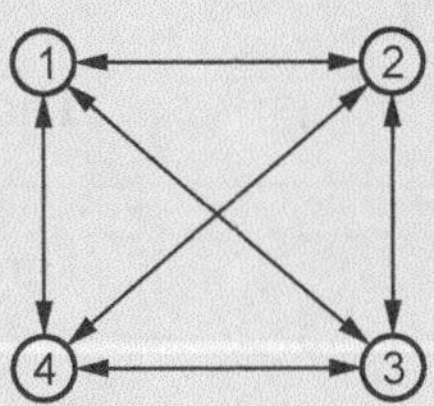

$$\begin{bmatrix} 0 & 10 & 15 & 20 \\ 5 & 0 & 9 & 10 \\ 6 & 13 & 0 & 12 \\ 8 & 8 & 9 & 0 \end{bmatrix}$$

Fig. 7.6.13

Solution : Step 1 : We will find the minimum value from each row and subtract it from corresponding row.

∞	10	15	20	10
5	∞	9	10	5
6	13	∞	12	6
8	8	9	∞	8
				29

⇒

∞	0	5	10
0	∞	4	5
0	7	∞	6
0	0	1	∞

Reduced Matrix

Now we will obtain min value from each column. If some column contains 0 value then ignore that column. The fully reduced matrix can be obtained as -

∞	0	5	10
0	∞	4	5
0	7	∞	6
0	0	1	∞
↑ ignore	↑ ignore	1	5

⇒

∞	0	4	5
0	∞	3	0
0	7	∞	1
0	0	0	∞

Total reduced cost = Total reduced row cost + Total reduced column cost

= 29 + 6 = 35

The 35 is now set as optimum cost

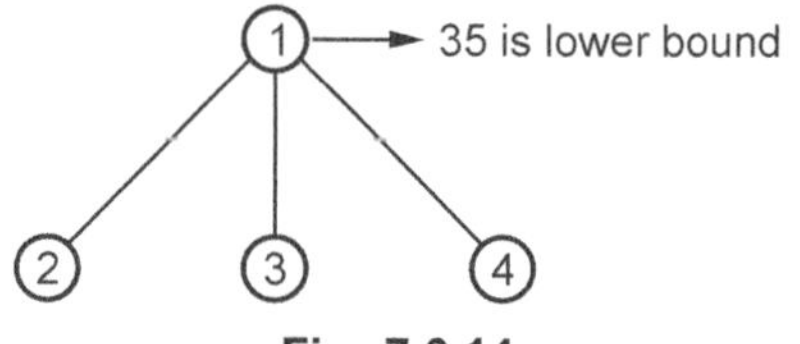

Fig. 7.6.14

Step 2 : Now consider path [1, 2]. Mark 1st row and 2nd column as ∞. Also set M[2][1] = ∞. Then we will find min from each row.

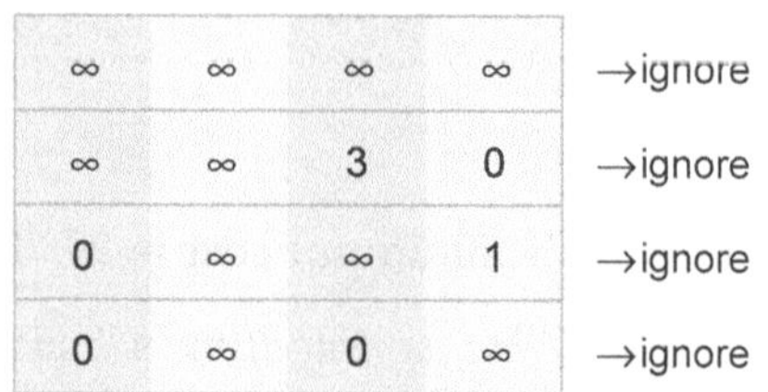

∞	∞	∞	∞	→ignore
∞	∞	3	0	→ignore
0	∞	∞	1	→ignore
0	∞	0	∞	→ignore

Now we will find min from each column

Hence total reduced cost for node 2 is

= Optimum cost + Old value of M[1][2]

= 35 + 0 = 35

∞	∞	∞	∞
∞	∞	3	0
0	∞	∞	1
0	∞	0	∞
↑ ignore	↑ ignore	↑ ignore	↑ ignore

There is no min value from any column

Now consider path (1, 3). Make 1st row and 3rd column to be ∞. set M[3][1] = ∞.

∞	∞	∞	∞	→ignore
0	∞	∞	0	→ignore
∞	7	∞	1	→1
0	0	∞	∞	→ignore

⇒

∞	∞	∞	∞
0	∞	∞	0
∞	6	∞	0
0	0	∞	∞
↑ ignore	↑ ignore		

Total cost for node 3 is

= Optimum cost + Old value of M[1][3] + Reduced cost

= 35 + 4 + 1 = 40

Now consider path (1, 4). Marks 1st row and 4th column to be ∞. Set M[4][1] = ∞.

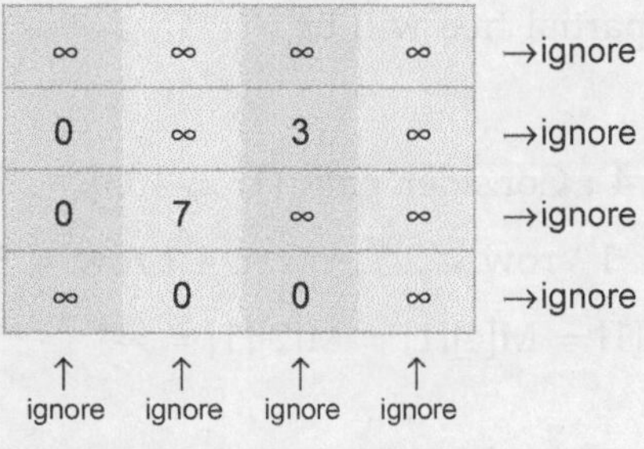

∞	∞	∞	∞	→ignore
0	∞	3	∞	→ignore
0	7	∞	∞	→ignore
∞	0	0	∞	→ignore
↑ ignore	↑ ignore	↑ ignore	↑ ignore	

Optimum cost for node 3 is =

Optimum cost + Old value of M[1][4]

= 35 + 5 = 40

The partial tree will be

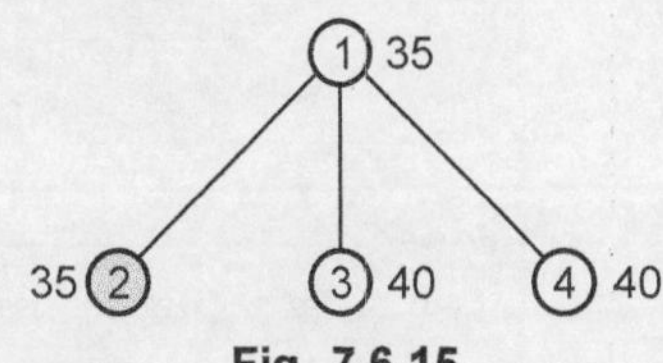

Fig. 7.6.15

Node 2 with minimum cost. Hence it will be expanded further.

Step 3 : Consider paths [1, 2, 3] , [1, 2, 4].

Consider path 1, 2, 3. Make 1st row, 2nd row and 3rd column as ∞. Mark M[2][1] and M[3][1] = ∞.

∞	∞	∞	∞	→X
∞	∞	∞	∞	→X
∞	7	∞	1	→1
0	0	∞	∞	→X

⇒

∞	∞	∞	∞
∞	∞	∞	∞
∞	6	∞	0
0	0	∞	∞

Hence total cost for node 5 will be

= Optimum cost at node 2 + Reduced cost + M[2][3]

= 35 + 1 + 3 = 39

Consider path [1, 2, 4]. Make 1st row, 2nd row and 4th column as ∞.

M[2][1] = M[4][1] = ∞

∞	∞	∞	∞	→X
∞	∞	∞	∞	→X
∞	7	∞	0	→X
0	0	∞	∞	
↑ X	↑ X	↑ X	↑ X	

No minimum value

∴ Optimum cost at node 6 will be

= Optimum cost at node 2 + Reduced cost + M[2][4]

= 35 + 0 + 0 = 35

The partial tree will be

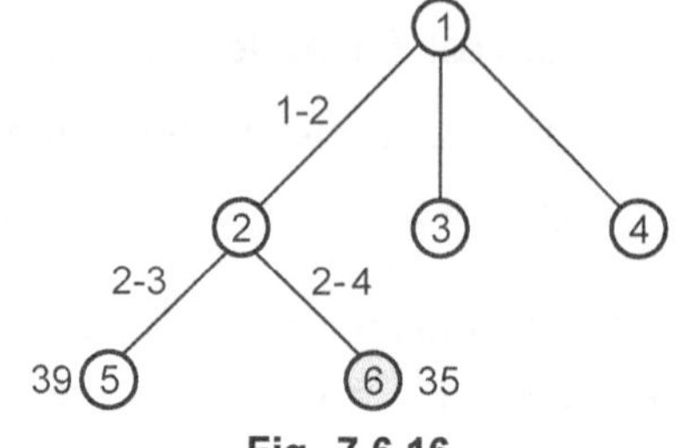

Fig. 7.6.16

Step 4 : Consider path [1, 2, 4, 3].

Mark 1st row = 2nd row = 4th row = 3rd column = ∞

M[3][1] = M[4][1] = M[2][1] = ∞

∞	∞	∞	∞	→X
∞	∞	∞	∞	→X
∞	7	∞	1	→1
∞	∞	∞	∞	→X

⇒

∞	∞	∞	∞
∞	∞	∞	∞
∞	6	∞	0
∞	∞	∞	∞

Subtract 6 from 2nd column.

⇒

∞	∞	∞	∞
∞	∞	∞	∞
∞	0	∞	0
∞	∞	∞	∞

Optimum cost = Optimum cost at node 6 + M[4][3]

= 35 + 0 = 35

Final state space tree will be

The path will be **1 - 2 - 4 - 3 - 1.**

The tour with minimum cost is 35.

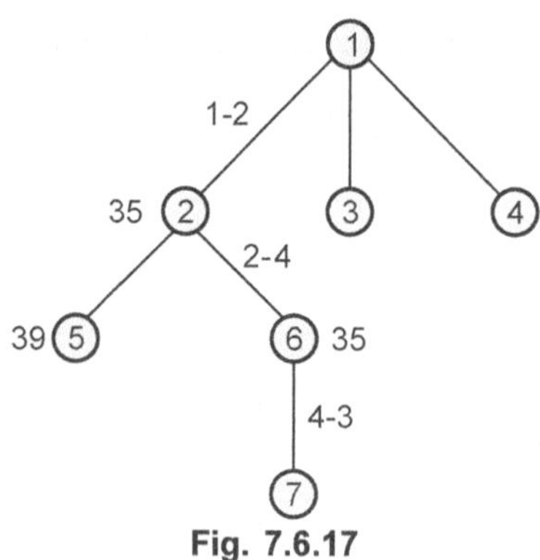

Fig. 7.6.17

Example 7.6.3 *Explain branch and bound strategy. Take an example of travelling salesman problem using branch and bound.* **Dec.-13**

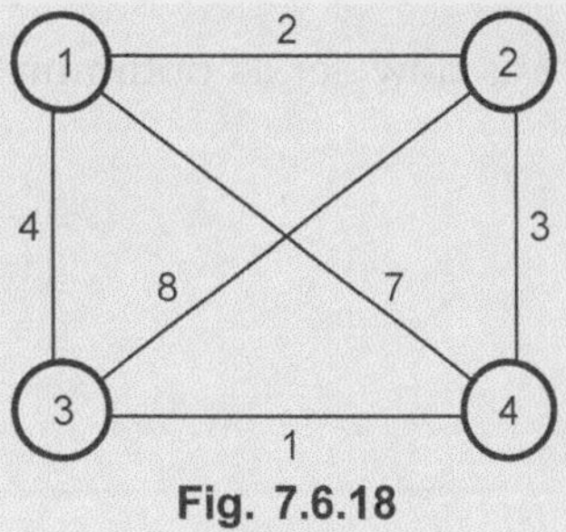

Fig. 7.6.18

Solution : Branch and bound strategy -

Refer section 7.5.1.

We will create adjacency matrix for given graph.

	1	2	3	4
1	∞	2	4	7
2	2	∞	8	3
3	4	8	∞	1
4	7	3	1	∞

Step 1 : We will find the minimum value from each row and subtract it from corresponding row.

∞	2	4	7	2
2	∞	8	3	2
4	8	∞	1	1
7	3	1	∞	1

Total reduced row cost 6

⇒

∞	0	2	5
0	∞	6	1
3	7	∞	0
6	2	0	∞

Now we will obtain minimum value from each column. If some column contains 0 value the ignore that column. The fully reduced matrix can be -

Matrix M [Used in further steps]

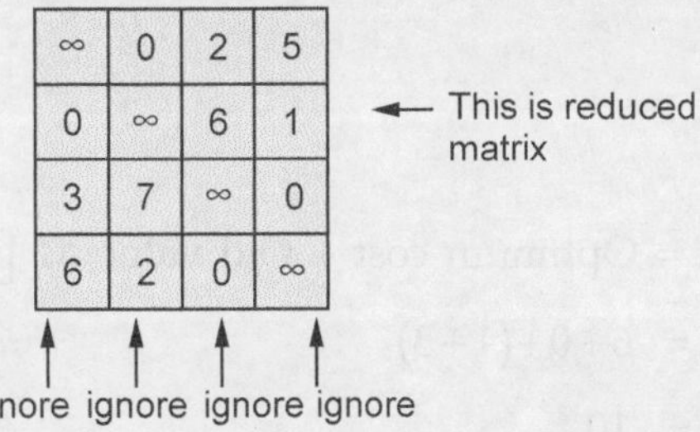

∞	0	2	5
0	∞	6	1
3	7	∞	0
6	2	0	∞

∴ Total reduced cost = Total reduced row cost + Total reduced column cost

= 6 + 0 = 6

∴ The 6 is now set as optimum cost.

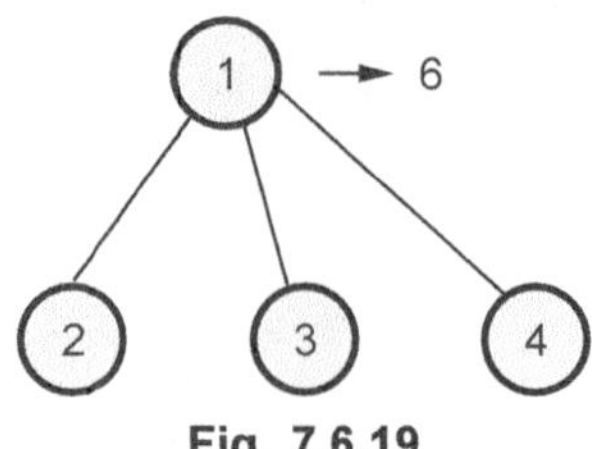

Fig. 7.6.19

Step 2 : Consider path $[1,2]$. Mark first row and 2nd column as ∞. Also set $M[2,1] = \infty$. We will then find minimum from each row.

The reduced matrix will be

∞	∞	∞	∞	→ ignore
∞	∞	6	1	→ 1
3	∞	∞	0	→ ignore
6	∞	0	∞	→ ignore

∞	∞	∞	∞
∞	∞	5	0
3	∞	∞	0
6	∞	0	∞
↓ 3	ignore		

The reduced matrix will be

∞	∞	∞	∞
∞	∞	5	0
0	∞	∞	0
3	∞	0	∞

∴ Reduced cost for node 2 = Optimum cost + Old value M $[1, 2]$ + Reduced cost

$$= 6 + 0 + (1 + 3)$$

$$= 10$$

Step 3 : Consider path (1, 3). Mark first row and 3rd column as ∞. Also set $M[3,1]=\infty$

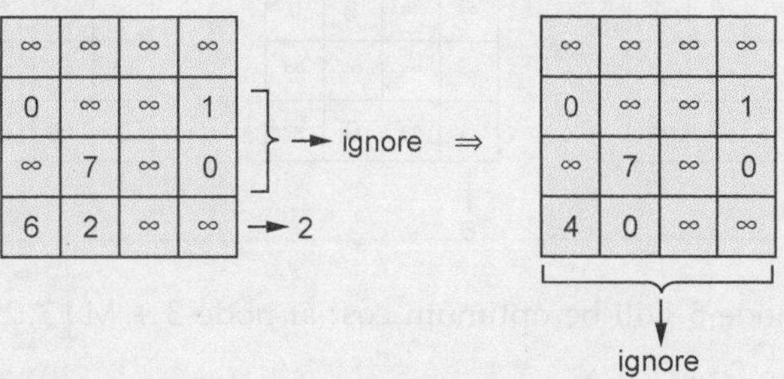

Cost for node 3 = Optimum cost + Old value $M[1, 3]$ + Reduced cost

$= 6+2+(2+0)$

$= 10$

Step 4 : Consider path $[1,4]$. Mark first row and 4th column as ∞. Set $M[4,1]=\infty$

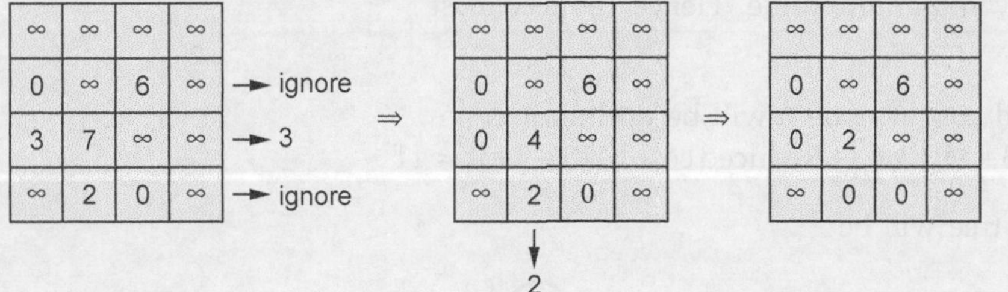

Reduced cost at node 4

= Optimum cost + Old value $M[1,4]$ + Reduced cost = 6 + 5 + (3 + 2) = 16

The partial tree will be

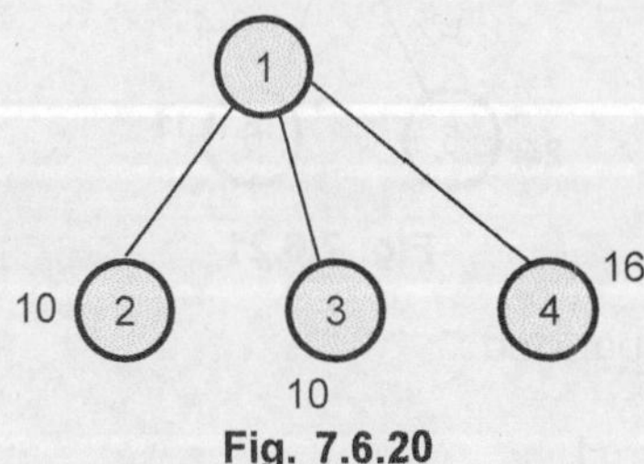

Fig. 7.6.20

We can choose either node 2 or node 3. Let us select node 3. We will expand it further.

Step 5 : Consider path $[1,3,4]$ and $[1,3,2]$ First consider path $[1,3,2]$. Mark 1st, 3rd row as ∞ and 2nd column as ∞ . Also $M[2,1]=M[3,1]=\infty$.

∞	∞	∞	∞
∞	∞	6	1
∞	∞	∞	∞
6	∞	0	∞

1 ⇒

∞	∞	∞	∞
∞	∞	5	0
∞	∞	∞	∞
6	∞	0	∞

↓ 6 ⇒

∞	∞	∞	∞
∞	∞	5	0
∞	∞	∞	∞
0	∞	0	∞

Reduced cost at node 5 will be optimum cost at node 3 + M $[3,2]$ + Reduced cost

$$= 10+7+(1+6)$$

$$= 24$$

Consider path $[1,3,4]$. Mark row 1 = row 3 = ∞ and column 4 = ∞. $M[4,1] = M[3,1] = \infty$

From Both row and column. we cannot obtain any minimum value. Hence reduced cost = 0.

∞	∞	∞	∞
0	∞	6	∞
∞	∞	∞	∞
∞	2	0	∞

∴ Reduced cost at node 6 will be optimum cost at node $3 + M[3,4] + \text{Reduced cost} = 10 + 1 + 0 = 11$

Partial tree will be

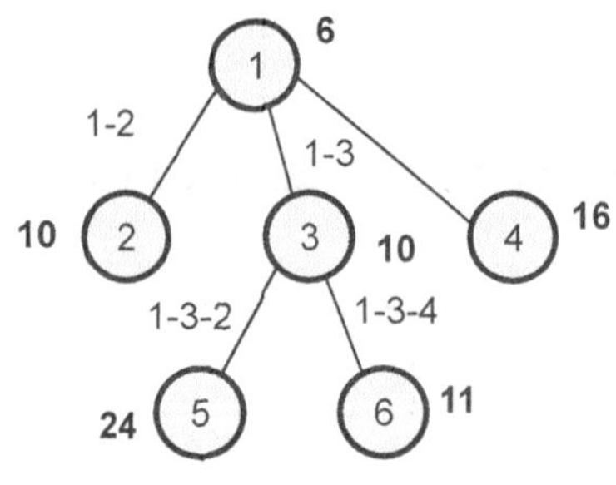

Fig. 7.6.21

Naturally node 6 will be expanded.

Step 6 : Consider path $[1,3,4,2]$

Mark 1st row = 3rd row = 4th row = ∞

Mark 2nd column = ∞

$M[2,1] = M[4,1] = M[3,1] = \infty$

$$\begin{array}{|c|c|c|c|}\hline \infty & \infty & \infty & \infty \\ \hline \infty & \infty & 6 & 1 \\ \hline \infty & \infty & \infty & \infty \\ \hline \infty & \infty & \infty & \infty \\ \hline \end{array}\ 1 \Rightarrow \begin{array}{|c|c|c|c|}\hline \infty & \infty & \infty & \infty \\ \hline \infty & \infty & 5 & 0 \\ \hline \infty & \infty & \infty & \infty \\ \hline \infty & \infty & \infty & \infty \\ \hline \end{array} \Rightarrow \begin{array}{|c|c|c|c|}\hline \infty & \infty & \infty & \infty \\ \hline \infty & \infty & 0 & 0 \\ \hline \infty & \infty & \infty & \infty \\ \hline \infty & \infty & \infty & \infty \\ \hline \end{array}$$

$$\uparrow 5$$

$\therefore$ Reduced cost at node 7

$$= \text{Optinum cost at node } 6 + M[4,2] + \text{Reduced cost}$$

$$= 11 + 2 + (1+5)$$

$$= 19$$

The tree will be

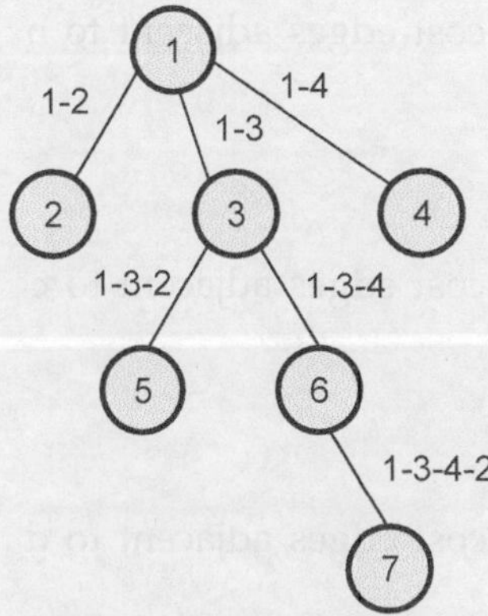

Fig. 7.6.22

Thus path with optinum tour length is **1-3-4-2-1.**

The cost of tour = 10.

7.6.5 Alternate Method to Solve TSP

In this method we consider computing of lower bounds. The lower bound is denoted by LB and can be obtained using following formula.

$$LB = \sum_{v \in V} \left(\begin{array}{l} \text{Sum of costs of the two least} \\ \text{cost edges adjacent to v} \end{array} \right)$$

This method can be well understood with the help of some examples.

Consider following graph for solving TSP. (Refer Fig. 7.6.22 (a))

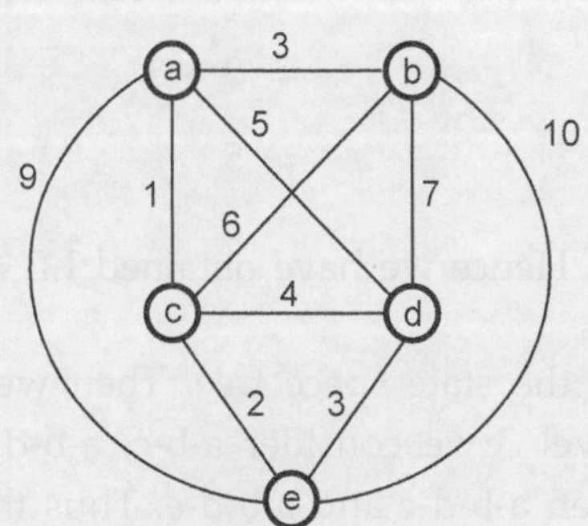

Fig. 7.6.22 (a)

We will first obtain Lower Bound LB as

$$\text{LB} = \left(\sum \begin{array}{l} \text{Sum of costs of the two least} \\ \text{cost edges adjacent to v} \end{array} \right)$$

$$= \lceil [\underset{\substack{\uparrow \\ a}}{(1+3)} + \underset{\substack{\uparrow \\ b}}{(3+6)} + \underset{\substack{\uparrow \\ c}}{(1+2)} + \underset{\substack{\uparrow \\ d}}{(3+4)} + \underset{\substack{\uparrow \\ e}}{(2+3)}]/2 \rceil$$

$$= 14$$

Because a = 2 Minimum cost edges adjacent to a

= ac + ab

a = 1 + 3 = 4

b = 2 Minimum cost edges adjacent to b

= ba + bc

b = 3 + 6 = 9

c = 2 Minimum cost edges adjacent to c

= ac + ce

c = 1 + 2 = 3

d = 2 Minimum cost edges adjacent to d

= de + dc

= 3 + 4

= 7

e = 2 Minimum cost edges adjacent to e

= ce + ed

= 2 + 3

= 5

Hence we have obtained LB $= \frac{1}{2}\sum_{v}$ adjacent distances of all vertices. This forms root of the state space tree. Then we consider a-b, a-c, a-d, a-e distances at level 1. Then at level 3 we consider a-b-c, a-b-d, a-b-e. Then at level 4 we consider a-b-c-d and a-b-c-e then a-b-d-c and a-b-d-e. Thus the state space tree can be

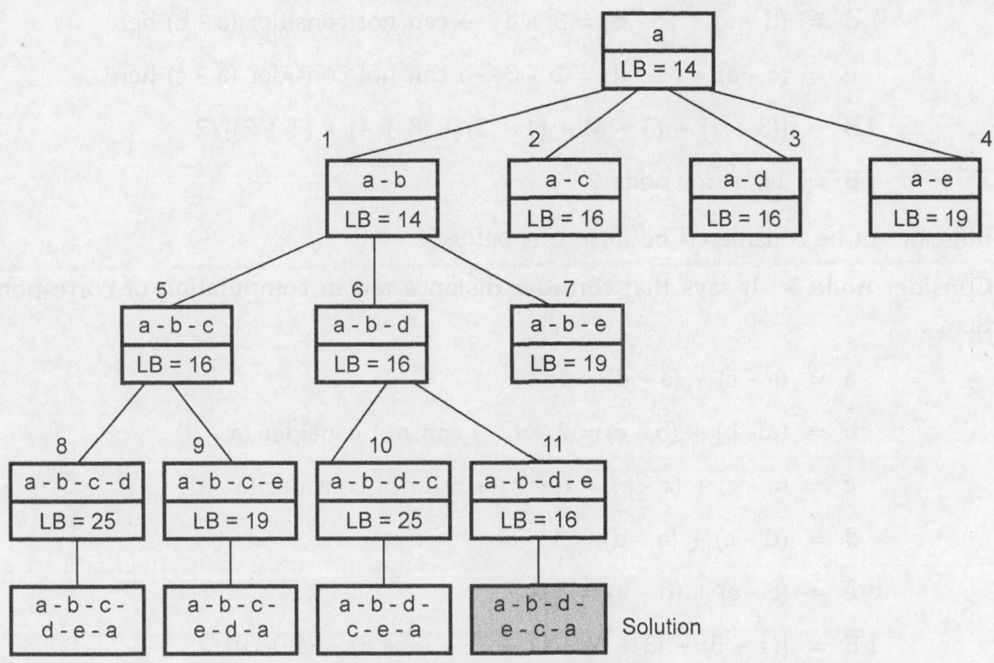

Fig. 7.6.23 State space tree

Consider node 1 : It says that consider distance a-b in computation of the corresponding vertices along with one minimum distance.

a = (a - b) + (a - c) = 3 + 1

b = (a - b) + (b - c) = 3 + 6

c = (a - c) + (c - e) = 1 + 2 → can not consider (a - b) because an edge (a - b) is not adjacent to c.

d = (d - e) + (c - d) = 3 + 4 → can not consider (a - b)

e = (c - e) + (d - e) = 2 + 3 → can not consider (a - b)

[(3 + 1) + (3 + 6) + (1 + 2) + (3 + 4) + (2 + 3)]/2

LB = 14 is for node 1.

Consider node 2 : It says that consider distance a-c in computation of corresponding vertices.

a = (a - b) + (a - c) = 3 + 1

b = (a - b) + (b - c) = 3 + 6 → can not consider (a - c) here because (a - c) is not adjacent to vertex b.

c = (a - c) + (c - e) = 1 + 2

d = (d - e) + (c - d) = 3 + 4 → can not consider (a - c) here

e = (c - e) + (d - d) = 2 + 3 → can not consider (a - c) here

LB = [(3 + 1) + (3 + 6) + (1 + 2) + (3 + 4) + (2 + 3)]/2

LB = 14 is for node 2.

But can not be considered because b is before c.

Consider node 3 : It says that consider distance a-d in computation of corresponding vertices.

a = (a - c) + (a - d) = 15

b = (a - b) + (b - c) = 3 + 6 → can not consider (a - d)

c = (a - c) + (c - e) = 1 + 2 → can not consider (a - d)

d = (d - e) + (a - d) = 3 + 5

e = (c - e) + (d - e) = 2 + 3

LB = [(1 + 5) + (3 + 6) + (1 + 2) + (3 + 5) + (2 + 3)]/2

= 32/2

LB = 16

Consider node 4 : This node say include edge a - e wherever possible.

a = (a - c) + (a - e) = 1 + 9 = 10

b = (a - b) + (b - c) = 3 + 6 = 9 → not possible to consider (a - e)

c = (a - c) + (c - e) = 1 + 2 = 3 → not possible to consider (a - e)

d = (c - d) + (d - e) = 4 + 3 = 7 → not possible to consider (a - e)

e = (c - e) + (a - e) = 2 + 9 = 11

LB = (10 + 9 + 3 + 7 + 11)/2

= 20

Consider node 5 : This node says path a-b-c i.e. include edges (a – b), (b – c) wherever possible.

a = (a - b) + (a - c)

= 3 + 1 → can not include (b - c) here because (b - c) is not

= 4 adjacent to a.

b = (a - b) + (b - c)

= 3 + 6

= 9

c = (a - c) + (b - c) → Min. distance (a - c) is included but (a - b)

= 1 + 6 but (a - b) can not be included as it is not adjacent to c.

= 7

d = (d - e) + (d - c)

= 3 + 4

= 7

e = (c - e) + (d - e)

= 2 + 3

= 5

LB = [4 + 9 + 7 + 7 + 5]/2

= 32/2

= 16

Similarly we can compute LB at node 6, 7, 8, 9, 10.

Consider node 8 : It says a-b-c-d that means include (a - b), (b - c), (c - d) whichever is minimum and whichever is applicable. As this is the leaf node and from this node we try to reach to source node. That is after a-b-c-d we go to e and from e-to-a. Hence

a → (a - b) + (a - e) = 3 + 9 = 12

b → (a - b) + (b - c) = 3 + 6 = 9

c → (b - c) + (c - d) = 6 + 4 = 10

d → (c - d) + (d - e) = 4 + 3 = 7

e → (a - e) + (d - e) = 9 + 3 = 12

LB = [12 + 9 + 10 + 7 + 12]/2

LB = 50/2

LB = 25

Consider node 11 : It says a-b-d-e. That means include (a - b), (b - d), (d - e) in computation.

a = (a - b) + (a - c) = 3 + 1 = 4

b = (a - b) + (b - d) = 3 + 7 = 10

$$c = (a - c) + (c - e) = 1 + 2 = 3$$

$$d = (b - d) + (d - e) = 7 + 3 = 10$$

$$e = (c - e) + (d - e) = 2 + 3 = 5$$

$$LB = (4 + 10 + 3 + 10 + 5)/2$$

$$= 32/2$$

$$= 16$$

At node 11 we get optimum tour i.e. a-b-d-e.

Hence the optimum cost tour of TSP is a-b-d-e-c-a with cost 16.

Example for Practice

Example 7.6.4 : *Solve TSP problem for following cost matrix.*

	A	B	C	D
A	X	5	2	3
B	4	X	2	3
C	4	2	X	3
D	7	6	8	X

Review Question

1. *Explain how to solve traveling salesman problem using branch and bound method.*

7.7 Minimax Principle

GTU : Dec.-10, June-12, Marks 3

Minimax (sometimes **minmax**) is a decision rule used in decision theory, game theory and philosophy for **minimizing** the possible **loss** and **maximizing** the total **profit**.

In game theory, the minimax principle can be used for playing the **tic-tac-toe** game. In this game, each player can win, lose or draw. If there are two players, A and B. If the player A wins by one move then that move is said to be best move. If player B knows that one move will lead to the situation where player A can win in one move, while another move will lead to the situation where player A can, at best draw, then player B's best move is the one leading to a draw.

The minimax algorithm helps find the best move, by working backwards from the end of the game.

At each step it assumes that player A is trying to **maximize** the chances of A winning, on the other hand, player B is trying to **minimize** the chance of A winning so that B can win. Thus minimax principle is applied in making out the decisions.

The representation of minimax principle in tic-tac-toe game playing is as shown by following figure -

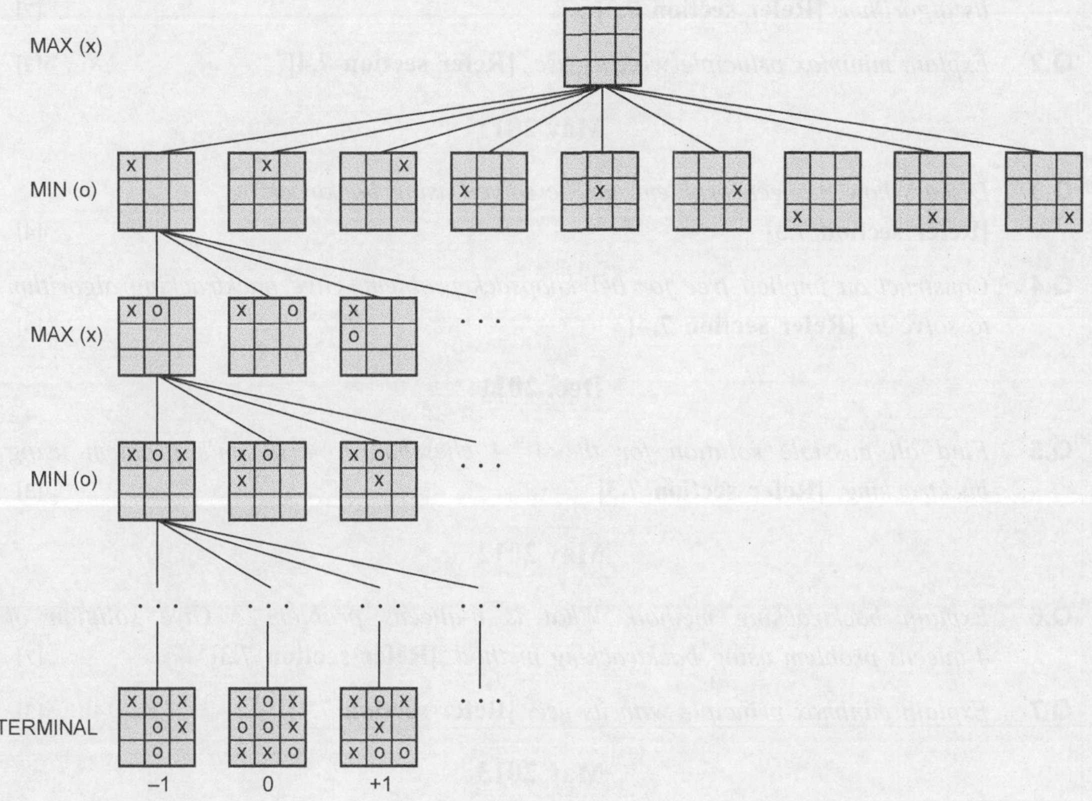

Fig. 7.7.1

Review Question

1. *Explain minimax principle with its use.* **GTU : Dec.-10, June-12, Marks 3**

7.8 University Questions with Answers

Regulation 2008

Dec. 2010

Q.1 *Explain the use of backtracking method for solving eight queens problem giving its algorithm.* **[Refer section 7.3]** [7]

Q.2 *Explain minimax principle with its use.* **[Refer section 7.4]** [3]

May 2011

Q.3 *Discuss how 8-queen problem can be solved using backtracking.* **[Refer section 7.3]** [4]

Q.4 *Construct an implicit tree for 0-1 knapsack problem. Give backtracking algorithm to solve it.* **[Refer section 7.4]** [6]

Dec. 2011

Q.5 *Find all possible solution for the 4 * 4 chessboard, 4 queen's problem using backtracking.* **[Refer section 7.3]** [3]

May 2012

Q.6 *Explain backtracking method. What is n-queens problem ? Give solution of 4-queens problem using backtracking method.* **[Refer section 7.3]** [7]

Q.7 *Explain minimax principle with its use.* **[Refer section 7.4]** [3]

May 2013

Q.8 *Find all possible solution for the 4 * 4 chessboard, 4 queen's problem using backtracking.* **[Refer section 7.3]** [3]

Dec. 2014

Q.9 *What is the central principle of backtracking taking n queens problem as an example, explain the solution process ?* **[Refer section 7.1]** [7]

Q.10 *Explain backtracking with knapsack problem.* **[Refer section 7.4]** [7]

Regulation 2013

Winter 2015

Q.11 *Explain backtracking method. What is n-queens problem ? Give solution of 4-queens problem using backtracking method.* **[Refer section 7.3]** [7]

7.9 Short Questions and Answers

Q.1 State the principle of backtracking.

Ans. : Backtracking is a method in which the desired solution is expressed as n tuple which is chosen from solution space, using backtrack formulation. The solution obtained i.e. can either minimizes or maximizes or satisfies the criteria function.

Q.2 What is state space tree ?

Ans. : A state space tree is a rooted tree whose nodes represent partially constructed solutions to given problem. In backtracking method the state space tree is built for finding the solution. This tree is built using depth first search fashion.

Q.3 What do the leaves of state space tree represent ?

Ans. : The leaves of state space tree represent either the solution (i.e. answer nodes) or the non promising dead ends.

Q.4 Define the term problem state in backtracking.

Ans. : Backtracking algorithm determines problem solutions by systematically searching for the solutions using tree structure. Each node in this tree is called problem state.

Q.5 What are the applications of backtracking ?

Ans. : Following are some applications of backtracking -

1. Eight queens problem 2. Sum of Subset problem
3. Finding Hamiltonian path 4. Knapsack problem.

Q.6 What is the advantage of backtracking algorithm ?

Ans. : The main advantage of backtracking algorithm is solving those problems in which the partial vector generated does not lead to an optimal solution. In such type of problem, the partial vector can be ignored.

Q.7 Give the formal definition of n-queen's problem.

Ans. : Definition : Consider a $n \times n$ chessboard on which we have to place n queens such that no two queens can attack each other by being in the same row or in the same column or on the same diagonal.

The diagonal conflicts can be checked by following formula -

Let, = (i, j) and (k, l) are two positions.

Then and are the positions that are on the same diagonal, if

$$i + j = k + l \quad \text{or}$$

$$i - j = k - l$$

Q.8 What type of constraints need to be satisfied by the solution in backtracking problem ?

Ans. : The implicit and explicit constraints need to be satisfied by the solution in backtracking.

Q.9 What type of searching method is adopted by the backtracking method ?

Ans. : The backtracking makes use of depth first searching method with some bounding function.

Q.10 Differentiate explicit and implicit constraints.

Ans. : Explicit constraints : Explicit constraints are rules, which restrict, each vector element to be chosen from given set.

Implicit constraints : Implicit constraints are rules which determine which of the tuples in the solution space satisfy the criterion function.

Q.11 Give the explicit constraint for 8-queen's problem.

Ans. : The explicit contraints show that the solution space Si must be = {1, 2, 3, 4, 5, 6, 7, 8} with $1 \leq i \leq 8$. Hence solution space consists of 88 8-tuples.

Q.12 Give the implicit constraint for the 8-queen's problem.

Ans. : The implicit constraint will be -

1) No two xi will be same. That means all the queens must lie in different columns.

2) No two queens can be on the same row, column or diagonal.

Q.13 What is the difference between live node and dead node ?

Ans. : Live node : The live node which is generated and whose children have not yet been generated is called live node. While tracing for the solution each internal node is a live node.

Dead node : The dead node is a generated node which is not to be expanded further or all of whose children have been generated.

Q.14 Describe the sum of subset problem.

Ans. : Let, S = be a set of n positive integers, then we have to find a subset whose sum is equal to given positive integer d.

It is always convenient to sort the set's elements in ascending order. That is,

s1<=s2<=...<=sn

Q.15 What is the principle behind branch and bound technique ?

Ans. : Principle - The branch and bound technique is a kind of technique in which state space tree is built and all the children of E node are generated before any other node can become a live node. The exploring can be done using BFS or D-search.

Q.16 What do you mean by the E-node ?

Ans. : The live nodes whose children are currently being expanded are called E-node.

Q.17 What is answer states ?

Ans. : The answer states are the leaf nodes which correspond to an element in the set of solutions. These are the states which satisfy the implicit constraint.

Q.18 State the usefulness of bounding function.

Ans. : The bounding functions are used to avoid the generation of subtrees that do not contain an answer node.

Notes

8 String Matching

Syllabus :

Introduction, The naive string matching algorithm, The Rabin-Karp algorithm, String matching with finite automata, The Knuth-Morris-Pratt algorithm.

Contents

8.1 Introduction

String matching algorithms are normally used in text processing. Normally text processing is done in compilation of program. In software design or in system design also text processing is a vital activity. And while processing the text, string matching is an important activity which is needed, most of the time. String matching means finding one or more generally all the occurrences of a string in the text. These occurrences are called as **pattern**. Hence sometimes string matching algorithms are also called as **pattern matching** algorithms.

Let,

Text T is denoted by t_o ......t_{n-1} and

pattern P is denoted by p_o ....p_{m-1}

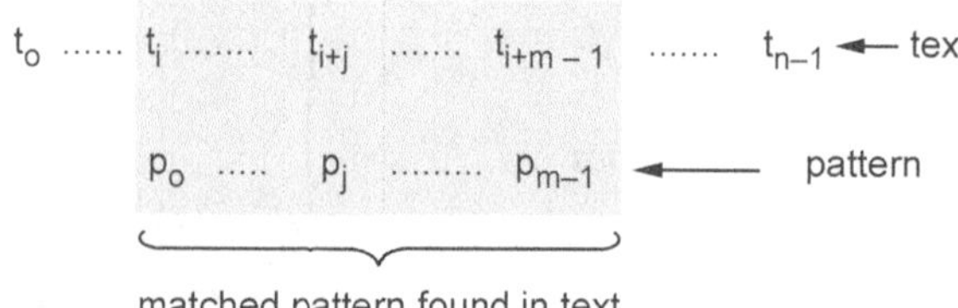

In this section we will discuss various string matching algorithms such as -

1. The naive method.
2. Rabin-Karp method.
3. Finite automaton for string matching.

Let us discuss these algorithms with the help of some examples.

8.2 The Naive String Matching Algorithm

This is the simplest method which works using **Brute Force** approach. The Brute force is a straightforward approach of solving the problem. This method has "Just do it" approach. This algorithm performs a checking at all positions in the text between o to n–m, whether an occurrence of the pattern starts there or not. Then after each attempt, it shifts the pattern by exactly one position to the right. If the match is found then it returns otherwise the matching process is continued by shifting one character to the right. If there is no match at all in the text for the given pattern even then we have to do n comparisons. Let us understand this method with the help of some example -

Example

Consider the text and pattern as given below.

0	1	2	3	4	5	6	7	8	9	10	11	12	13	14	15	16	
r	a	m	a	n		l	i	k	e	s		m	a	n	g	o	Text

0	1	2	3	4	
m	a	n	g	o	Pattern

We will start finding match for pattern from 0th location in **Text**. If the match is not found the shift to the right by 1 position.

0	1	2	3	4	5	6	7	8	9	10	11	12	13	14	15	16	
r	a	m	a	n		l	i	k	e	s		m	a	n	g	o	No match is found ∴ Shift to the right by 1 position
↕																	
m	a	n	g	o													

0	1	2	3	4	5	6	7	8	9	10	11	12	13	14	15	16	
r	a	m	a	n		l	i	k	e	s		m	a	n	g	o	No match
	↕																
	m	a	n	g	o												

0	1	2	3	4	5	6	7	8	9	10	11	12	13	14	15	16	
r	a	m	a	n		l	i	k	e	s		m	a	n	g	o	Three symbols are matching.
		↕	↕	↕													
		m	a	n	g	o											

0	1	2	3	4	5	6	7	8	9	10	11	12	13	14	15	16	
r	a	m	a	n		l	i	k	e	s		m	a	n	g	o	No match. ∴ Shift to the right by 1 position.
					↕												
		m	a	n	g	o											

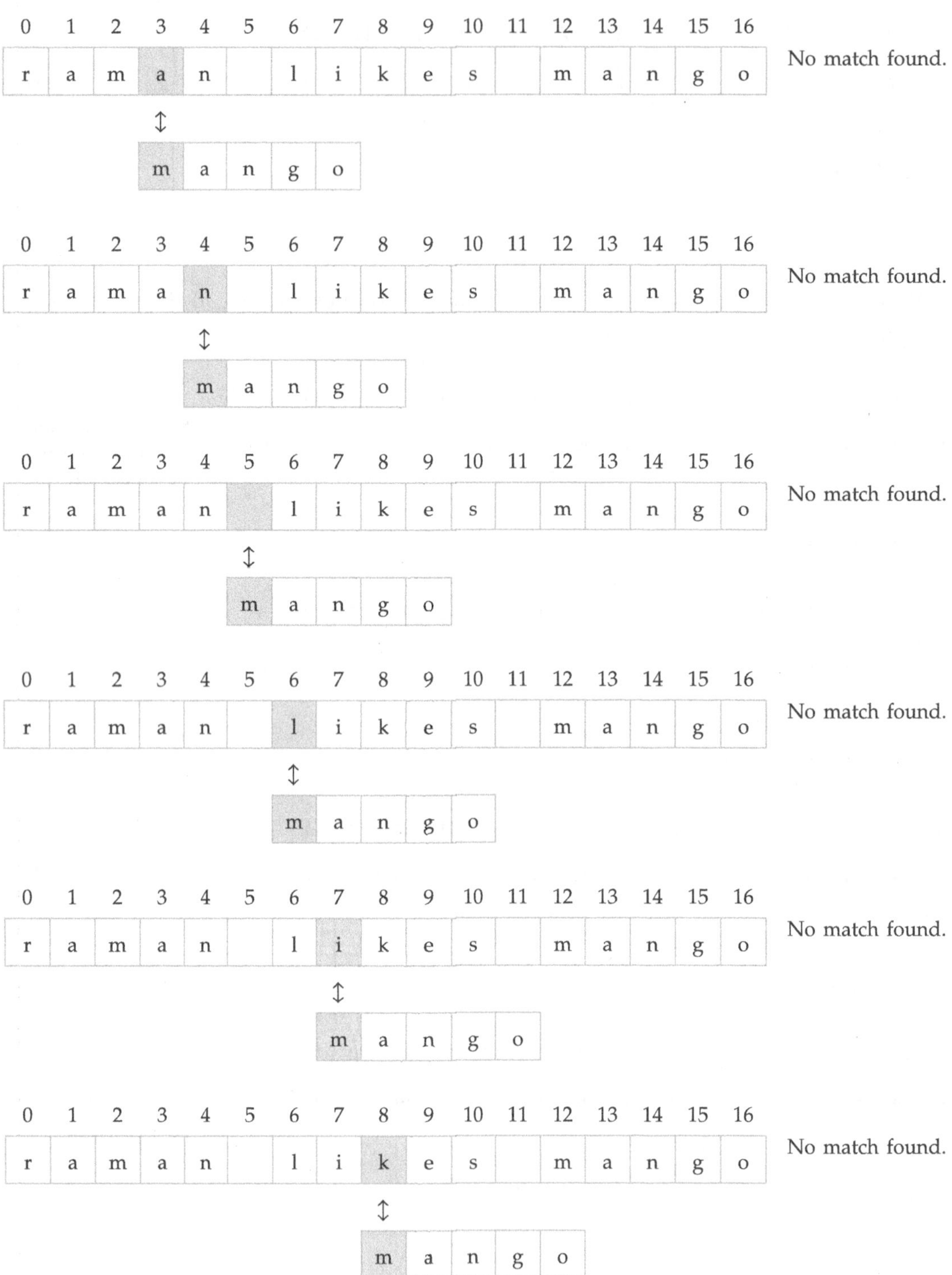
0 1 2 3 4 5 6 7 8 9 10 11 12 13 14 15 16
r a m a n l i k e s m a n g o
m a n g o
No match found.
No match found.
No match found.
No match found.
No match found.
No match found.

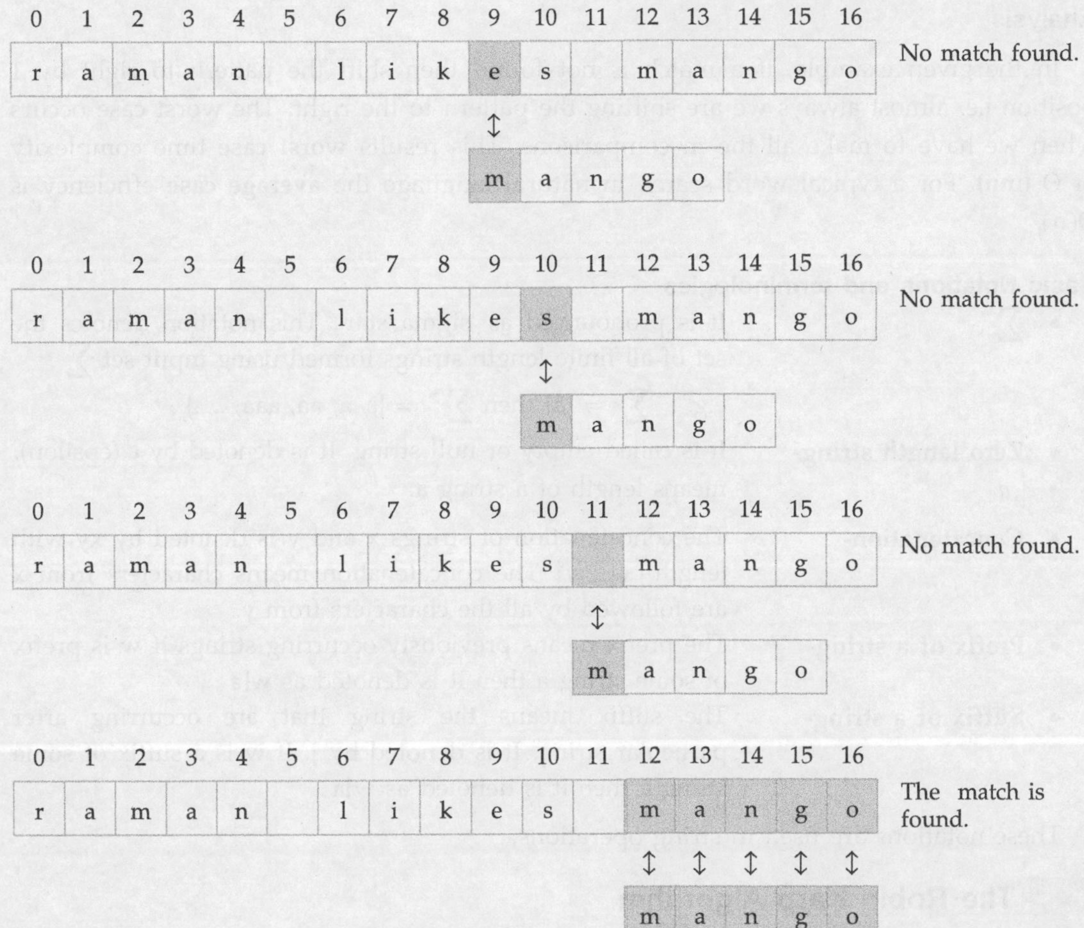

Hence return index 12, because a match with the pattern is found from that location in text.

Algorithm

```
Algorithm Naive (T[1....n], P[1.....m])
{
// Problem Description : This algorithm finds
// the string matching using Naive method.
// Input : The array text T and pattern P
for (s ← 0 to n–m) do
{
if (P[1......m] = T[s+1.......s+m] then
print ("pattern finding with shift", S);
}
} // end of algorithm
```

Analysis

In the given example, if a match is not found then shift the pattern to right by 1 position i.e. almost always we are shifting the pattern to the right. The worst case occurs when we have to make all the m comparisons. This results **worst case** time complexity of Θ **(mn)**. For a typical word search in natural language the **average case** efficiency is $\Theta(n)$.

Basic Notations and terminologies

- $\sum^*$ - It is pronounced as 'sigma star'. This notation denotes the set of all finite length strings formed using input set $\sum$
  e.g. : $\sum = \{a\}$ then $\sum^* = \{\varepsilon, a, aa, aaa, ...\}$
- **Zero length string-** It is called empty or null string. It is denoted by ε (epsilon).
- $|a|$ - means length of a string a.
- **Concatenation-** The concatenation of strings x and y is denoted by xy with length $|x|+|y|$. The concatenation means characters from x are followed by all the characters from y.
- **Prefix of a string-** The prefix means previously occurring strings if w is prefix of some string a then it is denoted as **w[a**
- **Suffix of a string-** The suffix means the string that are occurring **after** particular string. It is denoted by]. If w is a suffix of some string a then it is denoted as **w]a**

These notations are used in string operations.

8.3 The Robin Karp Algorithm

GTU : Dec.-10, June-11,12, Dec.-11, Winter-14, 15, Marks 7

The Rabin-Karp method is based on hashing technique. This algorithm assumes each character to be a digit in radix-d notation. It makes use of equivalence of two numbers modulo a third number. Let, p[1....m] be a pattern then p denotes its corresponding decimal value. The d = 10 for decimal number, d = 2 for binary number.

Similarly,

Let, T [1,...., n] be a text then t_s denotes the decimal value of the substring T[s+1, ... , s+m] for s= 0, 1, ... , n – m.

The method follows following steps-

1. Compute p in O(m) time.
2. Compute all t_i values in total of O(n) time.
3. Find all valid shifts s in total of O(n) time.

The computation of p can be done using Horner's rule as follows.

$$p = p[m] + d(p[m-1] + d(p[m-2] + ... + d(p[2] + d(p[1]))))$$

For example : To compute pattern

$$p[1, \ldots, m] = 41603 \text{ we have } m = 5 \text{ (i.e. length of pattern), } d = 10. \text{ Then}$$

$$p = p[m] + 10\,(p[m-1]) + 10^2(p[m-2]) + \ldots\ldots + 10^{m-1}(p[1])$$

$$= 3 + 10\,(0) + 100\,(6) + 1000\,(1) + 10000(4)$$

$$p = 41603$$

We can then compute to from T[1.....m] in O(m) time. Then remaining t_i can be computed in O(n–m) time as :

$$t_{s+1} = d(t_s - d^{m-1}\ T[s+1] + T[S+m+1])$$

where $d = 10.$

But these values of p and t_s may be too large hence we use **mod** value.

Example 8.3.1 *Using the Rabin - Karp algorithm for text T = 3141592653589793 find for pattern P = 26 with modulo q = 11.*

Solution :

Text	3	1	4	1	5	9	2	6	5	3	5	8	9	7	9	3

Pattern	2	6

The 26 mod 11 = **4**

We will now obtain mod 11 value for each text.

Step 1 :

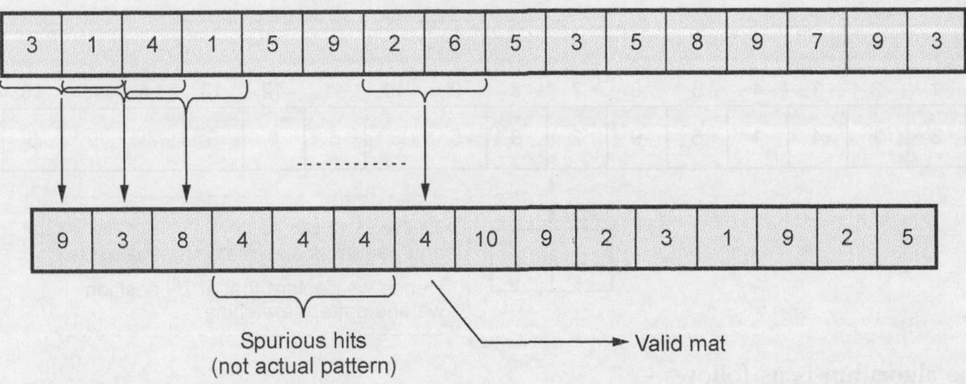

For m = 2, consider t_s = 26 then we can compute t_{s+1} as follows

$$t_{s+1} = 10\,(t_s - d_{10}^{m-1}.\ \text{old high order digit}) + \text{new low order digit}$$

$$= 10(26 - 10 \cdot 2) + 5$$

$$= 10(26 - 20) + 5$$

$$= 60 + 5$$

$$t_{s+1} = 65$$

Thus we can obtain every successive bit in text T.

According to Rabin-Karp method we start matching the pattern against text from beginning itself.

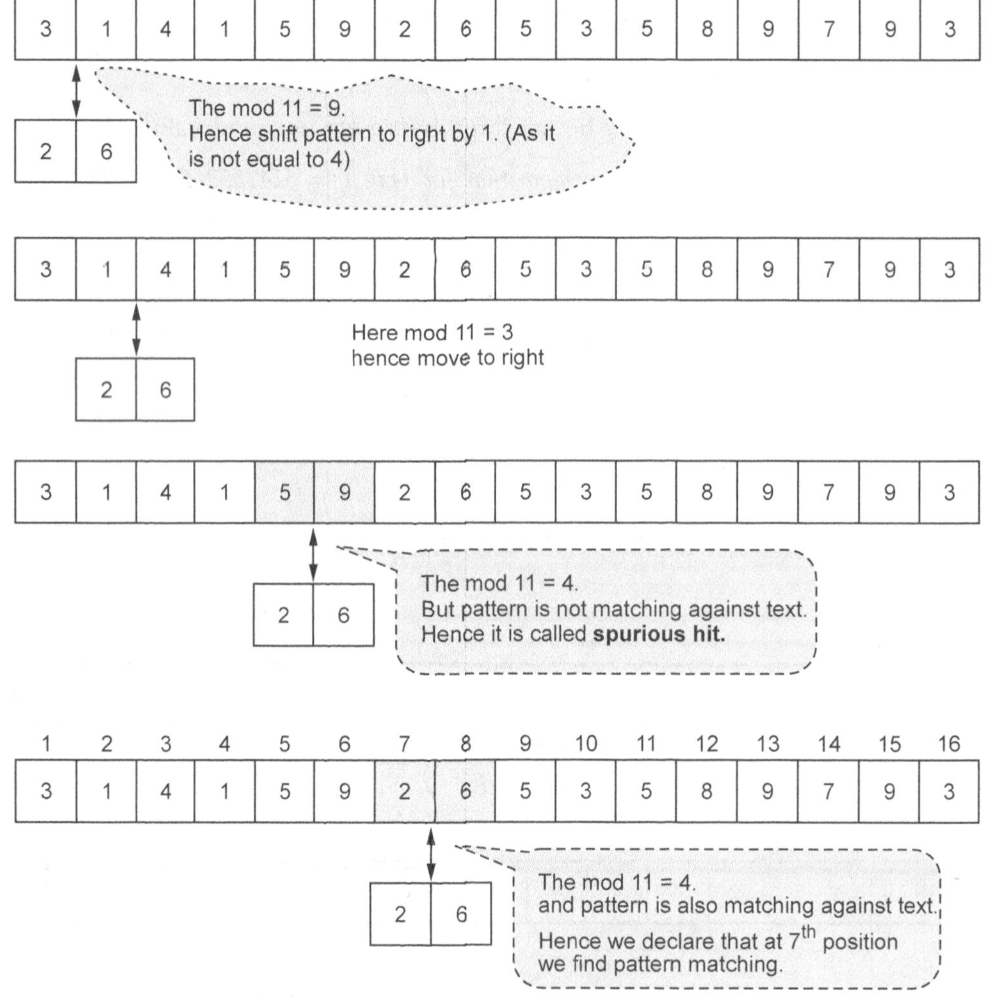

The algorithm is as follows -

Algorithm RabinKarp (T[1....n], P[1......m], d, q)
{
// **Problem Description :** This algorithm is

```
// for matching the pattern using Rabin-Karp method
    h ← pow (d, m–1) mod q ←  [high order digit position]
    p ← 0
    t0 ← 0
    for (i ← 1 to m)
    {
    p ← (dp + P[i]) mod q       }
    t0 ← (dt0 + T[i] mod q      } Θ (m) time
    }
    for (s← 0 to n – m)              // with shift value each time
    {                                // incremented by one we
                                     // go on matching pattern
        if (p = ts) then             // against text.
        {
            if (T[1.....m] = T [s+1 ....s+m] then
        write(" pattern found with shift," s)
        }                            [Yet end of text is not reached.]
        if (s<n – m)
        ts+1 ← (d (ts – T[s+1]h) + T(s+m+1)mod q
    } // end of for                  (Computing ts+1)
    } // end of algorithm
```

The matching time required by above algorithm is Θ ((n – m+1)m). Hence worst case running time of this algorithm is **Θ ((n – m+1)m)**.

Review Questions

1. *Explain Rabin-Karp method for string matching and also give the algorithm.*
   GTU : Winter-14, Dec.-10, June-12, Marks 7, Dec.-11, Marks 4
2. *Explain Rabin-Karp string matching algorithm with example.* **GTU : June-11, Marks 5**
3. *Give and explain Rabin-Carp string matching algorithm with example.*
   GTU : Winter-15, Marks 7

8.4 String Matching with Finite Automata

GTU : June-11,12,Summer-14, Dec.-11, Summer-15, Winter-15, Marks 7

Finite automata is a very effective tool which is used in string matching algorithms. Matching the pattern in this manner makes the process of string matching very efficient. In this method each character of the text is matched exactly once. Hence Θ**(n)** time is required for examining the text characters. But in this algorithm a large amount of time is needed to build a finite automaton. Before learning the actual string matching algorithm let us go through some basic concepts of finite automata.

Definition of Finite Automata :

A finite automaton is a collection of

1. Q a finite set of states.

2. $q_0 \in Q$ is a **start** state.

3. $q_f \in Q$ is a **Accept** state or a **final** state.

4. $\sum$ is a finite input set.

5. δ is a mapping function or a transition function from $Q \times \sum$.

For example

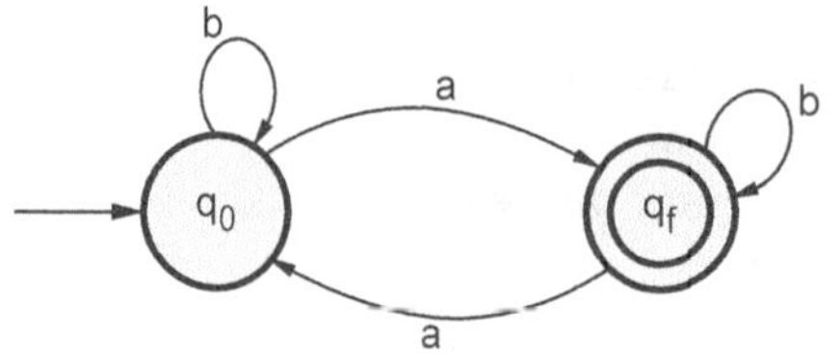

(a) Finite Automata

Input / State	a	b
q_0	q_f	q_0
q_f	q_0	q_f

(b) Transition Table

Fig. 8.4.1

Here q_0 is a start state and q_f is a final state. The above designed finite automata is for accepting a language which consists of odd number of a's and any number of b's. Hence for the pattern "aaabaa" the finite automata will reach final state. Hence input "aaabaa" is said to be **accepted**. But input "aabb" is said to be **rejected**. Let us now discuss, how finite automata is useful for pattern matching purpose.

For example : We can construct a finite automata for matching the pattern P = aabab for text string T = aaababaabaababaab.

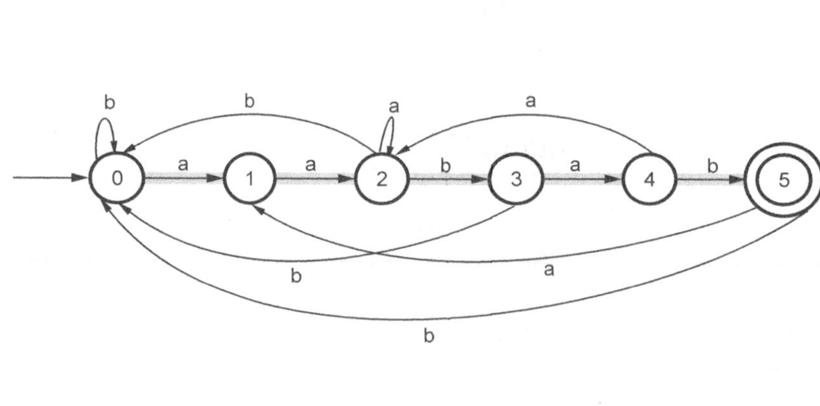

Transition table

Input / State	a	b
0	1	0
1	2	–
2	2	3
3	4	0
4	2	5
5	1	0

Matching Pattern

Fig. 8.4.2

In above Finite Automata (FA) the dark edge going from left to right represents a **spine**. It corresponds to successful match of the pattern. The edges from right to left are called **failing** edges. These edges are showing possible permutations of the string. Some of the failing edges are not shown.

	a	a	a	b	a	b	a	a	b	a	a	b	a	b	a	a	b
	a	a	b	a	b												
Match found →		a	a	b	a	b											
			a	a	b	a	b										
				a	a	b	a	b									
					a	a	b	a	b								
						a	a	b	a	b							
							a	a	b	a	b						
								a	a	b	a	b					
									a	a	b	a	b				
Match found →										a	a	b	a	b			
											a	a	b	a	b		
												a	a	b	a	b	
													a	a	b	a	b

Thus on accepting the pattern the FA should in final state. Then it is said that pattern is matched successfully. In above automata we have δ (4, a) = 2 because after reading the prefix "aaba" if the automata reads 'a' from text then there should be proper path so that the match for "aabab" can occur successfully, and should lead to final state on matching of pattern.

Algorithm

```
Algorithm FiniteAutomata (T, δ, m, n)
{
// Problem Description :
q ← 0
for (i ← 1 to n)
{
    q ← δ (q, T[i])          ← Obtaining next state after reading input text
    if (q = m) then          ← at final state
    write ("pattern matches with" , i – m)
} // end of for
} // end of algorithm
```

Review Questions

1. *What is finite automata ? How it can be used in string matching ?*
   GTU : June-11, Marks 5, GTU : June-12, Marks 6, Summer -14, Marks 7
2. *Explain string matching with finite automata.* **GTU : Dec.-11, Marks 4**
3. *What is finite automata ? Explain use of finite automata for string matching with suitable example.* **GTU : Winter-15, Summer-15, Marks 7**

8.5 Knuth Morris Pratt (KMP) Algorithm

In the pattern matching algorithms like naive method or Boyer-Moore, we often compare the pattern characters that do not match in the text, and on occurrence of mismatch we simply throw a way the information and restart the comparison, for another set of characters from the text. Thus again and again with next incremental position of text, the characters from pattern are matched. This ultimately reduces the efficiency of pattern matching algorithm. Hence the Knuth-Morris-Pratt algorithm came up which avoids the repeated comparison of characters. This algorithm is named after the scientists Knuth, Morris and Pratt. The **basic idea** behind this algorithm is to build a **prefix array**. Some times this array is also called π **array.** This prefix array is built using the **prefix** and **suffix** information of pattern. The overlapping prefix and suffix is used in K-M-P algorithm. The KMP algorithm achieves the efficiency of **O(m+n)** which is **optimal** in **worst case.** Let us first understand how to compute the prefix array for given **pattern.** Suppose the we have a pattern "abadab". The prefix or π array for this pattern can be built as follows.

Consider

Initially we will put 0 in 0th location of prefix array.

0	1	2	3	4	5
a	b	a	d	a	b
0					

Consider string
ab

Prefix : ε , a
Suffix : ε , b

No match of prefix and suffix. Hence we will put 0 in prefix array at 1st location.

0	1	2	3	4	5
a	b	a	d	a	b
0	**0**				

Consider string

aba

The length of matching prefix-suffix is 1. Hence make entry 1 in prefix table.

Prefix : ε , a, ab

Suffix : ε , a, ba

0	1	2	3	4	5
a	b	a	d	a	b
0	0	**1**			

Consider string

abad

The length of matching prefix-suffix is 0. Hence make entry 0 in prefix table.

Prefix : ε , a, ab, aba

Suffix : ε , d, ad, bad

0	1	2	3	4	5
a	b	a	d	a	b
0	0	1	**0**		

Consider string

abada

The length of matching prefix-suffix is 1. Hence make entry 1 in prefix table.

Prefix : ε, a, ab, aba, abad

Suffix : ε, a, da, ada, bada

0	1	2	3	4	5
a	b	a	d	a	b
0	0	1	0	**1**	

Consider string

abadab

The length of matching prefix-suffix is 2. Hence make entry 2 in prefix table.

Prefix : ε , a, ab, aba, abad, abada

Suffix : ε , b, ab, dab, adab, badab

0	1	2	3	4	5
a	b	a	d	a	b
0	0	1	0	1	**2**

Thus we have computed the prefix or π table before proceeding for the actual algorithm. The pseudo code for computing prefix array is as given below.

```
Algorithm Compute_Prefix (char p[size])
//Problem description : This algorithm computes prefix
//table for given pattern
//Input : pattern p
//Output : prefix table for given pattern
      prefix_table [0] ← 0
      for (q ← 1 to m) do //m is length of pattern
      {
            while (k > 0 AND p[k] ! = p[q])
                  k ← prefix_table [k-1]
            if (p[k] = p[q]) then
                  k ← k + 1
            prefix_table[q] ← k
      }
      return prefix_table ;
```

Now the next step is to compare the characters of pattern against text. It can be well understood with following example :

Consider

	0	1	2	3	4	5	6	7	8	9	10	11	12	13	14
Text	b	a	d	b	a	b	a	b	a	b	a	d	a	a	b
Pattern	a	b	a	b	a	d	a								

We will first compute the prefix table for the pattern abababada

0	1	2	3	4	5	6
a	b	a	b	a	d	a
0	0	1	2	3	0	1

	0	1	2	3	4	5	6	7	8	9	10	11	12	13	14
Text	b	a	d	b	a	b	a	b	a	b	a	d	a	a	b
Pattern	a	b	a	b	a	d	a								

↑

Comparing b and a, as it is not matching. We will compare Text [1] with Pattern [0].

	0	1	2	3	4	5	6	7	8	9	10	11	12	13	14
Text	b	a	d	b	a	b	a	b	a	b	a	d	a	a	b
Pattern	a	b	a	b	a	d	a								

As Text [1] is matching with Pattern [0], we will now compare Text [2] with Pattern [1].

	0	1	2	3	4	5	6	7	8	9	10	11	12	13	14
Text	b	a	d	b	a	b	a	b	a	b	a	d	a	a	b
Pattern	a	b	a	b	a	d	a								

As Text [2] is not matching with Pattern [1]. We will backtrack on Pattern and compare Pattern [0] with Text [3]. Because we consult prefix_table [1] which is 0. Hence Pattern [0] is compared with Text [3].

	0	1	2	3	4	5	6	7	8	9	10	11	12	13	14
Text	b	a	d	b	a	b	a	b	a	b	a	d	a	a	b
				i											

Pattern	a	b	a	b	a	d	a
	j						

Again Text [3] is not matching with Pattern [0]. We will then ask prefix_table [0] for the location of pattern. As prefix_table [0] is 0, we will compare Pattern [0] with Text [4].

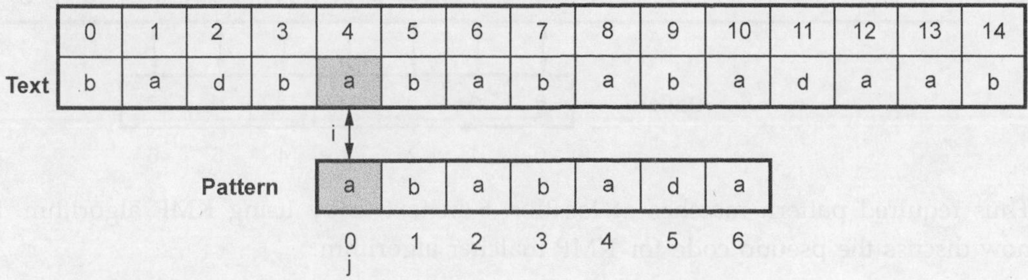

Text [4] matches with Pattern [0]. Increment i and j

Text [5] matches with Pattern [1]. Increment i and j

Text [6] matches with Pattern [2]. Increment i and j

Text [7] matches with Pattern [3]. Increment i and j

Text [8] matches with Pattern [4]. Increment i and j

But Text [9] is not matching with pattern [5] .

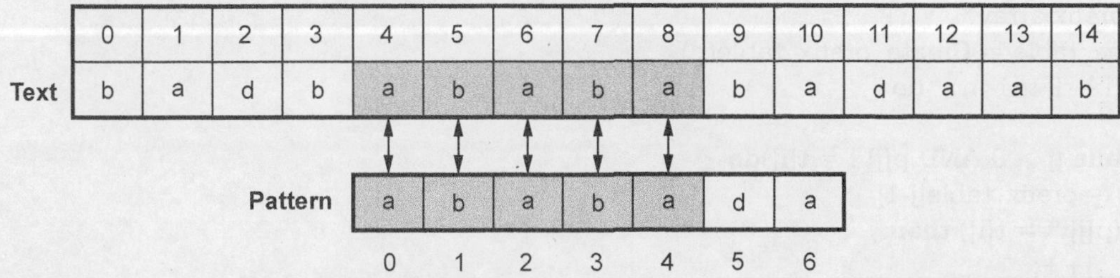

Hence we must backtrack on pattern array. That means j will be positioning on location 4. Consult prefix_table [4] which denotes the value 3. That indicates, compare Pattern [3] with current i position text array character. Hence we will compare Text [9] with Pattern [3], which is matching.

Text [10] with Pattern [4], matching ∴ Increment i and j

Text [11] with Pattern [5], matching ∴ Increment i and j

Text [12] with Pattern [6], matching ∴ Increment i and j

Thus we have reached on the last character of pattern, at the same time i is positioned at location 12 in the text array. The last character of pattern is also matching with Text [12], hence we can declare that a match of pattern is found in the text array at i – length of pattern + 1.

i.e. 12 – 7 + 1

i.e. 6

Hence

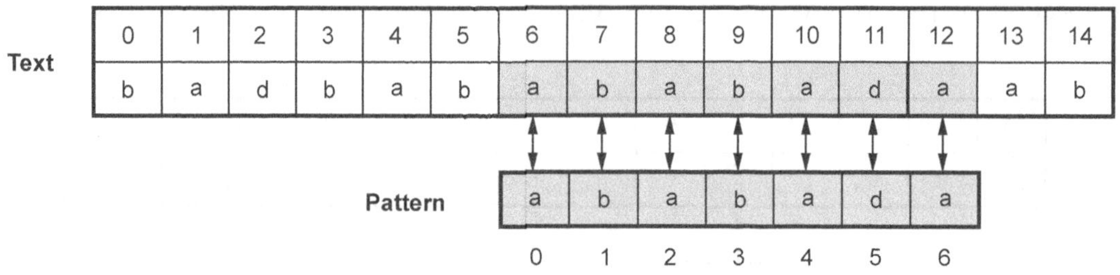

Text

0	1	2	3	4	5	6	7	8	9	10	11	12	13	14
b	a	d	b	a	b	a	b	a	b	a	d	a	a	b

Pattern

a	b	a	b	a	d	a
0	1	2	3	4	5	6

Thus required pattern matches at location 6 in text array using KMP algorithm. Let us now discuss the pseudo code for KMP matcher algorithm.

Algorithm

```
Algorithm kmp_match(char t[50], char p[10])
//Problem description : This is a KMP pattern matching algorithm
// Input : The array of Text and p denoted by t and p variables
//Output : The starting location at which the matched pattern is found
 j ← 0;
 n = strlen(t);
 m = strlen(p);
 // prefix array
Prefix_table = Create_prefix_table(p);
for (i ← 0 to i<n)  do
 {
  while (j > 0 AND p[j] ! = t[i])do
   j ← prefix_table[j-1]
  if (p[j] == t[i]) then
      j++;
  if (j == m) then
  {
   Write("\n\tPattern is present in the text at: ")
   Write(i-m+1)
  j ← prefix_table[j-1];//consult prefix table for
                          //positioning the pointer in pattern array
  }
 }
```

Analysis

The time complexity of the above algorithm is **O(n+m).** The n represents the length of text and m represents the length of pattern.

Review Question

1. *Explain KMP algorithm with suitable example.*

8.6 University Questions with Answers

Regulation 2008

Dec. 2010

Q.1 *Explain Rabin-Karp method for string matching and also give the algorithm.* **[Refer Section 8.3]** [7]

May 2011

Q.2 *Explain Rabin-Karp string matching algorithm with example.* **[Refer Section 8.3]** [5]

Q.3 *What is finite automata ? How it can be used in string matching ?* **[Refer Section 8.3]** [5]

Dec. 2011

Q.4 *Explain Rabin-Karp method for string matching and also give the algorithm.* **[Refer Section 8.3]** [4]

Q.5 *Explain string matching with finite automata.* **[Refer Section 8.4]** [4]

May 2012

Q.6 *Explain Rabin-Karp method for string matching and also give the algorithm.* **[Refer Section 8.3]** [7]

Q.7 *What is finite automata ? How it can be used in string matching ?* **[Refer Section 8.4]** [6]

May 2014

Q.8 *What is finite automata ? How it can be used in string matching ?* **[Refer Section 8.4]** [7]

Dec. 2014

Q.9 *Explain Rabin-Karp method for string matching and also give the algorithm.* **[Refer Section 8.3]** [7]

Regulation 2013

Winter 2015

Q.10 *What is finite automata ? Explain use of finite automata for string matching with suitable example.* **[Refer Section 8.4]** [7]

Q.11 *Give and explain Rabin-Carp string matching algorithm with example.* **[Refer Section 8.3]** [7]

8.7 Short Questions and Answers

Q.1 What is the applicability of string matching algorithm?

Ans. : String matching algorithm is used in text processing.

Q.2 Name few string matching algorithms.

Ans. : 1. Naïve Method 2. Rabin Karp Method 3. Finite automata for string matching

Q.3 Name the algorithmic technique on which the naïve method is used.

Ans. : The naïve method is based on Brute Force method.

Q.4 The hashing technique is used in which string matching algorithm?

Ans. : The Rabin Karp method is based on string matching algorithm.

Q.5 What is the principle idea behind the Knuth Morris Pratt algorithm?

Ans. : The basic idea behind this algorithm is to build a prefix array. Some times this array is also called π array. This prefix array is built using the prefix and suffix information of pattern. The overlapping prefix and suffix is used in K-M-P algorithm.

❑❑❑

9 Introduction to NP Completeness

Syllabus

The class P and NP, Polynomial reduction, NP-completeness problem, NP-hard problems. Travelling salesman problem, Hamiltonian problem, Approximation algorithms.

Contents

9.1 The Class P and NP

GTU : Dec.-10, Marks 6, Summer-15, Marks 4

There are two groups in which a problem can be classified. The first group consists of the problems that can be solved in polynomial time. For example : searching of an element from the list O(logn), sorting of elements O(logn).

The second group consists of problems that can be solved in non-deterministic polynomial time. For example : Knapsack problem $O(2^{n/2})$ and Travelling Salesperson problem $(O(n^2 2^n))$.

- Any problem for which answer is either yes or no is called decision problem. The algorithm for decision problem is called **decision algorithm.**
- Any problem that involves the identification of optimal cost (minimum or maximum) is called optimization problem. The algorithm for optimization problem is called **optimization algorithm.**
- **Definition of P** - Problems that can be solved in polynomial time. ("P" stands for polynomial).

  Examples - Searching of key element, Sorting of elements, All pair shortest path.
- **Definition of NP -** It stands for "non-deterministic polynomial time". Note that NP does not stand for "non-polynomial".

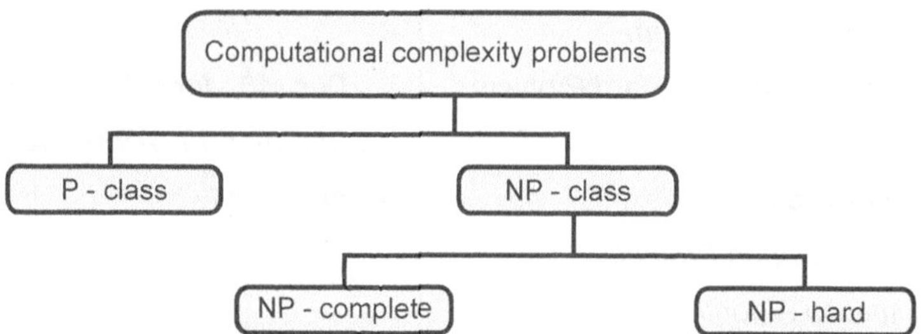

Fig. 9.1.1 Classification of problems

  Examples - Travelling Salesperson problem, Graph coloring problem, Knapsack problem, Hamiltonian circuit problems.
- The NP class problems can be further categorized into **NP-complete** and NP **hard problems.**
- A problem D is called **NP-complete** if -

  i) It belongs to class NP

  ii) Every problem in NP can also be solved in polynomial time.
- If an NP-hard problem can be solved in polynomial time then all NP-complete problems can also be solved in polynomial time.
- All NP-complete problems are NP-hard but all NP-hard problems cannot be NP-complete.

- The NP class problems are the decision problems that can be solved by non-deterministic polynomial algorithms.
- **Computational complexity** - The computational problems is an infinite collection of instances with a solution for every instance.

  In computational complexity the solution to the problem can be "yes" or "no" type. Such type of problems are called **decision problem.** The computational problems can be **function problem**. The function problem is a computational problem where single output is expected for every input. The output of such type of problems is more complex than the decision problem.

  The computational problems also consists of a class of problems, whose output can be obtained in polynomial time.
- **Complexity classes -** The complexity classes is a set of problems of related complexity. It includes function problems, P classes, NP classes, optimization problem.
- **Intractability** - Problems that can be solved by taking a long time for their solutions is known as intractable problems.

If NP is not same as P then NP complete problems are called intractable problems.

9.1.1 Example of P Class Problem

Kruskal's algorithm : In Kruskal's algorithm the minimum weight is obtained. In this algorithm also the circuit should not be formed. Each time the edge of minimum weight has to be selected, from the graph. It is not necessary in this algorithm to have edges of minimum weights to be adjacent. Let us solve one example by Kruskal's algorithm.

Example :

Find the minimum spanning tree for the following figure using Kruskal's algorithm.

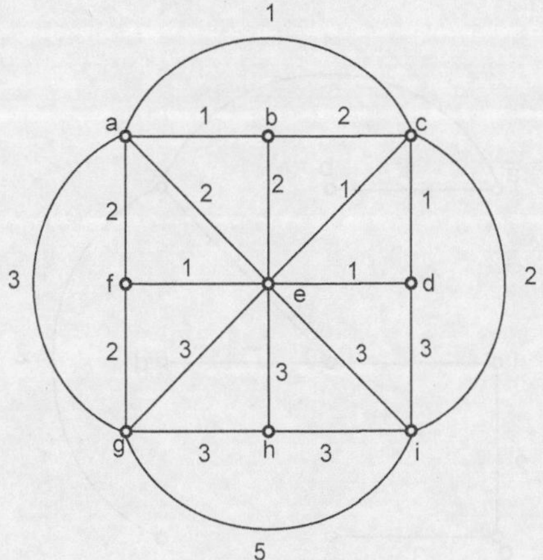

Fig. 9.1.2

In Kruskal's algorithm, we will start with some vertex and will cover all the vertices with minimum weight. The vertices need not be adjacent.

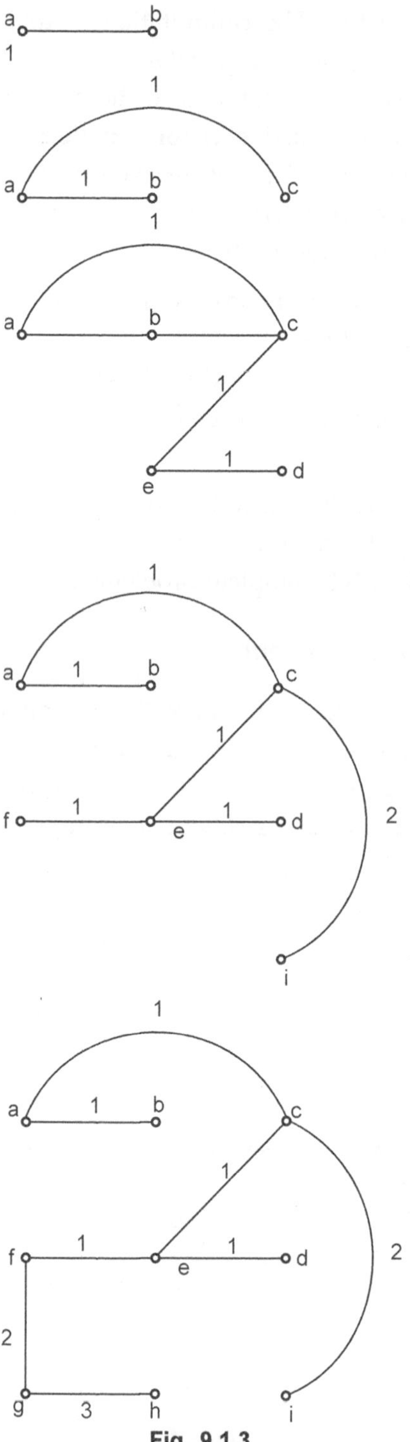

Fig. 9.1.3

9.1.2 Example of NP Class Problem

Travelling Salesman's Problem (TSP) : This problem can be stated as " Given a set of cities and cost to travel between each pair of cities, determine whether there is a path that visits every city once and returns to the first city. Such that the cost travelled is less".

For example :

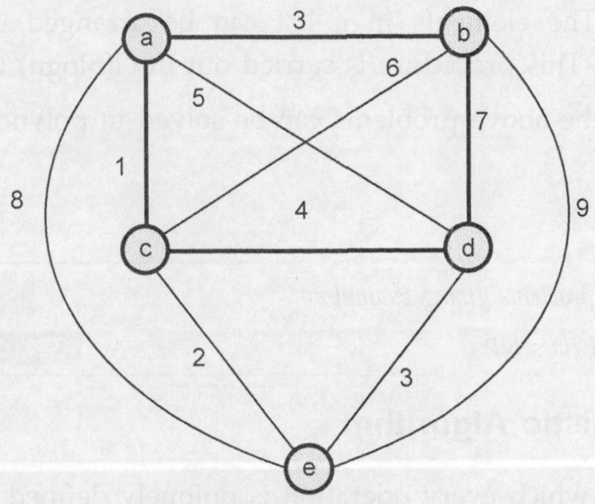

Fig. 9.1.4

The tour path will be **a-b-d-e-c-a** and total cost of tour will be **16.**

This problem is NP problem as there may exist some path with shortest distance between the cities. If you get the solution by applying certain algorithm then Travelling Salesman problem is **NP Complete Problem**. If we get no solution at all by applying an algorithm then the travelling salesman problem belongs to **NP hard class.**

Example 9.1.1 *Distinguish between deterministic and non-deterministic algorithms.*

Solution : **Deterministic algorithm :** An algorithm is called deterministic when for given input the same output gets generated, for a function. That means in deterministic algorithms the next state to be followed is fixed. The polynomial time algorithms are deterministic.

Non-deterministic algorithm : An algorithm is said to be non-deterministic when there are more than one paths that the algorithm can follow. Due to this one cannot determine which path is to be followed after a particular stage. All the NP class problems are basically non deterministic.

Example 9.1.2 *List three problems that have polynomial time algorithms. Justify your answer.*

Solution : The problems that can be solved in polynomial time are called P - class problems. For example -

1. **Binary search** - In searching an element using binary search method, the list is simply divided at the mid and either left or right sublist is searched for key element. This process is carried out in O(logn).
2. **Evaluation of polynomial** - In a polynomial evaluation we make out the summation of each term of polynomial. The evaluated result is simply an integer. This process is carried out in O(n) time.
3. **Sorting a list** - The elements in a list can be arranged either in ascending or descending order. This procedure is carried out in O(nlogn) time.

This shows that all the above problems can be solved in polynomial time.

Review Questions

1. *Explain P and NP problems giving examples.* **GTU : Dec.-10, Marks 6**
2. *Explain class P and class NP.* **GTU : Summer-15, Marks 4**

9.2 Non-deterministic Algorithm

- The algorithm in which every operation is uniquely defined is called **deterministic algorithm.**
- The algorithm in which every operation may not have unique result, rather there can be specified set of possibilities for every operation. Such an algorithm is called non-deterministic algorithm. Non-deterministic means that no particular rule is followed to make the guess.
- The non-deterministic algorithm is a two stage algorithm -
  - i) **Non-deterministic (Guessing) stage** - Generate an arbitrary string that can be thought of as a candidate solution.
  - ii) **Deterministic ("Verification") stage** - In this stage it takes as input the candidate solution and the instance to the problem and returns *yes* if the candidate solution represents actual solution.

```
Algorithm Non_Determin()
// A[1:n] is a set of elements
// we have to determine the index i of A at which element x is
//located.
{
  // The following for-loop is the guessing stage
        for i=1 to n do
          A[i] := choose(i);
```

```
 // Next is the verification(deterministic) stage
     if (A[i] = x) then
     {
           write(i);
           success();
     }
     write(0);
     fail();
}
```

In the above given non-deterministic algorithm there are three functions used -

1) Choose - Arbitrarily chooses one of the element from given input set.

2) Fail - Indicates the unsuccessful completion.

3) Success - Indicates successful completion.

The algorithm is of non-deterministic complexity O(1), when A is not ordered then the deterministic search algorithm has a complexity Ω (n).

Example 9.2.1 *Give the non-deterministic algorithm for sorting elements in non decreasing order.*

Solution :

```
Algorithm Non_DSort(A,n)
// A[1:n] is an array that stores n elements which are positive integers B[1:n] be an
auxiliary
// array in which elements are put at appropriate positions
{
// guessing stage
     for i←1 to n do
           B[i]←0;//initialize B to 0
     for i←1 to n do
     {
           j←choose(1,n)//select any element from the input set
           if(B[j]!=0) then
                 fail();
           B[j]←A[i];
     }
//verification stage
     for i←1 to n–1 do
           if(B[i]>B[i+1]) then
                 fail();// not sorted elements
           write(B[1:n]);// print the sorted list of elements
           success();
}
```

The time required by a non-deterministic algorithm with some input set is minimum number of steps needed to reach to a successful completion if there are multiple choices from input set leading to successful completion. In short, a non-deterministic algorithm is of complexity O(f(n)) where n is the total size of input.

9.3 Polynomial Reduction

GTU : June-11, Dec.-11, Winter-14, Marks 7

To prove whether particular problem is NP complete or not we use polynomial time reducibility. That means if

$A \xrightarrow{\text{Poly}} B$ and $B \xrightarrow{\text{Poly}} C$ then $A \xrightarrow{\text{Poly}} C$.

The **reduction** is an important task in NP completeness proofs. This can be illustrated by Fig. 9.3.1.

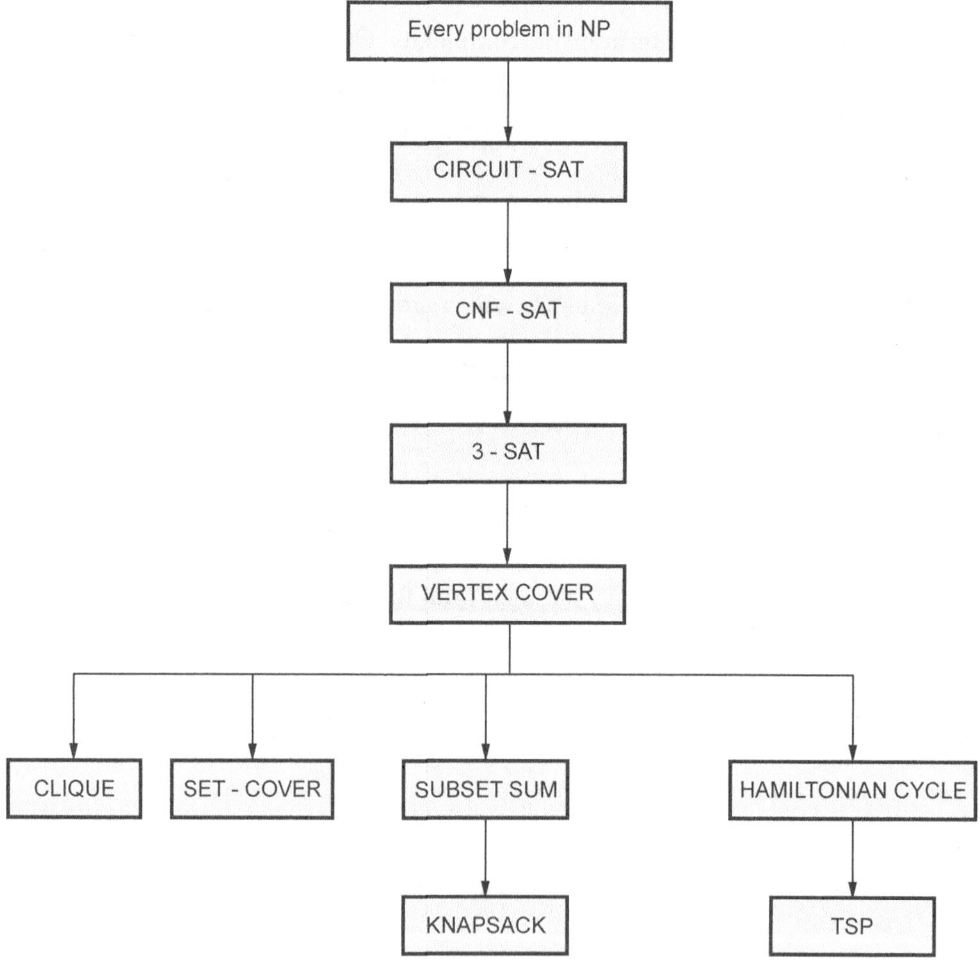

Fig. 9.3.1 Reduction in NP completeness

Various types of reductions are -

Local replacement - In this reduction A $\rightarrow$ B by dividing input to A in the form of components and then these components can be converted to components of B.

Component design - In this reduction A $\rightarrow$ B by building special component for input B that enforce propertied required by A.

Review Questions

1. *What is polynomially turing reducible problem ? Explain with example how problem A can be polynomially turing reduced to problem B.* **GTU : Winter-14, Marks 7, June-11, Marks 6**
2. *Explain polynomial reduction.* **GTU : Winter-14, Dec.-11, Marks 3**

9.4 NP Completeness Problem

In this section we will discuss various problems that can be proved to be NP complete. Their proofs of NP completeness is based on **reduction technique.** That means there are some problems which are already proved as NP complete problems. Using these problems we can prove the desired problems as NP complete.

9.4.1 Satisfiability Problem

1. CNF - SAT problem

This problem is based on Boolean formula. The Boolean formula has various Boolean operations such as OR(+), AND $(\cdot)$ and NOT. There are some notations such as $\rightarrow$ (means implies) and $\leftrightarrow$ (means if and only if).

A Boolean formula is in **Conjuctive Normal Form (CNF)** if it is formed as collection of subexpressions. These subexpressions are called **clauses.**

For example

$(\bar{a} + b + d + \bar{g})\ (c + \bar{e})\ (\bar{b} + d + \bar{f} + h)\ (a + c + e + \bar{h})$

This formula evaluates to 1 if b, c, d are 1.

The CNF - SAT is a problem which takes Boolean formula in CNF form and checks whether any assignment is there to Boolean values so that formula evaluates to 1.

Theorem : CIRCUIT-SAT is in NP

Proof :

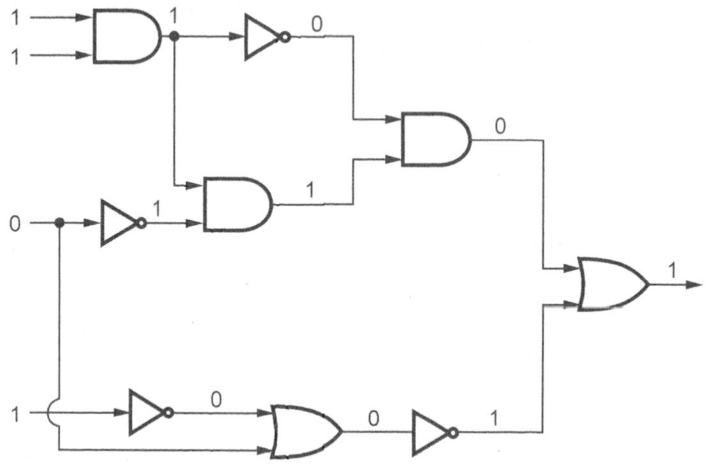

Fig. 9.4.1

The logic gates that used are -

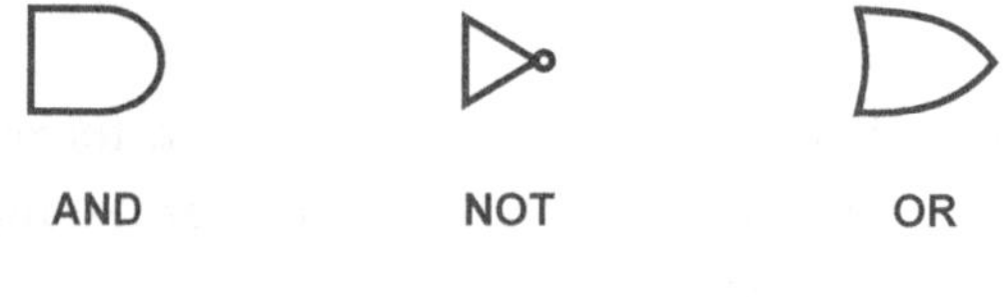

Fig. 9.4.2

Let us construct a non-deterministic algorithm. Which works in polynomial time. Then we should have **choose ( )** method which can guess the values of input node as well as the output, then the algorithm says "no" if we get output of Boolean circuit as 0. Similarly the algorithm says "yes" if we get output of Boolean circuit as 1.

Now from the output of algorithm we can guess the inputs to logic gates in the circuit. If the algorithm has output "yes" then we can say that Boolean circuit has satisfying input values. Thus we can say that CIRCUIT-SAT is in NP.

Theorem : CNF - SAT is in NP complete.

Proof : Let S be the Boolean formula for which we can construct a simple non-deterministic algorithm which can guess the values of variables in Boolean formula and then evaluates each clause of S. If all the clauses evaluate S to 1 then S is satisfied. Thus CNF - SAT is in NP-complete.

2. A 3SAT problem

A 3SAT problem is a problem which takes a Boolean formula S in CNF form with each clause having **exactly three literals** and check whether S is satisfied or not. [Note that CNF means each literal is ORed to form a clause and each clause is ANDed to form Boolean formula S].

Following formula is an instance of 3SAT problem :

$(\bar{a} + b + \bar{g})\ (c + \bar{e} + f)\ (\bar{b} + d + \bar{f})\ (a + e + \bar{h})$

Theorem : 3SAT is in NP complete.

Proof : Let S be the Boolean formula having 3 literals in each clause for which we can construct a simple non-deterministic algorithm which can guess an assignment of Boolean values to S. If the S is evaluated as 1 then S is satisfied. Thus we can prove that 3SAT is in NP-complete.

9.4.2 Clique Problem

Clique is nothing but a maximal complete subgraph of a graph G. The graph G is a set of (V, E) where V is a set of vertices and E is a set of edges. The size of Clique is number of vertices present in it.

For example :

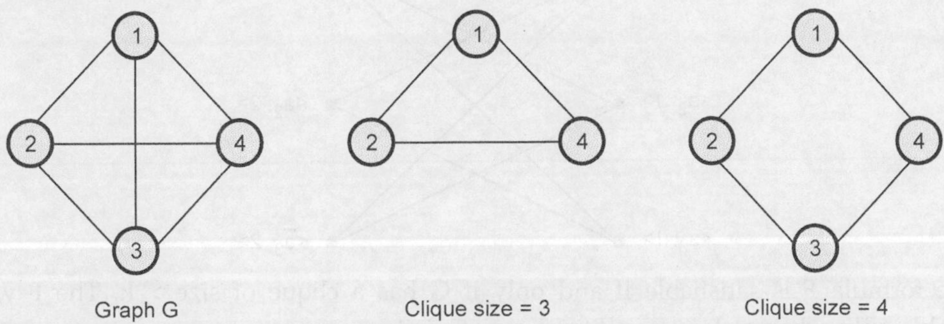

Graph G   Clique size = 3   Clique size = 4

Note that Clique of size = 3 and 4 are complete subgraph of graph G.

Max Clique Problem - It is an optimization problem in which the largest size Clique is to be obtained.

In the decision problem of Clique, we have to determine whether G has a Clique of size at least k for given k.

Let, DClique (G, k) is a deterministic decision algorithm for determining whether graph G has Clique or not of size atleast k. Then we have to apply DClique for k = n, n – 1, n – 2,... until the output is 1. The max Clique can be obtained in time $\leq n \cdot F(n)$

where F(n) is the time complexity of DClique. If Clique decision problem is solved in **polynomial time** then **max Clique** problem can be solved in **polynomial time**.

Theorem : The Clique Decision Problem (CDP) is NP-complete.

Proof : Let, F be a formula for CNF which is satisfiable.

$$F = C_1 \wedge C_2 \wedge \ldots C_k$$

where C is a clause. Every clause in CNF is denoted by a_i where $1 \leq i \leq n$. If length of F is F and is obtained in time O(m) then we can obtain polynomial time algorithm in CDP.

Let us design a graph G = (V, E) with set of vertices

$V = \{< \sigma, i > | \sigma$ is a literal in $C_i\}$ and set of edges

$E = \{ (< \sigma, i >, < \delta, j >) | i \neq j \text{ and } \sigma \neq \bar{\delta} \}$

For example

$$F = \left(\underbrace{(a_1 \vee a_2 \vee a_3)}_{C_1} \right) \wedge \left(\underbrace{(\bar{a}_1 \vee \bar{a}_2 \vee \bar{a}_3)}_{C_2} \right)$$

The graph G can be drawn as follows

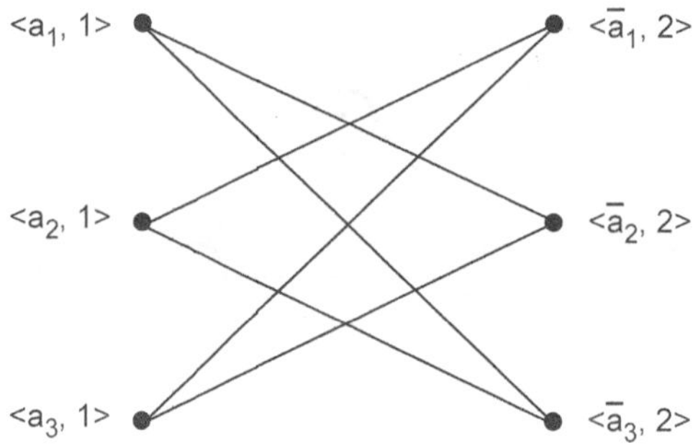

The formula F is satisfiable if and only if G has a clique of size > k. The F will be satisfiable only when at least one literal σ in C_i is true.

Thus the graph as six cliques of size two. Note that F is satisfiable as well.

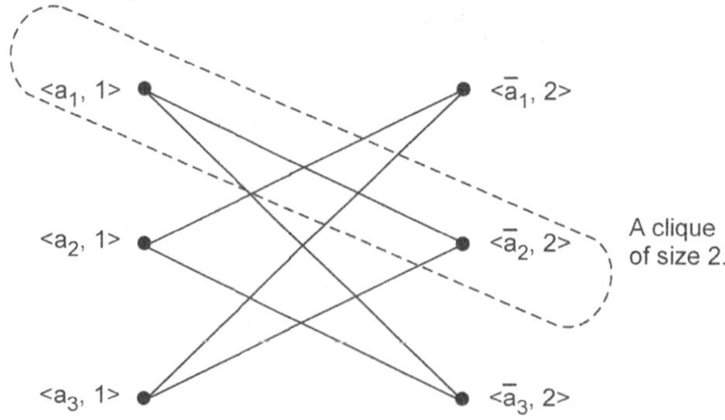

As CNF satisfiability is NP complete CDP is also NP complete.

9.4.3 Vertex Cover

The vertex cover problem is to find vertex cover of minimum size in a given graph. The word vertex cover means each vertex covers its incident edges. Thus by vertex cover we expect to choose the set of vertices which cover all the edges in a graph.

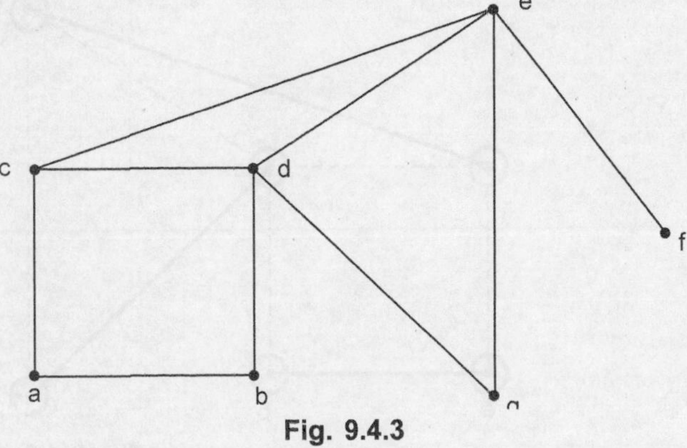

Fig. 9.4.3

For example : consider a graph G as given below.

Now we will select some arbitrary edge and delete all the incident edges. Repeat this process until all the incident edges get deleted.

Step 1 : Select an edge a-b and delete all the incident edges to vertex a or b.

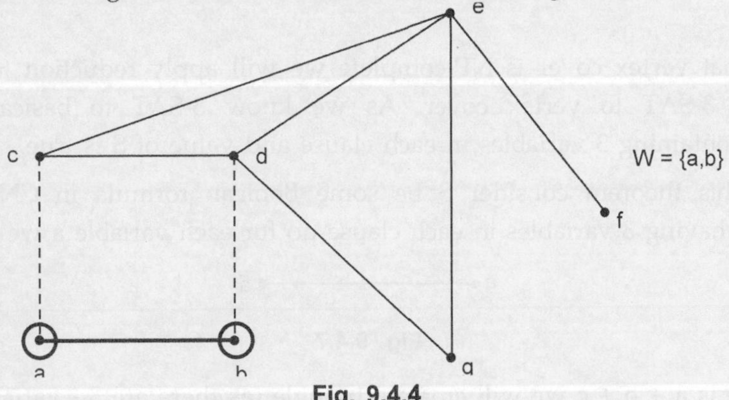

Fig. 9.4.4

Step 2 : Select an edge c-e and delete all the incident edges to vertex c or e.

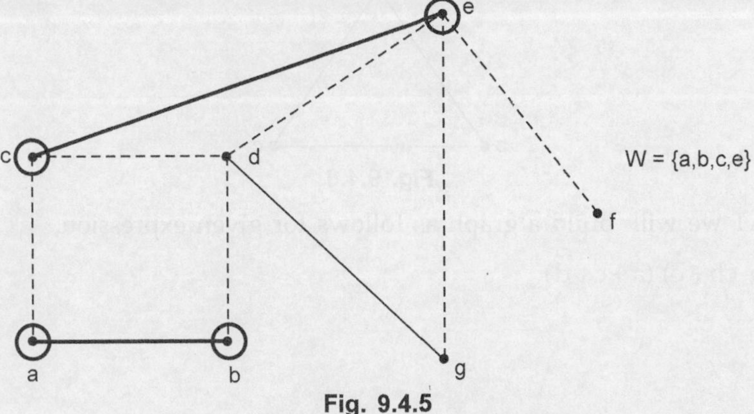

Fig. 9.4.5

Step 3 : Select an edge d-g. All the incident edges are already deleted.

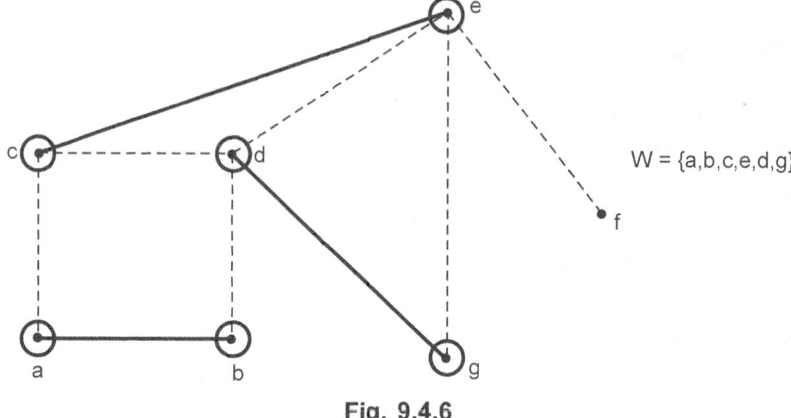

Fig. 9.4.6

Thus we obtain vertex cover as {a, b, c, d, e, g}.

Theorem :

The vertex cover is NP-complete.

Proof :

To prove that vertex cover is NP-complete we will apply reduction technique. That means reduce 3-SAT to vertex cover. As we know 3-SAT to basically a Boolean expression s containing 3 variables in each clause and value of S is true.

To prove this theorem consider S be some Boolean formula in CNF (conjunctive Normal Form) having 3 variables in each clause no for each variable a we will create,

$a \bullet \!\!-\!\!-\!\!-\!\!-\!\!-\!\!-\!\! \bullet \bar{a}$

Fig. 9.4.7

If the clause is a + b + c we will create a triangle (as there are 3 - variables)

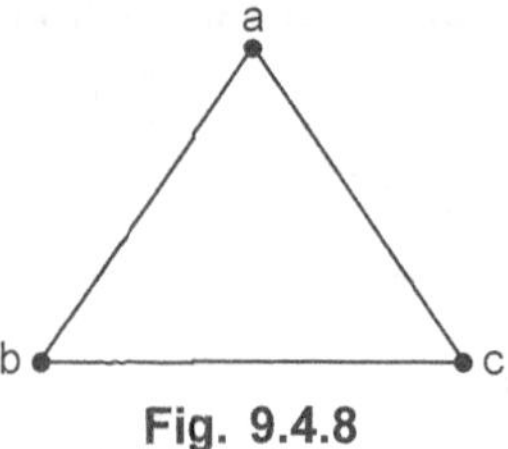

Fig. 9.4.8

Using 3-SAT we will build a graph as follows for given expression.

$(a+b+c)\ (a+b+\bar{c})\ (\bar{a}+c+\bar{d})$

The graph has vertex cover of size K = n + 2m, where n is number of variables in 3-SAT, m is number of clauses in CNF, K is total number of vertices that are present in the set of vertex cover.

For a clause (a + b + c) we can build a graph as :

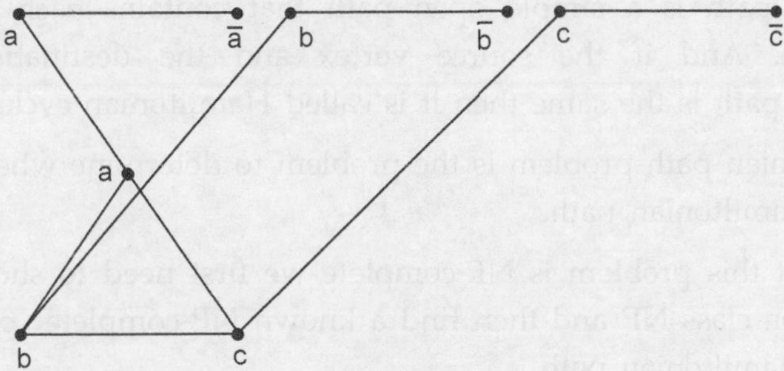

Fig. 9.4.9

Thus for given expression $(a+b+c)\ (a+b+\bar{c})\ (\bar{a}+c+\bar{d})$ we get following graph.

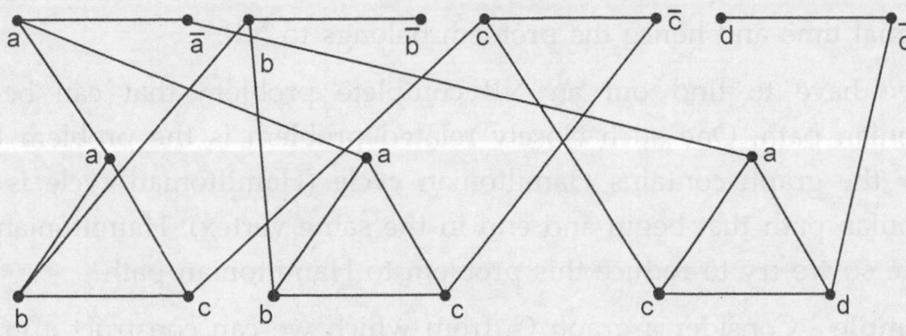

Fig. 9.4.10

Here n = Number of variable = 4

m = Number of clauses = 3

∴ K = n + 2m = 4 + 2(3) = 10

In vertex cover we get K = 10 vertices which cover all the vertices. The vertex cover is shown by following graph in which the covering vertices are rounded.

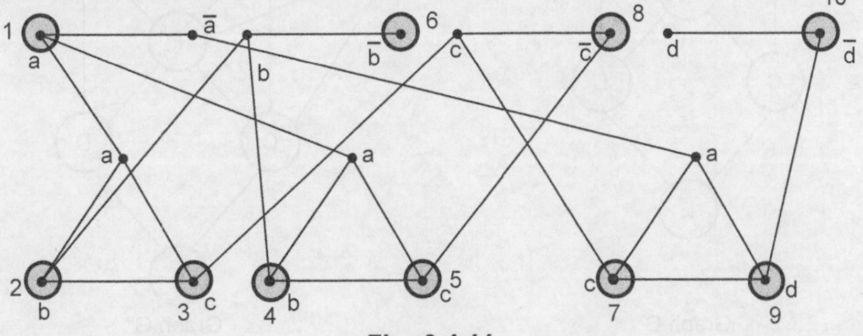

Fig. 9.4.11

Thus K = n + 2m is proved as K = 10. This is how 3-SAT can be reduced to vertex cover. The 3-SAT is NP-complete. Hence vertex is NP-complete is proved.

9.4.4 Hamiltonian Problem

- Hamiltonian path is a simple open path that contains each vertex in a graph exactly once. And if the source vertex and the destination vertex of this Hamiltonian path is the same then it is called Hamiltonian cycle.
- The Hamiltonian path problem is the problem to determine whether a given graph contains a Hamiltonian path.
- To show that this problem is NP-complete we first need to show that it actually belongs to the class NP and then find a known NP-complete problem that can be reduced to Hamiltonian path.
- For a given graph G we can solve Hamiltonian path by deterministically choosing edges from G that are to be included in the path. Then we traverse the path and make sure that we visit each vertex exactly once. This obviously can be done in polynomial time and hence the problem belongs to NP.
- Now we have to find out an NP complete problem that can be reduced to Hamiltonian path. One such closely related problem is the problem to determine whether the graph contains Hamiltonian cycle (Hamiltonian cycle is basically an Hamiltonian path that begin and end in the same vertex). Hamiltonian cycle is NP complete so we try to reduce this problem to Hamiltonian path.
- **For example** - Consider a graph G, from which we can construct a graph G'' such that G contains a Hamiltonian cycle if and only if G'' contains Hamiltonian path.

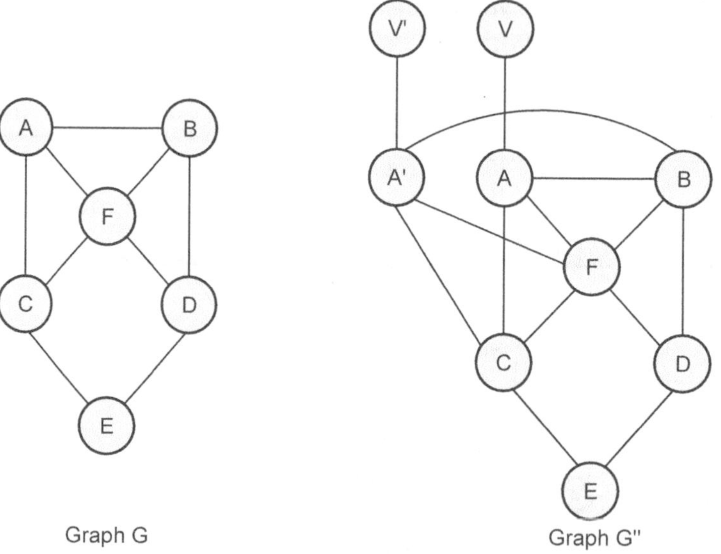

Fig. 9.4.12

- For instance in graph G the Hamiltonian cycle is A-B-D-E-C-F-A and G'' contains the Hamiltonian path V- A-B-D-E-C-F-A'-V'.
- Conversely if G'' contains Hamiltonian path then we can convert it to the Hamiltonian cycle present in G by removing the end points V and V' and mapping A' to A.
- Thus we can show that G contains Hamiltonian cycle if and only if G'' contains Hamiltonian path which concludes the proof that Hamiltonian path is NP Complete.

9.5 P, NP Complete and NP-Hard Problems

GTU : Dec.-10, June-11, Summer-13, Winter-15, Marks 7

- As we know, P denotes the class of all deterministic polynomial language problems and NP denotes the class of all non-deterministic polynomial language problems. Hence,

  $$P \subseteq NP.$$

- The question of whether or not

  $$P = NP$$

  holds, is the most famous outstanding problem in the computer science.
- Problems which are known to lie in P are often called as *tractable*. Problems which lie outside of P are often termed as *intractable*. Thus, the question of whether $P = NP$ or $P \neq NP$ is the same as that of asking whether there exist problems in NP which are intractable or not.

The relationship between P and NP is depicted by Fig. 9.5.1.

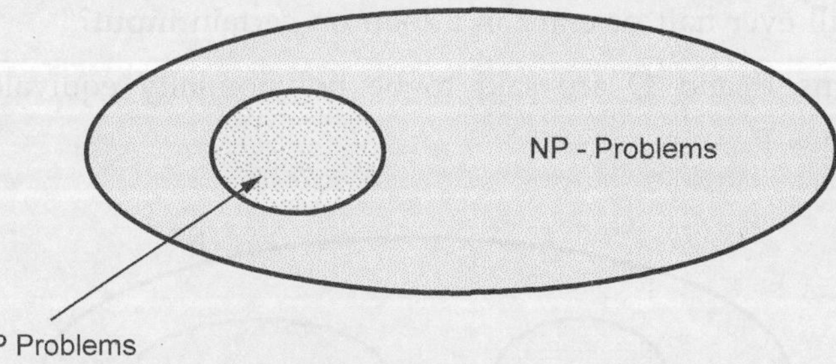

Fig. 9.5.1 P and NP problems assuming $P \neq NP$

- We don't know if $P = NP$. However in 1971, S. A. Cook proved that a particular NP problem known as SAT(Satisfiability of sets of Boolean clauses) has the property that, if it is solvable in polynomial time, so are all NP problems. This is called a "NP complete" problem.

- Let A and B are two problems then problem A reduces to B if and only if there is a way to solve A by deterministic polynomial time algorithm using a deterministic algorithm that solves B in polynomial time.

  A reduces to B can be denoted as $A \propto B$. In other words we can say that if there exists any polynomial time algorithm which solves B then we can solve A in polynomial time. We can also state that if $A \propto B$ and $B \propto C$ then $A \propto C$.

- A NP problem such that, if it is in P, then NP = P. If a (not necessarily NP) problem has this same property then it is called "NP-hard". Thus the class of NP-complete problem is the intersection of the NP and NP-hard classes.

- Normally the decision problems are NP-complete but optimization problems are NP-hard. However if problem A is a decision problem and B is optimization problem then it is possible that $A \propto B$. For instance the Knapsack decision problem can be Knapsack optimization problem.

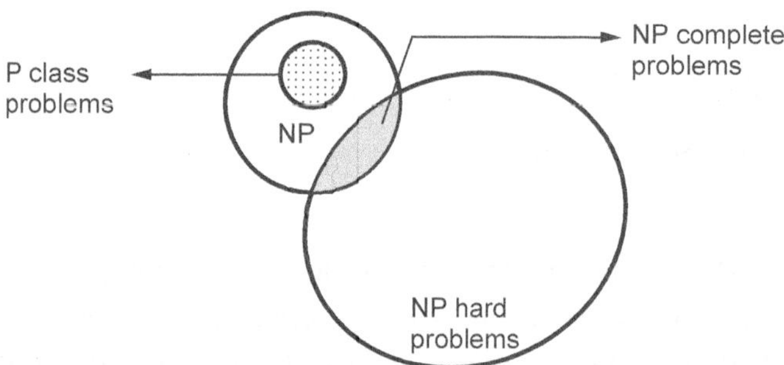

Fig. 9.5.2 Relationship between P, NP, NP-complete and NP-hard problems

- There are some NP-hard problems that are not NP-complete. For example *halting problem.* The halting problem states that : "Is it possible to determine whether an algorithm will ever halt or enter in a loop on certain input?"

- Two problems P and Q are said to be polynomially equivalent if and only if $P \propto Q$ and $Q \propto P$.

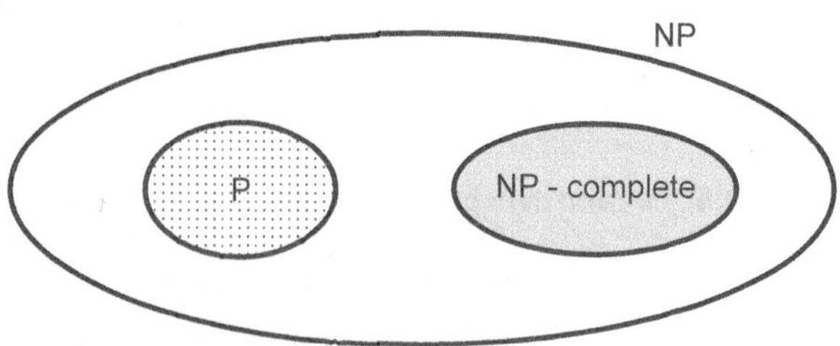

Fig. 9.5.3

Review Questions

1. *Compare NP-hard with NP-complete problems.* **GTU : Dec.-10, Marks 4**
2. *Define P, NP, NP complete and NP-hard problems.* **GTU : June-11, Marks 4**
3. *Explain P, Np and NP complete problems.* **GTU : Summer-13, Marks 3**
4. *Define P, NP, NP complete and NP-Hard problems. Give examples of each.* **GTU : Winter-15, Marks 7**

9.6 NP Hard Problem

GTU : Winter-14, Marks 3

Definition : A problem A is said to be NP hard if an algorithm for solving problem A can be translated into the problem which solves NP-problem. NP hard problems are atleast as hard as any NP - problem.

Difference between NP Complete and NP Hard Problems

The NP complete has a property that it can be solved in polynomial time if and only if all other NP complete problems can also be solved in polynomial time.

If an NP-hard problem can be solved in polynomial time then all the NP complete problems can be solved in polynomial time.

All the NP complete problems are NP-hard but there are some NP hard problems that are not known to be NP complete.

Review Question

1. *Explain in brief : NP hard problem* **GTU : Winter-14, Marks 3**

9.7 Traveling Salesman Problem

The travelling salesman decision problem can be stated as follows - Given n number of cities and a travelling salesman has to visit each city. Then find the shortest tour so that the travelling salesman can visit each and every city only once.

Theorem : Prove that a directed Hamiltonian cycle $\propto$ the travelling salesman decision problem. **PU : May-08, Marks 2, Dec.-11**

Proof

The directed Hamiltonian cycle is a cycle in which each vertex of a directed graph is visited only once. To prove that directed Hamiltonian cycle (DHC) $\propto$ Travelling Salesperson Problem (TSP) we will apply following steps -

If there are two problems A and B and if we wish to prove that B is NP complete then -

1) Pick up a known NP complete problem A

2) Reduce A to B. This can be done in following steps

a) Describe a transformation that maps the instance of A to instance of B in such a manner that "yes" for B = "yes" for A.

b) Prove that this transformation runs in polynomial time.

3) This proves that problem B is also NP complete.

To prove that DHC $\propto$ TSP we will reduce Directed Hamiltonian cycle to undirected Hamiltonian Cycle. The conversion is as follows -

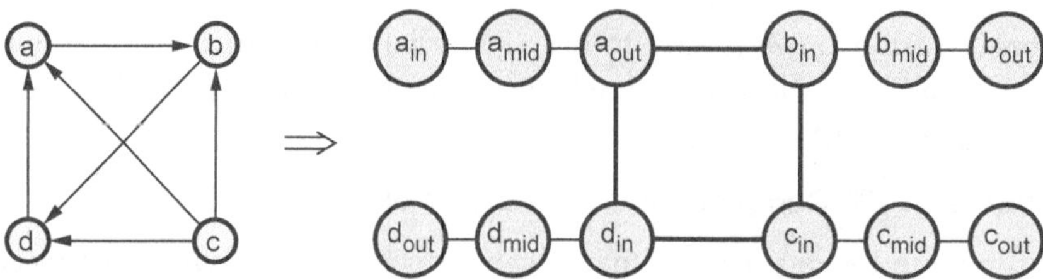

In this undirected graph if there exists a Hamiltonian cycle, then that denotes visiting cities in the order of nodes being visited in Hamiltonian cycle.

If no Hamiltonian cycle exists that means TSP has no solution. The Hamiltonian cycle problem is NP complete. This proves that TSP is also NP complete.

Review Question

1. *Prove that traveling salesman problem is NP complete.*

9.8 Approximation Algorithms

The approximation algorithms are algorithms used to find approximate solutions to optimization problems. Approximation algorithms are often associated with NP-hard problems because it is very difficult to get an efficient polynomial time exact algorithm for solving NP-hard problems. Note that approximate algorithms are mainly useful for solving those problems where exact polynomial algorithms are known but running such algorithm is too expensive because of their sizes of data sets. The philosophy behind approximation algorithm is *find 'good' solution fast.* That means you won't get the exact solution but you will get the approximate solution quickly. For approximation algorithm we start with inaccurate data, hence optimization may be as good as optimal solution. Hence approximation algorithms are based on heuristics (i.e. proceeding to solution by trial and error).

A **heuristics** can be defined as a collection of common sense rules defined from experience.

For example : In travelling salesperson problem going to next nearest city, or in knapsack problem start with highest value and minimum weight item.

Accuracy Ratio

It is always necessary to know the accuracy of approximation to the actual optimal solution. Hence accuracy ratio is defined as

$$r(s_a) = \frac{f(s_a)}{f(s^*)}$$

where s_a denotes approximate solution, $r(s_a)$ denotes accuracy ratio, $f(s_a)$ is a value of objective function for solution given by approximation algorithm, $f(s^*)$ is a value of objective function. Generally $r(s_a) >= 1$. When $r(s_a)$ reaches close to 1 then it is a better approximate solution.

Performance Ratio

The best upper bound on accuracy ratio taken over all instances of the problem is called performance ratio. It is denoted by R_A. By knowing performance ratio one can judge **quality** of approximation algorithm. The approximation algorithms with R_A value nearer to 1 is supposed to be a better approximation algorithm.

c-Approximation Algorithm

If there exists a value c which is $>= 1$ and $r(s_a) \leq c$ for all instances of problem then that algorithm is called c-approximation algorithm. If c value is 1 then corresponding c-approximation algorithms are good. For a c-approximation algorithm for any instance of problem is -

$$f(s_a) \leq c\, f(s^*)$$

9.8.1 Approximation Algorithms for the Travelling Salesperson Problem

The travelling salesman problem is based on the idea of obtaining optimum tour when travelling between many cities. The decision version of this algorithm belongs to a class of NP-complete problem and optimization version of this algorithm belongs to NP-hard class of problems. There are two approximation algorithms used for TSP : A NP-hard class of problem and those are

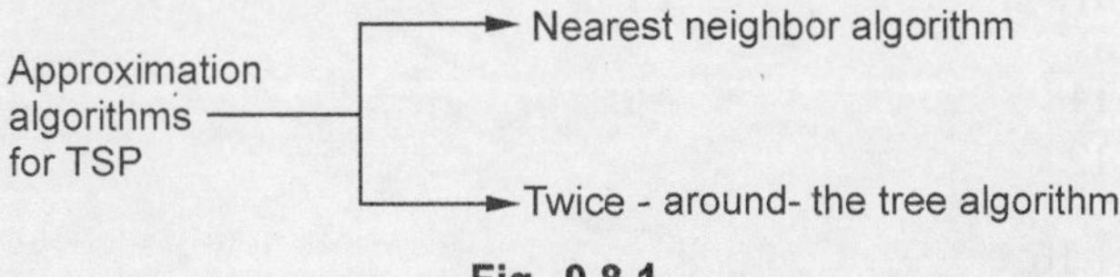

Fig. 9.8.1

Let us discuss each algorithm with some simple example.

1. Nearest neighbor algorithm

This algorithm is based on the idea of choosing nearest-neighbor while travelling from one city to another. This nearest neighbor should be unvisited one. Let see the algorithm.

1. Start at any arbitrary city.
2. Repeat until all the nodes are visited : Go to the nearest city (the unvisited one) each time.
3. Return to the starting city.

Let us apply this algorithm on some example.

Example 9.8.1 *Using nearest-neighbor algorithm, obtain the optimal solution for given travelling salesman problem. Also find the accuracy ratio for the same.*

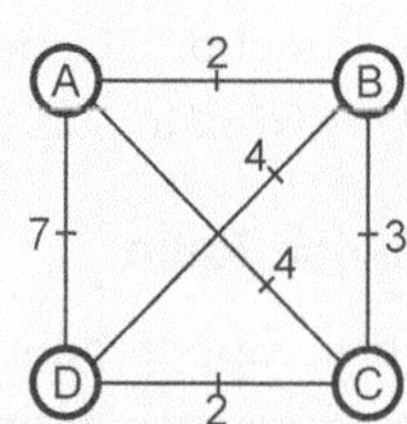

Fig. 9.8.2

Solution : We will apply nearest neighbor algorithm for the tour for given traveling salesman problem. Hence nearest neighbor will produce :

A-B-C-D-A.,

∴ $s_a = 2 + 3 + 2 + 7$

i.e. $s_a = \mathbf{14}$

Now the optimal solution can be obtained by exhaustive search. Then tour will be:

A-B-D-C-A

∴ $s^* = 2 + 4 + 2 + 4$

$s^* = \mathbf{12}$

The accuracy ratio $r(s_a)$ will be -

$$r(s_a) = \frac{f(s_a)}{f(s^*)}$$

$$= \frac{14}{12}$$

$$r(s_a) = 1.16$$

Hence the tour s_a is 16 % longer than optimum tour s*.

This algorithm is **simple** to use but it has some drawback. The major drawback of this method is that there may exist some **long path** which has to be traversed to return to the starting city (Note that we will go on choosing small distance of the neighbours but to return back to starting point there may not be short path and in such a case we have to traverse a long distance only !). For instance, in above discussed example in the tour A-B-C-D-A, the distance D-A will plays an important role (i.e. edge A-D), hence accuracy ratio $r(s_a)$ will be

$$r(s_a) = \frac{f(s_a)}{f(s^*)}$$

$$r(s_a) = \frac{7+w}{12} \quad \text{where w is the distance (A-D).}$$

As value of w increases, $r(s_a)$ increases. For larger value of w, $r(s_a)$ tends to ∞. Hence our approximation algorithm will fail to obtain the optimal solution.

2. Twice around-the-tree algorithm

This algorithm is based on important subset instance called **Euclidean** by which accuracy for the nearest neighbor algorithm can be obtained -

Eudidiean instances satisfy following conditions -

1. Triangle inequality

dist [i, j] ≤ dist [i, k] + dist [k, j]

where i, j and k denote cities.

2. Symmetry

dist [i, j] = dist [j, i]

The distance from city i to j should be same as distance between city j to i.

The Eudidiean instances satisfy following conditions about the accuracy ratio

$$r(s_a) \text{ i.e. } = \frac{f(s_a)}{f(s^*)} \leq \frac{1}{2}\left(\lceil \log_2 n \rceil + 1\right)$$

where n is total number of cities.

Now let us discuss another approximation algorithm i.e. twice-around-the tree algorithm. This is a 2-approximation (i.e. c-approximation with c to be 2) algorithm for travelling salesman problem with Euclidean distances.

Algorithm

1. Compute minimum spanning tree from the given graph.

2. Start at any arbitrary city and walk around the tree (i.e. depth first search) and record nodes visited.
3. Eliminate duplicates from the generated node list.

Example : Consider the graph as given below and apply the twice-around-the-tree algorithm.

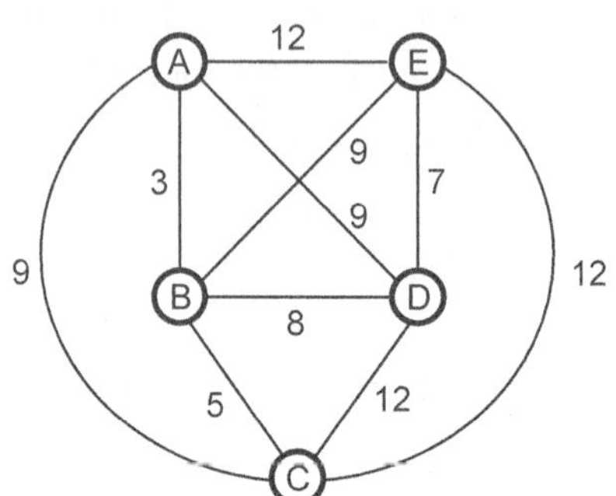

Fig. 9.8.3

Step 1 : Now we will obtain the Minimum Spanning Tree (MST) for given graph.

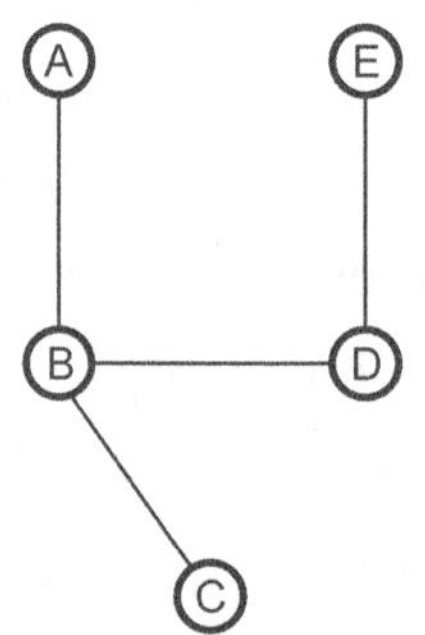

Fig. 9.8.4

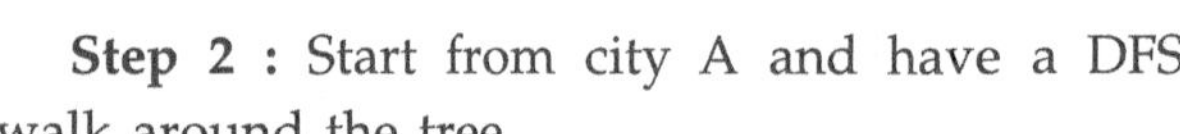

Step 2 : Start from city A and have a DFS walk around the tree.

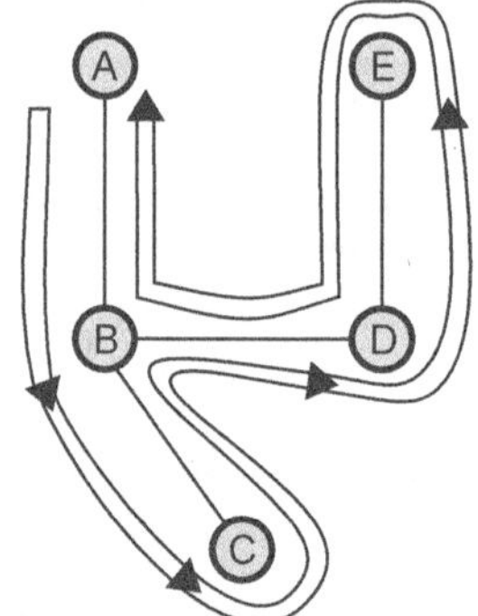

Fig. 9.8.5

Step 3 : Record the visited nodes A - B - C - B - D - E - D - B - A. Eliminate duplicates then A-B-C-D-E-A . This basically gives Hamiltonian circuit.

But the tour obtained is not the optimal tour.

9.9 University Questions with Answers

Regulation 2008

Dec. 2010

Q.1 *Explain P and NP problems giving examples.* **[Refer section 9.1]** [6]

Q.2 *Compare NP-hard with NP-complete problems.* **[Refer section 9.5]** [4]

May 2011

Q.3 *What is polynomially turing reducible problem ? Explain with example how problem A can be polynomially turing reduced to problem B.* **[Refer section 9.3]** [6]

Q.4 *Define P, NP, NP complete and NP-hard problems.* **[Refer section 9.5]** [4]

Dec. 2011

Q.5 *Explain polynomial reduction.* **[Refer section 9.3]** [3]

May 2013

Q.6 *Explain P, Np and NP complete problems.* **[Refer section 9.5]** [3]

Dec. 2014

Q.7 *What is polynomially turing reducible problem ? Explain with example how problem A can be polynomially turing reduced to problem B.* **[Refer section 9.3]** [7]

Q.8 *Explain polynomial reduction.* **[Refer section 9.3]** [3]

Q.9 *Explain in brief : NP hard problem.* **[Refer section 9.6]** [3]

Summer 2015

Q.10 *Explain class P and class NP.* **[Refer section 9.1]** [4]

Regulation 2013

Winter 2015

Q.11 *Define P, NP, NP complete and NP-Hard problems. Give examples of each.* **[Refer sections 9.1 and 9.6]** [7]

9.10 Short Questions and Answers

Q.1 What is decision problem ?

Ans. : Any problem for which answer is either yes or no is called decision problem.

Q.2 What is decision algorithm ?

Ans. : The algorithm used to solve the decision problem is called decision algorithm.

Q.3 What is optimization problem ?

Ans. : Any problem that involves the identification of optimal cost is called optimization problem.

Q.4 What is P class problems ?

Ans. : The problems that can be solved in polynomial time are called P class problems.

Q.5 What is NP class problems ?

Ans. : The problems that can be solved in non deterministic polynomial time are called NP class problems.

Q.6 Give examples of P and NP class problems.

Ans. : Examples of P class problems - Binary search method, sorting techniques.

Examples of NP class problems - Traveling Salesperson Problem, Hamiltonian circuit problem.

Q.7 Define NP Complete problems.

Ans. : A problem D is called NP-complete if - i) It belongs to class NP ii) Every problem in NP can also be solved in polynomial time.

Q.8 What is computational complexity?

Ans. : The computational problems is an infinite collection of instances with a solution for every instance. The computational complexity can be classified into P class and NP class problems.

Q.9 List out the type of problems involved in complexity classes

Ans. : The complexity classes involve functional problems, P classes, NP classes, optimization problems.

Q.10 What is the use of polynomial time reduction?

Ans. : To prove whether particular problem is NP complete or not we use polynomial time reducibility.

Q.11 What is Boolean Formula?

Ans. : The Boolean formula has various Boolean operations such as OR(+), AND ( ) and NOT.

Q.12 What is CNF-SAT ?

Ans. : The CNF-SAT stands for Conjuctive Normal Form Satisfiability. The CNF-SAT is a problem which takes Boolean formula in CNF form and checks whether any assignment is there to Boolean values so that formula evaluates to 1. For example -

$$(\bar{a} + b + d + \bar{g})\ (c + \bar{e})\ (\bar{b} + d + \bar{f} + h)\ (a + c + e + \bar{h})$$

This formula evaluates to 1 if b, c, d are 1.

Q.13 When a problem is said to be NP hard ?

Ans. : A problem A is said to be NP hard if an algorithm for solving problem A can be translated into the problem which solves NP-problem. NP hard problems are atleast as hard as any NP-problem.

Q.14 What is non deterministic polynomial time ?

Ans. : The polynomial time means the complexity of algorithm can be expressed in deterministic polynomial time. The nondeterministically polynomial time is the time required by the algorithm to execute which can not be expressed in polynomial time.

Example : Travelling salesperson problem, Knapsack problem.

Q.15 Differentiate between "polynomial" and "nondeterministically polynomial".

Ans. : Polynomial : An algorithm is called polynomial time algorithm (P-class) when for given input the same output is generated for a function. This is deterministic algorithm.

Non-deterministically polynomial : An algorithm is called non deterministically polynomial time algorithm (NP class) when for given input there are more than one paths that the algorithm can follow. Due to this one can not determine which path is to be followed after a particular stage. All the NP class problems are basically non deterministic.

Notes

Analysis & Design of Algorithms Lab

Contents

Experiment 1(a) : Implementation of Bubble Sort

Solution :

```
#include<stdio.h>
#include<conio.h>
int n;
void main( )
{
 int i,A[10];
 void bubble(int A[10]);
 clrscr( );
printf("\n\t\t Bubble Sort\n");
 printf("\n How many elements are there?");
 scanf("%d",&n);
 printf("\n Enter the elements\n");
 for(i=0;i<n;i++)
    scanf("%d",&A[i]);
    bubble(A);

 getch( );
}
void bubble(int A[10])
{
 int i,j,temp;
 for(i=0;i<=n-2;i++)
 {
    for(j=0;j<=n-2-i;j++)
    {
    if(A[j]>A[j+1])
    {
     temp=A[j];
     A[j]=A[j+1];
     A[j+1]=temp;
    }
 }
}
 printf("\n The sorted List is ...\n");
 for(i=0;i<n;i++)
```

```
    printf("  %d",A[i]);
}
```

Output

```
Bubble Sort
 How many elements are there?7

 Enter the elements
70
30
20
50
60
10
40

 The sorted List is ...
   10  20  30  40  50  60  70
```

Experiment 1(b) : Implementation of Insertion Sort

Solution :

```
/*************************************************************
Implementation of insertion sort
*************************************************************/
#include<stdio.h>
#include<conio.h>
void main( )
{
 int A[10],n,i;
 void Insert_sort(int A[10],int n);
 clrscr( );
 printf("\n\t\t Insertion Sort");
printf("\n How many elements are there?");
 scanf("%d",&n);
 printf("\n Enter the elements\n");
 for(i=0;i<n;i++)
    scanf("%d",&A[i]);
 Insert_sort(A,n);
 getch();
}
```

```
void Insert_sort(int A[10],int n)
{
 int i,j,temp;
 for(i=1;i<=n-1;i++)
 {
   temp=A[i];
   j=i-1;
   while( (j>=0)&&(A[j]>temp))
   {
    A[j+1]=A[j];
    j=j-1;
   }
   A[j+1]=temp;
 }
 printf("\n The sorted list of elements is...\n");
 for(i=0;i<n;i++)
   printf("\n%d",A[i]);
}
```

Output

```
Insertion Sort
How many elements are there?5

 Enter the elements
30
20
10
40
50
 The sorted list of elements is...
10
20
30
40
50
```

Experiment 1(c) : Implementation of Merge Sort

Solution :

```
#include<conio.h>
#include<stdio.h>
```

```
#include<stdlib.h>
int n;
void main()
{
    int i,low,high;
    int A[10];
    void MergeSort(int A[10],int low,int high);
    void Display(int A[10]);
    clrscr();
    printf("\n\t\t Merge Sort \n");
    printf("\n Enter the length of list:");
    scanf("%d",&n);
    printf("\n Enter list elements:");
    for(i=0;i<n;i++)
    scanf("%d",&A[i]);
    low=0;
    high=n-1;
    MergeSort(A,low,high);
    Display(A);
    getch();
}
/*
 This function is to split the list into sublists
*/
void MergeSort(int A[10],int low,int high)
{
    int mid;
    void Combine(int A[10],int low,int mid,int high);
    if(low < high)
    {
      mid = (low+high)/2;//split the list at mid
      MergeSort(A,low,mid);//first sublist
      MergeSort(A,mid+1,high);//second sublist
      Combine(A,low,mid,high);//merging of two sublists
    }
}
/* This function is for merging the two sublists*/
void Combine(int A[10],int low,int mid,int high)
```

```
{
    int i,j,k;
    int temp[10];
    k=low;
    i=low;
    j=mid+1;
    while(i <= mid && j <= high)
    {
     if(A[i]<=A[j])
   {
        temp[k]=A[i];
        i++;
        k++;
     }
     else
      {
          temp[k]=A[j];
          j++;
          k++;
      }
     }

     while(i<=mid)
     {
          temp[k]=A[i];
          i++;
          k++;
     }
     while(j<=high)
     {
          temp[k]=A[j];
          j++;
          k++;
     }
     //copy the elements from temp array to A
     for(k=low;k<=high;k++)
          A[k]=temp[k];
```

We compare elements from left sublist and right sublist. If element in the left sublist is lesser than the element in the right sublist then copy that smaller element of left sublist to **temp** array

We compare elements from left sublist and right sublist. If element in the right sublist is lesser than the element in the left sublist then copy that smaller element of right sublist to **temp** array

Reached at the end of right sublist and elements of left sublist are remaining, then copy the remaining elements of left sublist to **temp**

Reached at the end of left sublist and elements of right sublist are remaining, then copy the remaining elements of right sublist to **temp**

```
}
/* function to display sorted array */
void Display(int A[10])
{
        int i;
        printf("\n\n The Sorted Array Is ...\n");
        for(i=0;i<n;i++)
            printf("%d\t",A[i]);
}
```

Output

```
Merge Sort

 Enter the length of list :7

 Enter list elements :
70
20
30
40
10
50
60
 The Sorted Array Is ...
10      20      30      40      50      60      70
```

Experiment 1(d) : Implementation of Quick Sort

```
/*************************************************************
Program to sort the elements in ascending order using Quick Sort.
*************************************************************/
#include<stdio.h>
#include<conio.h>
#include<dos.h>
#include<stdlib.h>

#define SIZE 10
void Quick(int A[SIZE],int,int);
int Partition(int A[SIZE],int,int);
void swap(int A[SIZE],int *,int *);
```

```
int n;
int main()
{
        int i;
        int A[SIZE];
        printf("\n\t\t Quick Sort Method \n");
        printf("\n Generating the list using the random numbers");
        srand(10000);
        n=10;
        for (i = 0; i < n; i++)
        {
         int val = n * ((float)rand() / ((float)RAND_MAX +(float) 1));
         A[i] = val;
        }
        printf("\n The Original List is\n");
        for (i = 0; i < n; i++)
         printf(" %d",A[i]);
        Quick(A,0,n-1);

        printf("\n\n\t Sorted Array Is: \n");
        for(i=0;i<n;i++)
         printf(" %d",A[i]);
        return 0;
}

/*
This function is to sort the elements in a sublist
*/
void Quick(int A[SIZE],int low,int high)
{
        int m,i;
        if(low<high)
        {
          m=Partition(A,low,high);//setting pivot element
          Quick(A,low,m-1);//splitting of list
          Quick(A,m+1,high);//splitting  of list
        }
```

```
}
/*
This function is to partition a list and decide the pivot
element
*/
int Partition(int A[SIZE],int low,int high)
{
        int pivot=A[low],i=low,j=high;
        while(i<=j)
        {
         while(A[i]<=pivot)
            i++;
         while(A[j]>pivot)
            j—;
         if(i<j)
            swap(A,&i,&j);
        }
        swap(A,&low,&j);
        return j;
}

void swap(int A[SIZE],int *i,int *j)
{
        int temp;

        temp=A[*i];
        A[*i]=A[*j];
        A[*j]=temp;
}
```

Output

```
        Quick Sort Method

 Generating the list using the random numbers
 The Original List is
 6 1 7 6 4 1 8 6 7 2

        Sorted Array Is:
 1 1 2 4 6 6 6 7 7 8
```

Experiment 2(a) : Implementation of Linear Search

Solution :

```
#include<stdio.h>
#include<conio.h>
void Seq_Search(int a[10],int n,int key)
{
 int i,flag=0,mark;
 for(i=0;i<n;i++)
 { //searching element from beginning of array
  if(a[i]==key)
  {
   flag=1;//setting the flag if element found
   mark=i;//marking the location of key element
   break;
  }
 }
 if(flag==1)//flag=1 means element is found
  printf("\n The element is present at location: %d",mark+1);
 else
  printf("\n The element is not present in the array");

}
void main( )
{
 int key,a[10],i,n;
 clrscr( );
 printf("\n How Many Elements are there in an array? ");
 scanf("%d",&n);
 printf("\n Enter the elements ");
 for(i=0;i<n;i++)
  scanf("%d",&a[i]);
 printf("\n\t Enter the element which is to be searched ");
 scanf("%d",&key);
 Seq_Search(a,n,key);
 getch( );
}
```

Output

```
How Many Elements are there in an array? 7

Enter the elements
20
10
50
40
60
30
70

    Enter the element which is to be searched 60

The element is present at location: 5
```

Experiment 2(b) : Implementation of Binary Search

Solution :

(i) Recursive Binary Search

```
/*************************************************************
Implementation of recursive Binary Search algorithm
*************************************************************/
#include<stdio.h>
#include<conio.h>
#define SIZE 10
int n;
void main()
{
   int A[SIZE],KEY,i,flag,low,high;
   int BinSearch(int A[SIZE],int KEY,int low,int high);
   clrscr();
   printf("\n How Many elements in an array?");
   scanf("%d",&n);
   printf("\n Enter The Elements");
   for(i=0;i<n;i++)
      scanf("%d",&A[i]);
   printf("\n Enter the element which is to be searched");
```

```
    scanf("%d",&KEY);
    low=0;
    high=n-1;
    flag=BinSearch(A,KEY,low,high);
  printf("\n The element is at A[%d] location",flag);
  getch();
}
int BinSearch(int A[SIZE],int KEY,int low,int high)
{
  int m;
  m=(low+high)/2;    //mid of the array is obtained
  if(KEY==A[m])
       return m;
  else if(KEY<A[m])
       BinSearch(A,KEY,low,m-1);//search the left sub list
  else
        BinSearch(A,KEY,m+1,high);//search the right sub list
}
```

Output

```
How Many elements in an array? 5

Enter The Elements 10 20 30 40 50

Enter the element which is to be searched 20

The element is at A[1] location
```

(ii) Non Recursive Binary Search Program

```
/*****************************************************************
Implementation of non recursive Binary Search algorithm
*****************************************************************/
#include<stdio.h>
#include<conio.h>
#define SIZE 10
int n;
void main()
{
  int A[SIZE],KEY,i,flag;
  int BinSearch(int A[SIZE],int KEY);
```

```
 clrscr();
 printf("\n How Many elements in an array?");
 scanf("%d",&n);
 printf("\n Enter The Elements");
 for(i=0;i<n;i++)
   scanf("%d",&A[i]);
 printf("\n Enter the element which is to be searched");
 scanf("%d",&KEY);
 flag=BinSearch(A,KEY);
 if(flag==-1)
   printf("\n The Element is not present");
 else
   printf("\n The element is at A[%d] location",flag);
 getch();
}
int BinSearch(int A[SIZE],int KEY)
{
 int low,high,m;
 low=0;
 high=n-1;
 while(low<=high)
 {
       m=(low+high)/2; //mid of the array is obtained
       if(KEY==A[m])
           return m;
       else if(KEY<A[m])
           high=m-1;       //search the left sub list
       else
           low=m+1;        //search the right sub list
   }
   return-1; //if element is not present in the list
}
```

Output (Run 1)

How Many elements in an array? 6

Enter The Elements

10

20
30
40
50
60

Enter the element which is to be searched 50

The element is at A[4] location

(Run 2)

How Many elements in an array? 5

Enter The Elements
10
20
30
40
50
Enter the element which is to be searched 80

The Element is not present

Experiment 3 : Implementation of Max-heap Sort Algorithm

Soltion :

```
#include<stdio.h>
#include<stdlib.h>
#include<conio.h>
#define MAX 10
void main()
{
   int i,n;
   int arr[MAX];
   void makeheap(int arr[MAX],int n);
   void heapsort(int arr[MAX],int n);
   void display(int arr[MAX],int n);
   clrscr();
    for(i=0;i<MAX;i++)
```

```
        arr[i]=0;
    printf("\n How many elements you want to insert?");
    scanf("%d",&n);
    printf("\n Enter the elements");
    for(i=0;i<n;i++)
        scanf("%d",&arr[i]);
    printf("\n The Elements are ...");
    display(arr,n);
    makeheap(arr,n);
    printf("\n Heapified");
    display(arr,n);
    heapsort(arr,n);
    printf("\nElements sorted by Heap sort... ");
    display(arr,n);
    getch();
}

void makeheap(int arr[MAX],int n)
{
    int i,val,j,father;
    for(i=1;i<n;i++)
    {
        val=arr[i];
        j=i;
        father=(j-1)/2;//finding the parent of node j
        while(j>0&&arr[father]<val)//creating a MAX heap
        {
            arr[j]=arr[father];//preserving parent dominance
            j=father;
            father=(j-1)/2;
        }
        arr[j]=val;
    }
}
void heapsort(int arr[MAX],int n)
{
    int i,k,temp,j;
    for(i=n-1;i>0;i—)
```

```
        {
            temp=arr[i];
            arr[i]=arr[0];
            k=0;
            if(i==1)
               j=-1;
            else
              j=1;
        if(i>2&&arr[2]>arr[1])
             j=2;
        while(j>=0&& temp <arr[j])
        {
            arr[k]=arr[j];
            k=j;
            j=2*k+1;
            if(j+1<=i-1&&arr[j]<arr[j+1])
                j++;
            if(j>i-1)
                j=-1;
        }
            arr[k]=temp;
        }
}

void display(int arr[MAX],int n)
{
    int i;
    for(i=0;i<n;i++)
     printf("\n %d",arr[i]);

}
```

Output

```
 How many elements you want to insert?7

Enter the elements14
12
9
8
7
```

```
10
18

The Elements are ...
14
12
9
8
7
10
18
Heapified
18
12
14
8
7
9
10
Elements sorted by Heap sort...
  7
  8
  9
  10
  12
  14
  18
```

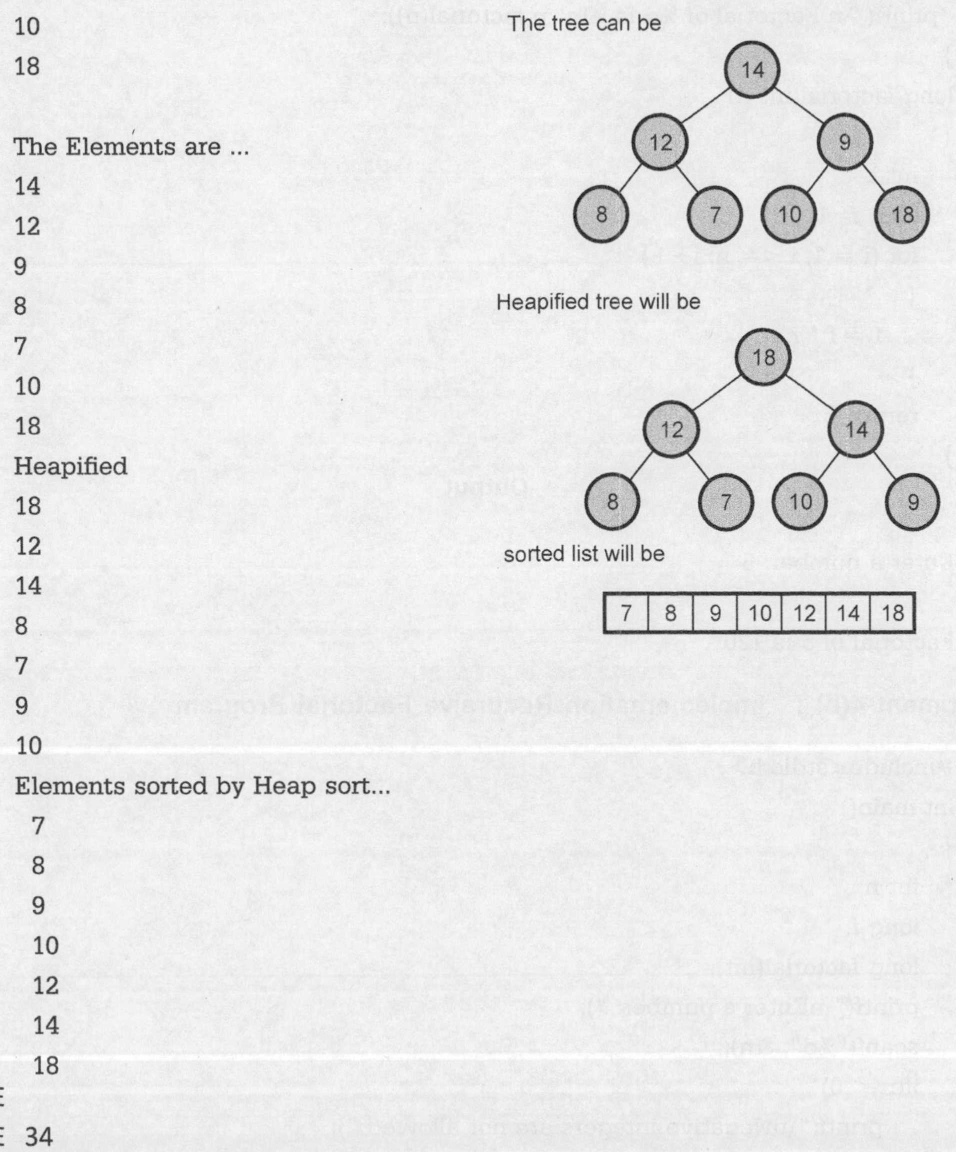

PAGE

PAGE 34

Experiment 4(a) : Implementation Iterative Factorial Program

```
#include <stdio.h>
void main(void)
{
  int n;
  long factorial(int n);
  printf("\nEnter a number: ");
  scanf("%d", &n);
```

```
    printf("\n Factorial of %d is %ld",n,factorial(n));
}
long factorial(int n)
{
    int i;
    long f=1;
    for (i = 1; i <= n; i++)
    {
        f = f * i;
    }
    return f;
}
```

Output

```
Enter a number: 5

Factorial of 5 is 120
```

Experiment 4(b) : Implementation Recursive Factorial Program

```
#include<stdio.h>
int main()
{
    int n;
    long f;
    long factorial(int);
    printf("\nEnter a number: ");
    scanf("%d", &n);
    if(n < 0)
        printf("\nNegative integers are not allowed.");
    else
    {
        f = factorial(n);
        printf("\n Factorial of %d = %ld",n,f);
    }
    return 0;
}
long factorial(int n)
{
 if (n == 0)
```

```
        return 1;
    else
        return(n * factorial(n-1));
}
```

Output

Enter a number: 5

Factorial of 5 = 120

Experiment 5 : Implementation of a Knapsack Problem using Dynamic Programming

```
/*****************************************************************
Implementation of 0/1 knapsack problem using Dynamic programming
*****************************************************************/
#include<stdio.h>
#include<conio.h>
#include<stdlib.h>
int table[5][6];

void main()
{
    int w[]={0,2,3,4,5};
    int v[]={0,3,4,5,6};
    int W=5;
    int n=4;
    int i;
    void DKP(int n,int W,int w[],int v[]);
    clrscr();
    printf("\n\t\t 0/1 Knapsack Problem using Dynamic Programming");
    printf("\n Given Data...\n");
    printf("\n w[i]    v[i]");
    printf("\n--------------------");
    for(i=1;i<=n;i++)
    printf("\n  %d       %d",w[i],v[i]);
    printf("\n\t\tCapacity=%d",W);
    printf("\n\n");
    /*initialization of table*/
    for(i=0;i<=n;i++)
```

```
    {
     for(int j=0;j<=W;j++)
     {
      table[i][j]=0;
     }
    DKP(n,W,w,v);
}
int max(int a,int b)
{
    if(a>b)
        return a;
     else
        return b;
}

void DKP(int n,int W,int w[5],int v[5])
{
      void find_item(int,int,int[]);
      int i,j;
      int val1,val2;
        for(i=0;i<=n;i++)
        {
         for(j=0;j<=W;j++)
         {
           table[i][0]=0;
           table[0][j]=0;
         }
        }
        for(i=1;i<=n;i++)
        {
         for(j=1;j<=W;j++)
         {
           if(j<w[i])
               table[i][j]=table[i-1][j];
           else if(j>=w[i])
           {
               val1=table[i-1][j];
```

```
          val2=v[i]+table[i-1][j-w[i]];
          table[i][j]=max(val1,val2);
        }
      }
      }
      printf("\n Table constructed using dynamic programming is ...\n");
      for(i=0;i<=n;i++)
      {
       for(j=0;j<=W;j++)
          printf(" %d",table[i][j]);
       printf("\n");
      }
   find_item(n,W,w);
}

void find_item(int i,int k,int w[5])
{
     printf("\nSolution for the Knapsack...");
     while(i>0 && k>0)
     {
       if(table[i][k]!=table[i-1][k])
       {
        printf("\nItem %d is selected",i);
        i=i-1;
        k=k-w[i];
       }
       else
          i=i-1;
     }
}
```

Output

```
          0/1 Knapsack Problem using Dynamic Programming
     Given Data...

     w[i]   v[i]
     ______________

     2      3
     3      4
```

```
4    5
5    6
          Capacity=5

Table constructed using dynamic programming is ...
0 0 0 0 0 0
0 0 3 3 3 3
0 0 3 4 4 7
0 0 3 4 5 7
0 0 3 4 5 7

Solution for the Knapsack...
Item 2 is selected
Item 1 is selected
```

Experiment 6 : Implementation of a Chain Matrix Multiplication using Dynamic Programming

Solution :

```
#include<stdio.h>
int main()
{
   int n,i,cost;
   int p[100];
   int s[20][20];
   int Matrix_chain(int s[20][20],int p[],int i,int j);
   void display_matrix_order(int s[20][20],int i,int j);

   printf("\nEnter the number of matrices: ");
   scanf("%d",&n);

   for(i=0;i<n+1;i++)
   {
      printf("\nEnter the dimension of the matrix: ");
      scanf("%d",&p[i]);
   }
   cost=Matrix_chain(s,p,1,n);
   printf("\nThe Optimal Cost: %d\n",cost);
   printf("\nThe Optimal Order :\t");
```

```
    display_matrix_order(s,1,n);

    return 0;

}


int Matrix_chain(int s[20][20],int p[],int i,int j)
{
  if(i==j)
    return 0;
  int k,count;
  int min=1000000;//infinity
  for (k=i;k<j;k++)
  {
    count=Matrix_chain(s,p,i,k)+Matrix_chain(s,p,k+1,j)+p[i-1]*p[k]*p[j];
    if(count<min)
    {
      min=count;
      s[i][j]=k;
    }
  }
  return min;//returns optimal cost
}
void display_matrix_order(int s[20][20],int i,int j)
{
  if(i==j)
   printf("A%d",i);
  else
  {
   printf("(");
   display_matrix_order(s,i,s[i][j]);
   display_matrix_order(s,s[i][j]+1,j);
   printf(")");
  }
```

```
}
```

Output

```
Enter the number of matrices: 4

Enter the dimension of the matrix: 5

Enter the dimension of the matrix: 4

Enter the dimension of the matrix: 6

Enter the dimension of the matrix: 2

Enter the dimension of the matrix: 7

The Optimal Cost: 158

The Optimal Order :    ((A1(A2A3))A4)
```

Experiment 7 : Implementation of a Making Change Problem using Dynamic Programming

Solution :

```
#include<stdio.h>
int main()
{
   int d[5];
   int NumberofCoins(int [5],int,int);
   int n,N;
   printf("\n Enter the number of Units(n): ");
   scanf("%d",&n);
   printf("\n Enter the value of coins:");
   for(int i=1;i<=n;i++)
      scanf("%d",&d[i]);
   printf("\n Enter total units for which the changes if required(N):");
   scanf("%d",&N);
   printf(" Minimum Number of coins %d ",NumberofCoins(d,n,N));
   return 0;
}
```

```
int minval(int x,int y)
{
    if(x<y)
        return x;
    else
        return y;
}
int NumberofCoins(int d[],int n,int N)
{
    int minval(int x,int y);
    int i,j;
    int c[10][10];
    for(i=0;i<=n;i++)
        for(j=0;j<=N;j++)
            c[i][j]=9999;//initialize table by infinity
    for (i=0;i<=n;i++)
        c[i][0]=0;
    for (j=1;j<=N;j++)
        c[0][j]=j;
    //Filling up table column by column
    for (j=1;j<=N;j++)
    {
        for (i=1;i<=n;i++)
        {
            if(i == 1 )
            {
                if(j<d[i])
                    c[i][j]=9999;//infinity
                else
                    c[i][j]=1+c[1][j-d[1]] ;
            }
            else if(j<d[i])
                c[i][j] = c[i-1][j];
            else
                c[i][j] =minval(c[i-1][j],1+c[i][j-d[i]])  ;
        }
    }
    printf("\n Printing the table for number of coins\n");
```

```
    for(i=0;i<=n;i++)
    {
        for(j=0;j<=N;j++)
        {
            printf(" %d",c[i][j]);
        }
        printf("\n");
    }
    return c[n][N]; //returning bottom most and rightmost element
}
```

Output

```
Enter the number of Units(n): 3
Enter the value of coins:1 4 6
Enter total units for which the changes if required(N):8
Printing the table for number of coins
0 1 2 3 4 5 6 7 8
0 1 2 3 4 5 6 7 8
0 1 2 3 1 2 3 4 2
0 1 2 3 1 2 1 2 2
Minimum Number of coins 2
```

Experiment 8 : Implementation of a Knapsack Problem using Greedy Algorithm

Solution :

```
/*************************************************************************
To implement knapsack problem using Greedy algorithm
*************************************************************************/
#include<stdio.h>
#include<conio.h>
void knapsack(int n,float m,float w[ ],float p[ ]);

void main( )
{
    int i,j,n;
    float p[15],w[15],c[15],temp,m;
    clrscr( );
    printf("\nEnter number of objects:");
    scanf("%d",&n);
```

```
printf("\nEnter weights:");
for(i=0;i<n;i++)
    scanf("%f",&w[i]);
flushall( );
printf("\nEnter profits:");
for(i=0;i<n;i++)
    scanf("%f",&p[i]);
printf("\nEnter knapsack size:");
scanf("%f",&m);

for(i=0;i<n;i++)
    c[i]=p[i]/w[i];
for(i=0;i<n;i++)
{
    for(j=0;j<n-1;j++)
    {
        if(c[j] < c[j+1])
        {
            temp=c[j];
            c[j]=c[j+1];
            c[j+1]=temp;

            temp=w[j];
            w[j]=w[j+1];
            w[j+1]=temp;

            temp=p[j];
            p[j]=p[j+1];
            p[j+1]=temp;
        }
    }
}
printf("\n The items are arranged as ...\n");
printf("\n\nItems\tweights \tProfits");

for(i=0;i<n;i++)
        printf("\nx[%d]\t%.0f\t\t%.0f",i,w[i],p[i]);
knapsack(n,m,w,p);
getch( );
```

```
}

void knapsack(int n,float m,float w[ ],float p[ ])
{
    float x[15],U,profit=0.0,weight=0.0;
    int i;
    U=m;

    for(i=0;i<n;i++)
        x[i]=0.0;

    for(i=0;i<n;i++)
    {
        if(w[i]>U)
            break;
        x[i]=1.0;
        U=U-w[i];
    }
    if(i<n)
        x[i]=U/w[i];//take fractional part of item to fulfil the size

    printf("\nThe solution vector is:");

    for(i=0;i<n;i++)
        printf("\n%d\t\%.2f",i,x[i]);

    for(i=0;i<n;i++)
    {
        w[i]=w[i]*x[i];
        p[i]=p[i]*x[i];
    }

    for(i=0;i<n;i++)
    {
        profit=profit+p[i];//computing total profit & wt.
        weight=weight+w[i];
    }

    printf("\nMaximum profit is:");
```

```
    printf("\n\t\t%.2f",profit);
    printf("\nMaximum weight is:");
    printf("\n\t\t%.2f",weight);
}
```

Output

```
Enter number of objects:7

Enter weights:2 3 5 7 1 4 1

Enter profits:10 5 15 7 6 18 3

Enter knapsack size:15

 The items are arranged as ...

Items        Weights      Profits
x[0]         1            6
x[1]         2            10
x[2]         4            18
x[3]         5            15
x[4]         1            3
x[5]         3            5
x[6]         7            7
The solution vector is :
0    1.00
1    1.00
2    1.00
3    1.00
4    1.00
5    0.67
6    0.00
Maximum profit is :
             55.33
Maximum weight is :
             15.00
```

Experiment 9(a) : Implementation Depth First Search for Graph

Solution :

```
#include<stdio.h>
#include<conio.h>
#include<stdlib.h>

/* List of defined constants */
#define MAX 20
#define TRUE 1
#define FALSE 0

/* Declare an adjacency matrix for storing the graph */

int g[MAX][MAX];
int v[MAX];
int n;

void main ( )
{
 /* Local declarations */
  int v1, v2;
  char ans;
  void create();
  void Dfs(int);
  clrscr();
  create();
  clrscr();
  printf("The Adjacency Matrix for the graph is \n");
  for ( v1 = 0; v1 < n; v1++)
  {
     for ( v2 = 0; v2 < n; v2++)
        printf(" %d ", g[v1][v2]);
     printf("\n");
}
getch();
```

```
do
{
  for ( v1 = 0; v1 < n; v1++)
     v[v1] = FALSE;
  clrscr();
  printf("Enter the Vertex from which you want to traverse :");
  scanf("%d", &v1);
  if ( v1 >= MAX )
  printf("Invalid Vertex\n");
  else
  {
    printf("The Depth First Search of the Graph is \n");
    Dfs(v1);
  }

  printf("\n Do U want To Taverse By any Other Node?");
  ans=getch();
 }while(ans=='y');
}

void  create()
{
    int ch,    v1, v2, flag;
    char ans='y';
    printf("\n\t\t This is a Progrm To Create a Graph");
    printf("\n\t\t The Display Is In Depth First Manner");
    getch();
    clrscr();
    flushall();
    for ( v1 = 0; v1 < n; v1++)
        for ( v2 = 0; v2 < n; v2++)
            g[v1][v2] = FALSE;
    printf("\nEnter no. of nodes");
    scanf("%d",&n);
    printf("\nEnter the vertices no. starting from 0");
    do
    {
```

```
        printf("\nEnter the vertices v1 & v2");
        scanf("%d%d", &v1, &v2);
        if ( v1 >= n || v2 >= n)
            printf("Invalid Vertex Value\n" );
        else
        {
            g[v1][v2] = TRUE;
            g[v2][v1] = TRUE;


        }
        printf("\n\nAdd more edges??(y/n)");
        ans=getche();
    }while(ans=='y');
}

void Dfs(int v1)
{
  int v2;
  printf("%d\n", v1);
  v[v1] = TRUE;
  for ( v2 = 0; v2 < MAX; v2++)
    if ( g[v1][v2] == TRUE &&  v[v2] == FALSE )
      Dfs(v2);
}
```

Output

```
This is a Program To Create a Graph
The Display Is In Depth First Manner
Enter no. of nodes 4
Enter the vertices no. starting from 0
Enter the vertices v1 & v2 0 1
Add more edges??(y/n)y
Enter the vertices v1 & v2 0 2
Add more edges??(y/n)y
Enter the vertices v1 & v2 1 3
Add more edges??(y/n)y
Enter the vertices v1 & v2 2 3
Add more edges??(y/n)
The Adjacency Matrix for the graph is
```

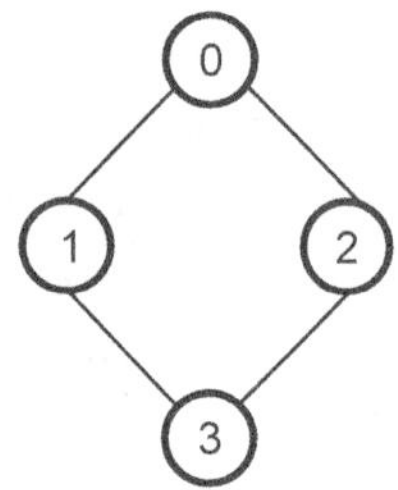

```
0 1 1 0
1 0 0 1
1 0 0 1
0 1 1 0
Enter the Vertex from which you want to traverse : 1
The Depth First Search of the Graph is
1
0
2
3
Do U want To Traverse By any Other Node?
```

Experiment 9(b) : Implementation Breadth First Search for Graph

Solution :

```
#include<stdio.h>
#include<conio.h>
#include<stdlib.h>
#define size    20
#define TRUE  1
#define FALSE 0

int g[size][size];
int visit[size];

int   Q[size];
int   front, rear;
int n;

void main()
{
    int v1, v2;
    char ans ='y';
    void create(),bfs();;
    clrscr();
    create();
    clrscr();
    printf("The Adjacency Matrix for the graph is \n");
```

```
        for ( v1 = 0; v1 < n; v1++)
        {
            for ( v2 = 0; v2 < n; v2++)
                printf(" %d ", g[v1][v2]);
            printf("\n");
        }
        getch();
        do
        {
            for ( v1 = 0; v1 < n; v1++)
                 visit[v1] = FALSE;
            clrscr();
            printf("Enter the Vertex from which you want to traverse ");
            scanf("%d", &v1);
            if ( v1 >= n )
                printf("Invalid Vertex\n");
            else
            {
            printf("The Breadth First Search of the Graph is \n");
            bfs(v1);
            getch();
            }
            printf("\nDo you want to traverse from any other node?");
            ans=getche();
        }while(ans=='y');
        exit(0);
    }

    void create()
    {
        int     v1, v2;
        char ans='y';
        printf("\n\t\t This is a Program To Create a Graph");
        printf("\n\t\t The Display Is In Breadth First Manner");
        printf("\nEnter no. of nodes");
        scanf("%d",&n);
        for ( v1 = 0; v1 < n; v1++)
            for ( v2 = 0; v2 < n; v2++)
```

```
        g[v1][v2] = FALSE;
    printf("\nEnter the vertices no. starting from 0");
    do
    {
        printf("\nEnter the vertices v1 & v2");
        scanf("%d%d", &v1, &v2);
        if ( v1 >= n || v2 >= n)
            printf("Invalid Vertex Value\n" );
        else
        {
            g[v1][v2] = TRUE;
            g[v2][v1] = TRUE;
        }
        printf("\n\nAdd more edges??(y/n)");
        ans=getche();
    }while(ans=='y');
}

void bfs(int v1)
{
    int v2;

    visit[v1] = TRUE;
    front = rear = -1;
    Q[++rear] = v1;
    while ( front != rear )
    {
        v1 = Q[++front];
        printf("%d\n", v1);
        for ( v2 = 0; v2 < n; v2++)
        {
            if ( g[v1][v2] == TRUE && visit[v2] == FALSE )
            {
                Q[++rear] = v2;
                visit[v2] = TRUE;
            }
        }
```

```
    }
}
```

Output

```
    This is a Program To Create a Graph
    The Display Is In Breadth First Manner
Enter no. of nodes 4
Enter the vertices no. starting from 0
Enter the vertices v1 & v2
0 1
Add more edges??(y/n)y
Enter the vertices v1 & v2
0 2
Add more edges??(y/n)y
Enter the vertices v1 & v2
1 3
Add more edges??(y/n)y
Enter the vertices v1 & v2
2 3
Add more edges??(y/n)
The Adjacency Matrix for the graph is
 0 1 1 0
 1 0 0 1
 1 0 0 1
 0 1 1 0

Enter the Vertex from which you want to traverse 0
The Breadth First Search of the Graph is
0
1
2
3
Do you want to traverse from any other node?
Enter the Vertex from which you want to traverse 1
The Breadth First Search of the Graph is
1
0
3
```

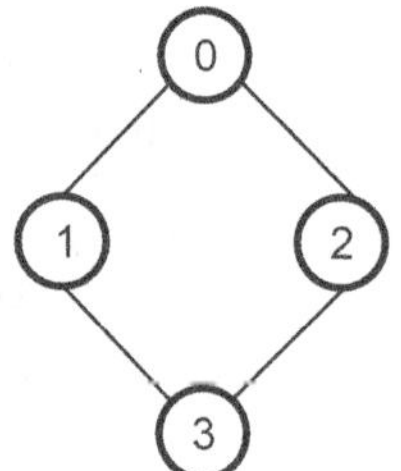

2

Do you want to traverse from any other node?

Experiment 10 : Implement Prim's Algorithm

Solution :

```
#include<stdio.h>
#include<conio.h>
#define SIZE 20
#define INFINITY 32767

/*This function finds the minimal spanning tree by Prim's Algorithm */

void Prim(int G[][SIZE],int nodes)
{
    int tree[SIZE],i,j,k;
    int min_dist,v1,v2,total=0;
  //Initialize the selected vertices list
  for (i=0; i<nodes; i++)
   tree[i] = 0;
  printf("\n\n The Minimal Spanning Tree Is :\n");
  tree[0] = 1;
  for (k=1; k<=nodes-1; k++)
  {

    min_dist = INFINITY;
  //initially assign minimum dist as infinity
      for (i=0; i<=nodes-1; i++)
      {
            for (j=0; j<=nodes-1; j++)
       {
           if (G[i][j]&&((tree[i]&&!tree[j])||
                         (!tree[i]&&tree[j])))
         {
           if (G[i][j]<min_dist)
            {
            min_dist=G[i][j];
```

```
                    v1 = i;
                    v2 = j;
                  }
                }
            }
        }

        printf("\n Edge (%d %d )and weight = %d",v1,v2,min_dist);
            tree[v1] = tree[v2] = 1;
        total =total+min_dist;
         }
        printf("\n\n\t Total Path Length Is = %d",total);
}
void main()
{
        int G[SIZE][SIZE],nodes;
        int v1,v2,length,i,j,n;

        clrscr();
        printf("\n\t Prim'S Algorithm\n");

        printf("\n Enter Number of Nodes in The Graph");

        scanf("%d",&nodes);
        printf("\n Enter Number of Edges in The Graph");
        scanf("%d",&n);

        for (i=0 ; i<nodes ; i++)// Initialize the graph
            for (j=0 ; j<nodes ; j++)
                G[i][j] = 0;
        //entering weighted graph
        printf("\n Enter edges and weights \n");
        for (i=0 ; i<n; i++)
        {
            printf("\n Enter Edge by V1 and V2:");
            printf("[Read the graph from starting node 0]");
            scanf("%d %d",&v1,&v2);
            printf("\n Enter corresponding weight:");
```

```
        scanf("%d",&length);
        G[v1][v2] = G[v2][v1] = length;
    }
    getch();
    printf("\n\t");
    clrscr();
    Prim(G,nodes);
    getch();
}
```

Output

```
    Prim'S Algorithm
Enter Number of Nodes in The Graph  5

Enter Number of Edges in The Graph  7

Enter edges and weights

  Enter Edge by V1 and V2 : [Read the graph from starting node 0 ]
  0 1

Enter corresponding weight : 10

Enter Edge by V1 and V2 : [Read the graph from
starting node 0]
  1 2

Enter corresponding weight : 1

Enter Edge by V1 and V2 :[Read the graph from
starting node 0]
  2 3

Enter corresponding weight :2

Enter Edge by V1 and V2 : [Read the graph from starting node 0]
  3 4

Enter corresponding weight : 3
```

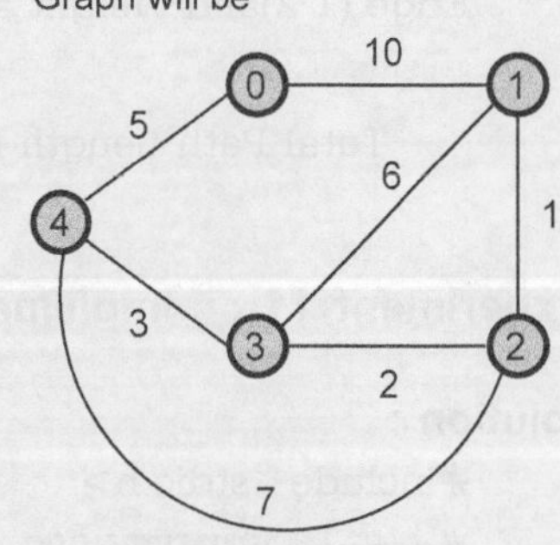

Enter Edge by V1 and V2 : [Read the graph from starting node 0]
4 0

Enter corresponding weight :5

Enter Edge by V1 and V2 : [Read the graph from starting node 0]
1 3

Enter corresponding weight : 6

Enter Edge by V1 and V2 : [Read the graph from starting node 0]
4 2

Enter corresponding weight : 7

The Minimal Spanning Tree Is :

Edge (0 4)and weight = 5
Edge (3 4)and weight = 3
Edge (2 3)and weight = 2
Edge (1 2)and weight = 1

Total Path Length Is = 11

The MST will be

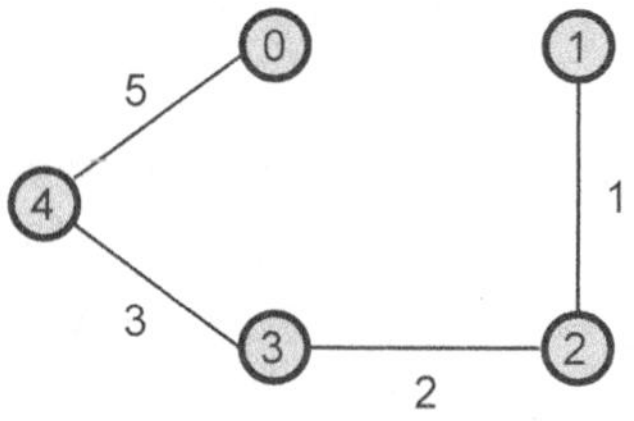

Experiment 11 : Implement Kruskal's Algorithm

Solution :

```
#include<stdio.h>
#define INFINITY 999
typedef struct Graph
{
 int v1;
 int v2;
 int cost;
}GR;
GR G[20];
int tot_edges,tot_nodes;
```

```
void create();
void spanning_tree();
int Minimum(int);
void main()
{
 printf("\n\t Graph Creation by adjacency matrix ");
 create();
 spanning_tree();
}
void create()
{

 int k;
 printf("\n Enter Total number of nodes: ");
 scanf("%d",&tot_nodes);
 printf("\n Enter Total number of edges: ");
 scanf("%d",&tot_edges);
 for(k=0;k<tot_edges;k++)
 {
        printf("\n Enter Edge in (V1 V2)form ");
        scanf("%d%d",&G[k].v1,&G[k].v2);
        printf("\n Enter Corresponding Cost ");
        scanf("%d",&G[k].cost);
 }
}
void spanning_tree()
{
 int count,k,v1,v2,i,j,tree[10][10],pos,parent[10];
 int sum;
 int Find(int v2,int parent[]);
 void Union(int i,int j,int parent[]);
 count=0;
 k=0;
 sum=0;
 for(i=0;i<tot_nodes;i++)
        parent[i]=i;
 while(count!=tot_nodes-1)
 {
```

```
        pos=Minimum(tot_edges);//finding the minimum cost edge
        if(pos==-1)//Perhaps no node in the graph
            break;
        v1=G[pos].v1;
        v2=G[pos].v2;
        i=Find(v1,parent);
        j=Find(v2,parent);
        if(i!=j)
        {
            tree[k][0]=v1;//storing the minimum edge in array
                              tree[]
            tree[k][1]=v2;
            k++;
            count++;
            sum+=G[pos].cost;//accumulating the total cost of MST
            Union(i,j,parent);
        }
        G[pos].cost=INFINITY;
      }
        if(count==tot_nodes-1)
        {
         printf("\n Spanning tree is...");
         printf("\n————————————————————\n");
         for(i=0;i<tot_nodes-1;i++)
         {
            printf("[%d",tree[i][0]);
            printf(" - ");
            printf("%d",tree[i][1]);
            printf("]");
         }
         printf("\n————————————————————");
         printf("\nCost of Spanning Tree is = %d",sum);
        }
        else
         {
            printf("There is no Spanning Tree");
         }
}
int Minimum(int n)
```

```
{
 int i,small,pos;
 small=INFINITY;
 pos=-1;
 for(i=0;i<n;i++)
 {
      if(G[i].cost<small)
      {
          small=G[i].cost;
          pos=i;
      }
 }
 return pos;
}
int Find(int v2,int parent[])
{
 while(parent[v2]!=v2)
 {
      v2=parent[v2];
   }
   return v2;
}
void Union(int i,int j,int parent[])
{
 if(i<j)
      parent[j]=i;
 else
      parent[i]=j;
}
```

Output

Graph Creation by adjacency matrix

Enter Total number of nodes: 4

Enter Total number of edges: 5

Enter Edge in (V1 V2)form 1 2

Graph to be taken as input

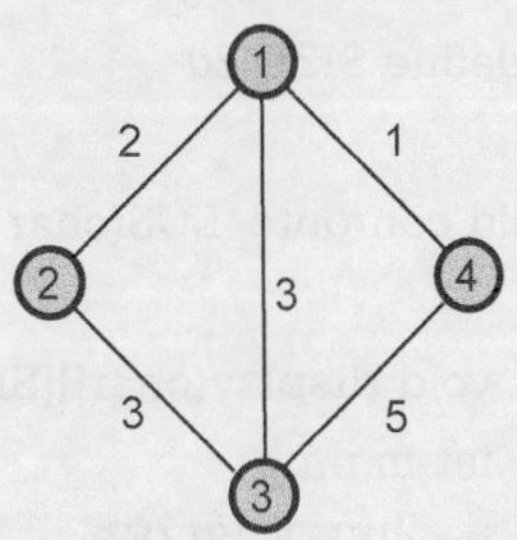

Enter Corresponding Cost 2

Enter Edge in (V1 V2)form 1 4

Enter Corresponding Cost 1

Enter Edge in (V1 V2)form 1 3

Enter Corresponding Cost 3

Enter Edge in (V1 V2)form 2 3

Enter Corresponding Cost 3

Enter Edge in (V1 V2)form 4 3

Enter Corresponding Cost 5

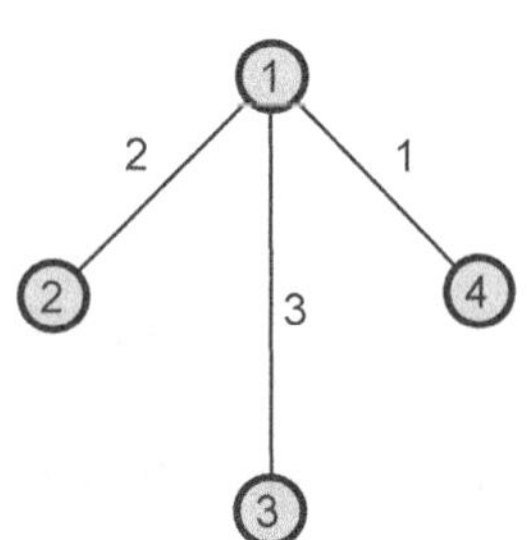

Spanning tree is...

[1 - 4][1 - 2][1 - 3]

Cost of Spanning Tree is = 6

Experiment 12 : Implement LCS Problem

Solution :

```
#include<stdio.h>
#include<conio.h>
#include<string.h>
#define SIZE 20

void compute_LCS(char A[],char B[])
{
   void display(char[][SIZE],char[],int,int);
   int m,n,i,j;
   int c[SIZE][SIZE];
   char d[SIZE][SIZE];
```

```
m=strlen(A);
n=strlen(B);

for(i=0;i<=m;i++)
 c[i][0]=0; // first column contains zero
for(i=0;i<=n;i++)
 c[0][i]=0; //first row contains zero

for(i=1;i<=m;i++) //buiding c[][] and d[]
{
 for(j=1;j<=n;j++)
 {
    if(A[i-1]==B[j-1])
    {
    c[i][j]=c[i-1][j-1]+1;
    d[i][j]='\ ';
    }
    else if(c[i-1][j]>=c[i][j-1])
    {
    c[i][j]=c[i-1][j];
    d[i][j]='^';
    }
    else
    {
    c[i][j]=c[i][j-1];
    d[i][j]='<-';
    }
 }
 }
 printf("\n Table is...\n");
 for(i=0;i<=m;i++)
 {
    for(j=0;j<=n;j++)
    {
       printf("%3d",c[i][j]);
    }
    printf("\n");
```

```
    }
    printf("\n The Longest Common Subsequence is... ");
    display(d,A,m,n);//print the result
}

void display(char d[][20],char A[],int i,int j)
{
    if(i==0 || j==0)
        return;
    if(d[i][j]=='\ ')
    {
        display(d,A,i-1,j-1);
        printf(" %c",A[i-1]);
    }
    else if(d[i][j]=='^')
        display(d,A,i-1,j);
    else
        display(d,A,i,j-1);
}
void main()
{
    char A[SIZE],B[SIZE];
    clrscr();
    printf("Enter First sequence:");
    scanf("%s",A);
    printf("Enter Second sequence:");
    scanf("%s",B);
    compute_LCS(A,B);
    getch();
}
```

Output

```
Enter First sequence:ABCDBACDF
Enter Second sequence:CBAF

Table is...
0 0 0 0 0
0 0 0 1 1
```

```
0 0 1 1 1
0 1 1 1 1
0 1 1 1 1
0 1 2 2 2
0 1 2 3 3
0 1 2 3 3
0 1 2 3 3
0 1 2 3 4

The Longest Common Subsequence is... C B A F
```

Notes

Winter - 2015
Analysis and Design of Algorithms

Semester - V (CE / CSE / IT/ I & CT) - 2013 Course

Gujarat Technological University
Solved Paper

Time : $2\frac{1}{2}$ Hours] **[Total Marks : 70**

Instructions :

1. ***Attempt all questions.***
2. ***Make suitable assumptions wherever necessary.***
3. ***Figures to the right indicate full marks.***

Q.1 a) *Define following terms*
i) Quantifier **(Refer section 1.5)**
ii) Algorithm **(Refer section 1.2)**
iii) Big 'Oh' Notation **(Refer section 2.4.1)**
iv) Big 'Omega' Notation **(Refer section 2.4.2)**
v) 'Theta' Notation **(Refer section 2.4.3)** **[7]**

b) *Explain an algorithm for Selection Sort Algorithm. Derive its best case, worst case and average case time complexity.* **(Refer section 2.8.1.2)** **[7]**

Q.2 a) *Write the Prim's Algorithm to find out Minimum Spanning Tree. Apply the same and find MST for the graph given below.* **(Refer example 5.7.5)** **[7]**

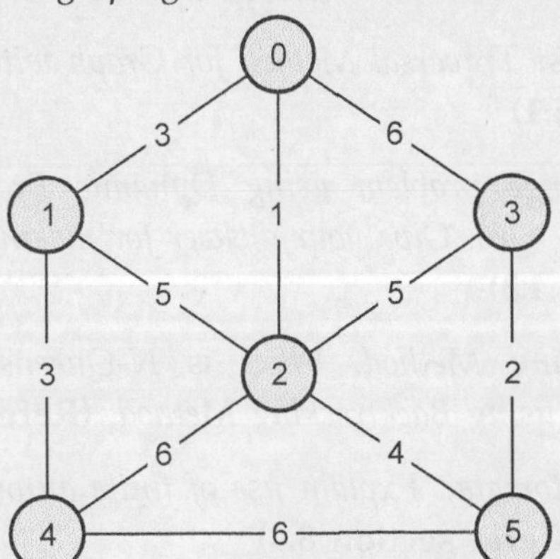

Fig. 1

b) *What is recurrence? Solve recurrence equation T (n) = T (n – 1) + n using forward substitution and backward substitution method.*
(Refer examples 2.5.1 and 2.5.2) **[7]**

OR

b) *Sort the given elements with Heap Sort Method: 20, 50, 30, 75, 90, 60, 25, 10, 40.*
(Refer example 2.8.3) **[7]**

Q.3 a) *Write Huffman code algorithm and Generate Huffman code for following* **[7]**

Letters	A	B	C	D	E
Frequency	24	12	10	8	8

(Refer example 5.11.4)

b) *Write an algorithm for quick sort and derive best case, worst case using divide and conquer technique also trace given data (3, 1, 4, 5, 9, 2, 6, 5).*
(Refer example 3.8.4) **[7]**

OR

Q.3 a) *Write equation for Chained matrix multiplication using Dynamic programming. Find out optimal sequence for multiplication : A1 [5 × 4], A2 [4 × 6], A3 [6 × 2], and A4 [2 × 7]. Also give the optimal parenthesization of matrices.*
(Refer example 4.8.1) **[7]**

b) *Using greedy algorithm find an optimal schedule for following jobs with n = 6.*
Profits : (Pl, P2, P3, P4, P5, P6) = (20, 15, 10, 7, 5, 3)
Deadline : (d1, d2, d3, d4, d5, d6) = (3 , 1, 1, 3, 1, 3) **(Refer example 5.10.3)** **[7]**

Q.4 a) *Explain Depth First Traversal Method for Graph with algorithm with example.*
(Refer section 6.5.2) **[7]**

b) *Explain how to find out Longest Common Subsequence of two strings using Dynamic Programming method. Find any one Longest Common Subsequence of given two strings using Dynamic Programming.*
X = abbacdcba, Y = bcdbbcaac **(Refer example 4.9.2)** **[7]**

OR

Q.4 a) *Explain Breath First Traversal Method for Graph with algorithm with example.*
(Refer section 6.5.1) **[7]**

b) *Solve making change problem using Dynamic Programming. (Denominations : d1 = 1, d2 = 4, d3 = 6). Give your answer for making change of Rs. 9.*
(Refer example 4.4.3) **[7]**

Q.5 a) *Explain Backtracking Method. What is N-Queens Problem? Give solution of 4-Queens Problem using Backtracking Method.* **(Refer section 7.3)** **[7]**

b) *What is Finite Automata? Explain use of finite automata for string matching with suitable example.* **(Refer section 8.4)** **[7]**

OR

Q.5 a) *Define P, NP, NP complete and NP-Hard problems. Give examples of each.*
(Refer sections 9.1 and 9.5) **[7]**

b) *Give and explain Rabin-Carp string matching algorithm with example.*
(Refer section 8.3) **[7]**

❑❑❑

Summer - 2016 **Analysis and Design of Algorithms** Semester - V (CE / CSE / IT / I & CT) - 2013 Course	**Gujarat Technological University** **Solved Paper**

Time : $2\frac{1}{2}$ Hours] **[Total Marks : 70**

Instructions :

1. ***Attempt all questions.***
2. ***Make suitable assumptions wherever necessary.***
3. ***Figures to the right indicate full marks.***

Q.1 a) *Why do we use asymptotic notations in the study of algorithms ? Briefly describe the commonly used asymptotic notations.* **(Refer section 2.4)** **[7]**

b) *Define MST. Explain Kruskal's algorithm with example for construction of MST.* **(Refer section 5.7.2)** **[7]**

Q.2 a) *Explain finite automata for string matching with example.* **(Refer section 8.4)** **[7]**

b) *Write a brief note on NP-completeness and the classes-P, NP and NPC.* **(Refer section 9.5)** **[7]**

OR

b) *What is the basic idea behind Rabin-Karp algorithm ? What is expected running time of this algorithm ? Explain it with example.* **(Refer section 8.3)** **[7]**

Q.3 a) *Explain in brief characteristics of Greedy algorithms. Compare Greedy method with dynamic programming method.* **[7]**

Ans. : **Characteristics of greedy algorithm :** Refer section 5.2.

Comparison with dynamic programming model : Refer section 5.3.

b) *Explain the use of divide and conquer technique for binary search method. What is the complexity of binary search method ? Explain it with example.* **(Refer section 3.5)** **[7]**

OR

Q.3 a) *Explain breadth first traversal method for graph with algorithm.* **(Refer section 6.5.1)** **[7]**

b) *Explain depth first traversal method for graph with algorithm.* **(Refer section 6.5.2)** **[7]**

Q.4 a) *What is an amortized analysis ? Explain aggregate method of amortized analysis using suitable example.* **(Refer section 2.7)** **[7]**

b) *Discuss assembly line scheduling problem using dynamic programming with example.* **(Refer section 4.5)** **[7]**

OR

Q.4 a) *Write a program / algorithm of Quick Sort method and analyze it with example.* **(Refer section 3.8)** **[7]**

b) *Explain Backtracking method. What is N-Queens problem ? Give solution of 4 queens problem using Backtracking method.*
(Refer section 7.3 and example 7.3.4) **[7]**

Q.5 a) *Explain chained matrix multiplication with example.* **(Refer section 4.8)** **[7]**

b) *Explain selection sort algorithm and give its best case, worst case and average case complexity with example.* **(Refer section 2.8.1.2)** **[7]**

OR

Q.5 a) *Discuss matrix multiplication problem using divide and conquer technique.* **(Refer section 3.9)** **[7]**

b) *Sort the letters of word "EDUCATION" in alphabetical order using insertion sort.* **[7]**

Ans. : Consider the list of elements as

E	D	U	C	A	T	I	O	N

The process starts with first element

0		1	2	3	4	5	6	7	8
E		D	U	C	A	T	I	O	N

Sorted zone

Compare E with D and insert it at appropriate position.

0	1		2	3	4	5	6	7	8
D	E		U	C	A	T	I	O	N

Sorted zone Unsorted zone

Compare U with D and E. Insert it at appropriate position.

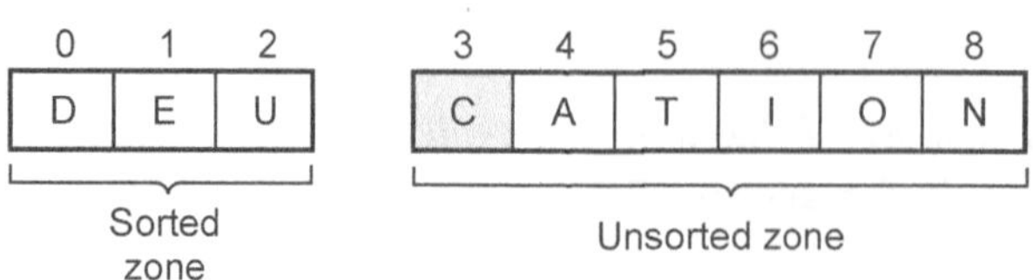

Compare C with **Sorted zone** elements. Insert it at appropriate position.

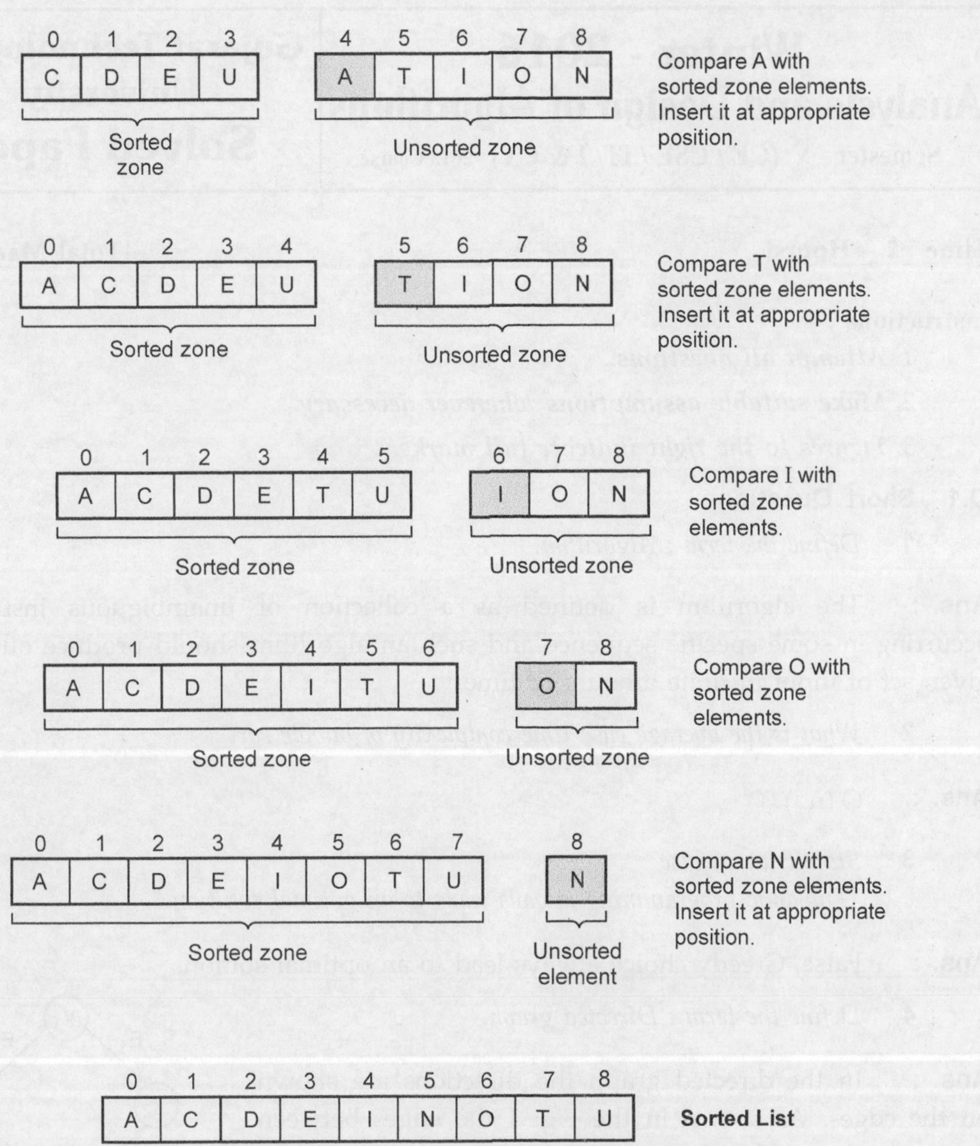

Thus we get the sorted list of elements using insertion sort.

❑❑❑

Winter - 2016 Analysis and Design of Algorithms Semester - V (CE / CSE / IT/ I & CT) - 2013 Course	Gujarat Technological University Solved Paper

Time : $2\frac{1}{2}$ Hours] [Total Marks : 70

Instructions :

1. *Attempt all questions.*
2. *Make suitable assumptions wherever necessary.*
3. *Figures to the right indicate full marks.*

Q.1 Short Questions. **[14]**

1 *Define the term : Algorithm.*

Ans. : The algorithm is defined as a collection of unambiguous instructions occurring in some specific sequence and such an algorithm should produce output for given set of input in finite amount of time.

2 *What is the average case time complexity of bubble sort ?*

Ans. : $O(n^2)$

3 *State true or false :*
"Dynamic programming always leads to an optimal solution."

Ans. : False. Greedy choice always lead to an optimal soltion.

4 *Define the term : Directed graph.*

Ans. : In the directed graph the directions are shown on the edges. As shown in the Fig. 1 the edges between the vertices are ordered.

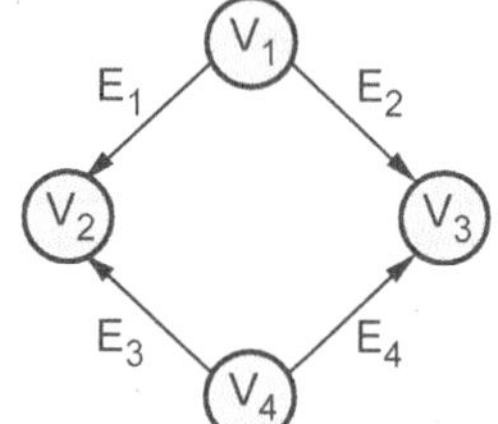

Fig. 1 Directed graph

5 *Give any two sorting methods which are based on divide and conquer strategy.*

Ans. : Merge sort and quick sort are the sorting techniques based on divide and conquer strategy.

6 *What is the basic nature of greedy strategy ?*

Ans. : In Greedy technique, the solution is constructed through a sequence of steps, each expanding a partially constructed solution obtained so far, until a complete solution to the problem is reached. At each step the choice made, while making a choice there should be a Greed for the optimum solution.

7 *What is meant by dead node in backtracking ?*

Ans. : A **dead node** is a generated node which is not to be expanded further or all of whose children have been generated.

8 *Write any one application of string matching.*

Ans. : String matching algorithms are normally used in text processing. Normally text processing is done in compilation of program. In software design or in system design also text processing is a vital activity.

9 *State true or false :*
"Hamiltonian problem is an example of NP-complete".

Ans. : True.

10 *Write the objective of making change problem.*

Ans. : The making change problem is to pay the desired amount of money by using as few coins as possible.

11 *State true or false :*
"Prim's algorithm is based on greedy strategy."

Ans. : True.

12 *What is meant by an optimal solution for a given problem ?*

Ans. : An optimal solution is a feasible solution where the objective function reaches its maximum (or minimum) value - for example, the most profit or the least cost.

13 *Time complexity of ______ is in linear time.*
(a) Bubble sort (b) Radix sort (c) Shell sort (d) Selection sort.

Ans. : Time complexity of **Radix sort** is in linear time.

14 *Which of the following case does not exist in complexity theory of an algorithm?*
(a) Average case (b) Worst case (c) Best case (d) Null case.

Ans. : Null case.

Q.2 a) *Check the correctness for the following equality.*
$5n^3 + 2n = O(n^3)$ **[3]**

Ans. : For big oh notation $f(n) \leq c * g(n)$ is true.

where f(n) and g(n) are functions and c is constant.

Here $f(n) = 5n^3 + 2n$

and $g(n) = n^3$

Also assume n = 1, c = 1 then

$$\text{L.H.S.} = f(n)$$
$$5n^3 + 2n$$
$$5(1)^3 + 2(1)$$
$$= 7$$

$$\text{R.H.S.} = c * g(n)$$
$$1 * (1)^3$$
$$= 1$$

Here $f(n) \leq c * g(n)$ is not true with c = 1 and n = 1.

Now if we assume c = 7 and n = 1 then

$$\text{L.H.S.} = 5n^3 + 2n$$
$$= 5(1)^3 + 2(1) = 7$$

$$\text{R.H.S.} = c * n^3$$
$$= 7 * 1 = 7$$

For c = 7 and n = 2

$$\text{L.H.S.} = 5n^3 + 2n$$
$$= 5(2)^3 + 2(2)$$
$$= 44$$

$$\text{R.H.S.} = c * g(n)$$
$$= 7 * (2)^3$$
$$= 56$$

Here f(n) < c * g(n) is true.

Thus $5n^3 + 2n = O(n^3)$ for $n \geq 0$ and c = 7.

b) *Briefly explain multiplying large integer problem with suitable example.* **(Refer section 2.4)** **[4]**

c) *Explain binary search with the suitable example.* **(Refer section 3.5)** **[7]**

OR

c) *Discuss insertion sort with its time complexity. Support your answer with suitable example.* **(Refer section 2.8.1.3)** **[7]**

Q.3 a) *Enlist various method(s) to solve recurrence equation and explain any one in brief.* **(Refer section 2.5)** **[3]**

b) *Sort the following numbers using heap sort.*
20, 10, 50, 40, 30 **[4]**

Ans. : **Stage I : Construction of Min heap**

Step 1 :

20

Step 2 :

20 → 10
10 → 20

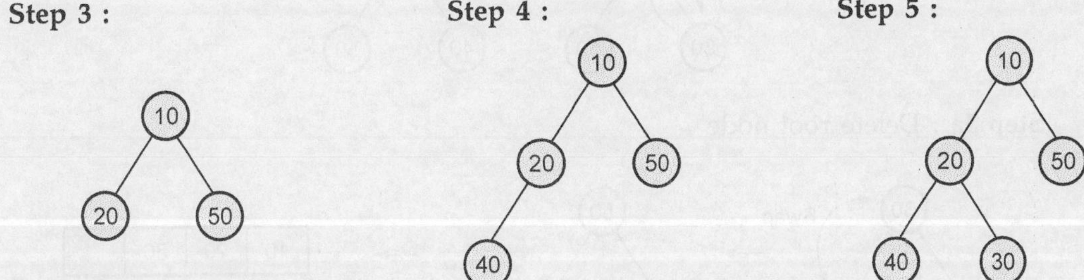

Stage II : Deletion of root

Step 1a :

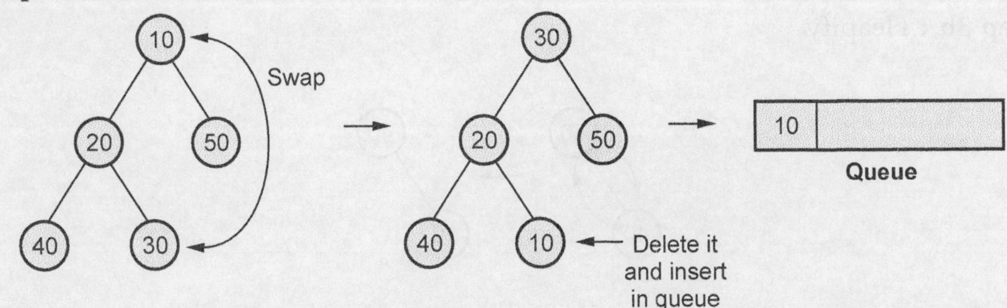

Step 1b : Heapify, for min heap construction

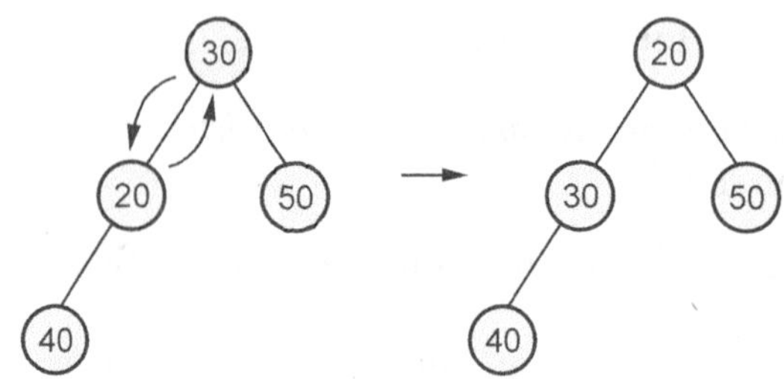

Step 2a : Delete root node

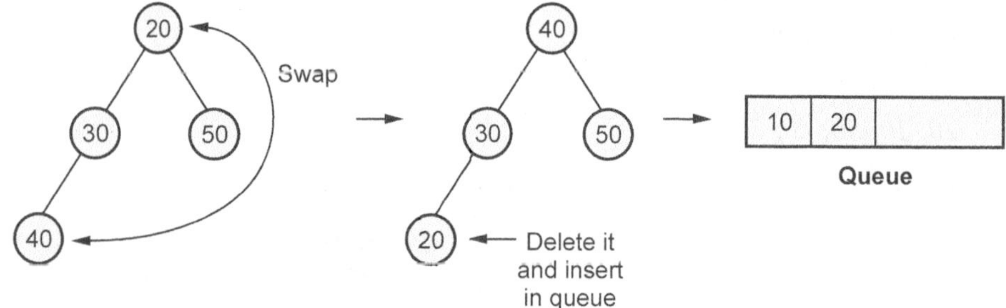

Step 2b : Heapify

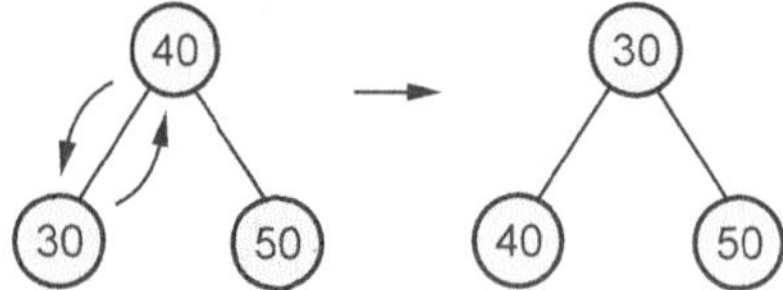

Step 3a : Delete root node

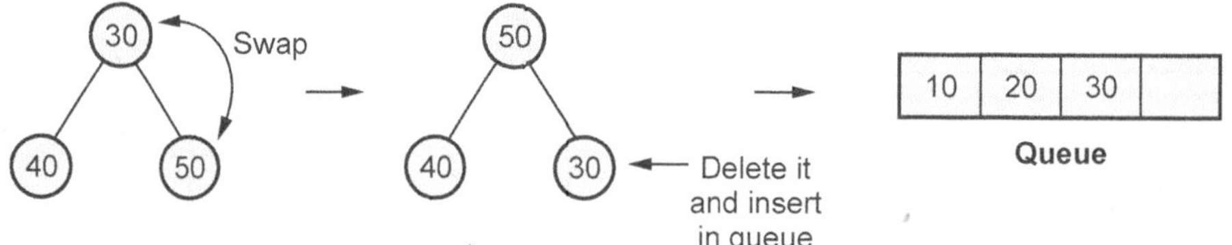

Step 3b : Heapify

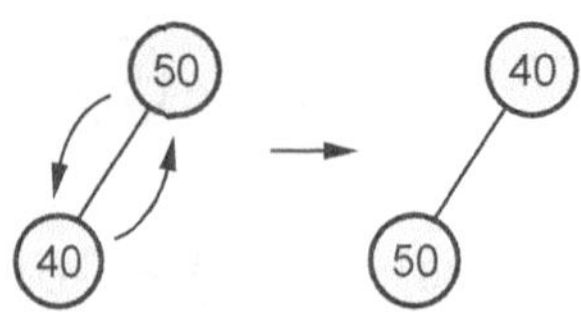

Step 4a : Delete root

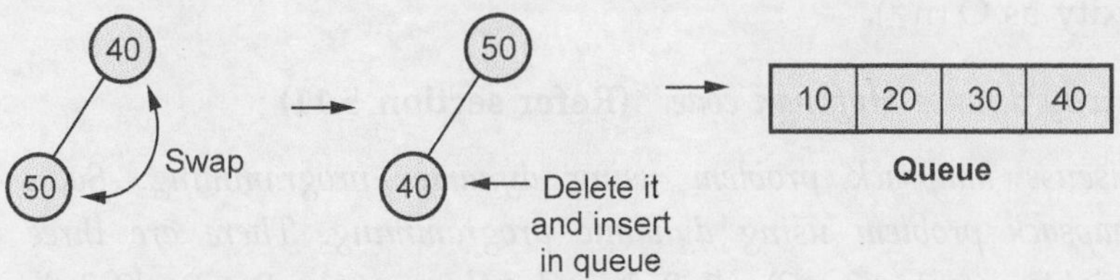

Step 4b : Heapify

Step 5 : Delete 50 and insert in queue

10	20	30	40	50

Sorted list

c) *Elaborate longest common subsequence problem with the help of dynamic programming. Support your answer with proper illustration.* **(Refer section 4.9)** **[7]**

OR

Q.3 a) *Find out time complexity for the following pseudo code using O-notation.* **[3]**

```
for (i = 0; i < n; i++)
{
    for (j = n; j > 0; j--)
    {
        if (i<j)
            c = c + 1;
    }
}
```

Ans. : The time complexity is computed step by step by considering the number of execution of each statement.

Code	Time complexity
for(i=0;i<n;i++)	O(n)
for(j=n;j>0;j--)	O(n*n)
If(i<j)	O(n*n)
c=c+1	O(n*n)
Total	$3\ O(n^2) + O(n)$

Thus considering the order of magnitude and neglecting the constants, we get the time complexity as $O(n^2)$.

b) *Briefly discuss Huffman code.* **(Refer section 5.11)** **[4]**

c) *Discuss knapsack problem using dynamic programming. Solve the following knapsack problem using dynamic programming. There are three objects, whose weights $w(w1, w2, w3) = \{1, 2, 3\}$ and values $v(v1, v2, v3) = \{2, 3, 4\}$ are given. The knapsack capacity M is 3 units.* **(Refer section 4.6)** **[7]**

Ans. : Let M = 3

w_i	v_i
1	2
2	3
3	4

Initially table [0, j] = 0 and table [i, 0] = 0

Thus there are 0 to n rows and 0 to M columns in table.

	0	1	2	3
0	0	0	0	0
1	0			
2	0			
3	0			

Now we will fill up table row by row using following formula

$$\text{table}[i, j] = \begin{cases} \max\{\text{table}[i-1, j],\ v_i + \text{table}[i-1, j-w_i]\} \\ \text{when } j \geq w_i \\ \text{or} \\ \text{table}[i-1, j] \text{ if } j < w_i \end{cases}$$

table [1, 1] with i = 1, j = 1, $w_i = 1$, $v_i = 2$

$j \geq w_i$ is satisfied here

$\therefore$ table [1, 1] = max {table [0, 1], 2 + table [0, 0]}

= max {0, 2}

$\therefore$ **table [1, 1] = 2**

table [1, 2] with i = 1, j = 2, $w_i = 1$, $v_i = 2$

$j \geq w_i$ is satisfied here.

$\therefore$ table [1, 2] = max {table [0, 2], 2 + table [0, 1]}

= max {0, 2}

table [1, 2] = 2

table [1, 3] with i = 1, j = 3, $w_i = 1$, $v_i = 2$

$j \geq w_i$ is satisfied here.

$\therefore$ table [1, 3] = max {table [0, 3], 2 + table [0, 2]}

= max {0, 2}

table [1, 3] = 2

The partially filled table will be

	0	1	2	3
0	0	0	0	0
1	0	2	2	2
2	0			
3	0			

Table [2, 1] with i = 2, j = 1, $w_i = 2$, $v_i = 3$

Here $j < w_i$ is satisfied.

$\therefore$ table [2, 1] = table [i – 1, j]

= table [1, 1]

table [2, 1] = 2

table [2, 2] with i = 2, j = 2, $w_i = 2$, $v_i = 3$

Here $j \geq w_i$ is satisfied.

$\therefore$ table [2, 2] = max {table [1, 2], 3 + table [1, 0]}

= max {2, 3 + 0]

table [2, 2] = 3

table [2, 3] with i = 2, j = 3, $w_i = 2$, $v_i = 3$

Here $j \geq w_i$ is satisfied.

$\therefore$ table [2, 3] = max {table [1, 3], 3+ table [1, 1]}

= max {2, 5}

table [2, 3] = 5

The partially filled table is as follows -

	0	1	2	3
0	0	0	0	0
1	0	2	2	2
2	0	2	3	5
3	0			

Table [3, 1] with i = 3, j = 1, $w_i = 3$, $v_i = 4$

As $j < w_i$ is satisfied

∴ table [3, 1] = table [i – 1, j]

= table [2, 1]

table [3, 1] = 2

table [3, 2] with i = 3, j = 2, $w_i = 3$, $v_i = 4$

As $j < w_i$ is satisfied

∴ table [3, 2] = table [i – 1, j]

= table [2, 2]

table [3, 2] = 3

table [3, 3] with i = 3, j = 3, $w_i = 3$, $v_i = 4$

As $j \geq w_i$ is satisfied

∴ table [3, 3] = max {table [i – 1, j], v_i + table [i – 1, $j - w_i$]}

= max {table [2, 3], 4 + table [2, 0]}

= max {5, 4}

table [3, 3] = 5

The completely filled table is

	0	1	2	3
0	0	0	0	0
1	0	2	2	2
2	0	2	3	5
3	0	2	3	5

Now we will find the actual items of knapsack

Step 1 : Consider i = n = 3

table [3, 3] = table [2, 3]

∴ Do not select i^{th} i.e. 3rd item.

Step 2 : Now i = i – 1

i.e. i = 2

$\text{table } [i, n] \stackrel{?}{=} \text{table } [i-1, n]$

i.e. $\text{table } [2, 3] \stackrel{?}{=} \text{table } [1, 3]$

table [2, 3] ≠ table [1, 3]

∴ Select i^{th} i.e. 2nd **item.**

Step 3 : Now i = i – 1 = 1

$j = j - w_i = 3 - 2 = 1$

Now check if table [i, j] = table [i – 1, j]

i.e. if $\text{table } [1, 1] \stackrel{?}{=} \text{table } [0, 1]$

As table [1, 1] ≠ table [0, 1]

Select i^{th} i.e. 1st item.

Step 4 : i = i – 1 = 0

$j = j - w_i = 1 - 1 = 0$

Thus we have selected **item1** and **item2** with total profit = 2+3 = 5.

Q.4 a) *Write brief note on topological sort.* **(Refer section 6.6)** **[3]**

b) *Explain breadth-first-search in brief with suitable example.* **(Refer section 6.5.1)** **[4]**

c) *Discuss Kruskal's algorithm for finding minimum spanning tree. Give proper example.* **(Refer section 5.7.2)** **[7]**

OR

Q.4 a) *Write a brief note on branch and bound strategy.* **(Refer section 7.5)** **[3]**

b) *Apply counting sort for the following numbers to sort in ascending order.* *4, 1, 3, 1, 3* **[4]**

Ans. : **Step 1 :** We will find the min and max values from given array. The min = 1 and max = 4.

Hence create an array A from 1 to 4.

A	1	2	3	4

Now create another array named **count.** Just count the number of occurrences of each element and store that count in count array at corresponding location of element i.e. element 1 appeared twice, element 2 is not present, element 3 appeared twice and element 4 appeared once.

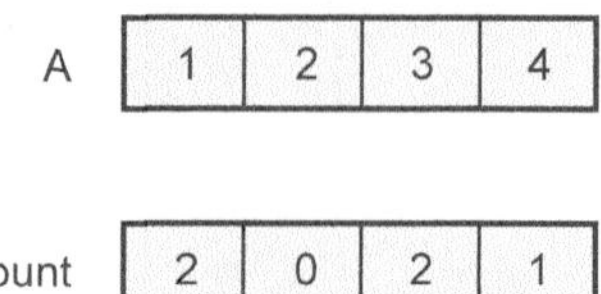

Step 2 : Now we will create another array B in which we will store sum of counts for given index.

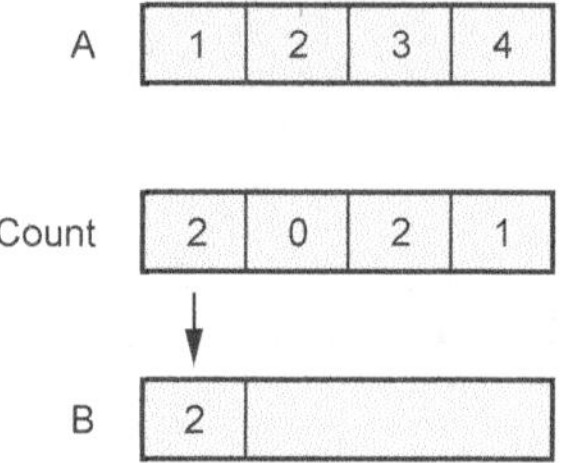

Simply copy first index value of count array to B.

For filling up rest of the elements to B array copy the sum of previous index value of B with current index value of count array.

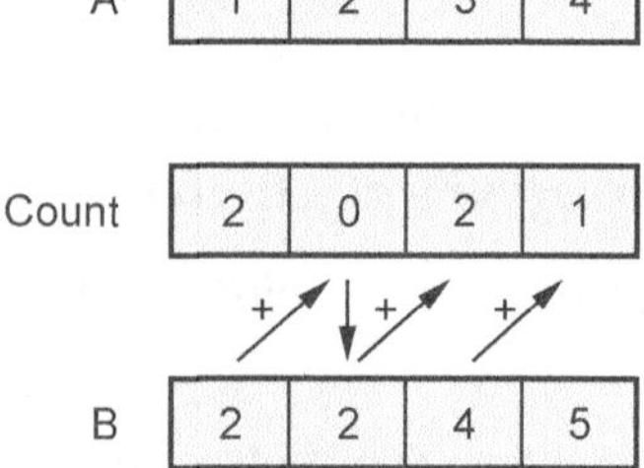

Step 3 : Now consider array A and B for creating two more arrays namely **Position** and **Element.**

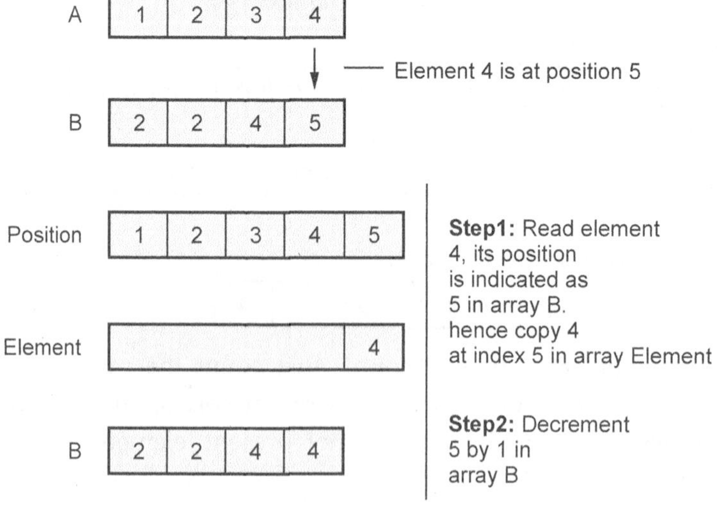

Step 4 : Next element is 1. The position of it is 2.

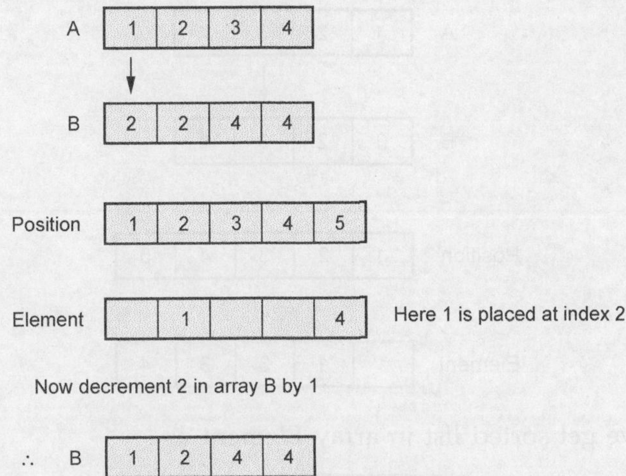

Step 5 : Next element is 3. The position of it is 4 in array B.

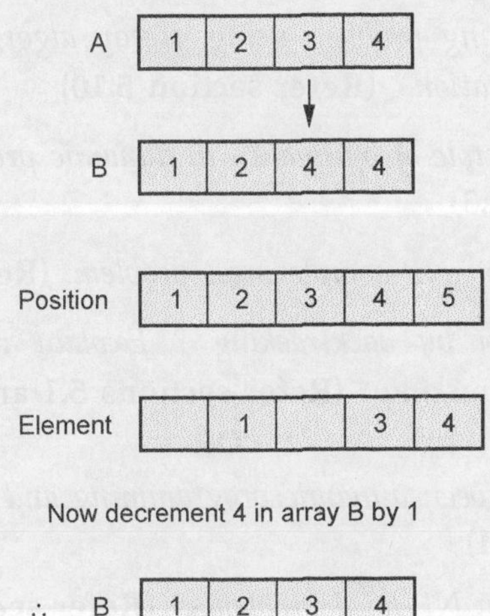

Step 6 : Next element is 1. The position of it in array B is 1.

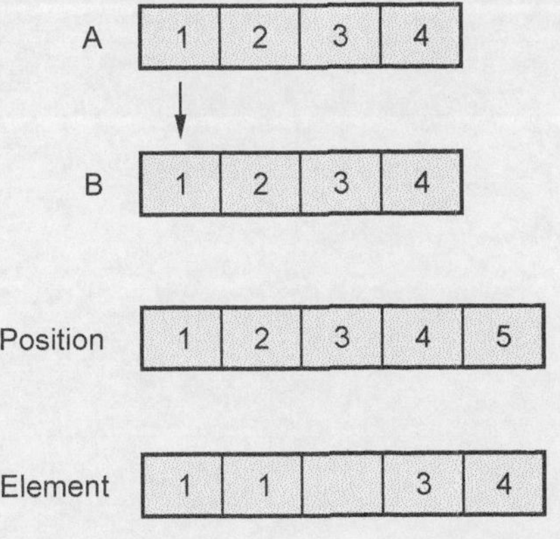

Step 7 : Next element is 3. In array B its position is 3.

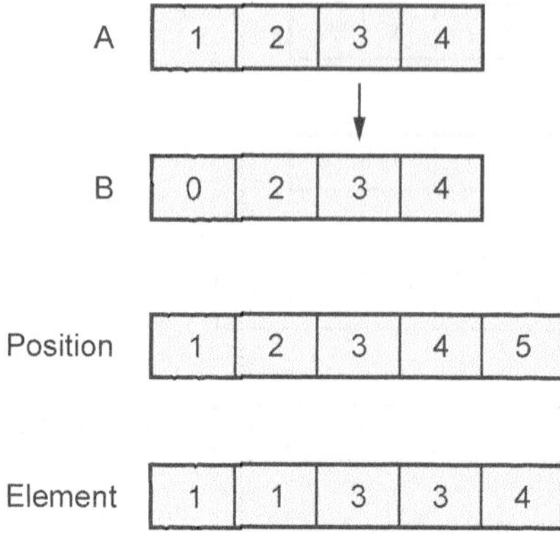

Step 8 : Thus we get sorted list in array **Element** as

1	1	3	3	4

c) *Explain job scheduling problem using greedy algorithm. Support your answer by taking proper illustration.* **(Refer section 5.10)** **[7]**

Q.5 a) *Briefly discuss principle of optimality in dynamic programming.* **(Refer section 4.2.3)** **[3]**

b) *Write a short note on NP-completeness problem.* **(Refer section 9.4)** **[4]**

c) *What do you mean by backtracking ? Explain in brief. Discuss eight queens problem using backtracking.* **(Refer sections 5.1 and 5.3)** **[7]**

OR

Q.5 a) *State differences between dynamic programming and divide and conquer strategy.* **(Refer section 4.2.1)** **[3]**

b) *Write a brief note on NP-hard problems.* **(Refer section 9.6)** **[4]**

c) *Discuss Rabin-Karp algorithm for string matching.* **(Refer section 8.3)** **[7]**

❑❑❑

Summer - 2017 **Analysis and Design of Algorithms** Semester - V (CE / CSE / IT / I & CT)	**Gujarat Technological University** **Solved Paper**

Time : 2 $\frac{1}{2}$ Hours] **[Total Marks : 70**

Instructions :

1. Attempt all questions.

2. Make suitable assumptions wherever necessary.

3. Figures to the right indicate full marks.

Q.1 Short Questions **[14]**

1) *What is an algorithm ?*

Ans. : Algorithm is a collection of unambiguous instructions occuring in some specific sequence.

2) *What is worst case time complexity ?*

Ans. : Worst case time complexity is a time complexity when algorirhtm runs for a longest time.

3) *Define space complexity.*

Ans. : Space complexity is an amount of space required by an algorithm to execute.

4) *Define big omega asymptotic notation.* **(Refer section 2.4.2)**

5) *Define feasible solution.* **(Refer short answers questions of Q.4 of Chapter - 4)**

6) *What is vector ? Which operations are performed on vector ?*
(Refer short answers questions of Q.11 of Chapter - 1)

7) *Define P - type problem.*
(Refer short answers questions of Q.4 of Chapter - 9)

8) *Write principal of optimality.*
(Refer short answers questions of Q.11 of Chapter - 4)

9) *Define directed acyclic graph.*
(Refer short answers questions of Q.3 of Chapter - 6)

10) *List types of algorithms.* **(Refer section 2.8)**

11) *Write down the best case, worst case and average case complexity for merge sort.*

Ans. : The best case, worst case and average case complexity of merge sort is **O (n/Og n)**.

12) *Define minimum spanning tree.*
(Refer short answers questions of Q.10 of Chapter - 5)

13) *Write down the small best case, worst case and average case complexity for slection sort.*

Ans. : The best case, worst case and average case complexity of selection sort is $O(n^2)$.

14) *Write down the best case, worst case and average case complexity for heap sort.*

Ans. : The average and worst case time complexity of heap sort is O (nlog n). While the best case time complexity is O (n).

Q.2 a) *Explain the difference between greedy and dynamic algorithm.*
(Refer section 5.3) **[3]**

b) *Apply the bubble sort algorithm for sorting {U, N, I, V, E, R, S}* **[4]**

Ans. : **Pass 1 :** **Pass 2 :**

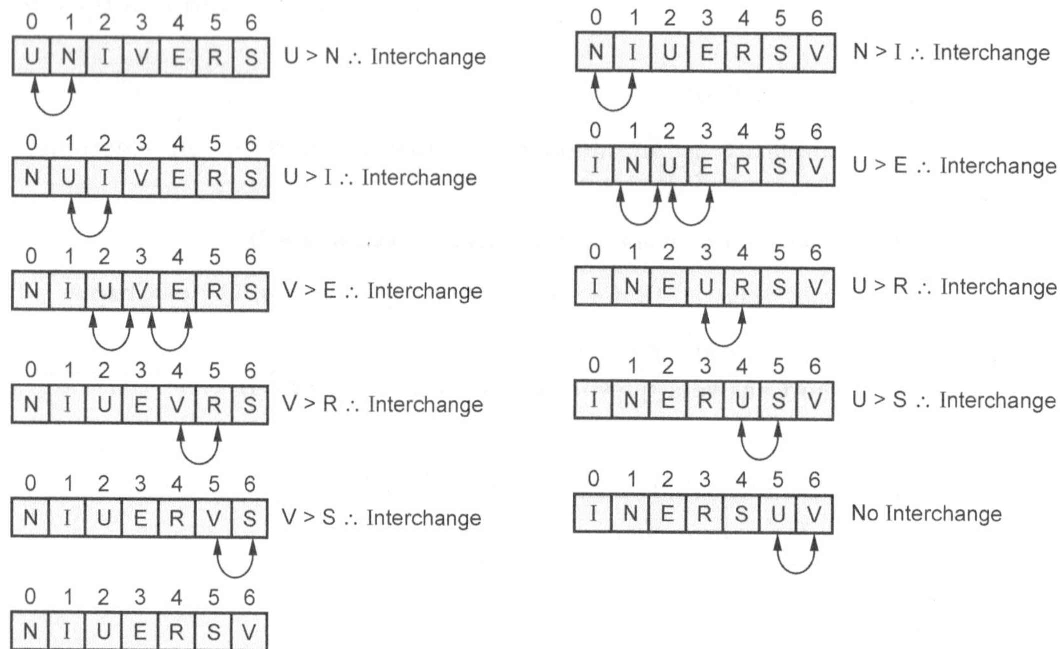

Pass 3 : **Pass 4 :**

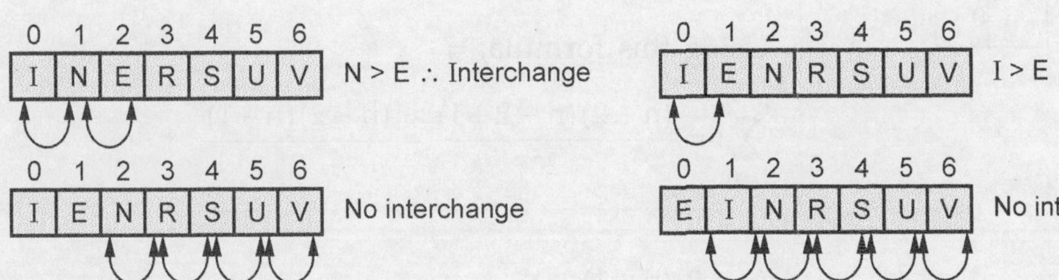

Pass 5 :

0	1	2	3	4	5	6
E	I	N	R	S	U	V

No interchange

Thus the sorted list is, **E, I, N, R, S, U, V.**

c) *Analyze selection sort algorithm in best case and worst case.* **[7]**

Ans. : The basic operation is comparison of elements A [i] and A [j].

In selection sort algorithm there are two nested for loops inside which the elements comparison (basic operation) is performed.

The recurrence relation will be

$$T(n) = \begin{matrix}\text{Outer for}\\ \text{loop with}\\ \text{variable } i\end{matrix} \times \begin{matrix}\text{Inner for}\\ \text{loop with}\\ \text{variable } j\end{matrix} \times \begin{matrix}\text{Basic}\\ \text{operation}\end{matrix}$$

$$= \sum_{i=0}^{n-2} \sum_{j=i+1}^{n-1} 1$$

$$\because \quad = \sum_{i=0}^{n-2}((n-1)-(i+1)+1)$$

Formula used

$$\because \sum_{i=0}^{n} 1 = (n - 0 + 1)$$

$$= \sum_{i=0}^{n-2}(n-1-i)$$

$$\sum_{i=0}^{n-2}(n-1) \quad \boxed{-\sum_{i=0}^{n-2} i} \longleftarrow$$

$$\sum_{i=1}^{n} j = \frac{n(n+1)}{2}$$

Using this formula, =

$$\sum_{i=0}^{n-2} i = \frac{(n-2)(n-2+1)}{2} = \frac{(n-2)(n-1)}{2}$$

$$= \sum_{i=0}^{n-2}(n-1) - \frac{(n-2)(n-1)}{2}$$

Now taking (n – 1) as common factor we get,

$$T(n) = (n-1)\boxed{\sum_{i=0}^{n-2} 1} - \frac{(n-2)(n-1)}{2}$$

As $\sum_{i=1}^{n} 1 = (n - 1 + 1)$ We get,

$$\sum_{i=0}^{n-2} 1 = ((n-2) - 0 + 1) = n - 1$$

$$T(n) = (n-1)(n-1) - \frac{(n-2)(n-1)}{2}$$

$$= (n-1)^2 - \frac{(n-2)(n-1)}{2}$$

Solving this, we get -

$$= \frac{2(n-1)^2 - (n-2)(n-1)}{2}$$

$$= \frac{2\,(n^2 - 2n + 1) - (n^2 - 3n + 2)}{2}$$

$$= \frac{n^2 - n}{2}$$

$$\approx \frac{1}{2}(n^2)$$

$$\mathbf{T(n) \approx O(n^2).}$$

OR

c) *Analyze quick sort algorithm in best case and worst case.*
(Refer section 3.8) **[7]**

Q.3 a) *Write down the characteristics of greedy algorithm.* **(Refer section 5.2)** [3]

b) *Solve following recurrence using master method* [4]

$T(n) = 9T(n/3) + n$ **(Refer example 2.5.15)**

c) *Solve making change problem using dynamic technique.* [7]

1 = 1, d2 = 3, d3 = 5, d4 = 6. Calculate for making change of ₹. 8.

Ans. : Let,

$$d1 = 1, d2 = 3, d3 = 5, d4 = 6$$

We will create a table with rows ranging from 1 to 4 and columns ranging from 0 to 8.

Initially c [i, 0] = 0

		0	1	2	3	4	5	6	7	8
i = 1	d1 = 1	0								
i = 2	d2 = 3	0								
i = 3	d3 = 5	0								
i = 4	d4 = 6	0								

Computations can be performed column by column and fill up the table.

c [1, 1] with i = 1, j = 1, d1 = 1.

As i = 1

$$c[1, 1] = 1 + c[1, j - d1]$$
$$= 1 + c[1, 0]$$
$$= 1 + 0$$
$$\mathbf{c[1, 1] = 1.}$$

c [2, 1] with i = 2, j = 1, d2 = 3.

Here j < di i.e. 1 < 3

$$\therefore \quad c[i, j] = c[i - 1, j]$$
$$c[2, 1] = c[2 - 1, 1]$$
$$= c[1, 1]$$
$$\mathbf{c[2, 1] = 1.}$$

c [3, 1] with i = 3, j = 1, d3 = 5.

j < di i.e. 1 < 5

∴ c [i, j] = c [i – 1, j]

c [3, 1] = c [3 – 1, 1]

= c [2, 1]

c [3, 1] = 1.

c [4, 1] with i = 4, j = 1, d4 = 6.

j < d4 i.e. 1 < 6

∴ c [i, j] = c [i – 1, j]

c [4, 1] = c [4 – 1, 1]

= c [3, 1]

c [4, 1] = 1.

c [1, 2] with i = 1, j = 2, d1 = 1.

Here As i = 1

∴ c [i, j] = 1 + c [1, j – d1]

= 1 + c [1, 1]

= 1 + 1

c [1, 2] = 2.

c [2, 2] with i = 2, j = 2, d2 = 3.

As j < di i.e. 2 < 3

∴ c [i, j] = c [i – 1, j]

= c [2 – 1, 2]

= c [1, 2]

c [2, 2] = 2

c [3, 2] with i = 3, j = 2, d3 = 5

As j < di i.e. 2 < 5

c [i, j] = c [i – 1, j]

$= c[3-1, 2]$

$= c[2, 2]$

c [3, 2] = 2.

c [4, 2] with i = 4, j = 2, d4 = 6.

As j < di i.e. 2 < 6

$\therefore$ $c[i, j] = c[i-1, j]$

$= c[4-1, 2]$

$= c[3, 2]$

c [4, 2] = 2.

c [1, 3] with i = 1, j = 3, d1 = 1.

As i = 1

$\therefore$ $c[i, j] = 1 + c[1, j - d1]$

$= 1 + c[1, 3-1]$

$= 1 + c[1, 2]$

c [1, 3] = 3.

c [2, 3] with i = 2, j = 3, d2 = 3.

$i \neq 1$ and $j = d_i$

$\therefore$ Formula used $c[i, j] = \min(c[i-1, j], 1 + c[i, j - di])$

$\therefore$ $c[2, 3] = \min(c[2-1, 3], 1 + c[2, 3-3])$

$= \min(c[1, 3], 1 + c[2, 0])$

$= \min(3, 1 + 0)$

c [2, 3] = 1.

c [3, 3] with i = 3, j = 3, d3 = 5.

j < di i.e. 3 < 5

$\therefore$ $c[i, j] = c[i-1, j]$

$= c[3-1, 3]$

$= c[2, 3]$

c [3, 3] = 1.

c [4, 3] with i = 4, j = 3, d4 = 6.

As j < d4

$$\therefore \quad c[i, j] = c[i-1, j]$$
$$= c[4-1, 3]$$
$$= c[3, 3]$$

c [4, 3] = 1.

Partially the table will be -

	0	1	2	3	4	5	6	7	8
d1 = 1	0	1	2	3					
d2 = 3	0	1	2	1					
d3 = 5	0	1	2	1					
d4 = 6	0	1	2	1					

c [1, 4] with i = 1, j = 4, d1 = 1.

As i = 1

$$\therefore \quad c[i, j] = 1 + c[1, j - d1]$$
$$= 1 + c[1, 4-1]$$
$$= 1 + c[1, 3]$$

c [1, 4] = 4.

c [2, 4] with i = 2, j = 4, d2 = 3.

As i ≠ 1 and j > d2

$$\therefore \quad c[i, j] = \min(c[i-1, j], 1 + c[i, j - d_i])$$
$$= \min(c[2-1, 4], 1 + c[2, 4-3])$$
$$= \min(c[1, 4], 1 + c[2, 1])$$
$$= \min(4, 1 + 1)$$

c [2, 4] = 2.

c [3, 4] with i = 3, j = 4, d3 = 5.

As $j < d_i$ i.e. 4 < 5

$\therefore$ c [i, j] = c [i – 1, j]

= c [3 – 1, 4]

= c [2, 4]

c [3, 4] = 2.

c [4, 4] with i = 4, j = 4, d4 = 6.

As j < di

$\therefore$ c [i, j] = c [i – 1, j]

= c [4 – 1, 4]

= c [3, 4]

c [4, 4] = 2.

c [1, 5] with i = 1, j = 5, d1 = 1.

As i = 1

$\therefore$ c [i, j] = 1 + c [i, j – d1]

= 1 + c [1, 5 – 1]

= 1 + c [1, 4]

c [1, 5] = 5.

c [2, 5] with i = 2, j = 5, d2 = 3

Here i ≠ 1 and j > di

$\therefore$ Formula used

c [i, j] = min (c [i – 1, j], 1 + c [i, j – di])

c [2, 5] = min (c [2 – 1, 5], 1 + c [2, 5 – 3])

= min (c [1, 5], 1 + c [2, 2])

= min (5, 1 + 2)

c [2, 5] = 3.

c [3, 5] with i = 3, j = 5, d3 = 5

c [3, 5] = min (c [i – 1, j], 1 + c [i, j – di])

= min (c [3 – 1, 5], 1 + c [3, 5 – 5])

= min (c [2, 5], 1 + c [3, 0])

$$= \min(3, 1 + 0)$$

$$\mathbf{c[3, 5] = 1.}$$

c [4, 5] with i = 4, j = 5, d4 = 6.

As j < d4

$$\therefore \quad c[i, j] = c[i - 1, j]$$

$$= c[4 - 1, 5]$$

$$= c[3, 5]$$

$$\mathbf{c[4, 5] = 1.}$$

c [1, 6] with i = 1, j = 6, d1 = 1.

As i = 1

$$\therefore \quad c[i, j] = 1 + c[i, j - d1]$$

$$= 1 + c[1, 6 - 1]$$

$$= 1 + c[1, 5]$$

$$\mathbf{c[1, 6] = 6.}$$

c [2, 6] with i = 2, j = 6, d2 = 3

Here i ≠ 1 and j > d2

$$c[i, j] = \min(c[i - 1, j], 1 + c[i, j - di])$$

$$= \min(c[2 - 1, 6], 1 + c[2, 6 - 3])$$

$$= \min(c[1, 6], 1 + c[2, 3])$$

$$= \min(6, 1 + 1)$$

$$\mathbf{c[2, 6] = 2.}$$

c [3, 6] with i = 3, j = 6, d3 = 5

$$c[i, j] = \min(c[i - 1, j], 1 + c[i, j - di])$$

$$= \min(c[3 - 1, 6], 1 + c[3, 6 - 5])$$

$$= \min(c[2, 6], 1 + c[3, 1])$$

$$= \min(2, 1 + 1)$$

$$\mathbf{c[3, 6] = 2.}$$

c [4, 6] with i = 4, j = 6, d4 = 6

$$c[i, j] = \min(c[i-1, j], 1 + c[i, j - di])$$
$$= \min(c[3, 6], 1 + c[4, 0])$$
$$= \min(2, 1 + 0)$$
$$c[4, 6] = 1.$$

Continuing in this fashion, we get -

	0	1	2	3	4	5	6	7	8
d1 = 1	0	1	2	3	4	5	6	7	8
d2 = 3	0	1	2	1	2	3	2	3	4
d3 = 5	0	1	2	1	2	1	2	3	2
d4 = 6	0	1	2	1	2	1	1	2	(2)
									↑ Total number of coins

The value c [4, 8] = 2 represents total number of coins to get sum of Rs. 8. The coins are,

d2 i.e. 3 units = 1 coin

\+ d3 i.e. 5 units = 1 coin

---

8 units (R.s.) = 2 coins

OR

Q.3 a) *Solve following recurrence using master method T(n) = T(2n/3) + 1.* **[3]**

Ans. : Let T(n) = T (2n/3) + 1

This recurrence can be rewritten as

$$T(n) = T(n/(3/2)) + 1$$

$$\therefore \quad a = 1, b = \frac{3}{2}, \; d = 0 \quad \because n^{o} = 1$$

$$\log_b a = \log_{\left(\frac{3}{2}\right)} 1 = 0 = d$$

$$\therefore \quad T(n) = \Theta(n^d \log n) \text{ is applicable}$$

$$\therefore \quad T(n) = \Theta(n^0 \log n)$$

$$T(n) = \Theta(\log n).$$

b) *Compute MST using PRIM's Algorithm.*
(Refer similar example 5.7.5) **[4]**

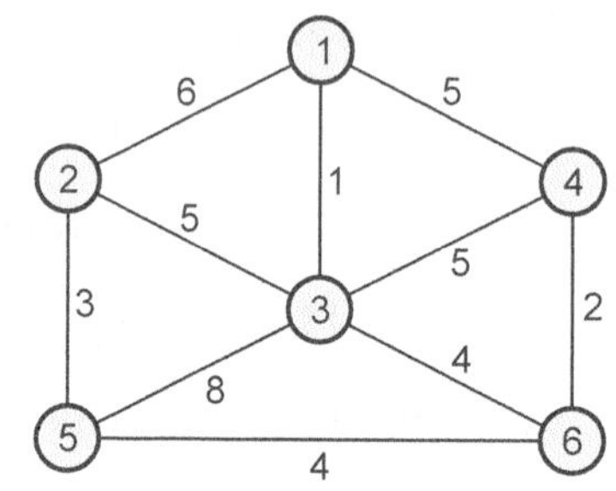

c) *Given two sequence of characters, X = {G, U, J, A, R, A, T}, Y = {J, R, A, T} obtain the longest common subsequence.* **[7]**

Ans. : Let,

	1	2	3	4	5	6	7
A [1]	G	U	J	A	R	A	T
B [j]	J	R	A	T			

The c [i, j] and d [i, j] table is as follows -

The longest common subsequence is J, R, A, T.

			(J)	(R)	(A)	(T)
		0	1	2	3	4
	0		0	0	0	0
G	1	0	0	0	0	0
U	2	0	0	0	0	0
(J)	3	0	↖1	1	1	1
A	4	0	↖1	1	2	2
(R)	5	0	1	↖2	2	2
(A)	6	0	1	2	↖3	3
(T)	7	0	1	2	4	↖4

Q.4 a) *Multiply 981 by 1234 by divide and conquer method.*
(Refer section 3.4) **[3]**

b) *Find an optimal Huffman code for the following set of frequency. a : 50, b : 20, c : 15, d : 30.* **[4]**

c : 15	b : 20	d : 30	a : 50

Ans. : We will arrange the characters in ascending order of frequencies.

c : 15	b : 20	d : 30	a : 50

Step 1 : Remove first two entries from table and form a node.

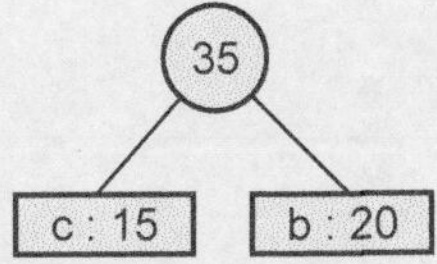

Insert this new entry in table at appropriate position.

d : 30	cb : 35	a : 50

Step 2 : Remove first two entries from the table and form a node.

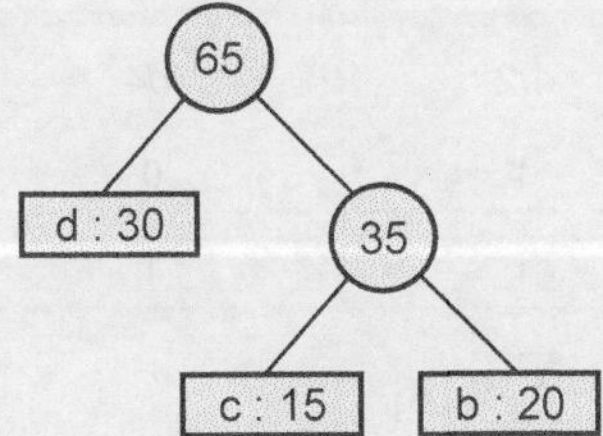

Insert this new entry in table at appropriate position.

a : 50	cbd : 65

Step 3 : Remove first two entries from the table and form a node.

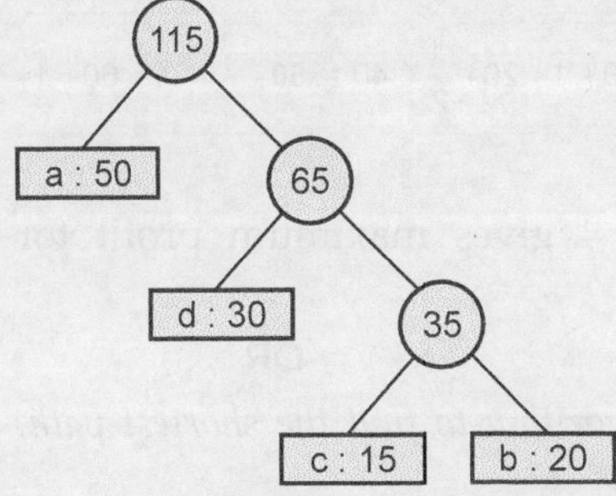

Step 4 : We will encode left branch as 0 and right branch as 1.

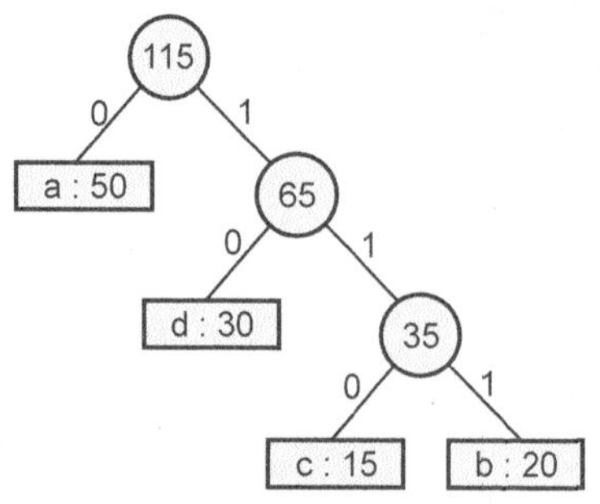

Frequency	Code
a : 50	0
b : 20	111
c : 15	110
d : 30	10

c) *Consider Kanpsack capacity W = 50, w = (10, 20, 40) and v = (60, 80, 100) find the maximum profit using greedy approach.* **[7]**

Ans. : The feasible solutions are -

Sr. No.	x_1	x_2	x_3
1.	0	1/2	1
2.	1/2	1/4	1
3.	1	0	1
4.	1	1	1/2

Let us compute $\sum w_i x_i$ and $\sum v_i x_i$

Sr. No.	$\sum w_i x_i$	$\sum v_i x_i$
1.	$0*10+\frac{1}{2}*20+1*40 = \mathbf{50}$	$0*60+\frac{1}{2}*80+1*100 = \mathbf{140}$
2.	$\frac{1}{2}*10+\frac{1}{4}*20+1*40 = \mathbf{50}$	$\frac{1}{2}*60+\frac{1}{4}*80+1*100 = \mathbf{150}$
3.	$1*10+0*20+1*40 = \mathbf{50}$	$1*60+0*80+1*100 = \mathbf{160}$
4.	$1*10+1*20+\frac{1}{2}*40 = \mathbf{50}$	$1*60+1*80+\frac{1}{2}*100 = \mathbf{190}$

This shows solution 4 gives maximum profit for capacity 50. Hence it is optimum solution.

OR

Q.4 a) *Explain Dijkstra algorithm to find the shortest path.* **(Refer section 5.8)** **[3]**

b) *Explain in brief breadth first search method.* **(Refer section 6.5.1)** **[4]**

c) *For the following chain of matrices find the order of parenthesization for the optimal chain multiplication (15, 5, 10, 20, 25).* **[7]**

Ans. : Here $P_0 = 15, P_1 = 5, P_2 = 10, P_3 = 20, P_4 = 25$.

For all $i, 1 \leq i \leq n$

$m[i, i] = 0$

Hence $m[1, 1] = 0, \quad m[3, 3] = 0$

$m[2, 2] = 0, \quad m[4, 4] = 0$

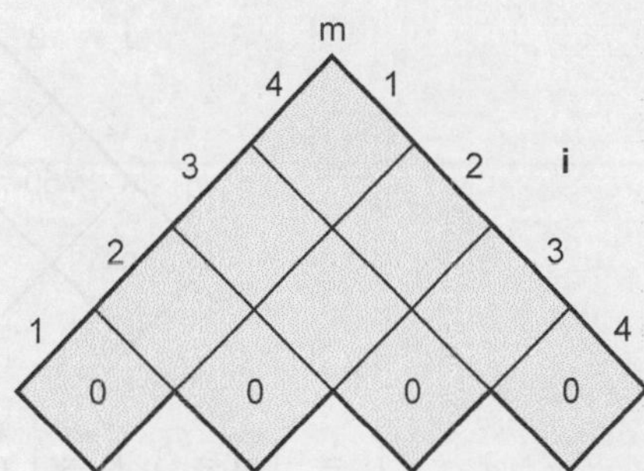

Now we will fill up the table horizontally from left to right assuming $i \leq k \leq j - 1$.

Let $i = 1, j = 2, k = 1$

$\therefore \quad m[1, 2] = m[i, k] + m[k + 1, j] + P_{i-1}P_kP_j$

$= m[1, 1] + m[2, 2] + P_0P_1P_2$

$= 0 + 0 + 15 * 5 * 10$

m [1, 2] = 750

Let $i = 2, j = 3, k = 2$

$\therefore \quad m[2, 3] = m[i, k] + m[k + 1, j] + P_{i-1}P_kP_j$

$= m[2, 2] + m[3, 3] + P_1P_2P_3$

$= 0 + 0 + 5 * 10 * 20$

m [2, 3] = 1000

Let $i = 3, j = 4, k = 3$

$\therefore \quad m[3, 4] = m[i, k] + m[k + 1, j] + P_{i-1}P_kP_j$

$= m[3, 3] + m[4, 4] + P_2P_3P_4$

$= 0 + 0 + 10 * 20 * 25$

m [3, 4] = 5000

The table can be represented partially as -

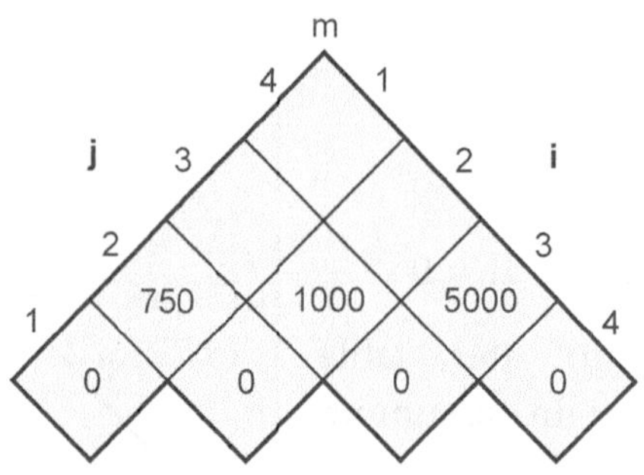

Let $i = 1, j = 3, k = 1$ or $k = 2$

$\therefore \quad m[i, j] = \min\{ m[i, k] + m[k+1, j] + P_{i-1}P_kP_j \}$

with **k = 1**

$m[1, 3] = m[1, 1] + m[2, 3] + P_0P_1P_3$

$= 0 + 1000 + 15 * 5 * 20$

$= 2500$

with **k = 2**

$m[1, 3] = m[1, 2] + m[3, 3] + P_0P_2P_3$

$= 750 + 0 + 15 * 10 * 20$

$= 3750$

m [1, 3] = 2500 with k = 1 as it gives minimum value.

Let $i = 2, j = 4, k = 2$ or $k = 3$

$m[2, 4] = \min\{ m[i, k] + m[k+1, j] + P_{i-1}P_kP_j \}$

$$= \min \begin{cases} m[2,2] + m[3,4] + P_1P_2P_4 \\ m[2,3] + m[4,4] + P_1P_3P_4 \end{cases}$$

$$= \min \begin{cases} 0 + 5000 + 5 * 10 * 25 \\ 1000 + 0 + 5 * 20 * 25 \end{cases}$$

$$= \min \begin{cases} 6250 \\ 3500 \end{cases}$$

m [2, 4] = 3500 with k = 3

The table can be partially filled up as -

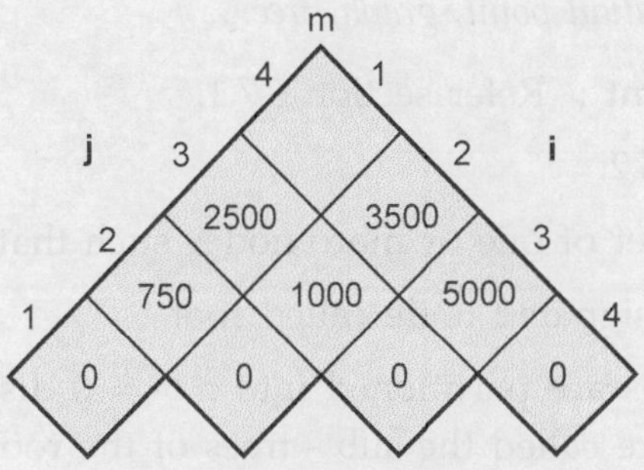

Let $i = 1, j = 4$, then $k = 1$ or 2 or 3

$$m[1,4] = \min \{ m[i,k] + m[k+1,j] + P_{i-1}P_kP_j \}$$

$$= \min \begin{cases} m[1,1] + m[2,4] + P_0P_1P_4 \\ m[1,2] + m[3,4] + P_0P_2P_4 \\ m[1,3] + m[4,4] + P_0P_3P_4 \end{cases}$$

$$= \min \begin{cases} 0 + 3500 + 15 * 5 * 25 \\ 750 + 5000 + 15 * 10 * 25 \\ 2500 + 0 + 15 * 20 * 25 \end{cases}$$

$$= \min \begin{cases} 5375 \\ 9500 \\ 10000 \end{cases}$$

m [1, 4] = 5375 with k = 1

The table can be represented as

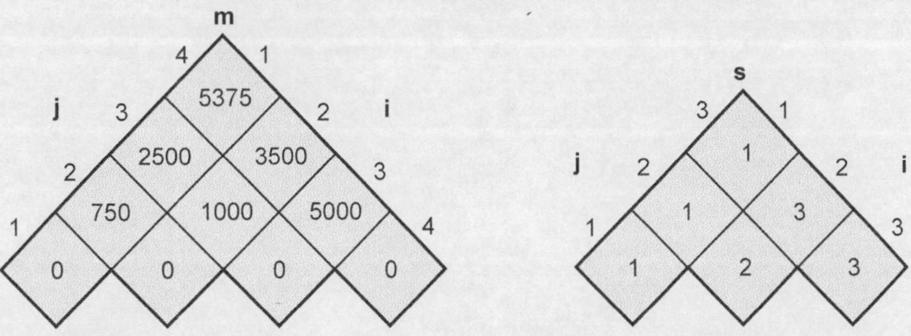

From above table,

The matrix chain order which we get is $(A_1((A_2A_3)A_4))$.

Q.5 a) *Explain : Articulation point, graph, tree.* **[3]**

Ans. : **Articulation point :** Refer section 6.7.1.

Graph : Refer section 6.2.

Tree : Tree is a finite set of one or more nodes such that,

i) There is specially designated node called root.

ii) The remaining nodes are partitioned into n > = 0 disjoint sets $T_1, T_2, T_3, \ldots, T_n$ where $T_1, T_2, T_3, \ldots, T_n$ are called the sub - trees of the root.

b) *Explain 4 queen problem with one of the solution.* **(Refer section 7.3)** **[4]**

c) *What is Rabin Karp algorithm ? Where it is used ? Explain the concept behind this algorithm and calculate its time complexity.* **(Refer section 8.3)** **[7]**

OR

Q.5 a) *What is finite automata ? Explain use of finite automata for string matching with suitable example.* **(Refer section 8.4)** **[3]**

b) *Explain naive string matching algorithm with example.* **(Refer section 8.2)** **[4]**

c) *Explain traveling salesman problem with example.* **(Refer section 9.7)** **[7]**

❑❑❑

Winter - 2017 **Analysis and Design of Algorithms** **Semester - V (CE / CSE / IT / I & CT)**	**Gujarat Technological University** **Solved Paper**

Time : $2\frac{1}{2}$ Hours] **[Total Marks : 70**

Instructions :

1. *Attempt all questions.*
2. *Make suitable assumptions wherever necessary.*
3. *Figures to the right indicate full marks.*

Q.1 a) *Define an algorithm. List various criteria used for analyzing an algorithm.* **(Refer section 2.1)** **[3]**

b) *What is smallest value of n such that an algorithm whose running time is $100n^2$ runs faster than an algorithm whose running time is 2^n on the same machine ?* **(Refer example 2.4.5)** **[4]**

c) *What do you mean by asymptotic notation ? Describe in brief any three asymptotic notations used for algorithm analysis.* **(Refer section 2.4)** **[7]**

Q.2 a) *What do you mean by divide and conquer approach ? List advantages and disadvantages of it.* **(Refer section 3.2)** **[3]**

b) *Left f(n) and g(n) be asymptotically nonnegative functions. Using the basic definition of notation, prove the max (f(n), g(n) = (Θ f(n) + g(n)).* **(Refer example 2.5.6)** **[4]**

c) *Solve the following recurrence relation using iteration method. $T(n) = 8T(n/2) + n^2$ Here $T(1) = 1$.* **[7]**

Ans. :

Let $$T(n) = 8T\left(\frac{n}{2}\right)+n^2$$

$$= 8\left(8T\left(\frac{n}{2^2}\right)+\left(\frac{n}{2}\right)^2\right)+n^2$$

$$= 8^2T\left(\frac{n}{2^2}\right)+8\left(\frac{n^2}{4}\right)+n^2$$

$$= 8^2 T\left(\frac{n}{2^2}\right) + 2n^2 + n^2$$

$$= 8^2\left(8T\left(\frac{n}{2^3}\right) + \left(\frac{n}{2^2}\right)^2\right)$$

$$= 8^3 T\left(\frac{n}{2^3}\right) + 8^2\left(\frac{n^2}{4^2}\right) + 2n^2 + n^2$$

$$= 8^3 T\left(\frac{n}{2^3}\right) + 2^2 n^2 + 2n^2 + n^2$$

$$= \ldots\ldots$$

$$= n^2 + 2n^2 + 2^2 n^2 + \cdots 2^{i-1} n^2 + 8^i T\left(\frac{n}{2^i}\right)$$

$$= n^2 + 2n^2 + 2^2 n^2 + 2^3 n^2 + \cdots + 2^{\log n - 1} n^2 + 8^{\log n}$$

$$= \sum_{k=0}^{\log n - 1} 2^k n^2 + 8^{\log n}$$

$$= n^2 \sum_{k=0}^{\log n - 1} 2^k + (2^3)^{\log n}$$

But $\displaystyle\sum_{k=0}^{\log n - 1} 2^k = \Theta(2^{\log n - 1}) = \Theta(n)$

$\therefore$ $(2^3)^{\log n} = (2^{\log n})^3 = n^3$

$\therefore$ $T(n) = n^3 \cdot \Theta(n) + n^3$

$\mathbf{T(n) \approx \Theta(n^3)}$

OR

c) *Solve the following recurrence relation using substitution method. T(n) = 2T(n/2) + n. Here T (1) = 1.* **(Refer section 3.7 (Analysis - substitution method))** **[7]**

Q.3 a) *Differentiate between greedy method and dynamic programming.* **(Refer section 5.3)** **[3]**

b) *Prove that the fractional knapsack problem has the greedy - choice property.* **(Refer section 5.9)** **[4]**

c) *Find optimal sequence of multiplication using dynamic programming of following matrices : A1 [10 × 100], A2 [100 × 5], A3 [5 × 50] and A4 [50 × 1]. List optimal number of multiplication and parenthesization of matrices.* **[7]**

Ans. :

Let, $P_0 = 10, P_1 = 100, P_2 = 5, P_3 = 50, P_4 = 1$

Let, m[1, 1], m[2, 2], m[3, 3] and [4, 4] = 0

Now let i = 1, j = 2, k = 1

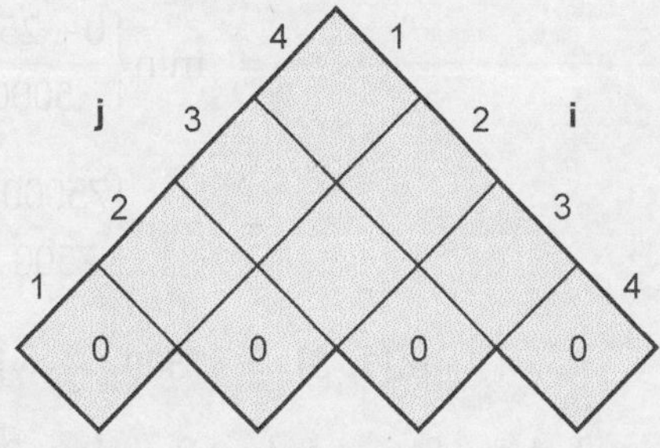

$$m[i, j] = m[i, k] + m[k+1, j] + P_{i-1}P_kP_j$$

$$= m[1,1] + m[2,2] + P_0\ P_1\ P_2$$

$$= 0 + 0 + 10*100*5$$

$$\mathbf{m[1, 2] = 5000}$$

Let i = 2, j = 3, k = 2

$$m[i, j] = m[i, k] + m[k+1, j] + P_{i-1}P_kP_j$$

$$= m[2,2] + m[3,3] + P_1\ P_2\ P_3$$

$$= 0 + 0 + 100*5*50$$

$$m[2, 3] = 25000$$

Let, i = 3, j = 4, k = 3

$$m[i, j] = m[i, k] + m[k+1, j] + P_{i-1}P_kP_j$$

$$m[3, 4] = m[3,3] + m[4,4] + P_2\ P_3\ P_4$$

$$= 0 + 0 + 5*50*1$$

$$\mathbf{m[3, 4] = 250}$$

The tables can be partially filled as

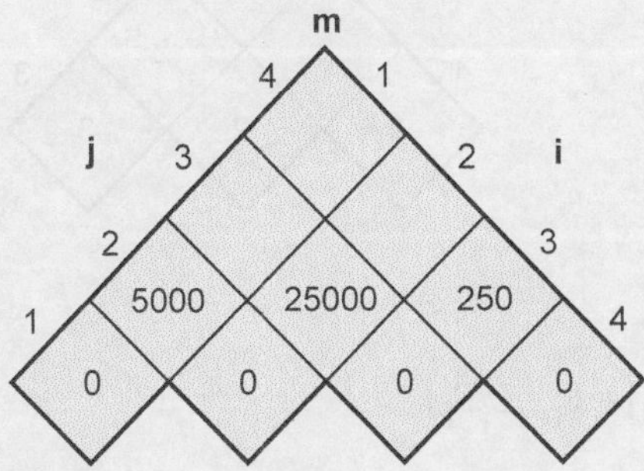

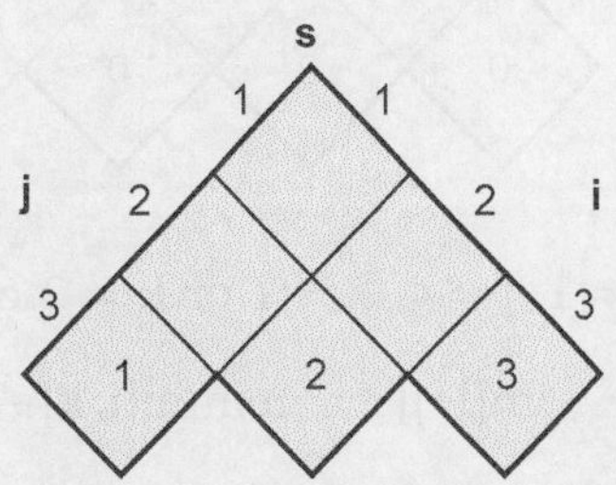

Let i = 1, j = 3, k = 1 or k = 2

$$m[i, j] = \min\{m[i,k] + m[k+1,j] + P_{i-1}P_kP_j\}$$

$$m[1, 3] = \min\begin{Bmatrix} m[1,1] + m[2,3] + P_0\ P_1\ P_3 \\ m[1,2] + m[3,3] + P_0\ P_2\ P_3 \end{Bmatrix}$$

$$= \min\begin{Bmatrix} 0 + 25000 + 10*100*50 \\ 5000 + 0 + 10*5*50 \end{Bmatrix}$$

$$= \min\begin{Bmatrix} 75000 \\ 7500 \end{Bmatrix}$$

m[1, 3] = 7500 with k = 2

Let i = 2, j = 4, k = 2 or k = 3

$$m[i, j] = \min\{m[i,k] + m[k+1,j] + P_{i-1}P_jP_k\}$$

$$m[2, 4] = \min\begin{Bmatrix} m[2,2] + m[3,4] + P_1\ P_4\ P_2 \\ m[2,3] + m[4,4] + P_1\ P_4\ P_3 \end{Bmatrix}$$

$$= \min\begin{Bmatrix} 0 + 250 + 100*1*5 \\ 25000 + 0 + 100*1*50 \end{Bmatrix}$$

$$= \min\begin{Bmatrix} 750 \\ 30{,}000 \end{Bmatrix}$$

m[2, 4] = 750 with k = 2

The tables can be partially filled as

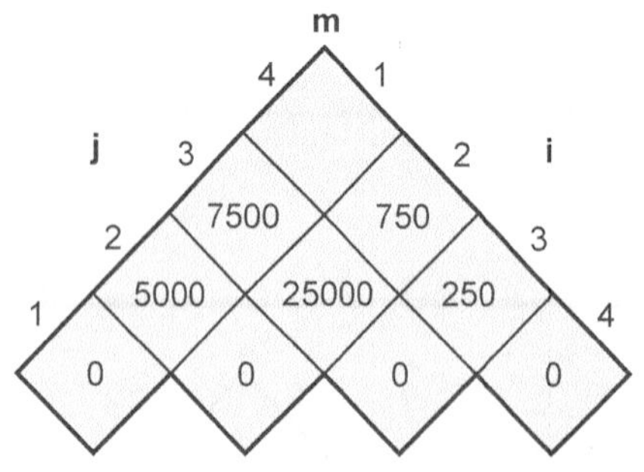

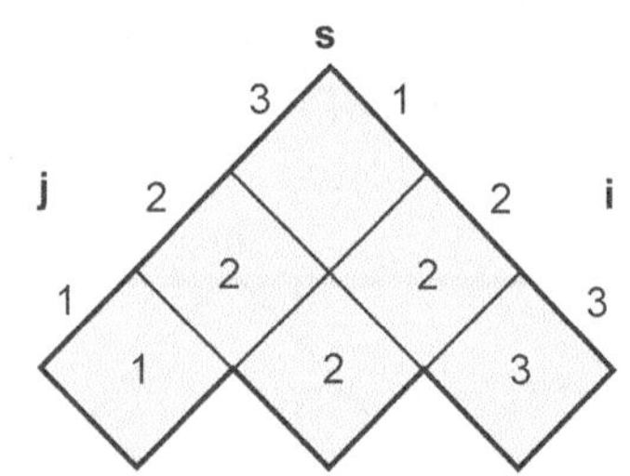

Let i = 1, j = 4, k = 1 or k = 2 or k = 3

$$m[i, j] = \min\{m[i,k] + m[k+1,j] + P_{i-1}P_jP_k\}$$

$$= \min \begin{Bmatrix} m[1,1]+m[2,4]+P_0 P_4 P_1 \\ m[1,2]+m[3,4]+P_0 P_4 P_2 \\ m[1,3]+m[4,4]+P_0 P_4 P_3 \end{Bmatrix}$$

$$m[1, 4] = \min \begin{Bmatrix} 0+750+10*1*100 \\ 5000+250+10*1*5 \\ 7500+0+10*1*50 \end{Bmatrix}$$

$$= \min \begin{Bmatrix} 1750 \\ 5300 \\ 8000 \end{Bmatrix}$$

m[1, 4] = 1750 with **k = 1**

The tables are as follows

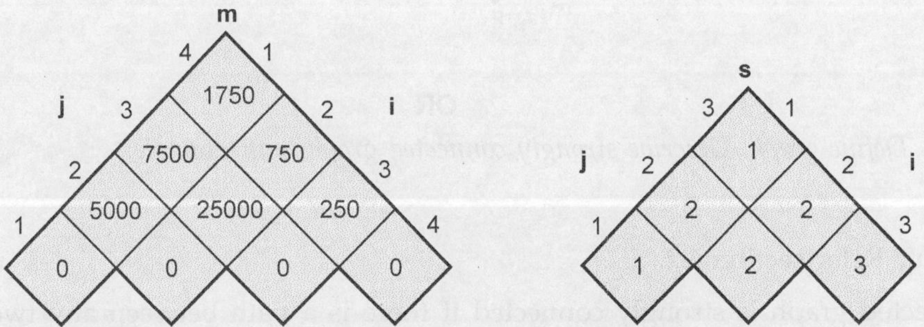

The optimal chained matrix order = **(A1(A2(A3A4)))**

OR

Q.3 a) *Briefly describe greedy choice property and optimal substructure.* **(Refer section 5.5)** **[3]**

b) *Suppose that we have a set of activities of schedule among a large number of lecture halls, where any activity can take place in any lecture hall. We wish to schedule all the activities using as few lecture halls as possible. Give an efficient greedy algorithm to determine which activity should use which lecture hall.* **(Refer section 5.6)** **[4]**

c) *Describe longest common subsequence problem. Find longest common subsequence of following two strings X and Y using dynamic programming. X = abbacdcba, Y = bcdbbcaac.* **(Refer example 4.9.2)** **[7]**

Q.4 a) *Differentiate between depth first search and breadth first search.* **(Refer section 6.5.2)** **[3]**

b) *Discuss and derive an equation for solving the 0/1 Knapsack problem using dynamic programming method.* **(Refer section 4.6)** **[4]**

c) *List applications of a minimum spanning tree. Find minimum spanning tree using Krushkal's algorithm of the following graph.*
(Refer section 5.7 and similar example 5.7.9) **[7]**

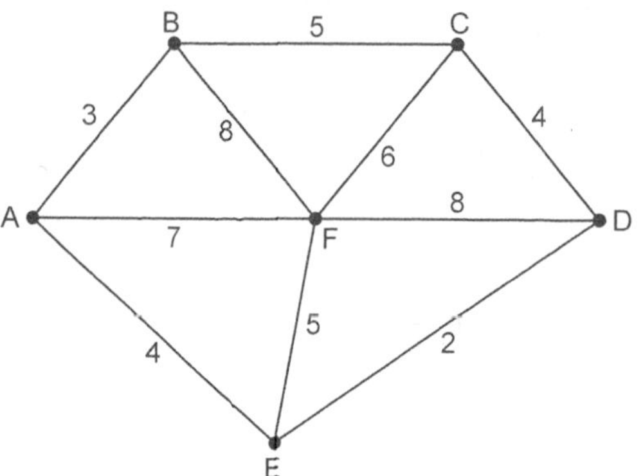

OR

Q.4 a) *Define graph. Describe strongly connected graph with example.* **[3]**

Ans. :

Graph : Refer section 6.2.

A directed graph is strongly connected if there is a path between any two pairs of vertices.

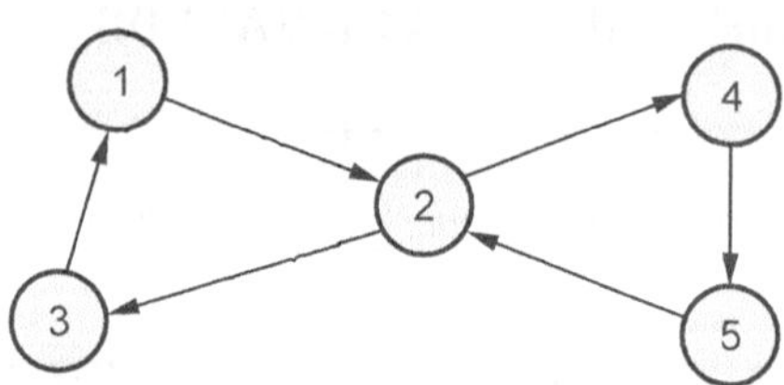

b) *Given an adjacency - list representation of a directed graph, how long does it take to compute the out - degree of every vertex ? How long does it take to compute the in - degrees ?* **(Refer section 6.4)** **[4]**

c) *Define minimum spanning tree. Find minimum spanning tree using Prim's algorithm of the following graph.* **(Refer similar example 5.7.4)** **[7]**

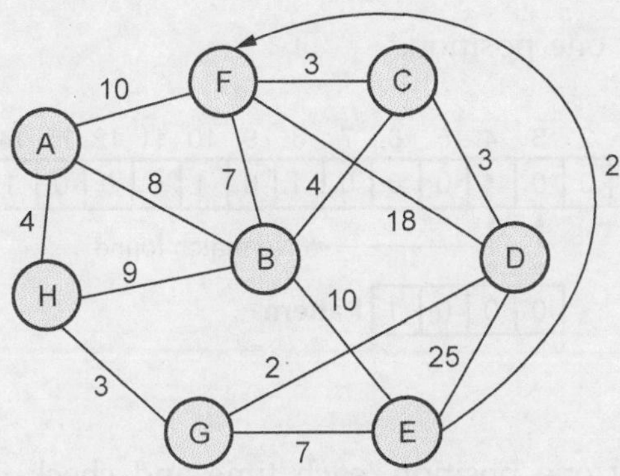

Q.5 a) *Define amortized analysis. Briefly explain its two techniques.* **(Refer section 2.7)** **[3]**

b) *Show the comparisons the native string matcher makes for the pattern P = 0001 in the text T = 0000 1000 1010001.* **[4]**

Ans. :

Let,

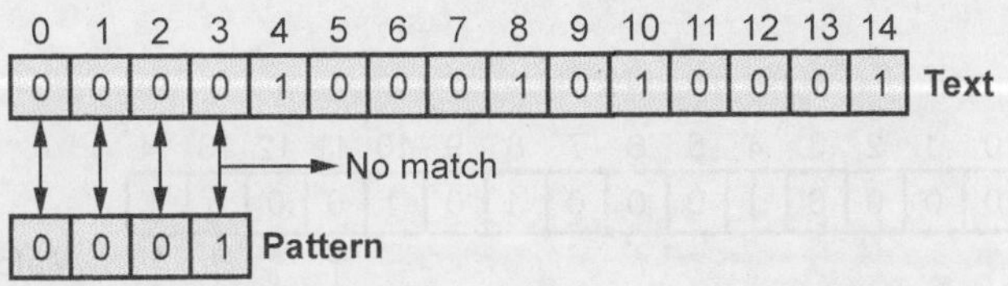

Shift to right by one position.

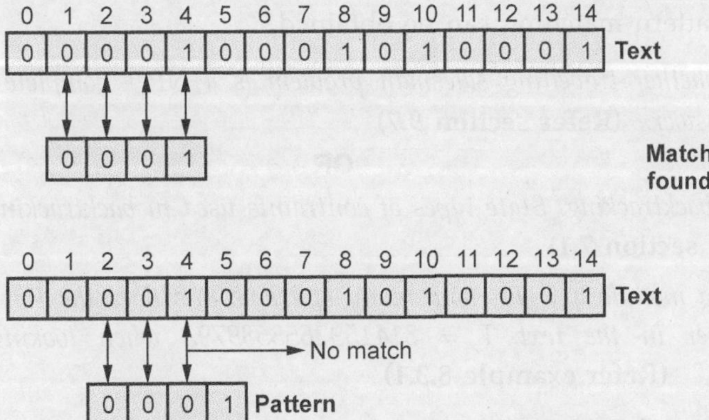

Shift pattern right by one position.

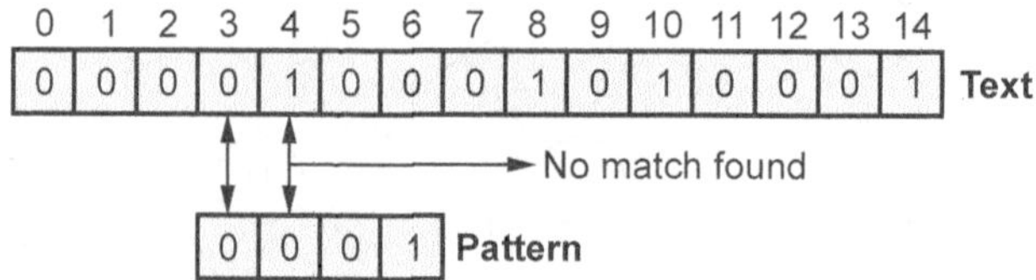

Shift pattern right by one position, each time and check pattern against text. The matched pattern will be

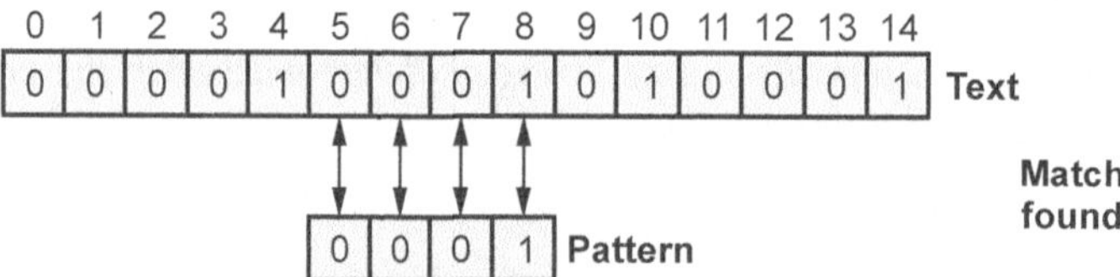

Similarly

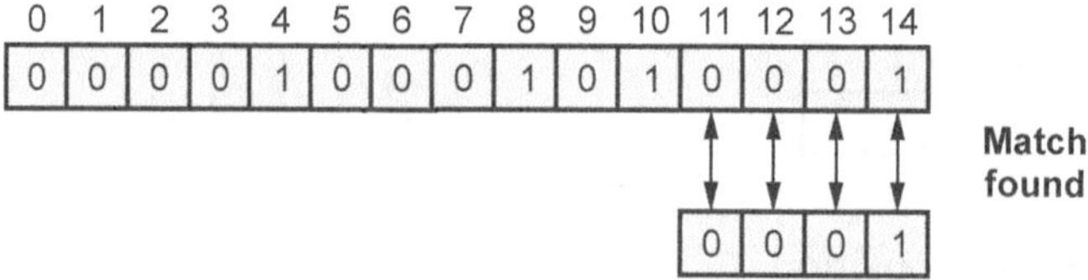

Thus pattern matching can be obtained.

c) *State whether travelling salesman problem is a NP - complete problem ? Justify your answer.* **(Refer section 9.7)** **[7]**

OR

Q.5 a) *Define backtracking. State types of contraints used in backtracking.* **(Refer section 7.1)** **[3]**

b) *Working modulo q = 11, how many spurious hits does the Rabin - Karp matcher encounter in the text T = 3141592653589793 when looking for the pattern P = 26 ?* **(Refer example 8.3.1)** **[4]**

c) *Prove that if G is an undirected biparitite graph with an odd number of vertices, then G is nonhamiltonian.* **(Refer section 9.4.4)** **[7]**

❑❑❑

Summer - 2018 **Analysis and Design of Algorithms** Semester - V (CE / CSE / IT / I & CT)	**Gujarat Technological University** **Solved Paper**

Time : $2\frac{1}{2}$ Hours] **[Total Marks : 70**

Q.1 a) *Define algorithm. Discuss key characteristics of algorithm.* **(Refer section 1.2)** **[3]**

b) *Prove or disprove that f(n) = 1 + 2 + 3 + ... + n ∈ Θ (n^2).* **[4]**

Ans. : Let, $f(n) = 1+2+3+.....n = \frac{n(n-1)}{2} \approx \frac{1}{2}n^2$

$g(n) = n^2$

- By definition $f(n) \in \Theta(g(n))$ if

  $c_1 * g(n) \le f(n) \le c_2 * g(n)$

- If $c_1 = \frac{1}{4}$ and n = 2 then

  $c_1 * g(n) \le f(n) \Rightarrow \frac{1}{4}(2^2) \le (2^2)$ is true

- If $c_2 = 1$ and n = 2

  $f(n) \le c_2 * g(n) \Rightarrow \frac{1}{2}(2^2) \le (2^2)$ is true

- As both the cases are true, it proves that.

  $1 + 2 + 3 + ... + n \in \Theta(n^2)$

c) *Which are the basic steps of counting sort ? Write counting sort algorithm. Derive its time complexity in worst case.* **(Refer section 2.8.2.3)** **[7]**

Q.2 a) *What are the advantages of dynamic programming method over devide-&-conquer method ?* **[3]**

Ans. : 1) In dynamic programming duplicating solutions are totally avoided.

2) The dynamic programming technique is efficient than the divide and conquer algorithm

3) In divide and conquer algorithm the input is split at its middle point. However, the dynamic programming method splits the input at every possible split points. After trying all split points it determines which split point is optimal.

b) *Solve following recurrence using reursion tree method :*
T(n) = 3T(n/3) + n ^ 3. **[4]**

Ans. : We Assume T(1) = 1

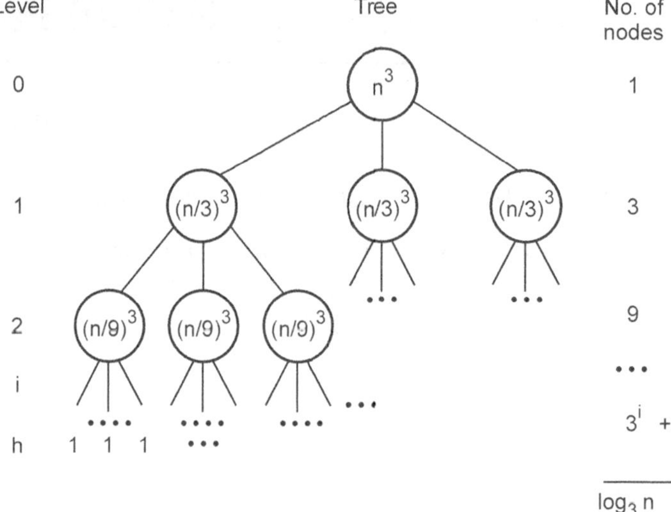

$$3^i \quad + 3^i\left(\frac{n}{3^i}\right)^3$$

$$\sum_{i=0}^{\log_3 n} 3^i\left(\frac{n}{3^i}\right)^3$$

$$\frac{n}{3^h} = 1 = n = 3^h = \log_3 n = h$$

Let, $\quad 3^i = x$

$$\therefore \quad \sum_{i=0}^{\log_3 n} x\left(\frac{n}{x}\right)^3 = \sum_{i=0}^{\log_3 n} x\left(\frac{n^3}{x^3}\right) = \sum_{i=0}^{\log_3 n} \frac{n^3}{x^2} = \sum_{i=0}^{\log_3 n} \frac{n^3}{(3^i)^2}$$

$$T(n) = \sum_{i=0}^{\log_3 n} n^3\left(\frac{1}{(3^i)^2}\right) \qquad \ldots(1)$$

Now we will use

$$\sum_{i=m}^{n} ar^i = a\frac{r^m - r^{n+1}}{1-r} \quad \text{where } r \neq 1$$

Consider equation (1), for above formula.

$$\underset{i=0\ (m)}{\overset{\log_3 n\ (n)}{\sum}} \underbrace{n^3}_{a} \underbrace{\left(\frac{1}{3^2}\right)^i}_{r} \xrightarrow{\text{implies}} n^3 \frac{\left(\frac{1}{3^2}\right)^0 - \left(\frac{1}{3^2}\right)^{\log_3 n + 1}}{1-\left(\frac{1}{3^2}\right)}$$

$$= n^3\left[\frac{1-\left(\frac{1}{9}\right)^{\log_3 n+1}}{\frac{8}{9}}\right] = \frac{9}{8}n^3\left[1-\left(\frac{1}{9}\right)^{\log_3 n}\cdot\left(\frac{1}{9}\right)\right]$$

Neglecting constants in the square bracket

$$\approx \frac{9}{8}n^3$$

$$T(n) = \Theta(\mathbf{n^3})$$

Hence, Time complexey of

$$T(n) = \Theta(\mathbf{n^3})$$

c) *Write standard (conventional) algorithm and Strassen's algorithm for matrix multiplication problem. What is the recurrence for Strassen's algorithm ? Solve it using master method to derive time complexity of Strassen's algorithm.* **(Refer section 3.9)** **[7]**

OR

c) *Discuss best case, average case and worst case time complexity of quick sort.* **(Refer section 3.8)** **[7]**

Q.3 a) *Justify with example that shortest path problem satisfies the principle of optimality.* **(Refer section 4.7)** **[3]**

b) *Which are the three basic steps of the development of the dynamic programming algorithm ? Mention any two examples of dynamic programming that we are using in real life.* **(Refer sections 4.2.2, 4.4 and 4.5)** **[4]**

c) *Solve the following making change problem using dynamic programming method : Amount ₹ 7 and Denominations : (₹ 1, ₹ 2 and ₹4).* **[7]**

Ans. : d1 = 1, d2 = 2 and d3 = 4 and N = 7

We will create a table with rows ranging from 1 to 3 and column ranging from 0 to 7.

Initially C[i,0]=0

C[1,0] = C[2,0] = C[3,0] = 0

		0	1	2	3	4	5	6	7
i = 1	d1 = 1	0							
i = 2	d2 = 2	0							
i = 3	d3 = 4	0							

Computations can be performed column by column and fill up the table accordingly.

We will use following formula

1. If i = 1 then C[i,j] = 1 + C[1,j – d1]
2. If j < di then C[i,j] = 1 + C[i – 1,j]
3. Otherwise C[i,j] = min(C[i –1,j],1 + C[I,j – d1])

Step 1	C[1,1] with i = 1, j = 1,d1 = 1 As i = 1, **Formula Used :** 1 + C[1,j – d1] = 1 + C[1,1 – 1] = 1 + C[1,0] = 1 + 0 = 1 ∴ **C[1,1] = 1**	C[2,1] with i = 2,j = 1,d2 = 2 As j<d2 **Formula Used :** C[i – 1,j] = C[1,1] = 1 ∴ **C[2,1] = 1**	C[3,1] with i = 3, j = 1, d3 = 4 As j<d3 **Formula Used :** C[i – 1,j] = C[3 – 1,1] = C[2,1] **C[3,1] = 1**
Step 2	C[1,2] with i = 1, j = 2, d1 = 1 As i = 1 **Formula Used:** 1+C[1,j – d1] = 1+C[1,1] = 1 + 1 ∴ **C[1,2] = 2**	C[2,2] with i = 2,j = 2, d2 = 2 As j = d2 and i ≠ 1 **Formula Used:** min(C[i – 1,j],1 + C[i,j – di]) = min(C[1,2] , 1 + C[2,0] = min (2, 1 + 0) ∴ **C[2,2] = 1**	C[3,2] with i = 3, j = 2, d 3 = 4 As j<d3 **Formula Used :** C[i – 1,j] = C[3 – 1,2] = C[2,2] ∴ **C[3,2] = 1**
Step 3	C[1,3] with i = 1, j = 3,d1 = 1 As i = 1 **Formula Used :** 1+C[1,j – d1] = 1+C[1,2] = 1 + 2 ∴ **C[1,3] = 3**	C[2,3] with i = 2, j = 3, d2 = 2 As j > d3 **Formula Used :** = min(C[i – 1,j], 1+C[i,j – di]) = min(C[1,3], 1+C[2,1]) = min (3, 2) ∴ **C[2,3] = 2**	C[3,3] with i = 3, j = 3, d 3 = 4 As j<d3 **Formula Used :** C[i – 1,j] = C[3 – 1,3] = C[2,3] ∴ **C[3,3] = 2**
Step 4	C[1,4] with i = 1, j = 4, d1 = 1 As i = 1 **Formula Used:** 1+C[1,j – d1] = 1+C[1,4 – 1] = 1 + C[1,3] ∴ **C[1,4] = 4**	C[2,4] with i = 2, j = 4, d2 = 2 As j > d2 **Formula Used :** = min(C[i – 1,j], 1+C[i,j – di]) = min(C[1,4], 1+C[2,2]) = min (4, 1+1) ∴ **C[2,4] = 2**	C[3,4] with i = 3, j = 4,d 3 = 4 As j=d3 and i **Formula Used :** = min(C[i – 1,j], 1+C[i,j – di]) = min(C[2,4], 1+C[3,0] = min (2,1+0) ∴ **C[3,4] = 1**

Step 5	C[1,5] with i = 1, j = 5, d1 = 1 As i = 1 Formula Used : 1+C[1,j – d1] = 1+C[1,5 – 1] = 1+C[1,4] ∴ **C[1,5] = 5**	C[2,5] with i = 2, j = 5, d2 = 2 As j > d2 **Formula Used :** = min(C[i – 1,j], 1+C[i,j-di]) = min(C[1,5], 1+C[2,3]) = min (5,1+2) ∴ **C[2,5] = 3**	C[3,5] with i = 3, j = 5, d3 = 4 As j > d2 **Formula Used :** = min(C[i – 1,j], 1+C[i, j – di]) = min(C[2,5], 1+C[3,1]) = min (3, 1+1) ∴ **C[3,5] = 2**
Step 6	C[1,6] with i = 1, j = 6,d1 = 1 As i = 1 **Formula Used :** 1+C[1,j – d1] = 1+C[1,6 – 1] = 1+C[1,5] ∴ **C[1,6] = 6**	C[2,6] with i = 2, j = 6,d2 = 2 As j > d2 **Formula Used :** = min(C[i – 1,j], 1+C[i,j – di]) = min(C[1,6], 1+C[2,4]) = min (6, 1+2) **C[2,6] = 3**	C[3,6] with i = 3, j = 6, d3 = 4 As j > d2 **Formula Used :** = min(C[i – 1,j], 1+C[i,j – di]) = min(C[2,6], 1+C[3,2]) = min (3, 1+2) **C[3,6] = 3**
Step 7	C[1,7] with i = 1, j = 7, d1 = 1 As i = 1 **Formula Used :** 1+C[1,j – d1] = 1+C[1,7 – 1] = 1+C[1,6] ∴ **C[1,7] = 7**	C[2,7] with i = 2, j = 7,d2 = 2 As j > d2 **Formula Used:** = min(C[i – 1,j], 1+C[i,j – di]) = min(C[1,7], 1+C[2,5]) = min (7, 1+3) ∴ **C[2,7] = 4**	C[3,7] with i = 3, j = 7,d3 = 4 As j > d2 **Formula Used :** = min(C[i – 1,j], 1+C[i,j – di]) = min(C[2,7], 1+C[3,3]) = min (4, 1+2) ∴ **C[3,7] = 3**

Thus we can represent the table filled up with above computations will be -

		0	**1**	**2**	**3**	**4**	**5**	**6**	**7**
i = 1	d1 = 1	0	1	2	3	4	5	6	7
i = 2	d2 = 2	0	1	1	2	2	3	3	4
i = 3	d3 = 4	0	1	2	2	1	2	3	3

Total number of coins

The value C[n,N] i.e C[3,7] = 3 which represents total number of coins required to get the sum 7 are 3.

Thus we get

₹ 1 -> 1 coin

₹ 2-> 1 coin

₹ 3 -> 1 coin

Sum=7

OR

Q.3 a) *Justify with example that longest path problem does not satisfy the principle of optimality.* **(Refer section 4.7)** **[3]**

b) *Discuss general characteristics of greedy method. Mention any two examples of greedy method that we are using in real life.* **(Refer sections 5.2, 5.6 and 5.10)** **[4]**

c) *Solve all pair shortest path problem for the following graph using Floyd's algorithm.* **[7]**

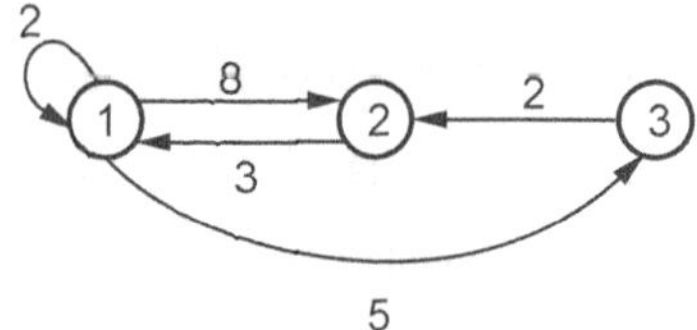

Ans. :

k = 1, i = 1, j = 1 compute **$D_{(1)}$[1,1]**	$D_{(1)}[1,1]$ = min $D_{(0)}[1,1], D_{(0)}[1,1] + D_{(0)}[1,1]$ = min{2,2+2} **$D_{(1)}$D(1)[1,1] = 2**
k = 1, i = 1, j = 2 compute **$D_{(1)}$ [1,2]**	$D_{(1)}[1,2]$ = min$D_{(0)}[1,2], D_{(0)}[1,1] + D_{(0)}[1,2]$ = min{8,2+8} **$D_{(1)}$ [1,2] = 8**
k = 1, i = 1, j = 3 compute **$D_{(1)}$ [1,3]**	$D_{(1)}[1,3]$ = min$D_{(0)}[1,3], D_{(0)}[1,1] + D_{(0)}[1,3]$ = min{5,2+5} **$D_{(1)}$ [1,3] = 5**
k = 1, i = 2, j = 1 compute **$D_{(1)}$ [2,1]**	$D_{(1)}[2,1]$ = min$D_{(0)}[2,1], D_{(0)}[2,1] + D_{(0)}[1,1]$ = min{3,3+2} **$D_{(1)}$ [2,1] = 3**
k = 1, i = 2, j = 2 compute **$D_{(1)}$ [2,2]**	$D_{(1)}[2,2]$ = min$D_{(0)}[2,2], D_{(0)}[2,1] + D_{(0)}[1,2]$ = min{0,3+5} **$D_{(1)}$ [2,2] = 0**

k = 1, i = 2, j = 3 compute **$D_{(1)}$[2,3]**	$D_{(1)}$[2,3] = min$D_{(0)}$[2,3], $D_{(0)}$[2,1] + $D_{(0)}$[1,3] = min{0,3+5} **$D_{(1)}$[2,3] = 8**
k = 1, i = 3, j = 1 compute **$D_{(1)}$[[3,1]**	$D_{(1)}$[3,1] = min$D_{(0)}$[3,1], $D_{(0)}$[3,1] + $D_{(0)}$[1,1] = min{∞,∞+2} **$D_{(1)}$[[3,1] = ∞**
k = 1, i = 3, j = 2 compute **$D_{(1)}$[3,2]**	$D_{(1)}$[3,2] = min$D_{(0)}$[3,2], $D_{(0)}$[3,1] + $D_{(0)}$[1,2] = min{2, ∞+5} **$D_{(1)}$[3,2] = 2**
k = 1, i = 3, j = 3 compute **$D_{(1)}$[3,3]**	$D_{(1)}$[3,3] = min {$D_{(0)}$[3,3], $D_{(0)}$ [3,1] + $D_{(0)}$ [1,3]} = min{∞,∞+5} **$D_{(1)}$[3,3] = ∞**

The matrix will be

D(1) =

2	8	5
3	0	8
∞	2	0

k = 2, i = 1, j = 1 compute **$D_{(2)}$[1,1]**	$D_{(2)}$[1,1] = min$D_{(1)}$[1,1], $D_{(1)}$[1,2] + $D_{(1)}$[2,1] = min{2,8+3} **$D_{(2)}$[1,1] = 2**
k = 2, i = 1, j = 2 compute **$D_{(2)}$[1,2]**	$D_{(2)}$[1,2] = min$D_{(1)}$[1,2], $D_{(1)}$[1,2] + $D_{(1)}$[2,2] = min{8,8+∞} **$D_{(2)}$[1,2] = 8**
k = 2, i = 1, j = 3 compute **$D_{(2)}$[1,3]**	$D_{(2)}$[1,3] = min$D_{(1)}$[1,3], $D_{(1)}$[1,2] + $D_{(1)}$[2,3] = min{5,8+8} **$D_{(2)}$[1,3] = 5**
k = 2, i = 2, j = 1 compute **$D_{(2)}$[2,1]**	$D_{(2)}$[2,1] = min$D_{(1)}$[2,1], $D_{(1)}$[2,2] + $D_{(1)}$[2,1] = min{3, 0+3} **$D_{(2)}$[2,1] = 3**
k = 2, i = 2, j = 2 compute **$D_{(2)}$[2,2]**	$D_{(2)}$[2,2] = min$D_{(1)}$[2,2], $D_{(1)}$[2,2] + $D_{(1)}$[2,2] = min{0,0+0} **$D_{(2)}$[[2,2] = 0**

k = 2, i = 2, j = 3	$D_{(2)}[2,3] = \min D_{(1)}[2,3], D_{(1)}[2,2] + D_{(1)}[2,3]$
compute	= min{8, 0+8}
$D_{(2)}$[2,3]	**$D_{(2)}$[2,3] = 8**
k = 2, i = 3, j = 1	$D_{(2)}[3,1] = \min D_{(1)}[3,1], D_{(1)}[3,2] + D_{(1)}[2,1]$
compute	= min{∞,2+3}
$D_{(2)}$[3,1]	**$D_{(2)}$[3,1]= 5**
k = 2, i = 3, j = 2	$D_{(2)}[3,2] = \min D_{(1)}[3,2], D_{(1)}[3,2] + D_{(1)}[2,2]$
compute	= min{2, 2+0}
$D_{(2)}$[3,2]	**$D_{(2)}$[3,2] = 2**
k = 2, i = 3, j = 3	$D_{(2)}[3,3] = \min D_{(1)}[3,3], D_{(1)}[3,2] + D_{(1)}[2,3]$
compute	= min{0,2+8}
$D_{(2)}$[3,3]	**$D_{(2)}$[3,3] = 0**

The matrix will be

D(2) =

2	8	5
3	0	8
5	2	0

k = 3, i = 1 ,j = 1	$D_{(3)}[1,1] = \min D_{(2)}[1,1], D_{(2)}[1,3] + D_{(2)}[3,1]$
compute	= min{2,5+5}
$D_{(3)}$[1,1]	**$D_{(3)}$[1,1] = 2**
k = 3, i = 1, j = 2	$D_{(3)}[1,2] = \min D_{(2)}[1,2], D_{(2)}[1,3] + D_{(2)}[3,2]$
compute	= min{8,5+2}
$D_{(3)}$[1,2]	**$D_{(3)}$[1,2] = 7**
k = 3, i = 1, j = 3	$D_{(3)}[1,3] = \min D_{(2)}[1,3], D_{(2)}[1,3] + D_{(2)}[3,3]$
compute	= min{5,5+0}
$D_{(3)}$[1,3]	**$D_{(3)}$[1,3] = 5**
k = 3, i = 2, j = 1	$D_{(3)}[2,1] = \min D_{(2)}[2,1], D_{(2)}[2,3] + D_{(2)}[3,1]$
compute	= min{3, 8+5}
$D_{(3)}$[2,1]	**$D_{(3)}$[2,1] = 3**

k = 3, i = 2, j = 2 compute **$D_{(3)}$ [2,2]**	$D_{(3)}[2,2] = \min D_{(2)}[2,2], D_{(2)}[2,3] + D_{(2)}[3,2]$ = min{0,8+2} **$D_{(3)}$ [2,2] = 0**
k = 3, i = 2, j = 3 compute **$D_{(3)}$ [2,3]**	$D_{(3)}[2,3] = \min D_{(2)}[2,3], D_{(2)}[2,3] + D_{(2)}[3,3]$ = min{8, 8+0} **$D_{(3)}$ [2,3] = 8**
k = 3, i = 3, j = 1 compute **$D_{(3)}$ [3,1]**	$D_{(3)}[3,1] = \min D_{(2)}[3,1], D_{(2)}[3,3] + D_{(2)}[3,1]$ = min{5,0+5} **$D_{(3)}$ [3,1] = 5**
k = 3, i = 3, j = 2 compute **$D_{(3)}$ [3,2]**	$D_{(3)}[3,2] = \min D_{(2)}[3,2], D_{(2)}[3,3] + D_{(2)}[3,2]$ = min{2, 0+2} **$D_{(3)}$ [3,2] = 2**
k = 3, i = 3, j = 3 compute **$D_{(2)}$ [3,3]**	$D_{(3)}[3,3] = \min D_{(2)}[3,3], D_{(2)}[3,3] + D_{(2)}[3,3]$ = min{0,0+0} **$D_{(3)}$ [3,3] = 0**

The matrix will be

D(3) =

2	7	5
3	0	8
5	2	0

Q.4 a) *What are the disadvantages of greedy method over dynamic programming method ?* **[3]**

Ans. : 1) In Greedy algorithm there is no guarantee of getting optimum solution.

2) The optimum selection is without revising previously generated solution.

3) Designing Greedy solution with right approach is hard.

4) Showing a Greedy algorithm correct is hard.

b) *What is DFS ? Explain with example. Show the ordering of vertices produced by Topological-sort for the following graph.* **[4]**

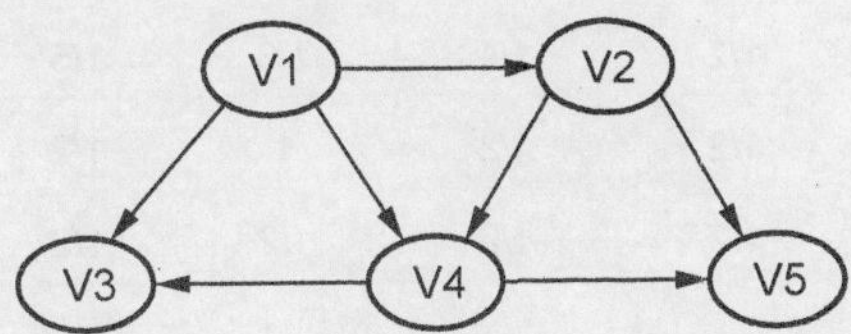

Ans. : We will find the node having no incoming edge. Such a vertex is V1. Hence delete it along with adjacent edges.

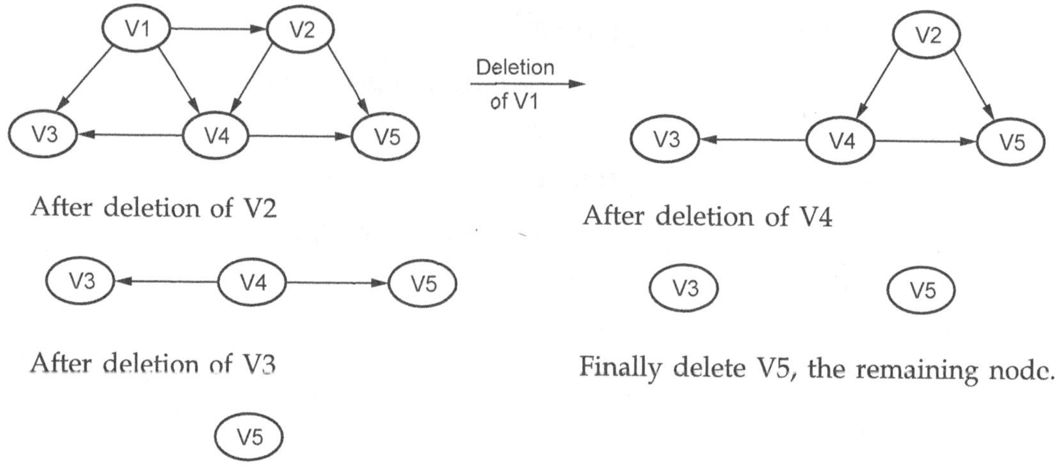

Thus the sequency in which we have deleted the nodes is V1, V2, V4, V3 and V5.

Hence the topological ordering is

V1, V2, V4, V3, V5

c) *Solve the following Knapsack problem using greedy method. Number of items = 5. Knapsack capacity W = 100, weight vector = {50, 40, 30, 20, 10} and profit vector = (1, 2, 3, 4, 5).* **[7]**

Ans. : For solving this problem, we will find out the fraction of weight that can be used to fill up the knapsack satisfying the given capacity with maximum weight. Various solutions are -

items	Profit	Weight	
1	1	50	with
2	2	40	W = 100
3	3	30	
4	4	20	
5	5	10	

Solution	x_1	x_2	x_3	x_4	x_5
1	1/2	1/2	1/3	1/2	1/2
2	1/2	1/4	1/3	1/5	1/5
3	1/2	1/2	1	1/2	1/2
4	1/2	1/2	1/2	1/2	1

Solution 1 :

$$\sum w_i x_i = \left(50*\frac{1}{2}\right)+\left(40*\frac{1}{2}\right)+\left(30*\frac{1}{3}\right)+\left(20*\frac{1}{2}\right)+\left(10*\frac{1}{2}\right) = 25 + 20 + 10 + 10 + 5$$

$$\sum w_i x_i = 70$$

$$\sum p_i x_i = \left(1*\frac{1}{2}\right)+\left(2*\frac{1}{2}\right)+\left(3*\frac{1}{3}\right)+\left(4*\frac{1}{2}\right)+\left(5*\frac{1}{2}\right) = 0.5 + 1 + 1 + 2 + 2.5$$

$$\sum p_i x_i = 7.0$$

Solution 2 :

$$\sum w_i x_i = \left(50*\frac{1}{2}\right)+\left(40*\frac{1}{4}\right)+\left(30*\frac{1}{3}\right)+\left(20*\frac{1}{5}\right)+\left(10*\frac{1}{5}\right) = 25 + 10 + 10 + 4 + 2$$

$$\sum w_i x_i = 51$$

$$\sum p_i x_i = \left(1*\frac{1}{2}\right)+\left(2*\frac{1}{4}\right)+\left(3*\frac{1}{3}\right)+\left(4*\frac{1}{5}\right)+\left(5*\frac{1}{5}\right) = 0.5 + 0.5 + 1 + 0.8 + 1$$

$$\sum p_i x_i = 3.8$$

Solution 3 :

$$\sum w_i x_i = \left(50*\frac{1}{2}\right)+\left(40*\frac{1}{2}\right)+(30*1)+\left(20*\frac{1}{2}\right)+\left(10*\frac{1}{2}\right) = 25 + 20 + 30 + 10 + 5$$

$$\sum w_i x_i = 90$$

$$\sum p_i x_i = \left(1*\frac{1}{2}\right)+\left(2*\frac{1}{2}\right)+(3*1)+\left(4*\frac{1}{2}\right)+\left(5*\frac{1}{2}\right) = 0.5 + 1 + 3 + 2 + 2.5$$

$$\sum p_i x_i = 9.0$$

Solution 4 :

$$\sum w_i x_i = \left(50*\frac{1}{2}\right)+\left(40*\frac{1}{2}\right)+\left(30*\frac{1}{2}\right)+\left(20*\frac{1}{2}\right)+(1*10) = 25 + 20 + 15 + 10 + 10$$

$$\sum w_i x_i = 80$$

$$\sum p_i x_i = \left(1*\frac{1}{2}\right)+\left(2*\frac{1}{2}\right)+\left(3*\frac{1}{2}\right)+\left(4*\frac{1}{2}\right)+(5*1) = 0.5 + 1 + 1.5 + 2 + 5$$

$$\sum p_i x_i = 10$$

From above solutions clearly solution 4 is **optimal solution.**

OR

Q.4 a) *Write an algorithm for Huffman code.* **(Refer section 5.11)** **[3]**

b) *What is an approximation algorithm ? Explain performance ratio for approximation algorithm.* **(Refer section 9.8)** **[4]**

c) *Explain use of branch and bound technique for solving assignment problem.* **[7]**

Ans. : **Problem statement :** There are n people to whom n jobs are to be assigned so that total cost of assignment is as small as possible. The assignment problem is specified by n by n matrix and each element in each row has to be selected in such a way that **no two** selected elements are in the **same column** and their **sum is smallest** as far as possible.

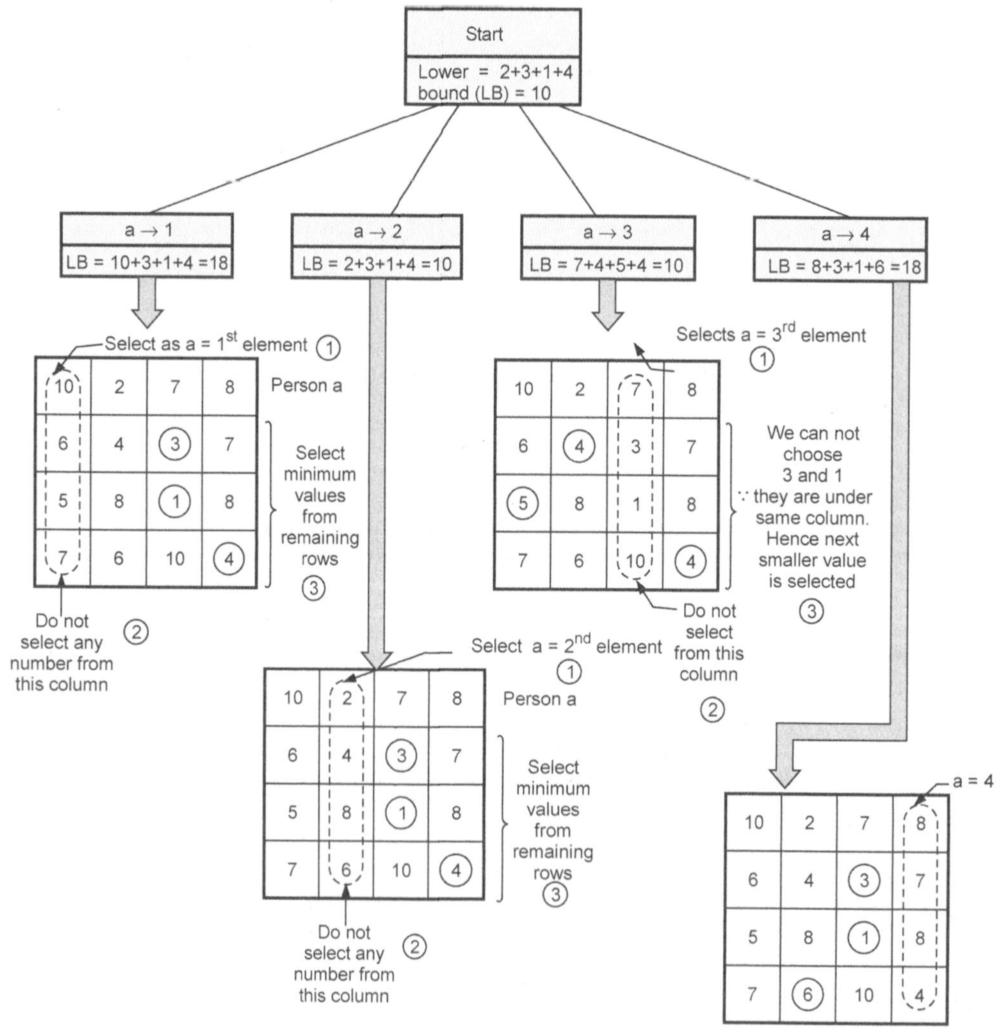

Fig. 1

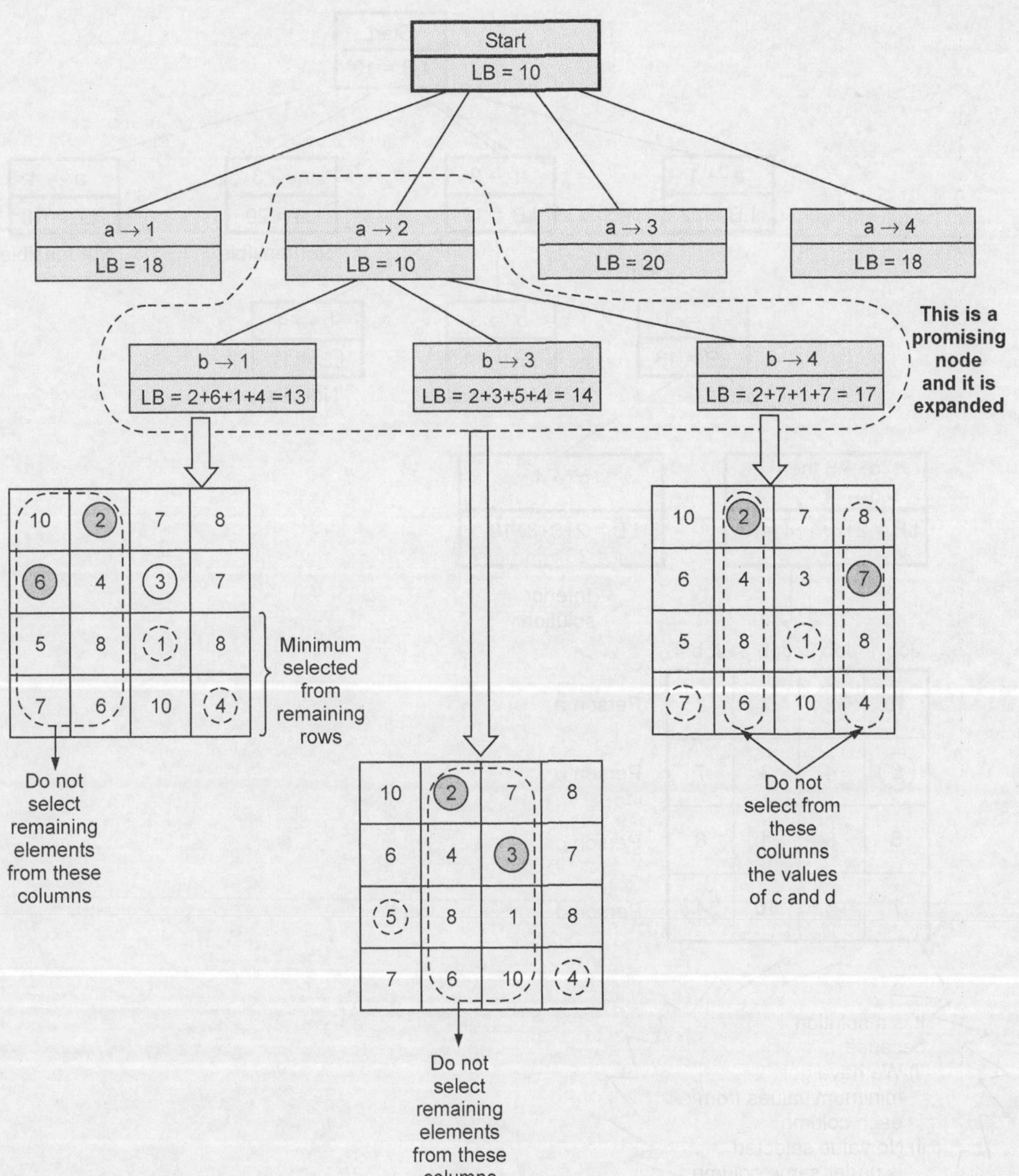
Start
LB = 10
a → 1
LB = 18
a → 2
LB = 10
a → 3
LB = 20
a → 4
LB = 18
b → 1
LB = 2+6+1+4 =13
b → 3
LB = 2+3+5+4 = 14
b → 4
LB = 2+7+1+7 = 17
This is a promising node and it is expanded
Minimum selected from remaining rows
Do not select remaining elements from these columns
Do not select from these columns the values of c and d
Do not select remaining elements from these columns

Fig. 2

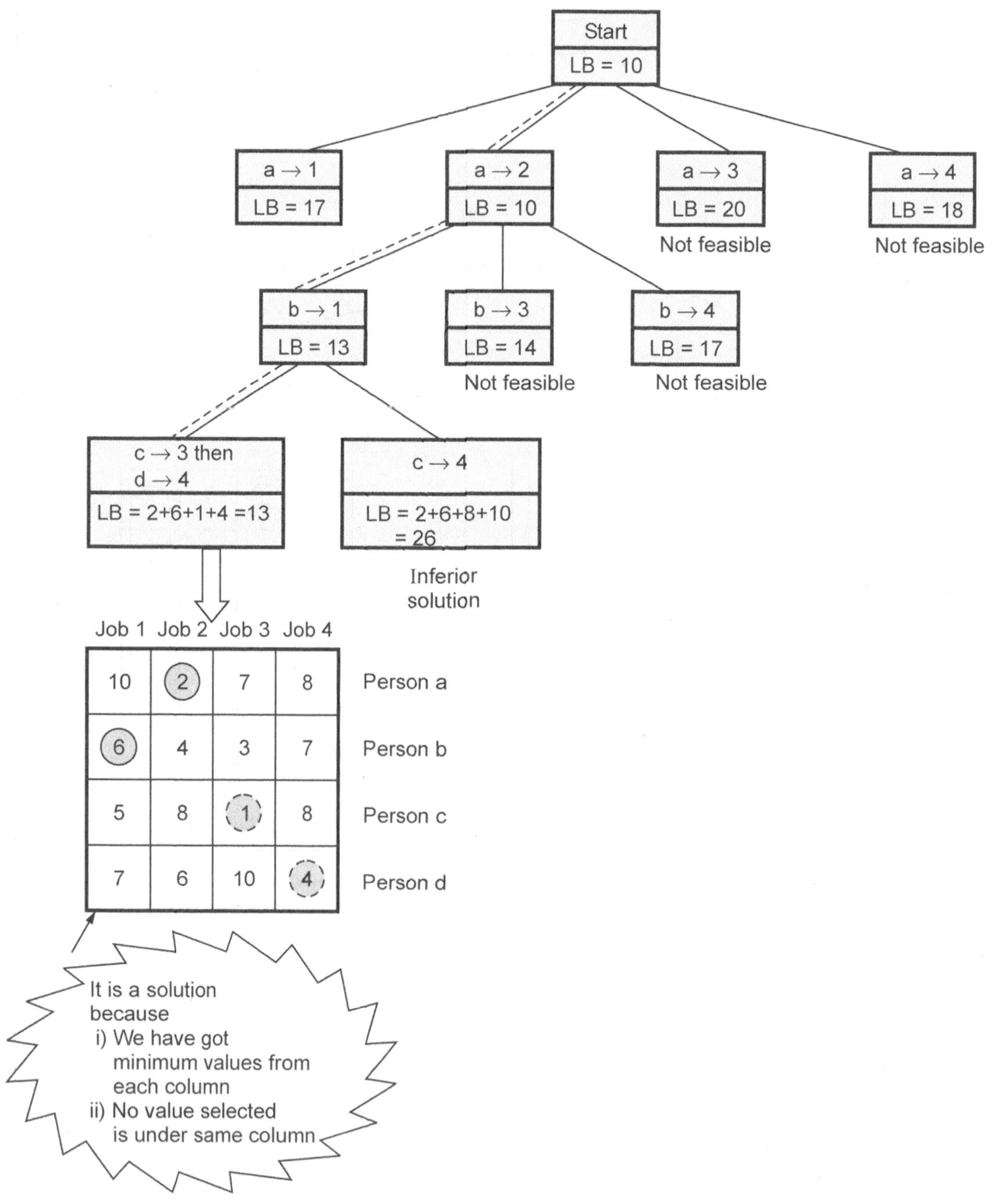
Start
LB = 10
a → 1
LB = 17
a → 2
LB = 10
a → 3
LB = 20
Not feasible
a → 4
LB = 18
Not feasible
b → 1
LB = 13
b → 3
LB = 14
Not feasible
b → 4
LB = 17
Not feasible
c → 3 then
d → 4
LB = 2+6+1+4 =13
c → 4
LB = 2+6+8+10
= 26
Inferior solution
Job 1 Job 2 Job 3 Job 4
10 2 7 8 Person a
6 4 3 7 Person b
5 8 1 8 Person c
7 6 10 4 Person d
It is a solution because
i) We have got minimum values from each column
ii) No value selected is under same column

Fig. 3

Let us take one example and understand this problem.

Job1	Job2	Job3	Job4	
10	2	7	8	Person a
6	4	3	7	Person b
5	8	1	8	Person c
7	6	10	4	Person d

If we select minimum value from each row then we get,

10	2	7	8
6	4	3	7
5	8	1	8
7	6	10	4

⇒ 2 + 3 + 1 + 4 = 10

Hence set lower bound = 10.

Now the state space tree can be drawn step by step.

Thus we have set jobs for person a, then we select jobs for person b then for person c and finally for person d.

Thus assignment problem can be solved with best fit branch and bound algorithm.

Q.5 a) *Write Naive string-matching algorithm. Explain notations used in the algorithm.* **(Refer section 8.2)** **[3]**

b) *Explain polynomial-time reduction algorithm.* **(Refer section 9.3)** **[4]**

c) *Working modulo q = 11. How many spurious hits does the Rabin-Karp matcher encounter in the text T = 3141592653589793 when looking for the pattern P = 26 ?* **(Refer example 8.3.1)** **[7]**

OR

Q.5 a) *Which are the three major concepts used to show that problem is an NP-complete problem ?* **(Refer section 9.5)** **[3]**

b) *Explain breadth first search with example.* **(Refer section 6.5.1)** **[4]**

c) *Find minimum spanning tree for the following undirected weighted graph using Kruskal's algorithm.* **[7]**

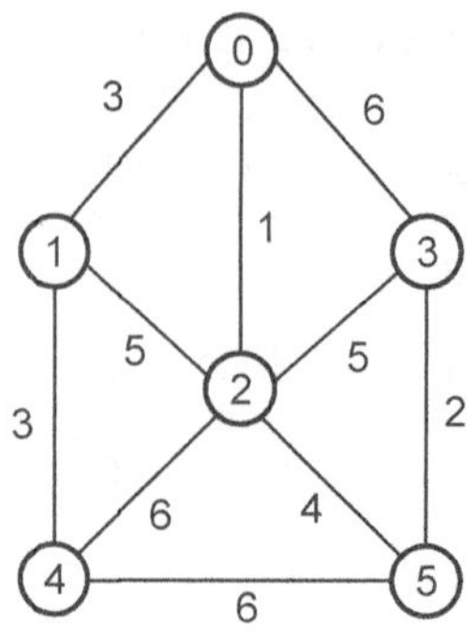

Fig. 4

Ans. :

Step 1 : Select edge 0-2

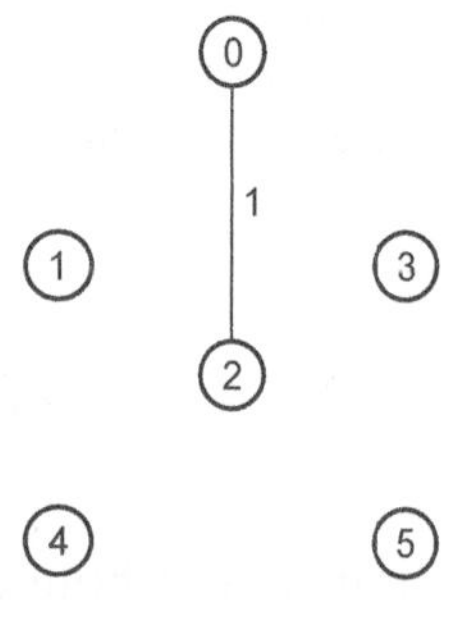

Step 2 : Select edge 3-5

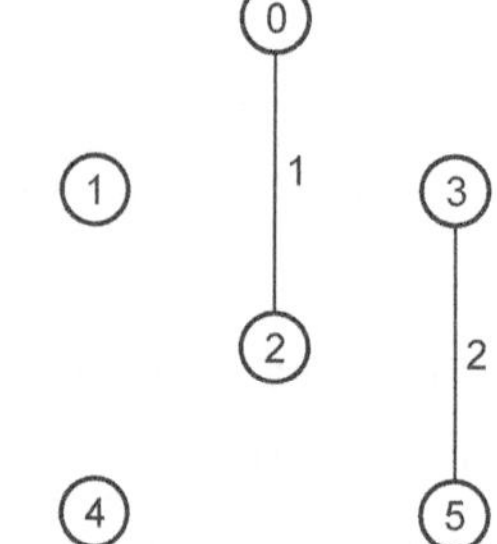

Step 3 : Select edge 0-1

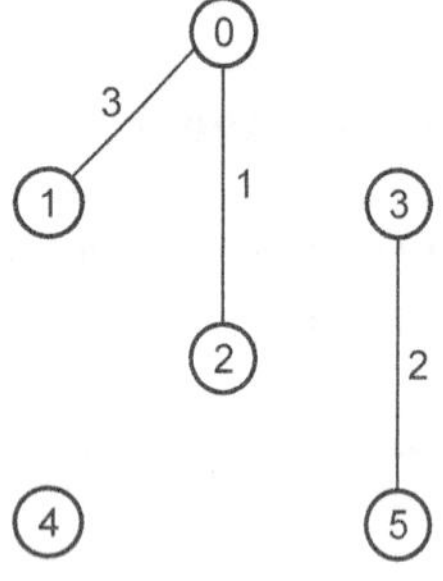

Step 4 : Select edge 1-4

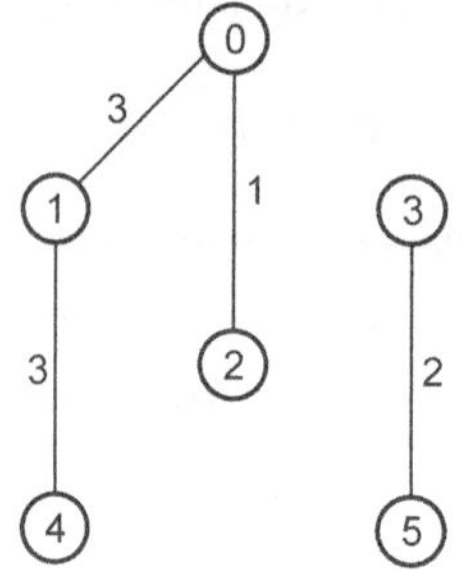

Step 5 : Select edge 2-5

This is required minimum spanning tree with total path length = **13**

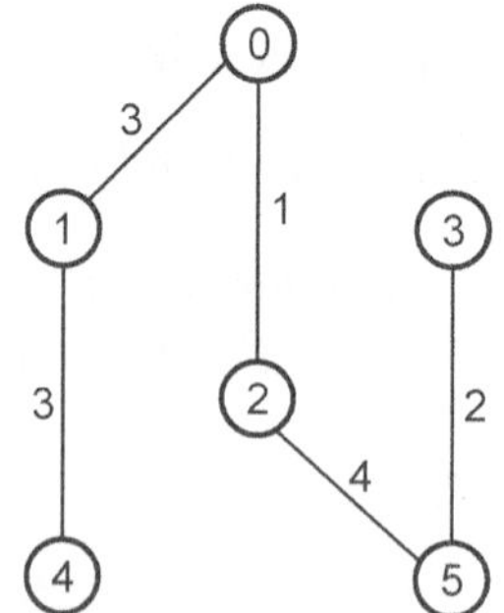

❑❑❑

Winter - 2018
Analysis and Design of Algorithms

Semester - V (CE / CSE / IT / I & CT)

Gujarat Technological University

Solved Paper

Time : $2\frac{1}{2}$ Hours] **[Total Marks : 70**

Q.1 a) *Define Algorithm. Time Complexity and Space Complexity.*
(Refer sections 1.2 and 1.3(5)) **[3]**

b) *Differentiate branch and bound and back tracking algorithm.* **[4]**

Ans. :

Sr. No.	Backtracking	Branch and Bound
1.	Solution for backtracking is traced using depth first search.	In this method, it is not necessary to use depth first search for obtaining the solution, even the breadth first search, best first search can be applied.
2.	Typically decision problems can be solved using backtracking.	Typically optimization problems can be solved using branch and bound.
3.	While finding the solution to the problem bad choices can be made.	It proceeds on better solutions. So there cannot be a bad solution.
4.	The state space tree is searched until the solution is obtained.	The state space tree needs to be searched completely as there may be chances of being an optimum solution any where in state space tree.
5.	Applications of backtracking are - M coloring, Knapsack.	Applications of branch and bound are - Job sequencing, TSP.

c) *Analyze selection sort algorithm in best case and worst case.*
(Refer section 2.8.1.2) **[7]**

Q.2 a) *Solve the recurrence $T(n) = 7T(n/2) + n^3$.* **[3]**

Ans. : Let, $T(n) = 7T\left(\frac{n}{2}\right) + n^3$

$$a = 7,\ b = 2,\ f(n) = n^3$$

$$n^{\log_2 7} = n^{2.803}$$

As $n^3 = \Omega(n^{\log_2 7} + \varepsilon)$ then

$$T(n) = \theta(f(n))$$

$\therefore$ $\mathbf{T(n) = \theta(n^3)}$

b) *Explain : Articulation Point, graph, tree.* **(Refer Q.5 (a) of Summer-2017)** **[3]**

Ans. : Tree : Tree is a collection of vertices and edges with specialized node called **root.**

c) *Write merge sort algorithm and compute its worst case and best-case time complexity. Sort the list G, U, J, A, R, A, T in alphabetical order using merge soft.* **[7]**

Ans. : Merge sort : Refer section 3.7.

Let us store the list G, U, J, A, R, A, T in an array

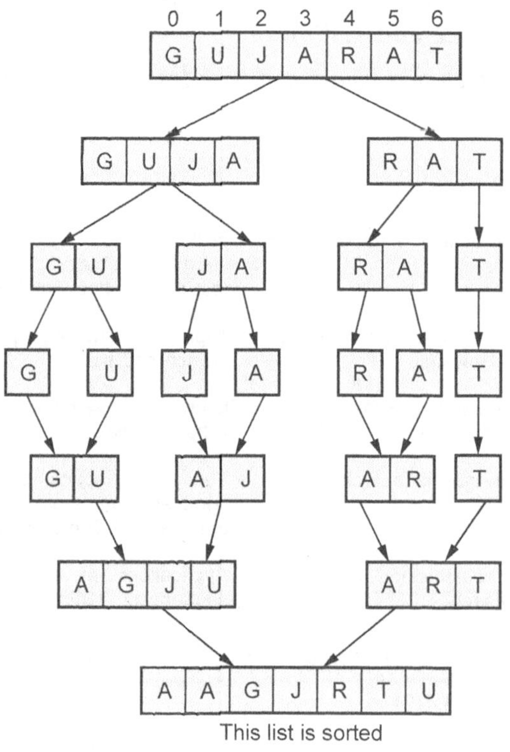

Fig. 1

OR

c) *Consider Knapsack capacity W = 9, w = (3,4,5,7) and v = (12,40,25,42) find the maximum profit using dynamic method.* **[7]**

Ans. : Let the instance of the problem be -

Item	w_i	v_i
1	3	12
2	4	40
3	5	25
4	7	42

Initially table[0, j] = 0 and the table[i, 0] = 0 There are 0 to n rows and 0 to W columns in the table. The n = 4 and W = 9. Hence partially the table is as follows -

	0	1	2	3	4	5	6	7	8	9
0	0	0	0	0	0	0	0	0	0	0
1	0									
2	0									
3	0									
4	0									

Now we will fill up the table row by row using following formula

table [i, j] = maximum{table[i-1, j], vi+table[i-1, j-wi] when j>=wi}

or table [i, j] = table[i-1, j] when j<wi

Step 1 : Computing next row

Computing table [1,1] with i = 1, j = 1 $w_i = w_1 = 3$ $v_i = v_1 = 12$	As $j < w_i$ i.e. 1 < 3 **Formula Used : table [i, j] = table[i −1, j]** ∴ table[1,1] = table[0,1] = 0 ∴ table[1,1] = 0
Computing table[1,2] with i = 1, j = 2 $w_i = w_1 = 3$ $v_i = v_1 = 12$	As $j < w_i$ i.e. 2 < 3 **Formula Used : table [i, j] = table[i −1, j]** ∴ table[1,1] = table[0,1] = 0 ∴ **table[1,2] = 0**
Computing table[1,3] with i = 1, j = 3 $w_i = w_1 = 3$ $v_i = v_1 = 12$	As $j > = w_i$ i.e. 3 = 3 **Formula Used : table [i, j] = maximum{table[i−1, j]], v_i + table[i − 1, j − w_i]}** ∴ table[1,3] = maximum{table[0,3],12+table[0,0] = 12 ∴ **table[1,3] = 12**
Computing table[1,4] with i = 1, j = 4 $w_i = w_1 = 3$ $v_i = v_1 = 12$	As $j > w_i$ i.e. 4 > 3 **Formula Used : table [i, j] = maximum{table[i −1, j], v_i + table[i −1, j −w_i]** ∴ table[1,4] = maximum{table[0,4],12 + table[0,1] = 12 ∴ **table[1,4] = 12**

Computing table[1,5] with i = 1, j = 4 $w_i = w_1 = 3$ $v_i = v_1 = 12$	As $j > w_i$ i.e. 5 > 3 **Formula Used : table [i, j] = maximum{table[i–1, j], v_i + table[i–1, j–w_i]** ∴ table[1,5] = maximum{table[0,5],12 + table[0,2] = 12 **∴ table[1,5] = 12**
Computing table[1,6] with i = 1, j = 4 $w_i = w_1 = 3$ $v_i = v_1 = 12$	As $j > w_i$ i.e. 6 > 3 **Formula Used : table [i, j] = maximum{table[i–1, j], v_i + table[i–1, j–w_i]** ∴ table[1,6] = maximum{table[0,6],12+table[0,3] = 12 **∴ table[1,6] = 12**
Computing table[1,7] with i = 1, j = 4 $w_i = w_1 = 3$ $v_i = v_1 = 12$	As $j > w_i$ i.e. 7 > 3 **Formula Used : table [i, j] = maximum{table[i–1, j], v_i + table[i–1, j–w_i]** ∴ table[1,7] = maximum{table[0,7],12 + table[0,4] = 12 **∴ table[1,7] = 12**
Computing table[1,8] with i = 1, j = 4 $w_i = w_1 = 3$ $v_i = v_1 = 12$	As $j > w_i$ i.e. 8 > 3 **Formula Used : table [i, j] = maximum{table[i–1, j], v_i + table[i–1, j–w_i]** ∴ table[1,8] = maximum{table[0,8],12 + table[0,5] = 12 ∴ table[1,8] = 12
Computing table[1,9] with i = 1, j = 4 $w_i = w_1 = 3$ $v_i = v_1 = 12$	As $j > w_i$ i.e. 9>3 **Formula Used : table [i, j] = maximum{table[i–1, j], v_i + table[i–1, j–w_i]** ∴ table[1,9] = maximum{table[0,9],12 + table[0,9] = 12 ∴ table[1,9] = 12

The partially filled table with above computed values is as follows

	0	1	2	3	4	5	6	7	8	9
0	0	0	0	0	0	0	0	0	0	0
1	0	0	0	12	12	12	12	12	12	12
2	0									
3	0									
4	0									

Step 2 : Computing next row

Computing table[2,1] with i = 2, j = 1 $w_i = w_2 = 4$ $v_i = v_2 = 40$	As j < w_i i.e. 1 < 4 **Formula Used : table [i, j] = table[i–1, j]** ∴ table[2,1] = table[1,1] = 0 **∴ table[2,1] = 0**
Computing table[2,2] with i = 2, j = 2 $w_i = w_2 = 4$ $v_i = v_2 = 40$	As j < w_i i.e. 2 < 4 **Formula Used : table [i, j] = table[i–1, j]** ∴ table[2,2] = table[1,2] = 0 **∴ table[2,2] = 0**
Computing table[2,3] with i = 2, j = 3 $w_i = w_2 = 4$ $v_i = v_2 = 40$	As j < w_i i.e. 3 < 4 **Formula Used : table [i, j] = table[i –1, j]** ∴ table[2,3] = table[1,3] = 12 **∴ table[2,3] = 12**
Computing table[2,4] with i = 2, j = 4 $w_i = w_2 = 4$ $v_i = v_2 = 40$	As j >= w_i i.e. 4 = 4 **Formula Used : table [i, j] = maximum{table[i–1, j], v_i + table[i–1, j–w_i]** ∴ table[2,4] = maximum{table[1,4],40+table[1,0] = maximum{12,40 + 0} **∴ table[2,4] = 40**
Computing table[2,5] with i = 2, j = 5 $w_i = w_2 = 4$ $v_i = v_2 = 40$	As j >= w_i i.e. 5 > 4 **Formula Used : table [i, j] = maximum{table[i–1, j], v_i + table[i–1, j–w_i]** ∴ table[2,5] = maximum{table[1,5],40 + table[1,1] = maximum{12,40 + 0} **∴ table[2,5] = 40**
Computing table[2,6] with i = 2, j = 6 $w_i = w_2 = 4$ $v_i = v_2 = 40$	As j >= w_i i.e. 6 = 4 **Formula Used : table [i, j] = maximum{table[i–1, j], v_i + table[i–1, j–w_i]** ∴ table[2,6] = maximum{table[1,6],40 + table[1,2] = maximum{12,40 + 0} **∴ table[2,6] = 40**

Computing table[2,7] with i = 2, j = 7 $w_i = w_2 = 4$ $v_i = v_2 = 40$	As j >= w_i i.e. 7 > 4 **Formula Used : table [i, j] = maximum{table[i–1, j], v_i + table[i–1, j–w_i]** ∴ table[2,7] = maximum{table[1,7],40 + table[1,3] = maximum{12,40 + 12} ∴ **table[2,7] = 52**
Computing table[2,8] with i = 2, j = 8 $w_i = w_2 = 4$ $v_i = v_2 = 40$	As j >= w_i i.e. 8 > 4 **Formula Used : table [i, j] = maximum{table[i–1, j], v_i + table[i–1, j–w_i]** ∴ table[2,8] = maximum{table[1,8],40 + table[1,4] = maximum{12,40 + 12} ∴ **table[2,8] = 52**
Computing table[2,9] with i = 2, j = 9 $w_i = w_2 = 4$ $v_i = v_2 = 40$	As j >= w_i i.e. 9 > 4 **Formula Used : table [i, j] = maximum{table[i–1, j], v_i + table[i–1, j–w_i]** ∴ table[2,9] = maximum{table[1,9],40 + table[1,5] = maximum{12,40 + 12} ∴ **table[2,9] = 52**

The partially filled table with above computed values is as follows

	0	1	2	3	4	5	6	7	8	9
0	0	0	0	0	0	0	0	0	0	0
1	0	0	0	12	12	12	12	12	12	12
2	0	0	0	12	40	40	40	52	52	52
3	0									
4	0									

Step 3 : Computing next row

Computing table[3,1] with i = 3, j = 1 $w_i = w_2 = 5$ $v_i = v_2 = 25$	As j < w_i i.e. 1 < 5 **Formula Used : table [i, j] = table[i–1, j]** ∴ table[3,1] = table[2,1] = 0 ∴ **table[3,1] = 0**
Computing table[3,2] with i = 3, j = 2 $w_i = w_2 = 5$ $v_i = v_2 = 25$	As j < w_i i.e. 2 < 5 **Formula Used : table [i, j] = table[i–1, j]** ∴ table[3,2] = table[2,2] = 0 ∴ **table[3,2] = 0**

Computing table[3,3] with i = 3, j = 3 $w_i = w_2 = 5$ $v_i = v_2 = 25$	As $j < w_i$ i.e. 3 < 5 **Formula Used : table [i, j] = table[i–1, j]** ∴ table[3,3] = table[2,3] = 12 **∴ table[3,3] = 12**
Computing table[3,4] with i = 3, j = 4 $w_i = w_2 = 5$ $v_i = v_2 = 25$	As $j < w_i$ i.e. 4 < 5 **Formula Used : table [i, j] = table[i–1, j]** ∴ table[3,4] = table[2,4] = 40 **∴ table[3,4] = 40**
Computing table[3,5] with i = 3, j = 5 $w_i = w_2 = 5$ $v_i = v_2 = 25$	As $j >= w_i$ i.e. 5 > 5 **Formula Used : table [i, j] = maximum{table[i–1, j], v_i + table[i–1, j–w_i]** ∴ table[3,5] = maximum{table[2,5],25 + table[2,0] = maximum{40,25 + 0} **∴ table[3,5] = 40**
Computing table[3,6] with i = 3, j = 6 $w_i = w_2 = 5$ $v_i = v_2 = 25$	As $j >= w_i$ i.e. 6 > 5 **Formula Used : table [i, j] = maximum{table[i–1, j], v_i + table[i–1,j–w_i]** ∴ table[3,6] = maximum{table[2,6],25 + table[2,1] = maximum{40, 25 + 0} **∴ table[3,6] = 40**
Computing table[3,7] with i = 3, j = 7 $w_i = w_2 = 5$ $v_i = v_2 = 25$	As $j >= w_i$ i.e. 7 > 5 **Formula Used : table [i, j] = maximum{table[i–1, j], v_i + table[i–1, j–w_i]** ∴ table[3,7] = maximum{table[2,7],25 + table[2,2] = maximum{52, 25 + 0} **∴ table[3,7] = 52**
Computing table[3,8] with i = 3, j = 8 $w_i = w_2 = 5$ $v_i = v_2 = 25$	As $j >= w_i$ i.e. 8 > 5 **Formula Used: table [i, j] = maximum{table[i–1, j], v_i + table[i–1, j–w_i]** ∴ table[3,8] = maximum{table[2,8],25 + table[2,3] = maximum{52, 25 + 12} **∴ table[3,8] = 52**
Computing table[3,9] with i = 3, j = 9 $w_i = w_2 = 5$ $v_i = v_2 = 25$	As j> = w_i i.e. 9 > 5 **Formula Used : table [i, j] = maximum{table[i-1,j], v_i + table[i–1, j–w_i]** ∴ table[3,9] = maximum{table[2,9],25 + table[2,4] = maximum{52,25 + 40} **∴ table[3,9] = 65**

The partially filled table with above computed values is as follows

	0	1	2	3	4	5	6	7	8	9
0	0	0	0	0	0	0	0	0	0	0
1	0	0	0	12	12	12	12	12	12	12
2	0	0	0	12	40	40	40	52	52	52
3	0	0	0	12	40	40	40	52	52	65
4	0									

Step 4 : Computing next row

Computing table[4,1] with i = 4, j = 1 $w_i = w_2 = 7$ $v_i = v_2 = 42$	As $j < w_i$ i.e. 1 < 7 **Formula Used : table [i, j] = table[i–1, j]** ∴ table[4,1] = table[3,1] = 0 **∴ table[4,1] = 0**
Computing table[4,2] with i = 4, j = 2 $w_i = w_2 = 7$ $v_i = v_2 = 42$	As $j < w_i$ i.e. 2 < 7 **Formula Used : table [i, j] = table[i–1, j]** ∴ table[4,2] = table[3,2] = 0 **∴ table[4,2] = 0**
Computing table[4,3] with i = 4, j = 3 $w_i = w_2 = 7$ $v_i = v_2 = 42$	As $j < w_i$ i.e. 3 < 7 **Formula Used : table [i, j] = table[i–1, j]** ∴ table[4,3] = table[3,3] = 12 **∴ table[4,3] = 12**
Computing table[4,4] with i = 4, j = 4 $w_i = w_2 = 7$ $v_i = v_2 = 42$	As $j < w_i$ i.e. 4 < 7 **Formula Used : table [i, j] = table[i–1, j]** ∴ table[4,4] = table[3,4] = 40 **∴ table[4,4] = 40**
Computing table[4,5] with i = 4, j = 5 $w_i = w_2 = 7$ $v_i = v_2 = 42$	As $j < w_i$ i.e. 5 < 7 **Formula Used : table [i, j] = table[i–1, j]** ∴ table[4,5] = table[3,5] = 40 **∴ table[4,5] = 40**

Computing table[4,6] with i = 4, j = 6 $w_i = w_2 = 7$ $v_i = v_2 = 42$	As $j < w_i$ i.e. 6 < 7 **Formula Used : table [i, j]=table[i–1, j]** ∴ table[4,6] = table[3,6] = 40 **∴ table[4,6] = 40**
Computing table[4,7] with i = 4, j = 7 $w_i = w_2 = 7$ $v_i = v_2 = 42$	As $j >= w_i$ i.e. 7 = 7 **Formula Used : table [i, j]= maximum{table[i–1, j], v_i + table[i–1, j–w_i]** ∴ table[4,7] = maximum{table[3,7],42 + table[3,0] = maximum{52,42+0} **∴ table[4,7] = 52**
Computing table[4,8] with i = 4, j = 8 $w_i = w_2 = 7$ $v_i = v_2 = 42$	As $j >= w_i$ i.e. 8 > 7 **Formula Used : table [i, j] = maximum{table[i–1, j], v_i + table[i–1,j–w_i]** ∴ table[4,8] = maximum{table[3,8],42 + table[3,1] = maximum{52,42 + 0} **∴ table[4,8] = 52**
Computing table[4,9] with i = 4, j = 9 $w_i = w_2 = 7$ $v_i = v_2 = 42$	As $j >= w_i$ i.e. 9 > 7 **Formula Used : table [i, j] = maximum{table[i–1, j], v_i + table[i–1, j–w_i]** ∴ table[4,9] = maximum{table[3,9],42 + table[3,2] = maximum{65,42 + 0} **∴ table[4,9] = 65**

The completely filled table with above computed values is as follows

	0	1	2	3	4	5	6	7	8	9
0	0	0	0	0	0	0	0	0	0	0
1	0	0	0	12	12	12	12	12	12	12
2	0	0	0	12	40	40	40	52	52	52
3	0	0	0	12	40	40	40	52	52	65
4	0	0	0	12	40	40	40	52	52	65

Now we will find actual items of Knapsack

Step 1 : Let i = n, k = j

∴ i = 4, k = 9

Compare table[i, k] and table[i–1, k]

table[4, 9] = table[3, 9]

∴ Do not select i^{th} i.e. 4th item

Step 2 : Set $i = i - 1$

$\therefore$ $i = 3, k = 9$

Compare table[i, k] and table[i–1, k]

table[3,9] $\neq$ table[2,9]

$\therefore$ Select i^{th} i.e. 3rd item

Step 3 : Set $i = i - 1, k = k - wi$

$\therefore$ $i = 2, k = 9 - 5 = 4$

Compare table[i, k] and table[i–1, k]

table[2,4] $\neq$ table[1,4]

$\therefore$ Select i^{th} i.e. 2nd item

Step 4 : Set $i = i - 1, k = k - w_i$

$\therefore$ $i = 1, k = 4 - 4 = 0$

Compare table[i, k] and table[i–1, k]

table[1, 0] $\neq$ table[0, 0]

$\therefore$ Do not select i^{th} i.e. 1st item

Thus the solution is : Select item 2 and item 3 with maximum profit of 65

Q.3 a) *Differentiate the Greedy And dynamic algorithm.* **(Refer section 5.3)** **[3]**

b) *Demonstrate binary Search method to search key = 14, form the array A = <2, 4, 7, 8, 10, 13, 14, 60>.* **[4]**

Ans. : Let us store the elements in an array

0	1	2	3	4	5	6	7
2	4	7	8	10	13	14	60

Step 1 : We will divide the array in the mid.

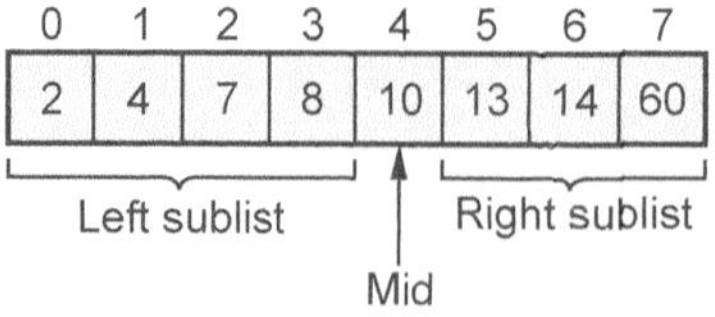

0	1	2	3	4	5	6	7
2	4	7	8	10	13	14	60

Left sublist (indices 0–3) | Mid (index 4) | Right sublist (indices 5–7)

Compare key with A [mid] i.e. 14 with 10

As 14 > 10 we will search right sublist.

Step 2 : As A [mid] = key. The element 14 is present at A [6].

5	6	7
13	14	60

↑ Mid

c) *Solve making change problem using dynamic technique.* $d_1 = 1$, $d_2 = 2$, $d_3 = 4$, $d_4 = 6$, *Calculate for making change of Rs. 10.* **(Refer similar example 4.4.3)** **[7]**

OR

Q.3 a) *Find out the NCR* $\binom{5}{3}$ *using dynamic method.* **[3]**

Ans. : Let us compute **C (5, 3)**

$$n = 5, k = 3$$

$$C(5, 3) = C(n-1, k-1) + C(n-1, k)$$

$$C(5, 3) = C(4, 2) + C(4, 3) \quad \text{...(1)}$$

Here there are two unknowns : C (4, 2) and C (4, 3). Let us compute them one by one we will compute **C (4, 2).**

$$\therefore \quad n = 4, k = 2$$

$$\therefore \quad C(4, 2) = C(n-1, k-1) + C(n-1, k)$$

$$C(4, 2) = C(3, 1) + C(3, 2) \quad \text{...(2)}$$

We will compute C (3, 1)

$$C(3, 1) = C(n-1, k-1) + C(n-1, k)$$

$$= C(2, 0) + C(2, 1) \qquad \because C(2, 0) = 1 \quad \text{...(3)}$$

Now we will compute C (2, 1)

$$C(2, 1) = C(n-1, k-1) + C(n-1, k) = C(1, 0) + C(1, 1)$$

As $C(n, 0) = 1$ and $C(n, n) = 1$

We get, $C(2, 1) = C(1, 0) + C(1, 1)$

$$= 1 + 1$$

$$\therefore \quad \boxed{C(2, 1) = 2} \quad \text{...(4)}$$

Put equation (4) in equation (3), we get -

$$C(3, 1) = 1 + C(2, 1) = 1 + 2$$

$\therefore$ $\boxed{C(3, 1) = 3}$ ...(5)

We will compute C (3, 2)

$$C(3, 2) = C(n-1, k-1) + C(n-1, k) = C(2, 1) + C(2, 2) = 2 + 1$$

$\therefore$ $\boxed{C(3, 2) = 3}$ ...(6)

Now put equation (5) and (6) in equation (2)

$$C(4, 2) = C(3, 1) + C(3, 2) = 3 + 3$$

$\therefore$ $\boxed{C(4, 2) = 6}$ ...(7)

Now let us compute C (4, 3)

$$C(4, 3) = C(n-1, k-1) + C(n-1, k) = C(3, 2) + C(3, 3) = 3 + 1$$

$\therefore$ $\boxed{C(4, 3) = 4}$ ...(8)

Let us put equation (7) and (8) in equation (1)

$\therefore$ $C(5, 3) = C(4, 2) + C(4, 3) = 6 + 4$

$\therefore$ $\boxed{C(5, 3) = 10}$

b) *Find single source shortest path using Dijkstra's algorithm form a to e.* **[4]**

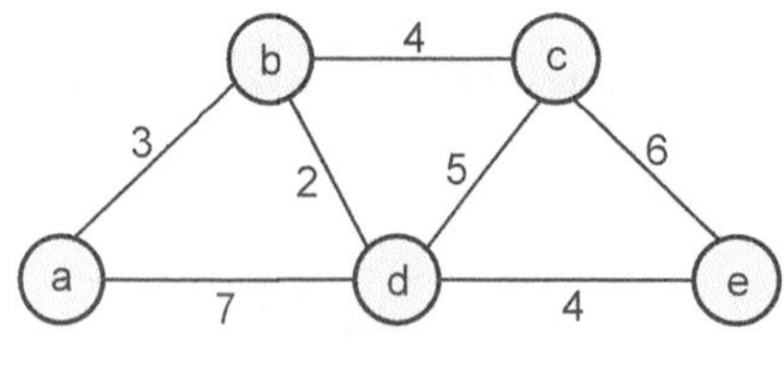

Fig. 2

Ans. :

Step 1 : Source = { a }, Target = {b, c, d, e}

d (a, b) = 3 d (a, c) = ∞

d (a, d) = 7 a (a, e) = ∞

The d (a, b) = 3 is minimum

∴ Select vertex b

Step 2 : Source {a, b}, Target = {c, d, e}

d (a, c) = 3 + 4 = 7d

d (a, d) = d (a, b) + d (b, d) = 3 + 2 = 5

d (a, e) = ∞

The d (a, d) = 5 is minimum distance. Hence select vertex d.

Step 3 : Source = { a, b, d }, Target = {c, e}

d (a, c) = 7

d (a, e) = d (a, d) + d (d, e) = 5 + 4 = 9

The d (a, c) = 7 is minimum

∴ Select vertex c

Step 4 : Source = {a, b, d, c}, Target = { e }

d (a, e) = 9

Step 5 : Thus we obtain single source shortest paths for all other vertices. The shortest path a-e = 5 i.e. **a-d-e.**

c) *For the following chain of matrices find the order of partenthesization for the optimal chain multiplication (13, 5, 89, 3, 34).* **(Refer example 4.8.4)** **[7]**

Q.4 a) *Explain tower of Hanoi problem, Derive its recursion equation and compute it's time complexity.* **[3]**

Ans. : The problem "Towers of Hanoi" is a classic example of recursive function. The initial setup is as shown in Fig. 3(a).

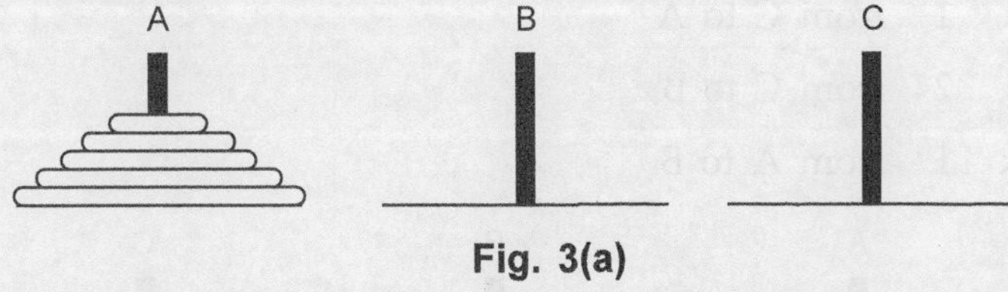

Fig. 3(a)

There are three pegs named as A, B and C. The five disks of different diameters are placed on peg A. The arrangement of the disks is such that every smaller disk is placed on the larger disk.

The problem of " Towers of Hanoi" states that move the five disks from peg A to peg C using peg B as an auxiliary.

The conditions are :

i) Only the top disk on any peg may be moved to any other peg.

ii) A larger disk should never rest on the smaller one.

First of all let us number out the disks for our comfort.

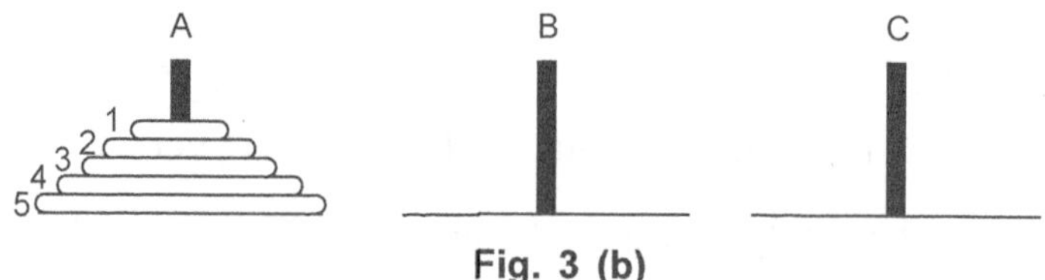

Fig. 3 (b)

The solution can be stated as

1. Move top n – 1 disks from A to B using C as auxiliary.
2. Move the remaining disk from A to C.
3. Move the n – 1 disks from B to C using A as auxiliary.

We can convert it to

move disk 1 from A to B.

move disk 2 from A to C.

move disk 1 from B to C.

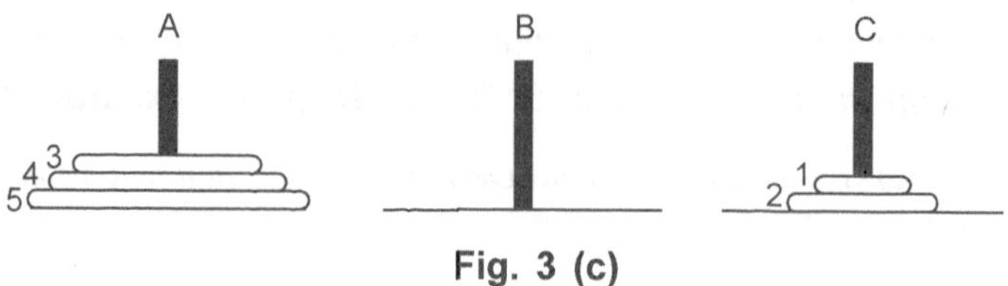

Fig. 3 (c)

move disk 3 from A to B

move disk 1 from C to A

move disk 2 from C to B

move disk 1 from A to B

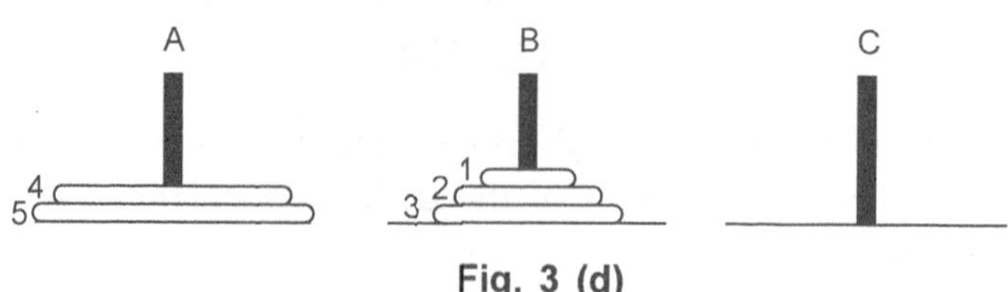

Fig. 3 (d)

move disk 4 from A to C

move disk 1 from B to C

move disk 2 from B to A

move disk 1 from C to A

move disk 3 from B to C

A B C

1 2 5 3 4

Fig. 3 (e)

move disk 1 from A to B

move disk 2 from A to C

move disk 1 from B to C

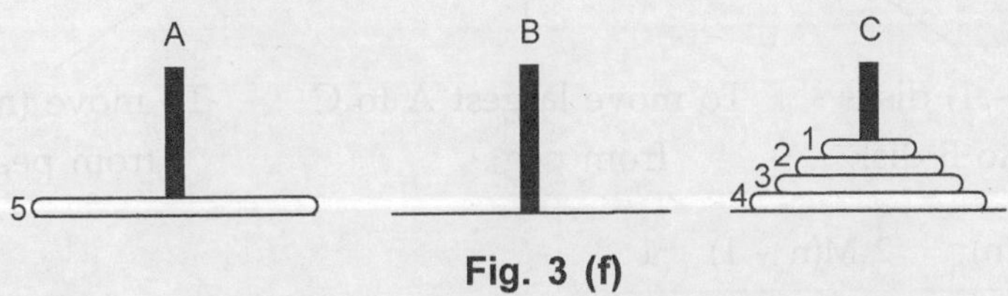

Fig. 3 (f)

Thus actually we have moved n – 1 disks from peg A to C.

```
Algorithm TOH(n,A,C,B)
{
//if only one disk has to be moved
 if (n=1) then
{
write("The peg moved from A to C")
return
}
else
 {
      //move top n-1 disks from A to B using C
      TOH(n-1,A,B,C);
      //move remaining disk from B to C using A
      TOH(n-1,B,C,A);
 }
}
```

Mathematical Analysis :

Step 1 : The input size is n i.e. total number of disks.

Step 2 : The basic operation in this problem is moving disks from one peg to another. When $n > 1$, then to move these disks from peg A to peg C using peg B, we first move recursively $n - 1$ disks from peg A to peg B using auxiliary peg C. Then we move the largest disk directly from peg A to peg C and finally move $n - 1$ disks from peg B to peg C (using peg A as auxiliary peg).

If $n = 1$ then we simply move the disk from peg A to peg C.

Step 3 : The moves of disks are denoted by M(n). M(n) depends on number of disks n. The recurrence relation can then set up as

$$M(1) = 1 \qquad \because \text{Only 1 move is needed TOH } (1, \cdot, \cdot, \cdot)$$

If $n > 1$ then we need two recursive calls plus one move. Hence

$$M(n) = M(n-1) + 1 + M(n-1)$$

To move (n – 1) disks from peg A to B disk | To move largest A to C from peg | To move (n – 1) disks from peg B to C

$$\therefore \quad \boxed{M(n) = 2\,M(n-1) + 1} \qquad \text{... (1)}$$

Step 4 : Solving recurrence $M(n) = 2M(n-1) + 1$ using two substitution methods.

- **Forward substitution :**

For $n > 1$

$$M(2) = 2\,M(1) + 1 = 2 + 1$$
$$M(2) = 3$$
$$M(3) = 2\,M(2) + 1 = 2\,(3) + 1$$
$$M(3) = 7$$
$$M(4) = 2\,M(3) + 1 = 2\,(7) + 1$$
$$M(4) = 15$$

- **Backward substitution :**

Put $M(n-1) = 2\,M(n-2) + 1$

$$M(n) = 2\,M(n-1) + 1$$
$$= 2\,[2M(n-2) + 1] + 1$$
$$= 4\,M(n-2) + 3$$

This is also written as $2^2 M(n-2) + 2 + 1$

Put $M(n-2) = 2\,M(n-3) + 1$

$$= 4\,[2\,M(n-3) + 1] + 3$$
$$= 8\,M(n-3) + 7$$

written as $2^3 M(n-3) + 2^2 + 2^1 + 1$

Above computations suggest us to compute next computation as

$$= 2^4 M(n-4) + 2^3 + 2^2 + 2 + 1$$

From this we can establish a general formula as

$$M(n) = 2^i M(n-i) + 2^{i-1} + 2^{i-2} + \ldots + 2 + 1$$

This can also be written as

Above computations suggest us to compute next computation as

$$= 2^4 M(n-4) + 2^3 + 2^2 + 2 + 1$$

From this we can establish a general formula as

$$M(n) = 2^i M(n-i) + 2^{i-1} + 2^{i-2} + \ldots + 2 + 1$$

This can also be written as

$$M(n) = 2^i M(n-i) + 2^i - 1 \quad \ldots (2)$$

Thus for obtaining M(n) we substitute n by n – i in the equation (2).

Let us use mathematical induction to establish correctness of equation (2).

- **Basis :**

As in equation (2) we can obtain M(n) by substituting n = n – i, assume initially n = 1 then

$$n - i = 1$$

i.e. $$i = n - 1$$

i.e. $$M(n) = 2^i M(n-i) + 2^i - 1 \quad \text{with } i = n - 1 \text{ can become}$$

$$= 2^{n-1} M(n-(n-1)) + 2^{n-1} - 1$$

$$= 2^{n-1} M(1) + 2^{n-1} - 1 \qquad \text{Put } M(1) = 1$$

$$= 2^{n-1} + 2^{n-1} - 1$$

$M(n) = 2^n - 1$ Now if n = 1 then

$M(1) = 2^1 - 1 = 1$ is proved.

- **Induction :**

From equation (1) we get,

$$M(n) = 2\,M\,(n-1)+1 \quad \text{... (3)}$$

But in basis of induction we have computed $M\,(n-1) = 2^{n-1}-1$ then substitute this value in equation (3) and we will get

$$M(n) = 2\,(2^{n-1}-1) + 1 = 2^n - 2 + 1$$

$$M(n) = 2^n - 1 \text{ is proved for } n = n-1$$

$\therefore$ We get recurrence as

$$M(n) = 2^n - 1$$

From this we can conclude that tower of Hanoi has a time complexity as $\Theta(2^n-1) = \Theta(2^n)$.

b) *Explain finite automata algorithm for string matching.* **(Refer section 8.4)** **[4]**

c) *Find out LCS of A = {K, A, N, D, L, A, P} and B = {A, N, D, L}.* **[7]**

Ans. : Refer similar example 4.9.3.

The table will be

		A	N	D	L
	0	0	0	0	0
K	0	0 ↑	0 ↑	0 ↑	0 ↑
(A)	0	1 ↖	1 ←	1 ←	1 ←
(N)	0	1 ↑	2 ↖	2 ←	2 ←
(D)	0	1 ↑	2 ↑	3 ↖	3 ←
(L)	0	1 ↑	2 ↑	3 ↑	4 ↖
A	0	1 ↖	2 ↑	3 ↑	4 ↑
P	0	1 ↑	2 ↑	3 ↑	4 ↑

Fig. 4

Thus the matching longest subsequence is **ANDL.**

OR

Q.4 a) *Explain principle of optimality with example.* **(Refer section 4.2.3)** **[3]**

b) *Define BFS. How it is differ from DFS.* **(Refer sections 6.5.1 and 6.5.2)** **[4]**

c) *Solve the following instance of knapsack problem using backtracking technique. The capacity of the knapsack W = 8 and w = (2, 3, 4, 5) and value v = (3, 5, 6, 10).* **[7]**

Ans. : The state space tree can be built as follows :

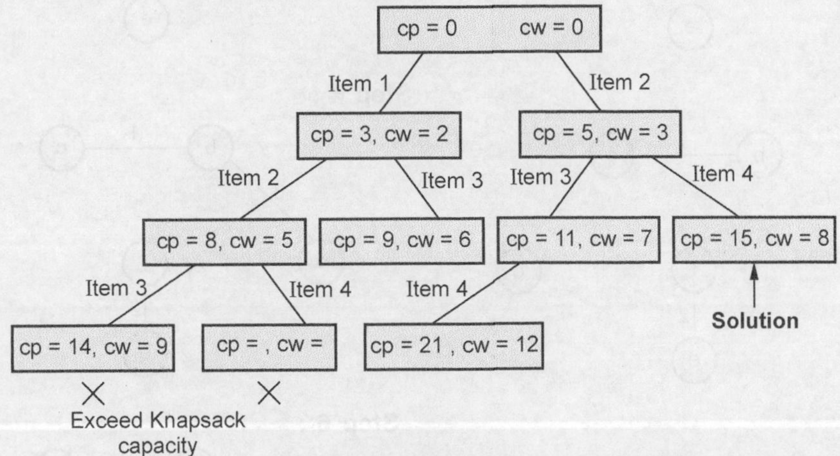

Fig. 5

Thus solution is { **item 2, item 4** } with profit **15.**

Q.5 a) *Draw the state space tree diagram for 4 Queen problem.* **(Refer Fig. 7.3.1)** **[3]**

b) *Define P, NP, NP-hard and NP-complete problem.* **(Refer sections 9.1 and 9.5)** **[4]**

c) *Find out the minimum spanning tree using Kruskal algorithm for given graph.* **[7]**

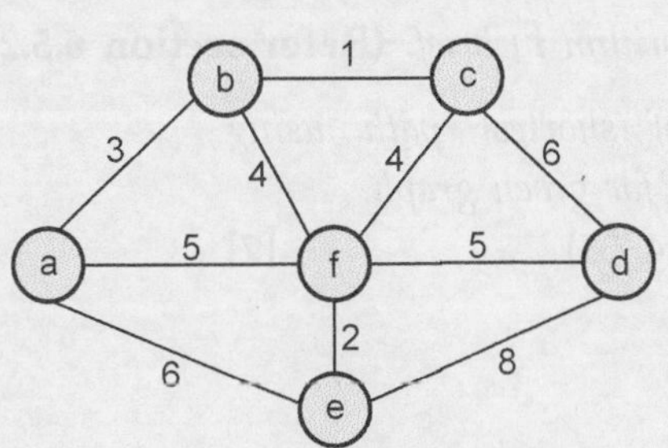

Fig. 6

Ans. :

Step 1 :

Step 2 :

Step 3 :

Step 4 :

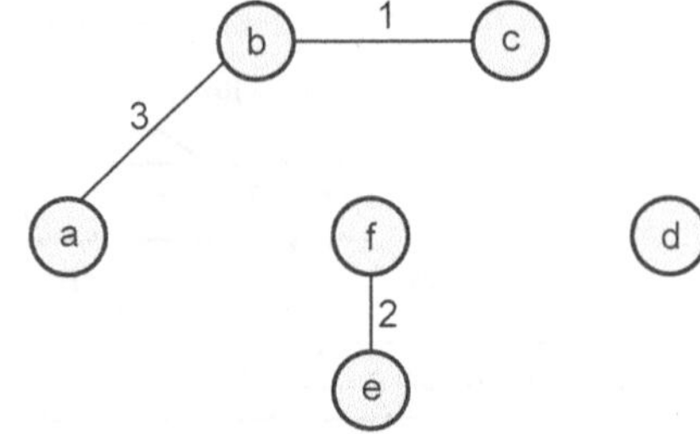

Step 5 :

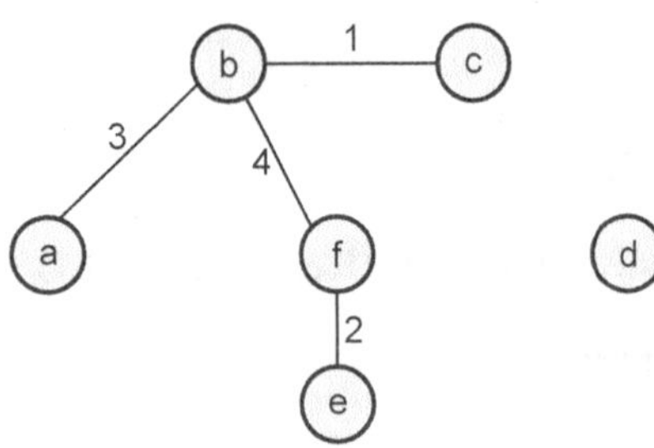

Step 6 :

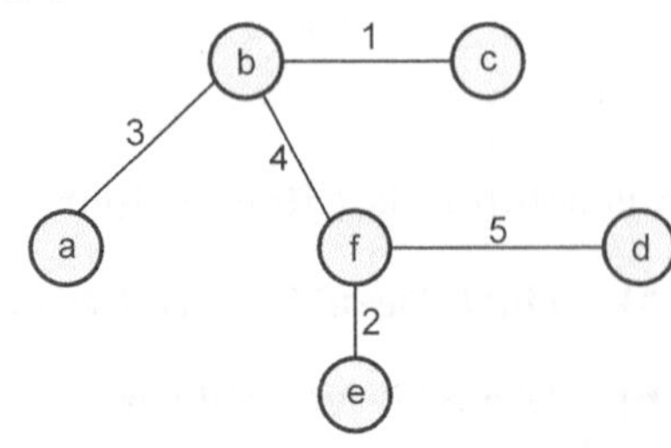

Total Path Length = 15

OR

Q.5 a) *Explain naïve string matching algorithm with example.* **(Refer section 8.2)** **[3]**

b) *Explain DFS algorithm in brief.* **(Refer section 6.5.2)** **[4]**

c) *Find all pair of shortest path using Floyd's algorithm for given graph.* **(Refer example 4.7.3)** **[7]**

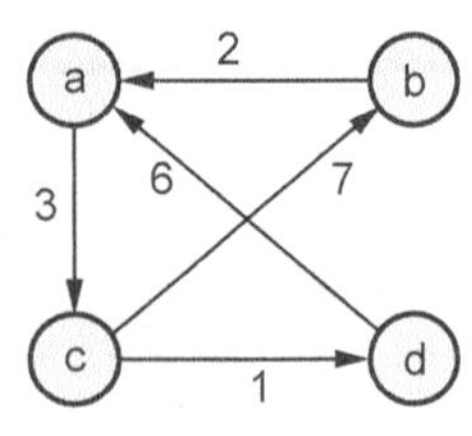

Fig. 7

❑❑❑